Collins English Thesaurus

HarperCollins Publishers
Westerhill Road
Bishopbriggs
Glasgow
G64 2QT

This edition 2013

ISBN 978-0-00-793586-4

www.collinslanguage.com

A catalogue record for this book is available from the British Library.

Typeset by Wordcraft

Printed in Great Britain by Clays Ltd, St Ives plc

Acknowledgements
We would like to thank those authors and publishers who kindly gave permission for copyright material to be used in the Collins Corpus. We would also like to thank Times Newspapers Ltd for providing valuable data.

Contents

EDITORIAL STAFF

EDITORS
Lorna Gilmour

FOR THE PUBLISHERS
Morven Dooner
Elaine Higgleton
Lorna Knight

USING THIS THESAURUS

Main entry words	Main entry words are printed in bold type: **altogether**
Parts of speech	Parts of speech are shown (in small capitals) when the entry has more than one part of speech. Where a word has several senses for one part of speech, the senses are numbered: **abandon** *verb* **1**
Alternatives	Alternatives are introduced by an equals sign: = The key synonym for each sense is underlined, with other alternatives given in roman: **absorb 1** = <u>soak up</u>, suck up, receive, digest, imbibe **2** = <u>engross</u>, involve, engage, fascinate, rivet, captivate
Opposites	Opposites are introduced by an equals sign with a line through it ≠ partially

ABBREVIATIONS USED IN THIS THESAURUS

AD	anno Domini
adj	adjective
adv	adverb
anat	anatomy
archit	architecture
astrol	astrology
Aust	Australia(n)
BC	before Christ
biol	biology
Brit	British
Canad	Canadian
chem	chemistry
C *of* E	Church of England
conj	conjunction
E	East
eg	for example
esp	especially
etc	et cetera
fem	feminine
foll	followed
geom	geometry
hist	history
interj	interjection
lit	literary
masc	masculine
med	medicine
NZ	New Zealand

a

abandon VERB **1** = leave, strand, ditch, forsake, run out on, desert, dump **2** = stop, give up, halt, pack in (*Brit. informal*), discontinue, leave off ≠ continue **3** = give up, yield, surrender, relinquish ≠ keep
• NOUN = recklessness, wildness ≠ restraint
abandonment = desertion, leaving, forsaking
abbey = monastery, convent, priory, nunnery, friary
abduct = kidnap, seize, carry off, snatch (*slang*)
abide VERB = tolerate, suffer, accept, bear, endure, put up with, take, stand
• PHRASES **abide by something** = obey, follow, agree to, carry out, observe, fulfil, act on, comply with
abiding = enduring, lasting, continuing, permanent, persistent, everlasting ≠ brief
ability **1** = capability, potential, competence, proficiency ≠ inability **2** = skill, talent, expertise, competence, aptitude, proficiency, cleverness
able = capable, qualified, efficient, accomplished, competent, skilful, proficient ≠ incapable
abnormal = unusual, different, odd, strange, extraordinary, remarkable, exceptional, peculiar ≠ normal
abnormality **1** = strangeness, peculiarity, irregularity, singularity **2** = anomaly, oddity, exception, peculiarity, deformity, irregularity
abolish = do away with, end, destroy, eliminate, cancel, get rid of, ditch (*slang*), throw out ≠ establish
abolition = eradication, ending, end, destruction, wiping out, elimination, cancellation, termination
abort **1** = terminate (*a pregnancy*), miscarry **2** = stop, end, finish, check, arrest, halt, cease, axe (*informal*)
abortion = termination, miscarriage, deliberate miscarriage
abound = be plentiful, thrive, flourish, be numerous, proliferate, be abundant, be thick on the ground
about PREPOSITION **1** = regarding, on, concerning, dealing with, referring to, relating to, as regards **2** = near, around, close to, nearby, beside, adjacent to, in the neighbourhood of
• ADVERB = approximately, around, almost, nearly, approaching, close to, roughly, just about
above **1** = over, upon, beyond, on top of, exceeding, higher than ≠ under **2** = senior to, over, ahead of, in charge of, higher than, superior to, more powerful than
abroad = overseas, out of the country, in foreign lands
abrupt **1** = sudden, unexpected, rapid, surprising, quick, rash, precipitate ≠ slow **2** = curt, brief, short, rude, impatient, terse, gruff, succinct ≠ polite
absence **1** = time off, leave, break, vacation, recess, truancy, absenteeism, nonattendance **2** = lack, deficiency, omission, scarcity, want, need, shortage, dearth
absent ADJECTIVE **1** = away, missing, gone, elsewhere, unavailable, nonexistent ≠ present **2** = absent-minded, blank, vague, distracted, vacant, preoccupied, oblivious, inattentive ≠ alert
• PHRASES **absent yourself** = stay away, withdraw, keep away, play truant
absolute **1** = complete, total, perfect, pure, sheer, utter, outright, thorough **2** = supreme, sovereign, unlimited, ultimate, full, unconditional, unrestricted, pre-eminent **3** = autocratic, supreme, all-powerful, imperious, domineering, tyrannical
absolutely = completely, totally, perfectly, fully, entirely, altogether, wholly, utterly ≠ somewhat
absorb **1** = soak up, suck up, receive, digest, imbibe **2** = engross, involve, engage, fascinate, rivet, captivate
absorbed = engrossed, lost, involved, gripped, fascinated, caught up, wrapped up, preoccupied
absorbing = fascinating, interesting, engaging, gripping, compelling, intriguing, enticing, riveting ≠ boring
absorption **1** = soaking up, consumption, digestion, sucking up **2** = immersion, involvement, concentration, fascination,

preoccupation, intentness

abstract ADJECTIVE = theoretical, general, academic, speculative, indefinite, hypothetical, notional, abstruse ≠ actual • NOUN = summary, résumé, outline, digest, epitome, rundown, synopsis, précis ≠ expansion • VERB = extract, draw, pull, remove, separate, withdraw, isolate, pull out ≠ add

absurd = ridiculous, crazy (*informal*), silly, foolish, ludicrous, unreasonable, irrational, senseless ≠ sensible

abundance = plenty, bounty, exuberance, profusion, plethora, affluence, fullness, fruitfulness ≠ shortage

abundant = plentiful, full, rich, liberal, generous, ample, exuberant, teeming ≠ scarce

abuse NOUN 1 = maltreatment, damage, injury, hurt, harm, exploitation, manhandling, ill-treatment 2 = insults, blame, slights, put-downs, censure, reproach, scolding, defamation 3 = misuse, misapplication • VERB 1 = ill-treat, damage, hurt, injure, harm, molest, maltreat, knock about *or* around ≠ care for 2 = insult, offend, curse, put down, malign, scold, disparage, castigate ≠ praise

abusive 1 = violent, rough, cruel, savage, brutal, vicious, destructive, harmful ≠ kind 2 = insulting, offensive, rude, degrading, scathing, contemptuous, disparaging, scurrilous ≠ complimentary

academic ADJECTIVE 1 = scholastic, educational 2 = scholarly, learned, intellectual, literary, erudite, highbrow, studious 3 = theoretical, abstract, speculative, hypothetical, impractical, notional, conjectural • NOUN = scholar, intellectual, don, master, professor, fellow, lecturer, tutor, acca (*Austral. slang*)

accelerate 1 = increase, grow, advance, extend, expand, raise, swell, enlarge ≠ fall 2 = expedite, further, speed up, hasten ≠ delay 3 = speed up, advance, quicken, gather momentum ≠ slow down

acceleration = hastening, hurrying, stepping up (*informal*), speeding up, quickening

accent NOUN = pronunciation, tone, articulation, inflection, brogue, intonation, diction, modulation • VERB = emphasize, stress, highlight, underline, underscore, accentuate

accept 1 = receive, take, gain, pick up, secure, collect, get, obtain 2 = acknowledge, believe, allow, admit, approve, recognize, yield, concede

acceptable = satisfactory, fair, all right, suitable, sufficient, good enough, adequate, tolerable ≠ unsatisfactory

acceptance 1 = accepting, taking, receiving, obtaining, acquiring, reception, receipt 2 = acknowledgement, agreement, approval, recognition, admission, consent, adoption, assent

accepted = agreed, common, established, traditional, approved, acknowledged, recognized, customary ≠ unconventional

access 1 = admission, entry, passage 2 = entrance, road, approach, entry, path, gate, opening, passage

accessible = handy, near, nearby, at hand, within reach, at your fingertips, reachable, achievable ≠ inaccessible

accessory 1 = extra, addition, supplement, attachment, adjunct, appendage 2 = accomplice, partner, ally, associate (*in crime*), assistant, helper, colleague, collaborator

accident 1 = crash, smash, wreck, collision 2 = misfortune, disaster, tragedy, setback, calamity, mishap, misadventure 3 = chance, fortune, luck, fate, hazard, coincidence, fluke, fortuity

accidental 1 = unintentional, unexpected, incidental, unforeseen, unplanned ≠ deliberate 2 = chance, random, casual, unplanned, fortuitous, inadvertent

accidentally = unintentionally, incidentally, by accident, by chance, inadvertently, unwittingly, randomly, haphazardly ≠ deliberately

acclaim VERB = praise, celebrate, honour, cheer, admire, hail, applaud, compliment • NOUN = praise, honour, celebration, approval, tribute, applause, kudos, commendation ≠ criticism

accommodate 1 = house, put up, take in, lodge, shelter, entertain, cater for 2 = help, support, aid, assist, cooperate with, abet, lend a hand to 3 = adapt, fit, settle, alter, adjust, modify, comply, reconcile

accommodating = obliging, willing,

kind, friendly, helpful, polite, cooperative, agreeable ≠ unhelpful
accommodation = housing, homes, houses, board, quarters, digs (*Brit. informal*), shelter, lodging(s)
accompaniment 1 = backing music, backing, support, obbligato 2 = supplement, extra, addition, companion, accessory, complement, decoration, adjunct
accompany 1 = go with, lead, partner, guide, attend, conduct, escort, shepherd 2 = occur with, belong to, come with, supplement, go together with, follow
accompanying = additional, extra, related, associated, attached, attendant, complementary, supplementary
accomplish = realize, produce, effect, finish, complete, manage, achieve, perform ≠ fail
accomplished = skilled, able, professional, expert, masterly, talented, gifted, polished ≠ unskilled
accomplishment 1 = achievement, feat, act, stroke, triumph, coup, exploit, deed 2 = accomplishing, finishing, carrying out, conclusion, bringing about, execution, completion, fulfilment
accord NOUN 1 = treaty, contract, agreement, arrangement, settlement, pact, deal (*informal*) 2 = sympathy, agreement, harmony, unison, rapport, conformity ≠ conflict
• PHRASES **accord with something** = agree with, match, coincide with, fit with, correspond with, conform with, tally with, harmonize with
accordingly 1 = consequently, so, thus, therefore, hence, subsequently, in consequence, ergo 2 = appropriately, correspondingly, properly, suitably, fitly
account NOUN 1 = description, report, story, statement, version, tale, explanation, narrative 2 = importance, standing, concern, value, note, worth, weight, honour
• PLURAL NOUN (*Commerce*) = ledgers, books, charges, bills, statements, balances, tallies, invoices
• VERB = consider, rate, value, judge, estimate, think, count, reckon
accountability = responsibility, liability, culpability, answerability, chargeability
accountable = answerable, subject, responsible, obliged, liable, amenable, obligated, chargeable
accountant = auditor, book-keeper, bean counter (*informal*)
accumulate = build up, increase, be stored, collect, gather, pile up, amass, hoard ≠ disperse
accumulation 1 = collection, increase, stock, store, mass, build-up, pile, stack 2 = growth, collection, gathering, build-up
accuracy = exactness, precision, fidelity, authenticity, correctness, closeness, veracity, truthfulness ≠ inaccuracy
accurate 1 = precise, close, correct, careful, strict, exact, faithful, explicit ≠ inaccurate 2 = correct, true, exact, spot-on (*Brit. informal*)
accurately 1 = precisely, correctly, closely, truly, strictly, exactly, faithfully, to the letter 2 = exactly, closely, correctly, precisely, strictly, faithfully, explicitly, scrupulously
accusation = charge, complaint, allegation, indictment, recrimination, denunciation, incrimination
accuse 1 = point a *or* the finger at, blame for, denounce, hold responsible for, impute blame to ≠ exonerate 2 = charge with, indict for, impeach for, censure with, incriminate for ≠ absolve
accustom = familiarize, train, discipline, adapt, instruct, school, acquaint, acclimatize
accustomed 1 = used, trained, familiar, given to, adapted, acquainted, in the habit of, familiarized ≠ unaccustomed 2 = usual, established, expected, common, standard, traditional, normal, regular ≠ unusual
ace NOUN 1 (*Cards, dice*) = one, single point 2 (*Informal*) = expert, star, champion, authority, professional, master, specialist, guru
• ADJECTIVE (*Informal*) = great, brilliant, fine, wonderful, excellent, outstanding, superb, fantastic (*informal*), booshit (*Austral. slang*), exo (*Austral. slang*), sik (*Austral. slang*), ka pai (*N.Z.*)
ache VERB = hurt, suffer, burn, pain, smart, sting, pound, throb
• NOUN = pain, discomfort, suffering, hurt, throbbing, irritation, tenderness, pounding
achieve = accomplish, fulfil, complete, gain, perform, do, get, carry out
achievement = accomplishment, effort,

feat, deed, stroke, triumph, coup, exploit

acid 1 = sour, tart, pungent, acerbic, acrid, vinegary ≠ sweet **2** = sharp, cutting, biting, bitter, harsh, barbed, caustic, vitriolic ≠ kindly

acknowledge 1 = admit, own up, allow, accept, reveal, grant, declare, recognize ≠ deny **2** = greet, address, notice, recognize, salute, accost ≠ snub **3** = reply to, answer, notice, recognize, respond to, react to, retort to ≠ ignore

acquaintance 1 = associate, contact, ally, colleague, comrade ≠ intimate **2** = relationship, connection, fellowship, familiarity ≠ unfamiliarity

acquire = get, win, buy, receive, gain, earn, secure, collect ≠ lose

acquisition 1 = acquiring, gaining, procurement, attainment **2** = purchase, buy, investment, property, gain, prize, asset, possession

acquit VERB = clear, free, release, excuse, discharge, liberate, vindicate ≠ find guilty
• PHRASES **acquit yourself** = behave, bear yourself, conduct yourself, comport yourself

act VERB **1** = do something, perform, function **2** = perform, mimic
• NOUN **1** = deed, action, performance, achievement, undertaking, exploit, feat, accomplishment **2** = pretence, show, front, performance, display, attitude, pose, posture **3** = law, bill, measure, resolution, decree, statute, ordinance, enactment **4** = performance, show, turn, production, routine, presentation, gig (*informal*), sketch

acting NOUN = performance, playing, performing, theatre, portrayal, impersonation, characterization, stagecraft
• ADJECTIVE = temporary, substitute, interim, provisional, surrogate, stopgap, pro tem

action 1 = deed, act, performance, achievement, exploit, feat, accomplishment **2** = measure, act, manoeuvre **3** = lawsuit, case, trial, suit, proceeding, dispute, prosecution, litigation **4** = energy, activity, spirit, force, vitality, vigour, liveliness, vim **5** = effect, working, process, operation, activity, movement, functioning, motion **6** = battle, fight, conflict, clash, contest, encounter, combat, engagement

activate = start, move, initiate, rouse, mobilize, set in motion, galvanize ≠ stop

active 1 = busy, involved, occupied, lively, energetic, bustling, on the move, strenuous ≠ sluggish **2** = energetic, quick, alert, dynamic, lively, vigorous, animated, forceful ≠ inactive **3** = in operation, working, acting, at work, in action, operative, in force, effectual

activist = militant, partisan

activity 1 = action, labour, movement, energy, exercise, spirit, motion, bustle ≠ inaction **2** = pursuit, project, scheme, pleasure, interest, hobby, pastime

actor *or* **actress** = performer, player, Thespian, luvvie (*informal*)

actual = real, substantial, concrete, definite, tangible

actually = really, in fact, indeed, truly, literally, genuinely, in reality, in truth

acute 1 = serious, important, dangerous, critical, crucial, severe, grave, urgent **2** = sharp, shooting, powerful, violent, severe, intense, fierce, piercing **3** = perceptive, sharp, keen, smart, sensitive, clever, astute, insightful ≠ slow

adamant = determined, firm, fixed, stubborn, uncompromising, resolute, unbending, obdurate ≠ flexible

adapt 1 = adjust, change, alter, modify, accommodate, conform, acclimatize **2** = convert, change, transform, alter, modify, tailor, remodel

adaptation 1 = acclimatization, naturalization, familiarization **2** = conversion, change, variation, adjustment, transformation, modification, alteration

add 1 = count up, total, reckon, compute, add up, tot up ≠ take away **2** = include, attach, supplement, adjoin, augment, affix, append

addict 1 = junkie (*informal*), freak (*informal*), fiend (*informal*) **2** = fan, lover, nut (*slang*), follower, enthusiast, admirer, buff (*informal*), junkie (*informal*)

addicted
• PHRASES **addicted to** = hooked on, dependent on, accustomed to (*slang*), habituated to

addiction = dependence, habit, obsession, craving, enslavement *with* ***to*** = love of, passion for, attachment to

addition NOUN **1** = extra, supplement, increase, gain, bonus, extension, accessory, additive **2** = inclusion, adding, increasing, extension, attachment, insertion, incorporation, augmentation ≠ removal **3** = counting up, totalling, adding up, computation, totting up ≠ subtraction • PHRASES **in addition to** = as well as, along with, on top of, besides, to boot, additionally, over and above, to say nothing of

additional = extra, new, other, added, further, fresh, spare, supplementary

address NOUN **1** = location, home, place, house, point, position, situation, site **2** = speech, talk, lecture, discourse, sermon, dissertation, homily, oration • VERB = speak to, talk to, greet, hail, approach, converse with, korero (*N.Z.*)

adept ADJECTIVE = skilful, able, skilled, expert, practised, accomplished, versed, proficient ≠ unskilled • NOUN = expert, master, genius, hotshot (*informal*), dab hand (*Brit. informal*)

adequate **1** = passable, acceptable, average, fair, satisfactory, competent, mediocre, so-so (*informal*) ≠ inadequate **2** = sufficient, enough ≠ insufficient

adhere to = stick to, attach to, cling to, glue to, fix to, fasten to, hold fast to, paste to

adjacent ADJECTIVE = adjoining, neighbouring, nearby ≠ far away • PREPOSITION *with* ***to*** = next to, touching, close to, neighbouring, beside, near to, adjoining, bordering on

adjoin = connect with *or* to, join, link with, touch on, border on

adjoining = connecting, touching, bordering, neighbouring, next door, adjacent, abutting

adjourn = postpone, delay, suspend, interrupt, put off, defer, discontinue ≠ continue

adjust **1** = adapt, change, alter, accustom, conform **2** = change, reform, alter, adapt, revise, modify, amend, make conform **3** = modify, alter, adapt

adjustable = alterable, flexible, adaptable, malleable, movable, modifiable

adjustment **1** = alteration, change, tuning, repair, conversion, modifying, adaptation, modification **2** = acclimatization, orientation, change, regulation, amendment, adaptation, revision, modification

administer **1** = manage, run, control, direct, handle, conduct, command, govern **2** = dispense, give, share, provide, apply, assign, allocate, allot **3** = execute, give, provide, apply, perform, carry out, impose, implement

administration **1** = management, government, running, control, handling, direction, conduct, application **2** = directors, board, executive(s), employers **3** = government, leadership, regime

administrative = managerial, executive, directing, regulatory, governmental, organizational, supervisory, directorial

administrator = manager, head, official, director, executive, boss (*informal*), governor, supervisor, baas (*S. African*)

admirable = praiseworthy, good, great, fine, wonderful, excellent, brilliant, outstanding, booshit (*Austral. slang*), exo (*Austral. slang*), sik (*Austral. slang*), ka pai (*N.Z.*) ≠ deplorable

admiration = regard, wonder, respect, praise, approval, recognition, esteem, appreciation

admire **1** = respect, value, prize, honour, praise, appreciate, esteem, approve of ≠ despise **2** = adore, like, love, take to, fancy (*Brit. informal*), treasure, cherish, glorify **3** = marvel at, look at, appreciate, delight in, wonder at, be amazed by, take pleasure in, gape at

admirer **1** = fan, supporter, follower, enthusiast, partisan, disciple, devotee **2** = suitor, lover, boyfriend, sweetheart, beau, wooer

admission **1** = admittance, access, entry, introduction, entrance, acceptance, initiation, entrée **2** = confession, declaration, revelation, allowance, disclosure, acknowledgement, unburdening, divulgence

admit **1** = confess, confide, own up, come clean (*informal*) **2** = allow, agree, accept, reveal, grant, declare, acknowledge, recognize ≠ deny **3** = let in, allow, receive, accept, introduce, take in, initiate, give access to ≠ keep out

adolescence = teens, youth, minority, boyhood, girlhood

adolescent ADJECTIVE **1** = young, junior,

teenage, juvenile, youthful, childish, immature, boyish **2** = teenage, young, teen (*informal*)
• NOUN = teenager, girl, boy, kid (*informal*), youth, lad, minor, young man

adopt **1** = take on, follow, choose, maintain, assume, take up, engage in, become involved in **2** = take in, raise, nurse, mother, rear, foster, bring up, take care of ≠ abandon

adoption **1** = fostering, adopting, taking in **2** = embracing, choice, taking up, selection, assumption, endorsement, appropriation, espousal

adore = love, honour, admire, worship, esteem, cherish, revere, dote on ≠ hate

adoring = admiring, loving, devoted, fond, affectionate, doting ≠ hating

adorn = decorate, array, embellish, festoon

adrift ADJECTIVE **1** = drifting, afloat, unmoored, unanchored **2** = aimless, goalless, directionless, purposeless
• ADVERB = wrong, astray, off course, amiss, off target, wide of the mark

adult NOUN = grown-up, mature person, person of mature age, grown *or* grown-up person, man *or* woman
• ADJECTIVE **1** = fully grown, mature, grown-up, of age, ripe, fully fledged, fully developed, full grown **2** = pornographic, blue, dirty, obscene, filthy, indecent, lewd, salacious

advance VERB **1** = progress, proceed, come forward, make inroads, make headway ≠ retreat **2** = accelerate, speed, promote, hasten, bring forward **3** = improve, rise, develop, pick up, progress, upgrade, prosper, make strides **4** = suggest, offer, present, propose, advocate, submit, prescribe, put forward ≠ withhold **5** = lend, loan, supply on credit ≠ withhold payment
• NOUN **1** = down payment, credit, loan, fee, deposit, retainer, prepayment **2** = attack, charge, strike, assault, raid, invasion, offensive, onslaught **3** = improvement, development, gain, growth, breakthrough, step, headway, inroads
• ADJECTIVE = prior, early, beforehand
• PHRASES **in advance** = beforehand, earlier, ahead, previously

advanced = sophisticated, foremost, modern, revolutionary, up-to-date, higher, leading, recent ≠ backward

advancement = promotion, rise, gain, progress, improvement, betterment, preferment

advantage **1** = benefit, help, profit, favour ≠ disadvantage **2** = lead, sway, dominance, precedence **3** = superiority, good

adventure **1** = venture, experience, incident, enterprise, undertaking, exploit, occurrence, caper **2** = excitement, action, passion, thrill, animation, commotion

adventurous = daring, enterprising, bold, reckless, intrepid, daredevil ≠ cautious

adversary = opponent, rival, enemy, competitor, foe, contestant, antagonist ≠ ally

adverse **1** = harmful, damaging, negative, destructive, detrimental, hurtful, injurious, inopportune ≠ beneficial **2** = unfavourable, hostile, unlucky **3** = negative, opposing, hostile, contrary, dissenting, unsympathetic, ill-disposed

advert (*Brit. informal*) = advertisement, notice, commercial, ad (*informal*), announcement, poster, plug (*informal*), blurb

advertise = publicize, promote, plug (*informal*), announce, inform, hype, notify, tout

advertisement = advert (*Brit. informal*), notice, commercial, ad (*informal*), announcement, poster, plug (*informal*), blurb

advice = guidance, help, opinion, direction, suggestion, instruction, counsel, counselling

advise **1** = recommend, suggest, urge, counsel, advocate, caution, prescribe, commend **2** = notify, tell, report, announce, warn, declare, inform, acquaint

adviser = counsellor, guide, consultant, aide, guru, mentor, helper, confidant

advisory = advising, helping, recommending, counselling, consultative

advocate VERB = recommend, support, champion, encourage, propose, promote, advise, endorse ≠ oppose
• NOUN **1** = supporter, spokesman, champion, defender, campaigner, promoter, counsellor, proponent **2** (*Law*) = lawyer, attorney, solicitor, counsel, barrister

affair **1** = matter, business, happening, event, activity, incident, episode, topic

2 = relationship, romance, intrigue, fling, liaison, flirtation, amour, dalliance

affect¹ 1 = influence, concern, alter, change, manipulate, act on, bear upon, impinge upon 2 = emotionally move, touch, upset, overcome, stir, disturb, perturb

affect² = put on, assume, adopt, pretend, imitate, simulate, contrive, aspire to

affected = pretended, artificial, contrived, put-on, mannered, unnatural, feigned, insincere ≠ genuine

affection = fondness, liking, feeling, love, care, warmth, attachment, goodwill, aroha (*N.Z.*)

affectionate = fond, loving, kind, caring, friendly, attached, devoted, tender ≠ cool

affiliate = associate, unite, join, link, ally, combine, incorporate, amalgamate

affinity 1 = attraction, liking, leaning, sympathy, inclination, rapport, fondness, partiality, aroha (*N.Z.*) ≠ hostility 2 = similarity, relationship, connection, correspondence, analogy, resemblance, closeness, likeness ≠ difference

affirm 1 = declare, state, maintain, swear, assert, testify, pronounce, certify ≠ deny 2 = confirm, prove, endorse, ratify, verify, validate, bear out, substantiate ≠ refute

affirmative = agreeing, confirming, positive, approving, consenting, favourable, concurring, assenting ≠ negative

afflict = torment, trouble, pain, hurt, distress, plague, grieve, harass

affluent = wealthy, rich, prosperous, loaded (*slang*), well-off, opulent, well-heeled (*informal*), well-to-do ≠ poor

afford 1 = have the money for, manage, bear, pay for, spare, stand, stretch to 2 = bear, stand, sustain, allow yourself 3 = give, offer, provide, produce, supply, yield, render

affordable = inexpensive, cheap, reasonable, moderate, modest, low-cost, economical ≠ expensive

afraid 1 = scared, frightened, nervous, terrified, shaken, startled, fearful, cowardly ≠ unafraid 2 = reluctant, frightened, scared, unwilling, hesitant, loath, disinclined, unenthusiastic 3 = sorry, apologetic, regretful, sad, distressed, unhappy ≠ pleased

after PREPOSITION = at the end of, following, subsequent to ≠ before
• ADVERB = following, later, next, succeeding, afterwards, subsequently, thereafter

RELATED WORD
prefix: post-

aftermath = effects, results, wake, consequences, outcome, sequel, end result, upshot

again 1 = once more, another time, anew, afresh 2 = also, in addition, moreover, besides, furthermore

against 1 = beside, on, up against, in contact with, abutting 2 = opposed to, anti (*informal*), hostile to, in opposition to, averse to, opposite to 3 = in opposition to, resisting, versus, counter to, in the opposite direction of 4 = in preparation for, in case of, in anticipation of, in expectation of, in provision for

RELATED WORDS
prefixes: anti-, counter-

age NOUN 1 = years, days, generation, lifetime, length of existence 2 = old age, experience, maturity, seniority, majority, senility, decline (*of life*), advancing years ≠ youth 3 = time, day(s), period, generation, era, epoch
• VERB 1 = grow old, decline, weather, fade, deteriorate, wither 2 = mature, season, condition, soften, mellow, ripen

aged = old, getting on, grey, ancient, antique, elderly, antiquated ≠ young

agency 1 = business, company, office, firm, department, organization, enterprise, establishment 2 (*Old-fashioned*) = medium, means, activity, vehicle, instrument, mechanism

agenda = programme, list, plan, schedule, diary, calendar, timetable

agent 1 = representative, rep (*informal*), negotiator, envoy, surrogate, go-between 2 = author, worker, vehicle, instrument, operator, performer, catalyst, doer 3 = force, means, power, cause, instrument

aggravate 1 = make worse, exaggerate, intensify, worsen, exacerbate, magnify, inflame, increase ≠ improve 2 (*Informal*) = annoy, bother, provoke, irritate, nettle, get on your nerves (*informal*) ≠ please

aggregate NOUN = total, body, whole, amount, collection, mass, sum, combination
• ADJECTIVE = collective, mixed, combined,

collected, accumulated, composite, cumulative
• VERB = combine, mix, collect, assemble, heap, accumulate, pile, amass

aggression 1 = hostility, malice, antagonism, antipathy, ill will, belligerence, destructiveness, pugnacity 2 = attack, campaign, injury, assault, raid, invasion, offensive, onslaught

aggressive 1 = hostile, offensive, destructive, belligerent, unfriendly, contrary, antagonistic, pugnacious, aggers (*Austral. slang*), biffo (*Austral. slang*) ≠ friendly 2 = forceful, powerful, convincing, effective, enterprising, dynamic, bold, militant ≠ submissive

agitate 1 = stir, beat, shake, disturb, toss, rouse 2 = upset, worry, trouble, excite, distract, unnerve, disconcert, fluster ≠ calm

agony = suffering, pain, distress, misery, torture, discomfort, torment, hardship

agree 1 = concur, be as one, sympathize, assent, see eye to eye, be of the same opinion ≠ disagree 2 = correspond, match, coincide, tally, conform 3 = suit, get on, befit

agreement 1 = treaty, contract, arrangement, alliance, deal (*informal*), understanding, settlement, bargain 2 = concurrence, harmony, compliance, union, agreeing, consent, unison, assent ≠ disagreement 3 = correspondence, similarity, consistency, correlation, conformity, compatibility, congruity ≠ difference

agricultural = farming, country, rural, rustic, agrarian

agriculture = farming, culture, cultivation, husbandry, tillage

ahead 1 = in front, in advance, towards the front, frontwards 2 = at an advantage, in advance, in the lead 3 = in the lead, winning, leading, at the head, to the fore, at an advantage 4 = in front, before, in advance, in the lead

aid NOUN = help, backing, support, benefit, favour, relief, promotion, assistance ≠ hindrance
• VERB 1 = help, support, serve, sustain, assist, avail, subsidize, be of service to ≠ hinder 2 = promote, help, further, forward, encourage, favour, facilitate, pave the way for

aide = assistant, supporter, attendant, helper, right-hand man, second

ailing 1 = weak, failing, poor, flawed, unstable, unsatisfactory, deficient 2 = ill, poorly, sick, weak, crook (*Austral. & N.Z. informal*), unwell, infirm, under the weather (*informal*), indisposed

ailment = illness, disease, complaint, disorder, sickness, affliction, malady, infirmity

aim VERB 1 = try for, seek, work for, plan for, strive, set your sights on 2 = point
• NOUN = intention, point, plan, goal, design, target, purpose, desire

air NOUN 1 = wind, breeze, draught, gust, zephyr 2 = atmosphere, sky, heavens, aerosphere 3 = tune, song, theme, melody, strain, lay, aria 4 = manner, appearance, look, aspect, atmosphere, mood, impression, aura
• PLURAL NOUN = affectation, arrogance, pretensions, pomposity, swank (*informal*), hauteur, haughtiness, superciliousness
• VERB 1 = publicize, reveal, exhibit, voice, express, display, circulate, make public 2 = ventilate, expose, freshen, aerate

RELATED WORD
adjective: aerial

airborne = flying, floating, in the air, hovering, gliding, in flight, on the wing

airing 1 = ventilation, drying, freshening, aeration 2 = exposure, display, expression, publicity, vent, utterance, dissemination

airplane (*U.S. & Canad.*) = plane, aircraft, jet, aeroplane, airliner

aisle = passageway, path, lane, passage, corridor, alley, gangway

alarm NOUN 1 = fear, panic, anxiety, fright, apprehension, nervousness, consternation, trepidation ≠ calmness 2 = danger signal, warning, bell, alert, siren, alarm bell, hooter, distress signal
• VERB = frighten, scare, panic, distress, startle, dismay, daunt, unnerve ≠ calm

alarming = frightening, shocking, scaring, disturbing, distressing, startling, horrifying, menacing

alcoholic NOUN = drunkard, drinker, drunk, toper, lush (*slang*), tippler, wino (*informal*), inebriate, alko *or* alco (*Austral. slang*)
• ADJECTIVE = intoxicating, hard, strong, stiff, brewed, fermented, distilled

alert ADJECTIVE 1 = attentive, awake,

vigilant, watchful, on the lookout, circumspect, observant, on guard ≠ careless **2** = quick-witted, bright, sharp
• NOUN = warning, signal, alarm, siren ≠ all clear
• VERB = warn, signal, inform, alarm, notify, tip off, forewarn ≠ lull

alien ADJECTIVE **1** = foreign, strange, imported, unknown, exotic, unfamiliar **2** = strange, new, foreign, novel, unknown, exotic, unfamiliar, untried ≠ similar
• NOUN = foreigner, incomer, immigrant, stranger, outsider, newcomer, asylum seeker ≠ citizen

alienate = antagonize, anger, annoy, offend, irritate, hassle (*informal*), estrange

alienation = estrangement, setting against, separation, turning away, disaffection, remoteness

alight[1] **1** = get off, descend, get down, disembark, dismount **2** = land, light, settle, come down, descend, perch, touch down, come to rest ≠ take off

alight[2] = lit up, bright, brilliant, shining, illuminated, fiery

align **1** = ally, side, join, associate, affiliate, cooperate, sympathize **2** = line up, order, range, regulate, straighten, even up

alike ADJECTIVE = similar, close, the same, parallel, resembling, identical, corresponding, akin ≠ different
• ADVERB = similarly, identically, equally, uniformly, correspondingly, analogously ≠ differently

alive **1** = living, breathing, animate, subsisting, existing, functioning, in the land of the living (*informal*) ≠ dead **2** = in existence, existing, functioning, active, operative, in force, on-going, prevalent ≠ inoperative **3** = lively, active, vital, alert, energetic, animated, agile, perky ≠ dull

all PRONOUN **1** = the whole amount, everything, the total, the aggregate, the totality, the sum total, the entirety, the entire amount **2** = every, each, every single, every one of, each and every
• ADJECTIVE = complete, greatest, full, total, perfect, entire, utter
• ADVERB = completely, totally, fully, entirely, absolutely, altogether, wholly, utterly

allegation = claim, charge, statement, declaration, accusation, assertion, affirmation

allege = claim, charge, challenge, state, maintain, declare, assert, uphold ≠ deny

alleged = claimed, supposed, declared, assumed, so-called, apparent, stated, described

allegiance = loyalty, devotion, fidelity, obedience, constancy, faithfulness ≠ disloyalty

allergic = sensitive, affected by, susceptible, hypersensitive

allergy = sensitivity, reaction, susceptibility, antipathy, hypersensitivity, sensitiveness

alleviate = ease, reduce, relieve, moderate, soothe, lessen, lighten, allay

alley = passage, walk, lane, pathway, alleyway, passageway, backstreet

alliance = union, league, association, agreement, marriage, connection, combination, coalition ≠ division

allied **1** = united, linked, related, combined, integrated, affiliated, cooperating, in league **2** = connected, linked, associated

allocate = assign, grant, distribute, designate, set aside, earmark, give out, consign

allocation **1** = allowance, share, portion, quota, lot, ration **2** = assignment, allowance, allotment

allow VERB **1** = permit, approve, enable, sanction, endure, license, tolerate, authorize ≠ prohibit **2** = let, permit, sanction, authorize, license, tolerate, consent to, assent to ≠ forbid **3** = give, provide, grant, spare, devote, assign, allocate, set aside **4** = acknowledge, accept, admit, grant, recognize, yield, concede, confess
• PHRASES **allow for something** = take something into account, consider, plan for, accommodate, provide for, make provision for, make allowances for, make concessions for

allowance **1** = portion, lot, share, amount, grant, quota, allocation, stint **2** = pocket money, grant, fee, payment, ration, handout, remittance **3** = concession, discount, reduction, repayment, deduction, rebate

all right **1** = satisfactory, O.K. *or* okay (*informal*), average, fair, sufficient, standard, acceptable, good enough ≠ unsatisfactory **2** = well, O.K. *or* okay (*informal*), whole, sound, fit, safe, healthy, unharmed ≠ ill

ally NOUN = partner, friend, colleague, associate, mate, comrade, helper, collaborator, cobber (*Austral. & N.Z. old-fashioned informal*), E hoa (*N.Z.*) ≠ opponent

• PHRASES **ally yourself with something** *or* **someone** = unite with, associate with, unify, collaborate with, join forces with, band together with

almost = nearly, about, close to, virtually, practically, roughly, just about, not quite

alone ADJECTIVE 1 = solitary, isolated, separate, apart, by yourself, unaccompanied, on your tod (*slang*) ≠ accompanied 2 = lonely, abandoned, isolated, solitary, desolate, forsaken, forlorn, destitute

• ADVERB 1 = solely, only, individually, singly, exclusively, uniquely 2 = by yourself, independently, unaccompanied, without help, on your own, without assistance ≠ with help

aloud = out loud, clearly, plainly, distinctly, audibly, intelligibly

already = before now, before, previously, at present, by now, by then, even now, just now

also = and, too, further, in addition, as well, moreover, besides, furthermore

alter 1 = modify, change, reform, vary, transform, adjust, adapt, revise 2 = change, turn, vary, transform, adjust, adapt

alternate VERB 1 = interchange, change, fluctuate, take turns, oscillate, chop and change 2 = intersperse, interchange, exchange, swap, stagger, rotate

• ADJECTIVE = alternating, interchanging, every other, rotating, every second, sequential

alternative NOUN = substitute, choice, other (*of two*), option, preference, recourse

• ADJECTIVE = different, other, substitute, alternate

alternatively = or, instead, otherwise, on the other hand, if not, then again, as an alternative, as another option

although = though, while, even if, even though, whilst, albeit, despite the fact that, notwithstanding

altogether 1 = absolutely, quite, completely, totally, perfectly, fully, thoroughly, wholly 2 = completely, fully, entirely, thoroughly, wholly, in every respect ≠ partially 3 = on the whole, generally, mostly, in general, collectively, all things considered, on average, for the most part 4 = in total, in all, all told, taken together, in sum, everything included

always 1 = habitually, regularly, every time, consistently, invariably, perpetually, without exception, customarily ≠ seldom 2 = forever, for keeps, eternally, for all time, evermore, till the cows come home (*informal*), till Doomsday 3 = continually, constantly, all the time, forever, repeatedly, persistently, perpetually, incessantly

amass = collect, gather, assemble, compile, accumulate, pile up, hoard

amateur = nonprofessional, outsider, layman, dilettante, layperson, non-specialist, dabbler

amaze = astonish, surprise, shock, stun, alarm, stagger, startle, bewilder

amazement = astonishment, surprise, wonder, shock, confusion, admiration, awe, bewilderment

amazing = astonishing, surprising, brilliant, stunning, overwhelming, staggering, sensational (*informal*), bewildering

ambassador = representative, minister, agent, deputy, diplomat, envoy, consul, attaché

ambiguity = vagueness, doubt, uncertainty, obscurity, equivocation, dubiousness

ambiguous = unclear, obscure, vague, dubious, enigmatic, indefinite, inconclusive, indeterminate ≠ clear

ambition 1 = goal, hope, dream, target, aim, wish, purpose, desire 2 = enterprise, longing, drive, spirit, desire, passion, enthusiasm, striving

ambitious = enterprising, spirited, daring, eager, intent, enthusiastic, hopeful, striving ≠ unambitious

ambush VERB = trap, attack, surprise, deceive, dupe, ensnare, waylay, bushwhack (*U.S.*)

• NOUN = trap, snare, lure, waylaying

amend VERB = change, improve, reform, fix, correct, repair, edit, alter

• PLURAL NOUN (usually in *make amends*) = compensation, redress, reparation, restitution, atonement, recompense

amendment 1 = addition, change, adjustment, attachment, adaptation, revision, modification, alteration 2 = change, improvement, repair, edit, remedy, correction, revision, modification
amenity = facility, service, advantage, comfort, convenience
amid *or* **amidst** 1 = during, among, at a time of, in an atmosphere of 2 = in the middle of, among, surrounded by, amongst, in the midst of, in the thick of
ammunition = munitions, rounds, shot, shells, powder, explosives, armaments
amnesty = general pardon, mercy, pardoning, immunity, forgiveness, reprieve, remission (*of penalty*), clemency
among *or* **amongst** 1 = in the midst of, with, together with, in the middle of, amid, surrounded by, amidst, in the thick of 2 = in the group of, one of, part of, included in, in the company of, in the class of, in the number of 3 = between, to
amount NOUN = quantity, measure, size, supply, mass, volume, capacity, extent
• PHRASES **amount to something** 1 = add up to, mean, total, equal, constitute, comprise, be equivalent to 2 = come to, become, develop into, advance to, progress to, mature into
ample 1 = plenty of, generous, lavish, abundant, plentiful, expansive, copious, profuse ≠ insufficient 2 = large, full, extensive, generous, abundant, bountiful
amply = fully, completely, richly, generously, abundantly, profusely, copiously ≠ insufficiently
amuse 1 = entertain, please, delight, charm, cheer, tickle ≠ bore 2 = occupy, interest, involve, engage, entertain, absorb, engross
amusement 1 = enjoyment, entertainment, cheer, mirth, merriment ≠ boredom 2 = diversion, fun, pleasure, entertainment 3 = pastime, game, sport, joke, entertainment, hobby, recreation, diversion
amusing = funny, humorous, comical, droll, interesting, entertaining, comic, enjoyable ≠ boring
anaesthetic NOUN = painkiller, narcotic, sedative, opiate, anodyne, analgesic, soporific
• ADJECTIVE = pain-killing, dulling, numbing, sedative, deadening, anodyne, analgesic, soporific
analogy = similarity, relation, comparison, parallel, correspondence, resemblance, correlation, likeness
analyse 1 = examine, test, study, research, survey, investigate, evaluate, inspect 2 = break down, separate, divide, resolve, dissect, think through
analysis = examination, test, inquiry, investigation, interpretation, breakdown, scanning, evaluation
analytical *or* **analytic** = rational, organized, exact, precise, logical, systematic, inquiring, investigative
anarchy = lawlessness, revolution, riot, disorder, confusion, chaos, disorganization ≠ order
anatomy 1 = structure, build, make-up, frame, framework, composition 2 = examination, study, division, inquiry, investigation, analysis, dissection
ancestor = forefather, predecessor, precursor, forerunner, forebear, antecedent, tupuna *or* tipuna (*N.Z.*) ≠ descendant
ancient 1 = classical, old, former, past, bygone, primordial, primeval, olden 2 = very old, aged, antique, archaic, timeworn 3 = old-fashioned, dated, outdated, obsolete, out of date, unfashionable, outmoded, passé ≠ up-to-date
and 1 = also, including, along with, together with, in addition to, as well as 2 = moreover, plus, furthermore
anecdote = story, tale, sketch, short story, yarn, reminiscence, urban myth, urban legend
angel 1 = divine messenger, cherub, archangel, seraph 2 (*Informal*) = dear, beauty, saint, treasure, darling, jewel, gem, paragon
anger NOUN = rage, outrage, temper, fury, resentment, wrath, annoyance, ire ≠ calmness
• VERB = enrage, outrage, annoy, infuriate, incense, gall, madden, exasperate ≠ soothe
angle 1 = gradient, bank, slope, incline, inclination 2 = intersection, point, edge, corner, bend, elbow, crook, nook 3 = point of view, position, approach, direction, aspect, perspective, outlook, viewpoint
angry = furious, cross, mad (*informal*),

outraged, annoyed, infuriated, incensed, enraged, tooshie (*Austral. slang*), off the air (*Austral. slang*) ≠ calm
angst = anxiety, worry, unease, apprehension ≠ peace of mind
anguish = suffering, pain, distress, grief, misery, agony, torment, sorrow
animal NOUN **1** = creature, beast, brute **2** = brute, devil, monster, savage, beast, bastard (*informal, offensive*), villain, barbarian
• ADJECTIVE = physical, gross, bodily, sensual, carnal, brutish, bestial
animate ADJECTIVE = living, live, moving, alive, breathing, alive and kicking
• VERB = enliven, excite, inspire, move, fire, stimulate, energize, kindle ≠ inhibit
animated = lively, spirited, excited, enthusiastic, passionate, energetic, ebullient, vivacious ≠ listless
animation = liveliness, energy, spirit, passion, enthusiasm, excitement, verve, zest
announce = make known, tell, report, reveal, declare, advertise, broadcast, disclose ≠ keep secret
announcement **1** = statement, communication, broadcast, declaration, advertisement, bulletin, communiqué, proclamation **2** = declaration, report, reporting, revelation, proclamation
annoy = irritate, trouble, anger, bother, disturb, plague, hassle (*informal*), madden ≠ soothe
annoying = irritating, disturbing, troublesome, maddening, exasperating ≠ delightful
annual **1** = once a year, yearly **2** = yearlong, yearly
annually **1** = once a year, yearly, every year, per year, by the year, every twelve months, per annum **2** = per year, yearly, every year, by the year, per annum
anomaly = irregularity, exception, abnormality, inconsistency, eccentricity, oddity, peculiarity, incongruity
anonymous **1** = unnamed, unknown, unidentified, nameless, unacknowledged, incognito ≠ identified **2** = unsigned, uncredited, unattributed ≠ signed
answer VERB = reply, explain, respond, resolve, react, return, retort ≠ ask
• NOUN **1** = reply, response, reaction, explanation, comeback, retort, return, defence ≠ question **2** = solution, resolution, explanation **3** = remedy, solution
anthem = song of praise, carol, chant, hymn, psalm, paean, chorale, canticle
anthology = collection, selection, treasury, compilation, compendium, miscellany
anticipate **1** = expect, predict, prepare for, hope for, envisage, foresee, bank on, foretell **2** = await, look forward to, count the hours until
anticipation = expectancy, expectation, foresight, premonition, prescience, forethought
antics = clowning, tricks, mischief, pranks, escapades, playfulness, horseplay, tomfoolery
antique NOUN = period piece, relic, bygone, heirloom, collector's item, museum piece
• ADJECTIVE = vintage, classic, antiquarian, olden
anxiety = uneasiness, concern, worry, doubt, tension, angst, apprehension, misgiving ≠ confidence
anxious **1** = eager, keen, intent, yearning, impatient, itching, desirous ≠ reluctant **2** = uneasy, concerned, worried, troubled, nervous, uncomfortable, tense, fearful ≠ confident
apart **1** = to pieces, to bits, asunder **2** = away from each other, distant from each other **3** = aside, away, alone, isolated, to one side, by yourself **4** *with* ***from*** = except for, excepting, other than, excluding, besides, not including, aside from, but
apartment **1** (*U.S.*) = flat, room, suite, penthouse, crib **2** = rooms, quarters, accommodation, living quarters
apathy = lack of interest, indifference, inertia, coolness, passivity, nonchalance, torpor, unconcern ≠ interest
apiece = each, individually, separately, for each, to each, respectively, from each ≠ all together
apologize = say sorry, express regret, ask forgiveness, make an apology, beg pardon
apology NOUN = regret, explanation, excuse, confession
• PHRASES **apology for something** *or* **someone** = mockery of, excuse for, imitation of, caricature of, travesty of, poor

substitute for

appal = horrify, shock, alarm, frighten, outrage, disgust, dishearten, revolt

appalling 1 = horrifying, shocking, alarming, awful, terrifying, horrible, dreadful, fearful ≠ reassuring **2** = awful, dreadful, horrendous

apparatus 1 = organization, system, network, structure, bureaucracy, hierarchy, setup (*informal*), chain of command **2** = equipment, tackle, gear, device, tools, mechanism, machinery, appliance

apparent 1 = seeming, outward, superficial, ostensible ≠ actual **2** = obvious, marked, visible, evident, distinct, manifest, noticeable, unmistakable ≠ unclear

apparently = seemingly, outwardly, ostensibly

appeal VERB = plead, ask, request, pray, beg, entreat ≠ refuse
• NOUN **1** = plea, call, application, request, prayer, petition, overture, entreaty ≠ refusal **2** = attraction, charm, fascination, beauty, allure ≠ repulsiveness
• PHRASES **appeal to someone** = attract, interest, draw, please, charm, fascinate, tempt, lure

appealing = attractive, engaging, charming, desirable, alluring, winsome ≠ repellent

appear 1 = look (like *or* as if), seem, occur, look to be, come across as, strike you as **2** = come into view, emerge, occur, surface, come out, turn up, be present, show up (*informal*) ≠ disappear

appearance 1 = look, form, figure, looks, manner, expression, demeanour, mien (*literary*) **2** = arrival, presence, introduction, emergence **3** = impression, air, front, image, illusion, guise, façade, pretence

appease 1 = pacify, satisfy, calm, soothe, quiet, placate, mollify, conciliate ≠ anger **2** = ease, calm, relieve, soothe, alleviate, allay

appendix = supplement, postscript, adjunct, appendage, addendum, addition

appetite 1 = hunger **2** = desire, liking, longing, demand, taste, passion, stomach, hunger ≠ distaste

applaud 1 = clap, encourage, praise, cheer, acclaim ≠ boo **2** = praise, celebrate, approve, acclaim, compliment, salute, commend, extol ≠ criticize

applause = ovation, praise, cheers, approval, clapping, accolade, big hand

appliance = device, machine, tool, instrument, implement, mechanism, apparatus, gadget

applicable = appropriate, fitting, useful, suitable, relevant, apt, pertinent ≠ inappropriate

applicant = candidate, claimant, inquirer

application 1 = request, claim, appeal, inquiry, petition, requisition **2** = effort, work, industry, trouble, struggle, pains, commitment, hard work

apply VERB **1** = request, appeal, put in, petition, inquire, claim, requisition **2** = be relevant, relate, refer, be fitting, be appropriate, fit, pertain, be applicable **3** = use, exercise, carry out, employ, implement, practise, exert, enact **4** = put on, work in, cover with, lay on, paint on, spread on, rub in, smear on
• PHRASES **apply yourself to something** = work hard at, concentrate on, try at, commit yourself to, buckle down to (*informal*), devote yourself to, be diligent in, dedicate yourself to

appoint 1 = assign, name, choose, commission, select, elect, delegate, nominate ≠ fire **2** = decide, set, choose, establish, fix, arrange, assign, designate ≠ cancel

appointed 1 = decided, set, chosen, established, fixed, arranged, assigned, designated **2** = assigned, named, chosen, selected, elected, delegated, nominated **3** = equipped, provided, supplied, furnished, fitted out

appointment 1 = selection, naming, election, choice, nomination, assignment **2** = job, office, position, post, situation, place, employment, assignment **3** = meeting, interview, date, arrangement, engagement, fixture, rendezvous, assignation

appraisal = assessment, opinion, estimate, judgment, evaluation, estimation

appreciate 1 = enjoy, like, value, respect, prize, admire, treasure, rate highly ≠ scorn **2** = be aware of, understand, realize, recognize, perceive, take account of, be sensitive to, sympathize with ≠ be unaware of **3** = be grateful, be obliged, be thankful, give thanks, be indebted, be in debt, be appreciative ≠ be ungrateful for **4** = increase, rise, grow, gain, improve, enhance, soar ≠ fall

appreciation **1** = admiration, enjoyment **2** = gratitude, thanks, recognition, obligation, acknowledgment, indebtedness, thankfulness, gratefulness ≠ ingratitude **3** = awareness, understanding, recognition, perception, sympathy, consciousness, sensitivity, realization ≠ ignorance **4** = increase, rise, gain, growth, improvement, escalation, enhancement ≠ fall

apprehension **1** = anxiety, concern, fear, worry, alarm, suspicion, dread, trepidation ≠ confidence **2** = arrest, catching, capture, taking, seizure ≠ release **3** = awareness, understanding, perception, grasp, comprehension ≠ incomprehension

apprentice = trainee, student, pupil, novice, beginner, learner, probationer ≠ master

approach **VERB** **1** = move towards, reach, near, come close, come near, draw near **2** = make a proposal to, speak to, apply to, appeal to, proposition, solicit, sound out, make overtures to **3** = set about, tackle, undertake, embark on, get down to, launch into, begin work on, commence on
• **NOUN** **1** = advance, coming, nearing, appearance, arrival, drawing near **2** = access, way, drive, road, passage, entrance, avenue, passageway **3** *often plural* = proposal, offer, appeal, advance, application, invitation, proposition, overture **4** = way, means, style, method, technique, manner

appropriate **ADJECTIVE** = suitable, fitting, relevant, to the point, apt, pertinent, befitting, well-suited ≠ unsuitable
• **VERB** **1** = seize, claim, acquire, confiscate, usurp, impound, commandeer, take possession of ≠ relinquish **2** = allocate, allow, budget, devote, assign, designate, set aside, earmark ≠ withhold **3** = steal, take, nick (*slang, chiefly Brit.*), pocket, pinch (*informal*), lift (*informal*), embezzle, pilfer

approval **1** = consent, agreement, sanction, blessing, permission, recommendation, endorsement, assent **2** = favour, respect, praise, esteem, acclaim, appreciation, admiration, applause ≠ disapproval

approve **VERB** = agree to, allow, pass, recommend, permit, sanction, endorse, authorize ≠ veto
• **PHRASES** **approve of something** *or* **someone** = favour, like, respect, praise, admire, commend, have a good opinion of, regard highly

apt **1** = appropriate, fitting, suitable, relevant, to the point, pertinent ≠ inappropriate **2** = inclined, likely, ready, disposed, prone, liable, given, predisposed **3** = gifted, skilled, quick, talented, sharp, capable, smart, clever ≠ slow

arbitrary = random, chance, subjective, inconsistent, erratic, personal, whimsical, capricious ≠ logical

arbitration = decision, settlement, judgment, determination, adjudication

arc = curve, bend, bow, arch, crescent, half-moon

arcade = gallery, cloister, portico, colonnade

arch¹ **NOUN** **1** = archway, curve, dome, span, vault **2** = curve, bend, bow, crook, arc, hunch, sweep, hump
• **VERB** = curve, bridge, bend, bow, span, arc

arch² = playful, sly, mischievous, saucy, pert, roguish, frolicsome, waggish

archetypal = typical, standard, model, original, classic, ideal, prototypic *or* prototypical

architect = designer, planner, draughtsman, master builder

architecture **1** = design, planning, building, construction **2** = construction, design, style **3** = structure, design, shape, make-up, construction, framework, layout, anatomy

archive **NOUN** = record office, museum, registry, repository
• **PLURAL NOUN** = records, papers, accounts, rolls, documents, files, deeds, chronicles

arctic (*Informal*) = freezing, cold, frozen, icy, chilly, glacial, frigid

Arctic = polar, far-northern, hyperborean

ardent **1** = enthusiastic, keen, eager, avid, zealous ≠ indifferent **2** = passionate, intense, impassioned, lusty, amorous, hot-blooded ≠ cold

area **1** = region, quarter, district, zone, neighbourhood, locality **2** = part, section, sector, portion **3** = realm, part, department, field, province, sphere, domain

arena 1 = ring, ground, field, theatre, bowl, pitch, stadium, enclosure 2 = scene, world, area, stage, field, sector, territory, province

argue 1 = quarrel, fight, row, clash, dispute, disagree, squabble, bicker 2 = discuss, debate, dispute 3 = claim, reason, challenge, insist, maintain, allege, assert, uphold

argument 1 = reason, case, reasoning, ground(s), defence, logic, polemic, dialectic 2 = debate, questioning, claim, discussion, dispute, controversy, plea, assertion 3 = quarrel, fight, row, clash, dispute, controversy, disagreement, feud ≠ agreement

arise 1 = happen, start, begin, follow, result, develop, emerge, occur 2 (*Old-fashioned*) = get to your feet, get up, rise, stand up, spring up, leap up 3 = get up, wake up, awaken, get out of bed

aristocrat = noble, lord, lady, peer, patrician, grandee, aristo (*informal*), peeress

aristocratic = upper-class, lordly, titled, elite, gentlemanly, noble, patrician, blue-blooded ≠ common

arm[1] = upper limb, limb, appendage

arm[2] VERB = equip, provide, supply, array, furnish, issue with, deck out, accoutre
• PLURAL NOUN = weapons, guns, firearms, weaponry, armaments, ordnance, munitions, instruments of war

armed = carrying weapons, protected, equipped, primed, fitted out

armour = protection, covering, shield, sheathing, armour plate, chain mail, protective covering

armoured = protected, mailed, reinforced, toughened, bulletproof, armour-plated, steel-plated, ironclad

army 1 = soldiers, military, troops, armed force, legions, infantry, military force, land force 2 = vast number, host, gang, mob, flock, array, legion, swarm

aroma = scent, smell, perfume, fragrance, bouquet, savour, odour, redolence

around PREPOSITION 1 = surrounding, about, enclosing, encompassing, framing, encircling, on all sides of, on every side of 2 = approximately, about, nearly, close to, roughly, just about, in the region of, circa (*used with dates*)
• ADVERB 1 = everywhere, about, throughout, all over, here and there, on all sides, in all directions, to and fro 2 = near, close, nearby, at hand, close at hand

arouse 1 = stimulate, encourage, inspire, prompt, spur, provoke, rouse, stir up ≠ quell 2 = inflame, move, excite, spur, provoke, stir up, agitate 3 = awaken, wake up, rouse, waken

arrange 1 = plan, agree, prepare, determine, organize, construct, devise, contrive, jack up (*N.Z. informal*) 2 = put in order, group, order, sort, position, line up, organize, classify, jack up (*N.Z. informal*) ≠ disorganize 3 = adapt, score, orchestrate, harmonize, instrument

arrangement 1 *often plural* = plan, planning, provision, preparation 2 = agreement, contract, settlement, appointment, compromise, deal (*informal*), pact, compact 3 = display, system, structure, organization, exhibition, presentation, classification, alignment 4 = adaptation, score, version, interpretation, instrumentation, orchestration, harmonization

array NOUN 1 = arrangement, show, supply, display, collection, exhibition, line-up, mixture 2 (*Poetic*) = clothing, dress, clothes, garments, apparel, attire, finery, regalia
• VERB 1 = arrange, show, group, present, range, display, parade, exhibit 2 = dress, clothe, deck, decorate, adorn, festoon, attire

arrest VERB 1 = capture, catch, nick (*slang, chiefly Brit.*), seize, detain, apprehend, take prisoner ≠ release 2 = stop, end, limit, block, slow, delay, interrupt, suppress ≠ speed up 3 = fascinate, hold, occupy, engage, grip, absorb, entrance, intrigue
• NOUN 1 = capture, bust (*informal*), detention, seizure ≠ release 2 = stoppage, suppression, obstruction, blockage, hindrance ≠ acceleration

arresting = striking, surprising, engaging, stunning, impressive, outstanding, remarkable, noticeable ≠ unremarkable

arrival 1 = appearance, coming, arriving, entrance, advent, materialization 2 = coming, happening, taking place, emergence, occurrence, materialization 3 = newcomer, incomer, visitor, caller, entrant

arrive 1 = come, appear, turn up, show up (*informal*), draw near ≠ depart 2 = occur, happen, take place 3 (*Informal*) = succeed, make it (*informal*), triumph, do well, thrive, flourish, be successful, make good
arrogance = conceit, pride, swagger, insolence, high-handedness, haughtiness, superciliousness, disdainfulness ≠ modesty
arrogant = conceited, proud, cocky, overbearing, haughty, scornful, egotistical, disdainful ≠ modest
arrow 1 = dart, flight, bolt, shaft (*archaic*), quarrel 2 = pointer, indicator, marker
arsenal = armoury, supply, store, stockpile, storehouse, ammunition dump, arms depot, ordnance depot
art 1 = artwork, style of art, fine art, creativity 2 = skill, craft, expertise, competence, mastery, ingenuity, virtuosity, cleverness
article 1 = feature, story, paper, piece, item, creation, essay, composition 2 = thing, piece, unit, item, object, device, tool, implement 3 = clause, point, part, section, item, passage, portion, paragraph
articulate ADJECTIVE = expressive, clear, coherent, fluent, eloquent, lucid ≠ incoherent
● VERB 1 = express, say, state, word, declare, phrase, communicate, utter 2 = pronounce, say, talk, speak, voice, utter, enunciate
artificial 1 = synthetic, manufactured, plastic, man-made, non-natural 2 = insincere, forced, affected, phoney *or* phony (*informal*), false, contrived, unnatural, feigned ≠ genuine 3 = fake, mock, imitation, bogus, simulated, sham, counterfeit ≠ authentic
artillery = big guns, battery, cannon, ordnance, gunnery
artistic 1 = creative, cultured, original, sophisticated, refined, aesthetic, discerning, eloquent ≠ untalented 2 = beautiful, creative, elegant, stylish, aesthetic, tasteful ≠ unattractive
as CONJUNCTION = when, while, just as, at the time that
● PREPOSITION 1 = in the role of, being, under the name of, in the character of 2 = in the way that, like, in the manner that 3 = since, because, seeing that, considering that, on account of the fact that
ashamed 1 = embarrassed, sorry, guilty, distressed, humiliated, self-conscious, red-faced, mortified ≠ proud 2 = reluctant, embarrassed
ashore = on land, on the beach, on the shore, aground, to the shore, on dry land, shorewards, landwards
aside ADVERB = to one side, separately, apart, beside, out of the way, on one side, to the side
● NOUN = interpolation, parenthesis
ask 1 = inquire, question, quiz, query, interrogate ≠ answer 2 = request, appeal to, plead with, demand, beg 3 = invite, bid, summon
asleep = sleeping, napping, dormant, dozing, slumbering, snoozing (*informal*), fast asleep, sound asleep
aspect 1 = feature, side, factor, angle, characteristic, facet 2 = position, view, situation, scene, prospect, point of view, outlook 3 = appearance, look, air, condition, quality, bearing, attitude, cast
aspiration = aim, plan, hope, goal, dream, wish, desire, objective
aspire to = aim for, desire, hope for, long for, seek out, wish for, dream about, set your heart on
ass 1 = donkey, moke (*slang*) 2 = fool, idiot, twit (*informal, chiefly Brit.*), oaf, jackass, blockhead, halfwit, numbskull *or* numskull, dorba *or* dorb (*Austral. slang*), bogan (*Austral. slang*)
assassin = murderer, killer, slayer, liquidator, executioner, hit man (*slang*), hatchet man (*slang*)
assassinate = murder, kill, eliminate (*slang*), take out (*slang*), terminate, hit (*slang*), slay, liquidate
assault NOUN = attack, raid, invasion, charge, offensive, onslaught, foray ≠ defence
● VERB = strike, attack, beat, knock, bang, slap, smack, thump
assemble 1 = gather, meet, collect, rally, come together, muster, congregate ≠ scatter 2 = bring together, collect, gather, rally, come together, muster, amass, congregate 3 = put together, join, set up, build up, connect, construct, piece together, fabricate ≠ take apart
assembly 1 = gathering, group, meeting, council, conference, crowd,

congress, collection, hui (*N.Z.*), runanga (*N.Z.*) **2** = putting together, setting up, construction, building up, connecting, piecing together

assert VERB **1** = state, argue, maintain, declare, swear, pronounce, affirm, profess ≠ deny **2** = insist upon, stress, defend, uphold, put forward, press, stand up for ≠ retract

• PHRASES **assert yourself** = be forceful, put your foot down (*informal*), put yourself forward, make your presence felt, exert your influence

assertion **1** = statement, claim, declaration, pronouncement **2** = insistence, stressing, maintenance

assertive = confident, positive, aggressive, forceful, emphatic, insistent, feisty (*informal, chiefly U.S. & Canad.*), pushy (*informal*) ≠ meek

assess **1** = judge, estimate, analyse, evaluate, rate, value, check out, weigh up **2** = evaluate, rate, tax, value, estimate, fix, impose, levy

assessment **1** = judgment, analysis, evaluation, valuation, appraisal, rating, opinion, estimate **2** = evaluation, rating, charge, fee, toll, levy, valuation

asset NOUN = benefit, help, service, aid, advantage, strength, resource, attraction ≠ disadvantage

• PLURAL NOUN = property, goods, money, funds, effects, capital, riches, finance

assign **1** = give, set, grant, allocate, give out, consign, allot, apportion **2** = select for, post, commission, elect, appoint, delegate, nominate, name **3** = attribute, credit, put down, set down, ascribe, accredit

assignment = task, job, position, post, commission, exercise, responsibility, duty

assist **1** = help, support, aid, cooperate with, abet, lend a helping hand to **2** = facilitate, help, further, serve, aid, forward, promote, speed up ≠ hinder

assistance = help, backing, support, aid, cooperation, helping hand ≠ hindrance

assistant = helper, ally, colleague, supporter, aide, second, attendant, accomplice

associate VERB **1** = connect, link, ally, identify, join, combine, attach, fasten ≠ separate **2** = socialize, mix, accompany, mingle, consort, hobnob ≠ avoid

• NOUN = partner, friend, ally, colleague, mate (*informal*), companion, comrade, affiliate, cobber (*Austral. & N.Z. old-fashioned informal*), E hoa (*N.Z.*)

association **1** = group, club, society, league, band, set, pack, collection **2** = connection, union, joining, pairing, combination, mixture, blend, juxtaposition

assorted = various, different, mixed, varied, diverse, miscellaneous, sundry, motley ≠ similar

assume **1** = presume, think, believe, expect, suppose, imagine, fancy, take for granted ≠ know **2** = take on, accept, shoulder, take over, put on, enter upon **3** = simulate, affect, adopt, put on, imitate, mimic, feign, impersonate **4** = take over, take, appropriate, seize, commandeer ≠ give up

assumed = false, made-up, fake, bogus, counterfeit, fictitious, make-believe ≠ real

assumption **1** = presumption, belief, guess, hypothesis, inference, conjecture, surmise, supposition **2** = taking on, managing, handling, shouldering, putting on, taking up, takeover, acquisition **3** = seizure, taking, takeover, acquisition, appropriation, wresting, confiscation, commandeering

assurance **1** = promise, statement, guarantee, commitment, pledge, vow, declaration, assertion ≠ lie **2** = confidence, conviction, certainty, self-confidence, poise, faith, nerve, aplomb ≠ self-doubt

assure **1** = convince, encourage, persuade, satisfy, comfort, reassure, hearten, embolden **2** = make certain, ensure, confirm, guarantee, secure, make sure, complete, seal **3** = promise to, pledge to, vow to, guarantee to, swear to, confirm to, certify to, give your word to

assured **1** = confident, certain, positive, poised, fearless, self-confident, self-assured, dauntless ≠ self-conscious **2** = certain, sure, ensured, confirmed, settled, guaranteed, fixed, secure ≠ doubtful

astonish = amaze, surprise, stun, stagger, bewilder, astound, daze, confound

astounding = amazing, surprising, brilliant, impressive, astonishing, staggering, sensational (*informal*), bewildering

astute = intelligent, sharp, clever, subtle, shrewd, cunning, canny, perceptive

≠ stupid
asylum 1 (*Old-fashioned*) = mental hospital, hospital, institution, psychiatric hospital, madhouse (*informal*) 2 = refuge, haven, safety, protection, preserve, shelter, retreat, harbour
athlete = sportsperson, player, runner, competitor, sportsman, contestant, gymnast, sportswoman
athletic ADJECTIVE = fit, strong, powerful, healthy, active, trim, strapping, energetic ≠ feeble
• PLURAL NOUN = sports, games, races, exercises, contests, sporting events, gymnastics, track and field events
atmosphere 1 = air, sky, heavens, aerosphere 2 = feeling, character, environment, spirit, surroundings, tone, mood, climate
atom = particle, bit, spot, trace, molecule, dot, speck
atrocity 1 = act of cruelty, crime, horror, evil, outrage, abomination 2 = cruelty, horror, brutality, savagery, wickedness, barbarity, viciousness, fiendishness
attach 1 = affix, stick, secure, add, join, couple, link, tie ≠ detach 2 = ascribe, connect, attribute, assign, associate
attached ADJECTIVE = spoken for, married, partnered, engaged, accompanied
• PHRASES **attached to** = fond of, devoted to, affectionate towards, full of regard for
attachment 1 = fondness, liking, feeling, relationship, regard, attraction, affection, affinity, aroha (*N.Z.*) ≠ aversion 2 = accessory, fitting, extra, component, extension, supplement, fixture, accoutrement
attack VERB 1 = assault, strike (at), mug, ambush, tear into, set upon, lay into (*informal*) ≠ defend 2 = invade, occupy, raid, infringe, storm, encroach 3 = criticize, blame, abuse, condemn, knock (*informal*), put down, slate (*informal*), have a go (at) (*informal*)
• NOUN 1 = assault, charge, campaign, strike, raid, invasion, offensive, blitz ≠ defence 2 = criticism, censure, disapproval, abuse, bad press, vilification, denigration, disparagement 3 = bout, fit, stroke, seizure, spasm, convulsion, paroxysm
attacker = assailant, assaulter, raider, intruder, invader, aggressor, mugger
attain 1 = obtain, get, reach, complete, gain, achieve, acquire, fulfil 2 = reach, achieve, acquire, accomplish
attempt VERB = try, seek, aim, struggle, venture, undertake, strive, endeavour
• NOUN 1 = try, go (*informal*), shot (*informal*), effort, trial, bid, crack (*informal*), stab (*informal*) 2 = attack
attend VERB 1 = be present, go to, visit, frequent, haunt, appear at, turn up at, patronize ≠ be absent 2 = pay attention, listen, hear, mark, note, observe, heed, pay heed ≠ ignore
• PHRASES **attend to something** = apply yourself to, concentrate on, look after, take care of, see to, get to work on, devote yourself to, occupy yourself with
attendance 1 = presence, being there, attending, appearance 2 = turnout, audience, gate, congregation, house, crowd, throng, number present
attendant NOUN = assistant, guard, servant, companion, aide, escort, follower, helper
• ADJECTIVE = accompanying, related, associated, accessory, consequent, resultant, concomitant
attention 1 = thinking, thought, mind, consideration, scrutiny, heed, deliberation, intentness 2 = care, support, concern, treatment, looking after, succour, ministration 3 = awareness, regard, notice, recognition, consideration, observation, consciousness ≠ inattention
attic = loft, garret, roof space
attitude 1 = opinion, view, position, approach, mood, perspective, point of view, stance 2 = position, bearing, pose, stance, carriage, posture
attract 1 = allure, draw, persuade, charm, appeal to, win over, tempt, lure (*informal*) ≠ repel 2 = pull, draw, magnetize
attraction 1 = appeal, pull (*informal*), charm, lure, temptation, fascination, allure, magnetism 2 = pull, magnetism
attractive 1 = seductive, charming, tempting, pretty, fair, inviting, lovely, pleasant ≠ unattractive 2 = appealing, pleasing, inviting, tempting, irresistable ≠ unappealing
attribute VERB = ascribe, credit, refer, trace, assign, charge, allocate, put down
• NOUN = quality, feature, property,

character, element, aspect, characteristic, distinction
audience 1 = spectators, company, crowd, gathering, gallery, assembly, viewers, listeners 2 = interview, meeting, hearing, exchange, reception, consultation
aura = air, feeling, quality, atmosphere, tone, mood, ambience
austerity 1 = plainness, simplicity, starkness 2 = asceticism, self-discipline, sobriety, puritanism, self-denial
authentic 1 = real, pure, genuine, valid, undisputed, lawful, bona fide, dinkum (*Austral. & N.Z. informal*), true-to-life ≠ fake 2 = accurate, legitimate, authoritative
authenticity 1 = genuineness, purity 2 = accuracy, certainty, validity, legitimacy, faithfulness, truthfulness
author 1 = writer, composer, novelist, hack, creator, scribbler, scribe, wordsmith 2 = creator, father, producer, designer, founder, architect, inventor, originator
authoritarian ADJECTIVE = strict, severe, autocratic, dictatorial, dogmatic, tyrannical, doctrinaire ≠ lenient
• NOUN = disciplinarian, dictator, tyrant, despot, autocrat, absolutist
authoritative 1 = commanding, masterly, imposing, assertive, imperious, self-assured ≠ timid 2 = reliable, accurate, valid, authentic, definitive, dependable, trustworthy ≠ unreliable
authority 1 *usually plural* = powers that be, government, police, officials, the state, management, administration, the system 2 = prerogative, influence, power, control, weight, direction, command, licence, mana (*N.Z.*) 3 = expert, specialist, professional, master, guru, virtuoso, connoisseur, fundi (*S. African*) 4 = command, power, control, rule, management, direction, mastery
authorize 1 = empower, commission, enable, entitle, mandate, accredit, give authority to 2 = permit, allow, grant, approve, sanction, license, warrant, consent to ≠ forbid
automatic 1 = mechanical, automated, mechanized, push-button, self-propelling ≠ done by hand 2 = involuntary, natural, unconscious, mechanical, spontaneous, reflex, instinctive, unwilled ≠ conscious
autonomous = self-ruling, free, independent, sovereign, self-sufficient, self-governing, self-determining
autonomy = independence, freedom, sovereignty, self-determination, self-government, self-rule, self-sufficiency, home rule, rangatiratanga (*N.Z.*) ≠ dependency
availability = accessibility, readiness, handiness, attainability
available = accessible, ready, to hand, handy, at hand, free, to be had, achievable ≠ in use
avalanche 1 = snow-slide, landslide, landslip 2 = large amount, barrage, torrent, deluge, inundation
avant-garde = progressive, pioneering, experimental, innovative, unconventional, ground-breaking ≠ conservative
avenue = street, way, course, drive, road, approach, route, path
average NOUN = standard, normal, usual, par, mode, mean, medium, norm
• ADJECTIVE 1 = usual, standard, general, normal, regular, ordinary, typical, commonplace ≠ unusual 2 = mean, middle, medium, intermediate, median ≠ minimum
• VERB = make on average, be on average, even out to, do on average, balance out to
• PHRASES **on average** = usually, generally, normally, typically, for the most part, as a rule
avert 1 = ward off, avoid, prevent, frustrate, fend off, preclude, stave off, forestall 2 = turn away, turn aside
avoid 1 = prevent, stop, frustrate, hamper, foil, inhibit, avert, thwart 2 = refrain from, bypass, dodge, eschew, escape, duck (out of) (*informal*), fight shy of, shirk from 3 = keep away from, dodge, shun, evade, steer clear of, bypass
await 1 = wait for, expect, look for, look forward to, anticipate, stay for 2 = be in store for, wait for, be ready for, lie in wait for, be in readiness for
awake ADJECTIVE = not sleeping, sleepless, wide-awake, aware, conscious, aroused, awakened, restless ≠ asleep
• VERB 1 = wake up, come to, wake, stir, awaken, rouse 2 = alert, stimulate, provoke, revive, arouse, stir up, kindle
awaken 1 = stimulate, provoke, alert, stir up, kindle 2 = awake, wake, revive, arouse, rouse

award NOUN = prize, gift, trophy, decoration, grant, bonsela (*S. African*), koha (*N.Z.*)
• VERB 1 = present with, give, grant, hand out, confer, endow, bestow 2 = grant, give, confer

aware = informed, enlightened, knowledgeable, learned, expert, versed, up to date, in the picture ≠ ignorant

awareness
• PHRASES **awareness of** = knowledge of, understanding of, recognition of, perception of, consciousness of, realization of, familiarity with

away ADJECTIVE = absent, out, gone, elsewhere, abroad, not here, not present, on vacation
• ADVERB 1 = off, elsewhere, abroad, hence, from here 2 = aside, out of the way, to one side 3 = at a distance, far, apart, remote, isolated 4 = continuously, repeatedly, relentlessly, incessantly, interminably, unremittingly, uninterruptedly

awe NOUN = wonder, fear, respect, reverence, horror, terror, dread, admiration ≠ contempt
• VERB = impress, amaze, stun, frighten, terrify, astonish, horrify, intimidate

awesome = awe-inspiring, amazing, stunning, impressive, astonishing, formidable, intimidating, breathtaking

awful 1 = disgusting, offensive, gross, foul, dreadful, revolting, sickening, frightful, festy (*Austral. slang*), yucko (*Austral. slang*) 2 = bad, poor, terrible, appalling, foul, rubbish (*slang*), dreadful, horrendous ≠ wonderful, ka pai (*N.Z.*) 3 = shocking, dreadful 4 = unwell, poorly (*informal*), ill, terrible, sick, crook (*Austral. & N.Z. informal*), unhealthy, off-colour, under the weather (*informal*)

awfully 1 (*Informal*) = very, extremely, terribly, exceptionally, greatly, immensely, exceedingly, dreadfully 2 = badly, woefully, dreadfully, disgracefully, wretchedly, unforgivably, reprehensibly

awkward 1 = embarrassing, difficult, sensitive, delicate, uncomfortable, humiliating, disconcerting, inconvenient, barro (*Austral. slang*) ≠ comfortable 2 = inconvenient, difficult, troublesome, cumbersome, unwieldy, unmanageable, clunky (*informal*) ≠ convenient 3 = clumsy, lumbering, bumbling, unwieldy, ponderous, ungainly, gauche, gawky, unco (*Austral. slang*) ≠ graceful

axe NOUN = hatchet, chopper, tomahawk, cleaver, adze
• VERB 1 (*Informal*) = abandon, end, eliminate, cancel, scrap, cut back, terminate, dispense with 2 (*Informal*) = dismiss, fire (*informal*), sack (*informal*), remove, get rid of
• PHRASES **the axe** (*Informal*) = the sack (*informal*), dismissal, the boot (*slang*), termination, the chop (*slang*)

axis = pivot, shaft, axle, spindle, centre line

b

baas (*S. African*) = master, bo (*informal*), chief, ruler, commander, head, overlord, overseer

baby NOUN = child, infant, babe, bairn (*Scot.*), newborn child, babe in arms, ankle-biter (*Austral. slang*), tacker (*Austral. slang*)
• ADJECTIVE = small, little, minute, tiny, mini, wee, miniature, petite

back NOUN 1 = spine, backbone, vertebrae, spinal column, vertebral column 2 = rear ≠ front 3 = reverse, rear, other side, wrong side, underside, flip side
• ADJECTIVE 1 = rear ≠ front 2 = rearmost, hind, hindmost 3 = previous, earlier, former, past, elapsed ≠ future 4 = tail, end, rear, posterior
• VERB 1 = support, help, aid, champion, defend, promote, assist, advocate ≠ oppose 2 = subsidize, help, support, sponsor, assist

backbone 1 = spinal column, spine, vertebrae, vertebral column 2 = strength of character, character, resolution, nerve, daring, courage, determination, pluck

backer 1 = supporter, second, angel (*informal*), patron, promoter, subscriber, helper, benefactor 2 = advocate, supporter, patron, sponsor, promoter

backfire = fail, founder, flop (*informal*), rebound, boomerang, miscarry, misfire
background 1 = upbringing, history, culture, environment, tradition, circumstances 2 = experience, grounding, education 3 = circumstances, history, conditions, situation, atmosphere, environment, framework, ambience
backing 1 = support, encouragement, endorsement, moral support 2 = assistance, support, help, aid, sponsorship, patronage
backlash = reaction, response, resistance, retaliation, repercussion, counterblast, counteraction
backward 1 = underdeveloped, undeveloped 2 = slow, behind, retarded, underdeveloped, subnormal, half-witted, slow-witted
backwards *or* **backward** = towards the rear, behind you, in reverse, rearwards
bacteria = microorganisms, viruses, bugs (*slang*), germs, microbes, pathogens, bacilli
bad 1 = harmful, damaging, dangerous, destructive, unhealthy, detrimental, hurtful, ruinous ≠ beneficial 2 = poor 3 = unfavourable, distressing, unfortunate, grim, unpleasant, gloomy, adverse 4 = inferior, poor, inadequate, faulty, unsatisfactory, defective, imperfect, substandard, bush-league (*Austral. & N.Z. informal*), half-pie (*N.Z. informal*), bodger *or* bodgie (*Austral. slang*) ≠ satisfactory 5 = incompetent, poor, useless, incapable, unfit, inexpert 6 = grim, severe, hard, tough 7 = wicked, criminal, evil, corrupt, immoral, sinful, depraved ≠ virtuous 8 = naughty, defiant, wayward, mischievous, wicked, unruly, impish, undisciplined ≠ well-behaved 9 = rotten, off, rank, sour, rancid, mouldy, putrid, festy (*Austral. slang*)
badge 1 = image, brand, stamp, identification, crest, emblem, insignia 2 = mark, sign, token
badger = pester, harry, bother, bug (*informal*), bully, plague, hound, harass
badly 1 = poorly, incorrectly, carelessly, inadequately, imperfectly, ineptly ≠ well 2 = severely, greatly, deeply, seriously, desperately, intensely, exceedingly 3 = unfavourably, unsuccessfully
baffle = puzzle, confuse, stump, bewilder, confound, perplex, mystify, flummox ≠ explain
bag NOUN = sack, container, sac, receptacle ● VERB 1 = get, land, score (*slang*), capture, acquire, procure 2 = catch, kill, shoot, capture, acquire, trap
baggage = luggage, things, cases, bags, equipment, gear, suitcases, belongings
baggy = loose, slack, bulging, sagging, sloppy, floppy, roomy, ill-fitting ≠ tight
bail NOUN (*Law*) = security, bond, guarantee, pledge, warranty, surety ● PHRASES **bail out** = escape, withdraw, get away, retreat, make your getaway, break free *or* out ◆ **bail something** *or* **someone out** (*Informal*) = save, help, release, aid, deliver, recover, rescue, get out
bait NOUN = lure, attraction, incentive, carrot (*informal*), temptation, snare, inducement, decoy ● VERB = tease, annoy, irritate, bother, mock, wind up (*Brit. slang*), hound, torment
baked = dry, desert, seared, scorched, barren, sterile, arid, torrid
bakkie (*S. African*) = truck, pick-up, van, lorry, pick-up truck
balance VERB 1 = stabilize, level, steady ≠ overbalance 2 = weigh, consider, compare, estimate, contrast, assess, evaluate, set against 3 (*Accounting*) = calculate, total, determine, estimate, settle, count, square, reckon ● NOUN 1 = equilibrium, stability, steadiness, evenness ≠ instability 2 = stability, equanimity, steadiness 3 = parity, equity, fairness, impartiality, equality, correspondence, equivalence 4 = remainder, rest, difference, surplus, residue 5 = composure, stability, restraint, self-control, poise, self-discipline, equanimity, self-restraint
balcony 1 = terrace, veranda 2 = upper circle, gods, gallery
bald 1 = hairless, depilated, baldheaded 2 = plain, direct, frank, straightforward, blunt, rude, forthright, unadorned
ball = sphere, drop, globe, pellet, orb, globule, spheroid
balloon = expand, rise, increase, swell, blow up, inflate, bulge, billow
ballot = vote, election, voting, poll, polling, referendum, show of hands

ban VERB **1** = prohibit, bar, block, veto, forbid, boycott, outlaw, banish ≠ permit **2** = bar, prohibit, exclude, forbid, disqualify, preclude, debar, declare ineligible
• NOUN = prohibition, restriction, veto, boycott, embargo, injunction, taboo, disqualification, rahui (*N.Z.*) ≠ permission

band¹ **1** = ensemble, group, orchestra, combo **2** = gang, company, group, party, team, body, crowd, pack

band² = headband, strip, ribbon

bandage NOUN = dressing, plaster, compress, gauze
• VERB = dress, cover, bind, swathe

bandit = robber, outlaw, raider, plunderer, mugger (*informal*), looter, highwayman, desperado

bang NOUN **1** = explosion, pop, clash, crack, blast, slam, discharge, thump **2** = blow, knock, stroke, punch, bump, sock (*slang*), smack, thump
• VERB **1** = resound, boom, explode, thunder, thump, clang **2** = bump, knock, elbow, jostle **3** *often with* ***on*** = hit, strike, knock, belt (*informal*), slam, thump, clatter
• ADVERB = exactly, straight, square, squarely, precisely, slap, smack, plumb (*informal*)

banish **1** = exclude, ban, dismiss, expel, throw out, eject, evict **2** = expel, exile, outlaw, deport ≠ admit **3** = get rid of, remove

bank¹ NOUN **1** = financial institution, repository, depository **2** = store, fund, stock, source, supply, reserve, pool, reservoir
• VERB = deposit, keep, save

bank² NOUN **1** = side, edge, margin, shore, brink **2** = mound, banking, rise, hill, mass, pile, heap, ridge, kopje *or* koppie (*S. African*) **3** = mass
• VERB = tilt, tip, pitch, heel, slope, incline, slant, cant

bank³ = row, group, line, range, series, file, rank, sequence

bankrupt = insolvent, broke (*informal*), ruined, wiped out (*informal*), impoverished, in the red, destitute, gone bust (*informal*) ≠ solvent

bankruptcy = insolvency, failure, disaster, ruin, liquidation

banner = flag, standard, colours, placard, pennant, ensign, streamer

banquet = feast, spread (*informal*), dinner, meal, revel, repast, hakari (*N.Z.*)

bar NOUN **1** = public house, pub (*informal, chiefly Brit.*), counter, inn, saloon, tavern, canteen, watering hole (*facetious slang*) **2** = rod, staff, stick, stake, rail, pole, paling, shaft **3** = obstacle, block, barrier, hurdle, hitch, barricade, snag, deterrent ≠ aid
• VERB **1** = lock, block, secure, attach, bolt, blockade, barricade, fortify **2** = block, restrict, restrain, hamper, thwart, hinder, obstruct, impede **3** = exclude, ban, forbid, prohibit, keep out of, disallow, shut out of, blackball ≠ admit

barbarian **1** = savage, monster, beast, brute, yahoo, swine, sadist **2** = lout, yahoo, bigot, philistine, hoon (*Austral. & N.Z.*), cougan (*Austral. slang*), scozza (*Austral. slang*), bogan (*Austral. slang*), boor, vulgarian

bare **1** = naked, nude, stripped, uncovered, undressed, unclothed, unclad, without a stitch on (*informal*) ≠ dressed **2** = simple, spare, stark, austere, spartan, unadorned, unembellished, unornamented ≠ adorned **3** = plain, simple, basic, obvious, sheer, patent, evident, stark

barely = only just, just, hardly, scarcely, at a push ≠ completely

bargain NOUN **1** = good buy, discount purchase, good deal, steal (*informal*), snip (*informal*), giveaway, cheap purchase **2** = agreement, deal (*informal*), promise, contract, arrangement, settlement, pledge, pact
• VERB = negotiate, deal, contract, mediate, covenant, stipulate, transact, cut a deal

barge = canal boat, lighter, narrow boat, flatboat

bark¹ VERB = yap, bay, howl, snarl, growl, yelp, woof
• NOUN = yap, bay, howl, snarl, growl, yelp, woof

bark² = covering, casing, cover, skin, layer, crust, cortex (*Anatomy, botany*), rind

barracks = camp, quarters, garrison, encampment, billet

barrage **1** = bombardment, attack, bombing, assault, shelling, battery, volley, blitz **2** = torrent, mass, burst, stream, hail, spate, onslaught, deluge

barren **1** = desolate, empty, desert, waste ≠ fertile **2** (*Old-fashioned*) = infertile, sterile, childless, unproductive

barricade NOUN = barrier, wall, fence,

blockade, obstruction, rampart, bulwark, palisade
• VERB = bar, block, defend, secure, lock, bolt, blockade, fortify

barrier = barricade, wall, bar, fence, boundary, obstacle, blockade, obstruction

base[1] NOUN **1** = bottom, floor, lowest part ≠ top **2** = support, stand, foot, rest, bed, bottom, foundation, pedestal **3** = foundation, institution, organization, establishment **4** = centre, post, station, camp, settlement, headquarters, starting point **5** = home, house, pad (*slang*), residence **6** = essence, source, basis, root, core
• VERB **1** = ground, found, build, establish, depend, construct, derive, hinge **2** = place, set, post, station, establish, locate, install

base[2] = dishonourable, evil, disgraceful, shameful, immoral, wicked, sordid, despicable, scungy (*Austral. & N.Z.*) ≠ honourable

bash NOUN (*Informal*) = attempt, go (*informal*), try, shot (*informal*), bid, crack (*informal*), stab (*informal*)
• VERB (*Informal*) = hit, beat, strike, knock, smash, belt (*informal*), slap, sock (*slang*)

basic ADJECTIVE **1** = fundamental, main, essential, primary, vital, principal, cardinal, elementary **2** = vital, needed, important, key, necessary, essential, primary, crucial **3** = essential, key, vital, fundamental ≠ secondary **4** = main, key, essential, primary **5** = plain, simple, classic, unfussy, unembellished
• PLURAL NOUN = essentials, principles, fundamentals, nuts and bolts (*informal*), nitty-gritty (*informal*), rudiments, brass tacks (*informal*)

basically = essentially, mainly, mostly, principally, fundamentally, primarily, at heart, inherently

basis 1 = arrangement, way, system, footing, agreement **2** = foundation, support, base, ground, footing, bottom, groundwork

bask = lie, relax, lounge, sprawl, loaf, lie about, swim in, sunbathe, outspan (*S. African*)

bass = deep, low, resonant, sonorous, low-pitched, deep-toned

batch = group, set, lot, crowd, pack, collection, quantity, bunch

bath NOUN = wash, cleaning, shower, soak, cleansing, scrub, scrubbing, douche
• VERB = clean, wash, shower, soak, cleanse, scrub, bathe, rinse

bathe 1 = swim **2** = wash, clean, bath, shower, soak, cleanse, scrub, rinse **3** = cleanse, clean, wash, soak, rinse **4** = cover, flood, steep, engulf, immerse, overrun, suffuse, wash over

baton = stick, club, staff, pole, rod, crook, cane, mace, mere (*N.Z.*), patu (*N.Z.*)

batter = beat, hit, strike, knock, bang, thrash, pound, buffet

battery = artillery, ordnance, gunnery, gun emplacement, cannonry

battle NOUN **1** = fight, attack, action, struggle, conflict, clash, encounter, combat, biffo (*Austral. slang*) ≠ peace **2** = conflict, campaign, struggle, dispute, contest, crusade **3** = campaign, drive, movement, push, struggle
• VERB **1** = wrestle, war, fight, argue, dispute, grapple, clamour, lock horns **2** = struggle, work, labour, strain, strive, toil, go all out (*informal*), give it your best shot (*informal*)

battlefield = battleground, front, field, combat zone, field of battle

batty = crazy, odd, mad, eccentric, peculiar, daft (*informal*), touched, potty (*Brit. informal*), off the air (*Austral. slang*), porangi (*N.Z.*)

bay[1] = inlet, sound, gulf, creek, cove, fjord, bight, natural harbour

bay[2] = recess, opening, corner, niche, compartment, nook, alcove

bay[3] VERB = howl, cry, roar (*used of hounds*), bark, wail, growl, bellow, clamour
• NOUN = cry, roar (*used of hounds*), bark, howl, wail, growl, bellow, clamour

bazaar 1 = market, exchange, fair, marketplace **2** = fair, fête, gala, bring-and-buy

be = be alive, live, exist, survive, breathe, be present, endure

beach = shore, coast, sands, seaside, water's edge, seashore

beached = stranded, grounded, abandoned, deserted, wrecked, ashore, marooned, aground

beacon = signal, sign, beam, flare, lighthouse, bonfire, watchtower

bead = drop, tear, bubble, pearl, dot, drip, blob, droplet

beam VERB **1** = smile, grin **2** = transmit,

show, air, broadcast, cable, send out, relay, televise **3** = radiate, flash, shine, glow, glitter, glare, gleam
• NOUN **1** = ray, flash, stream, glow, streak, shaft, gleam, glint **2** = rafter, support, timber, spar, plank, girder, joist **3** = smile, grin

bear VERB **1** = carry, take, move, bring, transfer, conduct, transport, haul ≠ put down **2** = support, shoulder, sustain, endure, uphold, withstand ≠ give up **3** = display, have, show, hold, carry, possess **4** = suffer, experience, go through, sustain, stomach, endure, brook, abide **5** = bring yourself to, allow, accept, permit, endure, tolerate **6** = produce, generate, yield, bring forth **7** = give birth to, produce, deliver, breed, bring forth, beget **8** = exhibit, hold, maintain **9** = conduct, carry, move, deport
• PHRASES **bear something out** = support, prove, confirm, justify, endorse, uphold, substantiate, corroborate

bearer **1** = agent, carrier, courier, herald, envoy, messenger, conveyor, emissary **2** = carrier, runner, servant, porter

bearing NOUN **1** *usually with **on** or **upon*** = relevance, relation, application, connection, import, reference, significance, pertinence ≠ irrelevance **2** = manner, attitude, conduct, aspect, behaviour, posture, demeanour, deportment
• PLURAL NOUN = way, course, position, situation, track, aim, direction, location

beast **1** = animal, creature, brute **2** = brute, monster, savage, barbarian, fiend, swine, ogre, sadist

beastly = unpleasant, mean, awful, nasty, rotten, horrid, disagreeable ≠ pleasant

beat VERB **1** = batter, hit, strike, knock, pound, smack, thrash, thump **2** = pound, strike, hammer, batter, thrash **3** = throb, thump, pound, quake, vibrate, pulsate, palpitate **4** = hit, strike, bang **5** = flap, thrash, flutter, wag **6** = defeat, outdo, trounce, overcome, crush, overwhelm, conquer, surpass
• NOUN **1** = throb, pounding, pulse, thumping, vibration, pulsating, palpitation, pulsation **2** = route, way, course, rounds, path, circuit
• PHRASES **beat someone up** (*Informal*) = assault, attack, batter, thrash, set about, set upon, lay into (*informal*), beat the living daylights out of (*informal*)

beaten **1** = stirred, mixed, whipped, blended, whisked, frothy, foamy **2** = defeated, overcome, overwhelmed, cowed, thwarted, vanquished

beautiful = attractive, pretty, lovely, charming, tempting, pleasant, handsome, fetching ≠ ugly

beauty **1** = attractiveness, charm, grace, glamour, elegance, loveliness, handsomeness, comeliness ≠ ugliness **2** = good-looker, lovely (*slang*), belle, stunner (*informal*)

because CONJUNCTION = since, as, in that
• PHRASES **because of** = as a result of, on account of, by reason of, thanks to, owing to

beckon = gesture, sign, wave, indicate, signal, nod, motion, summon

become **1** = come to be, develop into, be transformed into, grow into, change into, alter to, mature into, ripen into **2** = suit, fit, enhance, flatter, embellish, set off

becoming **1** = flattering, pretty, attractive, enhancing, neat, graceful, tasteful, well-chosen ≠ unflattering **2** = appropriate, seemly, fitting, suitable, proper, worthy, in keeping, compatible ≠ inappropriate

bed **1** = bedstead, couch, berth, cot, bunk, divan **2** = plot, area, row, strip, patch, ground, land, garden **3** = bottom, ground, floor **4** = base, footing, basis, bottom, foundation, underpinning, groundwork, bedrock

before PREPOSITION **1** = earlier than, ahead of, prior to, in advance of ≠ after **2** = in front of, ahead of, in advance of **3** = in the presence of, in front of **4** = ahead of, in front of, in advance of
• ADVERB **1** = previously, earlier, sooner, in advance, formerly ≠ after **2** = in the past, earlier, once, previously, formerly, hitherto, beforehand

RELATED WORDS
prefixes: ante-, fore-, pre-

beforehand = in advance, before, earlier, already, sooner, ahead, previously, in anticipation

beg **1** = implore, plead with, beseech, request, petition, solicit, entreat **2** = scrounge, bum (*informal*), touch (someone) for (*slang*), cadge, sponge on (someone) for, freeload (*slang*), seek charity, solicit charity ≠ give

beggar = tramp, bum (*informal*), derelict, drifter, down-and-out, pauper, vagrant, bag lady (*chiefly U.S.*), derro (*Austral. slang*)

begin 1 = start, commence, proceed ≠ stop 2 = commence, start, initiate, embark on, set about, instigate, institute, make a beginning 3 = start talking, start, initiate, commence 4 = come into existence, start, appear, emerge, arise, originate, come into being 5 = emerge, start, spring, stem, derive, originate ≠ end

beginner = novice, pupil, amateur, newcomer, starter, trainee, apprentice, learner ≠ expert

beginning 1 = start, opening, birth, origin, outset, onset, initiation, inauguration ≠ end 2 = outset, start, opening, birth, onset, commencement 3 = origins

behave 1 = act 2 *often reflexive* = be well-behaved, mind your manners, keep your nose clean, act correctly, conduct yourself properly ≠ misbehave

behaviour 1 = conduct, ways, actions, bearing, attitude, manner, manners, demeanour 2 = action, performance, operation, functioning

behind PREPOSITION 1 = at the rear of, at the back of, at the heels of 2 = after, following 3 = supporting, for, backing, on the side of, in agreement with 4 = causing, responsible for, initiating, at the bottom of, instigating 5 = later than, after

• ADVERB 1 = after, next, following, afterwards, subsequently, in the wake (of) ≠ in advance of 2 = behind schedule, delayed, running late, behind time ≠ ahead 3 = overdue, in debt, in arrears, behindhand

• NOUN (*Informal*) = bottom, butt (*U.S. & Canad. informal*), buttocks, posterior

being 1 = individual, creature, human being, living thing 2 = life, reality ≠ nonexistence 3 = soul, spirit, substance, creature, essence, organism, entity

beleaguered 1 = harassed, troubled, plagued, hassled (*informal*), badgered, persecuted, pestered, vexed 2 = besieged, surrounded, blockaded, beset, encircled, assailed, hemmed in

belief 1 = trust, confidence, conviction ≠ disbelief 2 = faith, principles, doctrine, ideology, creed, dogma, tenet, credo 3 = opinion, feeling, idea, impression, assessment, notion, judgment, point of view

believe 1 = think, judge, suppose, estimate, imagine, assume, gather, reckon 2 = accept, trust, credit, depend on, rely on, have faith in, swear by, be certain of ≠ disbelieve

believer = follower, supporter, convert, disciple, devotee, apostle, adherent, zealot ≠ sceptic

bellow VERB = shout, cry (out), scream, roar, yell, howl, shriek, bawl

• NOUN = shout, cry, scream, roar, yell, howl, shriek, bawl

belly = stomach, insides (*informal*), gut, abdomen, tummy, paunch, potbelly, corporation (*informal*), puku (*N.Z.*)

belong = go with, fit into, be part of, relate to, be connected with, pertain to

belonging = fellowship, relationship, association, loyalty, acceptance, attachment, inclusion, affinity

belongings = possessions, goods, things, effects, property, stuff, gear, paraphernalia

beloved = dear, loved, valued, prized, admired, treasured, precious, darling

below PREPOSITION 1 = under, underneath, lower than 2 = less than, lower than 3 = subordinate to, subject to, inferior to, lesser than

• ADVERB 1 = lower, down, under, beneath, underneath 2 = beneath, following, at the end, underneath, at the bottom, further on

belt 1 = waistband, band, sash, girdle, girth, cummerbund 2 = conveyor belt, band, loop, fan belt, drive belt 3 (*Geography*) = zone, area, region, section, district, stretch, strip, layer

bemused = puzzled, confused, baffled, at sea, bewildered, muddled, perplexed, mystified

bench NOUN 1 = seat, stall, pew 2 = worktable, stand, table, counter, trestle table, workbench

• PHRASES **the bench** = court, judges, magistrates, tribunal, judiciary, courtroom

benchmark = reference point, gauge, yardstick, measure, level, standard, model, par

bend VERB = twist, turn, wind, lean, hook, bow, curve, arch

• NOUN = curve, turn, corner, twist, angle, bow, loop, arc

beneath PREPOSITION **1** = under, below, underneath, lower than ≠ over **2** = inferior to, below **3** = unworthy of, unfitting for, unsuitable for, inappropriate for, unbefitting
• ADVERB = underneath, below, in a lower place
RELATED WORD
prefix: sub-
beneficial = favourable, useful, valuable, helpful, profitable, benign, wholesome, advantageous ≠ harmful
beneficiary 1 = recipient, receiver, payee **2** = heir, inheritor
benefit NOUN **1** = good, help, profit, favour ≠ harm **2** = advantage, aid, favour, assistance
• VERB **1** = profit from, make the most of, gain from, do well out of, reap benefits from, turn to your advantage **2** = help, aid, profit, improve, enhance, assist, avail ≠ harm
benign 1 = benevolent, kind, kindly, warm, friendly, obliging, sympathetic, compassionate ≠ unkind **2** (*Medical*) = harmless, innocent, innocuous, curable, inoffensive, remediable ≠ malignant
bent ADJECTIVE **1** = misshapen, twisted, angled, bowed, curved, arched, crooked, distorted ≠ straight **2** = stooped, bowed, arched, hunched
• NOUN = inclination, ability, leaning, tendency, preference, penchant, propensity, aptitude
• PHRASES **bent on** = intent on, set on, fixed on, predisposed to, resolved on, insistent on
bequeath 1 = leave, will, give, grant, hand down, endow, bestow, entrust **2** = give, accord, grant, afford, yield, lend, pass on, confer
berth NOUN **1** = bunk, bed, hammock, billet **2** (*Nautical*) = anchorage, haven, port, harbour, dock, pier, wharf, quay
• VERB (*Nautical*) = anchor, land, dock, moor, tie up, drop anchor
beside PREPOSITION = next to, near, close to, neighbouring, alongside, adjacent to, at the side of, abreast of
• PHRASES **beside yourself** = distraught, desperate, distressed, frantic, frenzied, demented, unhinged, overwrought
besides PREPOSITION = apart from, barring, excepting, other than, excluding, as well (as), in addition to, over and above
• ADVERB = also, too, further, otherwise, in addition, as well, moreover, furthermore
besiege 1 = harass, harry, plague, hound, hassle (*informal*), badger, pester **2** = surround, enclose, blockade, encircle, hem in, shut in, lay siege to
best ADJECTIVE = finest, leading, supreme, principal, foremost, pre-eminent, unsurpassed, most accomplished
• NOUN = finest, top, prime, pick, flower, cream, elite, crème de la crème (*French*)
• ADVERB = most highly, most fully, most deeply
bestow = present, give, award, grant, commit, hand out, lavish, impart ≠ obtain
bet VERB = gamble, chance, stake, venture, hazard, speculate, wager, risk money
• NOUN = gamble, risk, stake, venture, speculation, flutter (*informal*), punt, wager
betray 1 = be disloyal to, dob in (*Austral. slang*), double-cross (*informal*), stab in the back, be unfaithful to, inform on *or* against **2** = give away, reveal, expose, disclose, uncover, divulge, unmask, let slip
betrayal = disloyalty, sell-out (*informal*), deception, treason, treachery, trickery, double-cross (*informal*), breach of trust ≠ loyalty
better ADVERB **1** = to a greater degree, more completely, more thoroughly **2** = in a more excellent manner, more effectively, more attractively, more advantageously, more competently, in a superior way ≠ worse
• ADJECTIVE **1** = well, stronger, recovering, cured, fully recovered, on the mend (*informal*) ≠ worse **2** = superior, finer, higher-quality, surpassing, preferable, more desirable ≠ inferior
between = amidst, among, mid, in the middle of, betwixt
RELATED WORD
prefix: inter-
beverage = drink, liquid, liquor, refreshment
beware 1 = be careful, look out, watch out, be wary, be cautious, take heed, guard against something **2** = avoid, mind
bewilder = confound, confuse, puzzle, baffle, perplex, mystify, flummox, bemuse
bewildered = confused, puzzled, baffled, at sea, muddled, perplexed, at a loss, mystified

beyond 1 = on the other side of 2 = after, over, past, above 3 = past 4 = except for, but, save, apart from, other than, excluding, besides, aside from 5 = exceeding, surpassing, superior to, out of reach of 6 = outside, over, above

bias NOUN = prejudice, leaning, tendency, inclination, favouritism, partiality ≠ impartiality
• VERB = influence, colour, weight, prejudice, distort, sway, warp, slant

biased = prejudiced, weighted, one-sided, partial, distorted, slanted

bid NOUN 1 = attempt, try, effort, go (*informal*), shot (*informal*), stab (*informal*), crack (*informal*) 2 = offer, price, amount, advance, proposal, sum, tender
• VERB 1 = make an offer, offer, propose, submit, tender, proffer 2 = wish, say, call, tell, greet 3 = tell, ask, order, require, direct, command, instruct

bidding = order, request, command, instruction, summons, beck and call

big 1 = large, great, huge, massive, vast, enormous, substantial, extensive ≠ small 2 = important, significant, urgent, far-reaching ≠ unimportant 3 = powerful, important, prominent, dominant, influential, eminent 4 = grown-up, adult, grown, mature, elder, full-grown ≠ young 5 = generous, good, noble, gracious, benevolent, altruistic, unselfish, magnanimous

bill[1] NOUN 1 = charges, rate, costs, score, account, statement, reckoning, expense 2 = act of parliament, measure, proposal, piece of legislation, projected law 3 = list, listing, programme, card, schedule, agenda, catalogue, inventory 4 = advertisement, notice, poster, leaflet, bulletin, circular, handout, placard
• VERB 1 = charge, debit, invoice, send a statement to, send an invoice to 2 = advertise, post, announce, promote, plug (*informal*), tout, publicize, give advance notice of

bill[2] = beak, nib, neb (*archaic, dialect*), mandible

bind VERB 1 = oblige, make, force, require, engage, compel, constrain, necessitate 2 = tie, join, stick, secure, wrap, knot, strap, lash ≠ untie
• NOUN (*Informal*) = nuisance, inconvenience, hassle (*informal*), drag (*informal*), spot (*informal*), difficulty, bore, dilemma, uphill (*S. African*)

binding = compulsory, necessary, mandatory, obligatory, irrevocable, unalterable, indissoluble ≠ optional

binge (*Informal*) = bout, spell, fling, feast, stint, spree, orgy, bender (*informal*)

biography = life story, life, record, account, profile, memoir, CV, curriculum vitae

bird = feathered friend, fowl, songbird

RELATED WORDS
adjective: avian
male: cock
female: hen
young: chick, fledg(e)ling, nestling
collective nouns: flock, flight
habitation: nest

birth 1 = childbirth, delivery, nativity, parturition ≠ death 2 = ancestry, stock, blood, background, breeding, pedigree, lineage, parentage

RELATED WORD
adjective: natal

bit[1] 1 = slice, fragment, crumb, morsel 2 = piece, scrap 3 = jot, iota 4 = part

bit[2] = curb, check, brake, restraint, snaffle

bite VERB = nip, cut, tear, wound, snap, pierce, pinch, chew
• NOUN 1 = snack, food, piece, taste, refreshment, mouthful, morsel, titbit 2 = wound, sting, pinch, nip, prick

biting 1 = piercing, cutting, sharp, frozen, harsh, penetrating, arctic, icy 2 = sarcastic, cutting, stinging, scathing, acrimonious, incisive, virulent, caustic

bitter 1 = resentful, angry, offended, sour, sore, acrimonious, sullen, miffed (*informal*) ≠ happy 2 = freezing, biting, severe, intense, raw, fierce, chill, stinging ≠ mild 3 = sour, sharp, acid, harsh, tart, astringent, acrid, unsweetened ≠ sweet

bitterness 1 = resentment, hostility, indignation, animosity, acrimony, rancour, ill feeling, bad blood 2 = sourness, acidity, sharpness, tartness, acerbity

bizarre = strange, unusual, extraordinary, fantastic, weird, peculiar, eccentric, ludicrous ≠ normal

black 1 = dark, raven, ebony, sable, jet, dusky, pitch-black, swarthy ≠ light 2 = gloomy, sad, depressing, grim, bleak, hopeless, dismal, ominous ≠ happy 3 = terrible, bad, devastating, tragic, fatal, catastrophic, ruinous, calamitous **4** = wicked, bad, evil, corrupt, vicious, immoral, depraved, villainous ≠ good **5** = angry, cross, furious, hostile, sour, menacing, moody, resentful ≠ happy

blackmail NOUN = threat, intimidation, ransom, extortion, hush money (*slang*) • VERB = threaten, squeeze, compel, intimidate, coerce, dragoon, extort, hold to ransom

blame VERB **1** = hold responsible, accuse, denounce, indict, impeach, incriminate, impute ≠ absolve **2** = attribute to, credit to, assign to, put down to, impute to **3** (used in negative constructions) = criticize, condemn, censure, reproach, chide, find fault with ≠ praise • NOUN = responsibility, liability, accountability, onus, culpability, answerability ≠ praise

bland 1 = dull, boring, plain, flat, dreary, run-of-the-mill, uninspiring, humdrum ≠ exciting **2** = tasteless, insipid, flavourless, thin

blank ADJECTIVE **1** = unmarked, white, clear, clean, empty, plain, bare, void ≠ marked **2** = expressionless, empty, vague, vacant, deadpan, impassive, poker-faced (*informal*) ≠ expressive • NOUN **1** = empty space, space, gap **2** = void, vacuum, vacancy, emptiness, nothingness

blanket NOUN **1** = cover, rug, coverlet **2** = covering, sheet, coat, layer, carpet, cloak, mantle, thickness • VERB = coat, cover, hide, mask, conceal, obscure, cloak

blast NOUN **1** = explosion, crash, burst, discharge, eruption, detonation **2** = gust, rush, storm, breeze, puff, gale, tempest, squall **3** = blare, blow, scream, trumpet, wail, resound, clamour, toot • VERB = blow up, bomb, destroy, burst, ruin, break up, explode, shatter

blatant = obvious, clear, plain, evident, glaring, manifest, noticeable, conspicuous ≠ subtle

blaze VERB **1** = burn, glow, flare, be on fire, go up in flames, be ablaze, fire, flame **2** = shine, flash, beam, glow, flare, glare, gleam, radiate • NOUN **1** = inferno, fire, flames, bonfire, combustion, conflagration **2** = flash, glow, glitter, flare, glare, gleam, brilliance, radiance

bleach = lighten, wash out, blanch, whiten

bleak 1 = dismal, dark, depressing, grim, discouraging, gloomy, hopeless, dreary ≠ cheerful **2** = exposed, empty, bare, barren, desolate, windswept, weather-beaten, unsheltered ≠ sheltered **3** = stormy, severe, rough, harsh, tempestuous, intemperate

bleed 1 = lose blood, flow, gush, spurt, shed blood **2** = blend, run, meet, unite, mix, combine, flow, fuse **3** (*Informal*) = extort, milk, squeeze, drain, exhaust, fleece

blend VERB **1** = mix, join, combine, compound, merge, unite, mingle, amalgamate **2** = go well, match, fit, suit, go with, correspond, complement, coordinate **3** = combine, mix, link, integrate, merge, unite, amalgamate • NOUN = mixture, mix, combination, compound, brew, union, synthesis, alloy

bless 1 = sanctify, dedicate, ordain, exalt, anoint, consecrate, hallow ≠ curse **2** = endow, give to, provide for, grant for, favour, grace, bestow to ≠ afflict

blessed = holy, sacred, divine, adored, revered, hallowed, sanctified, beatified

blessing 1 = benefit, help, service, favour, gift, windfall, kindness, good fortune ≠ disadvantage **2** = approval, backing, support, agreement, favour, sanction, permission, leave ≠ disapproval **3** = benediction, grace, dedication, thanksgiving, invocation, commendation, consecration, benison ≠ curse

blight NOUN **1** = curse, suffering, evil, corruption, pollution, plague, hardship, woe ≠ blessing **2** = disease, pest, fungus, mildew, infestation, pestilence, canker • VERB = frustrate, destroy, ruin, crush, mar, dash, wreck, spoil, crool *or* cruel (*Austral. slang*)

blind 1 = sightless, unsighted, unseeing, eyeless, visionless ≠ sighted **2** *often with **to*** = unaware of, unconscious of, ignorant of, indifferent to, insensitive to, oblivious of, unconcerned about, inconsiderate of ≠ aware **3** = unquestioning, prejudiced, wholesale, indiscriminate, uncritical, unreasoning, undiscriminating

blindly 1 = thoughtlessly, carelessly, recklessly, indiscriminately, senselessly,

heedlessly **2** = wildly, aimlessly
blink VERB **1** = flutter, wink, bat **2** = flash, flicker, wink, shimmer, twinkle, glimmer
• PHRASES **on the blink** (*Slang*) = not working (properly), faulty, defective, playing up, out of action, malfunctioning, out of order
bliss **1** = joy, ecstasy, euphoria, rapture, nirvana, felicity, gladness, blissfulness ≠ misery **2** = beatitude, blessedness
blister = sore, boil, swelling, cyst, pimple, carbuncle, pustule
blitz = attack, strike, assault, raid, offensive, onslaught, bombardment, bombing campaign
bloc = group, union, league, alliance, coalition, axis
block NOUN **1** = piece, bar, mass, brick, lump, chunk, hunk, ingot **2** = obstruction, bar, barrier, obstacle, impediment, hindrance
• VERB **1** = obstruct, close, stop, plug, choke, clog, stop up, bung up (*informal*) ≠ clear **2** = obscure, bar, obstruct **3** = shut off, stop, bar, hamper, obstruct
blockade = stoppage, block, barrier, restriction, obstacle, barricade, obstruction, impediment
bloke (*Informal*) = man, person, individual, character (*informal*), guy (*informal*), fellow, chap
blonde *or* **blond** **1** = fair, light, flaxen **2** = fair-haired, golden-haired, tow-headed
blood **1** = lifeblood, gore, vital fluid **2** = family, relations, birth, descent, extraction, ancestry, lineage, kinship
bloodshed = killing, murder, massacre, slaughter, slaying, carnage, butchery, blood-letting
bloody **1** = cruel, fierce, savage, brutal, vicious, ferocious, cut-throat, warlike **2** = bloodstained, raw, bleeding, blood-soaked, blood-spattered
bloom NOUN **1** = flower, bud, blossom **2** = prime, flower, beauty, height, peak, flourishing, heyday, zenith **3** = glow, freshness, lustre, radiance ≠ pallor
• VERB **1** = flower, blossom, open, bud ≠ wither **2** = grow, develop, wax **3** = succeed, flourish, thrive, prosper, fare well ≠ fail
blossom NOUN = flower, bloom, bud, efflorescence, floret
• VERB **1** = bloom, grow, develop, mature **2** = succeed, progress, thrive, flourish, prosper **3** = flower, bloom, bud
blow[1] VERB **1** = move, carry, drive, sweep, fling, buffet, waft **2** = be carried, flutter **3** = exhale, breathe, pant, puff **4** = play, sound, pipe, trumpet, blare, toot
• PHRASES **blow something up** **1** = explode, bomb, blast, detonate, blow sky-high **2** = inflate, pump up, fill, expand, swell, enlarge, puff up, distend **3** = magnify, increase, extend, expand, widen, broaden, amplify ◆ **blow up** **1** = explode, burst, shatter, erupt, detonate **2** (*Informal*) = lose your temper, rage, erupt, see red (*informal*), become angry, hit the roof (*informal*), fly off the handle (*informal*), go crook (*Austral. & N.Z. slang*), blow your top
blow[2] **1** = knock, stroke, punch, bang, sock (*slang*), smack, thump, clout (*informal*) **2** = setback, shock, disaster, reverse, disappointment, catastrophe, misfortune, bombshell
bludge (*Austral. & N.Z. informal*) = slack, skive (*Brit. informal*), idle, shirk
blue ADJECTIVE **1** = depressed, low, sad, unhappy, melancholy, dejected, despondent, downcast ≠ happy **2** = smutty, obscene, indecent, lewd, risqué, X-rated (*informal*) ≠ respectable
• PLURAL NOUN = depression, gloom, melancholy, unhappiness, low spirits, the dumps (*informal*), doldrums
blueprint **1** = scheme, plan, design, system, programme, proposal, strategy, pattern **2** = plan, scheme, pattern, draft, outline, sketch
bluff[1] NOUN = deception, fraud, sham, pretence, deceit, bravado, bluster, humbug
• VERB = deceive, trick, fool, pretend, cheat, con, fake, mislead
bluff[2] NOUN = precipice, bank, peak, cliff, ridge, crag, escarpment, promontory
• ADJECTIVE = hearty, open, blunt, outspoken, genial, ebullient, jovial, plain-spoken ≠ tactful
blunder NOUN = mistake, slip, fault, error, oversight, gaffe, slip-up (*informal*), indiscretion ≠ correctness
• VERB **1** = make a mistake, blow it (*slang*), err, slip up (*informal*), foul up, put your foot in it (*informal*) ≠ be correct **2** = stumble, fall, reel, stagger, lurch

blunt ADJECTIVE **1** = frank, forthright, straightforward, rude, outspoken, bluff, brusque, plain-spoken ≠ tactful **2** = dull, rounded, dulled, edgeless, unsharpened ≠ sharp
• VERB = dull, weaken, soften, numb, dampen, water down, deaden, take the edge off ≠ stimulate

blur NOUN = haze, confusion, fog, obscurity, indistinctness
• VERB **1** = become indistinct, become vague, become hazy, become fuzzy **2** = obscure, make indistinct, mask, obfuscate, make vague, make hazy

blush VERB = turn red, colour, glow, flush, redden, go red (as a beetroot), turn scarlet ≠ turn pale
• NOUN = reddening, colour, glow, flush, pink tinge, rosiness, ruddiness, rosy tint

board NOUN **1** = plank, panel, timber, slat, piece of timber **2** = council, directors, committee, congress, advisers, panel, assembly, trustees **3** = meals, provisions, victuals, daily meals
• VERB = get on, enter, mount, embark ≠ get off

boast VERB **1** = brag, crow, vaunt, talk big (*slang*), blow your own trumpet, show off, be proud of, congratulate yourself on, skite (*Austral. & N.Z. informal*) ≠ cover up **2** = possess, exhibit
• NOUN = bragging ≠ disclaimer

bob = bounce, duck, hop, oscillate

bodily = physical, material, actual, substantial, tangible, corporal, carnal, corporeal

body **1** = physique, build, form, figure, shape, frame, constitution **2** = torso, trunk **3** = corpse, dead body, remains, stiff (*slang*), carcass, cadaver **4** = organization, company, group, society, association, band, congress, institution **5** = main part, matter, material, mass, substance, bulk, essence **6** = expanse, mass, sweep

RELATED WORDS
adjectives: corporal, physical

bog = marsh, swamp, slough, wetlands, fen, mire, quagmire, morass, pakihi (*N.Z.*)

bogey = bugbear, bête noire, horror, nightmare, bugaboo

bogus = fake, false, artificial, forged, imitation, sham, fraudulent, counterfeit ≠ genuine

Bohemian ADJECTIVE *often not cap.* = unconventional, alternative, artistic, unorthodox, arty (*informal*), offbeat, left bank, nonconformist ≠ conventional
• NOUN *often not cap.* = nonconformist, rebel, radical, eccentric, maverick, hippy, dropout, individualist

boil[1] = simmer, bubble, foam, seethe, fizz, froth, effervesce

boil[2] = pustule, gathering, swelling, blister, carbuncle

bold **1** = fearless, enterprising, brave, daring, heroic, adventurous, courageous, audacious ≠ timid **2** = impudent, forward, confident, rude, cheeky, brazen, shameless, insolent ≠ shy

bolster = support, help, boost, strengthen, reinforce, shore up, augment

bolt NOUN **1** = pin, rod, peg, rivet **2** = bar, catch, lock, latch, fastener, sliding bar
• VERB **1** = lock, close, bar, secure, fasten, latch **2** = dash, fly **3** = gobble, stuff, wolf, cram, gorge, devour, gulp, guzzle

bomb NOUN = explosive, mine, shell, missile, device, rocket, grenade, torpedo
• VERB = blow up, attack, destroy, assault, shell, blitz, bombard, torpedo

bombard **1** = attack, assault, besiege, beset, assail **2** = bomb, shell, blitz, open fire, strafe, fire upon

bombardment = bombing, attack, assault, shelling, blitz, barrage, fusillade

bond NOUN **1** = tie, union, coupling, link, association, relation, connection, alliance **2** = fastening, tie, chain, cord, shackle, fetter, manacle **3** = agreement, word, promise, contract, guarantee, pledge, obligation, covenant
• VERB **1** = form friendships, connect **2** = fix, hold, bind, connect, glue, stick, paste, fasten

bonus **1** = extra, prize, gift, reward, premium, dividend **2** = advantage, benefit, gain, extra, plus, asset, icing on the cake

book NOUN **1** = work, title, volume, publication, tract, tome **2** = notebook, album, journal, diary, pad, notepad, exercise book, jotter
• VERB = reserve, schedule, engage, organize, charter, arrange for, make reservations
• PHRASES **book in** = register, enter

booklet = brochure, leaflet, hand-out, pamphlet, folder, mailshot, handbill

boom NOUN **1** = expansion, increase,

development, growth, jump, boost, improvement, upsurge ≠ decline 2 = bang, crash, clash, blast, burst, explosion, roar, thunder
• VERB 1 = increase, flourish, grow, develop, expand, strengthen, swell, thrive ≠ fall 2 = bang, roll, crash, blast, explode, roar, thunder, rumble

boon 1 = benefit, blessing, godsend, gift 2 = gift, favour

boost VERB = increase, develop, raise, expand, add to, heighten, enlarge, amplify ≠ decrease
• NOUN 1 = rise, increase, jump, addition, improvement, expansion, upsurge, upturn ≠ fall 2 = encouragement, help

boot = kick, punt, put the boot in(to) (*slang*), drop-kick

border NOUN 1 = frontier, line, limit, bounds, boundary, perimeter, borderline 2 = edge, margin, verge, rim
• VERB = edge, bound, decorate, trim, fringe, rim, hem

bore¹ = drill, mine, sink, tunnel, pierce, penetrate, burrow, puncture

bore² VERB = tire, fatigue, weary, wear out, jade, be tedious, pall on, send to sleep ≠ excite
• NOUN = nuisance, pain (*informal*), yawn (*informal*), anorak (*informal*)

bored = fed up, tired, wearied, uninterested, sick and tired (*informal*), listless, brassed off (*Brit. slang*), hoha (*N.Z.*)

boredom = tedium, apathy, weariness, monotony, sameness, ennui, flatness, world-weariness ≠ excitement

boring = uninteresting, dull, tedious, tiresome, monotonous, flat, humdrum, mind-numbing

borrow 1 = take on loan, touch (someone) for (*slang*), scrounge (*informal*), cadge, use temporarily ≠ lend 2 = steal, take, copy, adopt, pinch (*informal*)

boss NOUN = manager, head, leader, director, chief, master, employer, supervisor, baas (*S. African*)
•PHRASES **boss someone around** (*Informal*) = order around, dominate, bully, oppress, push around (*slang*)

bother VERB 1 = trouble, concern, worry, alarm, disturb, disconcert, perturb 2 = pester, plague, harass, hassle (*informal*), inconvenience ≠ help
• NOUN = trouble, problem, worry, difficulty, fuss, irritation, hassle (*informal*), nuisance, uphill (*S. African*) ≠ help

bottle shop (*Austral. & N.Z.*) = off-licence (*Brit.*), liquor store (*U.S. & Canad.*), bottle store (*S. African*), package store (*U.S. & Canad.*), offie *or* offy (*Brit. informal*)

bottle store (*S. African*) = off-licence (*Brit.*), liquor store (*U.S. & Canad.*), bottle shop (*Austral. & N.Z.*), package store (*U.S. & Canad.*), offie *or* offy (*Brit. informal*)

bottom NOUN 1 = lowest part, base, foot, bed, floor, foundation, depths ≠ top 2 = underside, sole, underneath, lower side 3 = buttocks, behind (*informal*), rear, backside, rump, seat, posterior
• ADJECTIVE = lowest, last ≠ higher

bounce VERB 1 = rebound, recoil, ricochet 2 = bound, spring, jump, leap, skip, gambol
• NOUN 1 = springiness, give, spring, resilience, elasticity, recoil 2 (*Informal*) = life, go (*informal*), energy, zip (*informal*), vigour, exuberance, dynamism, vivacity

bound¹ 1 = compelled, obliged, forced, committed, pledged, constrained, beholden, duty-bound 2 = tied, fixed, secured, attached, tied up, fastened, pinioned 3 = certain, sure, fated, doomed, destined

bound² 1 = surround, confine, enclose, encircle, hem in, demarcate 2 = limit, restrict, confine, restrain, circumscribe

bound³ VERB = leap, bob, spring, jump, bounce, skip, vault
• NOUN = leap, bob, spring, jump, bounce, hurdle, skip, vault

boundary 1 = frontier, edge, border, barrier, margin, brink 2 = edges, limits, fringes, extremities 3 = dividing line, borderline

bounds = boundary, limit, edge, border, confine, verge, rim, perimeter

bouquet 1 = bunch of flowers, spray, garland, wreath, posy, buttonhole, corsage, nosegay 2 = aroma, smell, scent, perfume, fragrance, savour, odour, redolence

bourgeois = middle-class, traditional, conventional, materialistic, hidebound

bout 1 = period, term, fit, spell, turn, interval 2 = round, series, session, cycle, sequence, stint 3 = fight, match, competition, struggle, contest, set-to, encounter, engagement

bow[1] VERB = bend, bob, nod, stoop, droop, genuflect
• NOUN = bending, bob, nod, obeisance, kowtow, genuflection
bow[2] (*Nautical*) = prow, head, stem, fore, beak
bowels 1 = guts, insides (*informal*), intestines, innards (*informal*), entrails, viscera, vitals 2 = depths, hold, inside, deep, interior, core, belly
bowl[1] = basin, plate, dish, vessel
bowl[2] = throw, hurl, launch, cast, pitch, toss, fling, chuck (*informal*)
box[1] NOUN = container, case, chest, trunk, pack, package, carton, casket
• VERB = pack, package, wrap, encase, bundle up
box[2] = fight, spar, exchange blows
boxer = fighter, pugilist, prizefighter
boy = lad, kid (*informal*), youth, fellow, youngster, schoolboy, junior, stripling
boycott = embargo, reject, snub, black ≠ support
boyfriend = sweetheart, man, lover, beloved, admirer, suitor, beau, date
brace VERB 1 = steady, support, secure, stabilize 2 = support, strengthen, steady, reinforce, bolster, fortify, buttress
• NOUN = support, stay, prop, bolster, bracket, reinforcement, strut, truss
bracing = refreshing, fresh, stimulating, crisp, brisk, exhilarating, invigorating ≠ tiring
brain = intelligence, understanding, sense, intellect
brake NOUN = control, check, curb, restraint, constraint, rein
• VERB = slow, decelerate, reduce speed
branch 1 = bough, shoot, arm, spray, limb, sprig, offshoot 2 = office, department, unit, wing, chapter, bureau 3 = division, part, section, subdivision, subsection 4 = discipline, section, subdivision
brand NOUN 1 = trademark 2 = label, mark, sign, stamp, symbol, logo, trademark, marker
• VERB 1 = stigmatize, mark, expose, denounce, disgrace, discredit, censure 2 = mark, burn, label, stamp, scar
brash = bold, rude, cocky, pushy (*informal*), brazen, impertinent, insolent, impudent ≠ timid
brave ADJECTIVE = courageous, daring, bold, heroic, adventurous, fearless, resolute, audacious ≠ timid
• VERB = confront, face, suffer, tackle, endure, defy, withstand, stand up to ≠ give in to
bravery = courage, nerve, daring, pluck, spirit, fortitude, heroism, mettle ≠ cowardice
brawl NOUN = fight, clash, fray, skirmish, scuffle, punch-up (*Brit. informal*), fracas, altercation, biffo (*Austral. slang*)
• VERB = fight, scrap (*informal*), wrestle, tussle, scuffle
breach 1 = nonobservance, abuse, violation, infringement, trespass, transgression, contravention, infraction ≠ compliance 2 = opening, crack, split, gap, rift, rupture, cleft, fissure
bread 1 = food, fare, kai (*N.Z. informal*), nourishment, sustenance 2 (*Slang*) = money, cash, dough (*slang*)
breadth 1 = width, spread, span, latitude, broadness, wideness 2 = extent, range, scale, scope, compass, expanse
break VERB 1 = shatter, separate, destroy, crack, snap, smash, crush, fragment ≠ repair 2 = fracture, crack, smash 3 = burst, tear, split 4 = disobey, breach, defy, violate, disregard, flout, infringe, contravene ≠ obey 5 = stop, cut, suspend, interrupt, cut short, discontinue 6 = disturb, interrupt 7 = end, stop, cut, drop, give up, abandon, suspend, interrupt 8 = weaken, undermine, tame, subdue, demoralize, dispirit 9 = be revealed, be published, be announced, be made public, be proclaimed, be let out 10 = reveal, tell, announce, declare, disclose, proclaim, make known 11 = beat, top, better, exceed, go beyond, excel, surpass, outstrip
• NOUN 1 = fracture, opening, tear, hole, split, crack, gap, fissure 2 = interval, pause, interlude, intermission 3 = holiday, leave, vacation, time off, recess, awayday 4 (*Informal*) = stroke of luck, chance, opportunity, advantage, fortune, opening
• PHRASES **break off** = stop talking, pause ◆ **break out** = begin, start, happen, occur, arise, set in, commence, spring up ◆ **break something off** = detach, separate, divide, cut off, pull off, sever, part, remove ◆ **break something up** = stop, end, suspend, dismantle, terminate, disband, diffuse ◆ **break up** 1 = finish, be

suspended, adjourn **2** = split up, separate, part, divorce

breakdown = collapse

break-in = burglary, robbery, breaking and entering

breakthrough = development, advance, progress, discovery, find, invention, step forward, leap forwards

breast = bosom(s), front, chest, bust

breath = inhalation, breathing, pant, gasp, gulp, wheeze, exhalation, respiration

breathe 1 = inhale and exhale, pant, gasp, puff, gulp, wheeze, respire, draw in breath **2** = whisper, sigh, murmur

breathless 1 = out of breath, panting, gasping, gulping, wheezing, short-winded **2** = excited, curious, eager, enthusiastic, impatient, on tenterhooks, in suspense

breathtaking = amazing, exciting, stunning (*informal*), impressive, thrilling, magnificent, astonishing, sensational

breed NOUN **1** = variety, race, stock, type, species, strain, pedigree **2** = kind, sort, type, variety, brand, stamp

• VERB **1** = rear, tend, keep, raise, maintain, farm, look after, care for **2** = reproduce, multiply, propagate, procreate, produce offspring, bear young, bring forth young **3** = produce, cause, create, generate, bring about, arouse, give rise to, stir up

breeding = refinement, culture, taste, manners, polish, courtesy, sophistication, cultivation

breeze NOUN = light wind, air, draught, gust, waft, zephyr, breath of wind, current of air

• VERB = sweep, move briskly, pass, sail, hurry, glide, flit

brew VERB **1** = boil, make, soak, steep, stew, infuse (*tea*) **2** = make, ferment **3** = start, develop, gather, foment **4** = develop, form, gather, foment

• NOUN = drink, preparation, mixture, blend, liquor, beverage, infusion, concoction

bribe NOUN = inducement, pay-off (*informal*), sweetener (*slang*), kickback (*U.S.*), backhander (*slang*), enticement, allurement

• VERB = buy off, reward, pay off (*informal*), corrupt, suborn, grease the palm *or* hand of (*slang*)

bribery = corruption, inducement, buying off, payola (*informal*), palm-greasing (*slang*)

bridge NOUN = arch, span, viaduct, flyover, overpass

• VERB **1** = span, cross **2** = reconcile, resolve

brief ADJECTIVE = short, quick, fleeting, swift, short-lived, momentary, ephemeral, transitory ≠ long

• VERB = inform, prime, prepare, advise, fill in (*informal*), instruct, put in the picture (*informal*), keep (someone) posted

• NOUN = summary, résumé, outline, sketch, abstract, digest, epitome, rundown

briefing 1 = conference, priming **2** = instructions, information, priming, directions, preparation, guidance, rundown

briefly 1 = quickly, shortly, hastily, momentarily, hurriedly **2** = in outline, in brief, in a nutshell, concisely

brigade 1 = corps, company, force, unit, division, troop, squad, team **2** = group, band, squad, organization

bright 1 = vivid, rich, brilliant, glowing, colourful **2** = shining, glowing, dazzling, gleaming, shimmering, radiant, luminous, lustrous **3** = intelligent, smart, clever, aware, sharp, enlightened, astute, wide-awake ≠ stupid **4** = clever, smart, ingenious **5** = sunny, clear, fair, pleasant, lucid, cloudless, unclouded ≠ cloudy

brighten 1 = light up, shine, glow, gleam, lighten ≠ dim **2** = enliven, animate, make brighter, vitalize **3** = become brighter, light up, glow, gleam

brilliance *or* **brilliancy 1** = cleverness, talent, wisdom, distinction, genius, excellence, greatness, inventiveness ≠ stupidity **2** = brightness, intensity, sparkle, dazzle, lustre, radiance, luminosity, vividness ≠ darkness **3** = splendour, glamour, grandeur, magnificence, éclat, illustriousness

brilliant 1 = intelligent, sharp, intellectual, clever, profound, penetrating, inventive, perspicacious ≠ stupid **2** = expert, masterly, talented, gifted, accomplished ≠ untalented **3** = splendid, famous, celebrated, outstanding, superb, magnificent, glorious, notable **4** = bright, shining, intense, sparkling, glittering, dazzling, vivid, radiant ≠ dark

brim NOUN = rim, edge, border, lip, margin, verge, brink

• VERB **1** = be full, spill, well over, run over

2 = fill, well over, fill up, overflow
bring VERB 1 = fetch, take, carry, bear, transfer, deliver, transport, convey 2 = take, guide, conduct, escort 3 = cause, produce, create, effect, occasion, result in, contribute to, inflict
• PHRASES **bring someone up** = rear, raise, support, train, develop, teach, breed, foster ◆ **bring something about** = cause, produce, create, effect, achieve, generate, accomplish, give rise to ◆ **bring something off** = accomplish, achieve, perform, succeed, execute, pull off, carry off ◆ **bring something up** = mention, raise, introduce, point out, refer to, allude to, broach
brink = edge, limit, border, lip, margin, boundary, skirt, frontier
brisk 1 = quick, lively, energetic, active, vigorous, bustling, sprightly, spry ≠ slow 2 = short, brief, blunt, abrupt, terse, gruff, brusque, monosyllabic
briskly = quickly, smartly, promptly, rapidly, readily, actively, efficiently, energetically
bristle NOUN = hair, spine, thorn, whisker, barb, stubble, prickle
• VERB 1 = stand up, rise, stand on end 2 = be angry, rage, seethe, flare up, bridle, see red
brittle = fragile, delicate, crisp, crumbling, frail, crumbly, breakable, friable ≠ tough
broad 1 = wide, large, ample, generous, expansive 2 = large, huge, vast, extensive, ample, spacious, expansive, roomy ≠ narrow 3 = full, general, comprehensive, complete, wide, sweeping, wide-ranging, thorough 4 = universal, general, common, wide, sweeping, worldwide, widespread, wide-ranging 5 = general, loose, vague, approximate, indefinite, ill-defined, inexact, unspecific
broadcast NOUN = transmission, show, programme, telecast
• VERB 1 = transmit, show, air, radio, cable, beam, send out, relay 2 = make public, report, announce, publish, spread, advertise, proclaim, circulate
broaden = expand, increase, develop, spread, extend, stretch, swell, supplement ≠ restrict
brochure = booklet, advertisement, leaflet, hand-out, circular, pamphlet, folder, mailshot
broekies (*S. African informal*) = underpants, pants, briefs, drawers, knickers, panties, boxer shorts, Y-fronts®, underdaks (*Austral. slang*)
broke (*Informal*) = penniless, short, ruined, bust (*informal*), bankrupt, impoverished, in the red, insolvent ≠ rich
broken 1 = interrupted, incomplete, erratic, intermittent, fragmentary, spasmodic, discontinuous 2 = imperfect, halting, hesitating, stammering, disjointed 3 = smashed, burst, shattered, fragmented, fractured, severed, ruptured, separated 4 = defective, not working, imperfect, out of order, on the blink (*slang*), kaput (*informal*)
broker = dealer, agent, trader, supplier, merchant, negotiator, mediator, intermediary
bronze = reddish-brown, copper, tan, rust, chestnut, brownish
brood NOUN 1 = offspring, issue, clutch, litter, progeny 2 = children, family, nearest and dearest, flesh and blood, ainga (*N.Z.*)
• VERB = think, obsess, muse, ponder, agonize, mull over, mope, ruminate
brook = stream, burn (*Scot. & Northern English*), rivulet, beck, watercourse, rill
brother 1 = male sibling 2 = monk, cleric, friar, religious
RELATED WORD
adjective: fraternal
brotherly = fraternal, friendly, neighbourly, sympathetic, affectionate, benevolent, kind, amicable
brown ADJECTIVE 1 = brunette, bay, coffee, chocolate, chestnut, hazel, dun, auburn 2 = tanned, bronze, tan, sunburnt
• VERB = fry, cook, grill, sear, sauté
browse 1 = skim, scan, glance at, survey, look through, look round, dip into, leaf through 2 = graze, eat, feed, nibble
bruise NOUN = discoloration, mark, injury, blemish, contusion
• VERB 1 = hurt, injure, mark 2 = damage, mark, mar, discolour
brush[1] NOUN 1 = broom, sweeper, besom 2 = conflict, clash, confrontation, skirmish, tussle 3 = encounter, meeting, confrontation, rendezvous
• VERB 1 = clean, wash, polish, buff 2 = touch, sweep, kiss, stroke, glance, flick, scrape, graze
• PHRASES **brush someone off**

(*Slang*) = ignore, reject, dismiss, snub, disregard, scorn, disdain, spurn ◆ **brush something up** *or* **brush up on something** = revise, study, go over, cram, polish up, read up on, relearn, bone up on (*informal*)

brush² = shrubs, bushes, scrub, undergrowth, thicket, copse, brushwood

brutal **1** = cruel, savage, vicious, ruthless, callous, sadistic, heartless, inhuman ≠ kind **2** = harsh, tough, severe, rough, rude, indifferent, insensitive, callous ≠ sensitive

brutality = cruelty, atrocity, ferocity, savagery, ruthlessness, barbarism, inhumanity, viciousness

bubble NOUN = air ball, drop, bead, blister, blob, droplet, globule
• VERB **1** = boil, seethe **2** = foam, fizz, froth, percolate, effervesce **3** = gurgle, splash, murmur, trickle, ripple, babble, burble, lap

bubbly **1** = lively, happy, excited, animated, merry, bouncy, elated, sparky **2** = frothy, sparkling, fizzy, effervescent, carbonated, foamy

buckle NOUN = fastener, catch, clip, clasp, hasp
• VERB **1** = fasten, close, secure, hook, clasp **2** = distort, bend, warp, crumple, contort **3** = collapse, bend, twist, fold, give way, subside, cave in, crumple

bud NOUN = shoot, branch, sprout, sprig, offshoot
• VERB = develop, grow, shoot, sprout, burgeon, burst forth

budding = developing, beginning, growing, promising, potential, burgeoning, fledgling, embryonic

budge **1** = move, stir **2** = dislodge, move, push, transfer, shift, stir

budget NOUN = allowance, means, funds, income, finances, resources, allocation
• VERB = plan, estimate, allocate, cost, ration, apportion

buff¹ ADJECTIVE = fawn, tan, beige, yellowish, straw-coloured, sand-coloured, yellowish-brown
• VERB = polish, smooth, brush, shine, rub, wax, brighten, burnish

buff² (*Informal*) = expert, fan, addict, enthusiast, admirer, devotee, connoisseur, aficionado, fundi (*S. African*)

buffer = safeguard, screen, shield, cushion, intermediary, bulwark

buffet **1** = smorgasbord **2** = snack bar, café, cafeteria, brasserie, refreshment counter

bug NOUN **1** (*Informal*) = illness, disease, virus, infection, disorder, sickness, ailment, affliction **2** = fault, error, defect, flaw, glitch, gremlin
• VERB **1** = tap, eavesdrop, listen in on **2** (*Informal*) = annoy, bother, disturb, irritate, hassle (*informal*), pester, vex, get on your nerves (*informal*)

build VERB = construct, make, raise, put up, assemble, erect, fabricate, form ≠ demolish
• NOUN = physique, form, body, figure, shape, structure, frame

building = structure, house, construction, dwelling, erection, edifice, domicile

build-up = increase, development, growth, expansion, accumulation, enlargement, escalation

bulge VERB **1** = swell out, project, expand, stick out, protrude, puff out, distend **2** = stick out, stand out, protrude
• NOUN **1** = lump, swelling, bump, projection, hump, protuberance, protrusion ≠ hollow **2** = increase, rise, boost, surge, intensification

bulk **1** = size, volume, dimensions, magnitude, substance, immensity, largeness **2** = weight, size, mass, heaviness, poundage **3** = majority, mass, most, body, best part, lion's share, better part, preponderance

bullet = projectile, ball, shot, missile, slug, pellet

bulletin = report, account, statement, message, communication, announcement, dispatch, communiqué

bully NOUN = persecutor, tough, oppressor, tormentor, bully boy, browbeater, coercer, ruffian
• VERB **1** = persecute, intimidate, torment, oppress, pick on, victimize, terrorize, push around (*slang*) **2** = force, coerce, browbeat, hector, domineer

bump VERB **1** = knock, hit, strike, crash, smash, slam, bang **2** = jerk, shake, bounce, rattle, jog, lurch, jolt
• NOUN **1** = knock, blow, impact, collision, thump **2** = thud, crash, knock, bang, smack, thump **3** = lump, swelling, bulge, hump, nodule, protuberance, contusion

bumper = exceptional, excellent, exo (*Austral. slang*), massive, jumbo (*informal*),

abundant, whopping (*informal*), bountiful
bunch NOUN **1** = group, band, crowd, party, team, gathering, gang, flock **2** = bouquet, sheaf **3** = cluster, clump
• PHRASES **bunch together** *or* **up** = group, mass, collect, assemble, cluster, huddle
bundle NOUN = bunch, group, collection, mass, pile, stack, heap, batch
• VERB = push, thrust, shove, throw, rush, hurry, jostle, hustle
• PHRASES **bundle someone up** = wrap up, swathe
bungle = mess up, blow (*slang*), ruin, spoil, blunder, botch, make a mess of, muff, crool *or* cruel (*Austral. slang*) ≠ accomplish
bungling = incompetent, blundering, clumsy, inept, cack-handed (*informal*), maladroit, ham-fisted (*informal*), unco (*Austral. slang*)
bunk *or* **bunkum** (*Informal*) = nonsense, rubbish, garbage (*informal*), hot air (*informal*), twaddle, moonshine, baloney (*informal*), hogwash, bizzo (*Austral. slang*), bull's wool (*Austral. & N.Z. slang*), kak (*S. African taboo slang*)
buoy = float, guide, signal, marker, beacon
buoyant ADJECTIVE = cheerful, happy, upbeat (*informal*), carefree, jaunty, chirpy (*informal*), light-hearted ≠ gloomy
• ADJECTIVE = floating, light
burden NOUN **1** = trouble, worry, weight, responsibility, strain, affliction, onus, millstone **2** = load, weight, cargo, freight, consignment, encumbrance
• VERB = weigh down, worry, load, tax, bother, handicap, oppress, inconvenience
bureau **1** = agency **2** = office, department, section, branch, station, unit, division, subdivision **3** = desk, writing desk
bureaucracy **1** = government, officials, authorities, administration, the system, civil service, corridors of power **2** = red tape, regulations, officialdom
bureaucrat = official, officer, administrator, civil servant, public servant, functionary, mandarin
burglar = housebreaker, thief, robber, pilferer, filcher, cat burglar, sneak thief
burglary = breaking and entering, housebreaking, break-in
burial = funeral, interment, obsequies, entombment, exequies
burn **1** = be on fire, blaze, be ablaze, smoke, flame, glow, flare, go up in flames **2** = set on fire, light, ignite, kindle, incinerate **3** = scorch, toast, sear, char, singe **4** = be passionate, be aroused, be inflamed **5** = seethe, fume, be angry, simmer, smoulder
burning **1** = intense, passionate, eager, ardent, fervent, impassioned, vehement ≠ mild **2** = blazing, fiery, smouldering, glowing **3** = flashing, blazing, flaming, gleaming, fiery **4** = crucial, important, pressing, significant, essential, vital, critical, acute
burrow NOUN = hole, shelter, tunnel, den, lair, retreat
• VERB **1** = dig, tunnel, excavate **2** = delve, search, probe, ferret, rummage, forage, fossick (*Austral. & N.Z.*)
burst VERB **1** = explode, blow up, break, split, crack, shatter, puncture, rupture **2** = rush, run, break, break out, erupt, spout, gush forth **3** = barge, charge, rush, shove
• NOUN **1** = rush, surge, outbreak, outburst, spate, gush, torrent, spurt **2** = explosion, crack, blast, bang, discharge
• ADJECTIVE = ruptured, flat, punctured, split, rent
bury **1** = inter, lay to rest, entomb, consign to the grave, inhume ≠ dig up **2** = hide, cover, conceal, stash (*informal*), secrete, stow away ≠ uncover **3** = sink, embed, immerse, enfold **4** = forget
bush NOUN = shrub, plant, hedge, thicket, shrubbery
• PHRASES **the bush** = the wilds, brush, scrub, woodland, backwoods, scrubland
business **1** = trade, selling, industry, manufacturing, commerce, dealings **2** = establishment, company, firm, concern, organization, corporation, venture, enterprise **3** = profession, work, job, line, trade, career, function, employment **4** = matter, issue, subject, point, problem, responsibility, task, duty **5** = concern, affair
businessman = executive, director, manager, merchant, capitalist, administrator, entrepreneur, tycoon
bust[1] = bosom, breasts, chest, front
bust[2] (*Informal*) VERB **1** = break, smash, split, burst, shatter, fracture, rupture **2** = arrest, catch, raid
• PHRASES **go bust** = go bankrupt, fail, be

ruined, become insolvent

bustle VERB = hurry, rush, fuss, hasten, scuttle, scurry, scamper ≠ idle
• NOUN = activity, to-do, stir, excitement, fuss, flurry, commotion, ado ≠ inactivity

bustling = busy, full, crowded, active, lively, buzzing, humming, swarming

busy ADJECTIVE 1 = active, industrious, rushed off your feet ≠ idle 2 = occupied with, working, engaged in, on duty, employed in, hard at work ≠ unoccupied 3 = hectic, full, exacting, energetic
•PHRASES **busy yourself** = occupy yourself, be engrossed, immerse yourself, involve yourself, absorb yourself, employ yourself, engage yourself

but CONJUNCTION = however, still, yet, nevertheless
• PREPOSITION = except (for), save, bar, barring, excepting, excluding, with the exception of
• ADVERB = only, just, simply, merely

butcher NOUN = murderer, killer, slaughterer, slayer, destroyer, executioner, cut-throat, exterminator
• VERB 1 = slaughter, prepare, carve, cut up, dress, cut, clean, joint 2 = kill, slaughter, massacre, destroy, cut down, assassinate, slay, liquidate

butt¹ 1 = end, handle, shaft, stock, shank, hilt, haft 2 = stub, tip, leftover, fag end (*informal*)

butt² = target, victim, dupe, laughing stock, Aunt Sally

butt³ VERB = knock, push, bump, thrust, ram, shove, poke, prod
•PHRASES **butt in** 1 = interfere, meddle, intrude, heckle, barge in (*informal*), stick your nose in, put your oar in 2 = interrupt, cut in, break in, chip in (*informal*)

butt⁴ = cask, barrel

butterfly

RELATED WORDS
young: caterpillar, chrysalis *or* chrysalid
enthusiast: lepidopterist

buy VERB = purchase, get, pay for, obtain, acquire, invest in, shop for, procure ≠ sell
• NOUN = purchase, deal, bargain, acquisition, steal (*informal*), snip (*informal*), giveaway

by PREPOSITION 1 = through, through the agency of 2 = via, over, by way of 3 = near, past, along, close to, closest to, neighbouring, next to, beside
• ADVERB = nearby, close, handy, at hand, within reach

bypass 1 = get round, avoid 2 = go round, circumvent, depart from, deviate from, pass round, detour round ≠ cross

C

cab = taxi, minicab, taxicab, hackney carriage

cabin 1 = room, berth, quarters, compartment 2 = hut, shed, cottage, lodge, shack, chalet, shanty, whare (*N.Z.*)

cabinet 1 = cupboard, case, locker, dresser, closet, press, chiffonier 2 *often cap.* = council, committee, administration, ministry, assembly, board

cad (*Old-fashioned, informal*) = scoundrel (*slang*), rat (*informal*), bounder (*Brit. old-fashioned slang*), rotter (*slang, chiefly Brit.*), heel

café = snack bar, restaurant, cafeteria, coffee shop, brasserie, coffee bar, tearoom, lunchroom

cage = enclosure, pen, coop, hutch, pound

cake = block, bar, slab, lump, cube, loaf, mass

calculated = deliberate, planned, considered, intended, intentional, designed, aimed, purposeful ≠ unplanned

calculating = scheming, sharp, shrewd, cunning, sly, devious, manipulative, crafty ≠ direct

calculation 1 = computation, working out, reckoning, estimate, forecast, judgment, result, answer 2 = planning, intention, deliberation, foresight, contrivance, forethought, premeditation

calibre *or* (*U.S.*) **caliber** 1 = worth, quality, ability, talent, capacity, merit, distinction, stature 2 = standard, level, quality, grade 3 = diameter, bore, gauge, measure

call VERB 1 = name, entitle, dub, designate, term, style, label, describe as 2 = cry, shout,

scream, yell, whoop ≠ whisper **3** = phone, telephone, ring (up) (*informal*, *chiefly Brit.*) **4** = hail, summon **5** = summon, gather, rally, assemble, muster, convene ≠ dismiss **6** = waken, arouse, rouse
• **NOUN 1** = visit **2** = request, order, demand, appeal, notice, command, invitation, plea **3** (usually used in a negative construction) = need, cause, reason, grounds, occasion, excuse, justification **4** = attraction, pull (*informal*), appeal, lure, allure, magnetism **5** = cry, shout, scream, yell, whoop ≠ whisper
• **PHRASES call for someone** = fetch, pick up, collect ◆ **call for something 1** = demand, order, request, insist on, cry out for **2** = require, need, involve, demand, occasion, entail, necessitate

calling = profession, trade, career, mission, vocation, life's work

calm ADJECTIVE 1 = cool, relaxed, composed, sedate, collected, dispassionate, unemotional, self-possessed ≠ excited **2** = still, quiet, smooth, mild, serene, tranquil, balmy, windless ≠ rough
• **NOUN 1** = peacefulness, peace, serenity **2** = stillness, peace, quiet, hush, serenity, tranquillity, repose, peacefulness **3** = peace, calmness ≠ disturbance
• **VERB 1** = soothe, quiet, relax, appease, still, allay, assuage, quieten ≠ excite **2** = placate, hush, pacify, mollify ≠ aggravate

camouflage NOUN 1 = protective colouring **2** = disguise, cover, screen, blind, mask, cloak, masquerade, subterfuge
• **VERB** = disguise, cover, screen, hide, mask, conceal, obscure, veil ≠ reveal

camp[1] = camp site, tents, encampment, bivouac, camping ground

camp[2] (*Informal*) = affected, mannered, artificial, posturing, ostentatious, effeminate

campaign 1 = drive, appeal, movement, push (*informal*), offensive, crusade **2** = operation, drive, attack, movement, push, offensive, expedition, crusade

canal = waterway, channel, passage, conduit, duct, watercourse

cancel VERB 1 = call off, drop, forget about **2** = annul, abolish, repeal, abort, do away with, revoke, eliminate
• **PHRASES cancel something out** = counterbalance, offset, make up for, compensate for, neutralize, nullify, balance out

cancellation 1 = abandonment **2** = annulment, abolition, repeal, elimination, revocation

cancer 1 = growth, tumour, malignancy **2** = evil, corruption, sickness, pestilence

candidate = contender, competitor, applicant, nominee, entrant, claimant, contestant, runner

cannabis = marijuana, pot (*slang*), dope (*slang*), grass (*slang*), hemp, dagga (*S. African*)

cannon = gun, big gun, field gun, mortar

canon 1 = rule, standard, principle, regulation, formula, criterion, dictate, statute **2** = list, index, catalogue, roll

canopy = awning, covering, shade, sunshade

cap 1 (*Informal*) = beat, top, better, exceed, eclipse, surpass, transcend, outstrip **2** = top, crown **3** = complete, crown

capability = ability, means, power, potential, capacity, qualification(s), competence, proficiency ≠ inability

capable 1 = able ≠ incapable **2** = accomplished, qualified, talented, gifted, efficient, competent, proficient ≠ incompetent

capacity 1 = ability, facility, gift, genius, capability, aptitude, aptness, competence *or* competency **2** = size, room, range, space, volume, extent, dimensions, scope **3** = function, position, role, post, office

cape = headland, point, head, peninsula, promontory

capital NOUN = money, funds, investment(s), cash, finances, resources, assets, wealth
• **ADJECTIVE** (*Old-fashioned*) = first-rate, fine, excellent, superb

capitalism = private enterprise, free enterprise, private ownership, laissez faire *or* laisser faire

capsule 1 = pill, tablet, lozenge **2** (*Botany*) = pod, case, shell, vessel, sheath, receptacle, seed case

captain 1 = leader, boss, master, skipper, head, chief **2** = commander, skipper

captivate = charm, attract, fascinate, entrance, enchant, enthral, beguile, allure ≠ repel

captive ADJECTIVE = confined, caged,

imprisoned, locked up, enslaved, incarcerated, ensnared, subjugated
• NOUN = prisoner, hostage, convict, prisoner of war, detainee, internee

captivity = confinement, custody, detention, imprisonment, incarceration, internment

capture VERB = catch, arrest, take, bag, secure, seize, collar (*informal*), apprehend ≠ release
• NOUN = arrest, catching, trapping, imprisonment, seizure, apprehension, taking, taking captive

car 1 = vehicle, motor, wheels (*informal*), auto (*U.S.*), automobile, jalopy (*informal*), motorcar, machine 2 (*U.S. & Canad.*) = (railway) carriage, coach, cable car, dining car, sleeping car, buffet car, van

cardinal = principal, first, leading, chief, main, central, key, essential ≠ secondary

care VERB = be concerned, mind, bother, be interested, be bothered, give a damn, concern yourself
• NOUN 1 = custody, keeping, control, charge, management, protection, supervision, guardianship 2 = caution, attention, pains, consideration, heed, prudence, vigilance, forethought ≠ carelessness 3 = worry, concern, pressure, trouble, responsibility, stress, anxiety, disquiet ≠ pleasure
• PHRASES **care for someone** 1 = look after, mind, tend, attend, nurse, minister to, watch over 2 = love, desire, be fond of, want, prize ♦ **care for something** *or* **someone** = like, enjoy, take to, relish, be fond of, be keen on, be partial to ♦ **take care of** 1 = look after, mind, watch, protect, tend, nurse, care for, provide for 2 = deal with, manage, cope with, see to, handle

career NOUN = occupation, calling, employment, pursuit, vocation, livelihood, life's work
• VERB = rush, race, speed, tear, dash, barrel (along) (*informal*, (*chiefly U.S. & Canad.*), bolt, hurtle

careful 1 = cautious, scrupulous, circumspect, chary, thoughtful, discreet ≠ careless 2 = thorough, full, particular, precise, intensive, in-depth, meticulous, conscientious ≠ casual 3 = prudent, sparing, economical, canny, provident, frugal, thrifty

careless 1 = slapdash, irresponsible, sloppy (*informal*), cavalier, offhand, neglectful, slipshod, lackadaisical ≠ careful 2 = negligent, hasty, thoughtless, unthinking, forgetful, absent-minded, remiss ≠ careful 3 = nonchalant, casual, offhand, artless, unstudied ≠ careful

caretaker = warden, keeper, porter, superintendent, curator, custodian, watchman, janitor

cargo = load, goods, contents, shipment, freight, merchandise, baggage, consignment

caricature NOUN = parody, cartoon, distortion, satire, send-up (*Brit. informal*), travesty, takeoff (*informal*), lampoon
• VERB = parody, take off (*informal*), mock, distort, ridicule, mimic, send up (*Brit. informal*), lampoon

carnage = slaughter, murder, massacre, holocaust, havoc, bloodshed, shambles, mass murder

carnival = festival, fair, fête, celebration, gala, jubilee, jamboree, revelry

carol = song, hymn, Christmas song

carp = find fault, complain, criticize, reproach, quibble, cavil, pick holes ≠ praise

carpenter = joiner, cabinet-maker, woodworker

carriage 1 = vehicle, coach, trap, gig, cab, wagon, hackney, conveyance 2 = bearing, posture, gait, deportment, air

carry VERB 1 = convey, take, move, bring, bear, transfer, conduct, transport 2 = transport, take, transfer 3 = transmit, transfer, spread, pass on 4 = win, gain, secure, capture, accomplish
• PHRASES **carry on** 1 = continue, last, endure, persist, keep going, persevere 2 (*Informal*) = make a fuss, misbehave, create (*slang*), raise Cain ♦ **carry something on** = engage in, conduct, carry out, undertake, embark on, enter into ♦ **carry something out** = perform, effect, achieve, realize, implement, fulfil, accomplish, execute

carry-on (*Informal*, *chiefly Brit.*) = fuss, disturbance, racket, commotion

carton = box, case, pack, package, container

cartoon 1 = drawing, parody, satire, caricature, comic strip, takeoff (*informal*), lampoon, sketch 2 = animation, animated film, animated cartoon

carve **1** = sculpt, cut, chip, whittle, chisel, hew, fashion **2** = etch, engrave

cascade NOUN = waterfall, falls, torrent, flood, shower, fountain, avalanche, deluge
• VERB = flow, fall, flood, pour, plunge, surge, spill, tumble

case¹ **1** = situation, event, circumstance(s), state, position, condition, context, contingency **2** = instance, example, occasion, specimen, occurrence **3** (*Law*) = lawsuit, trial, suit, proceedings, dispute, action

case² **1** = cabinet, box, chest, holder **2** = container, carton, canister, casket, receptacle **3** = suitcase, bag, grip, holdall, portmanteau, valise **4** = crate, box **5** = covering, casing, shell, jacket, envelope, capsule, sheath, wrapper

cash = money, funds, notes, currency, silver, brass (*Northern English dialect*), dough (*slang*), coinage

cast NOUN **1** = actors, company, players, characters, troupe, dramatis personae **2** = type, sort, kind, style, stamp
• VERB **1** = choose, name, pick, select, appoint, assign, allot **2** = bestow, give, level, direct **3** = give out, spread, deposit, shed, distribute, scatter, emit, radiate **4** = throw, launch, pitch, toss, thrust, hurl, fling, sling **5** = mould, set, found, form, model, shape

caste = class, order, rank, status, stratum, social order

castle = fortress, keep, palace, tower, chateau, stronghold, citadel

casual **1** = careless, relaxed, unconcerned, blasé, offhand, nonchalant, lackadaisical ≠ serious **2** = chance, unexpected, random, accidental, incidental ≠ planned **3** = informal, leisure, sporty, non-dressy ≠ formal

casualty **1** = fatality, death, loss, wounded **2** = victim, sufferer

cat = feline, pussy (*informal*), moggy (*slang*), puss (*informal*), ballarat (*Austral. informal*), tabby

RELATED WORDS
adjective: feline
male: tom
female: tabby
young: kitten

catalogue *or* (*U.S.*) **catalog** NOUN = list, record, schedule, index, register, directory, inventory, gazetteer
• VERB = list, file, index, register, classify, inventory, tabulate, alphabetize

catastrophe = disaster, tragedy, calamity, cataclysm, trouble, adversity, fiasco

catch VERB **1** = capture, arrest, trap, seize, snare, apprehend, ensnare, entrap ≠ free **2** = trap, capture, snare, ensnare, entrap **3** = seize, get, grab, snatch **4** = grab, take, grip, seize, grasp, clutch, lay hold of ≠ release **5** = discover, surprise, find out, expose, detect, catch in the act, take unawares **6** = contract, get, develop, suffer from, incur, succumb to, go down with ≠ escape
• NOUN **1** = fastener, clip, bolt, latch, clasp **2** (*Informal*) = drawback, trick, trap, disadvantage, hitch, snag, stumbling block, fly in the ointment ≠ advantage
• PHRASES **catch on 1** (*Informal*) = understand, see, find out, grasp, see through, comprehend, twig (*Brit. informal*), get the picture **2** = become popular, take off, become trendy, come into fashion

catching = infectious, contagious, transferable, communicable, transmittable ≠ non-infectious

category = class, grouping, heading, sort, department, type, division, section

cater
• PHRASES **cater for something** *or* **someone 1** = provide for, supply, purvey **2** = take into account, consider, bear in mind, make allowance for, have regard for

cattle = cows, stock, beasts, livestock, bovines

RELATED WORDS
adjective: bovine
collective nouns: drove, herd

cause NOUN **1** = origin, source, spring, agent, maker, producer, root, beginning ≠ result **2** = reason, call, need, grounds, basis, incentive, motive, motivation **3** = aim, movement, principle, ideal, enterprise
• VERB = produce, create, lead to, result in, generate, induce, bring about, give rise to ≠ prevent

caution NOUN **1** = care, discretion, heed, prudence, vigilance, alertness, forethought, circumspection ≠ carelessness **2** = reprimand, warning, injunction, admonition

• VERB 1 = warn, urge, advise, alert, tip off, forewarn 2 = reprimand, warn, admonish, give an injunction to

cautious = careful, guarded, wary, tentative, prudent, judicious, circumspect, cagey (*informal*) ≠ careless

cavalry = horsemen, horse, mounted troops ≠ infantrymen

cave = hollow, cavern, grotto, den, cavity

cavity = hollow, hole, gap, pit, dent, crater

cease 1 = stop, end, finish, come to an end ≠ start 2 = discontinue, end, stop, finish, conclude, halt, terminate, break off ≠ begin

celebrate 1 = rejoice, party, enjoy yourself, carouse, live it up (*informal*), make merry, put the flags out, kill the fatted calf 2 = commemorate, honour, observe, toast, drink to, keep 3 = perform, observe, preside over, officiate at, solemnize

celebrated = renowned, popular, famous, distinguished, well-known, prominent, acclaimed, notable ≠ unknown

celebration 1 = party, festival, gala, jubilee, festivity, revelry, red-letter day, merrymaking 2 = commemoration, honouring, remembrance 3 = performance, observance, solemnization

celebrity 1 = personality, star, superstar, big name, dignitary, luminary, big shot (*informal*), V.I.P. ≠ nobody 2 = fame, reputation, distinction, prestige, prominence, stardom, renown, repute ≠ obscurity

cell 1 = room, chamber, lock-up, compartment, cavity, cubicle, dungeon, stall 2 = unit, group, section, core, nucleus, caucus, coterie

cement NOUN 1 = mortar, plaster, paste 2 = sealant, glue, gum, adhesive
• VERB = stick, join, bond, attach, seal, glue, plaster, weld

cemetery = graveyard, churchyard, burial ground, necropolis, God's acre

censor = expurgate, cut, blue-pencil, bowdlerize

censure VERB = criticize, blame, condemn, denounce, rebuke, reprimand, reproach, scold ≠ applaud
• NOUN = disapproval, criticism, blame, condemnation, rebuke, reprimand, reproach, stick (*slang*) ≠ approval

central 1 = inner, middle, mid, interior ≠ outer 2 = main, chief, key, essential, primary, principal, fundamental, focal ≠ minor

centre NOUN = middle, heart, focus, core, nucleus, hub, pivot, kernel ≠ edge
• VERB = focus, concentrate, cluster, revolve, converge

ceremonial ADJECTIVE = formal, public, official, ritual, stately, solemn, liturgical, courtly ≠ informal
• NOUN = ritual, ceremony, rite, formality, solemnity

ceremony 1 = ritual, service, rite, observance, commemoration, solemnities 2 = formality, ceremonial, propriety, decorum

certain 1 = sure, convinced, positive, confident, satisfied, assured ≠ unsure 2 = bound, sure, fated, destined ≠ unlikely 3 = inevitable, unavoidable, inescapable 4 = known, true, positive, conclusive, unequivocal, undeniable, irrefutable, unquestionable ≠ doubtful 5 = fixed, decided, established, settled, definite ≠ indefinite

certainly = definitely, surely, truly, undoubtedly, without doubt, undeniably, indisputably, assuredly

certainty 1 = confidence, trust, faith, conviction, assurance, sureness, positiveness ≠ doubt 2 = inevitability ≠ uncertainty 3 = fact, truth, reality, sure thing (*informal*), banker

certificate = document, licence, warrant, voucher, diploma, testimonial, authorization, credential(s)

certify = confirm, declare, guarantee, assure, testify, verify, validate, attest

chain NOUN 1 = tether, coupling, link, bond, shackle, fetter, manacle 2 = series, set, train, string, sequence, succession, progression
• VERB = bind, confine, restrain, handcuff, shackle, tether, fetter, manacle

chairman *or* **chairwoman** 1 = director, president, chief, executive, chairperson 2 = master of ceremonies, spokesman, chair, speaker, MC, chairperson

challenge NOUN 1 = dare, provocation, wero (*N.Z.*) 2 = test, trial, opposition, confrontation, ultimatum
• VERB 1 = dispute, question, tackle,

confront, defy, object to, disagree with, take issue with **2** = dare, invite, defy, throw down the gauntlet **3** = test **4** = question, interrogate

chamber **1** = hall, room **2** = council, assembly, legislature, legislative body **3** = room, bedroom, apartment, enclosure, cubicle **4** = compartment

champion NOUN **1** = winner, hero, victor, conqueror, title holder **2** = defender, guardian, patron, backer, protector, upholder

• VERB = support, back, defend, promote, advocate, fight for, uphold, espouse

chance NOUN **1** = probability, odds, possibility, prospect, likelihood ≠ certainty **2** = opportunity, opening, occasion, time **3** = accident, fortune, luck, fate, destiny, coincidence, providence ≠ design **4** = risk, speculation, gamble, hazard

• VERB = risk, try, stake, venture, gamble, hazard, wager

change NOUN **1** = alteration, innovation, transformation, modification, mutation, metamorphosis, difference, revolution **2** = variety, break (*informal*), departure, variation, novelty, diversion ≠ monotony **3** = exchange, trade, conversion, swap, substitution, interchange

• VERB **1** = alter, reform, transform, adjust, revise, modify, reorganize, restyle ≠ keep **2** = shift, vary, transform, alter, modify, mutate ≠ stay **3** = exchange, trade, replace, substitute, swap, interchange

channel NOUN **1** = means, way, course, approach, medium, route, path, avenue **2** = strait, sound, route, passage, canal, waterway **3** = duct, artery, groove, gutter, furrow, conduit

• VERB = direct, guide, conduct, transmit, convey

chant NOUN = song, carol, chorus, melody, psalm

• VERB = sing, chorus, recite, intone, carol

chaos = disorder, confusion, mayhem, anarchy, lawlessness, pandemonium, bedlam, tumult ≠ orderliness

chaotic = disordered, confused, uncontrolled, anarchic, tumultuous, lawless, riotous, topsy-turvy

chap (*Informal*) = fellow, man, person, individual, character, guy (*informal*), bloke (*Brit. informal*)

chapter **1** = section, part, stage, division, episode, topic, segment, instalment **2** = period, time, stage, phase

character **1** = personality, nature, attributes, temperament, complexion, disposition **2** = nature, kind, quality, calibre **3** = reputation, honour, integrity, good name, rectitude **4** = role, part, persona **5** = eccentric, card (*informal*), original, oddball (*informal*) **6** = symbol, mark, sign, letter, figure, device, rune, hieroglyph

characteristic NOUN = feature, mark, quality, property, attribute, faculty, trait, quirk

• ADJECTIVE = typical, special, individual, representative, distinguishing, distinctive, peculiar, singular ≠ rare

characterize = distinguish, mark, identify, brand, stamp, typify

charge VERB **1** = accuse, indict, impeach, incriminate, arraign ≠ acquit **2** = attack, assault, assail ≠ retreat **3** = rush, storm, stampede **4** = fill, load

• NOUN **1** = price, rate, cost, amount, payment, expense, toll, expenditure **2** = accusation, allegation, indictment, imputation ≠ acquittal **3** = care, trust, responsibility, custody, safekeeping **4** = duty, office, responsibility, remit **5** = ward, pupil, protégé, dependant **6** = attack, rush, assault, onset, onslaught, stampede, sortie ≠ retreat

charisma = charm, appeal, personality, attraction, lure, allure, magnetism, force of personality

charismatic = charming, appealing, attractive, influential, magnetic, enticing, alluring

charitable **1** = benevolent, liberal, generous, lavish, philanthropic, bountiful, beneficent ≠ mean **2** = kind, understanding, forgiving, sympathetic, favourable, tolerant, indulgent, lenient ≠ unkind

charity **1** = charitable organization, fund, movement, trust, endowment **2** = donations, help, relief, gift, contributions, assistance, hand-out, philanthropy, koha (*N.Z.*) ≠ meanness **3** = kindness, humanity, goodwill, compassion, generosity, indulgence, altruism, benevolence, aroha (*N.Z.*) ≠ ill will

charm NOUN **1** = attraction, appeal,

fascination, allure, magnetism ≠ repulsiveness **2** = talisman, trinket, amulet, fetish **3** = spell, magic, enchantment, sorcery, makutu (*N.Z.*)
• **VERB 1** = attract, delight, fascinate, entrance, win over, enchant, captivate, beguile ≠ repel **2** = persuade, seduce, coax, beguile, sweet-talk (*informal*)

charming = attractive, pleasing, appealing, fetching, delightful, cute, seductive, captivating ≠ unpleasant

chart **NOUN** = table, diagram, blueprint, graph, plan, map
• **VERB 1** = plot, map out, delineate, sketch, draft, tabulate **2** = monitor, follow, record, note, document, register, trace, outline

charter **NOUN 1** = document, contract, permit, licence, deed, prerogative **2** = constitution, laws, rules, code
• **VERB 1** = hire, commission, employ, rent, lease **2** = authorize, permit, sanction, entitle, license, empower, give authority

chase **VERB 1** = pursue, follow, track, hunt, run after, course **2** = drive away, drive, expel, hound, send away, send packing, put to flight **3** = rush, run, race, shoot, fly, speed, dash, bolt
• **NOUN** = pursuit, race, hunt, hunting

chat **VERB** = talk, gossip, jaw (*slang*), natter, blather, blether (*Scot.*)
• **NOUN** = talk, tête-à-tête, conversation, gossip, heart-to-heart, natter, blather, blether (*Scot.*), korero (*N.Z.*)

chatter **VERB** = prattle, chat, rabbit on (*Brit. informal*), babble, gab (*informal*), natter, blather, schmooze (*slang*)
• **NOUN** = prattle, chat, gossip, babble, gab (*informal*), natter, blather, blether (*Scot.*)

cheap **1** = inexpensive, reduced, keen, reasonable, bargain, low-priced, low-cost, cut-price ≠ expensive **2** = inferior, poor, worthless, second-rate, shoddy, tawdry, tatty, trashy, bodger *or* bodgie (*Austral. slang*) ≠ good **3** (*Informal*) = despicable, mean, contemptible, scungy (*Austral. & N.Z.*) ≠ decent

cheat **VERB** = deceive, trick, fool, con (*informal*), mislead, rip off (*slang*), fleece, defraud
• **NOUN** = deceiver, sharper, shark, charlatan, trickster, con man (*informal*), double-crosser (*informal*), swindler, rorter (*Austral. slang*)

check **VERB 1** *often with* ***out*** = examine, test, study, look at, research, investigate, monitor, vet ≠ overlook **2** = stop, limit, delay, halt, restrain, inhibit, hinder, obstruct ≠ further
• **NOUN 1** = examination, test, research, investigation, inspection, scrutiny, once-over (*informal*) **2** = control, limitation, restraint, constraint, obstacle, curb, obstruction, stoppage

cheek (*Informal*) = impudence, nerve, disrespect, audacity, lip (*slang*), temerity, chutzpah (*U.S. & Canad. informal*), insolence

cheeky = impudent, rude, forward, insulting, saucy, audacious, pert, disrespectful ≠ respectful

cheer **VERB 1** = applaud, hail, acclaim, clap ≠ boo **2** = hearten, encourage, comfort, uplift, brighten, cheer up, buoy up, gladden ≠ dishearten
• **NOUN** = applause, ovation, plaudits, acclamation
• **PHRASES cheer someone up** = comfort, encourage, hearten, enliven, gladden, gee up, jolly along (*informal*)
◆ **cheer up** = take heart, rally, perk up, buck up (*informal*)

cheerful **1** = happy, optimistic, enthusiastic, jolly, merry, upbeat (*informal*), buoyant, cheery ≠ sad **2** = pleasant ≠ gloomy

chemical = compound, drug, substance, synthetic substance, potion

chemist = pharmacist, apothecary (*obsolete*), dispenser

cherish **1** = cling to, prize, treasure, hold dear, cleave to ≠ despise **2** = care for, love, support, comfort, look after, shelter, nurture, hold dear ≠ neglect **3** = harbour, nurse, sustain, foster, entertain

chest **1** = breast, front **2** = box, case, trunk, crate, coffer, casket, strongbox

RELATED WORD
adjective: pectoral

chew = munch, bite, grind, champ, crunch, gnaw, chomp, masticate

chic = stylish, smart, elegant, fashionable, trendy (*Brit. informal*) ≠ unfashionable

chief **NOUN** = head, leader, director, manager, boss (*informal*), captain, master, governor, baas (*S. African*), ariki (*N.Z.*) ≠ subordinate
• **ADJECTIVE** = primary, highest, leading, main, prime, key, premier, supreme

≠ minor
chiefly **1** = especially, essentially, principally, primarily, above all **2** = mainly, largely, usually, mostly, in general, on the whole, predominantly, in the main
child **1** = youngster, baby, kid (*informal*), infant, babe, juvenile, toddler, tot, littlie (*Austral. informal*), ankle-biter (*Austral. slang*), tacker (*Austral. slang*) **2** = offspring
RELATED WORDS
adjective: filial
prefix: paedo-
childbirth = child-bearing, labour, delivery, lying-in, confinement, parturition
childhood = youth, minority, infancy, schooldays, immaturity, boyhood *or* girlhood
childish **1** = youthful, young, boyish *or* girlish **2** = immature, juvenile, foolish, infantile, puerile ≠ mature
chill **VERB** **1** = cool, refrigerate, freeze **2** = dishearten, depress, discourage, dismay, dampen, deject
• **NOUN** **1** = coldness, bite, nip, sharpness, coolness, rawness, crispness, frigidity **2** = shiver, frisson
• **ADJECTIVE** = chilly, biting, sharp, freezing, raw, bleak, chilly, wintry
chilly **1** = cool, fresh, sharp, crisp, penetrating, brisk, draughty, nippy ≠ warm **2** = unfriendly, hostile, unsympathetic, frigid, unresponsive, unwelcoming ≠ friendly
china[1] = pottery, ceramics, ware, porcelain, crockery, tableware, service
china[2] (*Brit. & S. African informal*) = friend, pal, mate (*informal*), buddy (*informal*), companion, best friend, intimate, comrade, cobber (*Austral. & N.Z. old-fashioned informal*), E hoa (*N.Z.*)
chip **NOUN** **1** = fragment, shaving, wafer, sliver, shard **2** = scratch, nick, notch **3** = counter, disc, token
• **VERB** **1** = nick, damage, gash **2** = chisel, whittle
choice **NOUN** **1** = range, variety, selection, assortment **2** = selection, preference, pick **3** = option, say, alternative
• **ADJECTIVE** = best, prime, select, excellent, exclusive, elite, booshit (*Austral. slang*), exo (*Austral. slang*), sik (*Austral. slang*)
choke **1** = suffocate, stifle, smother, overpower, asphyxiate **2** = strangle, throttle, asphyxiate **3** = block, clog, obstruct, bung, constrict, congest, stop, bar
choose **1** = pick, prefer, select, elect, adopt, opt for, designate, settle upon ≠ reject **2** = wish, want
chop = cut, fell, hack, sever, cleave, hew, lop
chore = task, job, duty, burden, hassle (*informal*), errand
chorus **NOUN** **1** = refrain, response, strain, burden **2** = choir, singers, ensemble, vocalists, choristers
• **PHRASES** **in chorus** = in unison, as one, all together, in concert, in harmony, in accord, with one voice
christen **1** = baptize, name **2** = name, call, term, style, title, dub, designate
Christmas = festive season, Noël, Xmas (*informal*), Yule (*archaic*), Yuletide (*archaic*)
chronicle **VERB** = record, tell, report, enter, relate, register, recount, set down
• **NOUN** = record, story, history, account, register, journal, diary, narrative
chuck (*Informal*) **1** = throw, cast, pitch, toss, hurl, fling, sling, heave **2** *often with* ***away*** or ***out*** = throw out, dump (*informal*), scrap, get rid of, ditch (*slang*), dispose of, dispense with, jettison **3** = give up *or* over, leave, abandon, cease, resign from, pack in **4** (*Austral. & N.Z. informal*) = vomit, throw up (*informal*), spew, heave (*slang*), puke (*slang*), barf (*U.S. slang*), chunder (*slang, chiefly Austral.*)
chuckle = laugh, giggle, snigger, chortle, titter
chum (*Informal*) = friend, mate (*informal*), pal (*informal*), companion, comrade, crony, cobber (*Austral. & N.Z. old-fashioned informal*), E hoa (*N.Z.*)
chunk = piece, block, mass, portion, lump, slab, hunk, nugget
churn **1** = stir up, beat, disturb, swirl, agitate **2** = swirl, toss
cinema **1** = pictures, movies, picture-house, flicks (*slang*) **2** = films, pictures, movies, big screen (*informal*), motion pictures, silver screen
circle **NOUN** **1** = ring, disc, hoop, halo **2** = group, company, set, club, society, clique, coterie
• **VERB** **1** = go round, ring, surround, enclose, envelop, encircle, circumscribe, circumnavigate **2** = wheel, spiral
circuit **1** = course, tour, track, route,

journey **2** = racetrack, course, track, racecourse **3** = lap, tour, revolution, orbit
circular ADJECTIVE **1** = round, ring-shaped **2** = circuitous, cyclical, orbital
• NOUN = advertisement, notice, ad (*informal*), announcement, advert (*Brit. informal*), press release
circulate 1 = spread, issue, publish, broadcast, distribute, publicize, disseminate, promulgate **2** = flow, revolve, rotate, radiate
circulation 1 = distribution, currency, readership **2** = bloodstream, blood flow **3** = flow, circling, motion, rotation **4** = spread, distribution, transmission, dissemination
circumstance 1 *usually plural* = situation, condition, contingency, state of affairs, lie of the land **2** *usually plural* = detail, event, particular, respect **3** *usually plural* = situation, state, means, position, station, status **4** = chance, the times, accident, fortune, luck, fate, destiny, providence
cite = quote, name, advance, mention, extract, specify, allude to, enumerate
citizen = inhabitant, resident, dweller, denizen, subject, townsman
RELATED WORD
adjective: civil
city = town, metropolis, municipality, conurbation
RELATED WORD
adjective: civic
civic = public, municipal, communal, local
civil 1 = civic, political, domestic, municipal ≠ state **2** = polite, obliging, courteous, considerate, affable, well-mannered ≠ rude
civilization 1 = society, people, community, nation, polity **2** = culture, development, education, progress, enlightenment, sophistication, advancement, cultivation
civilize = cultivate, educate, refine, tame, enlighten, sophisticate
civilized 1 = cultured, educated, sophisticated, enlightened, humane ≠ primitive **2** = polite, mannerly, tolerant, gracious, courteous, well-behaved, well-mannered
claim VERB **1** = assert, insist, maintain, allege, uphold, profess **2** = demand, call for, ask for, insist on
• NOUN **1** = assertion, statement, allegation, declaration, pretension, affirmation, protestation **2** = demand, application, request, petition, call **3** = right, title, entitlement
clamour = noise, shouting, racket, outcry, din, uproar, commotion, hubbub
clamp NOUN = vice, press, grip, bracket, fastener
• VERB = fasten, fix, secure, brace, make fast
clan 1 = family, group, society, tribe, fraternity, brotherhood, ainga (*N.Z.*), ngai (*N.Z.*) **2** = group, set, circle, gang, faction, coterie, cabal
clap = applaud, cheer, acclaim ≠ boo
clarify = explain, interpret, illuminate, clear up, simplify, make plain, elucidate, throw *or* shed light on
clarity 1 = clearness, precision, simplicity, transparency, lucidity, straightforwardness ≠ obscurity **2** = transparency, clearness ≠ cloudiness
clash VERB **1** = conflict, grapple, wrangle, lock horns, cross swords, war, feud, quarrel **2** = disagree, conflict, vary, counter, differ, contradict, diverge, run counter to **3** = not go, jar, not match **4** = crash, bang, rattle, jar, clatter, jangle, clang, clank
• NOUN **1** = conflict, fight, brush, confrontation, collision, showdown (*informal*) **2** = disagreement, difference, argument, dispute, dissent, difference of opinion
clasp VERB = grasp, hold, press, grip, seize, squeeze, embrace, clutch
• NOUN **1** = grasp, hold, grip, embrace, hug **2** = fastening, catch, grip, hook, pin, clip, buckle, brooch
class NOUN **1** = group, set, division, rank **2** = type, sort, kind, category, genre
• VERB = classify, group, rate, rank, brand, label, grade, designate
classic ADJECTIVE **1** = typical, standard, model, regular, usual, ideal, characteristic, definitive, dinki-di (*Austral. informal*) **2** = masterly, best, finest, world-class, consummate, first-rate ≠ second-rate **3** = lasting, enduring, abiding, immortal, undying, ageless, deathless
• NOUN = standard, masterpiece, prototype, paradigm, exemplar, model
classification = categorization, grading, taxonomy, sorting, analysis, arrangement
classify = categorize, sort, rank, arrange,

grade, catalogue, pigeonhole, tabulate
classy (*Informal*) = high-class, exclusive, superior, elegant, stylish, posh (*informal, chiefly Brit.*), up-market, top-drawer
clause = section, condition, article, chapter, passage, part, paragraph
claw NOUN 1 = nail, talon 2 = pincer
● VERB = scratch, tear, dig, rip, scrape, maul, mangulate (*Austral. slang*), lacerate
clean ADJECTIVE 1 = hygienic, fresh, sterile, pure, purified, antiseptic, sterilized, uncontaminated ≠ contaminated 2 = spotless, fresh, immaculate, impeccable, flawless, unblemished, unsullied ≠ dirty 3 = moral, good, pure, decent, innocent, respectable, upright, honourable ≠ immoral 4 = complete, final, whole, total, perfect, entire, decisive, thorough
● VERB = cleanse, wash, scrub, rinse, launder, scour, purify, disinfect ≠ dirty
cleanse = purify, clear, purge 1 = absolve, clear, purge, purify 2 = clean, wash, scrub, rinse, scour
clear ADJECTIVE 1 = comprehensible, explicit, understandable ≠ confused 2 = distinct ≠ indistinct 3 = obvious, plain, apparent, evident, distinct, pronounced, manifest, blatant ≠ ambiguous 4 = certain, sure, convinced, positive, satisfied, resolved, definite, decided ≠ confused 5 = transparent, see-through, translucent, crystalline, glassy, limpid, pellucid ≠ opaque 6 = unobstructed, open, free, empty, unhindered, unimpeded ≠ blocked 7 = bright, fine, fair, shining, sunny, luminous, cloudless, light ≠ cloudy 8 = untroubled, clean, pure, innocent, immaculate, unblemished, untarnished
● VERB 1 = unblock, free, loosen, extricate, open, disentangle 2 = remove, clean, wipe, cleanse, tidy (up), sweep away 3 = brighten, break up, lighten 4 = pass over, jump, leap, vault, miss 5 = absolve, acquit, vindicate, exonerate ≠ blame
clear-cut = straightforward, specific, plain, precise, black-and-white, explicit, definite, unequivocal
clearly 1 = obviously, undoubtedly, evidently, distinctly, markedly, overtly, undeniably, beyond doubt 2 = legibly, distinctly 3 = audibly, distinctly, intelligibly, comprehensibly
clergy = priesthood, ministry, clerics, clergymen, churchmen, the cloth, holy orders
clever 1 = intelligent, bright, talented, gifted, smart, knowledgeable, quick-witted ≠ stupid 2 = shrewd, bright, ingenious, resourceful, canny ≠ unimaginative 3 = skilful, talented, gifted ≠ inept
cliché = platitude, stereotype, commonplace, banality, truism, hackneyed phrase
client = customer, consumer, buyer, patron, shopper, patient
cliff = rock face, overhang, crag, precipice, escarpment, scar, bluff
climate = weather, temperature
climax = culmination, top, summit, height, highlight, peak, high point, zenith
climb VERB 1 = ascend, scale, mount, go up, clamber, shin up 2 = clamber, descend, scramble, dismount 3 = rise, go up, soar, ascend, fly up
● PHRASES **climb down** = back down, withdraw, yield, concede, retreat, surrender, give in, cave in (*informal*)
clinch 1 = secure, close, confirm, conclude, seal, sew up (*informal*), set the seal on 2 = settle, decide, determine
cling 1 = clutch, grip, embrace, grasp, hug, hold on to, clasp 2 = stick to, adhere to
clinical = unemotional, cold, scientific, objective, detached, analytic, impersonal, dispassionate
clip[1] VERB 1 = trim, cut, crop, prune, shorten, shear, snip, pare 2 (*Informal*) = smack, strike, knock, punch, thump, clout (*informal*), cuff, whack
● NOUN (*Informal*) = smack, strike, knock, punch, thump, clout (*informal*), cuff, whack
clip[2] = attach, fix, secure, connect, pin, staple, fasten, hold
cloak NOUN 1 = cape, coat, wrap, mantle 2 = covering, layer, blanket, shroud
● VERB 1 = cover, coat, wrap, blanket, shroud, envelop 2 = hide, cover, screen, mask, disguise, conceal, obscure, veil
clog = obstruct, block, jam, hinder, impede, congest
close[1] VERB 1 = shut, lock, fasten, secure ≠ open 2 = shut down, finish, cease 3 = wind up, finish, shut down, terminate 4 = block up, bar, seal ≠ open 5 = end, finish, complete, conclude, wind up,

terminate ≠ begin **6** = clinch, confirm, secure, conclude, seal, sew up (*informal*), set the seal on **7** = come together, join, connect ≠ separate
• **NOUN** = end, ending, finish, conclusion, completion, finale, culmination, denouement

close² **1** = near, neighbouring, nearby, handy, adjacent, adjoining, cheek by jowl ≠ far **2** = intimate, loving, familiar, thick (*informal*), attached, devoted, confidential, inseparable ≠ distant **3** = noticeable, marked, strong, distinct, pronounced **4** = careful, detailed, intense, minute, thorough, rigorous, painstaking **5** = even, level, neck and neck, fifty-fifty (*informal*), evenly matched **6** = imminent, near, impending, at hand, nigh ≠ far away **7** = stifling, oppressive, suffocating, stuffy, humid, sweltering, airless, muggy ≠ airy

closed **1** = shut, locked, sealed, fastened ≠ open **2** = shut down, out of service **3** = exclusive, select, restricted **4** = finished, over, ended, decided, settled, concluded, resolved, terminated

cloth = fabric, material, textiles

clothe = dress, array, robe, drape, swathe, attire, fit out, garb ≠ undress

clothes = clothing, wear, dress, gear (*informal*), outfit, costume, wardrobe, garments

clothing = clothes, wear, dress, gear (*informal*), outfit, costume, wardrobe, garments

cloud **NOUN** = mist, haze, vapour, murk, gloom
• **VERB** **1** = confuse, distort, impair, muddle, disorient **2** = darken, dim, be overshadowed

clout (*Informal*) **VERB** = hit, strike, punch, slap, sock (*slang*), smack, thump, clobber (*slang*)
• **NOUN** **1** = thump, blow, punch, slap, sock (*slang*), wallop (*informal*) **2** = influence, power, authority, pull, weight, prestige, mana (*N.Z.*)

clown **NOUN** **1** = comedian, fool, comic, harlequin, joker, jester, prankster, buffoon **2** = fool, idiot, twit (*informal, chiefly Brit.*), imbecile (*informal*), ignoramus, dolt, blockhead, dorba *or* dorb (*Austral. slang*), bogan (*Austral. slang*)
• **VERB** *usually with* ***around*** = play the fool, mess about, jest, act the fool

club **NOUN** **1** = association, company, group, union, society, lodge, guild, fraternity **2** = stick, bat, bludgeon, truncheon, cosh (*Brit.*), cudgel
• **VERB** = beat, strike, hammer, batter, bash, bludgeon, pummel, cosh (*Brit.*)

clue = indication, lead, sign, evidence, suggestion, trace, hint, suspicion

clump **NOUN** = cluster, group, bunch, bundle
• **VERB** = stomp, thump, lumber, tramp, plod, thud

clumsy = awkward, lumbering, bumbling, ponderous, ungainly, gauche, gawky, uncoordinated, unco (*Austral. slang*) ≠ skilful

cluster **NOUN** = gathering, group, collection, bunch, knot, clump, assemblage
• **VERB** = gather, group, collect, bunch, assemble, flock, huddle

clutch **VERB** **1** = hold, grip, embrace, grasp, cling to, clasp **2** = seize, catch, grab, grasp, snatch
• **PLURAL NOUN** = power, hands, control, grip, possession, grasp, custody, sway

clutter **NOUN** = untidiness, mess, disorder, confusion, litter, muddle, disarray, jumble ≠ order
• **VERB** = litter, scatter, strew, mess up ≠ tidy

coach **NOUN** **1** = instructor, teacher, trainer, tutor, handler **2** = bus, charabanc
• **VERB** = instruct, train, prepare, exercise, drill, tutor

coalition = alliance, union, association, combination, merger, conjunction, bloc, confederation

coarse **1** = rough, crude, unfinished, homespun, impure, unrefined, unprocessed, unpolished ≠ smooth **2** = vulgar, rude, indecent, improper, earthy, smutty, ribald, indelicate

coast **NOUN** = shore, border, beach, seaside, coastline, seaboard
• **VERB** = cruise, sail, drift, taxi, glide, freewheel

coat **NOUN** **1** = fur, hair, skin, hide, wool, fleece, pelt **2** = layer, covering, coating, overlay
• **VERB** = cover, spread, plaster, smear

coax = persuade, cajole, talk into, wheedle, sweet-talk (*informal*), prevail upon, entice, allure ≠ bully

cobber (*Austral. & N.Z. old-fashioned informal*) = friend, pal, mate (*informal*), buddy (*informal*), china (*Brit. & S. African informal*), best friend, intimate, comrade, E hoa (*N.Z.*)
cocktail = mixture, combination, compound, blend, mix
cocky *or* **cockie** (*Austral. & N.Z. informal*) = farmer, smallholder, crofter (*Scot.*), grazier, agriculturalist, rancher
code **1** = principles, rules, manners, custom, convention, ethics, maxim, etiquette, kawa (*N.Z.*), tikanga (*N.Z.*) **2** = cipher, cryptograph
coherent **1** = consistent, reasoned, organized, rational, logical, meaningful, systematic, orderly ≠ inconsistent **2** = articulate, lucid, comprehensible, intelligible ≠ unintelligible
coil **1** = wind, twist, curl, loop, spiral, twine **2** = curl, wind, twist, snake, loop, twine, wreathe
coin NOUN = money, change, cash, silver, copper, specie
• VERB = invent, create, make up, forge, originate, fabricate
coincide **1** = occur simultaneously, coexist, synchronize, be concurrent **2** = agree, match, accord, square, correspond, tally, concur, harmonize ≠ disagree
coincidence = chance, accident, luck, fluke, stroke of luck, happy accident
cold ADJECTIVE **1** = chilly, freezing, bleak, arctic, icy, frosty, wintry, frigid ≠ hot **2** = distant, reserved, indifferent, aloof, frigid, undemonstrative, standoffish ≠ emotional **3** = unfriendly, indifferent, frigid ≠ friendly
• NOUN = coldness, chill, frigidity, frostiness, iciness
collaborate **1** = work together, team up, join forces, cooperate, play ball (*informal*), participate **2** = conspire, cooperate, collude, fraternize
collaboration **1** = teamwork, partnership, cooperation, association, alliance **2** = conspiring, cooperation, collusion, fraternization
collaborator **1** = co-worker, partner, colleague, associate, team-mate, confederate **2** = traitor, turncoat, quisling, fraternizer
collapse VERB **1** = fall down, fall, give way, subside, cave in, crumple, fall apart at the seams **2** = fail, fold, founder, break down, fall through, come to nothing, go belly-up (*informal*)
• NOUN **1** = falling down, ruin, falling apart, cave-in, disintegration, subsidence **2** = failure, slump, breakdown, flop, downfall **3** = faint, breakdown, blackout, prostration
collar (*Informal*) = seize, catch, arrest, grab, capture, nail (*informal*), nab (*informal*), apprehend
colleague = fellow worker, partner, ally, associate, assistant, team-mate, comrade, helper
collect **1** = gather, save, assemble, heap, accumulate, amass, stockpile, hoard ≠ scatter **2** = assemble, meet, rally, cluster, come together, convene, converge, congregate ≠ disperse
collected = calm, cool, composed, poised, serene, unperturbed, unruffled, self-possessed ≠ nervous
collection **1** = accumulation, set, store, mass, pile, heap, stockpile, hoard **2** = compilation, accumulation, anthology **3** = group, company, crowd, assembly, cluster, assortment **4** = gathering **5** = contribution, donation, alms **6** = offering, offertory
collective **1** = joint, united, shared, combined, corporate, unified ≠ individual **2** = combined, aggregate, composite, cumulative ≠ separate
collide **1** = crash, clash, meet head-on, come into collision **2** = conflict, clash, be incompatible, be at variance
collision **1** = crash, impact, accident, smash, bump, pile-up (*informal*), prang (*informal*) **2** = conflict, opposition, clash, encounter, disagreement, incompatibility
colony = settlement, territory, province, possession, dependency, outpost, dominion, satellite state
colour *or* (*U.S.*) **color** NOUN **1** = hue, tone, shade, tint, colourway **2** = paint, stain, dye, tint, pigment, colorant
• VERB = blush, flush, redden
colourful **1** = bright, brilliant, psychedelic, variegated, multicoloured ≠ drab **2** = interesting, rich, graphic, lively, distinctive, vivid, picturesque ≠ boring

column 1 = pillar, support, post, shaft, upright, obelisk 2 = line, row, file, rank, procession, cavalcade
coma = unconsciousness, trance, oblivion, stupor
comb 1 = untangle, arrange, groom, dress 2 = search, hunt through, rake, sift, scour, rummage, ransack, forage, fossick (*Austral. & N.Z.*)
combat NOUN = fight, war, action, battle, conflict, engagement, warfare, skirmish ≠ peace
• VERB = fight, oppose, resist, defy, withstand, do battle with ≠ support
combination 1 = mixture, mix, blend, composite, amalgamation, coalescence 2 = association, union, alliance, coalition, federation, consortium, syndicate, confederation
combine 1 = amalgamate, mix, blend, integrate, merge ≠ separate 2 = join together, link, connect, integrate, merge, amalgamate 3 = unite, associate, team up, get together, collaborate, join forces, join together, pool resources ≠ split up
come VERB 1 = approach, near, advance, move towards, draw near 2 = arrive, turn up (*informal*), show up (*informal*) 3 = reach, extend, come up to, come as far as 4 = happen, fall, occur, take place, come about, come to pass 5 = be available, be made, be offered, be produced, be on offer
• PHRASES **come across as something** *or* **someone** = seem, look, seem to be, appear to be, give the impression of being ◆ **come across someone** = meet, encounter, run into, bump into (*informal*) ◆ **come across something** = find, discover, notice, unearth, stumble upon, chance upon = be obtained, be from, issue, emerge, flow, arise, originate, emanate
comeback 1 (*Informal*) = return, revival, rebound, resurgence, rally, recovery, triumph 2 = response, reply, retort, retaliation, riposte, rejoinder
comedian = comic, wit, clown, funny man, humorist, wag, joker, jester, dag (*N.Z. informal*)
comedy 1 = light entertainment ≠ tragedy, soapie (*Austral. slang*) 2 = humour, fun, joking, farce, jesting, hilarity ≠ seriousness
comfort NOUN 1 = ease, luxury, wellbeing, opulence 2 = consolation, succour, help, support, relief, compensation ≠ annoyance
• VERB = console, reassure, soothe, hearten, commiserate with ≠ distress
comfortable 1 = pleasant, homely, relaxing, cosy, agreeable, restful ≠ unpleasant 2 = at ease, happy, at home, contented, relaxed, serene ≠ uncomfortable 3 (*Informal*) = well-off, prosperous, affluent, well-to-do, comfortably-off, in clover (*informal*)
comforting = consoling, encouraging, cheering, reassuring, soothing, heart-warming ≠ upsetting
comic ADJECTIVE = funny, amusing, witty, humorous, farcical, comical, droll, jocular ≠ sad
• NOUN = comedian, funny man, humorist, wit, clown, wag, jester, dag (*N.Z. informal*), buffoon
coming ADJECTIVE = approaching, near, forthcoming, imminent, in store, impending, at hand, nigh
• NOUN = arrival, approach, advent
command VERB 1 = order, tell, charge, demand, require, direct, bid, compel ≠ beg 2 = have authority over, lead, head, control, rule, manage, handle, dominate ≠ be subordinate to
• NOUN 1 = order, demand, instruction, requirement, decree, directive, ultimatum, commandment 2 = domination, control, rule, mastery, power, government 3 = management, power, control, charge, authority, supervision
commander = leader, chief, officer, boss, head, captain, bass (*S. African*), ruler
commanding = dominant, controlling, dominating, superior, decisive, advantageous
commemorate = celebrate, remember, honour, recognize, salute, pay tribute to, immortalize ≠ ignore
commence 1 = embark on, start, open, begin, initiate, originate, instigate, enter upon ≠ stop 2 = start, open, begin, go ahead ≠ end
commend 1 = praise, acclaim, applaud, compliment, extol, approve, speak highly of ≠ criticize 2 = recommend, suggest, approve, advocate, endorse
comment VERB 1 = remark, say, note,

mention, point out, observe, utter **2** *usually with* ***on*** = remark on, explain, talk about, discuss, speak about, say something about, allude to, elucidate
• NOUN **1** = remark, statement, observation **2** = note, explanation, illustration, commentary, exposition, annotation, elucidation

commentary 1 = narration, report, review, explanation, description, voice-over **2** = analysis, notes, review, critique, treatise

commentator 1 = reporter, special correspondent, sportscaster **2** = critic, interpreter, annotator

commercial 1 = mercantile, trading **2** = materialistic, mercenary, profit-making

commission VERB = appoint, order, contract, select, engage, delegate, nominate, authorize
• NOUN **1** = duty, task, mission, mandate, errand **2** = fee, cut, percentage, royalties, rake-off (*slang*) **3** = committee, board, representatives, commissioners, delegation, deputation

commit 1 = do, perform, carry out, execute, enact, perpetrate **2** = put in custody, confine, imprison ≠ release

commitment 1 = dedication, loyalty, devotion ≠ indecisiveness **2** = responsibility, tie, duty, obligation, liability, engagement

common 1 = usual, standard, regular, ordinary, familiar, conventional, routine, frequent ≠ rare **2** = popular, general, accepted, standard, routine, widespread, universal, prevailing **3** = shared, collective **4** = ordinary, average, typical, dinki-di (*Austral. informal*) ≠ important **5** = vulgar, inferior, coarse, plebeian ≠ refined **6** = collective, public, community, social, communal ≠ personal

commonplace ADJECTIVE = everyday, common, ordinary, widespread, mundane, banal, run-of-the-mill, humdrum ≠ rare
• NOUN = cliché, platitude, banality, truism

common sense = good sense, sound judgment, level-headedness, prudence, gumption (*Brit. informal*), horse sense, native intelligence, wit

communal = public, shared, general, joint, collective ≠ private

commune = community, collective, cooperative, kibbutz

communicate 1 = contact, talk, speak, make contact, get in contact **2** = make known, declare, disclose, pass on, proclaim, transmit, convey, impart ≠ keep secret **3** = pass on, transfer, spread, transmit

communication 1 = contact, conversation, correspondence, link, relations **2** = passing on, circulation, transmission, disclosure, imparting, dissemination, conveyance **3** = message, news, report, word, information, statement, announcement, disclosure

communism *usually cap.* = socialism, Marxism, collectivism, Bolshevism, state socialism

communist *often cap.* = socialist, Red (*informal*), Marxist, Bolshevik, collectivist

community = society, people, public, residents, commonwealth, general public, populace, state

commuter = daily traveller, passenger, suburbanite

compact[1] ADJECTIVE **1** = closely packed, solid, thick, dense, compressed, condensed, pressed together ≠ loose **2** = concise, brief, to the point, succinct, terse ≠ lengthy
• VERB = pack closely, stuff, cram, compress, condense, tamp ≠ loosen

compact[2] = agreement, deal, understanding, contract, bond, arrangement, treaty, bargain

companion 1 = friend, partner, ally, colleague, associate, mate (*informal*), comrade, accomplice, cobber (*Austral. & N.Z. old-fashioned informal*) **2** = assistant, aide, escort, attendant

company 1 = business, firm, association, corporation, partnership, establishment, syndicate, house **2** = group, set, community, band, crowd, collection, gathering, assembly **3** = troop, unit, squad, team **4** = companionship, society, presence, fellowship **5** = guests, party, visitors, callers

comparable 1 = equal, equivalent, on a par, tantamount, a match for, proportionate, commensurate, as good as ≠ unequal **2** = similar, related, alike, corresponding, akin, analogous, of a piece, cognate

comparative = relative, qualified, by comparison
compare VERB = contrast, balance, weigh, set against, juxtapose
• PHRASES **compare to something** = liken to, parallel, identify with, equate to, correlate to, mention in the same breath as ◆ **compare with something** = be as good as, match, approach, equal, compete with, be on a par with, be the equal of, hold a candle to
comparison 1 = contrast, distinction, differentiation, juxtaposition 2 = similarity, analogy, resemblance, correlation, likeness, comparability
compartment 1 = section, carriage, berth 2 = bay, booth, locker, niche, cubicle, alcove, pigeonhole, cubbyhole
compass = range, field, area, reach, scope, limit, extent, boundary
compassion = sympathy, understanding, pity, humanity, mercy, sorrow, kindness, tenderness, aroha (*N.Z.*) ≠ indifference
compassionate = sympathetic, understanding, pitying, humanitarian, charitable, humane, benevolent, merciful ≠ uncaring
compatible 1 = consistent, in keeping, congruous ≠ inappropriate 2 = like-minded, harmonious, in harmony ≠ incompatible
compel = force, make, railroad (*informal*), oblige, constrain, coerce, impel, dragoon
compelling 1 = convincing, telling, powerful, forceful, conclusive, weighty, cogent, irrefutable 2 = pressing, binding, urgent, overriding, imperative, unavoidable, coercive, peremptory 3 = fascinating, gripping, irresistible, enchanting, enthralling, hypnotic, spellbinding, mesmeric ≠ boring
compensate 1 = recompense, repay, refund, reimburse, remunerate, make good 2 = make amends, make up for, atone, make it up to someone, pay for, do penance, cancel out, make reparation 3 = balance, cancel (out), offset, make up for, redress, counteract, counterbalance
compensation 1 = reparation, damages, recompense, remuneration, restitution, reimbursement 2 = recompense, amends, reparation, restitution, atonement
compete 1 = contend, fight, vie, challenge, struggle, contest, strive 2 = take part, participate, be in the running, be a competitor, be a contestant, play
competence 1 = ability, skill, talent, capacity, expertise, proficiency, capability ≠ incompetence 2 = fitness, suitability, adequacy, appropriateness ≠ inadequacy
competent 1 = able, skilled, capable, proficient ≠ incompetent 2 = fit, qualified, suitable, adequate ≠ unqualified
competition 1 = rivalry, opposition, struggle, strife 2 = opposition, field, rivals, challengers 3 = contest, event, championship, tournament, head-to-head
competitive 1 = cut-throat, aggressive, fierce, ruthless, relentless, antagonistic, dog-eat-dog 2 = ambitious, pushing, opposing, aggressive, vying, contentious, combative
competitor 1 = rival, adversary, antagonist 2 = contestant, participant, contender, challenger, entrant, player, opponent
compilation = collection, treasury, accumulation, anthology, assortment, assemblage
compile = put together, collect, gather, organize, accumulate, marshal, garner, amass
complacency = smugness, satisfaction, contentment, self-congratulation, self-satisfaction
complacent = smug, self-satisfied, pleased with yourself, resting on your laurels, contented, satisfied, serene, unconcerned ≠ insecure
complain = find fault, moan, grumble, whinge (*informal*), carp, groan, lament, whine
complaint 1 = protest, objection, grievance, charge 2 = grumble, criticism, moan, lament, grievance, grouse, gripe (*informal*) 3 = disorder, problem, disease, upset, illness, sickness, ailment, affliction
complement VERB = enhance, complete, improve, boost, crown, add to, set off, heighten
• NOUN 1 = accompaniment, companion, accessory, completion, finishing touch, rounding-off, adjunct, supplement 2 = total, capacity, quota, aggregate, contingent, entirety
complementary = matching,

companion, corresponding, compatible, reciprocal, interrelating, interdependent, harmonizing ≠ incompatible

complete ADJECTIVE **1** = total, perfect, absolute, utter, outright, thorough, consummate, out-and-out **2** = whole, full, entire ≠ partial **3** = entire, full, whole, intact, unbroken, faultless ≠ incomplete **4** = unabridged, full, entire **5** = finished, done, ended, achieved, concluded, fulfilled, accomplished ≠ unfinished **6** = perfect, finish off, round off, crown ≠ spoil
• VERB **1** = finish, conclude, end, close, settle, wrap up (*informal*), finalize ≠ start **2** = fill in, fill out

completely = totally, entirely, wholly, utterly, perfectly, fully, absolutely, altogether

completion = finishing, end, close, conclusion, fulfilment, culmination, fruition

complex ADJECTIVE **1** = compound, multiple, composite, manifold, heterogeneous, multifarious **2** = complicated, difficult, involved, elaborate, tangled, intricate, tortuous, convoluted ≠ simple
• NOUN **1** = structure, system, scheme, network, organization, aggregate, composite **2** (*Informal*) = obsession, preoccupation, phobia, fixation, fixed idea, idée fixe (*French*)

complexion **1** = skin, colour, colouring, hue, skin tone, pigmentation **2** = nature, character, make-up **3** = perspective, look, light, appearance, aspect, angle, slant

complexity = complication, involvement, intricacy, entanglement

complicate = make difficult, confuse, muddle, entangle, involve ≠ simplify

complicated **1** = involved, difficult, puzzling, troublesome, problematic, perplexing ≠ simple **2** = complex, involved, elaborate, intricate, convoluted, labyrinthine ≠ understandable

complication **1** = problem, difficulty, obstacle, drawback, snag, uphill (*S. African*) **2** = complexity, web, confusion, intricacy, entanglement

compliment NOUN = praise, honour, tribute, bouquet, flattery, eulogy ≠ criticism
• PLURAL NOUN **1** = greetings, regards, respects, good wishes, salutation ≠ insult **2** = congratulations, praise, commendation
• VERB = praise, flatter, salute, congratulate, pay tribute to, commend, extol, wax lyrical about ≠ criticize

complimentary **1** = flattering, approving, appreciative, congratulatory, commendatory ≠ critical **2** = free, donated, courtesy, honorary, on the house, gratuitous, gratis

comply = obey, follow, observe, submit to, conform to, adhere to, abide by, acquiesce with ≠ defy

component NOUN = part, piece, unit, item, element, ingredient, constituent
• ADJECTIVE = constituent, inherent, intrinsic

compose VERB **1** = put together, make up, constitute, comprise, make, build, form, fashion ≠ destroy **2** = create, write, produce, invent, devise, contrive **3** = arrange, make up, construct, put together, order, organize
• PHRASES **compose yourself** = calm, control, collect, quiet, soothe, pull yourself together

composed = calm, cool, collected, relaxed, poised, at ease, serene, sedate ≠ agitated

composition **1** = design, structure, make-up, organization, arrangement, formation, layout, configuration **2** = creation, work, piece, production, opus, masterpiece **3** = essay, exercise, treatise, literary work **4** = production, creation, making, fashioning, formation, putting together, compilation, formulation

compound NOUN = combination, mixture, blend, composite, fusion, synthesis, alloy, medley ≠ element
• ADJECTIVE = complex, multiple, composite, intricate ≠ simple
• VERB **1** = intensify, add to, complicate, worsen, heighten, exacerbate, aggravate, magnify ≠ lessen **2** = combine, unite, mix, blend, synthesize, amalgamate, intermingle ≠ divide

comprehend = understand, see, take in, perceive, grasp, conceive, make out, fathom ≠ misunderstand

comprehension = understanding,

grasp, conception, realization, intelligence, perception, discernment ≠ incomprehension
comprehensive = broad, full, complete, blanket, thorough, inclusive, exhaustive, all-inclusive ≠ limited
compress **1** = squeeze, crush, squash, press **2** = condense, contract, concentrate, shorten, abbreviate
comprise **1** = be composed of, include, contain, consist of, take in, embrace, encompass **2** = make up, form, constitute, compose
compromise NOUN = give-and-take, agreement, settlement, accommodation, concession, adjustment, trade-off ≠ disagreement
• VERB **1** = meet halfway, concede, make concessions, give and take, strike a balance, strike a happy medium, go fifty-fifty (*informal*) ≠ disagree **2** = undermine, expose, embarrass, weaken, prejudice, discredit, jeopardize, dishonour ≠ support
compulsive **1** = obsessive, confirmed, chronic, persistent, addictive, uncontrollable, incurable, inveterate **2** = fascinating, gripping, absorbing, compelling, captivating, enthralling, hypnotic, engrossing **3** = irresistible, overwhelming, compelling, urgent, neurotic, uncontrollable, driving
compulsory = obligatory, forced, required, binding, mandatory, imperative, requisite, de rigueur (*French*) ≠ voluntary
compute = calculate, total, count, reckon, figure out, add up, tally, enumerate
comrade = companion, friend, partner, ally, colleague, associate, fellow, co-worker, cobber (*Austral. & N.Z. old-fashioned informal*)
con (*Informal*) VERB = swindle, trick, cheat, rip off (*slang*), deceive, defraud, dupe, hoodwink
• NOUN = swindle, trick, fraud, deception, scam (*slang*), sting (*informal*)
conceal **1** = hide, bury, cover, screen, disguise, obscure, camouflage ≠ reveal **2** = keep secret, hide, disguise, mask, suppress, veil ≠ show
concede **1** = admit, allow, accept, acknowledge, own, grant, confess ≠ deny **2** = give up, yield, hand over, surrender, relinquish, cede ≠ conquer
conceive **1** = imagine, envisage, comprehend, visualize, think, believe, suppose, fancy **2** = think up, create, design, devise, formulate, contrive **3** = become pregnant, get pregnant, become impregnated
concentrate **1** = focus your attention on, focus on, pay attention to, be engrossed in, put your mind to, keep your mind on, apply yourself to, give your mind to ≠ pay no attention to **2** = focus, centre, converge, bring to bear **3** = gather, collect, cluster, accumulate, congregate ≠ scatter
concentrated **1** = condensed, rich, undiluted, reduced, evaporated, thickened, boiled down **2** = intense, hard, deep, intensive, all-out (*informal*)
concentration **1** = attention, application, absorption, single-mindedness, intentness ≠ inattention **2** = focusing, centring, consolidation, convergence, bringing to bear, intensification, centralization **3** = convergence, collection, mass, cluster, accumulation, aggregation ≠ scattering
concept = idea, view, image, theory, notion, conception, hypothesis, abstraction
conception **1** = idea, plan, design, image, concept, notion **2** = impregnation, insemination, fertilization, germination
concern NOUN **1** = anxiety, fear, worry, distress, unease, apprehension, misgiving, disquiet **2** = worry, care, anxiety **3** = affair, issue, matter, consideration **4** = care, interest, attentiveness **5** = business, job, affair, responsibility, task **6** = company, business, firm, organization, corporation, enterprise, establishment **7** = importance, interest, bearing, relevance
• VERB **1** = worry, trouble, bother, disturb, distress, disquiet, perturb, make anxious **2** = be about, cover, deal with, go into, relate to, have to do with **3** = be relevant to, involve, affect, regard, apply to, bear on, have something to do with, pertain to
concerned **1** = worried, troubled, upset, bothered, disturbed, anxious, distressed, uneasy ≠ indifferent **2** = involved, interested, active, mixed up, implicated, privy to
concerning = regarding, about, re, touching, respecting, relating to, on the subject of, with reference to
concession **1** = compromise, agreement, settlement, accommodation, adjustment,

trade-off, give-and-take **2** = privilege, right, permit, licence, entitlement, indulgence, prerogative **3** = reduction, saving, grant, discount, allowance **4** = surrender, yielding, conceding, renunciation, relinquishment

conclude **1** = decide, judge, assume, gather, work out, infer, deduce, surmise **2** = come to an end, end, close, finish, wind up ≠ begin **3** = bring to an end, end, close, finish, complete, wind up, terminate, round off ≠ begin **4** = accomplish, effect, bring about, carry out, pull off

conclusion **1** = decision, opinion, conviction, verdict, judgment, deduction, inference **2** = end, ending, close, finish, completion, finale, termination, bitter end **3** = outcome, result, upshot, consequence, culmination, end result

concrete **1** = specific, precise, explicit, definite, clear-cut, unequivocal ≠ vague **2** = real, material, actual, substantial, sensible, tangible, factual ≠ abstract

condemn **1** = denounce, damn, criticize, disapprove, censure, reprove, upbraid, blame ≠ approve **2** = sentence, convict, damn, doom, pass sentence on ≠ acquit

condemnation = denunciation, blame, censure, disapproval, reproach, stricture, reproof

condition **NOUN** **1** = state, order, shape, nick (*Brit. informal*), trim **2** = situation, state, position, status, circumstances **3** = requirement, terms, rider, restriction, qualification, limitation, prerequisite, proviso **4** = health, shape, fitness, trim, form, kilter, state of health, fettle **5** = ailment, problem, complaint, weakness, malady, infirmity

• **PLURAL NOUN** = circumstances, situation, environment, surroundings, way of life, milieu

• **VERB** = train, teach, adapt, accustom

conditional = dependent, limited, qualified, subject to, contingent, provisional, with reservations ≠ unconditional

condone = overlook, excuse, forgive, pardon, turn a blind eye to, look the other way, make allowance for, let pass ≠ condemn

conduct **VERB** **1** = carry out, run, control, manage, direct, handle, organize, administer **2** = accompany, lead, escort, guide, steer, convey, usher

• **NOUN** **1** = management, running, control, handling, administration, direction, organization, guidance **2** = behaviour, ways, bearing, attitude, manners, demeanour, deportment

• **PHRASES** **conduct yourself** = behave yourself, act, carry yourself, acquit yourself, deport yourself, comport yourself

confer **1** = discuss, talk, consult, deliberate, discourse, converse **2** = grant, give, present, accord, award, hand out, bestow

conference = meeting, congress, discussion, convention, forum, consultation, seminar, symposium, hui (*N.Z.*)

confess **1** = admit, acknowledge, disclose, confide, own up, come clean (*informal*), divulge ≠ cover up **2** = declare, allow, reveal, confirm, concede, assert, affirm, profess

confession = admission, revelation, disclosure, acknowledgment, exposure, unbosoming

confidant *or* **confidante** = close friend, familiar, intimate, crony, alter ego, bosom friend

confide = tell, admit, reveal, confess, whisper, disclose, impart, divulge

confidence **NOUN** **1** = trust, belief, faith, dependence, reliance, credence ≠ distrust **2** = self-assurance, courage, assurance, aplomb, boldness, self-possession, nerve ≠ shyness **3** = secret

• **PHRASES** **in confidence** = in secrecy, privately, confidentially, between you and me (and the gatepost), (just) between ourselves

confident **1** = certain, sure, convinced, positive, secure, satisfied, counting on ≠ unsure **2** = self-assured, positive, assured, bold, self-confident, self-reliant, sure of yourself ≠ insecure

confidential **1** = secret, private, intimate, classified, privy, off the record, hush-hush (*informal*) **2** = secretive, low, soft, hushed

confine **VERB** **1** = imprison, enclose, shut up, intern, incarcerate, hem in, keep, cage **2** = restrict, limit

• **PLURAL NOUN** = limits, bounds, boundaries, compass, precincts, circumference, edge

confirm **1** = prove, support, establish,

back up, verify, validate, bear out, substantiate **2** = ratify, establish, sanction, endorse, authorize **3** = strengthen, establish, fix, secure, reinforce, fortify

confirmation 1 = proof, evidence, testimony, verification, ratification, validation, corroboration, authentication ≠ repudiation **2** = affirmation, approval, acceptance, endorsement, ratification, assent, agreement ≠ disapproval

confirmed = long-established, seasoned, chronic, hardened, habitual, ingrained, inveterate, dyed-in-the-wool

confiscate = seize, appropriate, impound, commandeer, sequester ≠ give back

conflict NOUN **1** = dispute, difference, opposition, hostility, disagreement, friction, strife, fighting ≠ agreement **2** = struggle, battle, clash, strife **3** = battle, war, fight, clash, contest, encounter, combat, strife ≠ peace
• VERB = be incompatible, clash, differ, disagree, collide, be at variance ≠ agree

conflicting = incompatible, opposing, clashing, contrary, contradictory, inconsistent, paradoxical, discordant ≠ agreeing

conform 1 = fit in, follow, adjust, adapt, comply, obey, fall in with, toe the line **2** = fulfil, meet, match, suit, satisfy, agree with, obey, abide by

confound = bewilder, baffle, confuse, astound, perplex, mystify, flummox, dumbfound

confront 1 = tackle, deal with, cope with, meet head-on **2** = trouble, face, perturb, bedevil **3** = challenge, face, oppose, tackle, encounter, defy, stand up to, accost ≠ evade

confrontation = conflict, fight, contest, set-to (*informal*), encounter, showdown (*informal*), head-to-head

confuse 1 = mix up with, take for, muddle with **2** = bewilder, puzzle, baffle, perplex, mystify, fluster, faze, flummox **3** = obscure, cloud, make more difficult

confused 1 = bewildered, puzzled, baffled, at sea, muddled, perplexed, taken aback, disorientated ≠ enlightened **2** = disorderly, disordered, chaotic, mixed up, jumbled, untidy, in disarray, topsy-turvy ≠ tidy

confusing = bewildering, puzzling, misleading, unclear, baffling, contradictory, perplexing ≠ clear

confusion 1 = bewilderment, doubt, uncertainty ≠ enlightenment **2** = disorder, chaos, turmoil, upheaval, muddle, shambles, commotion ≠ order

congestion = overcrowding, crowding, jam, clogging, bottleneck

congratulate = compliment, pat on the back, wish joy to

congratulations PLURAL NOUN = good wishes, greetings, compliments, best wishes, felicitations
• INTERJECTION = good wishes, greetings, compliments, best wishes, felicitations

congregation = parishioners, brethren, crowd, assembly, flock, fellowship, multitude, throng

congress 1 = meeting, council, conference, assembly, convention, conclave, hui (*N.Z.*), runanga (*N.Z.*) **2** = legislature, council, parliament, House of Representatives (*N.Z.*)

conjure VERB = produce, generate, bring about, give rise to, make, create, effect, produce as if by magic
• PHRASES **conjure something up** = bring to mind, recall, evoke, recreate, recollect, produce as if by magic

connect 1 = link, join, couple, attach, fasten, affix, unite ≠ separate **2** = associate, join, link, identify, lump together

connected = linked, united, joined, coupled, related, allied, associated, combined

connection 1 = association, relationship, link, bond, relevance, tie-in **2** = communication, alliance, attachment, liaison, affinity, union **3** = link, coupling, junction, fastening, tie **4** = contact, friend, ally, associate, acquaintance

conquer 1 = seize, obtain, acquire, occupy, overrun, annex, win **2** = defeat, overcome, overthrow, beat, master, crush, overpower, quell ≠ lose to **3** = overcome, beat, defeat, master, overpower

conquest 1 = takeover, coup, invasion, occupation, annexation, subjugation **2** = defeat, victory, triumph, overthrow, rout, mastery

conscience 1 = principles, scruples, moral sense, sense of right and wrong, still small voice **2** = guilt, shame, regret, remorse, contrition, self-reproach

conscious 1 *often with* ***of*** = aware of, alert to, responsive to, sensible of ≠ unaware 2 = deliberate, knowing, studied, calculated, self-conscious, intentional, wilful, premeditated ≠ unintentional 3 = awake, wide-awake, sentient, alive ≠ asleep

consciousness = awareness, understanding, knowledge, recognition, sensibility, realization, apprehension

consecutive = successive, running, succeeding, in turn, uninterrupted, sequential, in sequence

consensus = agreement, general agreement, unanimity, common consent, unity, harmony, assent, concord, kotahitanga (*N.Z.*)

consent NOUN = agreement, sanction, approval, go-ahead (*informal*), permission, compliance, assent, acquiescence ≠ refusal
• VERB = agree, approve, permit, concur, assent, acquiesce ≠ refuse

consequence 1 = result, effect, outcome, repercussion, issue, sequel, end result, upshot 2 = importance, concern, moment, value, account, weight, import, significance

consequently = as a result, thus, therefore, hence, subsequently, accordingly, for that reason, thence

conservation 1 = preservation, saving, protection, maintenance, safeguarding, upkeep, guardianship, safekeeping 2 = economy, saving, thrift, husbandry

conservative ADJECTIVE = traditional, conventional, cautious, sober, reactionary, die-hard, hidebound ≠ radical
• NOUN = traditionalist, reactionary, die-hard, stick-in-the-mud (*informal*) ≠ radical

Conservative ADJECTIVE = Tory, Republican (*U.S.*), right-wing
• NOUN = Tory, Republican (*U.S.*), right-winger

conserve 1 = save, husband, take care of, hoard, store up, use sparingly ≠ waste 2 = protect, keep, save, preserve

consider 1 = think, see, believe, rate, judge, suppose, deem, view as 2 = think about, reflect on, weigh, contemplate, deliberate, ponder, meditate, ruminate 3 = bear in mind, remember, respect, think about, take into account, reckon with, take into consideration, make allowance for

considerable = large, goodly, great, marked, substantial, noticeable, plentiful, appreciable ≠ small

considerably = greatly, very much, significantly, remarkably, substantially, markedly, noticeably, appreciably

consideration 1 = thought, review, analysis, examination, reflection, scrutiny, deliberation 2 = thoughtfulness, concern, respect, kindness, tact, considerateness 3 = factor, point, issue, concern, element, aspect 4 = payment, fee, reward, remuneration, recompense, tip

considering = taking into account, in the light of, bearing in mind, in view of, keeping in mind, taking into consideration

consist VERB
• PHRASES **consist in something** = lie in, involve, reside in, be expressed by, subsist in, be found *or* contained in ◆ **consist of something** = be made up of, include, contain, incorporate, amount to, comprise, be composed of

consistency 1 = agreement, regularity, uniformity, constancy, steadiness, steadfastness, evenness 2 = texture, density, thickness, firmness, viscosity, compactness

consistent 1 = steady, even, regular, stable, constant, persistent, dependable, unchanging ≠ erratic 2 = compatible, agreeing, in keeping, harmonious, in harmony, consonant, in accord, congruous ≠ incompatible 3 = coherent, logical, compatible, harmonious, consonant ≠ contradictory

consolation = comfort, help, support, relief, cheer, encouragement, solace, succour

console = comfort, cheer, soothe, support, encourage, calm, succour, express sympathy for ≠ distress

consolidate 1 = strengthen, secure, reinforce, fortify, stabilize 2 = combine, unite, join, merge, unify, amalgamate, federate

conspicuous = obvious, clear, patent, evident, noticeable, blatant, salient ≠ inconspicuous

conspiracy = plot, scheme, intrigue, collusion, machination

conspire 1 = plot, scheme, intrigue,

manoeuvre, contrive, machinate, plan 2 = work together, combine, contribute, cooperate, concur, tend

constant 1 = continuous, sustained, perpetual, interminable, unrelenting, incessant, ceaseless, nonstop ≠ occasional 2 = unchanging, even, fixed, permanent, stable, steady, uniform, invariable ≠ changing 3 = faithful, true, devoted, loyal, stalwart, staunch, trustworthy, trusty ≠ undependable

constantly = continuously, always, all the time, invariably, continually, endlessly, perpetually, incessantly ≠ occasionally

constituent NOUN 1 = voter, elector, member of the electorate 2 = component, element, ingredient, part, unit, factor
• ADJECTIVE = component, basic, essential, integral, elemental

constitute 1 = represent, be, consist of, embody, exemplify, be equivalent to 2 = make up, form, compose, comprise

constitution 1 = state of health, build, body, frame, physique, physical condition 2 = structure, form, nature, make-up, composition, character, disposition

constitutional = legitimate, official, legal, chartered, statutory, vested

constrain 1 = restrict, confine, curb, restrain, constrict, straiten, check 2 = force, bind, compel, oblige, necessitate, coerce, impel, pressurize

constraint 1 = restriction, limitation, curb, rein, deterrent, hindrance, check 2 = force, pressure, necessity, restraint, compulsion, coercion

construct 1 = build, make, form, create, fashion, shape, manufacture, assemble ≠ demolish 2 = create, make, form, compose, put together

construction 1 = building, creation, composition 2 (*Formal*) = interpretation, reading, explanation, rendering, inference

constructive = helpful, positive, useful, practical, valuable, productive ≠ unproductive

consult 1 = ask, refer to, turn to, take counsel, pick (someone's) brains, question 2 = confer, talk, compare notes 3 = refer to, check in, look in

consultant = specialist, adviser, counsellor, authority

consultation 1 = discussion, talk, council, conference, dialogue 2 = meeting, interview, session, appointment, examination, deliberation, hearing

consume 1 = eat, swallow, devour, put away, gobble (up), eat up 2 = use up, spend, waste, absorb, exhaust, squander, dissipate, expend 3 = destroy, devastate, demolish, ravage, annihilate, lay waste 4 *often passive* = obsess, dominate, absorb, preoccupy, eat up, monopolize, engross

consumer = buyer, customer, user, shopper, purchaser

consumption 1 = using up, use, loss, waste, expenditure, exhaustion, depletion, dissipation 2 (*Old-fashioned*) = tuberculosis, T.B.

contact NOUN 1 = communication, link, association, connection, correspondence 2 = touch, contiguity 3 = connection, colleague, associate, liaison, acquaintance, confederate
• VERB = get *or* be in touch with, call, reach, approach, write to, speak to, communicate with

contain 1 = hold, incorporate, accommodate, enclose, have capacity for 2 = include, consist of, embrace, comprise, embody, comprehend 3 = restrain, control, hold in, curb, suppress, hold back, stifle, repress

container = holder, vessel, repository, receptacle

contaminate = pollute, infect, stain, corrupt, taint, defile, adulterate, befoul ≠ purify

contamination = pollution, infection, corruption, poisoning, taint, impurity, contagion, defilement

contemplate 1 = consider, plan, think of, intend, envisage, foresee 2 = think about, consider, ponder, reflect upon, ruminate (upon), muse over, deliberate over 3 = look at, examine, inspect, gaze at, eye up, view, study, regard

contemporary ADJECTIVE 1 = modern, recent, current, up-to-date, present-day, à la mode, newfangled, present ≠ old-fashioned 2 = coexisting, concurrent, contemporaneous
• NOUN = peer, fellow, equal

contempt = scorn, disdain, mockery, derision, disrespect, disregard ≠ respect

contend 1 = argue, hold, maintain, allege, assert, affirm 2 = compete, fight, struggle, clash, contest, strive, vie, jostle

content¹ NOUN 1 = subject matter, material, theme, substance, essence, gist 2 = amount, measure, size, load, volume, capacity
• PLURAL NOUN = constituents, elements, load, ingredients

content² ADJECTIVE = satisfied, happy, pleased, contented, comfortable, fulfilled, at ease, gratified
• NOUN = satisfaction, ease, pleasure, comfort, peace of mind, gratification, contentment
• PHRASES **content yourself with something** = satisfy yourself with, be happy with, be satisfied with, be content with

contented = satisfied, happy, pleased, content, comfortable, glad, thankful, gratified ≠ discontented

contentious = argumentative, wrangling, bickering, quarrelsome, querulous, cavilling, disputatious, captious

contest NOUN 1 = competition, game, match, trial, tournament 2 = struggle, fight, battle, conflict, dispute, controversy, combat
• VERB 1 = compete in, take part in, fight in, go in for, contend for, vie in 2 = oppose, question, challenge, argue, debate, dispute, object to, call in *or* into question

contestant = competitor, candidate, participant, contender, entrant, player

context 1 = circumstances, conditions, situation, ambience 2 = frame of reference, background, framework, relation, connection

contingency = possibility, happening, chance, event, incident, accident, emergency, eventuality

continual 1 = constant, interminable, incessant, unremitting ≠ erratic 2 = frequent, regular, repeated, recurrent ≠ occasional

continually 1 = constantly, always, all the time, forever, incessantly, nonstop, interminably 2 = repeatedly, often, frequently, many times, over and over, persistently

continuation 1 = continuing, lasting, carrying on, keeping up, endurance, perpetuation, prolongation 2 = addition, extension, supplement, sequel, resumption, postscript

continue 1 = keep on, go on, maintain, sustain, carry on, persist in, persevere, stick at ≠ stop 2 = go on, progress, proceed, carry on, keep going 3 = resume, return to, take up again, proceed, carry on, recommence, pick up where you left off ≠ stop 4 = remain, last, stay, survive, carry on, live on, endure, persist ≠ quit

continuing = lasting, sustained, enduring, ongoing, in progress

continuity = cohesion, flow, connection, sequence, succession, progression

continuous = constant, extended, prolonged, unbroken, uninterrupted, unceasing ≠ occasional

contract NOUN = agreement, commitment, arrangement, settlement, bargain, pact, covenant
• VERB 1 = agree, negotiate, pledge, bargain, undertake, come to terms, covenant, make a deal ≠ refuse 2 = constrict, confine, tighten, shorten, compress, condense, shrivel 3 = tighten, narrow, shorten ≠ stretch 4 = lessen, reduce, shrink, diminish, decrease, dwindle ≠ increase 5 = catch, get, develop, acquire, incur, be infected with, go down with, be afflicted with ≠ avoid

contraction 1 = tightening, narrowing, shortening, constricting, shrinkage 2 = abbreviation, reduction, shortening, compression

contradict 1 = dispute, deny, challenge, belie, fly in the face of, be at variance with 2 = negate, deny, rebut, controvert ≠ confirm

contradiction 1 = conflict, inconsistency, contravention, incongruity 2 = negation, opposite, denial

contradictory = inconsistent, conflicting, opposed, opposite, contrary, incompatible, paradoxical

contrary ADJECTIVE 1 = opposite, different, opposed, clashing, counter, reverse, adverse, contradictory ≠ in agreement 2 = perverse, difficult, awkward, intractable, obstinate, stroppy (*Brit. slang*), cantankerous, disobliging ≠ cooperative
• NOUN = opposite, reverse, converse, antithesis

contrast NOUN = difference, opposition, comparison, distinction, foil, disparity, divergence, dissimilarity
• VERB 1 = differentiate, compare, oppose, distinguish, set in opposition 2 = differ, be

contrary, be at variance, be dissimilar
contribute VERB = give, provide, supply, donate, subscribe, chip in (*informal*), bestow
• PHRASES **contribute to something** = be partly responsible for, lead to, be instrumental in, be conducive to, help
contribution = gift, offering, grant, donation, input, subscription, koha (*N.Z.*)
contributor = donor, supporter, patron, subscriber, giver
contrive 1 = devise, plan, fabricate, create, design, scheme, manufacture, plot 2 = manage, succeed, arrange, manoeuvre
contrived = forced, planned, laboured, strained, artificial, elaborate, unnatural, overdone ≠ natural
control NOUN 1 = power, authority, management, command, guidance, supervision, supremacy, charge 2 = restraint, check, regulation, brake, limitation, curb 3 = self-discipline, self-restraint, restraint, self-command 4 = switch, instrument, button, dial, lever, knob
• PLURAL NOUN = instruments, dash, dials, console, dashboard, control panel
• VERB 1 = have power over, manage, direct, handle, command, govern, administer, supervise 2 = limit, restrict, curb 3 = restrain, limit, check, contain, curb, hold back, subdue, repress
controversial = disputed, contentious, at issue, debatable, under discussion, open to question, disputable
controversy = argument, debate, row, dispute, quarrel, squabble, wrangling, altercation
convene 1 = call, gather, assemble, summon, bring together, convoke 2 = meet, gather, assemble, come together, congregate
convenience 1 = benefit, good, advantage 2 = suitability, fitness, appropriateness 3 = usefulness, utility ≠ uselessness 4 = accessibility, availability, nearness 5 = appliance, facility, comfort, amenity, labour-saving device, help
convenient 1 = suitable, fit, handy, satisfactory 2 = useful, practical, handy, serviceable, labour-saving ≠ useless 3 = nearby, available, accessible, handy, at hand, within reach, close at hand, just round the corner ≠ inaccessible 4 = appropriate, timely, suitable, helpful
convention 1 = custom, practice, tradition, code, usage, protocol, etiquette, propriety, kawa (*N.Z.*), tikanga (*N.Z.*) 2 = agreement, contract, treaty, bargain, pact, protocol 3 = assembly, meeting, council, conference, congress, convocation, hui (*N.Z.*), runanga (*N.Z.*)
conventional 1 = proper, conservative, respectable, genteel, conformist 2 = ordinary, standard, normal, regular, usual 3 = traditional, accepted, orthodox, customary 4 = unoriginal, routine, stereotyped, banal, prosaic, run-of-the-mill, hackneyed ≠ unconventional
converge VERB = come together, meet, join, combine, gather, merge, coincide, intersect
• PHRASES **converge on something** = close in on, arrive at, move towards, home in on, come together at
conversation = talk, discussion, dialogue, tête-à-tête, conference, chat, gossip, discourse, korero (*N.Z.*)
RELATED WORD
adjective: colloquial
conversion 1 = change, transformation, metamorphosis 2 = adaptation, reconstruction, modification, alteration, remodelling, reorganization
convert VERB 1 = change, turn, transform, alter, transpose 2 = adapt, modify, remodel, reorganize, customize, restyle 3 = reform, convince, proselytize
• NOUN = neophyte, disciple, proselyte
convey 1 = communicate, impart, reveal, relate, disclose, make known, tell 2 = carry, transport, move, bring, bear, conduct, fetch
convict VERB = find guilty, sentence, condemn, imprison, pronounce guilty
• NOUN = prisoner, criminal, lag (*slang*), felon, jailbird
conviction 1 = belief, view, opinion, principle, faith, persuasion, creed, tenet, kaupapa (*N.Z.*) 2 = certainty, confidence, assurance, firmness, certitude
convince 1 = assure, persuade, satisfy, reassure 2 = persuade, induce, coax, talk into, prevail upon, bring round to the idea of
convincing = persuasive, credible, conclusive, telling, powerful, impressive, plausible, cogent ≠ unconvincing

cool ADJECTIVE **1** = cold, chilled, refreshing, chilly, nippy ≠ warm **2** = calm, collected, relaxed, composed, sedate, self-controlled, unruffled, unemotional ≠ agitated **3** = unfriendly, distant, indifferent, aloof, lukewarm, offhand, unenthusiastic, unwelcoming ≠ friendly **4** = unenthusiastic, indifferent, lukewarm, unwelcoming
• VERB **1** = lose heat, cool off ≠ warm (up) **2** = make cool, freeze, chill, refrigerate, cool off ≠ warm (up)
• NOUN **1** = coldness, chill, coolness **2** (*Slang*) = calmness, control, temper, composure, self-control, poise, self-discipline, self-possession

cooperate = work together, collaborate, coordinate, join forces, conspire, pull together, pool resources, combine your efforts ≠ conflict

cooperation = teamwork, unity, collaboration, give-and-take, combined effort, esprit de corps, kotahitanga (*N.Z.*) ≠ opposition

cooperative **1** = shared, joint, combined, collective, collaborative **2** = helpful, obliging, accommodating, supportive, responsive, onside (*informal*)

cope VERB = manage, get by (*informal*), struggle through, survive, carry on, make the grade, hold your own
• PHRASES **cope with something** = deal with, handle, struggle with, grapple with, wrestle with, contend with, weather

copy NOUN = reproduction, duplicate, replica, imitation, forgery, counterfeit, likeness, facsimile ≠ original
• VERB **1** = reproduce, replicate, duplicate, transcribe, counterfeit ≠ create **2** = imitate, act like, emulate, behave like, follow, repeat, mirror, ape

cord = rope, line, string, twine

cordon NOUN = chain, line, ring, barrier, picket line
• PHRASES **cordon something off** = surround, isolate, close off, fence off, separate, enclose, picket, encircle

core **1** = centre **2** = heart, essence, nucleus, kernel, crux, gist, nub, pith

corner NOUN **1** = angle, joint, crook **2** = bend, curve **3** = space, hideaway, nook, hide-out
• VERB **1** = trap, catch, run to earth **2** (usually with *market* as object) = monopolize, take over, dominate, control, hog (*slang*), engross

corporation **1** = business, company, concern, firm, society, association, organization, enterprise **2** = town council, council, municipal authorities, civic authorities

corps = team, unit, regiment, detachment, company, band, division, troop

corpse = body, remains, carcass, cadaver, stiff (*slang*)

correct ADJECTIVE **1** = accurate, right, true, exact, precise, flawless, faultless, O.K. *or* okay (*informal*) ≠ inaccurate **2** = right, standard, appropriate, acceptable, proper, precise **3** = proper, seemly, standard, fitting, kosher (*informal*) ≠ inappropriate
• VERB **1** = rectify, remedy, redress, right, reform, cure, adjust, amend ≠ spoil **2** = rebuke, discipline, reprimand, chide, admonish, chastise, chasten, reprove ≠ praise

correction **1** = rectification, improvement, amendment, adjustment, modification, alteration, emendation **2** = punishment, discipline, reformation, admonition, chastisement, reproof, castigation

correctly = rightly, right, perfectly, properly, precisely, accurately

correctness **1** = truth, accuracy, precision, exactitude, exactness, faultlessness **2** = decorum, propriety, good manners, civility, good breeding

correspond **1** = be consistent, match, agree, accord, fit, square, tally, conform ≠ differ **2** = communicate, write, keep in touch, exchange letters

correspondence **1** = communication, writing, contact **2** = letters, post, mail **3** = relation, match, agreement, comparison, harmony, coincidence, similarity, correlation

correspondent **1** = reporter, journalist, contributor, hack **2** = letter writer, pen friend *or* pen pal

corresponding = equivalent, matching, similar, related, complementary, reciprocal, analogous

corridor = passage, alley, aisle, hallway, passageway

corrupt ADJECTIVE **1** = dishonest, bent (*slang*), crooked (*informal*), fraudulent, unscrupulous, venal, unprincipled

≠ honest **2** = depraved, vicious, degenerate, debased, profligate, dissolute **3** = distorted, doctored, altered, falsified
• **VERB 1** = bribe, fix (*informal*), buy off, suborn, grease (someone's) palm (*slang*) **2** = deprave, pervert, subvert, debauch ≠ reform **3** = distort, doctor, tamper with

corruption 1 = dishonesty, fraud, bribery, extortion, venality, shady dealings (*informal*) **2** = depravity, vice, evil, perversion, decadence, wickedness, immorality **3** = distortion, doctoring, falsification

cosmetic = superficial, surface, nonessential

cosmic 1 = extraterrestrial, stellar **2** = universal, general, overarching

cosmopolitan = sophisticated, cultured, refined, cultivated, urbane, well-travelled, worldly-wise ≠ unsophisticated

cost NOUN 1 = price, worth, expense, charge, damage (*informal*), amount, payment, outlay **2** = loss, suffering, damage, injury, penalty, hurt, expense, harm
• **PLURAL NOUN** = expenses, spending, expenditure, overheads, outgoings, outlay, budget
• **VERB 1** = sell at, come to, set (someone) back (*informal*), be priced at, command a price of **2** = lose, deprive of, cheat of

costly 1 = expensive, dear, stiff, steep (*informal*), highly-priced, exorbitant, extortionate ≠ inexpensive **2** = damaging, disastrous, harmful, catastrophic, loss-making, ruinous, deleterious

costume = outfit, dress, clothing, uniform, ensemble, livery, apparel, attire

cosy 1 = comfortable, homely, warm, intimate, snug, comfy (*informal*), sheltered **2** = snug, warm, comfortable, sheltered, comfy (*informal*), tucked up **3** = intimate, friendly, informal

cottage = cabin, lodge, hut, shack, chalet, whare (*N.Z.*)

cough VERB = clear your throat, bark, hack
• **NOUN** = frog *or* tickle in your throat, bark, hack

council 1 = committee, governing body, board **2** = governing body, parliament, congress, cabinet, panel, assembly, convention, conference, runanga (*N.Z.*)

counsel NOUN 1 = advice, information, warning, direction, suggestion, recommendation, guidance **2** = legal adviser, lawyer, attorney, solicitor, advocate, barrister
• **VERB** = advise, recommend, advocate, warn, urge, instruct, exhort

count VERB 1 *often with* ***up*** = add (up), total, reckon (up), tot up, calculate, compute, tally, number **2** = matter, be important, carry weight, tell, rate, weigh, signify **3** = consider, judge, regard, deem, think of, rate, look upon **4** = include, number among, take into account *or* consideration
• **NOUN** = calculation, poll, reckoning, sum, tally, numbering, computation, enumeration
• **PHRASES count on** *or* **upon something** *or* **someone** = depend on, trust, rely on, bank on, take for granted, lean on, reckon on, take on trust

counter VERB 1 = oppose, meet, block, resist, parry, deflect, repel, rebuff **2** = retaliate, answer, reply, respond, retort, hit back, rejoin, strike back ≠ yield
• **ADVERB** = opposite to, against, versus, conversely, in defiance of, at variance with, contrariwise ≠ in accordance with

counterpart = opposite number, equal, twin, equivalent, match, fellow, mate

countless = innumerable, legion, infinite, myriad, untold, limitless, incalculable, immeasurable ≠ limited

country 1 = nation, state, land, commonwealth, kingdom, realm, people **2** = people, community, nation, society, citizens, inhabitants, populace, public **3** = countryside, provinces, sticks (*informal*), farmland, outback (*Austral. & N.Z.*), green belt, backwoods, bush (*N.Z. & S. African*) ≠ town **4** = territory, land, region, terrain

countryside = country, rural areas, outback (*Austral. & N.Z.*), green belt, sticks (*informal*)

county = province, district, shire

coup = masterstroke, feat, stunt, action, exploit, manoeuvre, deed, accomplishment

couple NOUN = pair, two, brace, duo, twosome
• **PHRASES couple something to something** = link to, connect to, pair with, unite with, join to, hitch to, yoke to

coupon = slip, ticket, certificate, token,

voucher, card

courage = bravery, nerve, resolution, daring, pluck, heroism, mettle, gallantry ≠ cowardice

courageous = brave, daring, bold, gritty, fearless, gallant, intrepid, valiant ≠ cowardly

courier **1** = messenger, runner, carrier, bearer, envoy **2** = guide, representative, escort, conductor

course NOUN **1** = route, way, line, road, track, direction, path, passage **2** = procedure, plan, policy, programme, method, conduct, behaviour, manner **3** = progression, order, unfolding, development, movement, progress, flow, sequence **4** = classes, programme, schedule, lectures, curriculum **5** = racecourse, circuit **6** = period, time, duration, term, passing
• VERB **1** = run, flow, stream, gush, race, speed, surge **2** = hunt, follow, chase, pursue
• PHRASES **of course** = naturally, certainly, obviously, definitely, undoubtedly, needless to say, without a doubt, indubitably

court NOUN **1** = law court, bar, bench, tribunal **2** = palace, hall, castle, manor **3** = royal household, train, suite, attendants, entourage, retinue, cortege
• VERB **1** = cultivate, seek, flatter, solicit, pander to, curry favour with, fawn upon **2** = invite, seek, attract, prompt, provoke, bring about, incite **3** = woo, go (out) with, date, take out, run after, walk out with, set your cap at

courtesy **1** = politeness, good manners, civility, gallantry, graciousness, affability, urbanity **2** = favour, kindness, indulgence

courtyard = yard, square, piazza, quadrangle, plaza, enclosure, cloister, quad (*informal*)

cove = bay, sound, inlet, anchorage

covenant = promise, contract, agreement, commitment, arrangement, pledge, pact

cover VERB **1** = conceal, hide, mask, disguise, obscure, veil, cloak, shroud ≠ reveal **2** = clothe, dress, wrap, envelop ≠ uncover **3** = overlay, blanket **4** = coat, cake, plaster, smear, envelop, spread, encase, daub **5** = submerge, flood, engulf, overrun, wash over **6** = travel over, cross, traverse, pass through *or* over **7** = protect, guard, defend, shield **8** = consider, deal with, investigate, describe, tell of **9** = report on, write about, commentate on, relate, tell of, narrate, write up **10** = pay for, fund, provide for, offset, be enough for
• NOUN **1** = protection, shelter, shield, defence, guard, camouflage, concealment **2** = insurance, protection, compensation, indemnity, reimbursement **3** = covering, case, top, coating, envelope, lid, canopy, wrapper **4** = bedclothes, bedding, sheets, blankets, quilt, duvet, eiderdown **5** = jacket, case, wrapper **6** = disguise, front, screen, mask, veil, façade, pretext, smoke screen

covering NOUN = cover, coating, casing, wrapping, layer, blanket
• ADJECTIVE = explanatory, accompanying, introductory, descriptive

covet = long for, desire, envy, crave, aspire to, yearn for, lust after, set your heart on

coward = wimp, chicken (*slang*), scaredy-cat (*informal*), yellow-belly (*slang*)

cowardly = faint-hearted, scared, spineless, soft, yellow (*informal*), weak, chicken (*slang*), fearful, sookie (*N.Z.*) ≠ brave

cowboy = cowhand, drover, rancher, stockman, cattleman, herdsman, gaucho (*S. American*)

crack VERB **1** = break, split, burst, snap, fracture, splinter **2** = snap, ring, crash, burst, explode, pop, detonate **3** (*Informal*) = hit, clip (*informal*), slap, smack, clout (*informal*), cuff, whack **4** = break, cleave **5** = solve, work out, resolve, clear up, fathom, decipher, suss (out) (*slang*), get to the bottom of **6** = break down, collapse, yield, give in, give way, succumb, lose control, be overcome
• NOUN **1** = break, chink, gap, fracture, rift, cleft, crevice, fissure **2** = split, break, fracture **3** = snap, pop, crash, burst, explosion, clap, report **4** (*Informal*) = blow, slap, smack, clout (*informal*), cuff, whack, clip (*informal*) **5** (*Informal*) = joke, dig, gag (*informal*), quip, jibe, wisecrack, witticism, funny remark
• ADJECTIVE (*Slang*) = first-class, choice, excellent, ace, elite, superior, world-class, first-rate

crackdown = clampdown, crushing, repression, suppression

cracked = broken, damaged, split, chipped, flawed, faulty, defective, imperfect
cradle NOUN **1** = crib, cot, Moses basket, bassinet **2** = birthplace, beginning, source, spring, origin, fount, fountainhead, wellspring
• VERB = hold, support, rock, nurse, nestle
craft 1 = vessel, boat, ship, plane, aircraft, spacecraft **2** = occupation, work, business, trade, employment, pursuit, vocation, handicraft **3** = skill, art, ability, technique, know-how (*informal*), expertise, aptitude, artistry
craftsman = skilled worker, artisan, master, maker, wright, technician, smith
cram 1 = stuff, force, jam, shove, compress **2** = pack, fill, stuff **3** = squeeze, press, pack in **4** = study, revise, swot, bone up (*informal*), mug up (*slang*)
cramp[1] = spasm, pain, ache, contraction, pang, stitch, convulsion, twinge
cramp[2] = restrict, hamper, inhibit, hinder, handicap, constrain, obstruct, impede
cramped = restricted, confined, overcrowded, crowded, packed, uncomfortable, closed in, congested ≠ spacious
crash NOUN **1** = collision, accident, smash, wreck, prang (*informal*), bump, pile-up (*informal*) **2** = smash, clash, boom, bang, thunder, racket, din, clatter **3** = collapse, failure, depression, ruin, downfall
• VERB **1** = fall, plunge, topple, lurch, hurtle, overbalance, fall headlong **2** = plunge, hurtle **3** = collapse, fail, go under, be ruined, go bust (*informal*), fold up, go to the wall, go belly up (*informal*)
• PHRASES **crash into** = collide with, hit, bump into, drive into, plough into
crate = container, case, box, packing case, tea chest
crater = hollow, hole, depression, dip, cavity
crave 1 = long for, yearn for, hanker after, want, desire, hope for, lust after **2** (*Informal*) = beg, ask for, seek, petition, pray for, plead for, solicit, implore
craving = longing, hope, desire, yen (*informal*), hunger, appetite, yearning, thirst
crawl VERB = creep, slither, inch, wriggle, writhe, worm your way, advance slowly ≠ run
• PHRASES **crawl to someone** = grovel, creep, fawn, toady, humble yourself
craze = fad, fashion, trend, rage, enthusiasm, vogue, mania, infatuation
crazed = mad, crazy, raving, insane, lunatic, berko (*Austral. slang*), off the air (*Austral. slang*), porangi (*N.Z.*)
crazy 1 (*Informal*) = ridiculous, absurd, foolish, ludicrous, senseless, preposterous, idiotic, nonsensical, porangi (*N.Z.*) ≠ sensible **2** = insane, mad, unbalanced, deranged, nuts (*slang*), crazed, demented, off the air (*Austral. slang*), out of your mind, porangi (*N.Z.*) ≠ sane **3** = fanatical, wild (*informal*), mad, devoted, enthusiastic, passionate, infatuated ≠ uninterested
cream NOUN **1** = lotion, ointment, oil, essence, cosmetic, paste, emulsion, salve **2** = best, elite, prime, pick, flower, crème de la crème (*French*)
• NOUN *or* ADJECTIVE = off-white, ivory, yellowish-white
creamy 1 = milky, buttery **2** = smooth, soft, velvety, rich
crease NOUN **1** = fold, line, ridge, groove, corrugation **2** = wrinkle, line, crow's-foot
• VERB **1** = crumple, rumple, fold, double up, corrugate **2** = wrinkle, crumple, screw up
create 1 = cause, lead to, occasion, bring about **2** = make, produce, invent, compose, devise, originate, formulate, spawn ≠ destroy **3** = appoint, make, establish, set up, invest, install, constitute
creation 1 = universe, world, nature, cosmos **2** = invention, production, achievement, brainchild (*informal*), concoction, handiwork, pièce de résistance (*French*), magnum opus **3** = making, generation, formation, conception, genesis **4** = setting up, development, production, institution, foundation, establishment, formation, inception
creative = imaginative, gifted, artistic, inventive, original, inspired, clever, ingenious
creativity = imagination, inspiration, ingenuity, originality, inventiveness, cleverness
creator 1 = maker, father, author, designer, architect, inventor, originator **2** *usually with cap.* = God, Maker

creature 1 = living thing, being, animal, beast, brute **2** = person, man, woman, individual, soul, human being, mortal
credentials 1 = qualifications, ability, skill, fitness, attribute, capability, eligibility, aptitude **2** = certification, document, reference(s), papers, licence, passport, testimonial, authorization
credibility = believability, reliability, plausibility, trustworthiness
credible 1 = believable, possible, likely, reasonable, probable, plausible, conceivable, imaginable ≠ unbelievable **2** = reliable, honest, dependable, trustworthy, sincere, trusty ≠ unreliable
credit NOUN **1** = praise, honour, recognition, approval, tribute, acclaim, acknowledgment, kudos **2** = source of satisfaction *or* pride, asset, honour, feather in your cap **3** = prestige, reputation, standing, position, influence, regard, status, esteem **4** = belief, trust, confidence, faith, reliance, credence
• VERB = believe, rely on, have faith in, trust, accept
• PHRASES **credit someone with something** = attribute to, assign to, ascribe to, impute to
creed = belief, principles, doctrine, dogma, credo, catechism, articles of faith
creek 1 = inlet, bay, cove, bight, firth *or* frith (*Scot.*) **2** (*U.S., Canad., Austral., & N.Z.*) = stream, brook, tributary, bayou, rivulet, watercourse, runnel
creep VERB = sneak, steal, tiptoe, slink, skulk, approach unnoticed
• NOUN (*Slang*) = bootlicker (*informal*), sneak, sycophant, crawler (*slang*), toady
• PHRASES **give someone the creeps** (*Informal*) = disgust, frighten, scare, repel, repulse, make your hair stand on end, make you squirm
crescent = meniscus, sickle, new moon
crest 1 = top, summit, peak, ridge, highest point, pinnacle, apex, crown **2** = tuft, crown, comb, plume, mane **3** = emblem, badge, symbol, insignia, bearings, device
crew 1 = (ship's) company, hands, (ship's) complement **2** = team, squad, gang, corps, posse **3** (*Informal*) = crowd, set, bunch (*informal*), band, pack, gang, mob, horde
crime 1 = offence, violation, trespass, felony, misdemeanour, misdeed, transgression, unlawful act **2** = lawbreaking, corruption, illegality, vice, misconduct, wrongdoing
criminal NOUN = lawbreaker, convict, offender, crook (*informal*), villain, culprit, sinner, felon, rorter (*Austral. slang*), skelm (*S. African*)
• ADJECTIVE **1** = unlawful, illicit, lawless, wrong, illegal, corrupt, crooked (*informal*), immoral ≠ lawful **2** (*Informal*) = disgraceful, ridiculous, foolish, senseless, scandalous, preposterous, deplorable
cripple 1 = disable, paralyse, lame, maim, incapacitate, weaken, hamstring **2** = damage, destroy, ruin, spoil, impair, put paid to, put out of action ≠ help
crippled = disabled, handicapped, paralysed, lame, incapacitated
crisis 1 = emergency, plight, predicament, trouble, deep water, meltdown (*informal*), dire straits **2** = critical point, climax, height, crunch (*informal*), turning point, culmination, crux, moment of truth
crisp 1 = firm, crunchy, crispy, crumbly, fresh, brittle, unwilted ≠ soft **2** = bracing, fresh, refreshing, brisk, invigorating ≠ warm **3** = clean, smart, trim, neat, tidy, spruce, well-groomed, well-pressed
criterion = standard, test, rule, measure, principle, gauge, yardstick, touchstone
critic 1 = judge, authority, expert, analyst, commentator, pundit, reviewer, connoisseur **2** = fault-finder, attacker, detractor, knocker (*informal*)
critical 1 = crucial, decisive, pressing, serious, vital, urgent, all-important, pivotal ≠ unimportant **2** = grave, serious, acute, precarious ≠ safe **3** = disparaging, disapproving, scathing, derogatory, nit-picking (*informal*), censorious, fault-finding, captious ≠ complimentary **4** = analytical, penetrating, discriminating, discerning, perceptive, judicious ≠ undiscriminating
criticism 1 = fault-finding, censure, disapproval, disparagement, stick (*slang*), flak (*informal*), bad press, character assassination **2** = analysis, assessment, judgment, commentary, evaluation, appreciation, appraisal, critique
criticize = find fault with, censure, disapprove of, knock (*informal*), condemn, carp, put down, slate (*informal*) ≠ praise
crook NOUN (*Informal*) = criminal, rogue, cheat, thief, shark, villain, robber, racketeer,

skelm (*S. African*)
• ADJECTIVE (*Austral. & N.Z. informal*) = ill, sick, poorly (*informal*), unhealthy, seedy (*informal*), unwell, queasy, out of sorts (*informal*)
• PHRASES **go (off) crook** (*Austral. & N.Z. informal*) = lose your temper, be furious, rage, go mad, lose it (*informal*), crack up (*informal*), see red (*informal*), blow your top

crooked 1 = bent, twisted, curved, irregular, warped, out of shape, misshapen ≠ straight 2 = deformed, distorted 3 = zigzag, winding, twisting 4 = at an angle, uneven, slanting, squint, awry, lopsided, askew, off-centre 5 (*Informal*) = dishonest, criminal, illegal, corrupt, unlawful, shady (*informal*), fraudulent, bent (*slang*) ≠ honest

crop NOUN = yield, produce, gathering, fruits, harvest, vintage, reaping
• VERB 1 = graze, eat, browse, feed on, nibble 2 = cut, trim, clip, prune, shear, snip, pare, lop
• PHRASES **crop up** (*Informal*) = happen, appear, emerge, occur, arise, turn up, spring up

cross VERB 1 = go across, pass over, traverse, cut across, move across, travel across 2 = span, bridge, go across, extend over 3 = intersect, intertwine, crisscross 4 = oppose, interfere with, obstruct, block, resist, impede 5 = interbreed, mix, blend, cross-pollinate, crossbreed, hybridize, cross-fertilize, intercross
• NOUN 1 = crucifix 2 = trouble, worry, trial, load, burden, grief, woe, misfortune 3 = mixture, combination, blend, amalgam, amalgamation 4 = crossroads, crossing, junction, intersection
• ADJECTIVE = angry, annoyed, put out, grumpy, short, ill-tempered, irascible, tooshie (*Austral. slang*), in a bad mood, hoha (*N.Z.*) ≠ good-humoured
• PHRASES **cross something out** *or* **off** = strike off *or* out, eliminate, cancel, delete, blue-pencil, score off *or* out

crouch = bend down, kneel, squat, stoop, bow, duck, hunch

crow = gloat, triumph, boast, swagger, brag, exult, blow your own trumpet

crowd NOUN 1 = multitude, mass, throng, army, host, pack, mob, swarm 2 = group, set, lot, circle, gang, bunch (*informal*), clique 3 = audience, spectators, house, gate, attendance
• VERB 1 = flock, mass, collect, gather, stream, surge, swarm, throng 2 = squeeze, pack, pile, bundle, cram 3 = congest, pack, cram

crowded = packed, full, busy, cramped, swarming, teeming, congested, jam-packed

crown NOUN 1 = coronet, tiara, diadem, circlet 2 = laurel wreath, trophy, prize, honour, garland, laurels, wreath 3 = high point, top, tip, summit, crest, pinnacle, apex
• VERB 1 = install, honour, dignify, ordain, inaugurate 2 = top, cap, be on top of, surmount 3 = cap, finish, complete, perfect, round off, put the finishing touch to, be the climax *or* culmination of 4 (*Slang*) = strike, belt (*informal*), bash, hit over the head, box, punch, cuff, biff (*slang*)
• PHRASES **the Crown** 1 = monarch, ruler, sovereign, emperor *or* empress, king *or* queen 2 = monarchy, sovereignty, royalty

crucial 1 (*Informal*) = vital, important, pressing, essential, urgent, momentous, high-priority 2 = critical, central, key, psychological, decisive, pivotal

crude 1 = rough, basic, makeshift 2 = simple, rudimentary, basic, primitive, coarse, clumsy, rough-and-ready 3 = vulgar, dirty, rude, obscene, coarse, indecent, tasteless, smutty ≠ tasteful 4 = unrefined, natural, raw, unprocessed ≠ processed

crudely 1 = roughly, basically 2 = simply, roughly, basically, coarsely 3 = vulgarly, rudely, coarsely, crassly, obscenely, lewdly, impolitely, tastelessly

cruel 1 = brutal, ruthless, callous, sadistic, inhumane, vicious, monstrous, unkind ≠ kind 2 = bitter, ruthless, traumatic, grievous, unrelenting, merciless, pitiless

cruelly 1 = brutally, severely, mercilessly, in cold blood, callously, monstrously, sadistically, pitilessly 2 = bitterly, deeply, severely, ruthlessly, mercilessly, grievously, pitilessly, traumatically

cruelty = brutality, ruthlessness, depravity, inhumanity, barbarity, callousness, spitefulness, mercilessness

cruise NOUN = sail, voyage, boat trip, sea trip
• VERB 1 = sail, coast, voyage 2 = travel

along, coast, drift, keep a steady pace

crumb 1 = bit, grain, fragment, shred, morsel 2 = morsel, scrap, shred, snippet, soupçon (*French*)

crumble 1 = disintegrate, collapse, deteriorate, decay, fall apart, degenerate, tumble down, go to pieces 2 = crush, fragment, pulverize, pound, grind, powder, granulate 3 = collapse, deteriorate, decay, fall apart, degenerate, go to pieces, go to wrack and ruin

crumple 1 = crush, squash, screw up, scrumple 2 = crease, wrinkle, rumple, ruffle, pucker 3 = collapse, sink, go down, fall 4 = break down, fall, collapse, give way, cave in, go to pieces 5 = screw up

crunch VERB = chomp, champ, munch, chew noisily, grind
• NOUN (*Informal*) = critical point, test, crisis, emergency, crux, moment of truth

crusade NOUN 1 = campaign, drive, movement, cause, push 2 = holy war
• VERB = campaign, fight, push, struggle, lobby, agitate, work

crush VERB 1 = squash, break, squeeze, compress, press, pulverize 2 = crease, wrinkle, crumple 3 = overcome, overwhelm, put down, subdue, overpower, quash, quell, stamp out 4 = demoralize, depress, devastate, discourage, humble, put down (*slang*), humiliate, squash
• NOUN = crowd, mob, horde, throng, pack, mass, jam, huddle

crust = layer, covering, coating, skin, surface, shell

cry VERB 1 = weep, sob, shed tears, blubber, snivel ≠ laugh 2 = shout, scream, roar, yell, howl, call out, exclaim, shriek ≠ whisper
• NOUN 1 = weep, sob, bawl, blubber 2 = shout, call, scream, roar, yell, howl, shriek, bellow 3 = appeal, plea
• PLURAL NOUN = weeping, sobbing, blubbering, snivelling
• PHRASES **cry off** (*Informal*) = back out, withdraw, quit, excuse yourself

cuddle VERB 1 = hug, embrace, fondle, cosset 2 = pet, hug, bill and coo
• PHRASES **cuddle up** = snuggle

cue = signal, sign, hint, prompt, reminder, suggestion

culminate = end up, close, finish, conclude, wind up, climax, come to a head, come to a climax

culprit = offender, criminal, felon, guilty party, wrongdoer, miscreant, evildoer, transgressor

cult 1 = sect, faction, school, religion, clique, hauhau (*N.Z.*) 2 = craze, fashion, trend, fad 3 = obsession, worship, devotion, idolization

cultivate 1 = farm, work, plant, tend, till, plough 2 = develop, establish, foster 3 = court, seek out, run after, dance attendance upon 4 = improve, refine

cultural 1 = ethnic, national, native, folk, racial 2 = artistic, educational, aesthetic, enriching, enlightening, civilizing, edifying

culture 1 = the arts 2 = civilization, society, customs, way of life 3 = lifestyle, habit, way of life, mores 4 = refinement, education, enlightenment, sophistication, good taste, urbanity

cultured = refined, intellectual, educated, sophisticated, enlightened, well-informed, urbane, highbrow ≠ uneducated

cunning ADJECTIVE 1 = crafty, sly, devious, artful, sharp, wily, Machiavellian, shifty ≠ frank 2 = ingenious, imaginative, sly, devious, artful, Machiavellian 3 = skilful, clever ≠ clumsy
• NOUN 1 = craftiness, guile, trickery, deviousness, artfulness, slyness ≠ candour 2 = skill, subtlety, ingenuity, artifice, cleverness ≠ clumsiness

cup 1 = mug, goblet, chalice, teacup, beaker, bowl 2 = trophy

cupboard = cabinet, press

curb VERB = restrain, control, check, restrict, suppress, inhibit, hinder, retard
• NOUN = restraint, control, check, brake, limitation, rein, deterrent, bridle

cure VERB 1 = make better, correct, heal, relieve, remedy, mend, ease 2 = restore to health, restore, heal 3 = preserve, smoke, dry, salt, pickle
• NOUN = remedy, treatment, antidote, panacea, nostrum

curiosity 1 = inquisitiveness, interest, prying, snooping (*informal*), nosiness (*informal*) 2 = oddity, wonder, sight, phenomenon, spectacle, freak, novelty, rarity

curious ADJECTIVE 1 = inquisitive, interested, questioning, searching, inquiring, meddling, prying, nosy (*informal*) ≠ uninterested 2 = strange, unusual, bizarre, odd, novel, rare,

extraordinary, unexpected
• ADJECTIVE ≠ ordinary

curl NOUN 1 = ringlet, lock 2 = twist, spiral, coil, kink, whorl 3 = crimp, wave, perm
• VERB 1 = twirl, turn, bend, twist, curve, loop, spiral, coil 2 = wind

curly = wavy, curled, curling, fuzzy, frizzy

currency 1 = money, coinage, legal tender, notes, coins 2 = acceptance, popularity, circulation, vogue, prevalence

current NOUN 1 = flow, course, undertow, jet, stream, tide, progression, river 2 = draught, flow, breeze, puff 3 = mood, feeling, spirit, atmosphere, trend, tendency, undercurrent
• ADJECTIVE 1 = present, fashionable, up-to-date, contemporary, trendy (*Brit. informal*), topical, present-day, in fashion ≠ out-of-date 2 = prevalent, common, accepted, popular, widespread, customary, in circulation

curse VERB 1 = swear, cuss (*informal*), blaspheme, take the Lord's name in vain 2 = abuse, damn, scold, vilify
• NOUN 1 = oath, obscenity, blasphemy, expletive, profanity, imprecation, swearword 2 = malediction, jinx, anathema, hoodoo (*informal*), excommunication 3 = affliction, plague, scourge, trouble, torment, hardship, bane

cursed = under a curse, damned, doomed, jinxed, bedevilled, accursed, ill-fated

curtail = reduce, diminish, decrease, dock, cut back, shorten, lessen, cut short

curtain = hanging, drape (*chiefly U.S.*), portière

curve NOUN = bend, turn, loop, arc, curvature
• VERB = bend, turn, wind, twist, arch, snake, arc, coil

curved = bent, rounded, twisted, bowed, arched, serpentine, sinuous

cushion NOUN = pillow, pad, bolster, headrest, beanbag, hassock
• VERB 1 = protect 2 = soften, dampen, muffle, mitigate, deaden, suppress, stifle

custody 1 = care, charge, protection, supervision, safekeeping, keeping 2 = imprisonment, detention, confinement, incarceration

custom 1 = tradition, practice, convention, ritual, policy, rule, usage, kaupapa (*N.Z.*) 2 = habit, way, practice, procedure, routine, wont 3 = customers, business, trade, patronage

customary 1 = usual, common, accepted, established, traditional, normal, ordinary, conventional ≠ unusual 2 = accustomed, regular, usual

customer = client, consumer, regular (*informal*), buyer, patron, shopper, purchaser

customs = import charges, tax, duty, toll, tariff

cut VERB 1 = slit, score, slice, slash, pierce, penetrate 2 = chop, split, slice, dissect 3 = carve, slice 4 = sever, cut in two 5 = shape, carve, engrave, chisel, form, score, fashion, whittle 6 = slash, wound 7 = clip, mow, trim, prune, snip, pare, lop 8 = trim, shave, snip 9 = reduce, lower, slim (down), diminish, slash, decrease, cut back ≠ increase 10 = abridge, edit, shorten, curtail, condense, abbreviate ≠ extend 11 = delete, take out, expurgate 12 = hurt, wound, upset, sting, hurt someone's feelings 13 (*Informal*) = ignore, avoid, slight, blank (*slang*), snub, spurn, cold-shoulder, turn your back on ≠ greet 14 = cross, bisect
• NOUN 1 = incision, nick, stroke, slash, slit 2 = gash, nick, wound, slash, laceration 3 = reduction, fall, lowering, slash, decrease, cutback 4 (*Informal*) = share, piece, slice, percentage, portion 5 = style, look, fashion, shape

cutback = reduction, cut, retrenchment, economy, decrease, lessening

cute = appealing, sweet, attractive, engaging, charming, delightful, lovable, winsome

cutting = hurtful, wounding, bitter, malicious, scathing, acrimonious, barbed, sarcastic ≠ kind

cycle = series of events, circle, revolution, rotation

cynic = sceptic, doubter, pessimist, misanthrope, misanthropist, scoffer

cynical 1 = sceptical, mocking, pessimistic, scoffing, contemptuous, scornful, distrustful, derisive ≠ trusting 2 = unbelieving, sceptical, disillusioned, pessimistic, disbelieving, mistrustful ≠ optimistic

cynicism 1 = scepticism, pessimism, misanthropy 2 = disbelief, doubt, scepticism, mistrust

d

dab VERB **1** = pat, touch, tap **2** = apply, daub, stipple
• NOUN **1** = spot, bit, drop, pat, smudge, speck **2** = touch, stroke, flick

daft (*Informal, chiefly Brit.*) **1** = stupid, crazy, silly, absurd, foolish, idiotic, witless, crackpot (*informal*), off the air (*Austral. slang*) **2** = crazy, mad, touched, nuts (*slang*), crackers (*Brit. slang*), insane, demented, deranged, off the air (*Austral. slang*), porangi (*N.Z.*)

dag NOUN (*N.Z. informal*) = joker, comic, wag, wit, comedian, clown, humorist, prankster
• PHRASES **rattle your dags** (*N.Z. informal*) = hurry up, get a move on, step on it (*informal*), get your skates on (*informal*), make haste

dagga (*S. African*) = cannabis, marijuana, pot (*slang*), dope (*slang*), hash (*slang*), grass (*slang*), weed (*slang*), hemp

daily ADVERB = every day, day by day, once a day
• ADJECTIVE = everyday, diurnal, quotidian

dam NOUN = barrier, wall, barrage, obstruction, embankment
• VERB = block up, restrict, hold back, barricade, obstruct

damage VERB = spoil, hurt, injure, harm, ruin, crush, devastate, wreck ≠ fix
• NOUN **1** = destruction, harm, loss, injury, suffering, hurt, ruin, devastation ≠ improvement **2** (*Informal*) = cost, price, charge, bill, amount, payment, expense, outlay
• PLURAL NOUN (*Law*) = compensation, fine, satisfaction, amends, reparation, restitution, reimbursement, atonement

damaging = harmful, detrimental, hurtful, ruinous, deleterious, injurious, disadvantageous ≠ helpful

dame = lady, baroness, dowager, grande dame (*French*), noblewoman, peeress

damn = criticize, condemn, blast, denounce, put down, censure ≠ praise

damned (*Slang*) = infernal, detestable, confounded, hateful, loathsome

damp ADJECTIVE = moist, wet, soggy, humid, dank, sopping, clammy, dewy ≠ dry
• NOUN = moisture, liquid, drizzle, dampness, wetness, dankness ≠ dryness
• VERB = moisten, wet, soak, dampen, moisturize
• PHRASES **damp something down** = curb, reduce, check, diminish, inhibit, stifle, allay, pour cold water on

dampen **1** = reduce, check, moderate, dull, restrain, stifle, lessen **2** = moisten, wet, spray, make damp

dance VERB **1** = prance, trip, hop, skip, sway, whirl, caper, jig **2** = caper, trip, spring, jump, bound, skip, frolic, cavort
• NOUN = ball, social, hop (*informal*), disco, knees-up (*Brit. informal*), discotheque, B and S (*Austral. informal*)

dancer = ballerina, Terpsichorean

danger **1** = jeopardy, vulnerability **2** = hazard, risk, threat, menace, peril, pitfall

dangerous = perilous, risky, hazardous, vulnerable, insecure, unsafe, precarious, breakneck ≠ safe

dangerously = perilously, alarmingly, precariously, recklessly, riskily, hazardously, unsafely

dangle **1** = hang, swing, trail, sway, flap, hang down **2** = wave **3** = offer, flourish, brandish, flaunt

dare **1** = risk doing, venture, presume, make bold (*archaic*), hazard doing **2** = challenge, provoke, defy, taunt, goad, throw down the gauntlet

daring ADJECTIVE = brave, bold, adventurous, reckless, fearless, audacious, intrepid, daredevil ≠ timid
• NOUN = bravery, nerve (*informal*), courage, spirit, bottle (*Brit. slang*), pluck, audacity, boldness ≠ timidity

dark ADJECTIVE **1** = dim, murky, shady, shadowy, grey, dingy, unlit, poorly lit **2** = black, brunette, ebony, dark-skinned, sable, dusky, swarthy ≠ fair **3** = evil, foul, sinister, vile, wicked, infernal **4** = secret, hidden, mysterious, concealed **5** = gloomy, sad, grim, miserable, bleak, dismal, pessimistic, melancholy ≠ cheerful
• NOUN **1** = darkness, shadows, gloom, dusk, obscurity, murk, dimness, semi-

darkness **2** = night, twilight, evening, evo (*Austral. slang*), dusk, night-time, nightfall
darken **1** = cloud, obscure, dim, overshadow, blacken ≠ brighten **2** = make dark, blacken
darkness = dark, shadows, shade, gloom, blackness, murk, duskiness
darling NOUN = beloved, love, dear, dearest, angel, treasure, precious, sweetheart
• ADJECTIVE = beloved, dear, treasured, precious, adored, cherished
dart = dash, run, race, shoot, fly, speed, spring, tear
dash VERB **1** = rush, run, race, shoot, fly, career, speed, tear ≠ dawdle **2** = throw, cast, pitch, slam, toss, hurl, fling, chuck (*informal*) **3** = crash, break, smash, shatter, splinter
• NOUN **1** = rush, run, race, sprint, dart, spurt, sortie **2** = drop, little, bit, shot (*informal*), touch, spot, trace, hint ≠ lot **3** (*Old-fashioned*) = style, spirit, flair, flourish, verve, panache, élan, brio
dashing **1** (*Old-fashioned*) = stylish, smart, elegant, flamboyant, sporty, jaunty, showy **2** = bold, spirited, gallant, swashbuckling, debonair ≠ dull
data = information, facts, figures, details, intelligence, statistics
date NOUN **1** = time, stage, period **2** = appointment, meeting, arrangement, commitment, engagement, rendezvous, tryst, assignation **3** = partner, escort, friend
• VERB **1** = put a date on, assign a date to, fix the period of **2** = become dated, become old-fashioned
• PHRASES **date from** *or* **date back to** (with a *time* or *date* as object) = come from, belong to, originate in, exist from, bear a date of
dated = old-fashioned, outdated, out of date, obsolete, unfashionable, outmoded, passé, old hat ≠ modern
daunting = intimidating, alarming, frightening, discouraging, unnerving, disconcerting, demoralizing, off-putting (*Brit. informal*) ≠ reassuring
dawn NOUN **1** = daybreak, morning, sunrise, daylight, aurora (*poetic*), crack of dawn, sunup, cockcrow **2** (*Literary*) = beginning, start, birth, rise, origin, emergence, advent, genesis
• VERB **1** = begin, start, rise, develop, emerge, unfold, originate **2** = grow light, break, brighten, lighten
• PHRASES **dawn on** *or* **upon someone** = hit, strike, occur to, register (*informal*), become apparent, come to mind, come into your head
day **1** = twenty-four hours **2** = daytime, daylight **3** = date **4** = time, age, era, period, epoch
daylight = sunlight, sunshine, light of day
daze VERB = stun, shock, paralyse, numb, stupefy, benumb
• NOUN (usually used in the phrase *in a daze*) = shock, confusion, distraction, trance, bewilderment, stupor, trancelike state
dazzle VERB **1** = impress, amaze, overwhelm, astonish, overpower, bowl over (*informal*), take your breath away **2** = blind, confuse, daze, bedazzle
• NOUN = splendour, sparkle, glitter, brilliance, magnificence, razzmatazz (*slang*)
dazzling = splendid, brilliant, stunning, glorious, sparkling, glittering, sensational (*informal*), virtuoso ≠ ordinary
dead ADJECTIVE **1** = deceased, departed, late, perished, extinct, defunct, passed away ≠ alive **2** = boring, dull, dreary, flat, plain, humdrum, uninteresting **3** = not working, useless, inactive, inoperative ≠ working **4** = numb, frozen, paralysed, insensitive, inert, deadened, immobilized, unfeeling **5** (usually used of *centre, silence,* or *stop*) = total, complete, absolute, utter, outright, thorough, unqualified **6** (*Informal*) = exhausted, tired, worn out, spent, done in (*informal*), all in (*slang*), drained, knackered (*slang*)
• NOUN = middle, heart, depth, midst
• ADVERB (*Informal*) = exactly, completely, totally, directly, fully, entirely, absolutely, thoroughly
deadline = time limit, cutoff point, target date *or* time, limit
deadlock **1** = impasse, stalemate, standstill, gridlock, standoff **2** = tie, draw, stalemate, impasse, standstill, gridlock, standoff, dead heat
deadly **1** = lethal, fatal, deathly, dangerous, devastating, mortal, murderous, malignant **2** (*Informal*) = boring, dull, tedious, flat, monotonous,

uninteresting, mind-numbing, wearisome

deaf 1 = hard of hearing, without hearing, stone deaf 2 = oblivious, indifferent, unmoved, unconcerned, unsympathetic, impervious, unhearing

deal NOUN 1 (*Informal*) = agreement, understanding, contract, arrangement, bargain, transaction, pact 2 = amount, quantity, measure, degree, mass, volume, share, portion

• PHRASES **deal in something** = sell, trade in, stock, traffic in, buy and sell ◆ **deal something out** = distribute, give, share, assign, allocate, dispense, allot, mete out ◆ **deal with something** = be concerned with, involve, concern, touch, regard, apply to, bear on, pertain to ◆ **deal with something** *or* **someone** = handle, manage, treat, cope with, take care of, see to, attend to, get to grips with

dealer = trader, merchant, supplier, wholesaler, purveyor, tradesman

dear ADJECTIVE 1 = beloved, close, valued, favourite, prized, treasured, precious, intimate ≠ hated 2 (*Brit. informal*) = expensive, costly, high-priced, pricey (*informal*), at a premium, overpriced, exorbitant ≠ cheap

• NOUN = darling, love, dearest, angel, treasure, precious, beloved, loved one

dearly (*Formal*) 1 = very much, greatly, extremely, profoundly 2 = at great cost, at a high price

death 1 = dying, demise, end, passing, departure ≠ birth 2 = destruction, finish, ruin, undoing, extinction, downfall ≠ beginning

RELATED WORDS

adjectives: fatal, lethal, mortal

deathly = deathlike, white, pale, ghastly, wan, pallid, ashen

debacle *or* **débâcle** = disaster, catastrophe, fiasco

debate NOUN = discussion, talk, argument, dispute, analysis, conversation, controversy, dialogue

• VERB 1 = discuss, question, talk about, argue about, dispute, examine, deliberate 2 = consider, reflect, think about, weigh, contemplate, deliberate, ponder, ruminate

debris = remains, bits, waste, ruins, fragments, rubble, wreckage, detritus

debt NOUN = debit, commitment, obligation, liability

• PHRASES **in debt** = owing, liable, in the red (*informal*), in arrears

debtor = borrower, mortgagor

debut = entrance, beginning, launch, coming out, introduction, presentation, first appearance, initiation

decay VERB 1 = rot, spoil, crumble, deteriorate, perish, decompose, moulder, go bad 2 = decline, diminish, crumble, deteriorate, fall off, dwindle, lessen, wane ≠ grow

• NOUN 1 = rot, corruption, mould, blight, decomposition, gangrene, canker, caries 2 = decline, collapse, deterioration, failing, fading, degeneration ≠ growth

deceased = dead, late, departed, expired, defunct, lifeless

deceive = take in, trick, fool (*informal*), cheat, con (*informal*), mislead, dupe, swindle

decency 1 = propriety, correctness, decorum, respectability, etiquette 2 = courtesy, politeness, civility, graciousness, urbanity, courteousness

decent 1 = satisfactory, fair, all right, reasonable, sufficient, good enough, adequate, ample ≠ unsatisfactory 2 = proper, becoming, seemly, fitting, appropriate, suitable, respectable, befitting ≠ improper 3 (*Informal*) = good, kind, friendly, neighbourly, generous, helpful, obliging, accommodating 4 = respectable, pure, proper, modest, chaste, decorous

deception 1 = trickery, fraud, deceit, cunning, treachery, guile, legerdemain ≠ honesty 2 = trick, lie, bluff, hoax, decoy, ruse, subterfuge

decide 1 = make a decision, make up your mind, reach *or* come to a decision, choose, determine, conclude ≠ hesitate 2 = resolve, answer, determine, conclude, clear up, ordain, adjudicate, adjudge 3 = settle, determine, resolve

decidedly = definitely, clearly, positively, distinctly, downright, unequivocally, unmistakably

decision 1 = judgment, finding, ruling, sentence, resolution, conclusion, verdict, decree 2 = decisiveness, purpose, resolution, resolve, determination, firmness, forcefulness, strength of mind *or* will

decisive 1 = crucial, significant, critical,

influential, momentous, conclusive, fateful ≠ uncertain **2** = resolute, decided, firm, determined, forceful, incisive, trenchant, strong-minded ≠ indecisive

deck = decorate, dress, clothe, array, adorn, embellish, festoon, beautify

declaration 1 = announcement, proclamation, decree, notice, notification, edict, pronouncement **2** = affirmation, profession, assertion, revelation, disclosure, acknowledgment, protestation, avowal **3** = statement, testimony

declare 1 = state, claim, announce, voice, express, maintain, assert, proclaim **2** = testify, state, swear, assert, affirm, bear witness, vouch **3** = make known, reveal, show, broadcast, confess, communicate, disclose

decline VERB **1** = fall, drop, lower, sink, fade, shrink, diminish, decrease ≠ rise **2** = deteriorate, weaken, pine, decay, worsen, languish, degenerate, droop ≠ improve **3** = refuse, reject, turn down, avoid, spurn, abstain, say 'no' ≠ accept
• NOUN **1** = depression, recession, slump, falling off, downturn, dwindling, lessening ≠ rise **2** = deterioration, failing, weakening, decay, worsening, degeneration ≠ improvement

décor *or* **decor** = decoration, colour scheme, ornamentation, furnishing style

decorate 1 = adorn, trim, embroider, ornament, embellish, festoon, beautify, grace **2** = do up, paper, paint, wallpaper, renovate (*informal*), furbish **3** = pin a medal on, cite, confer an honour on *or* upon

decoration 1 = adornment, trimming, enhancement, elaboration, embellishment, ornamentation, beautification **2** = ornament, trimmings, garnish, frill, bauble **3** = medal, award, star, ribbon, badge

decorative = ornamental, fancy, pretty, attractive, for show, embellishing, showy, beautifying

decrease VERB **1** = drop, decline, lessen, lower, shrink, diminish, dwindle, subside **2** = reduce, cut, lower, moderate, weaken, diminish, cut down, shorten ≠ increase
• NOUN = lessening, decline, reduction, loss, falling off, dwindling, contraction, cutback ≠ growth

decree NOUN **1** = law, order, ruling, act, command, statute, proclamation, edict **2** = judgment, finding, ruling, decision, verdict, arbitration
• VERB = order, rule, command, demand, proclaim, prescribe, pronounce, ordain

dedicate 1 = devote, give, apply, commit, pledge, surrender, give over to **2** = offer, address, inscribe

dedicated = committed, devoted, enthusiastic, single-minded, zealous, purposeful, wholehearted ≠ indifferent

dedication 1 = commitment, loyalty, devotion, allegiance, adherence, single-mindedness, faithfulness, wholeheartedness ≠ indifference **2** = inscription, message, address

deduct = subtract, remove, take off, take away, reduce by, knock off (*informal*), decrease by ≠ add

deduction 1 = conclusion, finding, verdict, judgment, assumption, inference **2** = reasoning, thinking, thought, analysis, logic **3** = discount, reduction, cut, concession, decrease, rebate, diminution **4** = subtraction, reduction, concession

deed 1 = action, act, performance, achievement, exploit, feat **2** (*Law*) = document, title, contract

deep ADJECTIVE **1** = big, wide, broad, profound, yawning, bottomless, unfathomable ≠ shallow **2** = intense, great, serious (*informal*), acute, extreme, grave, profound, heartfelt ≠ superficial **3** = sound, profound, unbroken, undisturbed, untroubled **4** = absorbed, lost, gripped, preoccupied, immersed, engrossed, rapt **5** = dark, strong, rich, intense, vivid ≠ light **6** = low, booming, bass, resonant, sonorous, low-pitched ≠ high **7** = secret, hidden, mysterious, obscure, abstract, esoteric, mystifying, arcane **8** = far, a long way, a good way, miles, a great distance
• NOUN = middle, heart, midst, dead
• PHRASES **the deep** (*Poetic*) = the ocean, the sea, the waves, the main, the high seas, the briny (*informal*)

deepen 1 = intensify, increase, grow, strengthen, reinforce, escalate, magnify **2** = dig out, excavate, scoop out, hollow out

deeply = thoroughly, completely, seriously, sadly, severely, gravely, profoundly, intensely

de facto ADJECTIVE = actual, real, existing • ADVERB = in fact, really, actually, in effect, in reality
default VERB = fail to pay, dodge, evade, neglect • NOUN **1** (usually in phrase *by default* or *in default of*) = failure, neglect, deficiency, lapse, omission, dereliction **2** = nonpayment, evasion
defeat VERB **1** = beat, crush, overwhelm, conquer, master, rout, trounce, vanquish ≠ surrender **2** = frustrate, foil, thwart, ruin, baffle, confound, balk, get the better of • NOUN **1** = conquest, beating, overthrow, rout ≠ victory **2** = frustration, failure, reverse, setback, thwarting
defect NOUN = deficiency, failing, fault, error, flaw, imperfection • VERB = desert, rebel, quit, revolt, change sides
defence or (*U.S.*) **defense** NOUN **1** = protection, cover, security, guard, shelter, safeguard, immunity **2** = armaments, weapons **3** = argument, explanation, excuse, plea, justification, vindication, rationalization **4** = plea (*Law*), testimony, denial, alibi, rebuttal • PLURAL NOUN = shield, barricade, fortification, buttress, rampart, bulwark, fortified pa (*N.Z.*)
defend **1** = protect, cover, guard, screen, preserve, look after, shelter, shield **2** = support, champion, justify, endorse, uphold, vindicate, stand up for, speak up for
defendant = the accused, respondent, prisoner at the bar
defender **1** = supporter, champion, advocate, sponsor, follower **2** = protector, guard, guardian, escort, bodyguard
defensive **1** = protective, watchful, on the defensive, on guard **2** = oversensitive, uptight (*informal*)
defer = postpone, delay, put off, suspend, shelve, hold over, procrastinate, put on ice (*informal*)
defiance = resistance, opposition, confrontation, contempt, disregard, disobedience, insolence, insubordination ≠ obedience
defiant = resisting, rebellious, daring, bold, provocative, audacious, antagonistic, insolent ≠ obedient
deficiency **1** = lack, want, deficit, absence, shortage, scarcity, dearth ≠ sufficiency **2** = failing, fault, weakness, defect, flaw, drawback, shortcoming, imperfection
deficit = shortfall, shortage, deficiency, loss, arrears
define **1** = mark out, outline, limit, bound, delineate, circumscribe, demarcate **2** = describe, interpret, characterize, explain, spell out, expound **3** = establish, specify, designate
definite **1** = specific, exact, precise, clear, particular, fixed, black-and-white, cut-and-dried (*informal*) ≠ vague **2** = clear, black-and-white, unequivocal, unambiguous, guaranteed, cut-and-dried (*informal*) **3** = noticeable, marked, clear, decided, striking, particular, distinct, conspicuous **4** = certain, decided, sure, settled, convinced, positive, confident, assured ≠ uncertain
definitely = certainly, clearly, surely, absolutely, positively, without doubt, unquestionably, undeniably
definition **1** = description, interpretation, explanation, clarification, exposition, elucidation, statement of meaning **2** = sharpness, focus, clarity, contrast, precision, distinctness
definitive **1** = final, convincing, absolute, clinching, decisive, definite, conclusive, irrefutable **2** = authoritative, greatest, ultimate, reliable, exhaustive, superlative
deflect = turn aside, bend
defy = resist, oppose, confront, brave, disregard, stand up to, spurn, flout
degenerate VERB = decline, slip, sink, decrease, deteriorate, worsen, decay, lapse • ADJECTIVE = depraved, corrupt, low, perverted, immoral, decadent, debauched, dissolute
degrade = demean, disgrace, humiliate, shame, humble, discredit, debase, dishonour ≠ ennoble
degree = amount, stage, grade
delay VERB **1** = put off, suspend, postpone, shelve, defer, hold over **2** = hold up, detain, hold back, hinder, obstruct, impede, bog down, set back ≠ speed (up) • NOUN = hold-up, wait, setback, interruption, stoppage, impediment, hindrance
delegate NOUN = representative, agent, deputy, ambassador, commissioner, envoy, proxy, legate

• VERB 1 = entrust, transfer, hand over, give, pass on, assign, consign, devolve 2 = appoint, commission, select, contract, engage, nominate, designate, mandate

delegation 1 = deputation, envoys, contingent, commission, embassy, legation 2 = commissioning, assignment, devolution, committal

delete = remove, cancel, erase, strike out, obliterate, efface, cross out, expunge

deliberate ADJECTIVE 1 = intentional, meant, planned, intended, conscious, calculated, wilful, purposeful ≠ accidental 2 = careful, measured, slow, cautious, thoughtful, circumspect, methodical, unhurried ≠ hurried

• VERB = consider, think, ponder, discuss, debate, reflect, consult, weigh

deliberately = intentionally, on purpose, consciously, knowingly, wilfully, by design, in cold blood, wittingly

deliberation 1 = consideration, thought, reflection, calculation, meditation, forethought, circumspection 2 = discussion, talk, conference, debate, analysis, conversation, dialogue, consultation

delicacy 1 = fragility, flimsiness 2 = daintiness, charm, grace, elegance, neatness, prettiness, slenderness, exquisiteness 3 = difficulty 4 = sensitivity, understanding, consideration, diplomacy, discretion, tact, thoughtfulness, sensitiveness 5 = treat, luxury, savoury, dainty, morsel, titbit 6 = lightness, accuracy, precision, elegance, sensibility, purity, subtlety, refinement

delicate 1 = fine, elegant, exquisite, graceful 2 = subtle, fine, delicious, faint, refined, understated, dainty ≠ bright 3 = fragile, weak, frail, brittle, tender, flimsy, dainty, breakable 4 = skilled, precise, deft 5 = diplomatic, sensitive, thoughtful, discreet, considerate, tactful ≠ insensitive

delicious = delectable, tasty, choice, savoury, dainty, mouthwatering, scrumptious (*informal*), appetizing, lekker (*S. African slang*), yummo (*Austral. slang*) ≠ unpleasant

delight NOUN = pleasure, joy, satisfaction, happiness, ecstasy, enjoyment, bliss, glee ≠ displeasure

• VERB = please, satisfy, thrill, charm, cheer, amuse, enchant, gratify ≠ displease

• PHRASES **delight in** *or* **take (a) delight in something** *or* **someone** = like, love, enjoy, appreciate, relish, savour, revel in, take pleasure in

delightful = pleasant, charming, thrilling, enjoyable, enchanting, agreeable, pleasurable, rapturous ≠ unpleasant

deliver 1 = bring, carry, bear, transport, distribute, convey, cart 2 *sometimes with up* = hand over, commit, give up, yield, surrender, turn over, relinquish, make over 3 = give, read, present, announce, declare, utter 4 = strike, give, deal, launch, direct, aim, administer, inflict 5 (*Dated*) = release, free, save, rescue, loose, liberate, ransom, emancipate

delivery 1 = handing over, transfer, distribution, transmission, dispatch, consignment, conveyance 2 = consignment, goods, shipment, batch 3 = speech, utterance, articulation, intonation, elocution, enunciation 4 = childbirth, labour, confinement, parturition

delusion = misconception, mistaken idea, misapprehension, fancy, illusion, hallucination, fallacy, false impression

demand VERB 1 = request, ask (for), order, expect, claim, seek, insist on, exact 2 = challenge, ask, question, inquire 3 = require, want, need, involve, call for, entail, necessitate, cry out for ≠ provide

• NOUN 1 = request, order 2 = need, want, call, market, claim, requirement

demanding = difficult, trying, hard, taxing, wearing, challenging, tough, exacting ≠ easy

demise 1 = failure, end, fall, defeat, collapse, ruin, breakdown, overthrow 2 (*Euphemistic*) = death, end, dying, passing, departure, decease

democracy = self-government, republic, commonwealth

Democrat ADJECTIVE = left-wing, Labour

• NOUN = left-winger

democratic = self-governing, popular, representative, autonomous, populist, egalitarian

demolish 1 = knock down, level, destroy, dismantle, flatten, tear down, bulldoze, raze ≠ build 2 = destroy, wreck, overturn, overthrow, undo

demolition = knocking down, levelling, destruction, explosion, wrecking, tearing down, bulldozing, razing

demon 1 = evil spirit, devil, fiend, goblin, ghoul, malignant spirit, atua (*N.Z.*), wairua (*N.Z.*) 2 = wizard, master, ace (*informal*), fiend

demonstrate 1 = prove, show, indicate, make clear, manifest, testify to 2 = show, express, display, indicate, exhibit, manifest 3 = march, protest, rally, object, parade, picket, remonstrate, express disapproval, hikoi (*N.Z.*) 4 = describe, show, explain, teach, illustrate

demonstration 1 = march, protest, rally, sit-in, parade, picket, mass lobby, hikoi (*N.Z.*) 2 = display, show, performance, explanation, description, presentation, exposition 3 = indication, proof, testimony, confirmation, substantiation 4 = exhibition, display, expression, illustration

den 1 = lair, hole, shelter, cave, haunt, cavern, hide-out 2 (*Chiefly U.S.*) = study, retreat, sanctuary, hideaway, sanctum, cubbyhole

denial 1 = negation, contradiction, dissent, retraction, repudiation ≠ admission 2 = refusal, veto, rejection, prohibition, rebuff, repulse 3 = renunciation, giving up, rejection, abdication, repudiation, forswearing, disavowal, relinquishment

denomination 1 = religious group, belief, sect, persuasion, creed, school, hauhau (*N.Z.*) 2 = unit, value, size, grade

denounce 1 = condemn, attack, censure, revile, vilify, stigmatize 2 = report, dob in (*Austral. slang*)

dense 1 = thick, heavy, solid, compact, condensed, impenetrable, close-knit ≠ thin 2 = heavy, thick, opaque, impenetrable 3 = stupid (*Informal*), thick, dull, dumb (*informal*), dozy (*Brit. informal*), stolid, dopey (*informal*), moronic ≠ bright

density 1 = tightness, thickness, compactness, impenetrability, denseness 2 = mass, bulk, consistency, solidity

dent VERB = make a dent in, press in, gouge, hollow, push in
• NOUN = hollow, chip, indentation, depression, impression, pit, dip, crater, ding (*Austral. & N.Z. dated informal*)

deny 1 = contradict, disagree with, rebuff, negate, rebut, refute ≠ admit 2 = renounce, reject, retract, repudiate, disown, recant, disclaim 3 = refuse, forbid, reject, rule out, turn down, prohibit, withhold, preclude ≠ permit

depart 1 = leave, go, withdraw, retire, disappear, quit, retreat, exit ≠ arrive 2 = deviate, vary, differ, stray, veer, swerve, diverge, digress

department = section, office, unit, station, division, branch, bureau, subdivision

departure 1 = leaving, going, retirement, withdrawal, exit, going away, removal, exodus ≠ arrival 2 = retirement, going, withdrawal, exit, going away, removal 3 = shift, change, difference, variation, innovation, novelty, deviation, divergence

depend 1 = be determined by, be based on, be subject to, hang on, rest on, revolve around, hinge on, be subordinate to 2 = count on, turn to, trust in, bank on, lean on, rely upon, reckon on

dependent *or* (*U.S. sometimes*) **dependant** ADJECTIVE = reliant, vulnerable, helpless, powerless, weak, defenceless ≠ independent
• PHRASES **dependent on** *or* **upon** 1 = reliant on, relying on 2 = determined by, depending on, subject to, influenced by, conditional on, contingent on

depict 1 = illustrate, portray, picture, paint, outline, draw, sketch, delineate 2 = describe, present, represent, outline, characterize

deplete = use up, reduce, drain, exhaust, consume, empty, lessen, impoverish ≠ increase

deplore = disapprove of, condemn, object to, denounce, censure, abhor, take a dim view of

deploy (used of troops or military resources) = use, station, position, arrange, set out, utilize

deployment (used of troops or military resources) = use, stationing, spread, organization, arrangement, positioning, utilization

deport = expel, exile, throw out, oust, banish, expatriate, extradite, evict

depose = oust, dismiss, displace, demote, dethrone, remove from office

deposit NOUN 1 = down payment, security, stake, pledge, instalment, retainer, part payment 2 = accumulation, mass, build-up, layer 3 = sediment, grounds, residue,

lees, precipitate, silt, dregs
• VERB 1 = put, place, lay, drop 2 = store, keep, put, bank, lodge, entrust, consign

depot 1 = arsenal, warehouse, storehouse, repository, depository 2 (*Chiefly U.S. & Canad.*) = bus station, station, garage, terminus

depreciation = devaluation, fall, drop, depression, slump, deflation

depress 1 = sadden, upset, distress, discourage, grieve, oppress, weigh down, make sad ≠ cheer 2 = lower, cut, reduce, diminish, decrease, lessen ≠ raise 3 = devalue, depreciate, cheapen 4 = press down, push, squeeze, lower, flatten, compress, push down

depressed 1 = sad, blue, unhappy, discouraged, fed up, mournful, dejected, despondent 2 = poverty-stricken, poor, deprived, disadvantaged, run-down, impoverished, needy 3 = lowered, devalued, weakened, depreciated, cheapened 4 = sunken, hollow, recessed, indented, concave

depressing = bleak, sad, discouraging, gloomy, dismal, harrowing, saddening, dispiriting

depression 1 = despair, misery, sadness, dumps (*informal*), the blues, melancholy, unhappiness, despondency 2 = recession, slump, economic decline, stagnation, inactivity, hard *or* bad times 3 = hollow, pit, dip, bowl, valley, dent, cavity, indentation

deprivation 1 = lack, denial, withdrawal, removal, expropriation, dispossession 2 = want, need, hardship, suffering, distress, privation, destitution

deprive = dispossess, rob, strip, despoil, bereave

deprived = poor, disadvantaged, needy, in need, lacking, bereft, destitute, down at heel ≠ prosperous

depth 1 = deepness, drop, measure, extent 2 = insight, wisdom, penetration, profundity, discernment, sagacity, astuteness, profoundness ≠ superficiality 3 = breadth

deputy = substitute, representative, delegate, lieutenant, proxy, surrogate, second-in-command, legate

derelict ADJECTIVE = abandoned, deserted, ruined, neglected, discarded, forsaken, dilapidated
• NOUN = tramp, outcast, drifter, down-and-out, vagrant, bag lady, derro (*Austral. slang*)

descend VERB 1 = fall, drop, sink, go down, plunge, dive, tumble, plummet ≠ rise 2 = get off 3 = go down, come down, walk down, move down, climb down 4 = slope, dip, incline, slant
• PHRASES **be descended from** = originate from, derive from, spring from, proceed from, issue from

descent 1 = fall, drop, plunge, coming down, swoop 2 = slope, drop, dip, incline, slant, declivity 3 = decline, deterioration, degeneration 4 = origin, extraction, ancestry, lineage, family tree, parentage, genealogy, derivation

describe 1 = relate, tell, report, explain, express, recount, recite, narrate 2 = portray, depict 3 = trace, draw, outline, mark out, delineate

description 1 = account, report, explanation, representation, sketch, narrative, portrayal, depiction 2 = calling, naming, branding, labelling, dubbing, designation 3 = kind, sort, type, order, class, variety, brand, category

desert[1] = wilderness, waste, wilds, wasteland

desert[2] 1 = abandon, leave, quit (*informal*), forsake 2 = leave, abandon, strand, maroon, walk out on (*informal*), forsake, jilt, leave stranded ≠ take care of 3 = abscond

deserted 1 = empty, abandoned, desolate, neglected, vacant, derelict, unoccupied 2 = abandoned, neglected, forsaken

deserve = merit, warrant, be entitled to, have a right to, rate, earn, justify, be worthy of

deserved = well-earned, fitting, due, earned, justified, merited, proper, warranted

deserving = worthy, righteous, commendable, laudable, praiseworthy, meritorious, estimable ≠ undeserving

design VERB 1 = plan, draw, draft, trace, outline, devise, sketch, formulate 2 = create, plan, fashion, propose, invent, conceive, originate, fabricate 3 = intend, mean, plan, aim, purpose
• NOUN 1 = pattern, form, style, shape, organization, arrangement, construction

2 = plan, drawing, model, scheme, draft, outline, sketch, blueprint 3 = intention, end, aim, goal, target, purpose, object, objective

designate 1 = name, call, term, style, label, entitle, dub 2 = choose, reserve, select, label, flag, assign, allocate, set aside 3 = appoint, name, choose, commission, select, elect, delegate, nominate

designer 1 = couturier 2 = producer, architect, deviser, creator, planner, inventor, originator

desirable 1 = advantageous, useful, valuable, helpful, profitable, of service, convenient, worthwhile ≠ disadvantageous 2 = popular ≠ unpopular 3 = attractive, appealing, pretty, fair, inviting, lovely, charming, sexy (*informal*) ≠ unattractive

desire NOUN 1 = wish, want, longing, hope, urge, aspiration, craving, thirst 2 = lust, passion, libido, appetite, lasciviousness • VERB = want, long for, crave, hope for, ache for, wish for, yearn for, thirst for

despair NOUN = despondency, depression, misery, gloom, desperation, anguish, hopelessness, dejection • VERB = lose hope, give up, lose heart

desperate 1 = grave, pressing, serious, severe, extreme, urgent, drastic 2 = last-ditch, daring, furious, risky, frantic, audacious

desperately = gravely, badly, seriously, severely, dangerously, perilously

desperation 1 = misery, worry, trouble, despair, agony, anguish, unhappiness, hopelessness 2 = recklessness, madness, frenzy, impetuosity, rashness, foolhardiness

despise = look down on, loathe, scorn, detest, revile, abhor ≠ admire

despite = in spite of, in the face of, regardless of, even with, notwithstanding, in the teeth of, undeterred by

destination = stop, station, haven, resting-place, terminus, journey's end

destined = fated, meant, intended, certain, bound, doomed, predestined

destiny 1 = fate, fortune, lot, portion, doom, nemesis 2 *usually cap.* = fortune, chance, karma, providence, kismet, predestination, divine will

destroy 1 = ruin, crush, devastate, wreck, shatter, wipe out, demolish, eradicate 2 = slaughter, kill

destruction 1 = ruin, havoc, wreckage, demolition, devastation, annihilation 2 slaughter, extermination, eradication 3 = slaughter

destructive = devastating, fatal, deadly, lethal, harmful, damaging, catastrophic, ruinous

detach 1 = separate, remove, divide, cut off, sever, disconnect, tear off, disengage ≠ attach 2 = free, remove, separate, isolate, cut off, disengage

detached 1 = objective, neutral, impartial, reserved, impersonal, disinterested, unbiased, dispassionate ≠ subjective 2 = separate, disconnected, discrete, unconnected, undivided

detachment 1 = indifference, fairness, neutrality, objectivity, impartiality, coolness, remoteness, nonchalance 2 (*Military*) = unit, party, force, body, squad, patrol, task force

detail NOUN 1 = point, fact, feature, particular, respect, factor, element, aspect 2 = fine point, particular, nicety, triviality 3 (*Military*) = party, force, body, duty, squad, assignment, fatigue, detachment • VERB = list, relate, catalogue, recount, rehearse, recite, enumerate, itemize

detailed = comprehensive, full, complete, minute, particular, thorough, exhaustive, all-embracing ≠ brief

detain 1 = hold, arrest, confine, restrain, imprison, intern, take prisoner, hold in custody 2 = delay, hold up, hamper, hinder, retard, impede, keep back, slow up *or* down

detect 1 = discover, find, uncover, track down, unmask 2 = notice, see, spot, note, identify, observe, recognize, perceive

detective = investigator, cop (*slang*), private eye, sleuth (*informal*), private investigator, gumshoe (*U.S. slang*)

detention = imprisonment, custody, quarantine, confinement, incarceration ≠ release

deter 1 = discourage, inhibit, put off, frighten, intimidate, dissuade, talk out of 2 = prevent, stop

deteriorate = decline, worsen, degenerate, slump, go downhill ≠ improve

determination = resolution, purpose, resolve, dedication, fortitude, persistence, tenacity, perseverance ≠ indecision

determine **1** = affect, decide, regulate, ordain **2** = settle, learn, establish, discover, find out, work out, detect, verify **3** = decide on, choose, elect, resolve **4** = decide, conclude, resolve, make up your mind

determined = resolute, firm, dogged, intent, persistent, persevering, single-minded, tenacious

deterrent = discouragement, obstacle, curb, restraint, impediment, check, hindrance, disincentive ≠ incentive

devastate = destroy, ruin, sack, wreck, demolish, level, ravage, raze

devastation = destruction, ruin, havoc, demolition, desolation

develop **1** = grow, advance, progress, mature, evolve, flourish, ripen **2** = establish, set up, promote, generate, undertake, initiate, embark on, cultivate **3** = form, establish, breed, generate, originate **4** = expand, extend, work out, elaborate, unfold, enlarge, broaden, amplify

development **1** = growth, increase, advance, progress, spread, expansion, evolution, enlargement **2** = establishment, forming, generation, institution, invention, initiation, inauguration, instigation **3** = event, happening, result, incident, improvement, evolution, unfolding, occurrence

deviant ADJECTIVE = perverted, sick (*informal*), twisted, warped, kinky (*slang*) ≠ normal
• NOUN = pervert, freak, misfit

device **1** = gadget, machine, tool, instrument, implement, appliance, apparatus, contraption **2** = ploy, scheme, plan, trick, manoeuvre, gambit, stratagem, wile

devil NOUN **1** = evil spirit, demon, fiend, atua (*N.Z.*), wairua (*N.Z.*) **2** = brute, monster, beast, barbarian, fiend, terror, swine, ogre **3** = person, individual, soul, creature, thing, beggar **4** = scamp, rogue, rascal, scoundrel, scallywag (*informal*), nointer (*Austral. slang*)
• PHRASES **the Devil** = Satan, Lucifer, Prince of Darkness, Mephistopheles, Evil One, Beelzebub, Old Nick (*informal*)

devise = work out, design, construct, invent, conceive, formulate, contrive, dream up

devoid *with* ***of*** = lacking in, without, free from, wanting in, bereft of, empty of, deficient in

devote = dedicate, give, commit, apply, reserve, pledge, surrender, assign

devoted = dedicated, committed, true, constant, loyal, faithful, ardent, staunch ≠ disloyal

devotee = enthusiast, fan, supporter, follower, admirer, buff (*informal*), fanatic, adherent

devotion NOUN **1** = love, passion, affection, attachment, fondness **2** = dedication, commitment, loyalty, allegiance, fidelity, adherence, constancy, faithfulness ≠ indifference **3** = worship, reverence, spirituality, holiness, piety, godliness, devoutness ≠ irreverence
• PLURAL NOUN = prayers, religious observance, church service, divine office

devour **1** = eat, consume, swallow, wolf, gulp, gobble, guzzle, polish off (*informal*) **2** = enjoy, take in, read compulsively *or* voraciously

devout = religious, godly, pious, pure, holy, orthodox, saintly, reverent ≠ irreverent

diagnose = identify, determine, recognize, distinguish, interpret, pronounce, pinpoint

diagnosis = identification, discovery, recognition, detection

diagram = plan, figure, drawing, chart, representation, sketch, graph

dialogue **1** = discussion, conference, exchange, debate **2** = conversation, discussion, communication, discourse

diary **1** = journal, chronicle **2** = engagement book, Filofax®, appointment book

dictate VERB = speak, say, utter, read out
• NOUN **1** = command, order, decree, demand, direction, injunction, fiat, edict **2** = principle, law, rule, standard, code, criterion, maxim
• PHRASES **dictate to someone** = order (about), direct, lay down the law, pronounce to

dictator = absolute ruler, tyrant, despot, oppressor, autocrat, absolutist, martinet

dictatorship = absolute rule, tyranny, totalitarianism, authoritarianism, despotism, autocracy, absolutism

dictionary = wordbook, vocabulary,

glossary, lexicon

die VERB **1** = pass away, expire, perish, croak (*slang*), give up the ghost, snuff it (*slang*), peg out (*informal*), kick the bucket (*slang*), cark it (*Austral. & N.Z. slang*) ≠ live **2** = stop, fail, halt, break down, run down, stop working, peter out, fizzle out **3** = dwindle, decline, sink, fade, diminish, decrease, decay, wither ≠ increase
• PHRASES **be dying for something** = long for, want, desire, crave, yearn for, hunger for, pine for, hanker after

diet[1] NOUN **1** = food, provisions, fare, rations, kai (*N.Z. informal*), nourishment, sustenance, victuals **2** = fast, regime, abstinence, regimen
• VERB = slim, fast, lose weight, abstain, eat sparingly ≠ overindulge

diet[2] *often cap.* = council, meeting, parliament, congress, chamber, convention, legislature

differ **1** = be dissimilar, contradict, contrast with, vary, belie, depart from, diverge, negate ≠ accord **2** = disagree, clash, dispute, dissent ≠ agree

difference **1** = dissimilarity, contrast, variation, change, variety, diversity, alteration, discrepancy ≠ similarity **2** = remainder, rest, balance, remains, excess **3** = disagreement, conflict, argument, clash, dispute, quarrel, contretemps ≠ agreement

different **1** = dissimilar, opposed, contrasting, changed, unlike, altered, inconsistent, disparate **2** = various, varied, diverse, assorted, miscellaneous, sundry **3** = unusual, special, strange, extraordinary, distinctive, peculiar, uncommon, singular

differentiate **1** = distinguish, separate, discriminate, contrast, mark off, make a distinction, tell apart, set off *or* apart **2** = make different, separate, distinguish, characterize, single out, segregate, individualize, mark off **3** = become different, change, convert, transform, alter, adapt, modify

difficult **1** = hard, tough, taxing, demanding, challenging, exacting, formidable, uphill ≠ easy **2** = problematical, involved, complex, complicated, obscure, baffling, intricate, knotty ≠ simple **3** = troublesome, demanding, perverse, fussy, fastidious, hard to please, refractory, unaccommodating ≠ cooperative

difficulty **1** = problem, trouble, obstacle, hurdle, dilemma, complication, snag, uphill (*S. African*) **2** = hardship, strain, awkwardness, strenuousness, arduousness, laboriousness

dig VERB **1** = hollow out, mine, quarry, excavate, scoop out **2** = delve, tunnel, burrow **3** = turn over **4** = search, hunt, root, delve, forage, dig down, fossick (*Austral. & N.Z.*) **5** = poke, drive, push, stick, punch, stab, thrust, shove
• NOUN **1** = cutting remark, crack (*slang*), insult, taunt, sneer, jeer, barb, wisecrack (*informal*) **2** = poke, thrust, nudge, prod, jab, punch

digest VERB **1** = ingest, absorb, incorporate, dissolve, assimilate **2** = take in, absorb, grasp, soak up
• NOUN = summary, résumé, abstract, epitome, synopsis, précis, abridgment

dignity **1** = decorum, gravity, majesty, grandeur, respectability, nobility, solemnity, courtliness **2** = self-importance, pride, self-esteem, self-respect

dilemma = predicament, problem, difficulty, spot (*informal*), mess, puzzle, plight, quandary

dilute **1** = water down, thin (out), weaken, adulterate, make thinner, cut (*informal*) ≠ condense **2** = reduce, weaken, diminish, temper, decrease, lessen, diffuse, mitigate ≠ intensify

dim ADJECTIVE **1** = poorly lit, dark, gloomy, murky, shady, shadowy, dusky, tenebrous **2** = cloudy, grey, gloomy, dismal, overcast, leaden ≠ bright **3** = unclear, obscured, faint, blurred, fuzzy, shadowy, hazy, bleary ≠ distinct **4** = stupid (*Informal*), thick, dull, dense, dumb (*informal*), daft (*informal*), dozy (*Brit. informal*), obtuse ≠ bright
• VERB **1** = turn down, fade, dull **2** = grow *or* become faint, fade, dull, grow *or* become dim **3** = darken, dull, cloud over

dimension **1** = aspect, side, feature, angle, facet **2** = extent, size

diminish **1** = decrease, decline, lessen, shrink, dwindle, wane, recede, subside ≠ grow **2** = reduce, cut, decrease, lessen, lower, curtail ≠ increase

din = noise, row, racket, crash, clamour, clatter, uproar, commotion ≠ silence

dine = eat, lunch, feast, sup

dinkum (*Austral. & N.Z. informal*) = genuine, honest, natural, frank, sincere, candid, upfront (*informal*), artless

dinner 1 = meal, main meal, spread (*informal*), repast 2 = banquet, feast, repast, hakari (*N.Z.*)

dip VERB 1 = plunge, immerse, bathe, duck, douse, dunk 2 = drop (down), fall, lower, sink, descend, subside 3 = slope, drop (down), descend, fall, decline, sink, incline, drop away
• NOUN 1 = plunge, ducking, soaking, drenching, immersion, douche 2 = nod, drop, lowering, slump, sag 3 = hollow, hole, depression, pit, basin, trough, concavity
• PHRASES **dip into something** = sample, skim, glance at, browse, peruse

diplomacy 1 = statesmanship, statecraft, international negotiation 2 = tact, skill, sensitivity, craft, discretion, subtlety, delicacy, finesse ≠ tactlessness

diplomat = official, ambassador, envoy, statesman, consul, attaché, emissary, chargé d'affaires

diplomatic 1 = consular, official, foreign-office, ambassadorial, foreign-politic 2 = tactful, politic, sensitive, subtle, delicate, polite, discreet, prudent ≠ tactless

dire = desperate, pressing, critical, terrible, crucial, extreme, awful, urgent

direct ADJECTIVE = quickest, shortest
• ADVERB 1 = straight, through ≠ circuitous 2 = first-hand, personal, immediate ≠ indirect 3 = clear, specific, plain, absolute, definite, explicit, downright, point-blank ≠ ambiguous 4 = straightforward, open, straight, frank, blunt, honest, candid, forthright ≠ indirect 5 = verbatim, exact, word-for-word, strict, accurate, faithful, letter-for-letter 6 = non-stop, straight
• VERB 1 = aim, point, level, train, focus 2 = guide, show, lead, point the way, point in the direction of 3 = control, run, manage, lead, guide, handle, conduct, oversee 4 = order, command, instruct, charge, demand, require, bid 5 = address, send, mail, route, label

direction NOUN 1 = way, course, line, road, track, bearing, route, path 2 = management, control, charge, administration, leadership, command, guidance, supervision
• PLURAL NOUN = instructions, rules, information, plan, briefing, regulations, recommendations, guidelines

directive = order, ruling, regulation, command, instruction, decree, mandate, injunction

directly 1 = straight, unswervingly, without deviation, by the shortest route, in a beeline 2 = immediately, promptly, right away, straightaway 3 (*Old-fashioned*) = at once, as soon as possible, straightaway, forthwith 4 = honestly, openly, frankly, plainly, point-blank, unequivocally, truthfully, unreservedly

director = controller, head, leader, manager, chief, executive, governor, administrator, baas (*S. African*)

dirt 1 = filth, muck, grime, dust, mud, impurity, kak (*S. African taboo slang*) 2 = soil, ground, earth, clay, turf, loam

dirty ADJECTIVE 1 = filthy, soiled, grubby, foul, muddy, polluted, messy, grimy, festy (*Austral. slang*) ≠ clean 2 = dishonest, illegal, unfair, cheating, crooked, fraudulent, treacherous, unscrupulous ≠ honest 3 = obscene, indecent, blue, offensive, filthy, pornographic, sleazy, lewd ≠ decent
• VERB = soil, foul, stain, spoil, muddy, pollute, blacken, defile ≠ clean

disability = handicap, affliction, disorder, defect, impairment, infirmity

disable = handicap, cripple, damage, paralyse, impair, incapacitate, immobilize, enfeeble

disabled = differently abled, physically challenged, handicapped, weakened, crippled, paralysed, lame, incapacitated ≠ able-bodied

disadvantage 1 = drawback, trouble, handicap, nuisance, snag, inconvenience, downside ≠ advantage 2 = harm, loss, damage, injury, hurt, prejudice, detriment, disservice ≠ benefit

disagree 1 = differ (in opinion), argue, clash, dispute, dissent, quarrel, take issue with, cross swords ≠ agree 2 = make ill, upset, sicken, trouble, hurt, bother, distress, discomfort

disagreement = argument, row, conflict, clash, dispute, dissent, quarrel, squabble ≠ agreement

disappear 1 = vanish, recede, evanesce

≠ appear 2 = pass, fade away 3 = cease, dissolve, evaporate, perish, die out, pass away, melt away, leave no trace

disappearance 1 = vanishing, going, passing, melting, eclipse, evaporation, evanescence 2 = flight, departure 3 = loss, losing, mislaying

disappoint = let down, dismay, fail, disillusion, dishearten, disenchant, dissatisfy, disgruntle

disappointment 1 = regret, discontent, dissatisfaction, disillusionment, chagrin, disenchantment, dejection, despondency 2 = letdown, blow, setback, misfortune, calamity, choker (*informal*) 3 = frustration

disapproval = displeasure, criticism, objection, condemnation, dissatisfaction, censure, reproach, denunciation

disapprove = condemn, object to, dislike, deplore, frown on, take exception to, take a dim view of, find unacceptable ≠ approve

disarm 1 = demilitarize, disband, demobilize, deactivate 2 = win over, persuade

disarmament = arms reduction, demobilization, arms limitation, demilitarization, de-escalation

disarming = charming, winning, irresistible, persuasive, likable *or* likeable

disarray 1 = confusion, disorder, indiscipline, disunity, disorganization, unruliness ≠ order 2 = untidiness, mess, chaos, muddle, clutter, shambles, jumble, hotchpotch ≠ tidiness

disaster 1 = catastrophe, trouble, tragedy, ruin, misfortune, adversity, calamity, cataclysm 2 = failure, mess, flop (*informal*), catastrophe, debacle, cock-up (*Brit. slang*), washout (*informal*)

disastrous 1 = terrible, devastating, tragic, fatal, catastrophic, ruinous, calamitous, cataclysmic 2 = unsuccessful

disbelief = scepticism, doubt, distrust, mistrust, incredulity, unbelief, dubiety ≠ belief

discard = get rid of, drop, throw away *or* out, reject, abandon, dump (*informal*), dispose of, dispense with ≠ keep

discharge VERB 1 = release, free, clear, liberate, pardon, allow to go, set free 2 = dismiss, sack (*informal*), fire (*informal*), remove, expel, discard, oust, cashier 3 = carry out, perform, fulfil, accomplish, do, effect, realize, observe 4 = pay, meet, clear, settle, square (up), honour, satisfy, relieve 5 = pour forth, release, leak, emit, dispense, ooze, exude, give off 6 = fire, shoot, set off, explode, let off, detonate, let loose (*informal*)
• NOUN 1 = release, liberation, clearance, pardon, acquittal 2 = dismissal, notice, removal, the boot (*slang*), expulsion, the push (*slang*), marching orders (*informal*), ejection 3 = emission, ooze, secretion, excretion, pus, seepage, suppuration 4 = firing, report, shot, blast, burst, explosion, volley, salvo

disciple 1 = apostle 2 = follower, student, supporter, pupil, devotee, apostle, adherent ≠ teacher

discipline NOUN 1 = control, authority, regulation, supervision, orderliness, strictness 2 = punishment, penalty, correction, chastening, chastisement, castigation 3 = self-control, control, restraint, self-discipline, willpower, self-restraint, orderliness 4 = training, practice, exercise, method, regulation, drill, regimen 5 = field of study, area, subject, theme, topic, course, curriculum, speciality
• VERB 1 = punish, correct, reprimand, castigate, chastise, chasten, penalize, bring to book 2 = train, educate

disclose 1 = make known, reveal, publish, relate, broadcast, confess, communicate, divulge ≠ keep secret 2 = show, reveal, expose, unveil, uncover, lay bare, bring to light ≠ hide

disclosure 1 = revelation, announcement, publication, leak, admission, declaration, confession, acknowledgment 2 = uncovering, publication, revelation, divulgence

discomfort 1 = pain, hurt, ache, throbbing, irritation, tenderness, pang, malaise ≠ comfort 2 = uneasiness, worry, anxiety, doubt, distress, misgiving, qualms, trepidation ≠ reassurance 3 = inconvenience, trouble, difficulty, bother, hardship, irritation, nuisance, uphill (*S. African*)

discontent = dissatisfaction, unhappiness, displeasure, regret, envy, restlessness, uneasiness

discontented = dissatisfied, unhappy, fed up, disgruntled, disaffected, vexed, displeased ≠ satisfied

discount NOUN = deduction, cut, reduction, concession, rebate
• VERB 1 = mark down, reduce, lower 2 = disregard, reject, ignore, overlook, discard, set aside, dispel, pass over

discourage 1 = dishearten, depress, intimidate, overawe, demoralize, put a damper on, dispirit, deject ≠ hearten 2 = put off, deter, prevent, dissuade, talk out of ≠ encourage

discourse 1 = conversation, talk, discussion, speech, communication, chat, dialogue 2 = speech, essay, lecture, sermon, treatise, dissertation, homily, oration, whaikorero (*N.Z.*)

discover 1 = find out, learn, notice, realize, recognize, perceive, detect, uncover 2 = find, come across, uncover, unearth, turn up, dig up, come upon

discovery 1 = finding out, news, revelation, disclosure, realization 2 = invention, launch, institution, pioneering, innovation, inauguration 3 = breakthrough, find, development, advance, leap, invention, step forward, quantum leap 4 = finding, revelation, uncovering, disclosure, detection

discredit VERB 1 = disgrace, shame, smear, humiliate, taint, disparage, vilify, slander ≠ honour 2 = dispute, question, challenge, deny, reject, discount, distrust, mistrust
• NOUN = disgrace, scandal, shame, disrepute, stigma, ignominy, dishonour, ill-repute ≠ honour

discreet = tactful, diplomatic, guarded, careful, cautious, wary, prudent, considerate ≠ tactless

discrepancy = disagreement, difference, variation, conflict, contradiction, inconsistency, disparity, divergence

discretion 1 = tact, consideration, caution, diplomacy, prudence, wariness, carefulness, judiciousness ≠ tactlessness 2 = choice, will, pleasure, preference, inclination, volition

discriminate VERB = differentiate, distinguish, separate, tell the difference, draw a distinction
• PHRASES **discriminate against someone** = treat differently, single out, victimize, treat as inferior, show bias against, show prejudice against

discriminating = discerning, particular, refined, cultivated, selective, tasteful, fastidious ≠ undiscriminating

discrimination 1 = prejudice, bias, injustice, intolerance, bigotry, favouritism, unfairness 2 = discernment, taste, judgment, perception, subtlety, refinement

discuss = talk about, consider, debate, examine, argue about, deliberate about, converse about, confer about

discussion 1 = talk, debate, argument, conference, conversation, dialogue, consultation, discourse, korero (*N.Z.*) 2 = examination, investigation, analysis, scrutiny, dissection

disdain NOUN = contempt, scorn, arrogance, derision, haughtiness, superciliousness
• VERB = scorn, reject, slight, disregard, spurn, deride, look down on, sneer at

disease = illness, condition, complaint, infection, disorder, sickness, ailment, affliction

diseased = unhealthy, sick, infected, rotten, ailing, sickly, unwell, crook (*Austral. & N.Z. informal*), unsound

disgrace NOUN 1 = shame, degradation, disrepute, ignominy, dishonour, infamy, opprobrium, odium ≠ honour 2 = scandal, stain, stigma, blot, blemish
• VERB = shame, humiliate, discredit, degrade, taint, sully, dishonour, bring shame upon ≠ honour

disgraceful = shameful, shocking, scandalous, unworthy, ignominious, disreputable, contemptible, dishonourable

disgruntled = discontented, dissatisfied, annoyed, irritated, put out, grumpy, vexed, displeased, hoha (*N.Z.*)

disguise NOUN = costume, mask, camouflage
• VERB = hide, cover, conceal, screen, mask, suppress, withhold, veil

disguised 1 = in disguise, masked, camouflaged, undercover, incognito 2 = false, artificial, forged, fake, mock, imitation, sham, counterfeit

disgust NOUN 1 = loathing, revulsion, hatred, dislike, nausea, distaste, aversion, repulsion ≠ liking 2 = outrage, shock, anger, hurt, fury, resentment, wrath, indignation
• VERB = sicken, offend, revolt, put off, repel, nauseate ≠ delight

disgusting 1 = sickening, foul, revolting, gross, repellent, nauseating, repugnant, loathsome, festy (*Austral. slang*), yucko (*Austral. slang*) 2 = appalling, shocking, awful, offensive, dreadful, horrifying

dish 1 = bowl, plate, platter, salver 2 = food, fare, recipe

dishonest = deceitful, corrupt, crooked (*informal*), lying, bent (*slang*), false, cheating, treacherous ≠ honest

disintegrate = break up, crumble, fall apart, separate, shatter, splinter, break apart, go to pieces

dislike VERB = hate, object to, loathe, despise, disapprove of, detest, recoil from, take a dim view of ≠ like
• NOUN = hatred, hostility, disapproval, distaste, animosity, aversion, displeasure, antipathy ≠ liking

dismal 1 = bad, awful, dreadful, rotten (*informal*), terrible, poor, dire, abysmal 2 = sad, gloomy, dark, depressing, discouraging, bleak, dreary, sombre ≠ happy 3 = gloomy, depressing, dull, dreary ≠ cheerful

dismantle = take apart, strip, demolish, disassemble, take to pieces *or* bits

dismay NOUN 1 = alarm, fear, horror, anxiety, dread, apprehension, nervousness, consternation 2 = disappointment, frustration, dissatisfaction, disillusionment, chagrin, disenchantment, discouragement
• VERB 1 = alarm, frighten, scare, panic, distress, terrify, appal, startle 2 = disappoint, upset, discourage, daunt, disillusion, let down, dishearten, dispirit

dismiss 1 = reject, disregard 2 = banish, dispel, discard, set aside, cast out, lay aside, put out of your mind 3 = sack, fire (*informal*), remove (*informal*), axe (*informal*), discharge, lay off, cashier, give notice to 4 = let go, free, release, discharge, dissolve, liberate, disperse, send away

dismissal = the sack, removal, notice, the boot (*slang*), expulsion (*informal*), the push (*slang*), marching orders (*informal*)

disobey 1 = defy, ignore, rebel, disregard, refuse to obey 2 = infringe, defy, refuse to obey, flout, violate, contravene, overstep, transgress

disorder 1 = illness, disease, complaint, condition, sickness, ailment, affliction, malady 2 = untidiness, mess, confusion, chaos, muddle, clutter, shambles, disarray 3 = disturbance, riot, turmoil, unrest, uproar, commotion, unruliness, biffo (*Austral. slang*)

disorderly 1 = untidy, confused, chaotic, messy, jumbled, shambolic (*informal*), disorganized, higgledy-piggledy (*informal*) ≠ tidy 2 = unruly, disruptive, rowdy, turbulent, tumultuous, lawless, riotous, ungovernable

dispatch *or* **despatch** VERB 1 = send, consign 2 = kill, murder, destroy, execute, slaughter, assassinate, slay, liquidate 3 = carry out, perform, fulfil, effect, finish, achieve, settle, dismiss
• NOUN = message, news, report, story, account, communication, bulletin, communiqué

dispel = drive away, dismiss, eliminate, expel, disperse, banish, chase away

dispense VERB 1 = distribute, assign, allocate, allot, dole out, share out, apportion, deal out 2 = prepare, measure, supply, mix 3 = administer, operate, carry out, implement, enforce, execute, apply, discharge
• PHRASES **dispense with something** *or* **someone** 1 = do away with, give up, cancel, abolish, brush aside, forgo 2 = do without, get rid of, dispose of, relinquish

disperse 1 = scatter, spread, distribute, strew, diffuse, disseminate, throw about 2 = break up, separate, scatter, dissolve, disband ≠ gather 3 = dissolve, break up

displace 1 = replace, succeed, supersede, oust, usurp, supplant, take the place of 2 = move, shift, disturb, budge, misplace

display VERB 1 = show, present, exhibit, put on view ≠ conceal 2 = expose, show, reveal, exhibit, uncover 3 = demonstrate, show, reveal, register, expose, disclose, manifest 4 = show off, parade, exhibit, sport (*informal*), flash (*informal*), flourish, brandish, flaunt
• NOUN 1 = proof, exhibition, demonstration, evidence, expression, illustration, revelation, testimony 2 = exhibition, show, demonstration, presentation, array 3 = ostentation, show, flourish, fanfare, pomp 4 = show, exhibition, parade, spectacle, pageant

disposable 1 = throwaway, nonreturnable 2 = available, expendable, consumable

disposal NOUN = throwing away, dumping (*informal*), scrapping, removal, discarding, jettisoning, ejection, riddance
• PHRASES **at your disposal** = available, ready, to hand, accessible, handy, at hand, on tap, expendable

dispose VERB = arrange, put, place, group, order, distribute, array
• PHRASES **dispose of someone** = kill, murder, destroy, execute, slaughter, assassinate, slay, liquidate ◆ **dispose of something** 1 = get rid of, destroy, dump (*informal*), scrap, discard, unload, jettison, throw out *or* away 2 = deal with, manage, treat, handle, settle, cope with, take care of, see to

disposition 1 = character, nature, spirit, make-up, constitution, temper, temperament 2 = tendency, inclination, propensity, habit, leaning, bent, bias, proclivity 3 = arrangement, grouping, ordering, organization, distribution, placement

dispute NOUN 1 = disagreement, conflict, argument, dissent, altercation 2 = argument, row, clash, controversy, contention, feud, quarrel, squabble
• VERB 1 = contest, question, challenge, deny, doubt, oppose, object to, contradict 2 = argue, fight, clash, disagree, fall out (*informal*), quarrel, squabble, bicker

disqualify = ban, rule out, prohibit, preclude, debar, declare ineligible

disregard VERB = ignore, discount, overlook, neglect, pass over, turn a blind eye to, make light of, pay no heed to ≠ pay attention to
• NOUN = ignoring, neglect, contempt, indifference, negligence, disdain, disrespect

disrupt 1 = interrupt, stop, upset, hold up, interfere with, unsettle, obstruct, cut short 2 = disturb, upset, confuse, disorder, spoil, disorganize, disarrange

disruption = disturbance, interference, interruption, stoppage

disruptive = disturbing, upsetting, disorderly, unsettling, troublesome, unruly ≠ well-behaved

dissatisfaction = discontent, frustration, resentment, disappointment, irritation, unhappiness, annoyance, displeasure

dissatisfied = discontented, frustrated, unhappy, disappointed, fed up, disgruntled, displeased, unsatisfied ≠ satisfied

dissent = disagreement, opposition, protest, resistance, refusal, objection, discord, demur ≠ assent

dissident NOUN = protester, rebel, dissenter, demonstrator, agitator
• ADJECTIVE = dissenting, disagreeing, nonconformist, heterodox

dissolve 1 = melt, soften, thaw, liquefy, deliquesce 2 = end, suspend, break up, wind up, terminate, discontinue, dismantle, disband

distance 1 = space, length, extent, range, stretch, gap, interval, span 2 = aloofness, reserve, detachment, restraint, stiffness, coolness, coldness, standoffishness

distant 1 = far-off, far, remote, abroad, out-of-the-way, far-flung, faraway, outlying ≠ close 2 = remote 3 = reserved, withdrawn, cool, remote, detached, aloof, unfriendly, reticent ≠ friendly 4 = faraway, blank, vague, distracted, vacant, preoccupied, oblivious, absent-minded

distinct 1 = different, individual, separate, discrete, unconnected ≠ similar 2 = striking, dramatic, outstanding, noticeable, well-defined 3 = definite, marked, clear, decided, obvious, evident, noticeable, conspicuous ≠ vague

distinction 1 = difference, contrast, variation, differential, discrepancy, disparity, dissimilarity 2 = excellence, importance, fame, merit, prominence, greatness, eminence, repute 3 = feature, quality, characteristic, mark, individuality, peculiarity, distinctiveness, particularity 4 = merit, honour, integrity, excellence, rectitude

distinctive = characteristic, special, individual, unique, typical, peculiar, singular, idiosyncratic ≠ ordinary

distinctly 1 = definitely, clearly, obviously, plainly, patently, decidedly, markedly, noticeably 2 = clearly, plainly

distinguish 1 = differentiate, determine, separate, discriminate, decide, judge, ascertain, tell the difference 2 = characterize, mark, separate, single out, set apart 3 = make out, recognize, perceive, know, see, tell, pick out, discern

distinguished = eminent, noted, famous, celebrated, well-known, prominent, esteemed, acclaimed ≠ unknown

distort 1 = misrepresent, twist, bias, disguise, pervert, slant, colour, misinterpret 2 = deform, bend, twist, warp, buckle, mangle, mangulate (*Austral. slang*), disfigure, contort

distortion 1 = misrepresentation, bias, slant, perversion, falsification 2 = deformity, bend, twist, warp, buckle, contortion, malformation, crookedness

distract 1 = divert, sidetrack, draw away, turn aside, lead astray, draw *or* lead away from 2 = amuse, occupy, entertain, beguile, engross

distracted = agitated, troubled, puzzled, at sea, perplexed, flustered, in a flap (*informal*)

distraction 1 = disturbance, interference, diversion, interruption 2 = entertainment, recreation, amusement, diversion, pastime

distraught = frantic, desperate, distressed, distracted, worked-up, agitated, overwrought, out of your mind

distress NOUN 1 = suffering, pain, worry, grief, misery, torment, sorrow, heartache 2 = need, trouble, difficulties, poverty, hard times, hardship, misfortune, adversity
• VERB = upset, worry, trouble, disturb, grieve, torment, harass, agitate

distressed 1 = upset, worried, troubled, distracted, tormented, distraught, agitated, wretched 2 = poverty-stricken, poor, impoverished, needy, destitute, indigent, down at heel, straitened

distressing = upsetting, worrying, disturbing, painful, sad, harrowing, heart-breaking

distribute 1 = hand out, pass round 2 = circulate, deliver, convey 3 = share, deal, allocate, dispense, allot, dole out, apportion

distribution 1 = delivery, mailing, transportation, handling 2 = sharing, division, assignment, rationing, allocation, allotment, apportionment 3 = spread, organization, arrangement, placement

district = area, region, sector, quarter, parish, neighbourhood, vicinity, locality

distrust VERB = suspect, doubt, be wary of, mistrust, disbelieve, be suspicious of ≠ trust
• NOUN = suspicion, question, doubt, disbelief, scepticism, mistrust, misgiving, wariness ≠ trust

disturb 1 = interrupt, trouble, bother, plague, disrupt, interfere with, hassle, inconvenience 2 = upset, concern, worry, trouble, alarm, distress, unsettle, unnerve ≠ calm 3 = muddle, disorder, mix up, mess up, jumble up, disarrange

disturbance 1 = disorder, fray, brawl, fracas, commotion, rumpus 2 = upset, bother, distraction, intrusion, interruption, annoyance

disturbed 1 (*Psychiatry*) = unbalanced, troubled, disordered, unstable, neurotic, upset, deranged, maladjusted ≠ balanced 2 = worried, concerned, troubled, upset, bothered, nervous, anxious, uneasy ≠ calm

disturbing = worrying, upsetting, alarming, frightening, distressing, startling, unsettling, harrowing

ditch NOUN = channel, drain, trench, dyke, furrow, gully, moat, watercourse
• VERB 1 (*Slang*) = get rid of, dump (*informal*), scrap, discard, dispose of, dispense with, jettison, throw out *or* overboard 2 (*Slang*) = leave, drop, abandon, dump (*informal*), get rid of, forsake

dive VERB 1 = plunge, drop, duck, dip, descend, plummet 2 = go underwater 3 = nose-dive, plunge, crash, swoop, plummet
• NOUN = plunge, spring, jump, leap, lunge, nose dive

diverse 1 = various, mixed, varied, assorted, miscellaneous, several, sundry, motley 2 = different, unlike, varying, separate, distinct, disparate, discrete, dissimilar

diversify = vary, change, expand, spread out, branch out

diversion 1 = distraction, deviation, digression 2 = pastime, game, sport, entertainment, hobby, relaxation, recreation, distraction 3 (*Chiefly Brit.*) = detour, roundabout way, indirect course 4 (*Chiefly Brit.*) = deviation, departure, straying, divergence, digression

diversity 1 = difference, multiplicity, heterogeneity, diverseness 2 = range, variety, scope, sphere

divert 1 = redirect, switch, avert, deflect, deviate, turn aside 2 = distract, sidetrack, lead astray, draw *or* lead away from 3 = entertain, delight, amuse, please, charm, gratify, beguile, regale

divide 1 = separate, split, segregate, bisect ≠ join 2 *sometimes with* ***up*** = share, distribute, allocate, dispense, allot, mete, deal out 3 = split, break up, come between, estrange, cause to disagree

dividend = bonus, share, cut (*informal*), gain, extra, plus, portion, divvy (*informal*)

divine ADJECTIVE 1 = heavenly, spiritual, holy, immortal, supernatural, celestial, angelic, superhuman 2 = sacred, religious, holy, spiritual, blessed, revered, hallowed, consecrated 3 (*Informal*) = wonderful, perfect, beautiful, excellent, lovely, glorious, marvellous, splendid
• VERB = guess, suppose, perceive, discern, infer, deduce, apprehend, surmise

division 1 = separation, dividing, splitting up, partition, cutting up 2 = sharing, sharing, distribution, assignment, rationing, allocation, allotment, apportionment 3 = disagreement, split, rift, rupture, abyss, chasm, variance, discord ≠ unity 4 = department, group, branch 5 = part, bit, piece, section, class, category, fraction

divorce NOUN = separation, split, break-up, parting, split-up, rift, dissolution, annulment
• VERB = separate, split up, part company, dissolve your marriage

dizzy 1 = giddy, faint, light-headed, swimming, reeling, shaky, wobbly, off balance 2 = confused, dazzled, at sea, bewildered, muddled, bemused, dazed, disorientated

do VERB 1 = perform, achieve, carry out, complete, accomplish, execute, pull off 2 = make, prepare, fix, arrange, look after, see to, get ready 3 = solve, work out, resolve, figure out, decode, decipher, puzzle out 4 = be adequate, be sufficient, satisfy, suffice, pass muster, cut the mustard, meet requirements 5 = produce, make, create, develop, manufacture, construct, invent, fabricate
• NOUN (*Informal*, *chiefly Brit. & N.Z.*) = party, gathering, function, event, affair, occasion, celebration, reception
• PHRASES **do away with something** = get rid of, remove, eliminate, abolish, discard, put an end to, dispense with, discontinue ◆ **do without something** *or* **someone** = manage without, give up, dispense with, forgo, kick (*informal*), abstain from, get along without

dock[1] NOUN = port, haven, harbour, pier, wharf, quay, waterfront, anchorage
• VERB 1 = moor, land, anchor, put in, tie up, berth, drop anchor 2 (*of spacecraft*) = link up, unite, join, couple, rendezvous, hook up

dock[2] 1 = cut, reduce, decrease, diminish, lessen ≠ increase 2 = deduct, subtract 3 = cut off, crop, clip, shorten, curtail, cut short

doctor NOUN = physician, medic (*informal*), general practitioner, medical practitioner, G.P.
• VERB 1 = change, alter, interfere with, disguise, pervert, tamper with, tinker with, misrepresent 2 = add to, spike, cut, mix something with something, dilute, water down, adulterate

doctrine = teaching, principle, belief, opinion, conviction, creed, dogma, tenet, kaupapa (*N.Z.*)

document NOUN = paper, form, certificate, report, record, testimonial, authorization
• VERB = support, certify, verify, detail, validate, substantiate, corroborate, authenticate

dodge VERB 1 = duck, dart, swerve, sidestep, shoot, turn aside 2 = evade, avoid, escape, get away from, elude 3 = avoid, evade, shirk
• NOUN = trick, scheme, ploy, trap, device, fraud, manoeuvre, deception

dodgy 1 (*Brit., Austral., & N.Z*) = nasty, offensive, unpleasant, revolting, distasteful, repellent, obnoxious, repulsive 2 (*Brit., Austral., & N.Z*) = risky, difficult, tricky, dangerous, delicate, uncertain, dicey (*informal*, *chiefly Brit.*), chancy (*informal*) 3 = second rate, poor, inferior, mediocre, shoddy, bush-league (*Austral. & N.Z. informal*), half-pie (*N.Z. informal*), bodger *or* bodgie (*Austral. slang*)

dog NOUN = hound, canine, pooch (*slang*), cur, man's best friend, kuri *or* goorie (*N.Z.*), brak (*S. African*)
• VERB 1 = plague, follow, trouble, haunt, hound, torment 2 = pursue, follow, track, chase, trail, hound, stalk
• PHRASES **go to the dogs** (*Informal*) = deteriorate, degenerate, be in decline, go downhill (*informal*), go down the drain, go to pot, go to ruin

RELATED WORDS

adjective: canine
female: bitch
young: pup, puppy

dogged = determined, persistent, stubborn, resolute, tenacious, steadfast, obstinate, indefatigable ≠ irresolute

dole NOUN = share, grant, gift, allowance, handout, koha (*N.Z.*)
• PHRASES **dole something out** = give out, distribute, assign, allocate, hand out, dispense, allot, apportion

dolphin
RELATED WORD
collective noun: school

domestic ADJECTIVE **1** = home, internal, native, indigenous **2** = household, home, family, private **3** = home-loving, homely, housewifely, stay-at-home, domesticated **4** = domesticated, trained, tame, pet, house-trained
• NOUN = servant, help, maid, daily, char (*informal*), charwoman

dominant **1** = main, chief, primary, principal, prominent, predominant, pre-eminent ≠ minor **2** = controlling, ruling, commanding, supreme, governing, superior, authoritative

dominate **1** = control, rule, direct, govern, monopolize, tyrannize, have the whip hand over **2** = tower above, overlook, survey, stand over, loom over, stand head and shoulders above

domination = control, power, rule, authority, influence, command, supremacy, ascendancy

don = put on, get into, dress in, pull on, change into, get dressed in, clothe yourself in, slip on *or* into

donate = give, present, contribute, grant, subscribe, endow, entrust, impart

donation = contribution, gift, subscription, offering, present, grant, hand-out, koha (*N.Z.*)

donor = giver, contributor, benefactor, philanthropist, donator ≠ recipient

doom NOUN **1** = destruction, ruin, catastrophe, downfall **2** = fate, fortune
• VERB = condemn, sentence, consign, destine

doomed = hopeless, condemned, ill-fated, fated, unhappy, unfortunate, cursed, unlucky

door = opening, entry, entrance, exit, doorway

dope NOUN **1** (*Slang*) = drugs, narcotics, opiates, dadah (*Austral. slang*) **2** (*Informal*) = idiot, fool, twit (*informal, chiefly Brit.*), dunce, simpleton, dimwit (*informal*), nitwit (*informal*), dumb-ass (*slang*), dorba *or* dorb (*Austral. slang*), bogan (*Austral. slang*)
• VERB = drug, knock out, sedate, stupefy, anaesthetize, narcotize

dorp (*S. African*) = town, village, settlement, municipality, kainga *or* kaika (*N.Z.*)

dose **1** = measure, amount, allowance, portion, prescription, ration, draught, dosage **2** = quantity, measure, supply, portion

dot NOUN = spot, point, mark, fleck, jot, speck, speckle
• VERB = spot, stud, fleck, speckle
• PHRASES **on the dot** = on time, promptly, precisely, exactly (*informal*), to the minute, on the button (*informal*), punctually

double ADJECTIVE **1** = matching, coupled, paired, twin, duplicate, in pairs **2** = dual, enigmatic, twofold
• VERB **1** = multiply by two, duplicate, increase twofold, enlarge, magnify **2** = fold up *or* over
• NOUN = twin, lookalike, spitting image, clone, replica, dead ringer (*slang*), Doppelgänger, duplicate
• PHRASES **at** *or* **on the double** = at once, now, immediately, directly, quickly, promptly, straight away, right away
◆ **double as something** *or* **someone** = function as, serve as

doubt NOUN **1** = uncertainty, confusion, hesitation, suspense, indecision, hesitancy, lack of conviction, irresolution ≠ certainty **2** = suspicion, scepticism, distrust, apprehension, mistrust, misgivings, qualms ≠ belief
• VERB **1** = be uncertain, be sceptical, be dubious **2** = waver, hesitate, vacillate, fluctuate **3** = disbelieve, question, suspect, query, distrust, mistrust, lack confidence in ≠ believe

doubtful **1** = unlikely, unclear, dubious, questionable, improbable, debatable, equivocal ≠ certain **2** = unsure, uncertain, hesitant, suspicious, hesitating, sceptical, tentative, wavering ≠ certain

doubtless = probably, presumably, most

likely
down ADJECTIVE = depressed, low, sad, unhappy, discouraged, miserable, fed up, dejected
• VERB (*Informal*) = swallow, drink (down), drain, gulp (down), put away (*informal*), toss off
downfall = ruin, fall, destruction, collapse, disgrace, overthrow, undoing, comeuppance (*slang*)
downgrade = demote, degrade, take down a peg (*informal*), lower *or* reduce in rank ≠ promote
downright = complete, absolute, utter, total, plain, outright, unqualified, out-and-out
down-to-earth = sensible, practical, realistic, matter-of-fact, sane, no-nonsense, unsentimental, plain-spoken
downward = descending, declining, heading down, earthward
draft NOUN 1 = outline, plan, sketch, version, rough, abstract 2 = money order, bill (of exchange), cheque, postal order
• VERB = outline, write, plan, produce, create, design, draw, compose
drag VERB = pull, draw, haul, trail, tow, tug, jerk, lug
• NOUN (*Slang*) = nuisance, bore, bother, pest, hassle (*informal*), inconvenience, annoyance
drain VERB 1 = remove, draw, empty, withdraw, tap, pump, bleed 2 = empty 3 = flow out, leak, trickle, ooze, seep, exude, well out, effuse 4 = drink up, swallow, finish, put away (*informal*), quaff, gulp down 5 = exhaust, wear out, strain, weaken, fatigue, debilitate, tire out, enfeeble 6 = consume, exhaust, empty, use up, sap, dissipate
• NOUN 1 = sewer, channel, pipe, sink, ditch, trench, conduit, duct 2 = reduction, strain, drag, exhaustion, sapping, depletion
drama 1 = play, show, stage show, dramatization 2 = theatre, acting, stagecraft, dramaturgy 3 = excitement, crisis, spectacle, turmoil, histrionics
dramatic 1 = exciting, thrilling, tense, sensational, breathtaking, electrifying, melodramatic, climactic 2 = theatrical, Thespian, dramaturgical 3 = expressive 4 = powerful, striking, impressive, vivid, jaw-dropping ≠ ordinary
drape = cover, wrap, fold, swathe
drastic = extreme, strong, radical, desperate, severe, harsh
draught 1 = breeze, current, movement, flow, puff, gust, current of air 2 = drink
draw VERB 1 = sketch, design, outline, trace, portray, paint, depict, mark out 2 = pull, drag, haul, tow, tug 3 = extract, take, remove 4 = deduce, make, take, derive, infer 5 = attract 6 = entice
• NOUN 1 = tie, deadlock, stalemate, impasse, dead heat 2 (*Informal*) = appeal, pull (*informal*), charm, attraction, lure, temptation, fascination, allure
• PHRASES **draw on** *or* **upon something** = make use of, use, employ, rely on, exploit, extract, take from, fall back on
drawback = disadvantage, difficulty, handicap, deficiency, flaw, hitch, snag, downside ≠ advantage
drawing = picture, illustration, representation, cartoon, sketch, portrayal, depiction, study
drawn = tense, worn, stressed, tired, pinched, haggard
dread VERB = fear, shrink from, cringe at the thought of, quail from, shudder to think about, have cold feet about (*informal*), tremble to think about
• NOUN = fear, alarm, horror, terror, dismay, fright, apprehension, trepidation
dreadful 1 = terrible, shocking, awful, appalling, horrible, fearful, hideous, atrocious 2 = serious, terrible, awful, horrendous, monstrous, abysmal 3 = awful, terrible, horrendous, frightful
dream NOUN 1 = vision, illusion, delusion, hallucination 2 = ambition, wish, fantasy, desire, pipe dream 3 = daydream 4 = delight, pleasure, joy, beauty, treasure, gem, marvel, pearler (*Austral. slang*)
• VERB 1 = have dreams, hallucinate 2 = daydream, stargaze, build castles in the air *or* in Spain
• PHRASES **dream of something** *or* **someone** = daydream about, fantasize about
dreamer = idealist, visionary, daydreamer, utopian, escapist, Walter Mitty, fantasist
dreary = dull, boring, tedious, drab, tiresome, monotonous, humdrum, uneventful ≠ exciting
drench = soak, flood, wet, drown, steep, swamp, saturate, inundate
dress NOUN 1 = frock, gown, robe

2 = clothing, clothes, costume, garments, apparel, attire, garb, togs
• VERB 1 = put on clothes, don clothes, slip on *or* into something ≠ undress 2 = clothe
3 = bandage, treat, plaster, bind up
4 = arrange, prepare, get ready

dribble 1 = run, drip, trickle, drop, leak, ooze, seep, fall in drops 2 = drool, drivel, slaver, slobber

drift VERB 1 = float, go (aimlessly), bob, coast, slip, sail, slide, glide 2 = wander, stroll, stray, roam, meander, rove, range
3 = stray, wander, digress, get off the point
4 = pile up, gather, accumulate, amass, bank up
• NOUN 1 = pile, bank, mass, heap, mound, accumulation 2 = meaning, point, gist, direction, import, intention, tendency, significance

drill NOUN 1 = bit, borer, gimlet, boring tool 2 = training, exercise, discipline, instruction, preparation, repetition
3 = practice
• VERB 1 = bore, pierce, penetrate, sink in, puncture, perforate 2 = train, coach, teach, exercise, discipline, practise, instruct, rehearse

drink VERB 1 = swallow, sip, suck, gulp, sup, guzzle, imbibe, quaff 2 = booze (*informal*), tipple, tope, hit the bottle (*informal*)
• NOUN 1 = glass, cup, draught
2 = beverage, refreshment, potion, liquid
3 = alcohol, booze (*informal*), liquor, spirits, the bottle (*informal*), hooch *or* hootch (*informal*, *chiefly U.S. & Canad.*)

drip VERB = drop, splash, sprinkle, trickle, dribble, exude, plop
• NOUN 1 = drop, bead, trickle, dribble, droplet, globule, pearl 2 (*Informal*) = weakling, wet (*Brit. informal*), weed (*informal*), softie (*informal*), mummy's boy (*informal*), namby-pamby

drive VERB 1 = go (by car), ride (by car), motor, travel by car 2 = operate, manage, direct, guide, handle, steer 3 = push, propel 4 = thrust, push, hammer, ram
5 = herd, urge, impel 6 = force, press, prompt, spur, prod, constrain, coerce, goad
• NOUN 1 = run, ride, trip, journey, spin (*informal*), outing, excursion, jaunt
2 = initiative, energy, enterprise, ambition, motivation, zip (*informal*), vigour, get-up-and-go (*informal*) 3 = campaign, push (*informal*), crusade, action, effort, appeal

drop VERB 1 = fall, decline, diminish 2 *often with* ***away*** = decline, fall, sink 3 = plunge, fall, tumble, descend, plummet 4 = drip, trickle, dribble, fall in drops 5 = sink, fall, descend 6 = quit, give up, axe (*informal*), kick (*informal*), relinquish, discontinue
• NOUN 1 = decrease, fall, cut, lowering, decline, reduction, slump, fall-off
2 = droplet, bead, globule, bubble, pearl, drip 3 = dash, shot (*informal*), spot, trace, sip, tot, trickle, mouthful 4 = fall, plunge, descent
• PHRASES **drop off** 1 = fall asleep, nod (off), doze (off), snooze (*informal*), have forty winks (*informal*) 2 = decrease, lower, decline, shrink, diminish, dwindle, lessen, subside ♦ **drop out** = leave, stop, give up, withdraw, quit, pull out, fall by the wayside ♦ **drop out of something** = discontinue, give up, quit

drought = water shortage, dryness, dry spell, aridity ≠ flood

drove *often plural* = herd, company, crowds, collection, mob, flocks, swarm, horde

drown 1 = go down, go under 2 = drench, flood, soak, steep, swamp, saturate, engulf, submerge 3 = overwhelm, overcome, wipe out, overpower, obliterate, swallow up

drug NOUN 1 = medication, medicine, remedy, physic, medicament 2 = dope (*slang*), narcotic (*slang*), stimulant, opiate, dadah (*Austral. slang*)
• VERB = knock out, dope (*slang*), numb, deaden, stupefy, anaesthetize

drum VERB = pound, beat, tap, rap, thrash, tattoo, throb, pulsate
• PHRASES **drum something into someone** = drive into, hammer into, instil into, din into, harp on about to

drunk ADJECTIVE = intoxicated, plastered (*slang*), drunken, merry (*Brit. informal*), under the influence (*informal*), tipsy, legless (*informal*), inebriated, out to it (*Austral. & N.Z. slang*), babalas (*S. African*)
• NOUN = drunkard, alcoholic, lush (*slang*), boozer (*informal*), wino (*informal*), inebriate, alko *or* alco (*Austral. slang*)

dry ADJECTIVE 1 = dehydrated, dried-up, arid, parched, desiccated ≠ wet 2 = thirsty, parched 3 = sarcastic, cynical, low-key, sly, sardonic, deadpan, droll, ironical
4 = dull, boring, tedious, dreary, tiresome,

monotonous, run-of-the-mill, humdrum ≠ interesting **5** = plain, simple, bare, basic, stark, unembellished
• **VERB 1** = drain, make dry **2** *often with* ***out*** = dehydrate, make dry, desiccate, sear, parch, dehumidify ≠ wet
• **PHRASES dry up** *or* **out** = become dry, harden, wither, shrivel up, wizen

dual = twofold, double, twin, matched, paired, duplicate, binary, duplex

dubious 1 = suspect, suspicious, crooked, dodgy (*Brit., Austral., & N.Z. informal*), questionable, unreliable, fishy (*informal*), disreputable ≠ trustworthy **2** = unsure, uncertain, suspicious, hesitating, doubtful, sceptical, tentative, wavering ≠ sure

duck 1 = bob, drop, lower, bend, bow, dodge, crouch, stoop **2** (*Informal*) = dodge, avoid, escape, evade, elude, sidestep, shirk **3** = dunk, wet, plunge, dip, submerge, immerse, douse, souse

due ADJECTIVE 1 = expected, scheduled **2** = fitting, deserved, appropriate, justified, suitable, merited, proper, rightful **3** = payable, outstanding, owed, owing, unpaid, in arrears
• **ADVERB** = directly, dead, straight, exactly, undeviatingly
• **NOUN** = right(s), privilege, deserts, merits, comeuppance (*informal*)
• **PLURAL NOUN** = membership fee, charges, fee, contribution, levy

duel NOUN 1 = single combat, affair of honour **2** = contest, fight, competition, clash, encounter, engagement, rivalry
• **VERB** = fight, struggle, clash, compete, contest, contend, vie with, lock horns

duff (*Brit., Austral., & N.Z. informal*) = bad, poor, useless, inferior, unsatisfactory, defective, imperfect, substandard, bodger *or* bodgie (*Austral. slang*)

dull ADJECTIVE 1 = boring, tedious, dreary, flat, plain, monotonous, run-of-the-mill, humdrum ≠ exciting **2** = lifeless, indifferent, apathetic, listless, unresponsive, passionless ≠ lively **3** = cloudy, dim, gloomy, dismal, overcast, leaden ≠ bright **4** = blunt, blunted, unsharpened ≠ sharp
• **VERB** = relieve, blunt, lessen, moderate, soften, alleviate, allay, take the edge off

duly 1 = properly, fittingly, correctly, appropriately, accordingly, suitably, deservedly, rightfully **2** = on time, promptly, punctually, at the proper time

dumb 1 = unable to speak, mute ≠ articulate **2** = silent, mute, speechless, tongue-tied, wordless, voiceless, soundless, mum **3** (*Informal*) = stupid, thick, dull, foolish, dense, unintelligent, asinine, dim-witted (*informal*) ≠ clever

dummy NOUN 1 = model, figure, mannequin, form, manikin **2** = imitation, copy, duplicate, sham, counterfeit, replica **3** (*Slang*) = fool, idiot, dunce, oaf, simpleton, nitwit (*informal*), blockhead, dumb-ass (*slang*), dorba *or* dorb (*Austral. slang*), bogan (*Austral. slang*)
• **ADJECTIVE** = imitation, false, fake, artificial, mock, bogus, simulated, sham

dump VERB 1 = drop, deposit, throw down, let fall, fling down **2** = get rid of, tip, dispose of, unload, jettison, empty out, throw away *or* out **3** = scrap, get rid of, abolish, put an end to, discontinue, jettison, put paid to
• **NOUN 1** = rubbish tip, tip, junkyard, rubbish heap, refuse heap **2** (*Informal*) = pigsty, hole (*informal*), slum, hovel

dunny (*Austral. & N.Z. old-fashioned informal*) = toilet, lavatory, bathroom, loo (*Brit. informal*), W.C., bog (*slang*), Gents *or* Ladies, can (*U.S. & Canad. slang*), bogger (*Austral. slang*), brasco (*Austral. slang*)

duplicate VERB 1 = repeat, reproduce, copy, clone, replicate **2** = copy
• **ADJECTIVE** = identical, matched, matching, twin, corresponding, twofold
• **NOUN 1** = copy, facsimile **2** = photocopy, copy, reproduction, replica, carbon copy

durable 1 = hard-wearing, strong, tough, reliable, resistant, sturdy, long-lasting ≠ fragile **2** = enduring, continuing, dependable, unwavering, unfaltering

duration = length, time, period, term, stretch, extent, spell, span

dusk = twilight, evening, evo (*Austral. slang*), nightfall, sunset, dark, sundown, eventide, gloaming (*Scot. poetic*) ≠ dawn

dust NOUN 1 = grime, grit, powder **2** = particles
• **VERB** = sprinkle, cover, powder, spread, spray, scatter, sift, dredge

dusty = dirty, grubby, unclean, unswept

duty NOUN 1 = responsibility, job, task, work, role, function, obligation, assignment **2** = tax, toll, levy, tariff, excise
• **PHRASES on duty** = at work, busy,

engaged, on active service
dwarf VERB **1** = tower above *or* over, dominate, overlook, stand over, loom over, stand head and shoulders above **2** = eclipse, tower above *or* over, put in the shade, diminish
• ADJECTIVE = miniature, small, baby, tiny, diminutive, bonsai, undersized
• NOUN = gnome, midget, Lilliputian, Tom Thumb, pygmy *or* pigmy
dwell (*Formal or literary*) = live, reside, lodge, abide
dwelling (*Formal* or *literary*) = home, house, residence, abode, quarters, lodging, habitation, domicile, whare (*N.Z.*)
dwindle = lessen, decline, fade, shrink, diminish, decrease, wane, subside ≠ increase
dye VERB = colour, stain, tint, tinge, pigment
• NOUN = colouring, colour, pigment, stain, tint, tinge, colorant
dying **1** = near death, moribund, in extremis (*Latin*), at death's door, not long for this world **2** = final, last, parting, departing **3** = failing, declining, foundering, diminishing, decreasing, dwindling, subsiding
dynamic = energetic, powerful, vital, go-ahead, lively, animated, high-powered, forceful ≠ apathetic
dynasty = empire, house, rule, regime, sovereignty

e

each DETERMINER = every, every single
• PRONOUN = every one, all, each one, each and every one, one and all
• ADVERB = apiece, individually, for each, to each, respectively, per person, per head, per capita
eager **1** = anxious, keen, hungry, impatient, itching, thirsty ≠ unenthusiastic **2** = keen, interested, intense, enthusiastic, passionate, avid (*informal*), fervent ≠ uninterested
ear = sensitivity, taste, discrimination, appreciation
RELATED WORD
adjective: aural
early ADVERB **1** = in good time, beforehand, ahead of schedule, in advance, with time to spare ≠ late **2** = too soon, before the usual time, prematurely, ahead of time ≠ late
• ADJECTIVE **1** = first, opening, initial, introductory **2** = premature, forward, advanced, untimely, unseasonable ≠ belated **3** = primitive, first, earliest, young, original, undeveloped, primordial, primeval ≠ developed
earmark **1** = set aside, reserve, label, flag, allocate, designate, mark out **2** = mark out, identify, designate
earn **1** = be paid, make, get, receive, gain, net, collect, bring in **2** = deserve, win, gain, attain, justify, merit, warrant, be entitled to
earnest **1** = serious, grave, intense, dedicated, sincere, thoughtful, solemn, ardent ≠ frivolous **2** = determined, dogged, intent, persistent, persevering, resolute, wholehearted ≠ half-hearted
earnings = income, pay, wages, revenue, proceeds, salary, receipts, remuneration
earth **1** = world, planet, globe, sphere, orb, earthly sphere **2** = ground, land, dry land, terra firma **3** = soil, ground, land, dust, clay, dirt, turf, silt
earthly **1** = worldly, material, secular, mortal, temporal, human ≠ spiritual **2** = sensual, worldly, physical, fleshly, bodily, carnal **3** (*Informal*) = possible, likely, practical, feasible, conceivable, imaginable
ease NOUN **1** = straightforwardness, simplicity, readiness **2** = comfort, luxury, leisure, relaxation, prosperity, affluence, rest, repose ≠ hardship **3** = peace of mind, peace, content, quiet, comfort, happiness, serenity, tranquillity ≠ agitation
• VERB **1** = relieve, calm, soothe, lessen, alleviate, lighten, lower, relax ≠ aggravate **2** = reduce, diminish, lessen, slacken **3** = move carefully, edge, slip, inch, slide, creep, manoeuvre
easily = without difficulty, smoothly, readily, comfortably, effortlessly, with ease, straightforwardly

easy 1 = simple, straightforward, no trouble, not difficult, effortless, painless, uncomplicated, child's play (*informal*) ≠ hard 2 = untroubled, relaxed, peaceful, serene, tranquil, quiet 3 = carefree, comfortable, leisurely, trouble-free, untroubled, cushy (*informal*) ≠ difficult 4 = tolerant, soft, mild, laid-back (*informal*), indulgent, easy-going, lenient, permissive ≠ strict

eat 1 = consume, swallow, chew, scoff (*slang*), devour, munch, tuck into (*informal*), put away 2 = have a meal, lunch, breakfast, dine, snack, feed, graze (*informal*), have lunch

ebb VERB 1 = flow back, go out, withdraw, retreat, wane, recede 2 = decline, flag, diminish, decrease, dwindle, lessen, subside, fall away
• NOUN = flowing back, going out, withdrawal, retreat, wane, low water, low tide, outgoing tide

eccentric ADJECTIVE = odd, strange, peculiar, irregular, quirky, unconventional, idiosyncratic, outlandish ≠ normal
• NOUN = crank (*informal*), character (*informal*), oddball (*informal*), nonconformist, weirdo *or* weirdie (*informal*)

echo NOUN 1 = reverberation, ringing, repetition, answer, resonance, resounding 2 = copy, reflection, clone, reproduction, imitation, duplicate, double, reiteration
• VERB 1 = reverberate, repeat, resound, ring, resonate 2 = recall, reflect, copy, mirror, resemble, imitate, ape

eclipse NOUN = obscuring, covering, blocking, shading, dimming, extinction, darkening, blotting out
• VERB = surpass, exceed, overshadow, excel, transcend, outdo, outclass, outshine

economic 1 = financial, industrial, commercial 2 = profitable, successful, commercial, rewarding, productive, lucrative, worthwhile, viable 3 (*Informal*) = economical, cheap, reasonable, modest, low-priced, inexpensive

economical 1 = thrifty, sparing, careful, prudent, provident, frugal, parsimonious, scrimping ≠ extravagant 2 = efficient, sparing, cost-effective, money-saving, time-saving ≠ wasteful

economy 1 = financial system, financial state 2 = thrift, restraint, prudence, husbandry, frugality, parsimony

ecstasy = rapture, delight, joy, bliss, euphoria, fervour, elation ≠ agony

ecstatic = rapturous, entranced, joyous, elated, overjoyed, blissful, euphoric, enraptured

edge NOUN 1 = border, side, limit, outline, boundary, fringe, verge, brink 2 = verge, point, brink, threshold 3 = advantage, lead, dominance, superiority, upper hand, head start, ascendancy, whip hand 4 = power, force, bite, effectiveness, incisiveness, powerful quality 5 = sharpness, point, bitterness, keenness
• VERB 1 = inch, ease, creep, slink, steal, sidle, move slowly 2 = border, fringe, hem, pipe
• PHRASES **on edge** = tense, nervous, impatient, irritable, apprehensive, edgy, ill at ease, on tenterhooks

edit = revise, improve, correct, polish, adapt, rewrite, condense, redraft

edition = version, copy, issue, programme (*TV, Radio*), printing, volume, impression, publication

educate = teach, school, train, develop, improve, inform, discipline, tutor

educated 1 = cultured, intellectual, learned, sophisticated, refined, cultivated, enlightened, knowledgeable ≠ uncultured 2 = taught, schooled, coached, informed, tutored, instructed, nurtured, well-informed ≠ uneducated

education 1 = teaching, schooling, training, development, discipline, instruction, nurture, tuition 2 = learning, schooling, cultivation, refinement

educational 1 = academic, school, learning, teaching, scholastic, pedagogical, pedagogic 2 = instructive, useful, cultural, illuminating, enlightening, informative, instructional, edifying

eerie = uncanny, strange, frightening, ghostly, weird, mysterious, scary (*informal*), sinister

effect NOUN 1 = result, consequence, conclusion, outcome, event, end result, upshot 2 = impression, feeling, impact, influence 3 = purpose, impression, sense, intent, essence, thread, tenor
• PLURAL NOUN = belongings, goods, things, property, stuff, gear, possessions, paraphernalia
• VERB = bring about, produce, complete,

achieve, perform, fulfil, accomplish, execute
effective 1 = efficient, successful, useful, active, capable, valuable, helpful, adequate ≠ ineffective 2 = powerful, strong, convincing, persuasive, telling, impressive, compelling, forceful ≠ weak 3 = virtual, essential, practical, implied, implicit, tacit, unacknowledged 4 = in operation, official, current, legal, active, in effect, valid, operative ≠ inoperative
efficiency 1 = effectiveness, power, economy, productivity, organization, cost-effectiveness, orderliness 2 = competence, expertise, capability, professionalism, proficiency, adeptness
efficient 1 = effective, successful, structured, productive, systematic, streamlined, cost-effective, methodical ≠ inefficient 2 = competent, professional, capable, organized, productive, proficient, businesslike, well-organized ≠ incompetent
effort 1 = attempt, try, endeavour, shot (*informal*), bid, essay, go (*informal*), stab (*informal*) 2 = exertion, work, trouble, energy, struggle, application, graft, toil
egg NOUN = ovum, gamete, germ cell
• PHRASES **egg someone on** = incite, push, encourage, urge, prompt, spur, provoke, prod
eject 1 = throw out, remove, turn out, expel (*slang*), oust, banish, drive out, evict 2 = bail out, escape, get out
elaborate ADJECTIVE 1 = complicated, detailed, studied, complex, precise, thorough, intricate, painstaking 2 = ornate, involved, complex, fancy, complicated, intricate, baroque, ornamented ≠ plain
• VERB 1 = develop, flesh out 2 = expand (upon), extend, enlarge (on), amplify, embellish, flesh out, add detail (to) ≠ simplify
elastic 1 = flexible, supple, rubbery, pliable, plastic, springy, pliant, tensile ≠ rigid 2 = adaptable, yielding, variable, flexible, accommodating, tolerant, adjustable, supple ≠ inflexible
elbow = joint, angle, curve
elder ADJECTIVE = older, first, senior, first-born
• NOUN = older person, senior
elect 1 = vote for, choose, pick, determine, select, appoint, opt for, settle on 2 = choose, decide, prefer, select, opt
election 1 = vote, poll, ballot, referendum, franchise, plebiscite, show of hands 2 = appointment, picking, choice, selection
electric 1 = electric-powered, powered, cordless, battery-operated, electrically-charged, mains-operated 2 = charged, exciting, stirring, thrilling, stimulating, dynamic, tense, rousing
elegance = style, taste, grace, dignity, sophistication, grandeur, refinement, gracefulness
elegant = stylish, fine, sophisticated, delicate, handsome, refined, chic, exquisite ≠ inelegant
element NOUN 1 = component, part, unit, section, factor, principle, aspect, foundation 2 = group, faction, clique, set, party, circle 3 = trace, suggestion, hint, dash, suspicion, tinge, smattering, soupçon
• PLURAL NOUN = weather conditions, climate, the weather, wind and rain, atmospheric conditions, powers of nature
• PHRASES **be in your element** = be in a situation you enjoy, be in your natural environment, be in familiar surroundings
elementary = simple, clear, easy, plain, straightforward, rudimentary, uncomplicated, undemanding ≠ complicated
elevate 1 = promote, raise, advance, upgrade, exalt, kick upstairs (*informal*), aggrandize, give advancement to 2 = increase, lift, raise, step up, intensify, move up, hoist, raise high 3 = raise, lift, heighten, uplift, hoist, lift up, raise up, hike up
elevated 1 = exalted, important, august, grand, superior, noble, dignified, high-ranking 2 = high-minded, fine, grand, noble, inflated, dignified, sublime, lofty ≠ humble 3 = raised, high, lifted up, upraised
elicit 1 = bring about, cause, derive, bring out, evoke, give rise to, draw out, bring forth 2 = obtain, extract, exact, evoke, wrest, draw out, extort
eligible 1 = entitled, fit, qualified, suitable ≠ ineligible 2 = available, free, single, unmarried, unattached
eliminate = remove, end, stop, withdraw,

get rid of, abolish, cut out, dispose of
elite = aristocracy, best, pick, cream, upper class, nobility, crème de la crème (*French*), flower ≠ rabble
eloquent 1 = silver-tongued, moving, powerful, effective, stirring, articulate, persuasive, forceful ≠ inarticulate 2 = expressive, telling, pointed, significant, vivid, meaningful, indicative, suggestive
elsewhere = in *or* to another place, away, abroad, hence (*archaic*), somewhere else, not here, in other places, in *or* to a different place
elude 1 = evade, escape, lose, avoid, flee, duck (*informal*), dodge, get away from 2 = escape, baffle, frustrate, puzzle, stump, foil, be beyond (someone), thwart
elusive 1 = difficult to catch, tricky, slippery, difficult to find, evasive, shifty 2 = indefinable, fleeting, subtle, indefinite, transient, intangible, indescribable, transitory
emanate = flow, emerge, spring, proceed, arise, stem, derive, originate
embargo NOUN = ban, bar, restriction, boycott, restraint, prohibition, moratorium, stoppage, rahui (*N.Z.*)
• VERB = block, stop, bar, ban, restrict, boycott, prohibit, blacklist
embark VERB = go aboard, climb aboard, board ship, step aboard, go on board, take ship ≠ get off
• PHRASES **embark on something** = begin, start, launch, enter, take up, set out, set about, plunge into
embarrass = shame, distress, show up (*informal*), humiliate, disconcert, fluster, mortify, discomfit
embarrassed = ashamed, shamed, uncomfortable, awkward, abashed, humiliated, uneasy, unsettled
embarrassing = humiliating, upsetting, compromising, delicate, uncomfortable, awkward, sensitive, troublesome, barro (*Austral. slang*)
embarrassment 1 = shame, distress, showing up (*informal*), humiliation, discomfort, unease, self-consciousness, awkwardness 2 = problem, difficulty, nuisance, source of trouble, thorn in your flesh 3 = predicament, problem, difficulty (*informal*), mess, jam (*informal*), plight, scrape (*informal*), pickle (*informal*)
embody 1 = personify, represent, stand for, manifest, exemplify, symbolize, typify, actualize 2 = incorporate, include, contain, combine, collect, take in, encompass
embrace VERB 1 = hug, hold, cuddle, seize, squeeze, clasp, envelop, canoodle (*slang*) 2 = accept, support, welcome, adopt, take up, seize, espouse, take on board 3 = include, involve, cover, contain, take in, incorporate, comprise, encompass
• NOUN = hug, hold, cuddle, squeeze, clinch (*slang*), clasp
embroil = involve, mix up, implicate, entangle, mire, ensnare, enmesh
embryo 1 = foetus, unborn child, fertilized egg 2 = germ, beginning, source, root, seed, nucleus, rudiment
emerge 1 = come out, appear, surface, rise, arise, turn up, spring up, emanate ≠ withdraw 2 = become apparent, come out, become known, come to light, crop up, transpire, become evident, come out in the wash
emergence 1 = coming, development, arrival, surfacing, rise, appearance, arising, turning up 2 = disclosure, publishing, broadcasting, broadcast, publication, declaration, revelation, becoming known
emergency NOUN = crisis, danger, difficulty, accident, disaster, necessity, plight, scrape (*informal*)
• ADJECTIVE 1 = urgent, crisis, immediate 2 = alternative, extra, additional, substitute, replacement, temporary, makeshift, stopgap
emigrate = move abroad, move, relocate, migrate, resettle, leave your country
eminent = prominent, noted, respected, famous, celebrated, distinguished, well-known, esteemed ≠ unknown
emission = giving off *or* out, release, shedding, leak, radiation, discharge, transmission, ejaculation
emit 1 = give off, release, leak, transmit, discharge, send out, radiate, eject ≠ absorb 2 = utter, produce, voice, give out, let out
emotion 1 = feeling, spirit, soul, passion, excitement, sensation, sentiment, fervour 2 = instinct, sentiment, sensibility, intuition, tenderness, gut feeling, soft-heartedness
emotional 1 = psychological, private, personal, hidden, spiritual, inner 2 = moving, touching, affecting, stirring,

sentimental, poignant, emotive, heart-rending **3** = passionate, sentimental, temperamental, excitable, demonstrative, hot-blooded **4** = emotive, sensitive, controversial, delicate, contentious, heated, inflammatory, touchy

emphasis **1** = importance, attention, weight, significance, stress, priority, prominence **2** = stress, accent, force, weight

emphasize **1** = highlight, stress, underline, draw attention to, dwell on, play up, make a point of, give priority to ≠ minimize **2** = stress, accentuate, lay stress on

emphatic **1** = forceful, positive, definite, vigorous, unmistakable, insistent, unequivocal, vehement ≠ hesitant **2** = significant, pronounced, decisive, resounding, conclusive

empire **1** = kingdom, territory, province, federation, commonwealth, realm, domain **2** = organization, company, business, firm, concern, corporation, consortium, syndicate

RELATED WORD
adjective: imperial

empirical *or* **empiric** = first-hand, direct, observed, practical, actual, experimental, pragmatic, factual ≠ hypothetical

employ **1** = hire, commission, appoint, take on, retain, engage, recruit, sign up **2** = use, apply, exercise, exert, make use of, utilize, ply, bring to bear **3** = spend, fill, occupy, involve, engage, take up, make use of, use up

employed **1** = working, in work, having a job, in employment, in a job, earning your living ≠ out of work **2** = busy, active, occupied, engaged, hard at work, in harness, rushed off your feet ≠ idle

employee = worker, labourer, workman, staff member, member of staff, hand, wage-earner, white-collar worker

employer **1** = boss (*informal*), manager, head, leader, director, chief, owner, master, baas (*S. African*) **2** = company, business, firm, organization, establishment, outfit (*informal*)

employment **1** = job, work, position, trade, post, situation, profession, occupation **2** = taking on, commissioning, appointing, hire, hiring, retaining, engaging, appointment **3** = use, application, exertion, exercise, utilization

empower **1** = authorize, allow, commission, qualify, permit, sanction, entitle, delegate **2** = enable, equip, emancipate, give means to, enfranchise

empty **ADJECTIVE 1** = bare, clear, abandoned, deserted, vacant, free, void, desolate ≠ full **2** = meaningless, cheap, hollow, vain, idle, futile, insincere **3** = worthless, meaningless, hollow, pointless, futile, senseless, fruitless, inane ≠ meaningful

• **VERB 1** = clear, drain, void, unload, pour out, unpack, remove the contents of ≠ fill **2** = exhaust, consume the contents of, void, deplete, use up ≠ replenish **3** = evacuate, clear, vacate

emulate = imitate, follow, copy, mirror, echo, mimic, model yourself on

enable **1** = allow, permit, empower, give someone the opportunity, give someone the means ≠ prevent **2** = authorize, allow, permit, qualify, sanction, entitle, license, warrant ≠ stop

enact **1** = establish, order, command, approve, sanction, proclaim, decree, authorize **2** = perform, play, present, stage, represent, put on, portray, depict

enchant = fascinate, delight, charm, entrance, dazzle, captivate, enthral, beguile

enclose *or* **inclose** **1** = surround, circle, bound, fence, confine, close in, wall in, encircle **2** = send with, include, put in, insert

encompass **1** = include, hold, cover, admit, deal with, contain, take in, embrace **2** = surround, circle, enclose, close in, envelop, encircle, fence in, ring

encounter **VERB 1** = experience, meet, face, suffer, have, go through, sustain, endure **2** = meet, confront, come across, bump into (*informal*), run across, come upon, chance upon, meet by chance

• **NOUN 1** = meeting, brush, confrontation, rendezvous, chance meeting **2** = battle, conflict, clash, contest, run-in (*informal*), confrontation, head-to-head

encourage **1** = inspire, comfort, cheer, reassure, console, hearten, cheer up, embolden ≠ discourage **2** = urge, persuade, prompt, spur, coax, egg on ≠ dissuade **3** = promote, back, support, increase, foster, advocate, stimulate, endorse ≠ prevent

encouragement 1 = inspiration, support, comfort, comforting, cheer, cheering, reassurance, morale boosting 2 = urging, prompting, stimulus, persuasion, coaxing, egging on, incitement 3 = promotion, backing, support, endorsement, stimulation, furtherance

end NOUN 1 = close, ending, finish, expiry, expiration ≠ beginning 2 = conclusion, ending, climax, completion, finale, culmination, denouement, consummation ≠ start 3 = finish, close, stop, resolution, conclusion, closure, completion, termination 4 = extremity, limit, edge, border, extent, extreme, margin, boundary 5 = tip, point, head, peak, extremity 6 = purpose, point, reason, goal, target, aim, object, mission 7 = outcome, resolution, conclusion 8 = death, dying, ruin, destruction, passing on, doom, demise, extinction 9 = remnant, butt, stub, scrap, fragment, stump, remainder, leftover

• VERB 1 = stop, finish, halt, cease, wind up, terminate, call off, discontinue ≠ start 2 = finish, close, conclude, wind up, culminate, terminate, come to an end, draw to a close ≠ begin

RELATED WORDS

adjectives: final, terminal, ultimate

endanger = put at risk, risk, threaten, compromise, jeopardize, imperil, put in danger, expose to danger ≠ save

endearing = attractive, winning, pleasing, appealing, sweet, engaging, charming, pleasant

endeavour (*Formal*) VERB = try, labour, attempt, aim, struggle, venture, strive, aspire

• NOUN = attempt, try, effort, trial, bid, venture, enterprise, undertaking

ending = finish, end, close, conclusion, summing up, completion, finale, culmination ≠ start

endless = eternal, infinite, continual, unlimited, interminable, incessant, boundless, everlasting ≠ temporary

endorse 1 = approve, back, support, champion, promote, recommend, advocate, uphold 2 = sign, initial, countersign, sign on the back of

endorsement = approval, backing, support, favour, recommendation, acceptance, agreement, upholding

endow 1 = provide, favour, grace, bless, supply, furnish, endue 2 = finance, fund, pay for, award, confer, bestow, bequeath, donate money to 3 = imbue

endowment = provision, funding, award, grant, gift, contribution, subsidy, donation, koha (*N.Z.*)

endurance 1 = staying power, strength, resolution, determination, patience, stamina, fortitude, persistence 2 = permanence, stability, continuity, duration, longevity, durability, continuance

endure 1 = experience, suffer, bear, meet, encounter, cope with, sustain, undergo 2 = last, continue, remain, stay, stand, go on, survive, live on

enemy = foe, rival, opponent, the opposition, competitor, the other side, adversary, antagonist ≠ friend

energetic 1 = forceful, determined, active, aggressive, dynamic, vigorous, hard-hitting, strenuous 2 = lively, active, dynamic, vigorous, animated, tireless, bouncy, indefatigable ≠ lethargic 3 = strenuous, hard, taxing, demanding, tough, exhausting, vigorous, arduous

energy 1 = strength, might, stamina, forcefulness 2 = liveliness, drive, determination, pep, vitality, vigour, verve, resilience 3 = power

enforce 1 = carry out, apply, implement, fulfil, execute, administer, put into effect, put into action 2 = impose, force, insist on

engage 1 *with **in*** = participate in, join in, take part in, undertake, embark on, enter into, become involved in, set about 2 = captivate, catch, arrest, fix, capture 3 = occupy, involve, draw, grip, absorb, preoccupy, immerse, engross 4 = employ, appoint, take on, hire, retain, recruit, enlist, enrol ≠ dismiss 5 = set going, apply, trigger, activate, switch on, energize, bring into operation 6 (*Military*) = begin battle with, attack, take on, encounter, fall on, battle with, meet, assail

engaged 1 = occupied, working, employed, busy, tied up 2 = betrothed, promised, pledged, affianced, promised in marriage ≠ unattached 3 = in use, busy, tied up, unavailable ≠ free

engagement 1 = appointment, meeting, interview, date, commitment, arrangement, rendezvous **2** = betrothal, marriage contract, troth (*archaic*), agreement to marry **3** = battle, fight, conflict, action, struggle, clash, encounter, combat **4** = participation, joining, taking part, involvement

engaging = charming, interesting, pleasing, attractive, lovely, entertaining, winning, fetching (*informal*) ≠ unpleasant

engine = machine, motor, mechanism, generator, dynamo

engineer NOUN **1** = designer, producer, architect, developer, deviser, creator, planner, inventor **2** = worker, specialist, operator, practitioner, operative, driver, conductor, technician
• VERB **1** = design, plan, create, construct, devise **2** = bring about, plan, effect, set up (*informal*), scheme, arrange, plot, mastermind

engraving = print, carving, etching, inscription, plate, woodcut, dry point

engulf 1 = immerse, swamp, submerge, overrun, inundate, envelop, swallow up **2** = overwhelm, overcome, crush, swamp

enhance = improve, better, increase, lift, boost, add to, strengthen, reinforce ≠ reduce

enjoy 1 = take pleasure in *or* from, like, love, appreciate, relish, delight in, be pleased with, be fond of ≠ hate **2** = have, use, own, experience, possess, have the benefit of, reap the benefits of, be blessed *or* favoured with

enjoyable = pleasurable, good, great, fine, nice, satisfying, lovely, entertaining ≠ unpleasant

enjoyment 1 = pleasure, liking, fun, delight, entertainment, joy, happiness, relish **2** = benefit, use, advantage, favour, possession, blessing

enlarge VERB **1** = expand, increase, extend, add to, build up, widen, intensify, broaden ≠ reduce **2** = grow, increase, extend, expand, swell, become bigger, puff up, grow larger
• PHRASES **enlarge on something** = expand on, develop, add to, fill out, elaborate on, flesh out, expatiate on, give further details about

enlighten = inform, tell, teach, advise, counsel, educate, instruct, illuminate

enlightened = informed, aware, reasonable, educated, sophisticated, cultivated, open-minded, knowledgeable ≠ ignorant

enlightenment = understanding, learning, education, knowledge, instruction, awareness, wisdom, insight

enlist 1 = join up, join, enter (into), register, volunteer, sign up, enrol **2** = recruit, take on, hire, sign up, call up, muster, mobilize, conscript **3** = obtain, get, gain, secure, engage, procure

enormous = huge, massive, vast, extensive, tremendous, gross, immense, gigantic ≠ tiny

enough DETERMINER = sufficient, adequate, ample, abundant, as much as you need, as much as is necessary
• PRONOUN = sufficiency, plenty, sufficient, abundance, adequacy, right amount, ample supply
• ADVERB = sufficiently, amply, reasonably, adequately, satisfactorily, abundantly, tolerably

enrage = anger, infuriate, incense, madden, inflame, exasperate, antagonize, make you angry ≠ calm

enrich 1 = enhance, develop, improve, boost, supplement, refine, heighten, augment **2** = make rich, make wealthy, make affluent, make prosperous, make well-off

enrol 1 = enlist, register, be accepted, be admitted, join up, put your name down for, sign up *or* on **2** = recruit, take on, enlist

en route = on *or* along the way, travelling, on the road, in transit, on the journey

ensemble 1 = group, company, band, troupe, cast, orchestra, chorus **2** = collection, set, body, whole, total, sum, combination, entity **3** = outfit, suit, get-up (*informal*), costume

ensue = follow, result, develop, proceed, arise, stem, derive, issue ≠ come first

ensure 1 = make certain, guarantee, secure, make sure, confirm, warrant, certify **2** = protect, defend, secure, safeguard, guard, make safe

entail = involve, require, produce, demand, call for, occasion, need, bring about

enter 1 = come *or* go in *or* into, arrive, set foot in somewhere, cross the threshold of somewhere, make an entrance ≠ exit **2** = penetrate, get in, pierce, pass into, perforate **3** = join, start work at, begin work at, enrol in, enlist in ≠ leave **4** = participate in, join (in), be involved in, get involved in, play a part in, partake in, associate yourself with, start to be in **5** = begin, start, take up, move into, commence, set out on, embark upon **6** = compete in, contest, join in, fight, sign up for, go in for **7** = record, note, register, log, list, write down, take down, inscribe

enterprise **1** = firm, company, business, concern, operation, organization, establishment, commercial undertaking **2** = venture, operation, project, adventure, undertaking, programme, pursuit, endeavour **3** = initiative, energy, daring, enthusiasm, imagination, drive, ingenuity, originality

enterprising = resourceful, original, spirited, daring, bold, enthusiastic, imaginative, energetic

entertain **1** = amuse, interest, please, delight, charm, enthral, cheer, regale **2** = show hospitality to, receive, accommodate, treat, put up, lodge, be host to, have company of **3** = consider, imagine, think about, contemplate, conceive of, bear in mind, keep in mind, give thought to

entertainment **1** = enjoyable, fun, pleasure, leisure, relaxation, recreation, enjoyment, amusement **2** = pastime, show, sport, performance, treat, presentation, leisure activity

enthusiasm = keenness, interest, passion, motivation, relish, zeal, zest, fervour

enthusiast = fan, supporter, lover, follower, addict, buff (*informal*), fanatic, devotee

enthusiastic = keen, committed, eager, passionate, vigorous, avid, fervent, zealous ≠ apathetic

entice = lure, attract, invite, persuade, tempt, induce, seduce, lead on

entire = whole, full, complete, total, gross

entirely = completely, totally, absolutely, fully, altogether, thoroughly, wholly, utterly ≠ partly

entitle **1** = give the right to, allow, enable, permit, sanction, license, authorize, empower **2** = call, name, title, term, label, dub, christen, give the title of

entity = thing, being, individual, object, substance, creature, organism

entrance[1] **1** = way in, opening, door, approach, access, entry, gate, passage ≠ exit **2** = appearance, coming in, entry, arrival, introduction ≠ exit **3** = admission, access, entry, entrée, admittance, permission to enter, right of entry

entrance[2] **1** = enchant, delight, charm, fascinate, dazzle, captivate, enthral, beguile ≠ bore **2** = mesmerize, bewitch, hypnotize, put a spell on, cast a spell on, put in a trance

entrant = competitor, player, candidate, entry, participant, applicant, contender, contestant

entrenched *or* **intrenched** = fixed, set, rooted, well-established, ingrained, deep-seated, deep-rooted, unshakeable *or* unshakable

entrepreneur = businessman *or* businesswoman, tycoon, executive, industrialist, speculator, magnate, impresario, business executive

entrust *or* **intrust** **1** = give custody of, deliver, commit, delegate, hand over, turn over, confide **2** = assign

entry **1** = admission, access, entrance, admittance, entrée, permission to enter, right of entry **2** = coming in, entering, appearance, arrival, entrance ≠ exit **3** = introduction, presentation, initiation, inauguration, induction, debut, investiture **4** = record, listing, account, note, statement, item **5** = way in, opening, door, approach, access, gate, passage, entrance

envelope = wrapping, casing, case, covering, cover, jacket, sleeve, wrapper

environment **1** = surroundings, setting, conditions, situation, medium, circumstances, background, atmosphere **2** = habitat, home, surroundings, territory, terrain, locality, natural home

environmental = ecological, green

environmentalist = conservationist, ecologist, green

envisage **1** = imagine, contemplate, conceive (of), visualize, picture, fancy, think up, conceptualize **2** = foresee, see, expect, predict, anticipate, envision

envoy **1** = ambassador, diplomat, emissary **2** = messenger, agent, representative, delegate, courier, intermediary, emissary

envy NOUN = covetousness, resentment, jealousy, bitterness, resentfulness, enviousness (*informal*)

• VERB 1 = be jealous (of), resent, begrudge, be envious (of) 2 = covet, desire, crave, aspire to, yearn for, hanker after

epidemic 1 = outbreak, plague, growth, spread, scourge, contagion 2 = spate, plague, outbreak, wave, rash, eruption, upsurge

episode 1 = event, experience, happening, matter, affair, incident, adventure, occurrence 2 = instalment, part, act, scene, section, chapter, passage 3 = period, attack, spell, phase, bout

equal ADJECTIVE 1 = identical, the same, matching, equivalent, uniform, alike, corresponding ≠ unequal 2 = fair, just, impartial, egalitarian, unbiased, even-handed ≠ unfair 3 = even, balanced, fifty-fifty (*informal*), evenly matched ≠ uneven

• NOUN = match, equivalent, twin, counterpart

• VERB 1 = amount to, make, come to, total, level, parallel, tie with, equate ≠ be unequal to 2 = be equal to, match, reach 3 = be as good as, match, compare with, equate with, measure up to, be as great as

equality 1 = fairness, equal opportunity, equal treatment, egalitarianism, fair treatment, justness ≠ inequality 2 = sameness, balance, identity, similarity, correspondence, parity, likeness, uniformity ≠ disparity

equate 1 = identify, associate, connect, compare, relate, mention in the same breath, think of in connection with 2 = make equal, match, even up 3 = be equal to, parallel, compare with, liken, be commensurate with, correspond with *or* to

equation = equating, comparison, parallel, correspondence

equilibrium = stability, balance, symmetry, steadiness, evenness, equipoise

equip 1 = supply, provide for, stock, arm, array, furnish, fit out, kit out 2 = prepare, qualify, educate, get ready

equipment = apparatus, stock, supplies, stuff, tackle, gear, tools, provisions

equitable = even-handed, just, fair, reasonable, proper, honest, impartial, unbiased

equivalent NOUN = equal, counterpart, twin, parallel, match, opposite number

• ADJECTIVE = equal, same, comparable, parallel, identical, alike, corresponding, tantamount ≠ different

era = age, time, period, date, generation, epoch, day *or* days

eradicate = wipe out, eliminate, remove, destroy, get rid of, erase, extinguish, obliterate

erase 1 = delete, cancel out, wipe out, remove, eradicate, obliterate, blot out, expunge 2 = rub out, remove, wipe out, delete

erect VERB 1 = build, raise, set up, construct, put up, assemble, put together ≠ demolish 2 = found, establish, form, create, set up, institute, organize, put up

• ADJECTIVE = upright, straight, stiff, vertical, elevated, perpendicular, pricked-up ≠ bent

erode 1 = disintegrate, crumble, deteriorate, corrode, break up, grind down, waste away, wear down *or* away 2 = destroy, consume, crumble, eat away, corrode, break up, grind down, abrade 3 = weaken, destroy, undermine, diminish, impair, lessen, wear away

erosion 1 = disintegration, deterioration, wearing down *or* away, grinding down 2 = deterioration, undermining, destruction, weakening, attrition, eating away, abrasion, grinding down

erotic = sexual, sexy (*informal*), crude, explicit, sensual, seductive, vulgar, voluptuous

erratic = unpredictable, variable, unstable, irregular, inconsistent, uneven, unreliable, wayward ≠ regular

error = mistake, slip, blunder, oversight, howler (*informal*), bloomer (*Brit. informal*), miscalculation, solecism

erupt 1 = explode, blow up, emit lava 2 = discharge, expel, emit, eject, spout, throw off, pour forth, spew forth *or* out 3 = gush, burst out, pour forth, belch forth, spew forth *or* out 4 = start, break out, began, explode, flare up, burst out, boil over 5 (*Medical*) = break out, appear, flare up

escalate 1 = grow, increase, extend, intensify, expand, surge, mount, heighten ≠ decrease 2 = increase, develop, extend, intensify, expand, build up, heighten ≠ lessen

escape VERB 1 = get away, flee, take off, fly, bolt, slip away, abscond, make a break

for it **2** = avoid, miss, evade, dodge, shun, elude, duck, steer clear of **3** = leak out, flow out, gush out, emanate, seep out, exude, spill out, pour forth
• **NOUN 1** = getaway, break, flight, break-out **2** = avoidance, evasion, circumvention **3** = relaxation, recreation, distraction, diversion, pastime **4** = leak, emission, outpouring, seepage, issue, emanation

escort **NOUN 1** = guard, bodyguard, train, convoy, entourage, retinue, cortege **2** = companion, partner, attendant, guide, beau, chaperon
• **VERB** = accompany, lead, partner, conduct, guide, shepherd, usher, chaperon

especially 1 = notably, mostly, strikingly, conspicuously, outstandingly **2** = very, specially, extremely, remarkably, unusually, exceptionally, markedly, uncommonly

espionage = spying, intelligence, surveillance, counter-intelligence, undercover work

essay **NOUN** = composition, study, paper, article, piece, assignment, discourse, tract
• **VERB** (*Formal*) = attempt, try, undertake, endeavour

essence 1 = fundamental nature, nature, being, heart, spirit, soul, core, substance **2** = concentrate, spirits, extract, tincture, distillate

essential **ADJECTIVE 1** = vital, important, needed, necessary, critical, crucial, key, indispensable ≠ unimportant **2** = fundamental, main, basic, principal, cardinal, elementary, innate, intrinsic ≠ secondary
• **NOUN** = prerequisite, fundamental, necessity, must, basic, sine qua non (*Latin*), rudiment

establish 1 = set up, found, create, institute, constitute, inaugurate **2** = prove, confirm, demonstrate, certify, verify, substantiate, corroborate, authenticate **3** = secure, form, ground, settle

establishment **NOUN 1** = creation, founding, setting up, foundation, institution, organization, formation, installation **2** = organization, company, business, firm, concern, operation, institution, corporation
• **PHRASES** **the Establishment** = the authorities, the system, the powers that be, the ruling class

estate 1 = lands, property, area, grounds, domain, manor, holdings **2** = area, centre, park, development, site, zone, plot **3** (*Law*) = property, capital, assets, fortune, goods, effects, wealth, possessions

esteem **NOUN** = respect, regard, honour, admiration, reverence, estimation, veneration
• **VERB** = respect, admire, think highly of, love, value, prize, treasure, revere

estimate **VERB 1** = calculate roughly, value, guess, judge, reckon, assess, evaluate, gauge **2** = think, believe, consider, rate, judge, hold, rank, reckon
• **NOUN 1** = approximate calculation, guess, assessment, judgment, valuation, guesstimate (*informal*), rough calculation, ballpark figure (*informal*) **2** = assessment, opinion, belief, appraisal, evaluation, judgment, estimation

estuary = inlet, mouth, creek, firth, fjord

etch 1 = engrave, cut, impress, stamp, carve, imprint, inscribe **2** = corrode, eat into, burn into

etching = print, impression, carving, engraving, imprint, inscription

eternal 1 = everlasting, lasting, permanent, enduring, endless, perpetual, timeless, unending ≠ transitory **2** = interminable, endless, infinite, continual, immortal, never-ending, everlasting ≠ occasional

eternity 1 (*Theology*) = the afterlife, heaven, paradise, the next world, the hereafter **2** = perpetuity, immortality, infinity, timelessness, endlessness **3** = ages

ethical 1 = moral, behavioural **2** = right, morally acceptable, good, just, fair, responsible, principled ≠ unethical

ethics = moral code, standards, principles, morals, conscience, morality, moral values, moral principles, tikanga (*N.Z.*)

ethnic *or* **ethnical** = cultural, national, traditional, native, folk, racial, genetic, indigenous

euphoria = elation, joy, ecstasy, rapture, exhilaration, jubilation ≠ despondency

evacuate 1 = remove, clear, withdraw, expel, move out, send to a safe place **2** = abandon, leave, clear, desert, quit, withdraw from, pull out of, move out of

evade 1 = avoid, escape, dodge, get away from, elude, steer clear of, sidestep, duck ≠ face **2** = avoid answering, parry, fend off, fudge, hedge, equivocate

evaluate = assess, rate, judge, estimate, reckon, weigh, calculate, gauge

evaporate 1 = disappear, vaporize, dematerialize, vanish, dissolve, dry up, fade away, melt away 2 = dry up, dry, dehydrate, vaporize, desiccate 3 = fade away, disappear, vanish, dissolve, melt away

eve 1 = night before, day before, vigil 2 = brink, point, edge, verge, threshold

even 1 = regular, stable, constant, steady, smooth, uniform, unbroken, uninterrupted ≠ variable 2 = level, straight, flat, smooth, true, steady, uniform, parallel ≠ uneven 3 = equal, like, matching, similar, identical, comparable ≠ unequal 4 = equally matched, level, tied, on a par, neck and neck, fifty-fifty (*informal*), all square ≠ ill-matched 5 = square, quits, on the same level, on an equal footing 6 = calm, composed, cool, well-balanced, placid, unruffled, imperturbable, even-tempered ≠ excitable

evening = dusk (*archaic*), night, sunset, twilight, sundown, gloaming (*Scot. poetic*), close of day, evo (*Austral. slang*)

event 1 = incident, happening, experience, affair, occasion, proceeding, business, circumstance 2 = competition, game, tournament, contest, bout

eventual = final, overall, concluding, ultimate

eventually = in the end, finally, one day, after all, some time, ultimately, at the end of the day, when all is said and done

ever 1 = at any time, at all, in any case, at any point, by any chance, on any occasion, at any period 2 = always, for ever, at all times, evermore 3 = constantly, continually, perpetually

every = each, each and every, every single

everybody = everyone, each one, the whole world, each person, every person, all and sundry, one and all

everyday = ordinary, common, usual, routine, stock, customary, mundane, run-of-the-mill ≠ unusual

everyone = everybody, each one, the whole world, each person, every person, all and sundry, one and all

everything = all, the lot, the whole lot, each thing

everywhere 1 = all over, all around, the world over, high and low, in every nook and cranny, far and wide *or* near, to *or* in every place 2 = all around, all over, in every nook and cranny, ubiquitously, far and wide *or* near, to *or* in every place

evidence NOUN 1 = proof, grounds, demonstration, confirmation, verification, corroboration, authentication, substantiation 2 = sign(s), suggestion, trace, indication 3 = testimony, statement, submission, avowal
• VERB = show, prove, reveal, display, indicate, witness, demonstrate, exhibit

evident = obvious, clear, plain, apparent, visible, manifest, noticeable, unmistakable ≠ hidden

evidently 1 = obviously, clearly, plainly, undoubtedly, manifestly, without question, unmistakably 2 = apparently, seemingly, outwardly, ostensibly, so it seems, to all appearances

evil NOUN 1 = wickedness, bad, vice, sin, wrongdoing, depravity, badness, villainy 2 = harm, suffering, hurt, woe 3 = act of cruelty, crime, ill, horror, outrage, misfortune, mischief, affliction
• ADJECTIVE 1 = wicked, bad, malicious, immoral, sinful, malevolent, depraved, villainous 2 = harmful, disastrous, destructive, dire, catastrophic, pernicious, ruinous 3 = demonic, satanic, diabolical, hellish, devilish, infernal, fiendish 4 = offensive, nasty, foul, unpleasant, vile, noxious, disagreeable, pestilential 5 = unfortunate, unfavourable, ruinous, calamitous

evoke = arouse, cause, induce, awaken, give rise to, stir up, rekindle, summon up ≠ suppress

evolution 1 = rise, development, adaptation, natural selection, Darwinism, survival of the fittest 2 = development, growth, advance, progress, working out, expansion, extension, unfolding

evolve 1 = develop, metamorphose, adapt yourself 2 = grow, develop, advance, progress, mature 3 = work out, develop, progress, expand, unfold

exact ADJECTIVE = accurate, correct, true, right, specific, precise, definite, faultless ≠ approximate
• VERB 1 = demand, claim, force, command, extract, compel, extort 2 = inflict, apply, administer, mete out, deal out

exacting 1 = demanding, hard, taxing,

difficult, tough ≠ easy **2** = strict, severe, harsh, rigorous, stringent
exactly **1** = accurately, correctly, precisely, faithfully, explicitly, scrupulously, truthfully, unerringly **2** = precisely, specifically, bang on (*informal*), to the letter
exaggerate = overstate, enlarge, embroider, amplify, embellish, overestimate, overemphasize, pile it on about (*informal*)
examination **1** = checkup, analysis, going-over (*informal*), exploration, health check, check **2** = exam, test, research, paper, investigation, practical, assessment, quiz
examine **1** = inspect, study, survey, investigate, explore, analyse, scrutinize, peruse **2** = check, analyse, check over **3** = test, question, assess, quiz, evaluate, appraise **4** = question, quiz, interrogate, cross-examine, grill (*informal*), give the third degree to (*informal*)
example **1** = instance, specimen, case, sample, illustration, particular case, particular instance, typical case **2** = illustration, model, ideal, standard, prototype, paradigm, archetype, paragon **3** = warning, lesson, caution, deterrent
exceed **1** = surpass, better, pass, eclipse, beat, cap (*informal*), top, be over **2** = go over the limit of, go beyond, overstep
excel VERB = be superior, eclipse, beat, surpass, transcend, outdo, outshine
• PHRASES **excel in** *or* **at something** = be good at, shine at, be proficient in, show talent in, be skilful at, be talented at
excellence = high quality, merit, distinction, goodness, superiority, greatness, supremacy, eminence
excellent = outstanding, good, great, fine, cool (*informal*), brilliant, very good, superb, booshit (*Austral. slang*), exo (*Austral. slang*), sik (*Austral. slang*) ≠ terrible
except *or* **except for** PREPOSITION = apart from, but for, saving, barring, excepting, other than, excluding, omitting
• VERB = exclude, leave out, omit, disregard, pass over
exception = special case, freak, anomaly, inconsistency, deviation, oddity, peculiarity, irregularity
exceptional **1** = remarkable, special, excellent, extraordinary, outstanding, superior, first-class, marvellous ≠ average **2** = unusual, special, odd, strange, extraordinary, unprecedented, peculiar, abnormal ≠ ordinary
excerpt = extract, part, piece, section, selection, passage, fragment, quotation
excess **1** = surfeit, surplus, overload, glut, superabundance, superfluity ≠ shortage **2** = overindulgence, extravagance, profligacy, debauchery, dissipation, intemperance, indulgence, prodigality ≠ moderation
excessive **1** = immoderate, too much, extreme, exaggerated, unreasonable, disproportionate, undue, uncontrolled **2** = inordinate, unfair, unreasonable, disproportionate, undue, unwarranted, exorbitant, extortionate
exchange VERB = interchange, change, trade, switch, swap, barter, give to each other, give to one another
• NOUN **1** = conversation, talk, word, discussion, chat, dialogue, natter, powwow **2** = interchange, trade, switch, swap, trafficking, swapping, substitution, barter
excite **1** = thrill, inspire, stir, provoke, animate, rouse, exhilarate, inflame **2** = arouse, provoke, rouse, stir up **3** = titillate, thrill, stimulate, turn on (*slang*), arouse, get going (*informal*), electrify
excitement = exhilaration, action, activity, passion, thrill, animation, furore, agitation
exciting **1** = stimulating, dramatic, gripping, stirring, thrilling, sensational, rousing, exhilarating ≠ boring **2** = titillating, stimulating, arousing, erotic
exclaim = cry out, declare, shout, proclaim, yell, utter, call out
exclude **1** = keep out, bar, ban, refuse, forbid, boycott, prohibit, disallow ≠ let in **2** = omit, reject, eliminate, rule out, miss out, leave out ≠ include **3** = eliminate, reject, ignore, rule out, leave out, set aside, omit, pass over
exclusion **1** = ban, bar, veto, boycott, embargo, prohibition, disqualification **2** = elimination, missing out, rejection, leaving out, omission
exclusive **1** = select, fashionable, stylish, restricted, posh (*informal, chiefly Brit.*), chic, high-class, up-market ≠ unrestricted **2** = sole, full, whole, complete, total, entire,

absolute, undivided ≠ shared **3** = entire, full, whole, complete, total, absolute, undivided **4** = limited, unique, restricted, confined, peculiar

excursion = trip, tour, journey, outing, expedition, ramble, day trip, jaunt

excuse NOUN = justification, reason, explanation, defence, grounds, plea, apology, vindication ≠ accusation
• VERB **1** = justify, explain, defend, vindicate, mitigate, apologize for, make excuses for ≠ blame **2** = forgive, pardon, overlook, tolerate, acquit, turn a blind eye to, exonerate, make allowances for **3** = free, relieve, exempt, release, spare, discharge, let off, absolve ≠ convict

execute 1 = put to death, kill, shoot, hang, behead, decapitate, guillotine, electrocute **2** = carry out, effect, implement, accomplish, discharge, administer, prosecute, enact **3** = perform, carry out, accomplish

execution 1 = killing, hanging, the death penalty, the rope, capital punishment, beheading, the electric chair, the guillotine **2** = carrying out, performance, operation, administration, prosecution, enforcement, implementation, accomplishment

executive NOUN **1** = administrator, official, director, manager, chairman, managing director, controller, chief executive officer **2** = administration, government, directors, management, leadership, hierarchy, directorate
• ADJECTIVE = administrative, controlling, directing, governing, regulating, decision-making, managerial

exemplify = show, represent, display, demonstrate, illustrate, exhibit, embody, serve as an example of

exempt ADJECTIVE = immune, free, excepted, excused, released, spared, not liable to ≠ liable
• VERB = grant immunity, free, excuse, release, spare, relieve, discharge, let off

exemption = immunity, freedom, relief, exception, discharge, release, dispensation, absolution

exercise VERB **1** = put to use, use, apply, employ, exert, utilize, bring to bear, avail yourself of **2** = train, work out, practise, keep fit, do exercises
• NOUN **1** = use, practice, application, operation, discharge, implementation, fulfilment, utilization **2** = exertion, training, activity, work, labour, effort, movement, toil **3** = manoeuvre, campaign, operation, movement, deployment **4** = task, problem, lesson, assignment, practice

exert VERB = apply, use, exercise, employ, wield, make use of, utilize, bring to bear
• PHRASES **exert yourself** = make an effort, work, labour, struggle, strain, strive, endeavour, toil

exhaust 1 = tire out, fatigue, drain, weaken, weary, sap, wear out, debilitate **2** = use up, spend, consume, waste, go through, run through, deplete, squander

exhausted 1 = worn out, tired out, drained, spent, bushed (*informal*), done in (*informal*), all in (*slang*), fatigued ≠ invigorated **2** = used up, consumed, spent, finished, depleted, dissipated, expended ≠ replenished

exhaustion 1 = tiredness, fatigue, weariness, debilitation **2** = depletion, emptying, consumption, using up

exhibit 1 = show, reveal, display, demonstrate, express, indicate, manifest **2** = display, show, set out, parade, unveil, put on view

exhibition 1 = show, display, representation, presentation, spectacle, showcase, exposition **2** = display, show, performance, demonstration, revelation

exile NOUN **1** = banishment, expulsion, deportation, eviction, expatriation **2** = expatriate, refugee, outcast, émigré, deportee
• VERB = banish, expel, throw out, deport, drive out, eject, expatriate, cast out

exist 1 = live, be present, survive, endure, be in existence, be, have breath **2** = occur, be present **3** = survive, stay alive, make ends meet, subsist, eke out a living, scrape by, scrimp and save, support yourself

existence 1 = reality, being, life, subsistence, actuality **2** = life, situation, way of life, life style

existent = in existence, living, existing, surviving, standing, present, alive, extant

exit NOUN **1** = way out, door, gate, outlet, doorway, gateway, escape route ≠ entry **2** = departure, withdrawal, retreat, farewell, going, goodbye, exodus, decamping
• VERB = depart, leave, go out, withdraw,

retire, quit, retreat, go away ≠ enter
exodus = departure, withdrawal, retreat, leaving, flight, exit, migration, evacuation
exotic 1 = unusual, striking, strange, fascinating, mysterious, colourful, glamorous, unfamiliar ≠ ordinary 2 = foreign, alien, tropical, external, naturalized
expand VERB 1 = get bigger, increase, grow, extend, swell, widen, enlarge, become bigger ≠ contract 2 = make bigger, increase, develop, extend, widen, enlarge, broaden, magnify ≠ reduce 3 = spread (out), stretch (out), unfold, unravel, diffuse, unfurl, unroll
• PHRASES **expand on something** = go into detail about, embellish, elaborate on, develop, flesh out, expound on, enlarge on, expatiate on
expansion 1 = increase, development, growth, spread, magnification, amplification 2 = enlargement, increase, growth, opening out
expatriate NOUN = exile, refugee, emigrant, émigré
• ADJECTIVE = exiled, refugee, banished, emigrant, émigré, expat
expect 1 = think, believe, suppose, assume, trust, imagine, reckon, presume 2 = anticipate, look forward to, predict, envisage, await, hope for, contemplate 3 = require, demand, want, call for, ask for, hope for, insist on
expectation 1 = projection, supposition, assumption, belief, forecast, likelihood, probability, presumption 2 = anticipation, hope, promise, excitement, expectancy, apprehension, suspense
expedition = journey, mission, voyage, tour, quest, trek
expel 1 = throw out, exclude, ban, dismiss, kick out (*informal*), ask to leave, turf out (*informal*), debar ≠ let in 2 = banish, exile, deport, evict, force to leave ≠ take in 3 = drive out, discharge, force out, let out, eject, issue, spew, belch
expenditure 1 = spending, payment, expense, outgoings, cost, outlay 2 = consumption, using, output
expense = cost, charge, expenditure, payment, spending, outlay
expensive = costly, high-priced, lavish, extravagant, dear, stiff, steep (*informal*), pricey ≠ cheap
experience NOUN 1 = knowledge, practice, skill, contact, expertise, involvement, exposure, participation 2 = event, affair, incident, happening, encounter, episode, adventure, occurrence
• VERB = undergo, feel, face, taste, go through, sample, encounter, endure
experienced = knowledgeable, skilled, tried, tested, seasoned, expert, veteran, practised ≠ inexperienced
experiment NOUN 1 = test, trial, investigation, examination, procedure, demonstration, observation, try-out 2 = research, investigation, analysis, observation, research and development, experimentation
• VERB = test, investigate, trial, research, try, examine, pilot, sample
experimental 1 = test, trial, pilot, preliminary, provisional, tentative, speculative, exploratory 2 = innovative, new, original, radical, creative, ingenious, avant-garde, inventive
expert NOUN = specialist, authority, professional, master, genius, guru, pundit, maestro, fundi (*S. African*) ≠ amateur
• ADJECTIVE = skilful, experienced, professional, masterly, qualified, talented, outstanding, practised ≠ unskilled
expertise = skill, knowledge, know-how (*informal*), facility, judgment, mastery, proficiency, adroitness
expire 1 = become invalid, end, finish, conclude, close, stop, run out, cease 2 = die, depart, perish, kick the bucket (*informal*), depart this life, meet your maker, cark it (*Austral. & N.Z. slang*), pass away *or* on
explain 1 = make clear *or* plain, describe, teach, define, resolve, clarify, clear up, simplify 2 = account for, excuse, justify, give a reason for
explanation 1 = reason, answer, account, excuse, motive, justification, vindication 2 = description, report, definition, teaching, interpretation, illustration, clarification, simplification
explicit 1 = clear, obvious, specific, direct, precise, straightforward, definite, overt ≠ vague 2 = frank, specific, graphic, unambiguous, unrestricted, unrestrained, uncensored ≠ indirect
explode 1 = blow up, erupt, burst, go off, shatter 2 = detonate, set off, discharge,

let off **3** = lose your temper, rage, erupt, become angry, hit the roof (*informal*), go crook (*Austral. & N.Z. slang*) **4** = increase, grow, develop, extend, advance, shoot up, soar, boost **5** = disprove, discredit, refute, demolish, repudiate, put paid to, invalidate, debunk

exploit VERB **1** = take advantage of, abuse, use, manipulate, milk, misuse, ill-treat, play on *or* upon **2** = make the best use of, use, make use of, utilize, cash in on (*informal*), capitalize on, use to good advantage, profit by *or* from
• NOUN = feat, act, achievement, enterprise, adventure, stunt, deed, accomplishment

exploitation = misuse, abuse, manipulation, using, ill-treatment

exploration **1** = expedition, tour, trip, survey, travel, journey, reconnaissance **2** = investigation, research, survey, search, inquiry, analysis, examination, inspection

explore **1** = travel around, tour, survey, scout, reconnoitre **2** = investigate, consider, research, survey, search, examine, probe, look into

explosion **1** = blast, crack, burst, bang, discharge, report, blowing up, clap **2** = increase, rise, development, growth, boost, expansion, enlargement, escalation **3** = outburst, fit, storm, attack, surge, flare-up, eruption **4** = outbreak, flare-up, eruption, upsurge

explosive NOUN = bomb, mine, shell, missile, rocket, grenade, charge, torpedo
• ADJECTIVE **1** = unstable, dangerous, volatile, hazardous, unsafe, perilous, combustible, inflammable **2** = sudden, rapid, marked, unexpected, startling, swift, abrupt **3** = fiery, violent, volatile, stormy, touchy, vehement

expose **1** = uncover, show, reveal, display, exhibit, present, unveil, lay bare ≠ hide **2** = make vulnerable, subject, endanger, leave open, jeopardize, put at risk, imperil, lay open

exposure **1** = hypothermia, frostbite, extreme cold, intense cold **2** = uncovering, showing, display, exhibition, revelation, presentation, unveiling

express VERB **1** = state, communicate, convey, articulate, say, word, voice, declare **2** = show, indicate, exhibit, demonstrate, reveal, intimate, convey, signify
• ADJECTIVE **1** = explicit, clear, plain, distinct, definite, unambiguous, categorical **2** = specific, exclusive, particular, sole, special, singular, clear-cut, especial **3** = fast, direct, rapid, priority, prompt, swift, high-speed, speedy

expression **1** = statement, declaration, announcement, communication, utterance, articulation **2** = indication, demonstration, exhibition, display, showing, show, sign, symbol **3** = look, countenance, face, air, appearance, aspect **4** = phrase, saying, word, term, remark, maxim, idiom, adage

expressive = vivid, striking, telling, moving, poignant, eloquent ≠ impassive

expulsion **1** = ejection, exclusion, dismissal, removal, eviction, banishment **2** = discharge, emission, spewing, secretion, excretion, ejection, seepage, suppuration

exquisite **1** = beautiful, elegant, graceful, pleasing, attractive, lovely, charming, comely ≠ unattractive **2** = fine, beautiful, lovely, elegant, precious, delicate, dainty **3** = intense, acute, severe, sharp, keen, extreme

extend **1** = spread out, reach, stretch **2** = stretch, stretch out, spread out, straighten out **3** = last, continue, go on, stretch, carry on **4** = protrude, project, stand out, bulge, stick out, hang, overhang, jut out **5** = widen, increase, expand, add to, enhance, supplement, enlarge, broaden ≠ reduce **6** = make longer, prolong, lengthen, draw out, spin out, drag out ≠ shorten **7** = offer, present, confer, stick out, impart, proffer ≠ withdraw

extension **1** = annexe, addition, supplement, appendix, appendage **2** = lengthening, extra time, continuation, additional period of time **3** = development, expansion, widening, increase, broadening, enlargement, diversification

extensive ADJECTIVE = large, considerable, substantial, spacious, wide, broad, expansive
• ADJECTIVE ≠ confined **2** = comprehensive, complete, wide, pervasive ≠ restricted **3** = great, vast, widespread, large-scale, far-reaching, far-flung, voluminous ≠ limited

extent **1** = magnitude, amount, scale, level, stretch, expanse **2** = size, area, length,

width, breadth
exterior NOUN = outside, face, surface, covering, skin, shell, coating, façade
• ADJECTIVE = outer, outside, external, surface, outward, outermost ≠ inner
external 1 = outer, outside, surface, outward, exterior, outermost ≠ internal 2 = foreign, international, alien, extrinsic ≠ domestic 3 = outside, visiting ≠ inside
extinct = dead, lost, gone, vanished, defunct ≠ living
extinction = dying out, destruction, abolition, oblivion, extermination, annihilation, eradication, obliteration
extra ADJECTIVE 1 = additional, more, added, further, supplementary, auxiliary, ancillary ≠ vital 2 = surplus, excess, spare, redundant, unused, leftover, superfluous
• NOUN = addition, bonus, supplement, accessory ≠ necessity
• ADVERB 1 = in addition, additionally, over and above 2 = exceptionally, very, specially, especially, particularly, extremely, remarkably, unusually
extract VERB 1 = take out, draw, pull, remove, withdraw, pull out, bring out 2 = pull out, remove, take out, draw, uproot, pluck out 3 = elicit, obtain, force, draw, derive, glean, coerce
• NOUN 1 = passage, selection, excerpt, cutting, clipping, quotation, citation 2 = essence, solution, concentrate, juice, distillation
extraordinary 1 = remarkable, outstanding, amazing, fantastic, astonishing, exceptional, phenomenal, extremely good ≠ unremarkable 2 = unusual, strange, remarkable, uncommon ≠ ordinary
extravagant 1 = wasteful, lavish, prodigal, profligate, spendthrift ≠ economical 2 = excessive, outrageous, over the top (*slang*), unreasonable, preposterous ≠ moderate
extreme ADJECTIVE 1 = great, highest, supreme, acute, severe, maximum, intense, ultimate ≠ mild 2 = severe, radical, strict, harsh, rigid, drastic, uncompromising 3 = radical, excessive, fanatical, immoderate ≠ moderate 4 = farthest, furthest, far, remotest, far-off, outermost, most distant ≠ nearest
• NOUN = limit, end, edge, opposite, pole, boundary, antithesis, extremity
extremely = very, particularly, severely, terribly, unusually, exceptionally, extraordinarily, tremendously
extremist NOUN = radical, activist, militant, fanatic, die-hard, bigot, zealot
• ADJECTIVE = extreme, wild, passionate, frenzied, obsessive, fanatical, fervent, zealous
eye NOUN 1 = eyeball, optic (*informal*), organ of vision, organ of sight 2 *often plural* = eyesight, sight, vision, perception, ability to see, power of seeing 3 = appreciation, taste, recognition, judgment, discrimination, perception, discernment 4 = observance, observation, surveillance, vigil, watch, lookout 5 = centre, heart, middle, mid, core, nucleus
• VERB = look at, view, study, watch, survey, observe, contemplate, check out (*informal*)
RELATED WORDS
adjectives: ocular, ophthalmic, optic

f

fable 1 = legend, myth, parable, allegory, story, tale 2 = fiction, fantasy, myth, invention, yarn (*informal*), fabrication, urban myth, tall story (*informal*) ≠ fact
fabric 1 = cloth, material, stuff, textile, web 2 = framework, structure, make-up, organization, frame, foundations, construction, constitution 3 = structure, foundations, construction, framework
fabulous 1 (*Informal*) = wonderful, excellent, brilliant, superb, spectacular, fantastic (*informal*), marvellous, sensational (*informal*) ≠ ordinary 2 = astounding, amazing, extraordinary, remarkable, incredible, astonishing, unbelievable, breathtaking 3 = legendary, imaginary, mythical, fictitious, made-up, fantastic, invented, unreal
façade 1 = front, face, exterior 2 = show,

front, appearance, mask, exterior, guise, pretence, semblance

face NOUN **1** = countenance, features, profile, mug (*slang*), visage **2** = expression, look, air, appearance, aspect, countenance **3** = side, front, outside, surface, exterior, elevation, vertical surface
• VERB **1** = look onto, overlook, be opposite, look out on, front onto **2** = confront, meet, encounter, deal with, oppose, tackle, experience, brave **3** *often with **up to*** = accept, deal with, tackle, acknowledge, cope with, confront, come to terms with, meet head-on

facilitate = further, help, forward, promote, speed up, pave the way for, make easy, expedite ≠ hinder

facility 1 *often plural* = amenity, means, aid, opportunity, advantage, resource, equipment, provision **2** = opportunity, possibility, convenience **3** = ability, skill, efficiency, fluency, proficiency, dexterity, adroitness **4** = ease, fluency, effortlessness ≠ difficulty

fact 1 = truth, reality, certainty, verity ≠ fiction **2** = event, happening, act, performance, incident, deed, occurrence, fait accompli (*French*)

faction 1 = group, set, party, gang, bloc, contingent, clique, coterie **2** = dissension, division, conflict, rebellion, disagreement, variance, discord, infighting ≠ agreement

factor = element, part, cause, influence, item, aspect, characteristic, consideration

factory = works, plant, mill, workshop, assembly line, shop floor

factual = true, authentic, real, correct, genuine, exact, precise, dinkum (*Austral. & N.Z. informal*), true-to-life ≠ fictitious

faculty NOUN **1** = ability, power, skill, facility, capacity, propensity, aptitude ≠ failing **2** = department, school **3** = teaching staff, staff, teachers, professors, lecturers (*chiefly U.S.*)
• PLURAL NOUN = powers, reason, senses, intelligence, wits, capabilities, mental abilities, physical abilities

fad = craze, fashion, trend, rage, vogue, whim, mania

fade 1 = become pale, bleach, wash out, discolour, lose colour, decolour **2** = make pale, dim, bleach, wash out, blanch, discolour, decolour **3** = grow dim, fade away, become less loud **4** = dwindle, disappear, vanish, melt away, decline, dissolve, wane, die away

fail VERB **1** = be unsuccessful, founder, fall, break down, flop (*informal*), fizzle out (*informal*), come unstuck, miscarry ≠ succeed **2** = disappoint, abandon, desert, neglect, omit, let down, forsake, be disloyal to **3** = stop working, stop, die, break down, stall, cut out, malfunction, conk out (*informal*) **4** = wither, perish, sag, waste away, shrivel up **5** = go bankrupt, collapse, fold (*informal*), close down, go under, go bust (*informal*), go out of business, be wound up **6** = decline, deteriorate, degenerate **7** = give out, dim, peter out, die away, grow dim
• PHRASES **without fail** = without exception, regularly, constantly, invariably, religiously, unfailingly, conscientiously, like clockwork

failing NOUN = shortcoming, fault, weakness, defect, deficiency, flaw, drawback, blemish ≠ strength
• PREPOSITION = in the absence of, lacking, in default of

failure 1 = lack of success, defeat, collapse, breakdown, overthrow, miscarriage, fiasco, downfall ≠ success **2** = loser, disappointment, flop (*informal*), write-off, no-hoper (*chiefly Austral.*), dud (*informal*), black sheep, washout (*informal*), dead duck (*slang*) **3** = bankruptcy, crash, collapse, ruin, closure, winding up, downfall, going under ≠ prosperity

faint ADJECTIVE **1** = dim, low, soft, faded, distant, vague, unclear, muted ≠ clear **2** = slight, weak, feeble, unenthusiastic, remote, slim, vague, slender **3** = dizzy, giddy, light-headed, weak, exhausted, wobbly, muzzy, woozy (*informal*) ≠ energetic
• VERB = pass out, black out, lose consciousness, keel over (*informal*), go out, collapse, swoon (*literary*), flake out (*informal*)
• NOUN = blackout, collapse, coma, swoon (*literary*), unconsciousness

faintly 1 = slightly, rather, a little, somewhat, dimly **2** = softly, weakly, feebly, in a whisper, indistinctly, unclearly

fair[1] 1 = unbiased, impartial, even-handed, unprejudiced, just, reasonable, proper, legitimate ≠ unfair **2** = respectable, average, reasonable, decent, acceptable, moderate, adequate, satisfactory **3** = light, golden, blonde, blond, yellowish, fair-haired, light-coloured, flaxen-haired **4** = fine, clear, dry, bright, pleasant, sunny, cloudless, unclouded **5** = beautiful, pretty, attractive, lovely, handsome, good-looking, bonny, comely ≠ ugly

fair² = carnival, show, fête, festival, exhibition, mart, bazaar, gala

fairly **1** = equitably, objectively, legitimately, honestly, justly, lawfully, without prejudice, dispassionately **2** = moderately, rather, quite, somewhat, reasonably, adequately, pretty well, tolerably **3** = positively, really, simply, absolutely **4** = deservedly, objectively, honestly, justifiably, justly, impartially, equitably, without fear or favour

fairness = impartiality, justice, equity, legitimacy, decency, disinterestedness, rightfulness, equitableness

fairy = sprite, elf, brownie, pixie, puck, imp, leprechaun, peri

fairy tale *or* **fairy story** **1** = folk tale, romance, traditional story **2** = lie, fiction, invention, fabrication, untruth, urban myth, tall story, urban legend

faith **1** = confidence, trust, credit, conviction, assurance, dependence, reliance, credence ≠ distrust **2** = religion, church, belief, persuasion, creed, communion, denomination, dogma ≠ agnosticism

faithful **1** = loyal, true, committed, constant, devoted, dedicated, reliable, staunch ≠ disloyal **2** = accurate, close, true, strict, exact, precise

fake ADJECTIVE = artificial, false, forged, counterfeit, put-on, pretend (*informal*), mock, imitation ≠ genuine

● NOUN **1** = forgery, copy, fraud, reproduction, dummy, imitation, hoax, counterfeit **2** = charlatan, deceiver, sham, quack

● VERB **1** = forge, copy, reproduce, fabricate, counterfeit, falsify **2** = sham, put on, pretend, simulate, feign, go through the motions of

fall VERB **1** = drop, plunge, tumble, plummet, collapse, sink, go down, come down ≠ rise **2** = decrease, drop, decline, go down, slump, diminish, dwindle, lessen ≠ increase **3** = be overthrown, surrender, succumb, submit, capitulate, be conquered, pass into enemy hands ≠ triumph **4** = be killed, die, perish, meet your end ≠ survive **5** = occur, happen, come about, chance, take place, befall, come to pass

● NOUN **1** = drop, slip, plunge, dive, tumble, descent, plummet, nose dive **2** = decrease, drop, lowering, decline, reduction, slump, dip, lessening **3** = collapse, defeat, downfall, ruin, destruction, overthrow, submission, capitulation

false **1** = incorrect, wrong, mistaken, misleading, faulty, inaccurate, invalid, erroneous ≠ correct **2** = untrue, fraudulent, trumped up, fallacious, untruthful ≠ true **3** = artificial, forged, fake, reproduction, replica, imitation, bogus, simulated ≠ real

falter **1** = hesitate, delay, waver, vacillate ≠ persevere **2** = tumble, totter **3** = stutter, pause, stumble, hesitate, stammer

fame = prominence, glory, celebrity, stardom, reputation, honour, prestige, stature ≠ obscurity

familiar **1** = well-known, recognized, common, ordinary, routine, frequent, accustomed, customary ≠ unfamiliar **2** = friendly, close, dear, intimate, amicable ≠ formal **3** = relaxed, easy, friendly, comfortable, intimate, casual, amicable **4** = disrespectful, forward, bold, intrusive, presumptuous, impudent, overfamiliar

familiarity **1** = acquaintance, experience, understanding, knowledge, awareness, grasp ≠ unfamiliarity **2** = friendliness, intimacy, ease, openness, informality, sociability ≠ formality **3** = disrespect, forwardness, overfamiliarity, cheek, presumption, boldness ≠ respect

family **1** = relations, relatives, household, folk (*informal*), kin, nuclear family, next of kin, kith and kin, ainga (*N.Z.*) **2** = children, kids (*informal*), offspring, little ones, littlies (*Austral. informal*) **3** = ancestors, house, race, tribe, clan, dynasty, line of descent **4** = species, group, class, system, order, network, genre, subdivision

famine = hunger, want, starvation, deprivation, scarcity, dearth

famous = well-known, celebrated, acclaimed, noted, distinguished, prominent, legendary, renowned ≠ unknown

fan¹ NOUN = blower, ventilator, air

conditioner
• VERB = blow, cool, refresh, air-condition, ventilate

fan² = supporter, lover, follower, enthusiast, admirer, buff (*informal*), devotee, aficionado

fanatic = extremist, activist, militant, bigot, zealot

fancy ADJECTIVE = elaborate, decorative, extravagant, intricate, baroque, ornamental, ornate, embellished ≠ plain
• NOUN 1 = whim, thought, idea, desire, urge, notion, humour, impulse 2 = delusion, dream, vision, fantasy, daydream, chimera
• VERB 1 = wish for, want, desire, hope for, long for, crave, yearn for, thirst for 2 (*Informal*) = be attracted to, find attractive, lust after, like, take to, be captivated by, have a thing about (*informal*), have eyes for 3 = suppose, think, believe, imagine, reckon, conjecture, think likely

fantastic 1 (*Informal*) = wonderful, great, excellent, very good, smashing (*informal*), superb, tremendous (*informal*), magnificent, booshit (*Austral. slang*), exo (*Austral. slang*), sik (*Austral. slang*) ≠ ordinary 2 = strange, bizarre, grotesque, fanciful, outlandish 3 = implausible, unlikely, incredible, absurd, preposterous, cock-and-bull (*informal*)

fantasy or (*Archaic*) **phantasy**
1 = daydream, dream, wish, reverie, flight of fancy, pipe dream 2 = imagination, fancy, invention, creativity, originality

far ADVERB 1 = a long way, miles, deep, a good way, afar, a great distance 2 = much, greatly, very much, extremely, significantly, considerably, decidedly, markedly
• ADJECTIVE *often with* ***off*** = remote, distant, far-flung, faraway, out-of-the-way, far-off, outlying, off the beaten track ≠ near

farce 1 = comedy, satire, slapstick, burlesque, buffoonery 2 = mockery, joke, nonsense, parody, shambles, sham, travesty

fare NOUN 1 = charge, price, ticket price, ticket money 2 = food, provisions, board, rations, kai (*N.Z. informal*), nourishment, sustenance, victuals, nutriment
• VERB = get on, do, manage, make out, prosper, get along

farewell INTERJECTION = goodbye, bye (*informal*), so long, see you, take care, good morning, bye-bye (*informal*), good day, haere ra (*N.Z.*)
• NOUN = goodbye, parting, departure, leave-taking, adieu, valediction, sendoff (*informal*)

farm NOUN = smallholding, ranch (*chiefly U.S. & Canad.*), farmstead, station (*Austral. & N.Z.*), vineyard, plantation, croft (*Scot.*), grange, homestead
• VERB = cultivate, work, plant, grow crops on, keep animals on

fascinate = entrance, absorb, intrigue, rivet, captivate, enthral, beguile, transfix ≠ bore

fascinating = captivating, engaging, gripping, compelling, intriguing, very interesting, irresistible, enticing ≠ boring

fascination = attraction, pull, magic, charm, lure, allure, magnetism, enchantment

fashion NOUN 1 = style, look, trend, rage, custom, mode, vogue, craze 2 = method, way, style, manner, mode
• VERB = make, shape, cast, construct, form, create, manufacture, forge

fashionable = popular, in fashion, trendy (*Brit. informal*), in (*informal*), modern, with it (*informal*), stylish, chic ≠ unfashionable

fast¹ ADJECTIVE 1 = quick, flying, rapid, fleet, swift, speedy, brisk, hasty ≠ slow 2 = fixed, firm, sound, stuck, secure, tight, jammed, fastened ≠ unstable 3 = dissipated, wild, exciting, loose, extravagant, reckless, self-indulgent, wanton 4 = close, firm, devoted, faithful, steadfast
• ADVERB 1 = quickly, rapidly, swiftly, hastily, hurriedly, speedily, in haste, at full speed ≠ slowly 2 = securely, firmly, tightly, fixedly 3 = fixedly, firmly, soundly, deeply, securely, tightly

fast² VERB = go hungry, abstain, go without food, deny yourself
• NOUN = fasting, diet, abstinence

fasten 1 = secure, close, do up 2 = tie, bind, tie up 3 = fix, join, link, connect, attach, affix

fat ADJECTIVE 1 = overweight, large, heavy, plump, stout, obese, tubby, portly ≠ thin 2 = fatty, greasy, adipose, oleaginous, oily ≠ lean
• NOUN = fatness, flesh, bulk, obesity, flab, blubber, paunch, fatty tissue

fatal 1 = disastrous, devastating, crippling, catastrophic, ruinous, calamitous, baleful, baneful ≠ minor 2 = lethal, deadly, mortal, causing death, final, killing, terminal, malignant ≠ harmless

fate 1 = destiny, chance, fortune, luck, the stars, providence, nemesis, kismet 2 = fortune, destiny, lot, portion, cup, horoscope

fated = destined, doomed, predestined, preordained, foreordained

father NOUN 1 = daddy (*informal*), dad (*informal*), male parent, pop (*U.S. informal*), old man (*Brit. informal*), pa (*informal*), papa (*old-fashioned informal*), pater 2 = founder, author, maker, architect, creator, inventor, originator, prime mover 3 *usually cap.* = priest, minister, vicar, parson, pastor, cleric, churchman, padre (*informal*) 4 *usually plural* = forefather, predecessor, ancestor, forebear, progenitor, tupuna *or* tipuna (*N.Z.*)
• VERB = sire, parent, conceive, bring to life, beget, procreate, bring into being, give life to

RELATED WORD
adjective: paternal

fatherly = paternal, kindly, protective, supportive, benign, affectionate, patriarchal, benevolent

fatigue NOUN = tiredness, lethargy, weariness, heaviness, languor, listlessness ≠ freshness
• VERB = tire, exhaust, weaken, weary, drain, wear out, take it out of (*informal*), tire out ≠ refresh

fatty = greasy, fat, creamy, oily, adipose, oleaginous, suety, rich

fault NOUN 1 = responsibility, liability, guilt, accountability, culpability 2 = mistake, slip, error, blunder, lapse, oversight, indiscretion, howler (*informal*) 3 = failing, weakness, defect, deficiency, flaw, shortcoming, blemish, imperfection ≠ strength
• VERB = criticize, blame, complain, condemn, moan about, censure, hold (someone) responsible, find fault with
• PHRASES **find fault with something** *or* **someone** = criticize, complain about, whinge about (*informal*), whine about (*informal*), quibble, carp at, take to task, pick holes in ♦ **to a fault** = excessively, unduly, in the extreme, overmuch, immoderately

faulty 1 = defective, damaged, malfunctioning, broken, flawed, impaired, imperfect, out of order 2 = incorrect, flawed, unsound

favour NOUN 1 = approval, goodwill, commendation, approbation ≠ disapproval 2 = favouritism, preferential treatment 3 = support, backing, aid, assistance, patronage, good opinion 4 = good turn, service, benefit, courtesy, kindness, indulgence, boon, good deed ≠ wrong
• VERB 1 = prefer, opt for, like better, incline towards, choose, pick, desire, go for ≠ object to 2 = indulge, reward, side with, smile upon 3 = support, champion, encourage, approve, advocate, subscribe to, commend, stand up for ≠ oppose 4 = help, benefit

favourable 1 = positive, encouraging, approving, praising, reassuring, enthusiastic, sympathetic, commending ≠ disapproving 2 = affirmative, agreeing, confirming, positive, assenting, corroborative 3 = advantageous, promising, encouraging, suitable, helpful, beneficial, auspicious, opportune ≠ disadvantageous

favourite ADJECTIVE = preferred, favoured, best-loved, most-liked, special, choice, dearest, pet
• NOUN = darling, pet, blue-eyed boy (*informal*), beloved, idol, fave (*informal*), teacher's pet, the apple of your eye

fear NOUN 1 = dread, horror, panic, terror, fright, alarm, trepidation, fearfulness 2 = bugbear, bête noire, horror, nightmare, anxiety, terror, dread, spectre
• VERB 1 = be afraid of, dread, shudder at, be fearful of, tremble at, be terrified by, take fright at, shake in your shoes about 2 = regret, feel, suspect, have a feeling, have a hunch, have a sneaking suspicion, have a funny feeling
• PHRASES **fear for something** *or* **someone** = worry about, be anxious about, feel concern for

fearful 1 = scared, afraid, alarmed, frightened, nervous, terrified, petrified ≠ unafraid 2 = timid, afraid, frightened, scared, alarmed, nervous, uneasy, jumpy ≠ brave 3 = frightful, terrible, awful, dreadful, horrific, dire, horrendous, gruesome

feasible = practicable, possible, reasonable, viable, workable, achievable, attainable, likely ≠ impracticable

feast NOUN **1** = banquet, repast, spread (*informal*), dinner, treat, hakari (*N.Z.*) **2** = festival, holiday, fête, celebration, holy day, red-letter day, religious festival, saint's day
• VERB = eat your fill, wine and dine, overindulge, consume, indulge, gorge, devour, pig out (*slang*)

feat = accomplishment, act, performance, achievement, enterprise, undertaking, exploit, deed

feather NOUN = plume
• PLURAL NOUN = plumage, plumes, down

feature NOUN **1** = aspect, quality, characteristic, property, factor, trait, hallmark, facet **2** = article, report, story, piece, item, column **3** = highlight, attraction, speciality, main item
• PLURAL NOUN = face, countenance, physiognomy, lineaments
• VERB **1** = spotlight, present, emphasize, play up, foreground, give prominence to **2** = star, appear, participate, play a part

federation = union, league, association, alliance, combination, coalition, partnership, consortium

fed up = cheesed off, depressed, bored, tired, discontented, dissatisfied, glum, sick and tired (*informal*), hoha (*N.Z.*)

fee = charge, price, cost, bill, payment, wage, salary, toll

feeble **1** = weak, frail, debilitated, sickly, puny, weedy (*informal*), infirm, effete ≠ strong **2** = inadequate, pathetic, insufficient, lame **3** = unconvincing, poor, thin, tame, pathetic, lame, flimsy, paltry ≠ effective

feed VERB **1** = cater for, provide for, nourish, provide with food, supply, sustain, cook for, wine and dine **2** = graze, eat, browse, pasture **3** = eat, drink milk
• NOUN **1** = food, fodder, provender, pasturage **2** (*Informal*) = meal, spread (*informal*), dinner, lunch, tea, breakfast, feast, supper

feel VERB **1** = experience, bear **2** = touch, handle, manipulate, finger, stroke, paw, caress, fondle **3** = be aware of **4** = perceive, detect, discern, experience, notice, observe **5** = sense, be aware, be convinced, have a feeling, intuit **6** = believe, consider, judge, deem, think, hold
• NOUN **1** = texture, finish, touch, surface, surface quality **2** = impression, feeling, air, sense, quality, atmosphere, mood, aura

feeling **1** = emotion, sentiment **2** = opinion, view, attitude, belief, point of view, instinct, inclination **3** = passion, emotion, intensity, warmth **4** = ardour, love, care, warmth, tenderness, fervour **5** = sympathy, understanding, concern, pity, sensitivity, compassion, sorrow, sensibility **6** = sensation, sense, impression, awareness **7** = sense of touch, perception, sensation **8** = impression, idea, sense, notion, suspicion, hunch, inkling, presentiment **9** = atmosphere, mood, aura, ambience, feel, air, quality

fell **1** = cut down, cut, level, demolish, knock down, hew **2** = knock down

fellow **1** (*Old-fashioned*) = man, person, individual, character, guy (*informal*), bloke (*Brit. informal*), chap (*informal*) **2** = associate, colleague, peer, partner, companion, comrade, crony

fellowship **1** = society, club, league, association, organization, guild, fraternity, brotherhood **2** = camaraderie, brotherhood, companionship, sociability

feminine = womanly, pretty, soft, gentle, tender, delicate, ladylike ≠ masculine

fence NOUN = barrier, wall, defence, railings, hedge, barricade, hedgerow, rampart
• VERB *often with* ***in*** or ***off*** = enclose, surround, bound, protect, pen, confine, encircle

ferocious **1** = fierce, violent, savage, ravening, predatory, rapacious, wild ≠ gentle **2** = cruel, bitter, brutal, vicious, ruthless, bloodthirsty

ferry NOUN = ferry boat, boat, ship, passenger boat, packet boat, packet
• VERB = transport, bring, carry, ship, take, run, shuttle, convey

fertile = productive, rich, lush, prolific, abundant, plentiful, fruitful, teeming ≠ barren

fertility = fruitfulness, abundance, richness, fecundity, luxuriance, productiveness

fertilizer = compost, muck, manure, dung, bone meal, dressing

festival 1 = celebration, fair, carnival, gala, fête, entertainment, jubilee, fiesta 2 = holy day, holiday, feast, commemoration, feast day, red-letter day, saint's day, fiesta
festive = celebratory, happy, merry, jubilant, cheery, joyous, joyful, jovial ≠ mournful
fetch 1 = bring, pick up, collect, go and get, get, carry, deliver, transport 2 = sell for, make, raise, earn, realize, go for, yield, bring in
fetching = attractive, charming, cute, enticing, captivating, alluring, winsome
feud NOUN = hostility, row, conflict, argument, disagreement, rivalry, quarrel, vendetta
• VERB = quarrel, row, clash, dispute, fall out, contend, war, squabble
fever = excitement, frenzy, ferment, agitation, fervour, restlessness, delirium
few = not many, one or two, scarcely any, rare, meagre, negligible, sporadic, sparse
fiasco = flop, failure, disaster, mess (*informal*), catastrophe, debacle, cock-up (*Brit. slang*), washout (*informal*)
fibre = thread, strand, filament, tendril, pile, texture, wisp
fiction 1 = tale, story, novel, legend, myth, romance, narration, creative writing 2 = lie, invention, fabrication, falsehood, untruth, urban myth, tall story, urban legend
fictional = imaginary, made-up, invented, legendary, unreal, nonexistent
fiddle VERB 1 *usually with* ***with*** = fidget, play, finger, tamper, mess about *or* around 2 *usually with* ***with*** = tinker, adjust, interfere, mess about *or* around 3 (*Informal*) = cheat, cook (*informal*), fix, diddle (*informal*), wangle (*informal*)
• NOUN 1 (*Brit. informal*) = fraud, racket, scam (*slang*), fix, swindle 2 = violin
fiddling = trivial, small, petty, trifling, insignificant, unimportant, pettifogging, futile
fidelity 1 = loyalty, devotion, allegiance, constancy, faithfulness, dependability, trustworthiness, staunchness ≠ disloyalty 2 = accuracy, precision, correspondence, closeness, faithfulness, exactness, scrupulousness ≠ inaccuracy
field NOUN 1 = meadow, land, green, lea (*poetic*), pasture 2 = speciality, line, area, department, territory, discipline, province, sphere 3 = line, reach, sweep 4 = competitors, competition, candidates, runners, applicants, entrants, contestants
• VERB 1 (*Informal*) = deal with, answer, handle, respond to, reply to, deflect, turn aside 2 (*Sport*) = retrieve, return, stop, catch, pick up
fierce 1 = ferocious, wild, dangerous, cruel, savage, brutal, aggressive, menacing, aggers (*Austral. slang*), biffo (*Austral. slang*) ≠ gentle 2 = intense, strong, keen, relentless, cut-throat 3 = stormy, strong, powerful, violent, intense, raging, furious, howling ≠ tranquil
fiercely = ferociously, savagely, passionately, furiously, viciously, tooth and nail, tigerishly, with no holds barred
fiery 1 = burning, flaming, blazing, on fire, ablaze, aflame, afire 2 = excitable, fierce, passionate, irritable, impetuous, irascible, hot-headed
fight VERB 1 = oppose, campaign against, dispute, contest, resist, defy, contend, withstand 2 = battle, combat, do battle 3 = engage in, conduct, wage, pursue, carry on
• NOUN 1 = battle, campaign, movement, struggle 2 = conflict, clash, contest, encounter 3 = brawl, scrap (*informal*), confrontation, rumble (*U.S. & N.Z. slang*), duel, skirmish, tussle, biffo (*Austral. slang*) 4 = row, argument, dispute, quarrel, squabble 5 = resistance, spirit, pluck, militancy, belligerence, pluckiness
fighter 1 = boxer, wrestler, pugilist, prize fighter 2 = soldier, warrior, fighting man, man-at-arms
figure NOUN 1 = digit, character, symbol, number, numeral 2 = shape, build, body, frame, proportions, physique 3 = personage, person, individual, character, personality, celebrity, big name, dignitary 4 = diagram, drawing, picture, illustration, representation, sketch 5 = design, shape, pattern 6 = price, cost, value, amount, total, sum
• VERB 1 *usually with* ***in*** = feature, act, appear, contribute to, play a part, be featured 2 = calculate, work out, compute, tot up, total, count, reckon, tally
• PHRASES **figure something** *or* **someone out** = understand, make out, fathom, see, solve, comprehend, make sense of, decipher

figurehead = nominal head, titular head, front man, puppet, mouthpiece
file[1] NOUN **1** = folder, case, portfolio, binder **2** = dossier, record, information, data, documents, case history, report, case **3** = line, row, chain, column, queue, procession
• VERB **1** = arrange, order, classify, put in place, categorize, pigeonhole, put in order **2** = register, record, enter, log, put on record **3** = march, troop, parade, walk in line, walk behind one another
file[2] = smooth, shape, polish, rub, scrape, rasp, abrade
fill **1** = top up, fill up, make full, become full, brim over **2** = swell, expand, become bloated, extend, balloon, fatten **3** = pack, crowd, squeeze, cram, throng **4** = stock, supply, pack, load **5** = plug, close, stop, seal, cork, bung, block up, stop up **6** = saturate, charge, pervade, permeate, imbue, impregnate, suffuse **7** = fulfil, hold, perform, carry out, occupy, execute, discharge **8** *often with* ***up*** = satisfy, stuff, glut
filling NOUN = stuffing, padding, filler, wadding, inside, insides, contents
• ADJECTIVE = satisfying, heavy, square, substantial, ample
film NOUN **1** = movie, picture, flick (*slang*), motion picture **2** = cinema, the movies **3** = layer, covering, cover, skin, coating, dusting, tissue, membrane
• VERB **1** = photograph, record, shoot, video, videotape, take **2** = adapt for the screen, make into a film
filter VERB **1** = purify, treat, strain, refine, riddle, sift, sieve, winnow **2** = trickle, seep, percolate, escape, leak, penetrate, ooze, dribble
• NOUN = sieve, mesh, gauze, strainer, membrane, riddle, sifter
filthy **1** = dirty, foul, polluted, squalid, slimy, unclean, putrid, festy (*Austral. slang*) **2** = grimy, muddy, blackened, grubby, begrimed, festy (*Austral. slang*) **3** = obscene, corrupt, indecent, pornographic, lewd, depraved, impure, smutty
final **1** = last, latest, closing, finishing, concluding, ultimate, terminal ≠ first **2** = irrevocable, absolute, definitive, decided, settled, definite, conclusive, irrefutable
finale = climax, ending, close, conclusion, culmination, denouement, last part, epilogue ≠ opening
finally **1** = eventually, at last, in the end, ultimately, at length, at long last, after a long time **2** = lastly, in the end, ultimately **3** = in conclusion, lastly, in closing, to conclude, to sum up, in summary
finance VERB = fund, back, support, pay for, guarantee, invest in, underwrite, endow
• NOUN = economics, business, money, banking, accounts, investment, commerce
• PLURAL NOUN = resources, money, funds, capital, cash, affairs, budgeting, assets
financial = economic, business, commercial, monetary, fiscal, pecuniary
find VERB **1** = discover, uncover, spot, locate, detect, come across, hit upon, put your finger on ≠ lose **2** = encounter, meet, recognize **3** = observe, learn, note, discover, notice, realize, come up with, perceive
• NOUN = discovery, catch, asset, bargain, acquisition, good buy
• PHRASES **find something out** = learn, discover, realize, observe, perceive, detect, become aware, come to know
fine[1] **1** = excellent, good, striking, masterly, very good, impressive, outstanding, magnificent ≠ poor **2** = satisfactory, good, all right, suitable, acceptable, convenient, fair, O.K. *or* okay (*informal*) **3** = thin, light, narrow, wispy **4** = delicate, light, thin, sheer, flimsy, wispy, gossamer, diaphanous ≠ coarse **5** = stylish, expensive, elegant, refined, tasteful, quality **6** = exquisite, delicate, fragile, dainty **7** = minute, exact, precise, nice **8** = keen, minute, nice, sharp, acute, subtle, precise, hairsplitting **9** = brilliant, quick, keen, alert, clever, penetrating, astute **10** = sunny, clear, fair, dry, bright, pleasant, clement, balmy ≠ cloudy
fine[2] NOUN = penalty, damages, punishment, forfeit, financial penalty
• VERB = penalize, charge, punish
finger = touch, feel, handle, play with, manipulate, paw (*informal*), maul, toy with
finish VERB **1** = stop, close, complete, conclude, cease, wrap up (*informal*), terminate, round off ≠ start **2** = get done, complete, conclude **3** = end, stop, conclude, wind up, terminate

4 = consume, dispose of, devour, polish off, eat, get through 5 = use up, empty, exhaust 6 = coat, polish, stain, texture, wax, varnish, gild, veneer 7 *usually with* ***off*** = destroy, defeat, overcome, bring down, ruin, dispose of, rout, put an end to 8 *usually with* ***off*** = kill, murder, destroy, massacre, butcher, slaughter, slay, exterminate

• NOUN 1 = end, close, conclusion, run-in, completion, finale, culmination, cessation ≠ beginning 2 = surface, polish, shine, texture, glaze, veneer, lacquer, lustre

finished 1 = over, done, through, ended, closed, complete, executed, finalized ≠ begun 2 = ruined, done for (*informal*), doomed, through, lost, defeated, wiped out, undone

fire NOUN 1 = flames, blaze, combustion, inferno, conflagration, holocaust 2 = passion, energy, spirit, enthusiasm, excitement, intensity, sparkle, vitality 3 = bombardment, shooting, firing, shelling, hail, volley, barrage, gunfire

• VERB 1 = let off, shoot, shell, set off, discharge, detonate 2 = shoot, explode, discharge, detonate, pull the trigger 3 (*Informal*) = dismiss, sack (*informal*), get rid of, discharge, lay off, make redundant, cashier, give notice 4 *sometimes with* ***up*** = inspire, excite, stir, stimulate, motivate, awaken, animate, rouse

fireworks 1 = pyrotechnics, illuminations, feux d'artifice 2 (*Informal*) = trouble, row, storm, rage, uproar, hysterics

firm[1] 1 = hard, solid, dense, set, stiff, compacted, rigid, inflexible ≠ soft 2 = secure, fixed, rooted, stable, steady, fast, embedded, immovable ≠ unstable 3 = strong, close, tight, steady 4 = strict, unshakeable, resolute, inflexible, unyielding, unbending 5 = determined, resolved, definite, set on, adamant, resolute, inflexible, unyielding ≠ wavering 6 = definite, hard, clear, confirmed, settled, fixed, hard-and-fast, cut-and-dried (*informal*)

firm[2] = company, business, concern, association, organization, corporation, venture, enterprise

firmly 1 = securely, safely, tightly 2 = immovably, securely, steadily, like a rock, unflinchingly, unshakeably 3 = steadily, securely, tightly, unflinchingly 4 = resolutely, staunchly, steadfastly, definitely, unwaveringly, unchangeably

first ADJECTIVE 1 = earliest, original, primordial 2 = initial, opening, earliest, maiden, introductory 3 = top, best, winning, premier 4 = elementary, key, basic, primary, fundamental, cardinal, rudimentary, elemental 5 = foremost, highest, greatest, leading, head, ruling, chief, prime

• ADVERB = to begin with, firstly, initially, at the beginning, in the first place, beforehand, to start with, at the outset

• NOUN = novelty, innovation, originality, new experience

• PHRASES **from the first** = from the start, from the beginning, from the outset, from the very beginning, from the introduction, from the starting point, from the inception, from the commencement

fish = angle, net, cast, trawl

fit[1] VERB 1 = adapt, shape, arrange, alter, adjust, modify, tweak (*informal*), customize 2 = place, insert 3 = suit, meet, match, belong to, conform to, correspond to, accord with, be appropriate to 4 = equip, provide, arm, prepare, fit out, kit out

• ADJECTIVE 1 = appropriate, suitable, right, becoming, seemly, fitting, skilled, correct ≠ inappropriate 2 = healthy, strong, robust, sturdy, well, trim, strapping, hale ≠ unfit

fit[2] 1 = seizure, attack, bout, spasm, convulsion, paroxysm 2 = bout, burst, outbreak, outburst, spell

fitness 1 = appropriateness, competence, readiness, eligibility, suitability, propriety, aptness 2 = health, strength, good health, vigour, good condition, wellness, robustness

fitting NOUN = accessory, part, piece, unit, component, attachment

• ADJECTIVE = appropriate, suitable, proper, apt, right, becoming, seemly, correct ≠ unsuitable

fix VERB 1 = place, join, stick, attach, set, position, plant, link 2 = decide, set, choose, establish, determine, settle, arrange, arrive at 3 = arrange, organize, sort out, see to, fix up, make arrangements for 4 = repair, mend, service, correct, restore, see to, overhaul, patch up 5 = focus, direct at, fasten on 6 (*Informal*) = rig, set up

(*informal*), influence, manipulate, fiddle (*informal*)
• NOUN (*Informal*) = mess, corner, difficulty, dilemma, embarrassment, plight, pickle (*informal*), uphill (*S. African*)
• PHRASES **fix someone up** = provide, supply, bring about, lay on, arrange for ♦ **fix something up** = arrange, plan, settle, fix, organize, sort out, agree on, make arrangements for

fixed 1 = inflexible, set, steady, resolute, unwavering ≠ wavering 2 = immovable, set, established, secure, rooted, permanent, rigid ≠ mobile 3 = agreed, set, planned, decided, established, settled, arranged, resolved

fizz 1 = bubble, froth, fizzle, effervesce, produce bubbles 2 = sputter, buzz, sparkle, hiss, crackle

flag[1] NOUN = banner, standard, colours, pennant, ensign, streamer, pennon
• VERB = mark, identify, indicate, label, pick out, note
• PHRASES **flag something** *or* **someone down** = hail, stop, signal, wave down

flag[2] = weaken, fade, weary, falter, wilt, wane, sag, languish

flagging = weakening, declining, waning, fading, deteriorating, wearying, faltering, wilting

flair 1 = ability, feel, talent, gift, genius, faculty, mastery, knack 2 = style, taste, dash, chic, elegance, panache, discernment, stylishness

flake NOUN = chip, scale, layer, peeling, shaving, wafer, sliver
• VERB = chip, peel (off), blister

flamboyant 1 = camp (*informal*), dashing, theatrical, swashbuckling 2 = showy, elaborate, extravagant, ornate, ostentatious 3 = colourful, striking, brilliant, glamorous, stylish, dazzling, glitzy (*slang*), showy

flame NOUN 1 = fire, light, spark, glow, blaze, brightness, inferno 2 (*Informal*) = sweetheart, partner, lover, girlfriend, boyfriend, heart-throb (*Brit.*), beau
• VERB = burn, flash, shine, glow, blaze, flare, glare

flank 1 = side, hip, thigh, loin 2 = wing, side, sector, aspect

flap VERB 1 = flutter, wave, flail 2 = beat, wave, thrash, flutter, wag, vibrate, shake
• NOUN 1 = flutter, beating, waving, shaking, swinging, swish 2 (*Informal*) = panic, state (*informal*), agitation, commotion, sweat (*informal*), dither (*chiefly Brit.*), fluster, tizzy (*informal*)

flare NOUN = flame, burst, flash, blaze, glare, flicker
• VERB 1 = blaze, flame, glare, flicker, burn up 2 = widen, spread, broaden, spread out, dilate, splay

flash NOUN = blaze, burst, spark, beam, streak, flare, dazzle, glare
• VERB 1 = blaze, shine, beam, sparkle, flare, glare, gleam, light up 2 = speed, race, shoot, fly, tear, dash, whistle, streak 3 (*Informal*) = show quickly, display, expose, exhibit, flourish, show off, flaunt
• ADJECTIVE (*Informal*) = ostentatious, smart, trendy, showy

flat[1] ADJECTIVE 1 = even, level, levelled, smooth, horizontal ≠ uneven 2 = punctured, collapsed, burst, blown out, deflated, empty 3 = used up, finished, empty, drained, expired 4 = absolute, firm, positive, explicit, definite, outright, downright, unequivocal 5 = dull, dead, empty, boring, depressing, tedious, lacklustre, tiresome ≠ exciting 6 = without energy, empty, weak, tired, depressed, drained, weary, worn out 7 = monotonous, boring, dull, tedious, tiresome, unchanging
• ADVERB = completely, directly, absolutely, categorically, precisely, exactly, utterly, outright
• PHRASES **flat out** (*Informal*) = at full speed, all out, to the full, hell for leather (*informal*), as hard as possible, at full tilt, for all you are worth

flat[2] = apartment, rooms, quarters, digs, suite, penthouse, living quarters

flatly = absolutely, completely, positively, categorically, unequivocally, unhesitatingly

flatten 1 = level, squash, compress, trample, iron out, even out, smooth off 2 = destroy, level, ruin, demolish, knock down, pull down, raze

flatter 1 = praise, compliment, pander to, sweet-talk (*informal*), wheedle, soft-soap (*informal*), butter up 2 = suit, become, enhance, set off, embellish, do something for, show to advantage

flattering 1 = becoming, kind, effective, enhancing, well-chosen ≠ unflattering

2 = ingratiating, complimentary, fawning, fulsome, laudatory, adulatory ≠ uncomplimentary

flavour NOUN 1 = taste, seasoning, flavouring, savour, relish, smack, aroma, zest ≠ blandness 2 = quality, feeling, feel, style, character, tone, essence, tinge
• VERB = season, spice, add flavour to, enrich, infuse, imbue, pep up, leaven

flaw = weakness, failing, defect, weak spot, fault, blemish, imperfection, chink in your armour

flawed 1 = damaged, defective, imperfect, blemished, faulty 2 = erroneous, incorrect, invalid, wrong, mistaken, false, faulty, unsound

flee = run away, escape, bolt, fly, take off (*informal*), depart, run off, take flight

fleet = navy, task force, flotilla, armada

fleeting = momentary, passing, brief, temporary, short-lived, transient, ephemeral, transitory ≠ lasting

flesh NOUN 1 = fat, muscle, tissue, brawn 2 = fatness, fat, adipose tissue, corpulence, weight 3 = meat 4 = physical nature, carnality, human nature, flesh and blood, sinful nature
• PHRASES **your own flesh and blood** = family, blood, relations, relatives, kin, kith and kin, blood relations, kinsfolk, ainga (*N.Z.*)

flexibility 1 = elasticity, pliability, springiness, pliancy, give (*informal*) 2 = adaptability, openness, versatility, adjustability 3 = complaisance, accommodation, give and take, amenability

flexible 1 = pliable, plastic, elastic, supple, lithe, springy, pliant, stretchy ≠ rigid 2 = adaptable, open, variable, adjustable, discretionary ≠ inflexible

flick VERB 1 = jerk, pull, tug, lurch, jolt 2 = strike, tap, remove quickly, hit, touch, stroke, flip, whisk
• PHRASES **flick through something** = browse, glance at, skim, leaf through, flip through, thumb through, skip through

flicker VERB 1 = twinkle, flash, sparkle, flare, shimmer, gutter, glimmer 2 = flutter, waver, quiver, vibrate
• NOUN 1 = glimmer, flash, spark, flare, gleam 2 = trace, breath, spark, glimmer, iota

flight¹ 1 = journey, trip, voyage 2 = aviation, flying, aeronautics 3 = flock, group, unit, cloud, formation, squadron, swarm, flying group

flight² = escape, fleeing, departure, retreat, exit, running away, exodus, getaway

fling VERB = throw, toss, hurl, launch, cast, propel, sling, catapult
• NOUN = binge, good time, bash, party, spree, night on the town, rave-up (*Brit. slang*)

flip VERB 1 = flick, switch, snap, slick 2 = spin, turn, overturn, turn over, roll over 3 = toss, throw, flick, fling, sling
• NOUN = toss, throw, spin, snap, flick

flirt VERB 1 = chat up, lead on (*informal*), make advances at, make eyes at, philander, make sheep's eyes at 2 *usually with* ***with*** = toy with, consider, entertain, play with, dabble in, trifle with, give a thought to, expose yourself to
• NOUN = tease, philanderer, coquette, heart-breaker

float 1 = glide, sail, drift, move gently, bob, coast, slide, be carried 2 = be buoyant, hang, hover ≠ sink 3 = launch, offer, sell, set up, promote, get going ≠ dissolve

floating 1 = uncommitted, wavering, undecided, indecisive, vacillating, sitting on the fence (*informal*), unaffiliated, independent 2 = free, wandering, variable, fluctuating, unattached, movable

flock NOUN 1 = herd, group, flight, drove, colony, gaggle, skein 2 = crowd, company, group, host, collection, mass, gathering, herd
• VERB 1 = stream, crowd, mass, swarm, throng 2 = gather, crowd, mass, collect, assemble, herd, huddle, converge

flog = beat, whip, lash, thrash, whack, scourge, hit hard, trounce

flood NOUN 1 = deluge, downpour, inundation, tide, overflow, torrent, spate 2 = torrent, flow, rush, stream, tide, abundance, glut, profusion 3 = series, stream, avalanche, barrage, spate, torrent 4 = outpouring, rush, stream, surge, torrent
• VERB 1 = immerse, swamp, submerge, inundate, drown, cover with water 2 = pour over, swamp, run over, overflow, inundate 3 = engulf, sweep into, overwhelm, surge into, swarm into, pour into 4 = saturate, fill, choke, swamp, glut, oversupply, overfill 5 = stream, flow, rush,

pour, surge

floor NOUN **1** = ground **2** = storey, level, stage, tier
• VERB **1** (*Informal*) = disconcert, stump, baffle, confound, throw (*informal*), defeat, puzzle, bewilder **2** = knock down, fell, knock over, prostrate, deck (*slang*)

flop VERB **1** = slump, fall, drop, collapse, sink **2** = hang down, hang, dangle, sag, droop **3** (*Informal*) = fail, fold (*informal*), founder, fall flat, come unstuck, misfire, go belly-up (*slang*) ≠ succeed
• NOUN (*Informal*) = failure, disaster, fiasco, debacle, washout (*informal*), nonstarter ≠ success

floppy = droopy, soft, loose, limp, sagging, baggy, flaccid, pendulous

floral = flowery, flower-patterned

flounder 1 = falter, struggle, stall, slow down, run into trouble, come unstuck (*informal*), be in difficulties, hit a bad patch **2** = dither, struggle, blunder, be confused, falter, be in the dark, be out of your depth **3** = struggle, struggle, toss, thrash, stumble, fumble, grope

flourish VERB **1** = thrive, increase, advance, progress, boom, bloom, blossom, prosper ≠ fail **2** = succeed, move ahead, go places (*informal*) **3** = grow, thrive, flower, succeed, bloom, blossom, prosper **4** = wave, brandish, display, shake, wield, flaunt
• NOUN **1** = wave, sweep, brandish, swish, swing, twirl **2** = show, display, parade, fanfare **3** = curlicue, sweep, decoration, swirl, plume, embellishment, ornamentation

flourishing = thriving, successful, blooming, prospering, rampant, going places, in the pink

flow VERB **1** = run, course, rush, sweep, move, pass, roll, flood **2** = pour, move, sweep, flood, stream **3** = issue, follow, result, emerge, spring, proceed, arise, derive
• NOUN = stream, current, movement, motion, course, flood, drift, tide

flower NOUN **1** = bloom, blossom, efflorescence **2** = elite, best, prime, finest, pick, choice, cream, crème de la crème (*French*) **3** = height, prime, peak
• VERB **1** = bloom, open, mature, flourish, unfold, blossom **2** = blossom, grow, develop, progress, mature, thrive, flourish, bloom

RELATED WORD
adjective: floral

fluctuate 1 = change, swing, vary, alternate, waver, veer, seesaw **2** = shift, oscillate

fluent = effortless, natural, articulate, well-versed, voluble

fluid NOUN = liquid, solution, juice, liquor, sap
• ADJECTIVE = liquid, flowing, watery, molten, melted, runny, liquefied ≠ solid

flurry 1 = commotion, stir, bustle, flutter, excitement, fuss, disturbance, ado **2** = gust, shower, gale, swirl, squall, storm

flush[1] VERB **1** = blush, colour, glow, redden, turn red, go red **2** *often with* ***out*** = cleanse, wash out, rinse out, flood, swill, hose down **3** = expel, drive, dislodge
• NOUN = blush, colour, glow, reddening, redness, rosiness

flush[2] 1 = level, even, true, flat, square **2** (*Informal*) = wealthy, rich, well-off, in the money (*informal*), well-heeled (*informal*), replete, moneyed

flutter VERB **1** = beat, flap, tremble, ripple, waver, quiver, vibrate, palpitate **2** = flit
• NOUN **1** = tremor, tremble, shiver, shudder, palpitation **2** = vibration, twitching, quiver **3** = agitation, state (*informal*), confusion, excitement, flap (*informal*), dither (*chiefly Brit.*), commotion, fluster

fly 1 = take wing, soar, glide, wing, sail, hover, flutter, flit **2** = pilot, control, operate, steer, manoeuvre, navigate **3** = airlift, send by plane, take by plane, take in an aircraft **4** = flutter, wave, float, flap **5** = display, show, flourish, brandish **6** = rush, race, shoot, career, speed, tear, dash, hurry **7** = pass swiftly, pass, glide, slip away, roll on, flit, elapse, run its course **8** = leave, get away, escape, flee, run for it, skedaddle (*informal*), take to your heels

flying = hurried, brief, rushed, fleeting, short-lived, hasty, transitory

foam NOUN = froth, spray, bubbles, lather, suds, spume, head
• VERB = bubble, boil, fizz, froth, lather, effervesce

focus VERB **1** = concentrate, centre, spotlight, direct, aim, pinpoint, zoom in **2** = fix, train, direct, aim

• NOUN 1 = centre, focal point, central point 2 = focal point, heart, target, hub
foe = enemy, rival, opponent, adversary, antagonist ≠ friend
fog = mist, gloom, haze, smog, murk, miasma, peasouper (*informal*)
foil[1] = thwart, stop, defeat, disappoint, counter, frustrate, hamper, balk
foil[2] = complement, relief, contrast, antithesis
fold VERB 1 = bend, crease, double over 2 (*Informal*) = go bankrupt, fail, crash, collapse, founder, shut down, go under, go bust (*informal*)
• NOUN = crease, gather, bend, overlap, wrinkle, pleat, ruffle, furrow
folk 1 = people, persons, individuals, men and women, humanity, inhabitants, mankind, mortals 2 *usually plural* = family, parents, relations, relatives, tribe, clan, kin, kindred, ainga (*N.Z.*)
follow 1 = accompany, attend, escort, go behind, tag along behind, come behind 2 = pursue, track, dog, hunt, chase, shadow, trail, hound ≠ avoid 3 = come after, go after, come next ≠ precede 4 = result, issue, develop, spring, flow, proceed, arise, ensue 5 = obey, observe, adhere to, stick to, heed, conform to, keep to, pay attention to ≠ ignore 6 = succeed, replace, come after, take over from, come next, supersede, supplant, take the place of 7 = understand, realize, appreciate, take in, grasp, catch on (*informal*), comprehend, fathom 8 = keep up with, support, be interested in, cultivate, be a fan of, keep abreast of
follower = supporter, fan, disciple, devotee, apostle, pupil, adherent, groupie (*slang*) ≠ leader
following ADJECTIVE 1 = next, subsequent, successive, ensuing, later, succeeding, consequent 2 = coming, about to be mentioned
• NOUN = supporters, backing, train, fans, suite, clientele, entourage, coterie
folly = foolishness, nonsense, madness, stupidity, indiscretion, lunacy, imprudence, rashness ≠ wisdom
fond ADJECTIVE 1 = loving, caring, warm, devoted, tender, adoring, affectionate, indulgent ≠ indifferent 2 = unrealistic, empty, naive, vain, foolish, deluded, overoptimistic, delusive ≠ sensible
• PHRASES **fond of** 1 = attached to, in love with, keen on, attracted to, having a soft spot for, enamoured of 2 = keen on, into (*informal*), hooked on, partial to, having a soft spot for, addicted to
fondly 1 = lovingly, tenderly, affectionately, amorously, dearly, possessively, with affection, indulgently 2 = unrealistically, stupidly, vainly, foolishly, naively, credulously
food = nourishment, fare, diet, tucker (*Austral. & N.Z. informal*), rations, nutrition, cuisine, refreshment, nibbles, kai (*N.Z. informal*)
fool NOUN 1 = simpleton, idiot, mug (*Brit. slang*), dummy (*slang*), git (*Brit. slang*), twit (*informal*, *chiefly Brit.*), dunce, imbecile (*informal*), dorba *or* dorb (*Austral. slang*), bogan (*Austral. slang*) ≠ genius 2 = dupe, mug (*Brit. slang*), sucker (*slang*), stooge (*slang*), laughing stock, pushover (*informal*), fall guy (*informal*) 3 = jester, clown, harlequin, buffoon, court jester
• VERB = deceive, mislead, delude, trick, take in, con (*informal*), dupe, beguile
foolish = unwise, silly, absurd, rash, senseless, foolhardy, ill-judged, imprudent ≠ sensible
footing 1 = basis, foundation, base position, groundwork 2 = relationship, position, basis, standing, rank, status, grade
footpath (*Austral. & N.Z.*) = pavement, sidewalk (*U.S. & Canad.*)
footstep = step, tread, footfall
foray = raid, sally, incursion, inroad, attack, assault, invasion, swoop
forbid = prohibit, ban, disallow, exclude, rule out, veto, outlaw, preclude ≠ permit
forbidden = prohibited, banned, vetoed, outlawed, taboo, out of bounds, proscribed
forbidding = threatening, severe, frightening, hostile, menacing, sinister, daunting, ominous ≠ inviting
force VERB 1 = compel, make, drive, press, oblige, constrain, coerce, impel 2 = push, thrust, propel 3 = break open, blast, wrench, prise, wrest
• NOUN 1 = compulsion, pressure, violence, constraint, oppression, coercion, duress, arm-twisting (*informal*) 2 = power, might,

pressure, energy, strength, momentum, impulse, vigour ≠ weakness **3** = intensity, vigour, vehemence, fierceness, emphasis **4** = army, unit, company, host, troop, squad, patrol, regiment
• PHRASES **in force 1** = valid, working, current, effective, binding, operative, operational, in operation **2** = in great numbers, all together, in full strength

forced 1 = compulsory, enforced, mandatory, obligatory, involuntary, conscripted ≠ voluntary **2** = false, affected, strained, wooden, stiff, artificial, contrived, unnatural ≠ natural

forceful 1 = dynamic, powerful, assertive ≠ weak **2** = powerful, strong, convincing, effective, compelling, persuasive, cogent

forecast NOUN = prediction, prognosis, guess, prophecy, conjecture, forewarning
• VERB = predict, anticipate, foresee, foretell, divine, prophesy, augur, forewarn

forefront = lead, centre, front, fore, spearhead, prominence, vanguard, foreground

foreign = alien, exotic, unknown, strange, imported, remote, external, unfamiliar ≠ native

foreigner = alien, incomer, immigrant, non-native, stranger, settler

foremost = leading, best, highest, chief, prime, primary, supreme, most important

foresee = predict, forecast, anticipate, envisage, prophesy, foretell

forever 1 = evermore, always, ever, for good, for keeps, for all time, in perpetuity, till the cows come home (*informal*) **2** = constantly, always, all the time, continually, endlessly, persistently, eternally, perpetually

forfeit VERB = relinquish, lose, give up, surrender, renounce, be deprived of, say goodbye to, be stripped of
• NOUN = penalty, fine, damages, forfeiture, loss, mulct

forge 1 = form, build, create, establish, set up, fashion, shape, frame **2** = fake, copy, reproduce, imitate, counterfeit, feign, falsify **3** = create, make, work, found, form, model, fashion, shape

forget 1 = neglect, overlook, omit, not remember, be remiss, fail to remember **2** = leave behind, lose, lose sight of, mislay

forgive = excuse, pardon, not hold something against, understand, acquit, condone, let off (*informal*), turn a blind eye to ≠ blame

forgiveness = pardon, mercy, absolution, exoneration, amnesty, acquittal, remission

forgotten = unremembered, lost, past, left behind, omitted, bygone, past recall

fork = branch, part, separate, split, divide, diverge, subdivide, bifurcate

forked = branching, split, branched, divided, angled, pronged, zigzag, Y-shaped

form NOUN **1** = type, sort, kind, variety, class, style **2** = shape, formation, configuration, structure, pattern, appearance **3** = condition, health, shape, nick (*informal*), fitness, trim, fettle **4** = document, paper, sheet, questionnaire, application **5** = procedure, etiquette, use, custom, convention, usage, protocol, wont, kawa (*N.Z.*), tikanga (*N.Z.*) **6** = class, year, set, rank, grade, stream
• VERB **1** = arrange, combine, line up, organize, assemble, draw up **2** = make, produce, fashion, build, create, shape, construct, forge **3** = constitute, make up, compose, comprise **4** = establish, start, launch **5** = take shape, grow, develop, materialize, rise, appear, come into being, crystallize **6** = draw up, devise, formulate, organize **7** = develop, pick up, acquire, cultivate, contract

formal 1 = serious, stiff, detached, official, correct, conventional, remote, precise ≠ informal **2** = official, authorized, endorsed, certified, solemn **3** = ceremonial, traditional, solemn, ritualistic, dressy **4** = conventional, established, traditional

formality 1 = correctness, seriousness, decorum, protocol, etiquette **2** = convention, procedure, custom, ritual, rite

format = arrangement, form, style, make-up, look, plan, design, type

formation 1 = establishment, founding, forming, setting up, starting, production, generation, manufacture **2** = development, shaping, constitution, moulding, genesis **3** = arrangement, grouping, design, structure, pattern, organization, array, configuration

former = previous, one-time, erstwhile, earlier, prior, sometime, foregoing ≠ current

formerly = previously, earlier, in the past, at one time, before, lately, once

formidable 1 = impressive, great, powerful, tremendous, mighty, terrific, awesome, invincible 2 = intimidating, threatening, terrifying, menacing, dismaying, fearful, daunting, frightful ≠ encouraging

formula = method, plan, policy, rule, principle, procedure, recipe, blueprint

formulate 1 = devise, plan, develop, prepare, work out, invent, forge, draw up 2 = express, detail, frame, define, specify, articulate, set down, put into words

fort NOUN = fortress, keep, camp, tower, castle, garrison, stronghold, citadel, fortified pa (*N.Z.*)

• PHRASES **hold the fort** (*Informal*) = take responsibility, cover, stand in, carry on, take over the reins, deputize, keep things on an even keel

forte = speciality, strength, talent, strong point, métier, long suit (*informal*), gift ≠ weak point

forth 1 (*Formal or old-fashioned*) = forward, out, away, ahead, onward, outward 2 = out

forthcoming 1 = approaching, coming, expected, future, imminent, prospective, impending, upcoming 2 = available, ready, accessible, at hand, in evidence, obtainable, on tap (*informal*) 3 = communicative, open, free, informative, expansive, sociable, chatty, talkative

fortify 1 = protect, defend, strengthen, reinforce, support, shore up, augment, buttress 2 = strengthen, add alcohol to ≠ dishearten

fortitude = courage, strength, resolution, grit, bravery, backbone, perseverance, valour

fortress = castle, fort, stronghold, citadel, redoubt, fastness, fortified pa (*N.Z.*)

fortunate 1 = lucky, favoured, jammy (*Brit. slang*), in luck ≠ unfortunate 2 = well-off, rich, successful, wealthy, prosperous, affluent, opulent, well-heeled (*informal*) 3 = providential, fortuitous, felicitous, timely, helpful, convenient, favourable, advantageous

fortunately = luckily, happily, as luck would have it, providentially, by good luck, by a happy chance

fortune NOUN 1 = wealth, means, property, riches, resources, assets, possessions, treasure ≠ poverty 2 = luck, fluke (*informal*), stroke of luck, serendipity, twist of fate, run of luck 3 = chance, fate, destiny, providence, the stars, Lady Luck, kismet

• PLURAL NOUN = destiny, lot, experiences, history, condition, success, means, adventures

forward ADVERB 1 = forth, on, ahead, onwards ≠ backward(s) 2 = on, onward, onwards

• ADJECTIVE 1 = leading, first, head, front, advance, foremost 2 = future, advanced, premature, prospective 3 = presumptuous, familiar, bold, cheeky, brash, pushy (*informal*), brazen, shameless ≠ shy

• VERB 1 = further, advance, promote, assist, hurry, hasten, expedite 2 = send on, send, post, pass on, dispatch, redirect

fossick (*Austral. & N.Z.*) = search, hunt, explore, ferret, check, forage, rummage

foster 1 = bring up, mother, raise, nurse, look after, rear, care for, take care of 2 = develop, support, further, encourage, feed, promote, stimulate, uphold ≠ suppress

foul ADJECTIVE 1 = dirty, unpleasant, stinking, filthy, grubby, repellent, squalid, repulsive, festy (*Austral. slang*), yucko (*Austral. slang*) ≠ clean 2 = obscene, crude, indecent, blue, abusive, coarse, vulgar, lewd 3 = unfair, illegal, crooked, shady (*informal*), fraudulent, dishonest, unscrupulous, underhand 4 = offensive, bad, wrong, evil, corrupt, disgraceful, shameful, immoral ≠ admirable

• VERB = dirty, stain, contaminate, pollute, taint, sully, defile, besmirch ≠ clean

found = establish, start, set up, begin, create, institute, organize, constitute

foundation 1 = basis 2 *often plural* = substructure, underpinning, groundwork, bedrock, base, footing, bottom 3 = setting up, institution, instituting, organization, settlement, establishment, initiating, originating

founder[1] = initiator, father, author, architect, creator, beginner, inventor, originator

founder[2] 1 = fail, collapse, break down, fall through, be unsuccessful, come unstuck,

miscarry, misfire **2** = sink, go down, be lost, submerge, capsize, go to the bottom
fountain **1** = font, spring, reservoir, spout, fount, water feature, well **2** = jet, stream, spray, gush **3** = source, fount, wellspring, cause, origin, derivation, fountainhead
fowl = poultry
foyer = entrance hall, lobby, reception area, vestibule, anteroom, antechamber
fraction = percentage, share, section, slice, portion
fracture NOUN **1** = break, split, crack **2** = cleft, opening, split, crack, rift, rupture, crevice, fissure
• VERB **1** = break, crack **2** = split, separate, divide, rend, fragment, splinter, rupture
fragile **1** = unstable, weak, vulnerable, delicate, uncertain, insecure, precarious, flimsy **2** = fine, weak, delicate, frail, brittle, flimsy, dainty, easily broken ≠ durable **3** = delicate, fine, charming, elegant, neat, exquisite, graceful, petite **4** = unwell, poorly, weak, delicate, crook (*Austral. & N.Z. informal*), shaky, frail, feeble, sickly
fragment NOUN = piece, bit, scrap, particle, portion, shred, speck, sliver
• VERB **1** = break, shatter, crumble, disintegrate, splinter, come apart, break into pieces, come to pieces ≠ fuse **2** = break up, split up
fragrance **1** = scent, smell, perfume, bouquet, aroma, sweet smell, sweet odour, redolence ≠ stink **2** = perfume, scent, cologne, eau de toilette, eau de Cologne, toilet water, Cologne water
fragrant = aromatic, perfumed, balmy, redolent, sweet-smelling, sweet-scented, odorous ≠ stinking
frail **1** = feeble, weak, puny, infirm ≠ strong **2** = flimsy, weak, vulnerable, delicate, fragile, insubstantial
frame NOUN **1** = casing, framework, structure, shell, construction, skeleton, chassis **2** = physique, build, form, body, figure, anatomy, carcass
• VERB **1** = mount, case, enclose **2** = surround, ring, enclose, encompass, envelop, encircle, hem in **3** = devise, draft, compose, sketch, put together, draw up, formulate, map out
• PHRASES **frame of mind** = mood, state, attitude, humour, temper, outlook, disposition, mind-set
framework **1** = system, plan, order, scheme, arrangement, the bare bones **2** = structure, body, frame, foundation, shell, skeleton
frank = candid, open, direct, straightforward, blunt, sincere, outspoken, honest ≠ secretive
frankly **1** = honestly, sincerely, in truth, candidly, to tell you the truth, to be frank, to be frank with someone, to be honest **2** = openly, freely, directly, plainly, bluntly, candidly, without reserve
frantic **1** = frenzied, wild, furious, distracted, distraught, berserk, at the end of your tether, beside yourself, berko (*Austral. slang*) ≠ calm **2** = hectic, desperate, frenzied, fraught (*informal*), frenetic
fraternity **1** = companionship, fellowship, brotherhood, kinship, camaraderie **2** = circle, company, guild **3** = brotherhood, club, union, society, league, association
fraud **1** = deception, deceit, treachery, swindling, trickery, duplicity, double-dealing, chicanery ≠ honesty **2** = scam, deception (*slang*) **3** = hoax, trick, con (*informal*), deception, sham, spoof (*informal*), prank, swindle **4** (*Informal*) = impostor, fake, hoaxer, pretender, charlatan, fraudster, swindler, phoney *or* phony (*informal*)
fraudulent = deceitful, crooked (*informal*), untrue, sham, treacherous, dishonest, swindling, double-dealing ≠ genuine
fray = wear thin, wear, rub, wear out, chafe
freak ADJECTIVE = abnormal, chance, unusual, exceptional, unparalleled
• NOUN **1** (*Informal*) = enthusiast, fan, nut (*slang*), addict, buff (*informal*), fanatic, devotee, fiend (*informal*) **2** = aberration, eccentric, anomaly, oddity, monstrosity, malformation **3** = weirdo *or* weirdie (*informal*), eccentric, character (*informal*), oddball (*informal*), nonconformist
free ADJECTIVE **1** = complimentary, for free (*informal*), for nothing, unpaid, for love, free of charge, on the house, without charge **2** = allowed, permitted, unrestricted, unimpeded, clear, able **3** = at liberty, loose, liberated, at large, on the loose ≠ confined **4** = independent, unfettered, footloose **5** = available, empty, spare, vacant, unused, unoccupied,

untaken **6** = generous, liberal, lavish, unstinting, unsparing ≠ mean
• VERB **1** = clear, disengage, cut loose, release, rescue, extricate **2** = release, liberate, let out, set free, deliver, loose, untie, unchain ≠ confine **3** = disentangle, extricate, disengage, loose, unravel, disconnect, untangle

freedom 1 = independence, democracy, sovereignty, self-determination, emancipation, autarchy, rangatiratanga (*N.Z.*) **2** = liberty, release, discharge, emancipation, deliverance ≠ captivity **3** = licence, latitude, free rein, opportunity, discretion, carte blanche, blank cheque ≠ restriction

freely 1 = abundantly, liberally, lavishly, extravagantly, copiously, unstintingly, amply **2** = openly, frankly, plainly, candidly, unreservedly, straightforwardly, without reserve **3** = willingly, readily, voluntarily, spontaneously, without prompting, of your own free will, of your own accord

freeway (*U.S. & Austral.*) = motorway (*Brit.*), autobahn (*German*), autoroute (*French*), autostrada (*Italian*)

freeze 1 = ice over *or* up, harden, stiffen, solidify, become solid **2** = chill **3** = fix, hold, limit, hold up **4** = suspend, stop, shelve, curb, cut short, discontinue

freezing 1 = icy, biting, bitter, raw, chill, arctic, frosty, glacial **2** = frozen, very cold

freight 1 = transportation, traffic, delivery, carriage, shipment, haulage, conveyance, transport **2** = cargo, goods, load, delivery, burden, shipment, merchandise, consignment

French = Gallic

frenzied = uncontrolled, wild, crazy, furious, frantic, frenetic, feverish, rabid

frenzy = fury, passion, rage, seizure, hysteria, paroxysm, derangement ≠ calm

frequent ADJECTIVE = common, repeated, usual, familiar, everyday, persistent, customary, recurrent ≠ infrequent
• VERB = visit, attend, haunt, be found at, patronize, hang out at (*informal*), visit often, go to regularly ≠ keep away

frequently = often, commonly, repeatedly, many times, habitually, not infrequently, much ≠ infrequently

fresh 1 = additional, more, new, other, added, further, extra, supplementary **2** = natural, unprocessed, unpreserved ≠ preserved **3** = new, original, novel, different, recent, modern, up-to-date, unorthodox ≠ old **4** = invigorating, clean, pure, crisp, bracing, refreshing, brisk, unpolluted ≠ stale **5** = cool, cold, refreshing, brisk, chilly, nippy **6** = lively, keen, alert, refreshed, vigorous, energetic, sprightly, spry ≠ weary **7** = cheeky (*Informal*), impertinent, forward, familiar, audacious, disrespectful, presumptuous, insolent ≠ well-mannered

fret = worry, brood, agonize, obsess, lose sleep, upset yourself, distress yourself

friction 1 = conflict, hostility, resentment, disagreement, animosity, discord, bad blood, dissension **2** = resistance, rubbing, scraping, grating, rasping, chafing, abrasion **3** = rubbing, scraping, grating, rasping, chafing, abrasion

friend 1 = companion, pal, mate (*informal*), buddy (*informal*), best friend, close friend, comrade, chum (*informal*), cobber (*Austral. & N.Z.*), E hoa (*N.Z. old-fashioned informal*) ≠ foe **2** = supporter, ally, associate, sponsor, patron, well-wisher

friendly = amiable, welcoming, warm, neighbourly, pally (*informal*), helpful, sympathetic, affectionate = amicable, warm, familiar, pleasant, intimate, informal, cordial, congenial ≠ unfriendly

friendship 1 = attachment, relationship, bond, link, association, tie **2** = friendliness, affection, harmony, goodwill, intimacy, familiarity, rapport, companionship ≠ unfriendliness

fright 1 = fear, shock, alarm, horror, panic, dread, consternation, trepidation ≠ courage **2** = scare, start, turn, surprise, shock, jolt, the creeps (*informal*), the willies (*slang*)

frighten = scare, shock, alarm, terrify, startle, intimidate, unnerve, petrify ≠ reassure

frightened = afraid, alarmed, scared, terrified, shocked, startled, petrified, flustered

frightening = terrifying, shocking, alarming, startling, horrifying, menacing, scary (*informal*), fearful

fringe NOUN **1** = border, edging, edge, trimming, hem, frill, flounce **2** = edge, limits, border, margin, outskirts, perimeter, periphery, borderline
• ADJECTIVE = unofficial, alternative, radical,

innovative, avant-garde, unconventional, unorthodox

front NOUN **1** = head, start, lead, forefront **2** = exterior, face, façade, frontage **3** = foreground, fore, forefront, nearest part **4** = front line, trenches, vanguard, firing line **5** (*Informal*) = disguise, cover, blind, mask, cover-up, cloak, façade, pretext
• ADJECTIVE **1** = foremost, at the front ≠ back **2** = leading, first, lead, head, foremost, topmost
• VERB = face onto, overlook, look out on, have a view of, look over *or* onto

frontier = border, limit, edge, boundary, verge, perimeter, borderline, dividing line

frost = hoarfrost, freeze, rime

frown VERB = glare, scowl, glower, make a face, look daggers, knit your brows, lour *or* lower
• NOUN = scowl, glare, glower, dirty look

frozen 1 = icy, hard, solid, frosted, arctic, ice-covered, icebound **2** = chilled, cold, iced, refrigerated, ice-cold **3** = ice-cold, freezing, numb, very cold, frigid, frozen stiff

fruit 1 = produce, crop, yield, harvest **2** *often plural* = result, reward, outcome, end result, return, effect, benefit, profit

frustrate = thwart, stop, check, block, defeat, disappoint, counter, spoil, crool *or* cruel (*Austral. slang*) ≠ further

frustrated = disappointed, discouraged, infuriated, exasperated, resentful, embittered, disheartened

frustration 1 = annoyance, disappointment, resentment, irritation, grievance, dissatisfaction, exasperation, vexation **2** = obstruction, blocking, foiling, spoiling, thwarting, circumvention

fudge = misrepresent, hedge, stall, flannel (*Brit. informal*), equivocate

fuel = incitement, ammunition, provocation, incentive

fugitive = runaway, refugee, deserter, escapee

fulfil 1 = carry out, perform, complete, achieve, accomplish ≠ neglect **2** = achieve, realize, satisfy, attain, consummate, bring to fruition **3** = satisfy, please, content, cheer, refresh, gratify, make happy **4** = comply with, meet, fill, satisfy, observe, obey, conform to, answer

fulfilment = achievement, implementation, completion, accomplishment, realization, attainment, consummation

full 1 = filled, stocked, brimming, replete, complete, loaded, saturated ≠ empty **2** = satiated, having had enough, replete **3** = extensive, complete, generous, adequate, ample, abundant, plentiful ≠ incomplete **4** = comprehensive, complete, exhaustive, all-embracing **5** = rounded, strong, rich, powerful, intense, pungent **6** = plump, rounded, voluptuous, shapely, well-rounded, buxom, curvaceous **7** = voluminous, large, loose, baggy, billowing, puffy, capacious, loose-fitting ≠ tight **8** = rich, strong, deep, loud, distinct, resonant, sonorous, clear ≠ thin

full-scale = major, wide-ranging, all-out, sweeping, comprehensive, thorough, in-depth, exhaustive

fully 1 = completely, totally, perfectly, entirely, altogether, thoroughly, wholly, utterly **2** = in all respects, completely, totally, entirely, altogether, thoroughly, wholly

fumble = grope, flounder, scrabble, feel around

fume VERB = rage, seethe, see red (*informal*), storm, rant, smoulder, get hot under the collar (*informal*)
• PLURAL NOUN = smoke, gas, exhaust, pollution, vapour, smog

fun NOUN **1** = amusement, sport, pleasure, entertainment, recreation, enjoyment, merriment, jollity **2** = enjoyment, pleasure, mirth ≠ gloom
• ADJECTIVE = enjoyable, entertaining, pleasant, amusing, lively, diverting, witty, convivial
• PHRASES **make fun of something** *or* **someone** = mock, tease, ridicule, poke fun at, laugh at, mimic, parody, send up (*Brit. informal*)

function NOUN **1** = purpose, business, job, use, role, responsibility, task, duty **2** = reception, party, affair, gathering, bash (*informal*), social occasion, soiree, do (*informal*)
• VERB **1** = work, run, operate, perform, go **2** = act, operate, perform, behave, do duty, have the role of

functional 1 = practical, utilitarian, serviceable, hard-wearing, useful

2 = working, operative, operational, going, prepared, ready, viable, up and running

fund NOUN = reserve, stock, supply, store, collection, pool
• PLURAL NOUN = money, capital, cash, finance, means, savings, resources, assets
• VERB = finance, back, support, pay for, subsidize, provide money for, put up the money for

fundamental 1 = central, key, basic, essential, primary, principal, cardinal ≠ incidental 2 = basic, essential, underlying, profound, elementary, rudimentary

fundamentally 1 = basically, at heart, at bottom 2 = essentially, radically, basically, primarily, profoundly, intrinsically

fundi (*S. African*) = expert

funeral = burial, committal, laying to rest, cremation, interment, obsequies, entombment

funny 1 = humorous, amusing, comical, entertaining, comic, witty, hilarious, riotous ≠ unfunny 2 = comic, comical 3 = peculiar, odd, strange, unusual, bizarre, curious, weird, mysterious 4 = ill, poorly (*informal*), sick, odd, crook (*Austral. & N.Z. informal*), ailing, unhealthy, unwell, off-colour (*informal*)

furious 1 = angry, raging, fuming, infuriated, incensed, enraged, inflamed, very angry, tooshie (*Austral. slang*) ≠ pleased 2 = violent, intense, fierce, savage, turbulent, vehement, unrestrained

furnish 1 = decorate, fit out, stock, equip 2 = supply, give, offer, provide, present, grant, hand out

furniture = household goods, furnishings, fittings, house fittings, goods, things (*informal*), possessions, appliances

furore = commotion, to-do, stir, disturbance, outcry, uproar, hullabaloo

further *or* **farther** ADVERB = in addition, moreover, besides, furthermore, also, to boot, additionally, into the bargain
• ADJECTIVE = additional, more, new, other, extra, fresh, supplementary
• VERB = promote, help, develop, forward, encourage, advance, work for, assist ≠ hinder

furthermore = moreover, further, in addition, besides, too, as well, to boot, additionally

furthest *or* **farthest** = most distant, extreme, ultimate, remotest, furthermost, outmost

fury 1 = anger, passion, rage, madness, frenzy, wrath, impetuosity ≠ calmness 2 = violence, force, intensity, severity, ferocity, savagery, vehemence, fierceness ≠ peace

fuss NOUN 1 = commotion, to-do, bother, stir, excitement, ado, hue and cry, palaver 2 = bother, trouble, struggle, hassle (*informal*), nuisance, inconvenience, hindrance 3 = complaint, row, protest, objection, trouble, argument, squabble, furore
• VERB = worry, flap (*informal*), fret, fidget, take pains, be agitated, get worked up

futile = useless, vain, unsuccessful, pointless, worthless, fruitless, ineffectual, unprofitable ≠ useful

future NOUN 1 = time to come, hereafter, what lies ahead 2 = prospect, expectation, outlook
• ADJECTIVE = forthcoming, coming, later, approaching, to come, succeeding, fated, subsequent ≠ past

fuzzy 1 = frizzy, fluffy, woolly, downy 2 = indistinct, blurred, vague, distorted, unclear, bleary, out of focus, ill-defined ≠ distinct

g

gadget = device, thing, appliance, machine, tool, implement, invention, instrument

gag[1] NOUN = muzzle, tie, restraint
• VERB 1 = suppress, silence, muffle, curb, stifle, muzzle, quieten 2 = retch, heave

gag[2] (*Informal*) = joke, crack (*slang*), funny (*informal*), quip, pun, jest, wisecrack (*informal*), witticism

gain VERB 1 = acquire, get, receive, pick up, secure, collect, gather, obtain 2 = profit, get, land, secure, collect, gather, capture, acquire ≠ lose 3 = put on, increase in,

gather, build up **4** = attain, get, reach, get to, secure, obtain, acquire, arrive at
• NOUN **1** = rise, increase, growth, advance, improvement, upsurge, upturn, upswing **2** = profit, return, benefit, advantage, yield, dividend ≠ loss
• PLURAL NOUN = profits, earnings, revenue, proceeds, winnings, takings
• PHRASES **gain on something** *or* **someone** = get nearer to, close in on, approach, catch up with, narrow the gap on

gala = festival, fête, celebration, carnival, festivity, pageant, jamboree

gale 1 = storm, hurricane, tornado, cyclone, blast, typhoon, tempest, squall **2** (*Informal*) = outburst, scream, roar, fit, storm, shout, burst, explosion

gall = annoy, provoke, irritate, trouble, disturb, madden, exasperate, vex

gallop 1 = run, race, career, speed, bolt **2** = dash, run, race, career, speed, rush, sprint

gamble NOUN **1** = risk, chance, venture, lottery, speculation, uncertainty, leap in the dark ≠ certainty **2** = bet, flutter (*informal*), punt (*chiefly Brit.*), wager
• VERB **1** = take a chance, speculate, stick your neck out (*informal*) **2** = risk, chance, hazard, wager **3** = bet, play, game, speculate, punt, wager, have a flutter (*informal*)

game NOUN **1** = pastime, sport, activity, entertainment, recreation, distraction, amusement, diversion ≠ job **2** = match, meeting, event, competition, tournament, clash, contest, head-to-head **3** = amusement, joke, entertainment, diversion **4** = wild animals *or* birds, prey, quarry **5** = scheme, plan, design, trick, plot, tactic, manoeuvre, ploy
• ADJECTIVE **1** = willing, prepared, ready, keen, eager, interested, desirous **2** = brave, courageous, spirited, daring, persistent, gritty, intrepid, plucky ≠ cowardly

gang = group, crowd, pack, company, band, bunch, mob

gangster = hoodlum (*chiefly U.S.*), crook (*informal*), bandit, hood (*U.S. slang*), robber, mobster (*U.S. slang*), racketeer, ruffian, tsotsi (*S. African*)

gap 1 = opening, space, hole, break, crack, slot, aperture, cleft **2** = interval, pause, interruption, respite, lull, interlude, breathing space, hiatus **3** = difference, gulf, contrast, disagreement, discrepancy, inconsistency, disparity, divergence

gape 1 = stare, wonder, goggle, gawp (*Brit. slang*), gawk **2** = open, split, crack, yawn

gaping = wide, great, open, broad, vast, yawning, wide open, cavernous

garland NOUN = wreath, band, bays, crown, honours, laurels, festoon, chaplet
• VERB = adorn, crown, deck, festoon, wreathe

garment *often plural* = clothes, dress, clothing, gear (*slang*), uniform, outfit, costume, apparel

garnish NOUN = decoration, embellishment, adornment, ornamentation, trimming
• VERB = decorate, adorn, ornament, embellish, trim ≠ strip

garrison NOUN **1** = troops, group, unit, section, command, armed force, detachment **2** = fort, fortress, camp, base, post, station, stronghold, fortification, fortified pa (*N.Z.*)
• VERB = station, position, post, install, assign, put on duty

gas 1 = fumes, vapour **2** (*U.S., Canad., & N.Z.*) = petrol, gasoline

gasp VERB = pant, blow, puff, choke, gulp, catch your breath
• NOUN = pant, puff, gulp, sharp intake of breath

gate = barrier, opening, door, entrance, exit, gateway, portal

gather 1 = congregate, assemble, collect, meet, mass, come together, muster, converge ≠ scatter **2** = assemble, collect, bring together, muster, call together ≠ disperse **3** = collect, assemble, accumulate, mass, muster, garner, amass, stockpile **4** = pick, harvest, pluck, reap, garner, glean **5** = build up, rise, increase, grow, expand, swell, intensify, heighten **6** = understand, believe, hear, learn, assume, conclude, presume, infer **7** = fold, tuck, pleat

gathering 1 = assembly, group, crowd, meeting, conference, company, congress, mass, hui (*N.Z.*), runanga (*N.Z.*) **2** = collecting, obtaining, attainment

gauge VERB **1** = measure, calculate, evaluate, value, determine, count, weigh, compute **2** = judge, estimate, guess, assess, evaluate, rate, appraise, reckon

• **NOUN** = meter, dial, measuring instrument

gay **ADJECTIVE 1** = homosexual, lesbian, queer (*informal or derogatory*), moffie (*S. African slang*) **2** = cheerful, lively, sparkling, merry, upbeat (*informal*), buoyant, cheery, carefree ≠ sad **3** = colourful, rich, bright, brilliant, vivid, flamboyant, flashy, showy ≠ drab
• **NOUN** = homosexual, lesbian, auntie *or* aunty (*Austral. slang*), lily (*Austral. slang*) ≠ heterosexual

gaze **VERB** = stare, look, view, watch, regard, gape
• **NOUN** = stare, look, fixed look

gazette = newspaper, paper, journal, periodical, news-sheet

gear **NOUN 1** = mechanism, works, machinery, cogs, cogwheels, gearwheels **2** = equipment, supplies, tackle, tools, instruments, apparatus, paraphernalia, accoutrements **3** = clothing, wear, dress, clothes, outfit, costume, garments, togs
• **VERB** *with **to** or **towards*** = equip, fit, adjust, adapt

gem **1** = precious stone, jewel, stone **2** = treasure, prize, jewel, pearl, masterpiece, humdinger (*slang*), taonga (*N.Z.*)

general **1** = widespread, accepted, popular, public, common, broad, extensive, universal ≠ individual **2** = overall, complete, total, global, comprehensive, blanket, inclusive, all-embracing ≠ restricted **3** = universal, overall, widespread, collective, across-the-board ≠ exceptional **4** = vague, loose, blanket, sweeping, unclear, approximate, woolly, indefinite ≠ specific

generally **1** = usually, commonly, typically, normally, on the whole, by and large, ordinarily, as a rule ≠ occasionally **2** = commonly, widely, publicly, universally, extensively, popularly, conventionally, customarily ≠ individually

generate = produce, create, make, cause, give rise to, engender ≠ end

generation **1** = age group, peer group **2** = age, period, era, time, lifetime, span, epoch

generic = collective, general, common, wide, comprehensive, universal, blanket, inclusive ≠ specific

generosity **1** = liberality, charity, bounty, munificence, beneficence, largesse *or* largess **2** = magnanimity, goodness, kindness, selflessness, charity, unselfishness, high-mindedness, nobleness

generous **1** = liberal, lavish, charitable, hospitable, bountiful, open-handed, unstinting, beneficent ≠ mean **2** = magnanimous, kind, noble, good, high-minded, unselfish, big-hearted **3** = plentiful, lavish, ample, abundant, full, rich, liberal, copious ≠ meagre

genesis = beginning, origin, start, birth, creation, formation, inception ≠ end

genius **1** = brilliance, ability, talent, capacity, gift, bent, excellence, flair **2** = master, expert, mastermind, maestro, virtuoso, whiz (*informal*), hotshot (*informal*), brainbox, fundi (*S. African*) ≠ dunce

genre = type, group, order, sort, kind, class, style, species

gentle **1** = kind, kindly, tender, mild, humane, compassionate, meek, placid ≠ unkind **2** = slow, easy, slight, moderate, gradual, imperceptible **3** = moderate, light, soft, slight, mild, soothing ≠ violent

gentlemanly = chivalrous, refined, polite, civil, courteous, gallant, genteel, well-mannered

genuine **1** = authentic, real, actual, true, valid, legitimate, veritable, bona fide, dinkum (*Austral. & N.Z. informal*) ≠ counterfeit **2** = heartfelt, sincere, honest, earnest, real, true, frank, unaffected ≠ affected **3** = sincere, honest, frank, candid, dinkum (*Austral. & N.Z. informal*), guileless ≠ hypocritical

germ **1** = microbe, virus, bug (*informal*), bacterium, bacillus, microorganism **2** = beginning, root, seed, origin, spark, embryo, rudiment

gesture **NOUN** = sign, action, signal, motion, indication, gesticulation
• **VERB** = signal, sign, wave, indicate, motion, beckon, gesticulate

get **VERB 1** = become, grow, turn, come to be **2** = persuade, convince, induce, influence, entice, incite, impel, prevail upon **3** (*Informal*) = annoy, upset, anger, disturb, trouble, bug (*informal*), irritate, gall **4** = obtain, receive, gain, acquire, win, land, net, pick up **5** = fetch, bring, collect **6** = understand, follow, catch, see, realize,

take in, perceive, grasp **7** = catch, develop, contract, succumb to, fall victim to, go down with, come down with **8** = arrest, catch, grab, capture, seize, take, nab (*informal*), apprehend
• PHRASES **get at someone** = criticize, attack, blame, put down, knock (*informal*), nag, pick on, disparage ◆ **get at something 1** = reach, touch, grasp, get (a) hold of, stretch to **2** = find out, learn, reach, reveal, discover, acquire, detect, uncover **3** = imply, mean, suggest, hint, intimate, lead up to, insinuate ◆ **get by** = manage, survive, cope, fare, exist, get along, make do, muddle through ◆ **get something across** = communicate, pass on, transmit, convey, impart, bring home, make known, put over

ghastly = horrible, shocking, terrible, awful, dreadful, horrendous, hideous, frightful ≠ lovely

ghost 1 = spirit, soul, phantom, spectre, spook (*informal*), apparition, wraith, atua (*N.Z.*), kehua (*N.Z.*), wairua (*N.Z.*) **2** = trace, shadow, suggestion, hint, suspicion, glimmer, semblance
RELATED WORD
adjective: spectral

ghostly = unearthly, phantom, eerie, supernatural, spooky (*informal*), spectral

giant ADJECTIVE = huge, vast, enormous, tremendous, immense, titanic, gigantic, monumental ≠ tiny
• NOUN = ogre, monster, titan, colossus

gidday *or* **g'day** (*Austral. & N.Z.*) = hello, hi (*informal*), greetings, how do you do?, good morning, good evening, good afternoon, welcome, kia ora (*N.Z.*)

gift 1 = donation, offering, present, contribution, grant, legacy, hand-out, endowment, bonsela (*S. African*), koha (*N.Z.*) **2** = talent, ability, capacity, genius, power, capability, flair, knack

gifted = talented, able, skilled, expert, masterly, brilliant, capable, clever ≠ talentless

gigantic = huge, large, giant, massive, enormous, tremendous, immense, titanic ≠ tiny

giggle VERB = laugh, chuckle, snigger, chortle, titter, twitter
• NOUN = laugh, chuckle, snigger, chortle, titter, twitter

girl = female child, lass, lassie (*informal*), miss, maiden (*archaic*), maid (*archaic*)

give VERB **1** = perform, do, carry out, execute **2** = communicate, announce, transmit, pronounce, utter, issue **3** = produce, make, cause, occasion, engender **4** = present, contribute, donate, provide, supply, award, grant, deliver ≠ take **5** = concede, allow, grant **6** = surrender, yield, devote, hand over, relinquish, part with
• PHRASES **give in** = admit defeat, yield, concede, collapse, quit, submit, surrender, succumb ◆ **give something away** = reveal, expose, leak, disclose, betray, uncover, let out, divulge ◆ **give something off** *or* **out** = emit, produce, release, discharge, send out, throw out, exude ◆ **give something up** = abandon, stop, quit, cease, renounce, leave off, desist

glad 1 = happy, pleased, delighted, contented, gratified, joyful, overjoyed ≠ unhappy **2** (*Archaic*) = pleasing, happy, cheering, pleasant, cheerful, gratifying

gladly 1 = happily, cheerfully, gleefully **2** = willingly, freely, happily, readily, cheerfully, with pleasure ≠ reluctantly

glamorous 1 = attractive, elegant, dazzling ≠ unglamorous **2** = exciting, glittering, prestigious, glossy ≠ unglamorous

glamour 1 = charm, appeal, beauty, attraction, fascination, allure, enchantment **2** = excitement, magic, thrill, romance, prestige, glitz (*slang*)

glance VERB = peek, look, view, glimpse, peep ≠ scrutinize
• NOUN = peek, look, glimpse, peep, dekko (*slang*) ≠ good look

glare VERB **1** = scowl, frown, glower, look daggers, lour *or* lower **2** = dazzle, blaze, flare, flame
• NOUN **1** = scowl, frown, glower, dirty look, black look, lour *or* lower **2** = dazzle, glow, blaze, flame, brilliance

glaring 1 = obvious, gross, outrageous, manifest, blatant, conspicuous, flagrant, unconcealed ≠ inconspicuous **2** = dazzling, strong, bright, glowing, blazing ≠ subdued

glaze NOUN = coat, finish, polish, shine, gloss, varnish, enamel, lacquer
• VERB = coat, polish, gloss, varnish, enamel, lacquer

gleam VERB = shine, flash, glow, sparkle, glitter, shimmer, glint, glimmer
• NOUN **1** = glimmer, flash, beam, glow, sparkle **2** = trace, suggestion, hint, flicker, glimmer, inkling

glide = slip, sail, slide

glimpse NOUN = look, sighting, sight, glance, peep, peek
• VERB = catch sight of, spot, sight, view, spy, espy

glitter VERB = shine, flash, sparkle, glare, gleam, shimmer, twinkle, glint
• NOUN **1** = glamour, show, display, splendour, tinsel, pageantry, gaudiness, showiness **2** = sparkle, flash, shine, glare, gleam, sheen, shimmer, brightness

global **1** = worldwide, world, international, universal **2** = comprehensive, general, total, unlimited, exhaustive, all-inclusive ≠ limited

globe = planet, world, earth, sphere, orb

gloom **1** = darkness, dark, shadow, shade, twilight, dusk, obscurity, blackness ≠ light **2** = depression, sorrow, woe, melancholy, unhappiness, despondency, dejection, low spirits ≠ happiness

gloomy **1** = dark, dull, dim, dismal, black, grey, murky, dreary ≠ light **2** = miserable, sad, pessimistic, melancholy, glum, dejected, dispirited, downcast ≠ happy **3** = depressing, bad, dreary, sombre, dispiriting, disheartening, cheerless

glorious **1** = splendid, beautiful, brilliant, shining, superb, gorgeous, dazzling ≠ dull **2** = delightful, fine, wonderful, excellent, marvellous, gorgeous **3** = illustrious, famous, celebrated, distinguished, honoured, magnificent, renowned, eminent ≠ ordinary

glory NOUN **1** = honour, praise, fame, distinction, acclaim, prestige, eminence, renown ≠ shame **2** = splendour, majesty, greatness, grandeur, nobility, pomp, magnificence, pageantry
• VERB = triumph, boast, relish, revel, exult, take delight, pride yourself

gloss[1] = shine, gleam, sheen, polish, brightness, veneer, lustre, patina

gloss[2] NOUN = interpretation, comment, note, explanation, commentary, translation, footnote, elucidation
• VERB = interpret, explain, comment, translate, annotate, elucidate

glossy = shiny, polished, shining, glazed, bright, silky, glassy, lustrous ≠ dull

glow NOUN = light, gleam, splendour, glimmer, brilliance, brightness, radiance, luminosity ≠ dullness
• VERB **1** = shine, burn, gleam, brighten, glimmer, smoulder **2** = be pink

glowing **1** = complimentary, enthusiastic, rave (*informal*), ecstatic, rhapsodic, laudatory, adulatory ≠ scathing **2** = aglow, bright, radiant ≠ pale

glue NOUN = adhesive, cement, gum, paste
• VERB = stick, fix, seal, cement, gum, paste, affix

go VERB **1** = move, travel, advance, journey, proceed, pass, set off ≠ stay **2** = leave, withdraw, depart, move out, slope off, make tracks **3** = elapse, pass, flow, fly by, expire, lapse, slip away **4** = be given, be spent, be awarded, be allotted **5** = function, work, run, move, operate, perform ≠ fail **6** = match, blend, correspond, fit, suit, chime, harmonize **7** = serve, help, tend
• NOUN **1** = attempt, try, effort, bid, shot (*informal*), crack (*informal*) **2** = turn, shot (*informal*), stint **3** (*Informal*) = energy, life, drive, spirit, vitality, vigour, verve, force
• PHRASES **go off** **1** = depart, leave, quit, go away, move out, decamp, slope off **2** = explode, fire, blow up, detonate, come about **3** (*Informal*) = go bad, turn, spoil, rot, go stale ♦ **go out** **1** = see someone, court, date (*informal*, *chiefly U.S.*), woo, go steady (*informal*), be romantically involved with **2** = be extinguished, die out, fade out ♦ **go through something** **1** = suffer, experience, bear, endure, brave, undergo, tolerate, withstand **2** = search, look through, rummage through, rifle through, hunt through, fossick through (*Austral. & N.Z.*), ferret about in **3** = examine, check, search, explore, look through

goal = aim, end, target, purpose, object, intention, objective, ambition

god = deity, immortal, divinity, divine being, supreme being, atua (*N.Z.*)

godly = devout, religious, holy, righteous, pious, good, saintly, god-fearing

gogga (*S. African*) = insect, bug, creepy-crawly (*Brit. informal*)

golden **1** = yellow, blonde, blond, flaxen ≠ dark **2** = successful, glorious, prosperous, rich, flourishing, halcyon ≠ worst

3 = promising, excellent, favourable, opportune ≠ unfavourable

gone 1 = missing, lost, away, vanished, absent, astray 2 = past, over, ended, finished, elapsed

good ADJECTIVE 1 = excellent, great, fine, pleasing, acceptable, first-class, splendid, satisfactory, booshit (*Austral. slang*), exo (*Austral. slang*), sik (*Austral. slang*) ≠ bad 2 = proficient, able, skilled, expert, talented, clever, accomplished, first-class ≠ bad 3 = beneficial, useful, helpful, favourable, wholesome, advantageous ≠ harmful 4 = honourable, moral, worthy, ethical, upright, admirable, honest, righteous ≠ bad 5 = well-behaved, polite, orderly, obedient, dutiful, well-mannered ≠ naughty 6 = kind, kindly, friendly, obliging, charitable, humane, benevolent, merciful ≠ unkind 7 = true, real, genuine, proper, dinkum (*Austral. & N.Z. informal*) 8 = full, complete, extensive ≠ scant 9 = considerable, large, substantial, sufficient, adequate, ample 10 = valid, convincing, compelling, legitimate, authentic, persuasive, bona fide ≠ invalid 11 = convenient, timely, fitting, appropriate, suitable ≠ inconvenient
• NOUN 1 = benefit, interest, gain, advantage, use, profit, welfare, usefulness ≠ disadvantage 2 = virtue, goodness, righteousness, worth, merit, excellence, morality, rectitude ≠ evil
• PHRASES **for good** = permanently, finally, for ever, once and for all, irrevocably

goodbye NOUN = farewell, parting, leave-taking
• INTERJECTION = farewell, see you, see you later, ciao (*Italian*), cheerio, adieu, ta-ta, au revoir (*French*), haere ra (*N.Z.*)

goodness 1 = virtue, honour, merit, integrity, morality, honesty, righteousness, probity ≠ badness 2 = excellence, value, quality, worth, merit, superiority 3 = nutrition, benefit, advantage, wholesomeness, salubriousness 4 = kindness, charity, humanity, goodwill, mercy, compassion, generosity, friendliness

goods 1 = merchandise, stock, products, stuff, commodities, wares 2 = property, things, effects, gear, possessions, belongings, trappings, paraphernalia

goodwill = friendliness, friendship, benevolence, amity, kindliness

gore[1] = blood, slaughter, bloodshed, carnage, butchery

gore[2] = pierce, wound, transfix, impale

gorge NOUN = ravine, canyon, pass, chasm, cleft, fissure, defile, gulch
• VERB 1 = overeat, devour, gobble, wolf, gulp, guzzle 2 *usually reflexive* = stuff, feed, cram, glut

gorgeous 1 = magnificent, beautiful, superb, spectacular, splendid, dazzling, sumptuous ≠ shabby 2 = delightful, good, great, wonderful, excellent, lovely, fantastic, pleasant ≠ awful 3 (*Informal*) = beautiful, lovely, stunning (*informal*), elegant, handsome, exquisite, ravishing ≠ ugly

gospel 1 = doctrine, news, teachings, message, revelation, creed, credo, tidings 2 = truth, fact, certainty, the last word

gossip NOUN 1 = idle talk, scandal, hearsay, tittle-tattle, small talk, chitchat, blether, chinwag (*Brit. informal*) 2 = busybody, chatterbox (*informal*), chatterer, scandalmonger, gossipmonger
• VERB = chat, chatter, jaw (*slang*), blether

gourmet = connoisseur, foodie (*informal*), bon vivant (*French*), epicure, gastronome

govern 1 = rule, lead, control, command, manage, direct, guide, handle 2 = restrain, control, check, master, discipline, regulate, curb, tame

government 1 = administration, executive, ministry, regime, powers-that-be 2 = rule, authority, administration, sovereignty, governance, statecraft

governor = leader, administrator, ruler, head, director, manager, chief, executive, baas (*S. African*)

gown = dress, costume, garment, robe, frock, garb, habit

grab = snatch, catch, seize, capture, grip, grasp, clutch, snap up

grace NOUN 1 = elegance, poise, ease, polish, refinement, fluency, suppleness, gracefulness ≠ ungainliness 2 = manners, decency, etiquette, consideration, propriety, tact, decorum ≠ bad manners 3 = indulgence, mercy, pardon, reprieve 4 = benevolence, favour, goodness, goodwill, generosity, kindness, kindliness ≠ ill will 5 = prayer, thanks, blessing, thanksgiving, benediction 6 = favour,

regard, respect, approval, approbation, good opinion ≠ disfavour
• VERB 1 = adorn, enhance, decorate, enrich, set off, ornament, embellish 2 = honour, favour, dignify ≠ insult

graceful 1 = elegant, easy, pleasing, beautiful ≠ inelegant 2 = polite, mannerly, charming, gracious, civil, courteous, well-mannered

gracious = courteous, polite, civil, accommodating, kind, friendly, cordial, well-mannered ≠ ungracious

grade VERB = classify, rate, order, class, group, sort, range, rank
• NOUN 1 = class 2 degree 3 = level, rank, group, class, stage, category, echelon

gradual = steady, slow, regular, gentle, progressive, piecemeal, unhurried ≠ sudden

gradually = steadily, slowly, progressively, gently, step by step, little by little, by degrees, unhurriedly

graduate 1 = mark off, grade, proportion, regulate, gauge, calibrate, measure out 2 = classify, rank, grade, group, order, sort, arrange

graft NOUN 1 = shoot, bud, implant, sprout, splice, scion 2 (*Informal*) = labour, work, effort, struggle, sweat, toil, slog, exertion
• VERB 1 = join, insert, transplant, implant, splice, affix 2 = work, labour, struggle, sweat (*informal*), slave, strive, toil

grain 1 = seed, kernel, grist 2 = cereal, corn 3 = bit, piece, trace, scrap, particle, fragment, speck, morsel 4 = texture, pattern, surface, fibre, weave, nap

grand 1 = impressive, great, large, magnificent, imposing, splendid, regal, stately ≠ unimposing 2 = ambitious, great, grandiose 3 = superior, great, dignified, stately 4 = excellent, great (*informal*), fine, wonderful, outstanding, smashing (*informal*), first-class, splendid ≠ bad

grandeur = splendour, glory, majesty, nobility, pomp, magnificence, sumptuousness, sublimity

grant NOUN = award, allowance, donation, endowment, gift, subsidy, hand-out
• VERB 1 = give, allow, present, award, permit, assign, allocate, hand out 2 = accept, allow, admit, acknowledge, concede

graphic 1 = vivid, clear, detailed, striking, explicit, expressive ≠ vague 2 = pictorial, visual, diagrammatic ≠ impressionistic

grapple 1 = deal, tackle, struggle, take on, confront, get to grips, address yourself to 2 = struggle, fight, combat, wrestle, battle, clash, tussle, scuffle

grasp VERB 1 = grip, hold, catch, grab, seize, snatch, clutch, clinch 2 = understand, realize, take in, get, see, catch on, comprehend, catch *or* get the drift of
• NOUN 1 = grip, hold, possession, embrace, clutches, clasp 2 = understanding, knowledge, grip, awareness, mastery, comprehension 3 = reach, power, control, scope

grasping = greedy, acquisitive, rapacious, avaricious, covetous, snoep (*S. African informal*) ≠ generous

grate 1 = shred, mince, pulverize 2 = scrape, grind, rub, scratch, creak, rasp

grateful = thankful, obliged, in (someone's) debt, indebted, appreciative, beholden

grating[1] = grille, grid, grate, lattice, trellis, gridiron

grating[2] = irritating, harsh, annoying, jarring, unpleasant, raucous, strident, discordant ≠ pleasing

gratitude = thankfulness, thanks, recognition, obligation, appreciation, indebtedness, gratefulness ≠ ingratitude

grave[1] = tomb, vault, crypt, mausoleum, sepulchre, pit, burying place

grave[2] 1 = serious, important, critical, pressing, threatening, dangerous, acute, severe ≠ trifling 2 = solemn, sober, sombre, dour, unsmiling ≠ carefree

graveyard = cemetery, churchyard, burial ground, charnel house, necropolis

gravity 1 = seriousness, importance, significance, urgency, severity, acuteness, weightiness, momentousness ≠ triviality 2 = solemnity, seriousness, gravitas ≠ frivolity

graze[1] = feed, crop, browse, pasture

graze[2] VERB 1 = scratch, skin, scrape, chafe, abrade 2 = touch, brush, rub, scrape, shave, skim, glance off
• NOUN = scratch, scrape, abrasion

greasy = fatty, slippery, oily, slimy, oleaginous

great 1 = large, big, huge, vast, enormous, immense, gigantic, prodigious ≠ small 2 = important, serious, significant, critical, crucial, momentous ≠ unimportant

3 = famous, outstanding, remarkable, prominent, renowned, eminent, illustrious, noteworthy 4 (*Informal*) = excellent, fine, wonderful, superb, fantastic (*informal*), tremendous (*informal*), marvellous (*informal*), terrific (*informal*), booshit (*Austral. slang*), exo (*Austral. slang*), sik (*Austral. slang*) ≠ poor 5 = very, really, extremely, exceedingly

greatly = very much, hugely, vastly, considerably, remarkably, enormously, immensely, tremendously

greatness 1 = grandeur, glory, majesty, splendour, pomp, magnificence 2 = fame, glory, celebrity, distinction, eminence, note, renown, illustriousness

greed *or* **greediness** 1 = gluttony, voracity 2 = avarice, longing, desire, hunger, craving, selfishness, acquisitiveness, covetousness ≠ generosity

greedy 1 = gluttonous, insatiable, voracious, ravenous, piggish 2 = avaricious, grasping, selfish, insatiable, acquisitive, rapacious, materialistic, desirous ≠ generous

green ADJECTIVE 1 = verdant, leafy, grassy 2 = ecological, conservationist, environment-friendly, ozone-friendly, non-polluting 3 = inexperienced, new, raw, naive, immature, gullible, untrained, wet behind the ears (*informal*) 4 = jealous, grudging, resentful, envious, covetous
• NOUN = lawn, common, turf, sward

greet 1 = salute, hail, say hello to, address, accost 2 = welcome, meet, receive, karanga (*N.Z.*), mihi (*N.Z.*) 3 = receive, take, respond to, react to

greeting = welcome, reception, salute, address, salutation, hongi (*N.Z.*), kia ora (*N.Z.*)

grey 1 = dull, dark, dim, gloomy, drab 2 = boring, dull, anonymous, faceless, colourless, nondescript, characterless 3 = pale, wan, pallid, ashen 4 = ambiguous, uncertain, neutral, unclear, debatable

grief = sadness, suffering, regret, distress, misery, sorrow, woe, anguish ≠ joy

grievance = complaint, gripe (*informal*), axe to grind

grieve 1 = mourn, suffer, weep, lament 2 = sadden, hurt, injure, distress, wound, pain, afflict, upset ≠ gladden

grim = terrible, severe, harsh, forbidding, formidable, sinister

grind VERB 1 = crush, mill, powder, grate, pulverize, pound, abrade, granulate 2 = press, push, crush, jam, mash, force down 3 = grate, scrape, gnash 4 = sharpen, polish, sand, smooth, whet
• NOUN = hard work (*Informal*), labour, sweat (*informal*), chore, toil, drudgery

grip VERB 1 = grasp, hold, catch, seize, clutch, clasp, take hold of 2 = engross, fascinate, absorb, entrance, hold, compel, rivet, enthral
• NOUN 1 = clasp, hold, grasp 2 = control, rule, influence, command, power, possession, domination, mastery 3 = hold, purchase, friction, traction 4 = understanding, sense, command, awareness, grasp, appreciation, mastery, comprehension

gripping = fascinating, exciting, thrilling, entrancing, compelling, riveting, enthralling, engrossing

grit NOUN 1 = gravel, sand, dust, pebbles 2 = courage, spirit, resolution, determination, guts (*informal*), backbone, fortitude, tenacity
• VERB = clench, grind, grate, gnash

gritty 1 = rough, sandy, dusty, rasping, gravelly, granular 2 = courageous, dogged, determined, spirited, brave, resolute, tenacious, plucky

groan VERB 1 = moan, cry, sigh 2 (*Informal*) = complain, object, moan, grumble, gripe (*informal*), carp, lament, whine
• NOUN 1 = moan, cry, sigh, whine 2 (*Informal*) = complaint, protest, objection, grumble, grouse, gripe (*informal*)

groom NOUN 1 = stableman, stableboy, hostler *or* ostler (*archaic*) 2 = newly-wed, husband, bridegroom, marriage partner
• VERB 1 = brush, clean, tend, rub down, curry 2 = smarten up, clean, tidy, preen, spruce up, primp 3 = train, prime, prepare, coach, ready, educate, drill, nurture

groove = indentation, cut, hollow, channel, trench, flute, trough, furrow

grope = feel, search, fumble, flounder, fish, scrabble, cast about, fossick (*Austral. & N.Z.*)

gross ADJECTIVE 1 = flagrant, blatant, rank, sheer, utter, grievous, heinous, unmitigated ≠ qualified 2 = vulgar, offensive, crude, obscene, coarse,

indelicate ≠ decent **3** = fat, obese, overweight, hulking, corpulent ≠ slim **4** = total, whole, entire, aggregate, before tax, before deductions ≠ net
• VERB = earn, make, take, bring in, rake in (*informal*)

grotesque **1** = unnatural, bizarre, strange, fantastic, distorted, deformed, outlandish, freakish ≠ natural **2** = absurd, preposterous ≠ natural

ground NOUN **1** = earth, land, dry land, terra firma **2** = arena, pitch, stadium, park (*informal*), field, enclosure
• PLURAL NOUN **1** = estate, land, fields, gardens, territory **2** = reason, cause, basis, occasion, foundation, excuse, motive, justification **3** = dregs, lees, deposit, sediment
• VERB **1** = base, found, establish, set, settle, fix **2** = instruct, train, teach, initiate, tutor, acquaint with, familiarize with

group NOUN = crowd, party, band, pack, gang, bunch
• VERB = arrange, order, sort, class, classify, marshal, bracket

grove = wood, plantation, covert, thicket, copse, coppice, spinney

grow **1** = develop, get bigger ≠ shrink **2** = get bigger, spread, swell, stretch, expand, enlarge, multiply **3** = cultivate, produce, raise, farm, breed, nurture, propagate **4** = become, get, turn, come to be **5** = originate, spring, arise, stem, issue **6** = improve, advance, progress, succeed, thrive, flourish, prosper

grown-up NOUN = adult, man, woman
• ADJECTIVE = mature, adult, of age, fully-grown

growth **1** = increase, development, expansion, proliferation, enlargement, multiplication ≠ decline **2** = progress, success, improvement, expansion, advance, prosperity ≠ failure **3** (*Medical*) = tumour, cancer, swelling, lump, carcinoma (*Pathology*), sarcoma (*Medical*)

grudge NOUN = resentment, bitterness, grievance, dislike, animosity, antipathy, enmity, rancour ≠ goodwill
• VERB = resent, mind, envy, covet, begrudge ≠ welcome

gruelling = exhausting, demanding, tiring, taxing, severe, punishing, strenuous, arduous ≠ easy

gruesome = horrific, shocking, terrible, horrible, grim, ghastly, grisly, macabre ≠ pleasant

grumble VERB **1** = complain, moan, gripe (*informal*), whinge (*informal*), carp, whine, grouse, bleat **2** = rumble, growl, gurgle
• NOUN **1** = complaint, protest, objection, moan, grievance, grouse, gripe (*informal*), grouch (*informal*) **2** = rumble, growl, gurgle

guarantee VERB **1** = ensure, secure, assure, warrant, make certain **2** = promise, pledge, undertake
• NOUN **1** = promise, pledge, assurance, certainty, word of honour **2** = warranty, contract, bond

guard VERB = protect, defend, secure, mind, preserve, shield, safeguard, watch over
• NOUN **1** = sentry, warder, warden, custodian, watch, lookout, watchman, sentinel **2** = shield, security, defence, screen, protection, safeguard, buffer

guarded = cautious, reserved, careful, suspicious, wary, prudent, reticent, circumspect

guardian = keeper, champion, defender, guard, warden, curator, protector, custodian

guerrilla = freedom fighter, partisan, underground fighter

guess VERB **1** = estimate, predict, work out, speculate, conjecture, postulate, hypothesize ≠ know **2** = suppose, think, believe, suspect, judge, imagine, reckon, fancy
• NOUN **1** = estimate, speculation, judgment, hypothesis, conjecture, shot in the dark ≠ certainty **2** = supposition, idea, theory, hypothesis

guest = visitor, company, caller, manu(w)hiri (*N.Z.*)

guidance = advice, direction, leadership, instruction, help, management, teaching, counselling

guide NOUN **1** = handbook, manual, guidebook, instructions, catalogue **2** = directory, street map **3** = escort, leader, usher **4** = pointer, sign, landmark, marker, beacon, signpost, guiding light, lodestar **5** = model, example, standard, ideal, inspiration, paradigm
• VERB **1** = lead, direct, escort, conduct, accompany, shepherd, usher, show the way **2** = steer, control, manage,

direct, handle, command, manoeuvre **3** = supervise, train, teach, influence, advise, counsel, instruct, oversee

guild = society, union, league, association, company, club, order, organization

guilt **1** = shame, regret, remorse, contrition, guilty conscience, self-reproach ≠ pride **2** = culpability, blame, responsibility, misconduct, wickedness, sinfulness, guiltiness ≠ innocence

guilty **1** = ashamed, sorry, rueful, sheepish, contrite, remorseful, regretful, shamefaced ≠ proud **2** = culpable, responsible, to blame, offending, erring, at fault, reprehensible, blameworthy ≠ innocent

guise **1** = form, appearance, shape, aspect, mode, semblance **2** = pretence, disguise, aspect, semblance

gulf **1** = bay, bight, sea inlet **2** = chasm, opening, split, gap, separation, void, rift, abyss

gum NOUN = glue, adhesive, resin, cement, paste
• VERB = stick, glue, affix, cement, paste

gun = firearm, shooter (*slang*), piece (*slang*), handgun

gunman = armed man, gunslinger (*U.S. slang*)

guru **1** = authority, expert, leader, master, pundit, Svengali, fundi (*S. African*) **2** = teacher, mentor, sage, master, tutor

gush VERB **1** = flow, run, rush, flood, pour, stream, cascade, spurt **2** = enthuse, rave, spout, overstate, effuse
• NOUN = stream, flow, rush, flood, jet, cascade, torrent, spurt

gut NOUN = paunch (*Informal*), belly, spare tyre (*Brit. slang*), potbelly, puku (*N.Z.*)
• PLURAL NOUN **1** = intestines, insides (*informal*), stomach, belly, bowels, innards (*informal*), entrails **2** (*Informal*) = courage, spirit, nerve, daring, pluck, backbone, bottle (*slang*), audacity
• VERB **1** = disembowel, clean **2** = ravage, empty, clean out, despoil
• ADJECTIVE = instinctive, natural, basic, spontaneous, intuitive, involuntary, heartfelt, unthinking

gutter = drain, channel, ditch, trench, trough, conduit, sluice

guy (*Informal*) = man, person, fellow, lad, bloke (*Brit. informal*), chap

Gypsy *or* **Gipsy** = traveller, roamer, wanderer, Bohemian, rover, rambler, nomad, Romany

h

habit **1** = mannerism, custom, way, practice, characteristic, tendency, quirk, propensity **2** = addiction, dependence, compulsion

hack[1] = cut, chop, slash, mutilate, mangle, mangulate (*Austral. slang*), hew, lacerate

hack[2] = reporter, writer, correspondent, journalist, scribbler, contributor, literary hack

hail[1] VERB **1** = acclaim, honour, acknowledge, cheer, applaud ≠ condemn **2** = salute, greet, address, welcome, say hello to, halloo ≠ snub **3** = flag down, summon, signal to, wave down
• PHRASES **hail from somewhere** = come from, be born in, originate in, be a native of, have your roots in

hail[2] NOUN **1** = hailstones, sleet, hailstorm, frozen rain **2** = shower, rain, storm, battery, volley, barrage, bombardment, downpour
• VERB **1** = rain, shower, pelt **2** = batter, rain, bombard, pelt, rain down on, beat down upon

hair = locks, mane, tresses, shock, mop, head of hair

hairdresser = stylist, barber, coiffeur *or* coiffeuse

hairy **1** = shaggy, woolly, furry, stubbly, bushy, unshaven, hirsute **2** (*Slang*) = dangerous, risky, unpredictable, hazardous, perilous

hale (*Old-fashioned*) = healthy, well, strong, sound, fit, flourishing, robust, vigorous

half NOUN = fifty per cent, equal part
• ADJECTIVE = partial, limited, moderate, halved
• ADVERB = partially, partly, in part
RELATED WORDS
prefixes: bi-, demi-, hemi-, semi-

halfway ADVERB = midway, to *or* in the middle
• ADJECTIVE = midway, middle, mid, central, intermediate, equidistant

hall **1** = passage, lobby, corridor, hallway,

foyer, entry, passageway, entrance hall **2** = meeting place, chamber, auditorium, concert hall, assembly room

hallmark 1 = trademark, sure sign, telltale sign **2** (*Brit.*) = mark, sign, device, stamp, seal, symbol

halt VERB **1** = stop, break off, stand still, wait, rest ≠ continue **2** = come to an end, stop, cease **3** = hold back, end, check, block, curb, terminate, cut short, bring to an end ≠ aid

• NOUN = stop, end, close, pause, standstill, stoppage ≠ continuation

halting = faltering, stumbling, awkward, hesitant, laboured, stammering, stuttering

halve 1 = cut in half, reduce by fifty per cent, decrease by fifty per cent, lessen by fifty per cent **2** = split in two, cut in half, bisect, divide in two, share equally, divide equally

hammer 1 = hit, drive, knock, beat, strike, tap, bang **2** (*Informal*) = defeat, beat, thrash, trounce, run rings around (*informal*), wipe the floor with (*informal*), drub

hamper = hinder, handicap, prevent, restrict, frustrate, hamstring, interfere with, obstruct ≠ help

hand NOUN **1** = palm, fist, paw (*informal*), mitt (*slang*) **2** = worker, employee, labourer, workman, operative, craftsman, artisan, hired man **3** = round of applause, clap, ovation, big hand **4** = writing, script, handwriting, calligraphy

• VERB = give, pass, hand over, present to, deliver

handbook = guidebook, guide, manual, instruction book

handcuff VERB = shackle, secure, restrain, fetter, manacle

• PLURAL NOUN = shackles, cuffs (*informal*), fetters, manacles

handful = few, sprinkling, small amount, smattering, small number ≠ a lot

handicap NOUN **1** = disability, defect, impairment, physical abnormality **2** = disadvantage, barrier, restriction, obstacle, limitation, drawback, stumbling block, impediment ≠ advantage **3** = advantage, head start

• VERB = hinder, limit, restrict, burden, hamstring, hamper, hold back, impede ≠ help

handle NOUN = grip, hilt, haft, stock

• VERB **1** = manage, deal with, tackle, cope with **2** = deal with, manage **3** = control, manage, direct, guide, manipulate, manoeuvre **4** = hold, feel, touch, pick up, finger, grasp

handsome 1 = good-looking, attractive, gorgeous, elegant, personable, dishy (*informal*, *chiefly Brit.*), comely ≠ ugly **2** = generous, large, princely, liberal, considerable, lavish, ample, abundant ≠ mean

handy 1 = useful, practical, helpful, neat, convenient, easy to use, manageable, user-friendly ≠ useless **2** = convenient, close, available, nearby, accessible, on hand, at hand, within reach ≠ inconvenient **3** = skilful, skilled, expert, adept, deft, proficient, adroit, dexterous ≠ unskilled

hang VERB **1** = dangle, swing, suspend **2** = lower, suspend, dangle **3** = lean **4** = execute, lynch, string up (*informal*)

• PHRASES **get the hang of something** = grasp, understand, learn, master, comprehend, catch on to, acquire the technique of ◆ **hang back** = be reluctant, hesitate, hold back, recoil, demur

hangover = aftereffects, morning after (*informal*)

hang-up (*Informal*) = preoccupation, thing (*informal*), problem, block, difficulty, obsession, mania, inhibition

hank = coil, roll, length, bunch, piece, loop, clump, skein

happen 1 = occur, take place, come about, result, develop, transpire (*informal*), come to pass **2** = chance, turn out (*informal*)

happening = event, incident, experience, affair, proceeding, episode, occurrence

happily 1 = luckily, fortunately, providentially, opportunely **2** = joyfully, cheerfully, gleefully, blithely, merrily, gaily, joyously **3** = willingly, freely, gladly, with pleasure

happiness = pleasure, delight, joy, satisfaction, ecstasy, bliss, contentment, elation ≠ unhappiness

happy 1 = pleased, delighted, content, thrilled, glad, cheerful, merry, ecstatic **2** = contented, joyful, blissful ≠ sad **3** = fortunate, lucky, timely, favourable, auspicious, propitious, advantageous ≠ unfortunate

harass = annoy, trouble, bother, harry, plague, hound, hassle (*informal*), persecute
harassed = hassled, worried, troubled, strained, under pressure, tormented, distraught (*informal*), vexed
harassment = hassle, trouble, bother, irritation, persecution (*informal*), nuisance, annoyance, pestering
harbour NOUN = port, haven, dock, mooring, marina, pier, wharf, anchorage
• VERB 1 = hold, bear, maintain, nurse, retain, foster, entertain, nurture 2 = shelter, protect, hide, shield, provide refuge, give asylum to
hard ADJECTIVE 1 = tough, strong, firm, solid, stiff, rigid, resistant, compressed ≠ soft 2 = difficult, involved, complicated, puzzling, intricate, perplexing, impenetrable, thorny ≠ easy 3 = exhausting, tough, exacting, rigorous, gruelling, strenuous, arduous, laborious ≠ easy 4 = harsh, cold, cruel, stern, callous, unkind, unsympathetic, pitiless ≠ kind 5 = grim, painful, distressing, harsh, unpleasant, intolerable, grievous, disagreeable
• ADVERB 1 = strenuously, steadily, persistently, doggedly, diligently, energetically, industriously, untiringly 2 = intently, closely, carefully, sharply, keenly 3 = forcefully, strongly, heavily, sharply, severely, fiercely, vigorously, intensely ≠ softly
harden 1 = solidify, set, freeze, cake, bake, clot, thicken, stiffen 2 = accustom, season, toughen, train, inure, habituate
hardened 1 = habitual, chronic, shameless, inveterate, incorrigible ≠ occasional 2 = seasoned, experienced, accustomed, toughened, inured, habituated ≠ naive
hardly 1 = barely, only just, scarcely, just, with difficulty, with effort ≠ completely 2 = only just, just, barely, scarcely
hardship = suffering, need, difficulty, misfortune, adversity, tribulation, privation ≠ ease
hardy = strong, tough, robust, sound, rugged, sturdy, stout ≠ frail
harm VERB 1 = injure, hurt, wound, abuse, ill-treat, maltreat ≠ heal 2 = damage, hurt, ruin, spoil
• NOUN 1 = injury, suffering, damage, ill, hurt, distress 2 = damage, loss, ill, hurt, misfortune, mischief ≠ good
harmful = damaging, dangerous, negative, destructive, hazardous, unhealthy, detrimental, hurtful ≠ harmless
harmless 1 = safe, benign, wholesome, innocuous, nontoxic ≠ dangerous 2 = inoffensive, innocent, innocuous, gentle, tame, unobjectionable
harmony 1 = accord, peace, agreement, friendship, sympathy, cooperation, rapport, compatibility ≠ conflict 2 = tune, melody, unison, tunefulness, euphony ≠ discord
harness VERB = exploit, control, channel, employ, utilize, mobilize
• NOUN = equipment, tackle, gear, tack
harrowing = distressing, disturbing, painful, terrifying, traumatic, tormenting, agonizing, nerve-racking
harry = pester, bother, plague, harass, hassle (*informal*), badger, chivvy
harsh 1 = severe, hard, tough, stark, austere, inhospitable 2 = bleak, freezing, severe, icy 3 = cruel, savage, ruthless, barbarous, pitiless 4 = hard, severe, cruel, stern, pitiless ≠ kind 5 = drastic, punitive, Draconian 6 = raucous, rough, grating, strident, rasping, discordant, guttural, dissonant ≠ soft
harshly = severely, roughly, cruelly, strictly, sternly, brutally
harvest NOUN 1 = harvesting, picking, gathering, collecting, reaping, harvest-time 2 = crop, yield, year's growth, produce
• VERB = gather, pick, collect, bring in, pluck, reap
hassle (*Informal*) NOUN = trouble, problem, difficulty, bother, grief (*informal*), uphill (*S. African*), inconvenience
• VERB = bother, bug (*informal*), annoy, hound, harass, badger, pester
hasten = rush, race, fly, speed, dash, hurry (up), scurry, make haste ≠ dawdle
hastily 1 = quickly, rapidly, promptly, speedily 2 = hurriedly, rashly, precipitately, impetuously
hatch 1 = incubate, breed, sit on, brood, bring forth 2 = devise, design, invent, put together, conceive, brew, formulate, contrive
hate VERB 1 = detest, loathe, despise, dislike, abhor, recoil from, not be able to

bear ≠ love **2** = dislike, detest, shrink from, recoil from, not be able to bear ≠ like **3** = be unwilling, regret, be reluctant, hesitate, be sorry, be loath, feel disinclined
• **NOUN** = dislike, hostility, hatred, loathing, animosity, aversion, antipathy, enmity ≠ love

hatred = hate, dislike, animosity, aversion, revulsion, antipathy, enmity, repugnance ≠ love

haul VERB = drag, draw, pull, heave
• **NOUN** = yield, gain, spoils, catch, harvest, loot, takings, booty

haunt VERB = plague, trouble, obsess, torment, possess, stay with, recur, prey on
• **NOUN** = meeting place, hangout (*informal*), rendezvous, stamping ground

haunted 1 = possessed, ghostly, cursed, eerie, spooky (*informal*), jinxed **2** = preoccupied, worried, troubled, plagued, obsessed, tormented

haunting = evocative, poignant, unforgettable

have VERB 1 = own, keep, possess, hold, retain, boast, be the owner of **2** = get, obtain, take, receive, accept, gain, secure, acquire **3** = suffer, experience, undergo, sustain, endure, be suffering from **4** = give birth to, bear, deliver, bring forth, beget **5** = experience, go through, undergo, meet with, come across, run into, be faced with
• **PHRASES have someone on** = tease, kid (*informal*), wind up (*Brit. slang*), trick, deceive, take the mickey, pull someone's leg ♦ **have something on** = wear, be wearing, be dressed in, be clothed in, be attired in ♦ **have to 1** = must, should, be forced, ought, be obliged, be bound, have got to, be compelled **2** = have got to, must

haven = sanctuary, shelter, retreat, asylum, refuge, oasis, sanctum

havoc 1 = devastation, damage, destruction, ruin **2** (*Informal*) = disorder, confusion, chaos, disruption, mayhem, shambles

hazard NOUN = danger, risk, threat, problem, menace, peril, jeopardy, pitfall
• **VERB** = jeopardize, risk, endanger, threaten, expose, imperil, put in jeopardy
• **PHRASES hazard a guess** = guess, conjecture, presume, take a guess

hazardous = dangerous, risky, difficult, insecure, unsafe, precarious, perilous, dicey (*informal, chiefly Brit.*) ≠ safe

haze = mist, cloud, fog, obscurity, vapour

head NOUN 1 = skull, crown, pate, nut (*slang*), loaf (*slang*) **2** = mind, reasoning, understanding, thought, sense, brain, brains (*informal*), intelligence **3** = top, crown, summit, peak, crest, pinnacle **4** (*Informal*) = head teacher, principal **5** = leader, president, director, manager, chief, boss (*informal*), captain, master
• **ADJECTIVE** = chief, main, leading, first, prime, premier, supreme, principal
• **VERB 1** = lead, precede, be the leader of, be *or* go first, be *or* go at the front of, lead the way **2** = top, lead, crown, cap **3** = be in charge of, run, manage, lead, control, direct, guide, command
• **PHRASES go to your head 1** = intoxicate **2** = make someone conceited, puff someone up, make someone full of themselves ♦ **head over heels** = completely, thoroughly, utterly, intensely, wholeheartedly, uncontrollably

headache 1 = migraine, head (*informal*), neuralgia **2** = problem (*Informal*), worry, trouble, bother, nuisance, inconvenience, bane, vexation

heading = title, name, caption, headline, rubric

heady 1 = exciting, thrilling, stimulating, exhilarating, intoxicating **2** = intoxicating, strong, potent, inebriating

heal 1 *sometimes with* **up** = mend, get better, get well, cure, regenerate, show improvement **2** = cure, restore, mend, make better, remedy, make good, make well ≠ injure

health 1 = condition, state, shape, constitution, fettle **2** = wellbeing, strength, fitness, vigour, good condition, soundness, robustness, healthiness ≠ illness **3** = state, condition, shape

healthy 1 = well, fit, strong, active, robust, in good shape (*informal*), in the pink, in fine fettle ≠ ill **2** = wholesome, beneficial, nourishing, nutritious, salutary, hygienic, salubrious ≠ unwholesome **3** = invigorating, beneficial, salutary, salubrious

heap NOUN 1 = pile, lot, collection, mass, stack, mound, accumulation, hoard **2** *often plural* (*Informal*) = a lot, lots (*informal*), plenty, masses, load(s) (*informal*), great

deal, tons, stack(s)
• VERB *sometimes with **up*** = pile, collect, gather, stack, accumulate, amass, hoard
• PHRASES **heap something on someone** = load with, confer on, assign to, bestow on, shower upon

hear **1** = overhear, catch, detect **2** = listen to **3** (*Law*) = try, judge, examine, investigate **4** = learn, discover, find out, pick up, gather, ascertain, get wind of (*informal*)

hearing = inquiry, trial, investigation, industrial tribunal

heart NOUN **1** = emotions, feelings, love, affection **2** = nature, character, soul, constitution, essence, temperament, disposition **3** = root, core, centre, nucleus, hub, gist, nitty-gritty (*informal*), nub **4** = courage, will, spirit, purpose, bottle (*Brit. informal*), resolution, resolve, stomach
• PHRASES **by heart** = from *or* by memory, verbatim, word for word, pat, word-perfect, by rote, off by heart, off pat
RELATED WORD
adjective: cardiac

heat VERB *sometimes with **up*** = warm (up), cook, boil, roast, reheat, make hot ≠ chill
• NOUN **1** = warmth, hotness, temperature ≠ cold **2** = hot weather, warmth, closeness, high temperature, heatwave, warm weather, hot climate, mugginess **3** = passion, excitement, intensity, fury, fervour, vehemence ≠ calmness
RELATED WORD
adjective: thermal

heated **1** = impassioned, intense, spirited, excited, angry, furious, fierce, lively ≠ calm **2** = wound up, worked up, keyed up, het up (*informal*)

heaven NOUN **1** = paradise, next world, hereafter, nirvana (*Buddhism*, *Hinduism*), bliss, Zion (*Christianity*), life everlasting, Elysium *or* Elysian fields (*Greek myth*) **2** (*Informal*) = happiness, paradise, ecstasy, bliss, utopia, rapture, seventh heaven
• PHRASES **the heavens** (*Old-fashioned*) = sky, ether, firmament

heavenly **1** = celestial, holy, divine, blessed, immortal, angelic ≠ earthly **2** (*Informal*) = wonderful, lovely, delightful, beautiful, divine (*informal*), exquisite, sublime, blissful ≠ awful

heavily **1** = excessively, to excess, very much, a great deal, considerably, copiously, without restraint, immoderately **2** = densely, closely, thickly, compactly **3** = hard, clumsily, awkwardly, weightily

heavy **1** = weighty, large, massive, hefty, bulky, ponderous ≠ light **2** = intensive, severe, serious, concentrated, fierce, excessive, relentless **3** = considerable, large, huge, substantial, abundant, copious, profuse ≠ slight

hectic = frantic, chaotic, heated, animated, turbulent, frenetic, feverish ≠ peaceful

hedge VERB = prevaricate, evade, sidestep, duck, dodge, flannel (*Brit. informal*), equivocate, temporize
• PHRASES **hedge against something** = protect against, insure against, guard against, safeguard against, shield against, cover against

heed (*Formal*) VERB = pay attention to, listen to, take notice of, follow, consider, note, observe, obey ≠ ignore
• NOUN = thought, care, mind, attention, regard, respect, notice ≠ disregard

heel (*Slang*) = swine, cad (*Brit. informal*), bounder (*Brit. old-fashioned slang*), rotter (*slang, chiefly Brit.*)

hefty (*Informal*) = big, strong, massive, strapping, robust, muscular, burly, hulking ≠ small

height **1** = tallness, stature, highness, loftiness ≠ shortness **2** = altitude, measurement, highness, elevation, tallness ≠ depth **3** = peak, top, crown, summit, crest, pinnacle, apex ≠ valley **4** = culmination, climax, zenith, limit, maximum, ultimate ≠ low point

heighten = intensify, increase, add to, improve, strengthen, enhance, sharpen, magnify

heir = successor, beneficiary, inheritor, heiress (*fem.*), next in line

hell **1** = the underworld, the abyss, Hades (*Greek myth*), hellfire, the inferno, fire and brimstone, the nether world, the bad fire (*informal*) **2** (*Informal*) = torment, suffering, agony, nightmare, misery, ordeal, anguish, wretchedness

hello = hi (*informal*), greetings, how do you do?, good morning, good evening, good afternoon, welcome, kia ora (*N.Z.*), gidday *or* g'day (*Austral. & N.Z.*)

helm (*Nautical*) = tiller, wheel, rudder

help VERB **1** *sometimes with **out*** = aid,

support, assist, cooperate with, abet, lend a hand, succour ≠ hinder **2** = improve, ease, relieve, facilitate, alleviate, mitigate, ameliorate ≠ make worse **3** = assist, aid, support **4** = resist, refrain from, avoid, prevent, keep from
• **NOUN** = assistance, aid, support, advice, guidance, cooperation, helping hand ≠ hindrance

helper = assistant, ally, supporter, mate, second, aide, attendant, collaborator

helpful **1** = cooperative, accommodating, kind, friendly, neighbourly, sympathetic, supportive, considerate **2** = useful, practical, profitable, constructive **3** = beneficial, advantageous

helping = portion, serving, ration, piece, dollop (*informal*), plateful

helpless = powerless, weak, disabled, incapable, paralysed, impotent, infirm ≠ powerful

hem **NOUN** = edge, border, margin, trimming, fringe
• **PHRASES** **hem something** *or* **someone in** **1** = surround, confine, enclose, shut in **2** = restrict, confine, beset, circumscribe

hence = therefore, thus, consequently, for this reason, in consequence, ergo, on that account

herald **VERB** = indicate, promise, usher in, presage, portend, foretoken
• **NOUN** **1** (*Often literary*) = forerunner, sign, signal, indication, token, omen, precursor, harbinger **2** = messenger, courier, proclaimer, announcer, crier, town crier

herd = flock, crowd, collection, mass, drove, mob, swarm, horde

hereditary **1** = genetic, inborn, inbred, transmissible, inheritable **2** (*Law*) = inherited, passed down, traditional, ancestral

heritage = inheritance, legacy, birthright, tradition, endowment, bequest

hero **1** = protagonist, leading man **2** = star, champion, victor, superstar, conqueror **3** = idol, favourite, pin-up (*slang*), fave (*informal*)

heroic = courageous, brave, daring, fearless, gallant, intrepid, valiant, lion-hearted ≠ cowardly

heroine **1** = protagonist, leading lady, diva, prima donna **2** = idol, favourite, pin-up (*slang*), fave (*informal*)

hesitate **1** = waver, delay, pause, wait, doubt, falter, dither (*chiefly Brit.*), vacillate ≠ be decisive **2** = be reluctant, be unwilling, shrink from, think twice, scruple, demur, hang back, be disinclined ≠ be determined

hesitation = reluctance, reservation(s), misgiving(s), ambivalence, qualm(s), unwillingness, scruple(s), compunction

hidden **1** = secret, veiled, latent **2** = concealed, secret, covert, unseen, clandestine, secreted, under wraps

hide¹ **1** = conceal, stash (*informal*), secrete, put out of sight ≠ display **2** = go into hiding, take cover, keep out of sight, hole up, lie low, go underground, go to ground, go to earth **3** = keep secret, suppress, withhold, keep quiet about, hush up, draw a veil over, keep dark, keep under your hat ≠ disclose **4** = obscure, cover, mask, disguise, conceal, veil, cloak, shroud ≠ reveal

hide² = skin, leather, pelt

hideous = ugly, revolting, ghastly, monstrous, grotesque, gruesome, grisly, unsightly ≠ beautiful

hiding (*Informal*) = beating, whipping, thrashing, licking (*informal*), spanking, walloping (*informal*), drubbing

hierarchy = grading, ranking, social order, pecking order, class system, social stratum

high **ADJECTIVE** **1** = tall, towering, soaring, steep, elevated, lofty ≠ short **2** = extreme, great, acute, severe, extraordinary, excessive ≠ low **3** = strong, violent, extreme, blustery, squally, sharp **4** = important, chief, powerful, superior, eminent, exalted ≠ lowly **5** = high-pitched, piercing, shrill, penetrating, strident, sharp, acute, piping ≠ deep **6** (*Informal*) = intoxicated, stoned (*slang*), tripping (*informal*)
• **ADVERB** = way up, aloft, far up, to a great height

high-flown = extravagant, elaborate, pretentious, exaggerated, inflated, lofty, grandiose, overblown ≠ straightforward

highlight **VERB** = emphasize, stress, accent, show up, underline, spotlight, accentuate, call attention to ≠ play down
• **NOUN** = high point, peak, climax, feature, focus, focal point, high spot ≠ low point

highly = extremely, very, greatly, vastly, exceptionally, immensely, tremendously

hijack = seize, take over, commandeer, expropriate
hike NOUN = walk, march, trek, ramble, tramp, traipse
• VERB = walk, march, trek, ramble, tramp, back-pack
hilarious 1 = funny, entertaining, amusing, hysterical, humorous, comical, side-splitting 2 = merry, uproarious, rollicking ≠ serious
hill = mount, fell, height, mound, hilltop, tor, knoll, hillock, kopje *or* koppie (*S. African*)
hinder = obstruct, stop, check, block, delay, frustrate, handicap, interrupt ≠ help
hint NOUN 1 = clue, suggestion, implication, indication, pointer, allusion, innuendo, intimation 2 *often plural* = advice, help, tip(s), suggestion(s), pointer(s) 3 = trace, touch, suggestion, dash, suspicion, tinge, undertone
• VERB *sometimes with* ***at*** = suggest, indicate, imply, intimate, insinuate
hire VERB 1 = employ, commission, take on, engage, appoint, sign up, enlist 2 = rent, charter, lease, let, engage
• NOUN 1 = rental, hiring, rent, lease 2 = charge, rental, price, cost, fee
hiss VERB 1 = whistle, wheeze, whiz, whirr, sibilate 2 = jeer, mock, deride
• NOUN = fizz, buzz, hissing, fizzing, sibilation
historic = significant, notable, momentous, famous, extraordinary, outstanding, remarkable, ground-breaking ≠ unimportant
historical = factual, real, documented, actual, authentic, attested ≠ contemporary
history 1 = the past, antiquity, yesterday, yesteryear, olden days 2 = chronicle, record, story, account, narrative, recital, annals
hit VERB 1 = strike, beat, knock, bang, slap, smack, thump, clout (*informal*) 2 = collide with, run into, bump into, clash with, smash into, crash against, bang into 3 = affect, damage, harm, ruin, devastate, overwhelm, touch, impact on 4 = reach, gain, achieve, arrive at, accomplish, attain
• NOUN 1 = shot, blow 2 = blow, knock, stroke, belt (*informal*), rap, slap, smack, clout (*informal*) 3 = success, winner, triumph, smash (*informal*), sensation
• PHRASES **hit it off** (*Informal*) = get on (well) with, click (*slang*), be on good terms, get on like a house on fire (*informal*) ◆ **hit on** *or* **upon something** = think up, discover, arrive at, invent, stumble on, light upon, strike upon
hitch NOUN = problem, catch, difficulty, hold-up, obstacle, drawback, snag, uphill (*S. African*), impediment
• VERB 1 (*Informal*) = hitchhike, thumb a lift 2 = fasten, join, attach, couple, tie, connect, harness, tether
• PHRASES **hitch something up** = pull up, tug, jerk, yank
hitherto (*Formal*) = previously, so far, until now, thus far, heretofore
hobby = pastime, relaxation, leisure pursuit, diversion, avocation, (leisure) activity
hoist VERB = raise, lift, erect, elevate, heave
• NOUN = lift, crane, elevator, winch
hold VERB 1 = embrace, grasp, clutch, hug, squeeze, cradle, clasp, enfold 2 = restrain ≠ release 3 = accommodate, take, contain, seat, have a capacity for 4 = consider, think, believe, judge, regard, assume, reckon, deem ≠ deny 5 = occupy, have, fill, maintain, retain, possess, hold down (*informal*) 6 = conduct, convene, call, run, preside over ≠ cancel 7 = detain, confine, imprison, impound ≠ release
• NOUN 1 = grip, grasp, clasp 2 = foothold, footing 3 = control, influence, mastery, mana (*N.Z.*)
holder 1 = owner, bearer, possessor, keeper, proprietor 2 = case, cover, container
hold-up 1 = robbery, theft, mugging (*informal*), stick-up (*slang, chiefly U.S.*) 2 = delay, wait, hitch, setback, snag, traffic jam, stoppage, bottleneck
hole 1 = cavity, pit, hollow, chamber, cave, cavern 2 = opening, crack, tear, gap, breach, vent, puncture, aperture 3 = burrow, den, earth, shelter, lair 4 (*Informal*) = hovel, dump (*informal*), dive (*slang*), slum 5 (*Informal*) = predicament, spot (*informal*), fix (*informal*), mess, jam (*informal*), dilemma, scrape (*informal*), hot water (*informal*)
holiday 1 = vacation, leave, break, time off, recess 2 = festival, fête, celebration, feast, gala
hollow ADJECTIVE 1 = empty, vacant, void,

unfilled ≠ solid **2** = worthless, useless, vain, meaningless, pointless, futile, fruitless ≠ meaningful **3** = dull, low, deep, muted, toneless, reverberant ≠ vibrant
• NOUN **1** = cavity, hole, bowl, depression, pit, basin, crater, trough ≠ mound **2** = valley, dale, glen, dell, dingle ≠ hill
• VERB *often followed by* ***out*** = scoop out, dig out, excavate, gouge out

holocaust **1** = devastation, destruction, genocide, annihilation, conflagration **2** = genocide, massacre, annihilation

holy **1** = sacred, blessed, hallowed, venerable, consecrated, sacrosanct, sanctified ≠ unsanctified **2** = devout, godly, religious, pure, righteous, pious, virtuous, saintly ≠ sinful

homage = respect, honour, worship, devotion, reverence, deference, adulation, adoration ≠ contempt

home NOUN **1** = dwelling, house, residence, abode, habitation, pad (*slang*), domicile **2** = birthplace, homeland, home town, native land
• ADJECTIVE **1** = domestic, local, internal, native
• PHRASES **at home** **1** = in, present, available **2** = at ease, relaxed, comfortable, content, at peace ◆ **bring something home to someone** = make clear, emphasize, drive home, press home, impress upon

homeland = native land, birthplace, motherland, fatherland, country of origin, mother country

homeless = destitute, displaced, dispossessed, down-and-out

homely **1** = comfortable, welcoming, friendly, cosy, homespun **2** = plain, simple, ordinary, modest ≠ elaborate

homicide = murder, killing, manslaughter, slaying, bloodshed

hone **1** = improve, better, enhance, upgrade, refine, sharpen, help **2** = sharpen, point, grind, edge, file, polish, whet

honest **1** = trustworthy, upright, ethical, honourable, reputable, truthful, virtuous, law-abiding ≠ dishonest **2** = open, direct, frank, plain, sincere, candid, forthright, upfront (*informal*) ≠ secretive

honestly **1** = ethically, legally, lawfully, honourably, by fair means **2** = frankly, plainly, candidly, straight (out), truthfully, to your face, in all sincerity

honesty **1** = integrity, honour, virtue, morality, probity, rectitude, truthfulness, trustworthiness **2** = frankness, openness, sincerity, candour, bluntness, outspokenness, straightforwardness

honorary = nominal, unofficial, titular, in name *or* title only

honour NOUN **1** = integrity, morality, honesty, goodness, fairness, decency, probity, rectitude ≠ dishonour **2** = prestige, credit, reputation, glory, fame, distinction, dignity, renown ≠ disgrace **3** = reputation, standing, prestige, image, status, stature, good name, cachet **4** = acclaim, praise, recognition, compliments, homage, accolades, commendation ≠ contempt **5** = privilege, credit, pleasure, compliment
• VERB **1** = acclaim, praise, decorate, commemorate, commend **2** = respect, value, esteem, prize, appreciate, adore ≠ scorn **3** = fulfil, keep, carry out, observe, discharge, live up to, be true to **4** = pay, take, accept, pass, acknowledge ≠ refuse

honourable **1** = principled, moral, ethical, fair, upright, honest, virtuous, trustworthy **2** = proper, respectable, virtuous, creditable

hook NOUN = fastener, catch, link, peg, clasp
• VERB **1** = fasten, fix, secure, clasp **2** = catch, land, trap, entrap

hooked **1** = bent, curved, aquiline, hook-shaped **2** (*Informal*) = obsessed, addicted, taken, devoted, turned on (*slang*), enamoured **3** (*Informal*) = addicted, dependent, using (*informal*), having a habit

hooligan = delinquent, vandal, hoon (*Austral. & N.Z.*), ruffian, lager lout, yob *or* yobbo (*Brit. slang*), cougan (*Austral. slang*), scozza (*Austral. slang*), bogan (*Austral. slang*)

hoop = ring, band, loop, wheel, round, girdle, circlet

hop VERB = jump, spring, bound, leap, skip, vault, caper
• NOUN = jump, step, spring, bound, leap, bounce, skip, vault

hope VERB = believe, look forward to, cross your fingers
• NOUN = belief, confidence, expectation, longing, dream, desire, ambition, assumption ≠ despair

hopeful 1 = optimistic, confident, looking forward to, buoyant, sanguine, expectant ≠ despairing 2 = promising, encouraging, bright, reassuring, rosy, heartening, auspicious ≠ unpromising
hopefully = optimistically, confidently, expectantly, with anticipation
hopeless = impossible, pointless, futile, useless, vain, no-win, unattainable
horde = crowd, mob, swarm, host, band, pack, drove, gang
horizon = skyline, view, vista
horizontal = level, flat, parallel
horrible 1 (*Informal*) = dreadful, terrible, awful, nasty, cruel, mean, unpleasant, horrid ≠ wonderful 2 = terrible, appalling, terrifying, shocking, grim, dreadful, revolting, ghastly
horrific = horrifying, shocking, appalling, awful, terrifying, dreadful, horrendous, ghastly
horrify 1 = terrify, alarm, frighten, scare, intimidate, petrify, make your hair stand on end ≠ comfort 2 = shock, appal, dismay, sicken, outrage ≠ delight
horror 1 = terror, fear, alarm, panic, dread, fright, consternation, trepidation 2 = hatred, disgust, loathing, aversion, revulsion, repugnance, odium, detestation ≠ love
horse = nag, mount, mare, colt, filly, stallion, steed (*archaic or literary*), moke (*Austral. slang*), yarraman *or* yarramin (*Austral.*), gee-gee (*slang*)

RELATED WORDS
adjectives: equestrian, equine
male: stallion
female: mare
young: foal, colt, filly

hospitality = welcome, warmth, kindness, friendliness, sociability, conviviality, neighbourliness, cordiality
host[1] *or* **hostess** NOUN 1 = master of ceremonies, proprietor, innkeeper, landlord *or* landlady 2 = presenter, compere (*Brit.*), anchorman *or* anchorwoman
• VERB = present, introduce, compere (*Brit.*), front (*informal*)
host[2] 1 = multitude, lot, load (*informal*), wealth, array, myriad, great quantity, large number 2 = crowd, army, pack, drove, mob, herd, legion, swarm
hostage = captive, prisoner, pawn
hostile 1 = antagonistic, opposed, contrary, ill-disposed 2 = unfriendly, belligerent, antagonistic, rancorous, ill-disposed ≠ friendly 3 = inhospitable, adverse, uncongenial, unsympathetic, unwelcoming ≠ hospitable
hostility NOUN 1 = unfriendliness, hatred, animosity, spite, bitterness, malice, venom, enmity ≠ friendliness 2 = opposition, resentment, antipathy, aversion, antagonism, ill feeling, ill-will, animus ≠ approval
• PLURAL NOUN = warfare, war, fighting, conflict, combat, armed conflict ≠ peace
hot 1 = heated, boiling, steaming, roasting, searing, scorching, scalding 2 = warm, close, stifling, humid, torrid, sultry, sweltering, balmy ≠ cold 3 = spicy, pungent, peppery, piquant, biting, sharp ≠ mild 4 = intense, passionate, heated, spirited, fierce, lively, animated, ardent 5 = new, latest, fresh, recent, up to date, just out, up to the minute, bang up to date (*informal*) ≠ old 6 = popular, hip, fashionable, cool, in demand, sought-after, must-see, in vogue ≠ unpopular 7 = fierce, intense, strong, keen, competitive, cut-throat 8 = fiery, violent, raging, passionate, stormy ≠ calm
hound = harass, harry, bother, provoke, annoy, torment, hassle (*informal*), badger

RELATED WORD
collective noun: pack

house NOUN 1 = home, residence, dwelling, pad (*slang*), homestead, abode, habitation, domicile, whare (*N.Z.*) 2 = household, family 3 = firm, company, business, organization, outfit (*informal*) 4 = assembly, parliament, Commons, legislative body 5 = dynasty, tribe, clan
• VERB 1 = accommodate, quarter, take in, put up, lodge, harbour, billet 2 = contain, keep, hold, cover, store, protect, shelter 3 = take, accommodate, sleep, provide shelter for, give a bed to
• PHRASES **on the house** = free, for free (*informal*), for nothing, free of charge, gratis
household = family, home, house, family circle, ainga (*N.Z.*)
housing 1 = accommodation, homes, houses, dwellings, domiciles 2 = case, casing, covering, cover, shell, jacket, holder, container

hover 1 = float, fly, hang, drift, flutter 2 = linger, loiter, hang about *or* around (*informal*) 3 = waver, fluctuate, dither (*chiefly Brit.*), oscillate, vacillate

however = but, nevertheless, still, though, yet, nonetheless, notwithstanding, anyhow

howl VERB 1 = bay, cry 2 = cry, scream, roar, weep, yell, wail, shriek, bellow
• NOUN 1 = baying, cry, bay, bark, barking, yelping 2 = cry, scream, roar, bay, wail, shriek, clamour, bawl

hub = centre, heart, focus, core, middle, focal point, nerve centre

huddle VERB 1 = curl up, crouch, hunch up 2 = crowd, press, gather, collect, squeeze, cluster, flock, herd
• NOUN (*Informal*) = discussion, conference, meeting, hui (*N.Z.*), powwow, confab (*informal*), korero (*N.Z.*)

hue = colour, tone, shade, dye, tint, tinge

hug VERB = embrace, cuddle, squeeze, clasp, enfold, hold close, take in your arms
• NOUN = embrace, squeeze, bear hug, clinch (*slang*), clasp

huge = enormous, large, massive, vast, tremendous, immense, gigantic, monumental ≠ tiny

hui (*N.Z.*) = meeting, gathering, assembly, conference, congress, rally, convention, get-together (*informal*)

hull = framework, casing, body, covering, frame

hum 1 = drone, buzz, murmur, throb, vibrate, purr, thrum, whir 2 (*Informal*) = be busy, buzz, bustle, stir, pulse, pulsate

human ADJECTIVE = mortal, manlike ≠ nonhuman
• NOUN = human being, person, individual, creature, mortal, man *or* woman ≠ nonhuman

humane = kind, compassionate, understanding, forgiving, tender, sympathetic, benign, merciful ≠ cruel

humanitarian ADJECTIVE 1 = compassionate, charitable, humane, benevolent, altruistic 2 = charitable, philanthropic, public-spirited
• NOUN = philanthropist, benefactor, Good Samaritan, altruist

humanity 1 = the human race, man, mankind, people, mortals, humankind, Homo sapiens 2 = human nature, mortality 3 = kindness, charity, compassion, sympathy, mercy, philanthropy, fellow feeling, kind-heartedness

humble ADJECTIVE 1 = modest, meek, unassuming, unpretentious, self-effacing, unostentatious ≠ proud 2 = lowly, poor, mean, simple, ordinary, modest, obscure, undistinguished ≠ distinguished
• VERB = humiliate, disgrace, crush, subdue, chasten, put (someone) in their place, take down a peg (*informal*) ≠ exalt

humidity = damp, moisture, dampness, wetness, moistness, dankness, clamminess, mugginess

humiliate = embarrass, shame, humble, crush, put down, degrade, chasten, mortify ≠ honour

humiliating = embarrassing, shaming, humbling, mortifying, crushing, degrading, ignominious, barro (*Austral. slang*)

humiliation = embarrassment, shame, disgrace, humbling, put-down, degradation, indignity, ignominy

humorous = funny, comic, amusing, entertaining, witty, comical, droll, jocular ≠ serious

humour NOUN 1 = comedy, funniness, fun, amusement, funny side, jocularity, facetiousness, ludicrousness ≠ seriousness 2 = mood, spirits, temper, disposition, frame of mind 3 = joking, comedy, wit, farce, jesting, wisecracks (*informal*), witticisms
• VERB = indulge, accommodate, go along with, flatter, gratify, pander to, mollify ≠ oppose

hunch NOUN = feeling, idea, impression, suspicion, intuition, premonition, inkling, presentiment
• VERB = crouch, bend, curve, arch, draw in

hunger NOUN 1 = appetite, emptiness, hungriness, ravenousness 2 = starvation, famine, malnutrition, undernourishment 3 = desire, appetite, craving, ache, lust, yearning, itch, thirst
• PHRASES **hunger for** *or* **after something** = want, desire, crave, long for, wish for, yearn for, hanker after, ache for

hungry 1 = starving, ravenous, famished, starved, empty, voracious, peckish (*informal, chiefly Brit.*) 2 = eager, keen, craving, yearning, greedy, avid, desirous, covetous

hunk = lump, piece, chunk, block, mass, wedge, slab, nugget

hunt VERB = stalk, track, chase, pursue, trail, hound
• NOUN = search, hunting, investigation, chase, pursuit, quest
• PHRASES **hunt for something** *or* **someone** = search for, look for, seek for, forage for, scour for, fossick for (*Austral. & N.Z.*), ferret about for

hurdle 1 = obstacle, difficulty, barrier, handicap, hazard, uphill (*S. African*), obstruction, stumbling block 2 = fence, barrier, barricade

hurl = throw, fling, launch, cast, pitch, toss, propel, sling

hurricane = storm, gale, tornado, cyclone, typhoon, tempest, twister (*U.S. informal*), willy-willy (*Austral.*)

hurried 1 = hasty, quick, brief, rushed, short, swift, speedy 2 = rushed, perfunctory, speedy, hasty, cursory

hurry VERB 1 = rush, fly, dash, scurry, scoot ≠ dawdle 2 = make haste, rush, get a move on (*informal*), step on it (*informal*)
• NOUN = rush, haste, speed, urgency, flurry, quickness ≠ slowness

hurt VERB 1 = injure, damage, wound, cut, disable, bruise, scrape, impair ≠ heal 2 = ache, be sore, be painful, burn, smart, sting, throb, be tender 3 = harm, injure, ill-treat, maltreat 4 = upset, distress, pain, wound, annoy, grieve, sadden
• NOUN = distress, suffering, pain, grief, misery, sorrow, heartache, wretchedness ≠ happiness
• ADJECTIVE 1 = injured, wounded, damaged, harmed, cut, bruised, scarred ≠ healed 2 = upset, wounded, crushed, offended, aggrieved, tooshie (*Austral. slang*) ≠ calmed

hurtle = rush, charge, race, shoot, fly, speed, tear, crash

husband NOUN = partner, spouse, mate, better half (*humorous*)
• VERB = conserve, budget, save, store, hoard, economize on, use economically ≠ squander

hush VERB = quieten, silence, mute, muzzle, shush
• NOUN = quiet, silence, calm, peace, tranquillity, stillness

hut 1 = cabin, shack, shanty, hovel, whare (*N.Z.*) 2 = shed, outhouse, lean-to, lockup

hybrid 1 = crossbreed, cross, mixture, compound, composite, amalgam, mongrel, half-breed 2 = mixture, compound, composite, amalgam

hygiene = cleanliness, sanitation, disinfection, sterility

hymn 1 = religious song, song of praise, carol, chant, anthem, psalm, paean 2 = song of praise, anthem, paean

hype (*Slang*) = publicity, promotion, plugging (*informal*), razzmatazz (*slang*), brouhaha, ballyhoo (*informal*)

hypocrisy = insincerity, pretence, deception, cant, duplicity, deceitfulness ≠ sincerity

hypothesis = theory, premise, proposition, assumption, thesis, postulate, supposition

hysteria = frenzy, panic, madness, agitation, delirium, hysterics

hysterical 1 = frenzied, frantic, raving, distracted, distraught, crazed, overwrought, berko (*Austral. slang*) ≠ calm 2 (*Informal*) = hilarious, uproarious, side-splitting, comical ≠ serious

I

icy 1 = cold, freezing, bitter, biting, raw, chill, chilly, frosty ≠ hot 2 = slippery, glassy, slippy (*informal* or *dialect*), like a sheet of glass 3 = unfriendly, cold, distant, aloof, frosty, frigid, unwelcoming ≠ friendly

idea 1 = notion, thought, view, teaching, opinion, belief, conclusion, hypothesis 2 = understanding, thought, view, opinion, concept, impression, perception 3 = intention, aim, purpose, object, plan, objective

ideal NOUN 1 = epitome, standard, dream, pattern, perfection, last word, paragon 2 = model, prototype, paradigm
• ADJECTIVE = perfect, best, model, classic, supreme, ultimate, archetypal, exemplary

≠ imperfect
ideally = in a perfect world, all things being equal, if you had your way
identical = alike, matching, twin, duplicate, indistinguishable, interchangeable ≠ different
identification 1 = discovery, recognition, determining, establishment, diagnosis, confirmation, divination 2 = recognition, naming, distinguishing, confirmation, pinpointing 3 = connection, relationship, association 4 = understanding, relationship, involvement, unity, sympathy, empathy, rapport, fellow feeling
identify VERB 1 = recognize, place, name, remember, spot, diagnose, make out, pinpoint 2 = establish, spot, confirm, demonstrate, pick out, certify, verify, mark out
• PHRASES **identify something** *or* **someone with something** *or* **someone** = equate with, associate with ♦ **identify with someone** = relate to, respond to, feel for, empathize with
identity = individuality, self, character, personality, existence, originality, separateness
idiot = fool, moron, twit (*informal*, *chiefly Brit.*), chump, imbecile, cretin, simpleton, halfwit, galah (*Austral. & N.Z. informal*), dorba *or* dorb (*Austral. slang*), bogan (*Austral. slang*)
idle ADJECTIVE 1 = unoccupied, unemployed, redundant, inactive ≠ occupied 2 = unused, inactive, out of order, out of service 3 = lazy, slow, slack, sluggish, lax, negligent, inactive, inert ≠ busy 4 = useless, vain, pointless, unsuccessful, ineffective, worthless, futile, fruitless ≠ useful
• VERB *often with* ***away*** = fritter, lounge, potter, loaf, dally, loiter, dawdle, laze
idol 1 = hero, pin-up, favourite, pet, darling, beloved (*slang*), fave (*informal*) 2 = graven image, god, deity
if 1 = provided, assuming, given that, providing, supposing, presuming, on condition that, as long as 2 = when, whenever, every time, any time
ignite 1 = catch fire, burn, burst into flames, inflame, flare up, take fire 2 = set fire to, light, set alight, torch, kindle
ignorance 1 = lack of education, stupidity, foolishness ≠ knowledge
2 *with* ***of*** = unawareness of, inexperience of, unfamiliarity with, innocence of, unconsciousness of
ignorant 1 = uneducated, illiterate ≠ educated 2 = insensitive, rude, crass 3 *with* ***of*** = uninformed of, unaware of, oblivious to, innocent of, unconscious of, inexperienced of, uninitiated about, unenlightened about ≠ informed
ignore 1 = pay no attention to, neglect, disregard, slight, overlook, scorn, spurn, rebuff ≠ pay attention to 2 = overlook, discount, disregard, reject, neglect, shrug off, pass over, brush aside 3 = snub, slight, rebuff
ill ADJECTIVE 1 = unwell, sick, poorly (*informal*), diseased, weak, crook (*Austral. & N.Z. slang*), ailing, frail ≠ healthy 2 = harmful, bad, damaging, evil, foul, unfortunate, destructive, detrimental ≠ favourable
• NOUN = problem, trouble, suffering, worry, injury, hurt, strain, harm ≠ good
• ADVERB 1 = badly, unfortunately, unfavourably, inauspiciously 2 = hardly, barely, scarcely, just, only just, by no means, at a push ≠ well
illegal = unlawful, banned, forbidden, prohibited, criminal, outlawed, illicit, unlicensed ≠ legal
illicit 1 = illegal, criminal, prohibited, unlawful, illegitimate, unlicensed, unauthorized, felonious ≠ legal 2 = forbidden, improper, immoral, guilty, clandestine, furtive
illness = sickness, disease, infection, disorder, bug (*informal*), ailment, affliction, malady
illuminate 1 = light up, brighten ≠ darken 2 = explain, interpret, make clear, clarify, clear up, enlighten, shed light on, elucidate ≠ obscure
illuminating = informative, revealing, enlightening, helpful, explanatory, instructive ≠ confusing
illusion 1 = delusion, misconception, misapprehension, fancy, fallacy, false impression, false belief 2 = false impression, appearance, impression, deception, fallacy ≠ reality 3 = fantasy, vision, hallucination, trick, spectre, mirage, daydream, apparition
illustrate 1 = demonstrate, emphasize 2 = explain, sum up, summarize, bring

home, point up, elucidate

illustrated = pictured, decorated, pictorial

illustration **1** = example, case, instance, sample, specimen, exemplar **2** = picture, drawing, painting, image, print, plate, figure, portrait

image **1** = thought, idea, vision, concept, impression, perception, mental picture, conceptualization **2** = figure of speech **3** = reflection, likeness, mirror image **4** = figure, idol, icon, fetish, talisman **5** = replica, copy, reproduction, counterpart, clone, facsimile, spitting image (*informal*), Doppelgänger **6** = picture, photo, photograph, representation, reproduction, snapshot

imaginary = fictional, made-up, invented, imagined, unreal, hypothetical, fictitious, illusory ≠ real

imagination **1** = creativity, vision, invention, ingenuity, enterprise, originality, inventiveness, resourcefulness **2** = mind's eye, fancy

imaginative = creative, original, inspired, enterprising, clever, ingenious, inventive ≠ unimaginative

imagine **1** = envisage, see, picture, plan, think of, conjure up, envision, visualize **2** = believe, think, suppose, assume, suspect, guess (*informal*, *chiefly U.S. & Canad.*), take it, reckon

imitate **1** = copy, follow, repeat, echo, emulate, ape, simulate, mirror **2** = do an impression of, mimic, copy

imitation NOUN **1** = replica, fake, reproduction, sham, forgery, counterfeiting, likeness, duplication **2** = copying, resemblance, mimicry **3** = impression, impersonation

● ADJECTIVE = artificial, mock, reproduction, dummy, synthetic, man-made, simulated, sham ≠ real

immaculate **1** = clean, spotless, neat, spruce, squeaky-clean, spick-and-span ≠ dirty **2** = pure, perfect, impeccable, flawless, faultless, above reproach ≠ corrupt **3** = perfect, flawless, impeccable, faultless, unblemished, untarnished, unexceptionable ≠ tainted

immediate **1** = instant, prompt, instantaneous, quick, on-the-spot, split-second ≠ later **2** = nearest, next, direct, close, near ≠ far

immediately = at once, now, instantly, straight away, directly, promptly, right away, without delay

immense = huge, great, massive, vast, enormous, extensive, tremendous, very big ≠ tiny

immerse **1** = engross, involve, absorb, busy, occupy, engage **2** = plunge, dip, submerge, sink, duck, bathe, douse, dunk

immigrant = settler, incomer, alien, stranger, outsider, newcomer, migrant, emigrant

imminent = near, coming, close, approaching, gathering, forthcoming, looming, impending ≠ remote

immoral = wicked, bad, wrong, corrupt, indecent, sinful, unethical, depraved ≠ moral

immortal ADJECTIVE **1** = timeless, eternal, everlasting, lasting, traditional, classic, enduring, perennial ≠ ephemeral **2** = undying, eternal, imperishable, deathless ≠ mortal

● NOUN **1** = hero, genius, great **2** = god, goddess, deity, divine being, immortal being, atua (*N.Z.*)

immune

● PHRASES **immune from** = exempt from, free from ◆ **immune to** **1** = resistant to, free from, protected from, safe from, not open to, spared from, secure against, invulnerable to **2** = unaffected by, invulnerable to

immunity **1** = exemption, amnesty, indemnity, release, freedom, invulnerability **2** *with* ***to*** = resistance to, protection from, resilience to, inoculation against, immunization from ≠ susceptibility to

impact NOUN **1** = effect, influence, consequences, impression, repercussions, ramifications **2** = collision, contact, crash, knock, stroke, smash, bump, thump

● VERB = hit, strike, crash, clash, crush, ram, smack, collide

impair = worsen, reduce, damage, injure, harm, undermine, weaken, diminish ≠ improve

impaired = damaged, flawed, faulty, defective, imperfect, unsound

impasse = deadlock, stalemate, standstill, dead end, standoff

impatient **1** = cross, annoyed, irritated, prickly, touchy, bad-tempered, intolerant,

ill-tempered ≠ easy-going **2** = eager, longing, keen, anxious, hungry, enthusiastic, restless, avid ≠ calm
impeccable = faultless, perfect, immaculate, flawless, squeaky-clean, unblemished, unimpeachable, irreproachable ≠ flawed
impending = looming, coming, approaching, near, forthcoming, imminent, upcoming, in the pipeline
imperative = urgent, essential, pressing, vital, crucial ≠ unnecessary
imperial = royal, regal, kingly, queenly, princely, sovereign, majestic, monarchial
impetus **1** = incentive, push, spur, motivation, impulse, stimulus, catalyst, goad **2** = force, power, energy, momentum
implant **1** = insert, fix, graft **2** = instil, infuse, inculcate
implement VERB = carry out, effect, carry through, complete, apply, perform, realize, fulfil ≠ hinder
• NOUN = tool, machine, device, instrument, appliance, apparatus, gadget, utensil
implicate VERB = incriminate, involve, embroil, entangle, inculpate ≠ dissociate
• PHRASES **implicate something** *or* **someone in something** = involve in, associate with
implication NOUN = suggestion, hint, inference, meaning, significance, presumption, overtone, innuendo
• PLURAL NOUN = consequences, result, developments, upshot
implicit **1** = implied, understood, suggested, hinted at, taken for granted, unspoken, inferred, tacit ≠ explicit **2** = inherent, underlying, intrinsic, latent, ingrained, inbuilt **3** = absolute, full, complete, firm, fixed, constant, utter, outright
implied = suggested, indirect, hinted at, implicit, unspoken, tacit, undeclared, unstated
imply **1** = suggest, hint, insinuate, indicate, intimate, signify **2** = involve, mean, entail, require, indicate, point to, signify, presuppose
import VERB = bring in, buy in, ship in, introduce
• NOUN **1** (*Formal*) = significance, concern, value, weight, consequence, substance, moment, magnitude **2** = meaning, implication, significance, sense, intention, substance, drift, thrust
importance **1** = significance, interest, concern, moment, value, weight, import, consequence **2** = prestige, standing, status, rule, authority, influence, distinction, esteem, mana (*N.Z.*)
important **1** = significant, critical, substantial, urgent, serious, far-reaching, momentous, seminal ≠ unimportant **2** = powerful, prominent, commanding, dominant, influential, eminent, high-ranking, authoritative
impose
• PHRASES **impose something on** *or* **upon someone** **1** = levy, introduce, charge, establish, fix, institute, decree, ordain **2** = inflict, force, enforce, visit, press, apply, thrust, saddle (someone) with
imposing = impressive, striking, grand, powerful, commanding, awesome, majestic, dignified ≠ unimposing
imposition **1** = application, introduction, levying **2** = intrusion, liberty, presumption
impossible **1** = not possible, out of the question, impracticable, unfeasible **2** = unachievable, out of the question, vain, unthinkable, inconceivable, far-fetched, unworkable, implausible ≠ possible **3** = absurd, crazy (*informal*), ridiculous, outrageous, ludicrous, unreasonable, preposterous, farcical
impotence = powerlessness, inability, helplessness, weakness, incompetence, paralysis, frailty, incapacity ≠ powerfulness
impoverish **1** = bankrupt, ruin, beggar, break **2** = deplete, drain, exhaust, diminish, use up, sap, wear out, reduce
impoverished = poor, needy, destitute, bankrupt, poverty-stricken, impecunious, penurious ≠ rich
impress VERB = excite, move, strike, touch, affect, inspire, amaze, overcome
• PHRASES **impress something on** *or* **upon someone** = stress, bring home to, instil in, drum into, knock into, emphasize to, fix in, inculcate in
impression **1** = idea, feeling, thought, sense, view, assessment, judgment, reaction **2** = effect, influence, impact **3** = imitation, parody, impersonation, send-up (*Brit. informal*), takeoff (*informal*) **4** = mark, imprint, stamp, outline, hollow, dent, indentation

impressive = grand, striking, splendid, good, great (*informal*), fine, powerful, exciting ≠ unimpressive
imprint NOUN = mark, impression, stamp, indentation
• VERB = engrave, print, stamp, impress, etch, emboss
imprison = jail, confine, detain, lock up, put away, intern, incarcerate, send down (*informal*) ≠ free
imprisoned = jailed, confined, locked up, inside (*slang*), in jail, captive, behind bars, incarcerated
imprisonment = confinement, custody, detention, captivity, incarceration
improbable 1 = doubtful, unlikely, dubious, questionable, fanciful, far-fetched, implausible ≠ probable 2 = unconvincing, weak, unbelievable, preposterous ≠ convincing
improper 1 = inappropriate, unfit, unsuitable, out of place, unwarranted, uncalled-for ≠ appropriate 2 = indecent, vulgar, suggestive, unseemly, untoward, risqué, smutty, unbecoming ≠ decent
improve 1 = enhance, better, add to, upgrade, touch up, ameliorate ≠ worsen 2 = get better, pick up, develop, advance
improvement 1 = enhancement, advancement, betterment 2 = advance, development, progress, recovery, upswing
improvise 1 = devise, contrive, concoct, throw together 2 = ad-lib, invent, busk, wing it (*informal*), play it by ear (*informal*), extemporize, speak off the cuff (*informal*)
impulse = urge, longing, wish, notion, yearning, inclination, itch, whim
inaccurate = incorrect, wrong, mistaken, faulty, unreliable, defective, erroneous, unsound ≠ accurate
inadequacy 1 = shortage, poverty, dearth, paucity, insufficiency, meagreness, scantiness 2 = incompetence, inability, deficiency, incapacity, ineffectiveness 3 = shortcoming, failing, weakness, defect, imperfection
inadequate 1 = insufficient, meagre, poor, lacking, scant, sparse, sketchy ≠ adequate 2 = incapable, incompetent, faulty, deficient, unqualified, not up to scratch (*informal*) ≠ capable
inadvertently = unintentionally, accidentally, by accident, mistakenly, unwittingly, by mistake, involuntarily ≠ deliberately
inaugural = first, opening, initial, maiden, introductory
incarnation = embodiment, manifestation, epitome, type, personification
incense = anger, infuriate, enrage, irritate, madden, inflame, rile (*informal*), make your blood boil (*informal*)
incensed = angry, furious, fuming, infuriated, enraged, maddened, indignant, irate, tooshie (*Austral. slang*), off the air (*Austral. slang*)
incentive = inducement, encouragement, spur, lure, bait, motivation, carrot (*informal*), stimulus ≠ disincentive
incident 1 = disturbance, scene, clash, disorder, confrontation, brawl, fracas, commotion 2 = adventure, drama, excitement, crisis, spectacle 3 = happening, event, affair, business, fact, matter, occasion, episode
incidentally = by the way, in passing, en passant, parenthetically, by the bye
inclination 1 = desire, longing, aspiration, craving, hankering 2 = tendency, liking, disposition, penchant, propensity, predisposition, predilection, proclivity ≠ aversion
incline VERB = predispose, influence, persuade, prejudice, sway, dispose
• NOUN = slope, rise, dip, grade, descent, ascent, gradient
inclined 1 = disposed, given, prone, likely, liable, apt, predisposed 2 = willing, minded, disposed
include 1 = contain, involve, incorporate, cover, consist of, take in, embrace, comprise ≠ exclude 2 = count 3 = add, enter, put in, insert
inclusion = addition, incorporation, introduction, insertion ≠ exclusion
inclusive = comprehensive, general, global, sweeping, blanket, umbrella, across-the-board, all-embracing ≠ limited
income = revenue, earnings, pay, returns, profits, wages, yield, proceeds
incoming 1 = arriving, landing, approaching, entering, returning, homeward ≠ departing 2 = new
incompatible = inconsistent, conflicting, contradictory, incongruous, unsuited, mismatched ≠ compatible
incompetence = ineptitude, inability,

inadequacy, incapacity, ineffectiveness, uselessness, unfitness, incapability
incompetent = inept, useless, incapable, floundering, bungling, unfit, ineffectual, inexpert ≠ competent
incomplete = unfinished, partial, wanting, deficient, imperfect, fragmentary, half-pie (*N.Z. informal*) ≠ complete
inconsistency 1 = unreliability, instability, unpredictability, fickleness, unsteadiness **2** = incompatibility, discrepancy, disparity, disagreement, variance, divergence, incongruity
inconsistent 1 = changeable, variable, unpredictable, unstable, erratic, fickle, capricious, unsteady ≠ consistent **2** = incompatible, conflicting, at odds, contradictory, incongruous, discordant, out of step, irreconcilable ≠ compatible
inconvenience NOUN = trouble, difficulty, bother, fuss, disadvantage, disturbance, disruption, nuisance, uphill (*S. African*) • VERB = trouble, bother, disturb, upset, disrupt, put out, discommode
incorporate 1 = include, contain, take in, embrace, integrate, encompass, assimilate, comprise of **2** = integrate, include, absorb, merge, fuse, assimilate, subsume **3** = blend, combine, compound, mingle
incorrect = false, wrong, mistaken, flawed, faulty, inaccurate, untrue, erroneous ≠ correct
increase VERB **1** = raise, extend, boost, expand, develop, advance, strengthen, widen ≠ decrease **2** = grow, develop, spread, expand, swell, enlarge, escalate, multiply ≠ shrink • NOUN = growth, rise, development, gain, expansion, extension, proliferation, enlargement
increasingly = progressively, more and more
incredible 1 (*Informal*) = amazing, wonderful, stunning, extraordinary, overwhelming, astonishing, staggering, sensational (*informal*) **2** = unbelievable, unthinkable, improbable, inconceivable, preposterous, unconvincing, unimaginable, far-fetched
incumbent NOUN = holder, keeper, bearer • ADJECTIVE (*Formal*) = obligatory, required, necessary, essential, binding, compulsory, mandatory, imperative
incur = sustain, experience, suffer, gain, earn, collect, meet with, provoke
indecent 1 = obscene, lewd, dirty, inappropriate, rude, crude, filthy, improper ≠ decent **2** = unbecoming, unsuitable, vulgar, unseemly, undignified, indecorous ≠ proper
indeed 1 = certainly, yes, definitely, surely, truly, undoubtedly, without doubt, indisputably **2** = really, actually, in fact, certainly, genuinely, in truth, in actuality
indefinitely = endlessly, continually, for ever, ad infinitum
independence = freedom, liberty, autonomy, sovereignty, self-rule, self-sufficiency, self-reliance, rangatiratanga (*N.Z.*) ≠ subjugation
independent 1 = separate, unattached, uncontrolled, unconstrained ≠ controlled **2** = self-sufficient, free, liberated, self-contained, self-reliant, self-supporting **3** = self-governing, free, autonomous, liberated, sovereign, self-determining, nonaligned ≠ subject
independently = separately, alone, solo, on your own, by yourself, unaided, individually, autonomously
indicate 1 = show, suggest, reveal, display, demonstrate, point to, imply, manifest **2** = imply, suggest, hint, intimate, signify, insinuate **3** = point to, point out, specify, gesture towards, designate **4** = register, show, record, read, express, display, demonstrate
indication = sign, mark, evidence, suggestion, symptom, hint, clue, manifestation
indicator = sign, mark, measure, guide, signal, symbol, meter, gauge
indict = charge, accuse, prosecute, summon, impeach, arraign
indictment = charge, allegation, prosecution, accusation, impeachment, summons, arraignment
indifference = disregard, apathy, negligence, detachment, coolness, coldness, nonchalance, aloofness ≠ concern
indifferent 1 = unconcerned, detached, cold, cool, callous, aloof, unmoved, unsympathetic ≠ concerned **2** = mediocre, ordinary, moderate, so-so (*informal*), passable, undistinguished, no great shakes (*informal*), half-pie (*N.Z. informal*) ≠ excellent

indignation = resentment, anger, rage, exasperation, pique, umbrage
indirect 1 = related, secondary, subsidiary, incidental, unintended 2 = circuitous, roundabout, curving, wandering, rambling, deviant, meandering, tortuous ≠ direct
indispensable = essential, necessary, needed, key, vital, crucial, imperative, requisite ≠ dispensable
individual ADJECTIVE 1 = separate, independent, isolated, lone, solitary ≠ collective 2 = unique, special, fresh, novel, exclusive, singular, idiosyncratic, unorthodox ≠ conventional
• NOUN = person, being, human, unit, character, soul, creature
individually = separately, independently, singly, one by one, one at a time
induce 1 = cause, produce, create, effect, lead to, occasion, generate, bring about ≠ prevent 2 = persuade, encourage, influence, convince, urge, prompt, sway, entice ≠ dissuade
indulge VERB 1 = gratify, satisfy, feed, give way to, yield to, pander to, gladden 2 = spoil, pamper, cosset, humour, give in to, coddle, mollycoddle, overindulge
• PHRASES **indulge yourself** = treat yourself, splash out, spoil yourself, luxuriate in something, overindulge yourself
indulgence 1 = luxury, treat, extravagance, favour, privilege 2 = gratification, satisfaction, fulfilment, appeasement, satiation
industrialist = capitalist, tycoon, magnate, manufacturer, captain of industry, big businessman
industry 1 = business, production, manufacturing, trade, commerce 2 = trade, world, business, service, line, field, profession, occupation 3 = diligence, effort, labour, hard work, trouble, activity, application, endeavour
ineffective 1 = unproductive, useless, futile, vain, unsuccessful, pointless, fruitless, ineffectual ≠ effective 2 = inefficient, useless, poor, powerless, unfit, worthless, inept, impotent
inefficient 1 = wasteful, uneconomical, profligate 2 = incompetent, inept, weak, bungling, ineffectual, disorganized ≠ efficient
inequality = disparity, prejudice, difference, bias, diversity, irregularity, unevenness, disproportion
inevitable = unavoidable, inescapable, inexorable, sure, certain, fixed, assured, fated ≠ avoidable
inevitably = unavoidably, naturally, necessarily, surely, certainly, as a result, automatically, consequently
inexpensive = cheap, reasonable, budget, bargain, modest, economical ≠ expensive
inexperienced = new, green, raw, callow, immature, untried, unpractised, unversed ≠ experienced
infamous = notorious, ignominious, disreputable, ill-famed ≠ esteemed
infancy = beginnings, start, birth, roots, seeds, origins, dawn, outset ≠ end
infant = baby, child, babe, toddler, tot, bairn (*Scot.*), littlie (*Austral. informal*), ankle-biter (*Austral. slang*), tacker (*Austral. slang*)
infect 1 = contaminate 2 = pollute, poison, corrupt, contaminate, taint, defile 3 = affect, move, upset, overcome, stir, disturb
infection = disease, condition, complaint, illness, virus, disorder, corruption, poison
infectious = catching, spreading, contagious, communicable, virulent, transmittable
inferior ADJECTIVE = lower, minor, secondary, subsidiary, lesser, humble, subordinate, lowly ≠ superior
• NOUN = underling, junior, subordinate, lesser, menial, minion
infertility = sterility, barrenness, unproductiveness, infecundity
infiltrate = penetrate, pervade, permeate, percolate, filter through to, make inroads into, sneak into (*informal*), insinuate yourself
infinite 1 = vast, enormous, immense, countless, measureless 2 = limitless, endless, unlimited, eternal, never-ending, boundless, everlasting, inexhaustible ≠ finite
inflame = enrage, stimulate, provoke, excite, anger, arouse, rouse, infuriate ≠ calm
inflamed = swollen, sore, red, hot, infected, fevered
inflate 1 = blow up, pump up, swell, dilate,

distend, bloat, puff up *or* out ≠ deflate **2** = increase, expand, enlarge ≠ diminish **3** = exaggerate, embroider, embellish, enlarge, amplify, overstate, overestimate, overemphasize

inflated = exaggerated, swollen, overblown

inflation = increase, expansion, extension, swelling, escalation, enlargement

inflict = impose, administer, visit, apply, deliver, levy, wreak, mete *or* deal out

influence NOUN **1** = control, power, authority, direction, command, domination, supremacy, mastery, mana (*N.Z.*) **2** = power, authority, pull (*informal*), importance, prestige, clout (*informal*), leverage **3** = spell, hold, power, weight, magic, sway, allure, magnetism
• VERB **1** = affect, have an effect on, have an impact on, control, concern, direct, guide, bear upon **2** = persuade, prompt, urge, induce, entice, coax, incite, instigate

influential **1** = important, powerful, telling, leading, inspiring, potent, authoritative, weighty ≠ unimportant **2** = instrumental, important, significant, crucial

influx = arrival, rush, invasion, incursion, inundation, inrush

inform VERB = tell, advise, notify, instruct, enlighten, communicate to, tip someone off
• PHRASES **inform on someone** = betray, denounce, shop (*slang, chiefly Brit.*), give someone away, incriminate, blow the whistle on (*informal*), grass on (*Brit. slang*), double-cross (*informal*), dob someone in (*Austral. & N.Z. slang*)

informal **1** = natural, relaxed, casual, familiar, unofficial, laid-back, easy-going, colloquial **2** = relaxed, easy, comfortable, simple, natural, casual, cosy, laid-back (*informal*) ≠ formal **3** = casual, comfortable, leisure, everyday, simple **4** = unofficial, irregular ≠ official

information = facts, news, report, message, notice, knowledge, data, intelligence, drum (*Austral. informal*)

informative = instructive, revealing, educational, forthcoming, illuminating, enlightening, chatty, communicative

informed = knowledgeable, up to date, enlightened, learned, expert, familiar, versed, in the picture

infuriate = enrage, anger, provoke, irritate, incense, madden, exasperate, rile ≠ soothe

infuriating = annoying, irritating, provoking, galling, maddening, exasperating, vexatious

ingenious = creative, original, brilliant, clever, bright, shrewd, inventive, crafty ≠ unimaginative

ingredient = component, part, element, feature, piece, unit, item, aspect

inhabit = live in, occupy, populate, reside in, dwell in, abide in

inhabitant = occupant, resident, citizen, local, native, tenant, inmate, dweller

inhabited = populated, peopled, occupied, developed, settled, tenanted, colonized

inhale = breathe in, gasp, draw in, suck in, respire ≠ exhale

inherent = intrinsic, natural, essential, native, fundamental, hereditary, instinctive, innate ≠ extraneous

inherit = be left, come into, be willed, succeed to, fall heir to

inheritance = legacy, heritage, bequest, birthright, patrimony

inhibit **1** = hinder, check, frustrate, curb, restrain, constrain, obstruct, impede ≠ further **2** = prevent, stop, frustrate ≠ allow

inhibited = shy, reserved, guarded, subdued, repressed, constrained, self-conscious, reticent ≠ uninhibited

initial = opening, first, earliest, beginning, primary, maiden, introductory, embryonic ≠ final

initially = at first, first, firstly, originally, primarily, in the beginning, at *or* in the beginning

initiate VERB **1** = begin, start, open, launch, kick off (*informal*), embark on, originate, set about **2** = introduce, admit, enlist, enrol, launch, establish, invest, recruit
• NOUN = novice, member, pupil, convert, amateur, newcomer, beginner, trainee
• PHRASES **initiate someone into something** = instruct in, train in, coach in, acquaint with, drill in, make aware of, teach about, tutor in

initiative **1** = advantage, start, lead, upper hand **2** = enterprise, drive, energy, leadership, ambition, daring, enthusiasm, dynamism

inject **1** = vaccinate, administer, inoculate **2** = introduce, bring in, insert, instil, infuse, breathe
injection **1** = vaccination, shot (*informal*), jab (*informal*), dose, booster, immunization, inoculation **2** = introduction, investment, insertion, advancement, dose, infusion
injunction = order, ruling, command, instruction, mandate, precept, exhortation
injure **1** = hurt, wound, harm, damage, smash, crush, mar, shatter, mangulate (*Austral. slang*) **2** = damage, harm, ruin, wreck, spoil, impair, crool *or* cruel (*Austral. slang*) **3** = undermine, damage
injured = hurt, damaged, wounded, broken, cut, crushed, disabled, weakened, crook (*Austral. & N.Z. slang*)
injury **1** = wound, cut, damage, trauma (*Pathology*), gash, lesion, laceration **2** = harm, suffering, damage, ill, hurt, disability, misfortune, affliction **3** = wrong, offence, insult, detriment, disservice
injustice **1** = unfairness, discrimination, prejudice, bias, inequality, oppression, intolerance, bigotry ≠ justice **2** = wrong, injury, crime, error, offence, sin, misdeed, transgression
inland = interior, internal, upcountry
inner **1** = inside, internal, interior, inward ≠ outer **2** = central, middle, internal, interior **3** = hidden, deep, secret, underlying, obscure, repressed, unrevealed ≠ obvious
innocence **1** = naiveté, simplicity, inexperience, credulity, gullibility, ingenuousness, artlessness, unworldliness ≠ worldliness **2** = blamelessness, clean hands, uprightness, irreproachability, guiltlessness ≠ guilt **3** = chastity, virtue, purity, modesty, celibacy, continence, maidenhood
innocent **1** = not guilty, in the clear, blameless, clean, honest, uninvolved, irreproachable, guiltless ≠ guilty **2** = naive, open, trusting, simple, childlike, gullible, unsophisticated, unworldly ≠ worldly **3** = harmless, innocuous, inoffensive, well-meant, unobjectionable, well-intentioned
innovation **1** = change, revolution, departure, introduction, variation, transformation, upheaval, alteration **2** = newness, novelty, originality, freshness, modernization, uniqueness
inquest = inquiry, investigation, probe, inquisition
inquire *or* **enquire** VERB = ask, question, query, quiz
• PHRASES **inquire into something** = investigate, study, examine, research, explore, look into, probe into, make inquiries into
inquiry *or* **enquiry** **1** = question, query, investigation **2** = investigation, study, review, survey, examination, probe, inspection, exploration **3** = research, investigation, analysis, inspection, exploration, interrogation
insane **1** = mad, crazy, mentally ill, crazed, demented, deranged, out of your mind, off the air (*Austral. slang*), porangi (*N.Z.*) ≠ sane **2** = stupid, foolish, daft (*informal*), irresponsible, irrational, senseless, preposterous, impractical ≠ reasonable
insect = bug, creepy-crawly (*Brit. informal*), gogga (*S. African informal*)
insecure **1** = unconfident, worried, anxious, afraid, shy, uncertain, unsure, timid ≠ confident **2** = unsafe, exposed, vulnerable, wide-open, unprotected, defenceless, unguarded ≠ safe
insecurity = anxiety, fear, worry, uncertainty ≠ confidence
insert = put, place, position, slip, slide, slot, thrust, stick in
inside NOUN = interior, contents, core, nucleus
• PLURAL NOUN (*Informal*) = stomach, guts, belly, bowels, innards (*informal*), entrails, viscera, vitals
• ADJECTIVE **1** = inner, internal, interior, inward ≠ outside **2** = confidential, private, secret, internal, exclusive, restricted, privileged, classified
• ADVERB = indoors, in, within, under cover
insight **1** = understanding, perception, sense, knowledge, vision, judgment, awareness, grasp **2** *with* ***into*** = understanding of, perception of, awareness of, experience of, description of, introduction to, observation of, judgment of
insignificant = unimportant, minor, irrelevant, petty, trivial, meaningless, trifling, paltry ≠ important
insist **1** lay down the law, put your foot down (*informal*) **2** = demand, order, require, command, dictate, entreat

3 = assert, state, maintain, claim, declare, repeat, vow, swear
insistence 1 = demand, command, dictate, entreaty, importunity 2 = assertion, claim, statement, declaration, persistence, pronouncement
inspect 1 = examine, check, look at, view, survey, look over, scrutinize, go over *or* through 2 = check, examine, investigate, look at, survey, vet, look over, go over *or* through
inspection 1 = examination, investigation, scrutiny, once-over (*informal*) 2 = check, search, investigation, review, survey, examination, scrutiny, once-over (*informal*)
inspector = examiner, investigator, supervisor, monitor, superintendent, auditor, censor, surveyor
inspiration 1 = imagination, creativity, ingenuity, insight, originality, inventiveness, cleverness 2 = motivation, example, model, boost, spur, incentive, revelation, stimulus ≠ deterrent 3 = influence, spur, stimulus, muse
inspire 1 = motivate, stimulate, encourage, influence, spur, animate, enliven, galvanize ≠ discourage 2 = give rise to, produce, result in, engender
inspired 1 = brilliant, wonderful, impressive, outstanding, thrilling, memorable, dazzling, superlative 2 = stimulated, uplifted, exhilarated, enthused, elated
inspiring = uplifting, exciting, moving, stirring, stimulating, rousing, exhilarating, heartening ≠ uninspiring
instability 1 = uncertainty, insecurity, vulnerability, volatility, unpredictability, fluctuation, impermanence, unsteadiness ≠ stability 2 = imbalance, variability, unpredictability, unsteadiness, changeableness
install 1 = set up, put in, place, position, station, establish, lay, fix 2 = institute, establish, introduce, invest, ordain, inaugurate, induct 3 = settle, position, plant, establish, lodge, ensconce
installation 1 = setting up, fitting, instalment, placing, positioning, establishment 2 = appointment, ordination, inauguration, induction, investiture
instalment 1 = payment, repayment, part payment 2 = part, section, chapter, episode, portion, division
instance NOUN = example, case, occurrence, occasion, sample, illustration • VERB = name, mention, identify, point out, advance, quote, refer to, point to
instant NOUN 1 = moment, second, flash, split second, jiffy (*informal*), trice, twinkling of an eye (*informal*) 2 = time, point, hour, moment, stage, occasion, phase, juncture • ADJECTIVE 1 = immediate, prompt, instantaneous, direct, quick, on-the-spot, split-second 2 = ready-made, fast, convenience, ready-mixed, ready-cooked, precooked
instantly = immediately, at once, straight away, now, directly, right away, instantaneously, this minute
instead ADVERB = rather, alternatively, preferably, in preference, in lieu, on second thoughts • PHRASES **instead of** = in place of, rather than, in preference to, in lieu of, in contrast with
instinct 1 = natural inclination, talent, tendency, faculty, inclination, knack, predisposition, proclivity 2 = talent, skill, gift, capacity, bent, genius, faculty, knack 3 = intuition, impulse
instinctive = natural, inborn, automatic, unconscious, inherent, spontaneous, reflex, innate ≠ acquired
instinctively = intuitively, naturally, automatically, without thinking, involuntarily, by instinct
institute NOUN = establishment, body, centre, school, university, society, association, college • VERB = establish, start, found, launch, set up, introduce, fix, organize ≠ end
institution 1 = establishment, body, centre, school, university, society, association, college 2 = custom, practice, tradition, law, rule, procedure, convention, ritual
institutional = conventional, accepted, established, formal, routine, orthodox, procedural
instruct 1 = order, tell, direct, charge, bid, command, mandate, enjoin 2 = teach, school, train, coach, educate, drill, tutor
instruction NOUN 1 = order, ruling, command, rule, demand, regulation,

dictate, decree **2** = teaching, schooling, training, grounding, education, coaching, lesson(s), guidance
• PLURAL NOUN = information, rules, advice, directions, recommendations, guidance, specifications

instructor = teacher, coach, guide, adviser, trainer, demonstrator, tutor, mentor

instrument **1** = tool, device, implement, mechanism, appliance, apparatus, gadget, contraption (*informal*) **2** = agent, means, medium, agency, vehicle, mechanism, organ

instrumental = active, involved, influential, useful, helpful, contributory

insufficient = inadequate, scant, meagre, short, sparse, deficient, lacking ≠ ample

insulate = isolate, protect, screen, defend, shelter, shield, cut off, cushion

insult VERB = offend, abuse, wound, slight, put down, snub, malign, affront ≠ praise
• NOUN **1** = jibe, slight, put-down, abuse, snub, barb, affront, abusive remark **2** = offence, slight, snub, slur, affront, slap in the face (*informal*), kick in the teeth (*informal*), insolence

insulting = offensive, rude, abusive, degrading, contemptuous, disparaging, scurrilous, insolent ≠ complimentary

insurance **1** = assurance, cover, security, protection, safeguard, indemnity **2** = protection, security, guarantee, shelter, safeguard, warranty

insure **1** = assure, cover, protect, guarantee, warrant, underwrite, indemnify **2** = protect, cover, safeguard

intact = undamaged, whole, complete, sound, perfect, entire, unscathed, unbroken ≠ damaged

integral = essential, basic, fundamental, necessary, component, constituent, indispensable, intrinsic ≠ inessential

integrate = join, unite, combine, blend, incorporate, merge, fuse, assimilate ≠ separate

integrity **1** = honesty, principle, honour, virtue, goodness, morality, purity, probity ≠ dishonesty **2** = unity, unification, cohesion, coherence, wholeness, soundness, completeness

intellect = intelligence, mind, reason, understanding, sense, brains (*informal*), judgment

intellectual ADJECTIVE = scholarly, learned, academic, lettered, intelligent, cerebral, erudite, scholastic ≠ stupid
• NOUN = academic, expert, genius, thinker, master, mastermind, maestro, highbrow, fundi (*S. African*), acca (*Austral. slang*) ≠ idiot

intelligence **1** = intellect, understanding, brains (*informal*), sense, knowledge, judgment, wit, perception ≠ stupidity **2** = information, news, facts, report, findings, knowledge, data, notification ≠ misinformation

intelligent = clever, bright, smart, sharp, enlightened, knowledgeable, well-informed, brainy (*informal*) ≠ stupid

intend = plan, mean, aim, propose, purpose, have in mind *or* view

intense **1** = extreme, great, severe, fierce, deep, powerful, supreme, acute ≠ mild **2** = fierce, tough **3** = passionate, emotional, fierce, heightened, ardent, fanatical, fervent, heartfelt ≠ indifferent

intensify **1** = increase, raise, add to, strengthen, reinforce, widen, heighten, sharpen ≠ decrease **2** = escalate, increase, widen, deepen

intensity **1** = force, strength, fierceness **2** = passion, emotion, fervour, force, strength, fanaticism, ardour, vehemence

intensive = concentrated, thorough, exhaustive, full, demanding, detailed, complete, serious

intent ADJECTIVE = absorbed, intense, fascinated, preoccupied, enthralled, attentive, watchful, engrossed ≠ indifferent
• NOUN = intention, aim, purpose, meaning, end, plan, goal, design ≠ chance

intention = aim, plan, idea, goal, end, design, target, wish

inter = bury, lay to rest, entomb, consign to the grave

intercept = catch, stop, block, seize, cut off, interrupt, head off, obstruct

intercourse **1** = sexual intercourse, sex (*informal*), copulation, coitus, carnal knowledge **2** = contact, communication, commerce, dealings

interest NOUN **1** *often plural* = hobby, activity, pursuit, entertainment, recreation, amusement, preoccupation, diversion **2** *often plural* = advantage, good, benefit, profit **3** = stake, investment

• **VERB** = arouse your curiosity, fascinate, attract, grip, entertain, intrigue, divert, captivate ≠ bore

interested 1 = curious, attracted, excited, drawn, keen, gripped, fascinated, captivated ≠ uninterested 2 = involved, concerned, affected, implicated

interesting = intriguing, absorbing, appealing, attractive, engaging, gripping, entrancing, stimulating ≠ uninteresting

interface = connection, link, boundary, border, frontier

interfere **VERB** = meddle, intervene, intrude, butt in, tamper, pry, encroach, stick your oar in (*informal*)
• **PHRASES** **interfere with something** *or* **someone** = conflict with, check, clash, handicap, hamper, disrupt, inhibit, thwart

interference = intrusion, intervention, meddling, opposition, conflict, obstruction, prying

interim = temporary, provisional, makeshift, acting, caretaker, improvised, stopgap

interior **NOUN** = inside, centre, heart, middle, depths, core, nucleus
• **ADJECTIVE** 1 = inside, internal, inner ≠ exterior 2 = mental, emotional, psychological, private, personal, secret, hidden, spiritual

intermediary = mediator, agent, middleman, broker, go-between

intermediate = middle, mid, halfway, in-between (*informal*), midway, intervening, transitional, median

internal 1 = domestic, home, national, local, civic, in-house, intramural 2 = inner, inside, interior ≠ external

international = global, world, worldwide, universal, cosmopolitan, intercontinental

Internet
• **PHRASES** **the Internet** = the information superhighway, the net (*informal*), the web (*informal*), the World Wide Web, cyberspace

interpret 1 = take, understand, explain, construe 2 = translate, transliterate 3 = explain, make sense of, decode, decipher, elucidate 4 = understand, read, crack, solve, figure out (*informal*), comprehend, decode, deduce 5 = portray, present, perform, render, depict, enact, act out

interpretation 1 = explanation, analysis, exposition, elucidation 2 = performance, portrayal, presentation, reading, rendition 3 = reading, study, review, version, analysis, explanation, examination, evaluation

interpreter = translator

interrogation = questioning, inquiry, examination, grilling (*informal*), cross-examination, inquisition, third degree (*informal*)

interrupt 1 = intrude, disturb, intervene, interfere (with), break in, heckle, butt in, barge in (*informal*) 2 = suspend, stop, end, delay, cease, postpone, shelve, put off

interruption 1 = disruption, break, disturbance, hitch, intrusion 2 = stoppage, pause, suspension

interval 1 = period, spell, space, stretch, pause, span 2 = break, interlude, intermission, rest, gap, pause, respite, lull 3 = delay, gap, hold-up, stoppage 4 = stretch, space

intervene 1 = step in (*informal*), interfere, mediate, intrude, intercede, arbitrate, take a hand (*informal*) 2 = interrupt, involve yourself 3 = happen, occur, take place, follow, arise, ensue, befall, materialize

intervention = mediation, interference, intrusion, arbitration, conciliation, agency

interview **NOUN** 1 = meeting 2 = audience, talk, conference, exchange, dialogue, consultation, press conference
• **VERB** 1 = examine, talk to 2 = question, interrogate, examine, investigate, pump, grill (*informal*), quiz, cross-examine

interviewer = questioner, reporter, investigator, examiner, interrogator

intimacy = familiarity, closeness, confidentiality ≠ aloofness

intimate[1] **ADJECTIVE** 1 = close, dear, loving, near, familiar, thick (*informal*), devoted, confidential ≠ distant 2 = private, personal, confidential, special, individual, secret, exclusive ≠ public 3 = detailed, minute, full, deep, particular, immediate, comprehensive, profound 4 = cosy, relaxed, friendly, informal, harmonious, snug, comfy (*informal*), warm
• **NOUN** = friend, close friend, crony, cobber (*Austral. & N.Z. old-fashioned informal*), confidant *or* confidante, (constant) companion, E hoa (*N.Z.*) ≠ stranger

intimate[2] 1 = suggest, indicate, hint, imply, insinuate 2 = announce, state, declare, communicate, make known

intimately 1 = closely, personally, warmly, familiarly, tenderly, affectionately, confidentially, confidingly 2 = fully, very well, thoroughly, in detail, inside out

intimidate = frighten, pressure, threaten, scare, bully, plague, hound, daunt

intimidation = bullying, pressure, threat(s), menaces, coercion, arm-twisting (*informal*), browbeating, terrorization

intricate = complicated, involved, complex, fancy, elaborate, tangled, tortuous, convoluted ≠ simple

intrigue NOUN 1 = plot, scheme, conspiracy, manoeuvre, collusion, stratagem, chicanery, wile 2 = affair, romance, intimacy, liaison, amour
• VERB 1 = interest, fascinate, attract, rivet, titillate 2 = plot, scheme, manoeuvre, conspire, connive, machinate

intriguing = interesting, fascinating, absorbing, exciting, engaging, gripping, stimulating, compelling

introduce 1 = bring in, establish, set up, start, found, launch, institute, pioneer 2 = present, acquaint, make known, familiarize 3 = suggest, air, advance, submit, bring up, put forward, broach, moot 4 = add, insert, inject, throw in (*informal*), infuse

introduction 1 = launch, institution, pioneering, inauguration ≠ elimination 2 = opening, prelude, preface, lead-in, preamble, foreword, prologue, intro (*informal*) ≠ conclusion

introductory 1 = preliminary, first, initial, inaugural, preparatory ≠ concluding 2 = starting, opening, initial

intruder = trespasser, invader, prowler, interloper, infiltrator, gate-crasher (*informal*)

intrusion 1 = interruption, interference, infringement, trespass, encroachment 2 = invasion, breach, infringement, encroachment, infraction, usurpation

intuition 1 = instinct, perception, insight, sixth sense 2 = feeling, idea, impression, suspicion, premonition, inkling, presentiment

invade 1 = attack, storm, assault, capture, occupy, seize, raid, overwhelm 2 = infest, swarm, overrun, ravage, beset, pervade, permeate

invader = attacker, raider, plunderer, aggressor, trespasser

invalid[1] NOUN = patient, sufferer, convalescent, valetudinarian
• ADJECTIVE = disabled, ill, sick, ailing, frail, infirm, bedridden

invalid[2] 1 = null and void, void, worthless, inoperative ≠ valid 2 = unfounded, false, illogical, irrational, unsound, fallacious ≠ sound

invaluable = precious, valuable, priceless, inestimable, worth your *or* its weight in gold ≠ worthless

invariably = always, regularly, constantly, repeatedly, consistently, continually, eternally, habitually

invasion 1 = attack, assault, capture, takeover, raid, offensive, occupation, conquering 2 = intrusion, breach, violation, disturbance, disruption, infringement, encroachment, infraction

invent 1 = create, make, produce, design, discover, manufacture, devise, conceive 2 = make up, devise, concoct, forge, fake, fabricate, feign, falsify

invention 1 = creation, machine, device, design, instrument, discovery, innovation, gadget 2 = development, design, production, setting up, foundation, construction, creation, discovery 3 = fiction, fantasy, lie, yarn, fabrication, falsehood, untruth 4 = creativity, imagination, initiative, enterprise, genius, ingenuity, originality, inventiveness

inventive = creative, original, innovative, imaginative, inspired, fertile, ingenious, resourceful ≠ uninspired

inventor = creator, maker, author, designer, architect, coiner, originator

inventory = list, record, catalogue, listing, account, roll, file, register

invest VERB 1 = spend, expend, advance, venture, put in, devote, lay out, sink in 2 = empower, provide, charge, sanction, license, authorize, vest
• PHRASES **invest in something** = buy, get, purchase, pay for, obtain, acquire, procure

investigate = examine, study, research, go into, explore, look into, inspect, probe into

investigation = examination, study, inquiry, review, search, survey, probe, inspection

investigator = examiner, researcher,

monitor, detective, analyser, explorer, scrutinizer, inquirer

investment 1 = investing, backing, funding, financing, contribution, speculation, transaction, expenditure 2 = stake, interest, share, concern, portion, ante (*informal*) 3 = buy, asset, acquisition, venture, risk, gamble

invisible = unseen, imperceptible, indiscernible, unseeable ≠ visible

invitation = request, call, invite (*informal*), summons

invite 1 = ask 2 = request, look for, bid for, appeal for 3 = encourage, attract, cause, court, ask for (*informal*), generate, foster, tempt

inviting = tempting, appealing, attractive, welcoming, enticing, seductive, alluring, mouthwatering ≠ uninviting

invoke 1 = apply, use, implement, initiate, resort to, put into effect 2 = call upon, appeal to, pray to, petition, beseech, entreat, supplicate

involve 1 = entail, mean, require, occasion, imply, give rise to, necessitate 2 = concern, draw in, bear on

involved = complicated, complex, intricate, hard, confused, confusing, elaborate, tangled ≠ straightforward

involvement = connection, interest, association, commitment, attachment

inward 1 = incoming, entering, inbound, ingoing 2 = internal, inner, private, personal, inside, secret, hidden, interior ≠ outward

Ireland = Hibernia (*Latin*)

iron ADJECTIVE 1 = ferrous, ferric 2 = inflexible, hard, strong, tough, rigid, adamant, unconditional, steely ≠ weak
• PHRASES **iron something out** = settle, resolve, sort out, get rid of, reconcile, clear up, put right, straighten out

RELATED WORDS
adjectives: ferric, ferrous

ironic *or* **ironical** 1 = sarcastic, dry, acid, bitter, mocking, wry, satirical, tongue-in-cheek 2 = paradoxical, contradictory, puzzling, baffling, confounding, enigmatic, incongruous

irony 1 = sarcasm, mockery, ridicule, satire, cynicism, derision 2 = paradox, incongruity

irrational = illogical, crazy, absurd, unreasonable, preposterous, nonsensical ≠ rational

irregular 1 = variable, erratic, occasional, random, casual, shaky, sporadic, haphazard ≠ steady 2 = uneven, rough, ragged, crooked, jagged, bumpy, contorted, lopsided ≠ even 3 = inappropriate, unconventional, unethical, unusual, extraordinary, exceptional, peculiar, unofficial 4 = unofficial, underground, guerrilla, resistance, partisan, rogue, paramilitary, mercenary

irrelevant = unconnected, unrelated, unimportant, inappropriate, peripheral, immaterial, extraneous, beside the point ≠ relevant

irresistible = overwhelming, compelling, overpowering, urgent, compulsive

irresponsible = thoughtless, reckless, careless, unreliable, untrustworthy, shiftless, scatterbrained ≠ responsible

irritate 1 = annoy, anger, bother, needle (*informal*), infuriate, exasperate, nettle, irk ≠ placate 2 = inflame, pain, rub, scratch, scrape, chafe

irritated = annoyed, cross, angry, bothered, put out, exasperated, nettled, vexed, tooshie (*Austral. slang*), hoha (*N.Z.*)

irritating = annoying, trying, infuriating, disturbing, nagging, troublesome, maddening, irksome ≠ pleasing

irritation 1 = annoyance, anger, fury, resentment, gall, indignation, displeasure, exasperation ≠ pleasure 2 = nuisance, irritant, drag (*informal*), pain in the neck (*informal*), thorn in your flesh

island = isle, atoll, islet, ait *or* eyot (*dialect*), cay *or* key

RELATED WORD
adjective: insular

isolate 1 = separate, break up, cut off, detach, split up, insulate, segregate, disconnect 2 = quarantine

isolated = remote, far, distant, lonely, out-of-the-way, hidden, secluded, inaccessible

isolation = separation, segregation, detachment, solitude, seclusion, remoteness

issue NOUN 1 = topic, point, matter, problem, question, subject, theme 2 = point, question, bone of contention 3 = edition, printing, copy, publication, number, version 4 = children, offspring, babies, kids (*informal*), heirs, descendants,

progeny ≠ parent
• **VERB** = give out, release, publish, announce, deliver, spread, broadcast, distribute
• **PHRASES take issue with something** *or* **someone** = disagree with, question, challenge, oppose, dispute, object to, argue with, take exception to

itch VERB 1 = prickle, tickle, tingle **2** = long, ache, crave, pine, hunger, lust, yearn, hanker
• **NOUN 1** = irritation, tingling, prickling, itchiness **2** = desire, longing, craving, passion, yen (*informal*), hunger, lust, yearning

item 1 = article, thing, object, piece, unit, component **2** = matter, point, issue, case, question, concern, detail, subject **3** = report, story, piece, account, note, feature, notice, article

itinerary = schedule, programme, route, timetable

J

jab VERB = poke, dig, punch, thrust, tap, stab, nudge, prod
• **NOUN** = poke, dig, punch, thrust, tap, stab, nudge, prod

jacket = covering, casing, case, cover, skin, shell, coat, wrapping

jackpot = prize, winnings, award, reward, bonanza

jail NOUN = prison, penitentiary (*U.S.*), confinement, dungeon, nick (*Brit. slang*), slammer (*slang*), reformatory, boob (*Austral. slang*)
• **VERB** = imprison, confine, detain, lock up, put away, intern, incarcerate, send down

jam NOUN = predicament, tight spot, situation, trouble, hole (*slang*), fix (*informal*), mess, pinch
• **VERB 1** = pack, force, press, stuff, squeeze, ram, wedge, cram **2** = crowd, throng, crush, mass, surge, flock, swarm, congregate **3** = congest, block, clog, stick, stall, obstruct

jar[1] = pot, container, drum, vase, jug, pitcher, urn, crock

jar[2] 1 *usually with* ***on*** = irritate, annoy, offend, nettle, irk, grate on, get on your nerves (*informal*) **2** = jolt, rock, shake, bump, rattle, vibrate, convulse

jargon = parlance, idiom, usage, argot

jaw PLURAL NOUN = opening, entrance, mouth
• **VERB** (*Informal*) = talk, chat, gossip, chatter, spout, natter

jealous 1 = suspicious, protective, wary, doubtful, sceptical, vigilant, watchful, possessive ≠ trusting **2** = envious, grudging, resentful, green, green with envy, desirous, covetous ≠ satisfied

jealousy = suspicion, mistrust, possessiveness, doubt, spite, resentment, wariness, dubiety

jeer VERB = mock, deride, heckle, barrack, ridicule, taunt, scoff, gibe ≠ cheer
• **NOUN** = mockery, abuse, ridicule, taunt, boo, derision, gibe, catcall ≠ applause

jeopardy = danger, risk, peril, vulnerability, insecurity

jerk VERB = jolt, bang, bump, lurch
• **NOUN** = lurch, movement, thrust, twitch, jolt

jet NOUN = stream, current, spring, flow, rush, flood, burst, spray
• **VERB** = fly, wing, cruise, soar, zoom

jewel 1 = gemstone, gem, ornament, sparkler (*informal*), rock (*slang*) **2** = treasure, wonder, darling, pearl, gem, paragon, pride and joy, taonga (*N.Z.*)

jewellery = jewels, treasure, gems, trinkets, ornaments, finery, regalia

job 1 = position, work, calling, business, field, career, employment, profession **2** = task, duty, work, venture, enterprise, undertaking, assignment, chore

jobless = unemployed, redundant, out of work, inactive, unoccupied, idle

jog 1 = run, trot, canter, lope **2** = nudge, push, shake, prod **3** = stimulate, stir, prod

join 1 = enrol in, enter, sign up for, enlist in **2** = connect, unite, couple, link, combine, attach, fasten, add ≠ detach

joint ADJECTIVE = shared, mutual, collective, communal, united, joined, allied, combined
• **NOUN** = junction, connection, brace,

bracket, hinge, intersection, node, nexus
jointly = collectively, together, in conjunction, as one, in common, mutually, in partnership, in league ≠ separately
joke NOUN **1** = jest, gag (*informal*), wisecrack (*informal*), witticism, crack (*informal*), quip, pun, one-liner (*informal*) **2** = laugh, jest, jape **3** = prank, trick, practical joke, lark (*informal*), escapade, jape **4** = laughing stock, clown, buffoon
• VERB = jest, kid (*informal*), mock, tease, taunt, quip, banter, play the fool
joker = comedian, comic, wit, clown, wag, jester, prankster, buffoon
jolly = happy, cheerful, merry, upbeat (*informal*), playful, cheery, genial, chirpy (*informal*) ≠ miserable
jolt VERB **1** = jerk, push, shake, knock, jar, shove, jog, jostle **2** = surprise, stun, disturb, stagger, startle, perturb, discompose
• NOUN **1** = jerk, start, jump, shake, bump, jar, jog, lurch **2** = surprise, blow, shock, setback, bombshell, bolt from the blue
journal **1** = magazine, publication, gazette, periodical **2** = newspaper, paper, daily, weekly, monthly **3** = diary, record, history, log, notebook, chronicle, annals, yearbook
journalist = reporter, writer, correspondent, newsman *or* newswoman, commentator, broadcaster, hack (*derogatory*), columnist
journey NOUN **1** = trip, drive, tour, flight, excursion, trek, expedition, voyage **2** = progress, voyage, pilgrimage, odyssey
• VERB = travel, go, move, tour, progress, proceed, wander, trek, go walkabout (*Austral.*)
joy = delight, pleasure, satisfaction, ecstasy, enjoyment, bliss, glee, rapture ≠ sorrow
jubilee = celebration, holiday, festival, festivity
judge NOUN **1** = magistrate, justice, beak (*Brit. slang*), His, Her *or* Your Honour **2** = referee, expert, specialist, umpire, mediator, examiner, connoisseur, assessor **3** = critic, assessor, arbiter
• VERB **1** = adjudicate, referee, umpire, mediate, officiate, arbitrate **2** = evaluate, rate, consider, view, value, esteem **3** = estimate, guess, assess, calculate, evaluate, gauge

RELATED WORD
adjective: judicial

judgment **1** = opinion, view, estimate, belief, assessment, diagnosis, valuation, appraisal **2** = verdict, finding, ruling, decision, sentence, decree, arbitration, adjudication **3** = sense, good sense, understanding, discrimination, perception, wisdom, wit, prudence
judicial = legal, official
jug = container, pitcher, urn, carafe, creamer (*U.S. & Canad.*), vessel, jar, crock
juggle = manipulate, change, alter, modify, manoeuvre
juice **1** = liquid, extract, fluid, liquor, sap, nectar **2** = secretion
juicy **1** = moist, lush, succulent **2** (*Informal*) = interesting, colourful, sensational, vivid, provocative, spicy (*informal*), suggestive, racy
jumble NOUN = muddle, mixture, mess, disorder, confusion, clutter, disarray, mishmash
• VERB = mix, mistake, confuse, disorder, shuffle, muddle, disorganize
jumbo = giant, large, huge, immense, gigantic, oversized ≠ tiny
jump VERB **1** = leap, spring, bound, bounce, hop, skip **2** = vault, hurdle, go over, sail over, hop over **3** = spring, bound, bounce **4** = recoil, start, jolt, flinch, shake, jerk, quake, shudder **5** = increase, rise, climb, escalate, advance, soar, surge, spiral **6** = miss, avoid, skip, omit, evade
• NOUN **1** = leap, spring, skip, bound, hop, vault **2** = rise, increase, upswing, advance, upsurge, upturn, increment
jumped-up = conceited, arrogant, pompous, overbearing, presumptuous, insolent
jumper = sweater, top, jersey, cardigan, woolly, pullover
junior **1** = minor, lower, secondary, lesser, subordinate, inferior **2** = younger ≠ senior
junk = rubbish, refuse, waste, scrap, litter, debris, garbage (*chiefly U.S.*), trash
jurisdiction **1** = authority, power, control, rule, influence, command, mana (*N.Z.*) **2** = range, area, field, bounds, province, scope, sphere, compass
just ADVERB **1** = recently, lately, only now **2** = merely, only, simply, solely **3** = barely, hardly, by a whisker, by the skin of your

teeth **4** = exactly, really, quite, completely, totally, perfectly, entirely, truly
• **ADJECTIVE 1** = fair, good, legitimate, upright, honest, equitable, conscientious, virtuous ≠ unfair **2** = fitting, due, correct, deserved, appropriate, justified, decent, merited ≠ inappropriate

justice 1 = fairness, equity, integrity, honesty, decency, rightfulness, right ≠ injustice **2** = justness, fairness, legitimacy, right, integrity, honesty, legality, rightfulness **3** = judge, magistrate, beak (*Brit. slang*), His, Her *or* Your Honour

justification = reason, grounds, defence, basis, excuse, warrant, rationale, vindication

justify = explain, support, warrant, defend, excuse, uphold, vindicate, exonerate

juvenile NOUN = child, youth, minor, girl, boy, teenager, infant, adolescent ≠ adult
• **ADJECTIVE 1** = young, junior, adolescent, youthful, immature ≠ adult **2** = immature, childish, infantile, puerile, young, youthful, inexperienced, callow

k

kai (*N.Z. informal*) = food, grub (*slang*), provisions, fare, tucker (*Austral. & N.Z. informal*), refreshment, foodstuffs

kak (*S. African taboo*) **1** = faeces, excrement, manure, dung, droppings, waste matter **2** = rubbish, nonsense, garbage (*informal*), rot, drivel, tripe (*informal*), bizzo (*Austral. slang*), bull's wool (*Austral. & N.Z. slang*)

keen 1 = eager, intense, enthusiastic, passionate, ardent, avid, fervent, impassioned ≠ unenthusiastic **2** = earnest, fierce, intense, vehement, passionate, heightened, ardent, fanatical **3** = sharp, incisive, cutting, edged, razor-like ≠ dull **4** = perceptive, quick, sharp, acute, smart, wise, clever, shrewd ≠ obtuse **5** = intense, strong, fierce, relentless, cut-throat

keep[1] **VERB 1** *usually with **from*** = prevent, restrain, hinder, keep back **2** = hold on to, maintain, retain, save, preserve, nurture, cherish, conserve ≠ lose **3** = store, put, place, house, hold, deposit, stack, stow **4** = carry, stock, sell, supply, handle **5** = support, maintain, sustain, provide for, mind, fund, finance, feed **6** = raise, own, maintain, tend, farm, breed, look after, rear **7** = manage, run, administer, be in charge (of), direct, handle, supervise **8** = delay, detain, hinder, impede, obstruct, set back ≠ release
• **NOUN** = board, food, maintenance, living, kai (*N.Z. informal*)
• **PHRASES keep something up 1** = continue, make, maintain, carry on, persist in, persevere with **2** = maintain, sustain, perpetuate, retain, preserve, prolong ◆ **keep up** = keep pace

keep[2] = tower, castle

keeper = curator, guardian, steward, attendant, caretaker, preserver

keeping NOUN = care, charge, protection, possession, custody, guardianship, safekeeping
• **PHRASES in keeping with** = in agreement with, in harmony with, in accord with, in compliance with, in conformity with, in balance with, in correspondence with, in proportion with

key NOUN 1 = opener, door key, latchkey **2** = answer
• **ADJECTIVE** = essential, leading, major, main, important, necessary, vital, crucial ≠ minor

kia ora (*N.Z.*) = hello, hi (*informal*), greetings, gidday *or* g'day (*Austral. & N.Z.*), how do you do?, good morning, good evening, good afternoon

kick VERB 1 = boot, knock, punt **2** (*Informal*) = give up, break, stop, abandon, quit, cease, eschew, leave off
• **NOUN** (*Informal*) = thrill, buzz (*slang*), tingle, high (*slang*)
• **PHRASES kick off** (*Informal*) = begin, start, open, commence, initiate, get on the road ◆ **kick someone out** (*Informal*) = dismiss, remove, get rid of, expel, eject, evict, sack (*informal*)

kid[1] (*Informal*) = child, baby, teenager, youngster, infant, adolescent, juvenile, toddler, littlie (*Austral. informal*), ankle-

biter (*Austral. slang*), tacker (*Austral. slang*)
kid² = tease, joke, trick, fool, pretend, wind up (*Brit. slang*), hoax, delude
kidnap = abduct, capture, seize, snatch (*slang*), hijack, hold to ransom
kill **1** = slay, murder, execute, slaughter, destroy, massacre, butcher, cut down **2** (*Informal*) = destroy, crush, scotch, stop, halt, wreck, shatter, suppress
killer = murderer, slayer, hit man (*slang*), butcher, gunman, assassin, terminator, executioner
killing NOUN = murder, massacre, slaughter, dispatch, manslaughter, elimination, slaying, homicide
• ADJECTIVE (*Informal*) = tiring, taxing, exhausting, punishing, fatiguing, gruelling, sapping, debilitating
• PHRASES **make a killing** (*Informal*) = profit, gain, clean up (*informal*), be lucky, be successful, make a fortune, strike it rich (*informal*), make a bomb (*slang*)
kind¹ **1** = class, sort, type, variety, brand, category, genre **2** = sort, set, type, family, species, breed
kind² = considerate, kindly, concerned, friendly, generous, obliging, charitable, benign ≠ unkind
kindly ADJECTIVE = benevolent, kind, caring, warm, helpful, pleasant, sympathetic, benign ≠ cruel
• ADVERB = benevolently, politely, generously, thoughtfully, tenderly, lovingly, cordially, affectionately ≠ unkindly
kindness = goodwill, understanding, charity, humanity, compassion, generosity, philanthropy, benevolence ≠ malice
king = ruler, monarch, sovereign, leader, lord, Crown, emperor, head of state
kingdom = country, state, nation, territory, realm
kiss VERB **1** = peck (*informal*), osculate, neck (*informal*) **2** = brush, touch, shave, scrape, graze, glance off, stroke
• NOUN = peck (*informal*), snog (*Brit. slang*), smacker (*slang*), French kiss, osculation
kit NOUN **1** = equipment, materials, tackle, tools, apparatus, paraphernalia **2** = gear, things, stuff, equipment, uniform
• PHRASES **kit something** *or* **someone out** *or* **up** = equip, fit, supply, provide with, arm, stock, costume, furnish
knack = skill, art, ability, facility, talent, gift, capacity, trick ≠ ineptitude
kneel = genuflect, stoop
knickers = underwear, smalls, briefs, drawers, panties, bloomers
knife NOUN = blade, carver, cutter
• VERB = cut, wound, stab, slash, thrust, pierce, spear, jab
knit **1** = join, unite, link, tie, bond, combine, bind, weave **2** = heal, unite, join, link, bind, fasten, intertwine **3** = furrow, tighten, knot, wrinkle, crease, screw up, pucker, scrunch up
knob = ball, stud, knot, lump, bump, projection, hump, protrusion
knock VERB **1** = bang, strike, tap, rap, thump, pummel **2** = hit, strike, punch, belt (*informal*), smack, thump, cuff **3** (*Informal*) = criticize, condemn, put down, run down, abuse, slate (*informal*), censure, denigrate
• NOUN **1** = knocking, pounding, beating, tap, bang, banging, rap, thump **2** = bang, blow, impact, jar, collision, jolt, smash **3** = blow, hit, punch, crack, clip, slap, bash, smack **4** (*Informal*) = setback, check, defeat, blow, reverse, disappointment, hold-up, hitch
• PHRASES **knock about** *or* **around** = wander, travel, roam, rove, range, drift, stray, ramble, go walkabout (*Austral.*)
◆ **knock about** *or* **around with someone** = mix with, associate with, mingle with, consort with, hobnob with, socialize with, accompany ◆ **knock off** (*Informal*) = stop work, get out, call it a day (*informal*), finish work, clock off, clock out ◆ **knock someone about** *or* **around** = hit, attack, beat, strike, abuse, injure, assault, batter ◆ **knock someone down** = run over, hit, run down, knock over, mow down ◆ **knock something down** = demolish, destroy, flatten, tear down, level, fell, dismantle, bulldoze
◆ **knock something off** (*Slang*) = steal, take, nick (*slang, chiefly Brit.*), thieve, rob, pinch
knockout **1** = killer blow, coup de grâce (*French*), KO *or* K.O. (*slang*) **2** (*Informal*) = success, hit, winner, triumph, smash, sensation, smash hit ≠ failure
knot NOUN = connection, tie, bond, joint, loop, ligature
• VERB = tie, secure, bind, loop, tether
know **1** = have knowledge of, see,

understand, recognize, perceive, be aware of, be conscious of **2** = be acquainted with, recognize, be familiar with, be friends with, be friendly with, have knowledge of, have dealings with, socialize with ≠ be unfamiliar with **3** *sometimes with* ***about*** *or* ***of*** = be familiar with, understand, comprehend, have knowledge of, be acquainted with, feel certain of, have dealings in, be versed in ≠ be ignorant of

know-how (*Informal*) = expertise, ability, skill, knowledge, facility, talent, command, capability

knowing = meaningful, significant, expressive, enigmatic, suggestive

knowledge **1** = understanding, sense, judgment, perception, awareness, insight, grasp, appreciation **2** = learning, education, intelligence, instruction, wisdom, scholarship, enlightenment, erudition ≠ ignorance **3** = acquaintance, intimacy, familiarity ≠ unfamiliarity

knowledgeable **1** = well-informed, conversant, au fait (*French*), experienced, aware, familiar, in the know (*informal*), cognizant **2** = intelligent, learned, educated, scholarly, erudite

known = famous, well-known, celebrated, noted, acknowledged, recognized, avowed ≠ unknown

kopje *or* **koppie** (*S. African*) = hill, down (*archaic*), fell, mount, hilltop, knoll, hillock, brae (*Scot.*)

l

label NOUN = tag, ticket, tab, marker, sticker
• VERB = tag, mark, stamp, ticket, tab

labour NOUN **1** = workers, employees, workforce, labourers, hands **2** = work, effort, employment, toil, industry **3** = childbirth, birth, delivery, parturition
• VERB **1** = work, toil, strive, work hard, sweat (*informal*), slave, endeavour, slog away (*informal*) ≠ rest **2** = struggle, work, strain, work hard, strive, grapple, toil, make an effort **3** = overemphasize, stress, elaborate, exaggerate, strain, dwell on, overdo, go on about **4** *usually with* ***under*** = be disadvantaged by, suffer from, be a victim of, be burdened by

Labour = left-wing, Democrat (*U.S.*)

laboured = difficult, forced, strained, heavy, awkward

labourer = worker, manual worker, hand, blue-collar worker, drudge, navvy (*Brit. informal*)

lace NOUN **1** = netting, net, filigree, meshwork, openwork **2** = cord, tie, string, lacing, shoelace, bootlace
• VERB **1** = fasten, tie, tie up, do up, secure, bind, thread **2** = mix, drug, doctor, add to, spike, contaminate, fortify, adulterate **3** = intertwine, interweave, entwine, twine, interlink

lack NOUN = shortage, want, absence, deficiency, need, inadequacy, scarcity, dearth ≠ abundance
• VERB = miss, want, need, require, not have, be without, be short of, be in need of ≠ have

lad = boy, kid (*informal*), guy (*informal*), youth, fellow, youngster, juvenile, nipper (*informal*)

laden = loaded, burdened, full, charged, weighed down, encumbered

lady **1** = gentlewoman, duchess, noble, dame, baroness, countess, aristocrat, viscountess **2** = woman, female, girl, damsel, charlie (*Austral. slang*), chook (*Austral. slang*), wahine (*N.Z.*)

lag = hang back, delay, trail, linger, loiter, straggle, dawdle, tarry

laid-back = relaxed, calm, casual, easy-going, unflappable (*informal*), unhurried, free and easy ≠ tense

lake = pond, pool, reservoir, loch (*Scot.*), lagoon, mere, lough (*Irish*), tarn

lame **1** = disabled, handicapped, crippled, limping, hobbling, game **2** = unconvincing, poor, pathetic, inadequate, thin, weak, feeble, unsatisfactory

lament VERB = bemoan, grieve, mourn, weep over, complain about, regret, wail

about, deplore
• NOUN 1 = complaint, moan, wailing, lamentation 2 = dirge, requiem, elegy, threnody

land NOUN 1 = ground, earth, dry land, terra firma 2 = soil, ground, earth, clay, dirt, sod, loam 3 = countryside, farmland 4 (*Law*) = property, grounds, estate, real estate, realty, acreage 5 = country, nation, region, state, district, territory, province, kingdom
• VERB 1 = arrive, dock, put down, moor, alight, touch down, disembark, come to rest 2 (*Informal*) = gain, get, win, secure, acquire
• PHRASES **land up** = end up, turn up, wind up, finish up, fetch up (*informal*)
RELATED WORD
adjective: terrestrial

landlord 1 = owner, landowner, proprietor, freeholder, lessor, landholder 2 = innkeeper, host, hotelier

landmark 1 = feature, spectacle, monument 2 = milestone, turning point, watershed, critical point

landscape = scenery, country, view, land, scene, prospect, countryside, outlook

landslide = landslip, avalanche, rockfall

lane = road, street, track, path, way, passage, trail, pathway

language 1 = tongue, dialect, vernacular, patois 2 = speech, communication, expression, speaking, talk, talking, discourse, parlance

languish 1 = decline, fade away, wither away, flag, weaken, wilt ≠ flourish 2 (*Literary*) = waste away, suffer, rot, be abandoned, be neglected ≠ thrive 3 *often with* **for** = pine, long, desire, hunger, yearn, hanker

lap¹ = circuit, tour, leg, stretch, circle, orbit, loop

lap² VERB 1 = ripple, wash, splash, swish, gurgle, slosh, purl, plash 2 = drink, sip, lick, swallow, gulp, sup
• PHRASES **lap something up** = relish, like, enjoy, delight in, savour, revel in, wallow in, accept eagerly

lapse NOUN 1 = decline, fall, drop, deterioration 2 = mistake, failing, fault, failure, error, slip, negligence, omission 3 = interval, break, gap, pause, interruption, lull, breathing space, intermission
• VERB 1 = slip, fall, decline, sink, drop, slide, deteriorate, degenerate 2 = end, stop, run out, expire, terminate

lapsed = expired, ended, finished, run out, invalid, out of date, discontinued

large ADJECTIVE 1 = big, great, huge, heavy, massive, vast, enormous, tall ≠ small 2 = massive, great, big, huge, vast, enormous, considerable, substantial ≠ small
• PHRASES **at large** 1 = in general, generally, chiefly, mainly, as a whole, in the main 2 = free, on the run, fugitive, at liberty, on the loose, unchained, unconfined ♦ **by and large** = on the whole, generally, mostly, in general, all things considered, predominantly, in the main, all in all

largely = mainly, generally, chiefly, mostly, principally, primarily, predominantly, by and large

large-scale = wide-ranging, global, sweeping, broad, wide, vast, extensive, wholesale

lash¹ VERB 1 = pound, beat, strike, hammer, drum, smack (*dialect*) 2 = censure, attack, blast, put down, criticize, slate (*informal, chiefly Brit.*), scold, tear into (*informal*) 3 = whip, beat, thrash, birch, flog, scourge
• NOUN = blow, hit, strike, stroke, stripe, swipe (*informal*)

lash² = fasten, tie, secure, bind, strap, make fast

last¹ ADJECTIVE 1 = most recent, latest, previous 2 = hindmost, final, at the end, remotest, furthest behind, most distant, rearmost ≠ foremost 3 = final, closing, concluding, ultimate ≠ first
• ADVERB = in *or* at the end, after, behind, in the rear, bringing up the rear
• PHRASES **the last word** 1 = final decision, final say, final statement, conclusive comment 2 = leading, finest, cream, supreme, elite, foremost, pre-eminent, unsurpassed

last² = continue, remain, survive, carry on, endure, persist, keep on, abide ≠ end

lasting = continuing, long-term, permanent, enduring, remaining, abiding, long-standing, perennial ≠ passing

latch NOUN = fastening, catch, bar, lock, hook, bolt, hasp
• VERB = fasten, bar, secure, bolt, make fast

late ADJECTIVE **1** = overdue, delayed, last-minute, belated, tardy, behind time, behindhand ≠ early **2** = dead, deceased, departed, passed on, former, defunct ≠ alive **3** = recent, new, advanced, fresh ≠ old
• ADVERB = behind time, belatedly, tardily, behindhand, dilatorily ≠ early

lately = recently, of late, just now, in recent times, not long ago, latterly

later ADVERB = afterwards, after, eventually, in time, subsequently, later on, thereafter, in a while
• ADJECTIVE = subsequent, next, following, ensuing

latest = up-to-date, current, fresh, newest, modern, most recent, up-to-the-minute

latitude = scope, liberty, freedom, play, space, licence, leeway, laxity

latter PRONOUN = second, last, last-mentioned, second-mentioned
• ADJECTIVE = last, ending, closing, final, concluding ≠ earlier

laugh VERB = chuckle, giggle, snigger, cackle, chortle, guffaw, titter, be in stitches
• NOUN **1** = chortle, giggle, chuckle, snigger, guffaw, titter **2** (*Informal*) = joke, scream (*informal*), hoot (*informal*), lark, prank **3** (*Informal*) = clown, character (*informal*), scream (*informal*), entertainer, card (*informal*), joker, hoot (*informal*)
• PHRASES **laugh something off** = disregard, ignore, dismiss, overlook, shrug off, minimize, brush aside, make light of

laughter = amusement, entertainment, humour, glee, fun, mirth, hilarity, merriment

launch VERB **1** = propel, fire, dispatch, discharge, project, send off, set in motion, send into orbit **2** = begin, start, open, initiate, introduce, found, set up, originate
• PHRASES **launch into something** = start enthusiastically, begin, initiate, embark on, instigate, inaugurate, embark upon

laurel
• PHRASES **rest on your laurels** = sit back, relax, take it easy, relax your efforts

lavatory = toilet, bathroom, loo (*Brit. informal*), privy, cloakroom (*Brit.*), urinal, latrine, washroom, dunny (*Austral. & N.Z. old-fashioned informal*), bogger (*Austral. slang*), brasco (*Austral. slang*)

lavish ADJECTIVE **1** = grand, magnificent, splendid, abundant, copious, profuse ≠ stingy **2** = extravagant, wild, excessive, exaggerated, wasteful, prodigal, unrestrained, immoderate ≠ thrifty **3** = generous, free, liberal, bountiful, open-handed, unstinting, munificent ≠ stingy
• VERB = shower, pour, heap, deluge, dissipate ≠ stint

law **1** = constitution, code, legislation, charter **2** = statute, act, bill, rule, order, command, regulation, resolution **3** = principle, code, canon, precept, axiom, kaupapa (*N.Z.*) **4** = the legal profession, the bar, barristers

RELATED WORDS
adjectives: legal, judicial

lawsuit = case, action, trial, suit, proceedings, dispute, prosecution, legal action

lawyer = legal adviser, attorney, solicitor, counsel, advocate, barrister, counsellor, legal representative

lay[1] VERB **1** = place, put, set, spread, plant, leave, deposit, put down **2** = devise, plan, design, prepare, work out, plot, hatch, contrive **3** = produce, bear, deposit **4** = arrange, prepare, make, organize, position, set out, devise, put together **5** = attribute, assign, allocate, allot, ascribe, impute **6** = put forward, offer, present, advance, lodge, submit, bring forward **7** = bet, stake, venture, gamble, chance, risk, hazard, wager
• PHRASES **lay someone off** = dismiss, fire (*informal*), release, sack (*informal*), pay off, discharge, let go, make redundant ◆ **lay someone out** (*Informal*) = knock out, fell, floor, knock unconscious, knock for six ◆ **lay something out** **1** = arrange, order, design, display, exhibit, put out, spread out **2** (*Informal*) = spend, pay, invest, fork out (*slang*), expend, shell out (*informal*), disburse

lay[2] **1** = nonclerical, secular, non-ordained **2** = nonspecialist, amateur, unqualified, untrained, inexpert, nonprofessional

layer = tier, level, seam, stratum

layout = arrangement, design, outline, format, plan, formation

lazy 1 = idle, inactive, indolent, slack, negligent, inert, workshy, slothful ≠ industrious 2 = lethargic, languorous, slow-moving, languid, sleepy, sluggish, drowsy, somnolent ≠ quick

leach = extract, strain, drain, filter, seep, percolate

lead VERB 1 = go in front (of), head, be in front, be at the head (of), walk in front (of) 2 = guide, conduct, steer, escort, precede, usher, pilot, show the way 3 = connect to, link, open onto 4 = be ahead (of), be first, exceed, be winning, excel, surpass, come first, transcend 5 = command, rule, govern, preside over, head, control, manage, direct 6 = live, have, spend, experience, pass, undergo 7 = result in, cause, produce, contribute, generate, bring about, bring on, give rise to 8 = cause, prompt, persuade, move, draw, influence, motivate, prevail
• NOUN 1 = first place, winning position, primary position, vanguard 2 = advantage, start, edge, margin, winning margin 3 = example, direction, leadership, guidance, model, pattern 4 = clue, suggestion, hint, indication, pointer, tip-off 5 = leading role, principal, protagonist, title role, principal part 6 = leash, line, cord, rein, tether
• ADJECTIVE = main, prime, top, leading, first, head, chief, premier
• PHRASES **lead someone on** = entice, tempt, lure, mislead, draw on, seduce, deceive, beguile ◆ **lead up to something** = introduce, prepare for, pave the way for

leader = principal, president, head, chief, boss (*informal*), director, manager, chairman, baas (*S. African*) ≠ follower

leadership 1 = authority, control, influence, command, premiership, captaincy, governance, headship 2 = guidance, government, authority, management, direction, supervision, domination, superintendency

leading = principal, top, major, main, first, highest, greatest, chief ≠ minor

leaf NOUN 1 = frond, blade, cotyledon 2 = page, sheet, folio
• PHRASES **leaf through something** (with *book, magazine* etc. as object) = skim, glance, scan, browse, look through, dip into, flick through, flip through

leaflet = booklet, notice, brochure, circular, flyer, tract, pamphlet, handout

leafy = green, shaded, shady, verdant

league 1 = association, union, alliance, coalition, group, corporation, partnership, federation 2 (*Informal*) = class, group, level, category

leak VERB 1 = escape, pass, spill, release, drip, trickle, ooze, seep 2 = disclose, tell, reveal, pass on, give away, make public, divulge, let slip
• NOUN 1 = leakage, discharge, drip, seepage, percolation 2 = hole, opening, crack, puncture, aperture, chink, crevice, fissure 3 = disclosure, exposé, exposure, admission, revelation, uncovering, betrayal, unearthing

lean[1] VERB 1 = bend, tip, slope, incline, tilt, heel, slant 2 = rest, prop, be supported, recline, repose 3 = tend, prefer, favour, incline, be prone to, be disposed to
• PHRASES **lean on someone** = depend on, trust, rely on, cling to, count on, have faith in

lean[2] = thin, slim, slender, skinny, angular, trim, spare, gaunt ≠ fat

leaning = tendency, bias, inclination, bent, disposition, penchant, propensity, predilection

leap VERB = jump, spring, bound, bounce, hop, skip
• NOUN 1 = jump, spring, bound, vault 2 = rise, change, increase, soaring, surge, escalation, upsurge, upswing
• PHRASES **leap at something** = accept eagerly, seize on, jump at

learn 1 = master, grasp, pick up, take in, familiarize yourself with 2 = discover, hear, understand, find out about, become aware, discern, ascertain, come to know 3 = memorize, commit to memory, learn by heart, learn by rote, learn parrot-fashion, get off pat

learned = scholarly, academic, intellectual, versed, well-informed, erudite, highbrow, well-read ≠ uneducated

learner = student, novice, beginner, apprentice, neophyte, tyro ≠ expert

learning = knowledge, study, education, scholarship, enlightenment

lease = hire, rent, let, loan, charter, rent out, hire out

least = smallest, meanest, fewest, lowest,

tiniest, minimum, slightest, minimal

leave VERB **1** = depart from, withdraw from, go from, escape from, quit, flee, exit, pull out of ≠ arrive **2** = quit, give up, get out of, resign from, drop out of **3** = give up, abandon, dump (*informal*), drop, surrender, ditch (*informal*), chuck (*informal*), discard ≠ stay with **4** = entrust, commit, delegate, refer, hand over, assign, consign, allot **5** = bequeath, will, transfer, endow, confer, hand down **6** = forget, leave behind, mislay **7** = cause, produce, result in, generate, deposit
• NOUN **1** = holiday, break, vacation, time off, sabbatical, leave of absence, furlough **2** = permission, freedom, sanction, liberty, concession, consent, allowance, warrant ≠ refusal **3** = departure, parting, withdrawal, goodbye, farewell, retirement, leave-taking, adieu ≠ arrival
• PHRASES **leave something** *or* **someone out** = omit, exclude, miss out, forget, reject, ignore, overlook, neglect

lecture NOUN **1** = talk, address, speech, lesson, instruction, presentation, discourse, sermon **2** = telling-off (*informal*), rebuke, reprimand, talking-to (*informal*), scolding, dressing-down (*informal*), reproof
• VERB **1** = talk, speak, teach, address, discourse, spout, expound, hold forth **2** = tell off (*informal*), berate, scold, reprimand, censure, castigate, admonish, reprove

lees = sediment, grounds, deposit, dregs

left **1** = left-hand, port, larboard (*Nautical*) **2** (*of politics*) = socialist, radical, left-wing, leftist

left-wing = socialist, communist, red (*informal*), radical, revolutionary, militant, Bolshevik, Leninist

leg NOUN **1** = limb, member, shank, lower limb, pin (*informal*), stump (*informal*) **2** = support, prop, brace, upright **3** = stage, part, section, stretch, lap, segment, portion
• PHRASES **pull someone's leg** (*Informal*) = tease, trick, fool, kid (*informal*), wind up (*Brit. slang*), hoax, make fun of, lead up the garden path

legacy = bequest, inheritance, gift, estate, heirloom

legal **1** = judicial, judiciary, forensic, juridical, jurisdictive **2** = lawful, allowed, sanctioned, constitutional, valid, legitimate, authorized, permissible

legend **1** = myth, story, tale, fiction, saga, fable, folk tale, folk story **2** = celebrity, star, phenomenon, genius, prodigy, luminary, megastar (*informal*) **3** = inscription, title, caption, device, motto, rubric

legendary **1** = famous, celebrated, well-known, acclaimed, renowned, famed, immortal, illustrious ≠ unknown **2** = mythical, fabled, traditional, romantic, fabulous, fictitious, storybook, apocryphal ≠ factual

legion **1** = army, company, force, division, troop, brigade **2** = multitude, host, mass, drove, number, horde, myriad, throng

legislation **1** = law, act, ruling, rule, bill, measure, regulation, charter **2** = lawmaking, regulation, prescription, enactment

legislative = law-making, judicial, law-giving

legislator = lawmaker, lawgiver

legislature = parliament, congress, senate, assembly, chamber

legitimate ADJECTIVE **1** = lawful, legal, genuine, authentic, authorized, rightful, kosher (*informal*), dinkum (*Austral. & N.Z. informal*), licit ≠ unlawful **2** = reasonable, correct, sensible, valid, warranted, logical, justifiable, well-founded ≠ unreasonable
• VERB = legitimize, allow, permit, sanction, authorize, legalize, pronounce lawful

leisure = spare, free, rest, ease, relaxation, recreation ≠ work

lekker (*S. African slang*) = delicious, tasty, luscious, palatable, delectable, mouthwatering, scrumptious (*informal*), appetizing, yummo (*Austral. slang*)

lemon

RELATED WORDS
adjectives: citric, citrous

lend VERB **1** = loan, advance, sub (*Brit. informal*) **2** = give, provide, add, supply, grant, confer, bestow, impart
• PHRASES **lend itself to something** = be appropriate for, suit, be suitable for, be appropriate to, be serviceable for

length NOUN **1** = distance, reach, measure, extent, span, longitude **2** = duration, term, period, space, stretch, span, expanse **3** = piece, measure, section, segment, portion
• PHRASES **at length** **1** = at last, finally, eventually, in time, in the end, at long

last **2** = for a long time, completely, fully, thoroughly, for hours, in detail, for ages, in depth

lengthen **1** = extend, continue, increase, stretch, expand, elongate ≠ shorten **2** = protract, extend, prolong, draw out, spin out, make longer ≠ cut down

lengthy **1** = protracted, long, prolonged, tedious, drawn-out, interminable, long-winded, long-drawn-out **2** = very long, rambling, interminable, long-winded, wordy, discursive, extended ≠ brief

lesbian = homosexual, gay, les (*slang*), sapphic, lesbo (*slang*)

less **DETERMINER** = smaller, shorter, not so much

• **PREPOSITION** = minus, without, lacking, excepting, subtracting

lessen **1** = reduce, lower, diminish, decrease, ease, narrow, minimize ≠ increase **2** = grow less, diminish, decrease, contract, ease, shrink

lesser = lower, secondary, subsidiary, inferior, less important ≠ greater

lesson **1** = class, schooling, period, teaching, coaching, session, instruction, lecture **2** = example, warning, message, moral, deterrent **3** = Bible reading, reading, text, Bible passage, Scripture passage

let **VERB** **1** = allow, permit, authorize, give the go-ahead, give permission **2** = lease, hire, rent, rent out, hire out, sublease

• **PHRASES** **let on** (*Informal*) **1** = reveal, disclose, say, tell, admit, give away, divulge, let slip ◆ **let someone down** = disappoint, fail, abandon, desert, disillusion, fall short, leave stranded, leave in the lurch ◆ **let someone off** = excuse, release, discharge, pardon, spare, forgive, exempt, exonerate ◆ **let something** *or* **someone in** = admit, include, receive, welcome, greet, take in, incorporate, give access to ◆ **let something down** = deflate, empty, exhaust, flatten, puncture ◆ **let something off** **1** = fire, explode, set off, discharge, detonate **2** = emit, release, leak, exude, give off ◆ **let something out** **1** = release, discharge **2** = emit, make, produce, give vent to ◆ **let up** = stop, diminish, decrease, subside, relax, ease (up), moderate, lessen

lethal = deadly, terminal, fatal, dangerous, devastating, destructive, mortal, murderous ≠ harmless

letter **1** = message, line, note, communication, dispatch, missive, epistle **2** = character, mark, sign, symbol

level **NOUN** = position, standard, degree, grade, standing, stage, rank, status

• **ADJECTIVE** **1** = equal, balanced, at the same height **2** = horizontal, even, flat, smooth, uniform ≠ slanted **3** = even, tied, equal, drawn, neck and neck, all square, level pegging

• **VERB** **1** = equalize, balance, even up **2** = destroy, devastate, demolish, flatten, knock down, pull down, tear down, bulldoze ≠ build **3** = direct, point, turn, train, aim, focus **4** = flatten, plane, smooth, even off *or* out

• **PHRASES** **on the level** (*Informal*) = honest, genuine, straight, fair, square, dinkum (*Austral. & N.Z. informal*), above board

lever **NOUN** = handle, bar

• **VERB** = prise, force

leverage **1** = influence, authority, pull (*informal*), weight, clout (*informal*) **2** = force, hold, pull, strength, grip, grasp

levy **NOUN** = tax, fee, toll, tariff, duty, excise, exaction

• **VERB** = impose, charge, collect, demand, exact

liability **1** = disadvantage, burden, drawback, inconvenience, handicap, nuisance, hindrance, millstone **2** = responsibility, accountability, culpability, answerability

liable **1** = likely, tending, inclined, disposed, prone, apt **2** = vulnerable, subject, exposed, prone, susceptible, open, at risk of **3** = responsible, accountable, answerable, obligated

liaison **1** = contact, communication, connection, interchange **2** = intermediary, contact, hook-up **3** = affair, romance, intrigue, fling, love affair, amour, entanglement

liar = falsifier, perjurer, fibber, fabricator

libel **NOUN** = defamation, misrepresentation, denigration, smear, calumny, aspersion

• **VERB** = defame, smear, slur, blacken, malign, denigrate, revile, vilify

liberal **1** = tolerant, open-minded, permissive, indulgent, easy-going, broad-minded ≠ intolerant **2** = progressive, radical, reformist, libertarian, forward-looking, free-thinking ≠ conservative **3** = abundant, generous, handsome, lavish, ample, rich, plentiful, copious ≠ limited **4** = generous, kind, charitable, extravagant, open-hearted, bountiful, magnanimous, open-handed ≠ stingy

liberate = free, release, rescue, save, deliver, let out, set free, let loose ≠ imprison

liberty NOUN = independence, sovereignty, liberation, autonomy, immunity, self-determination, emancipation, self-government ≠ restraint
• PHRASES **at liberty 1** = free, escaped, unlimited, at large, not confined, untied, on the loose, unchained **2** = able, free, allowed, permitted, entitled, authorized
◆ **take liberties** *or* **a liberty** = not show enough respect, show disrespect, act presumptuously, behave too familiarly, behave impertinently

licence NOUN **1** = certificate, document, permit, charter, warrant **2** = permission, the right, authority, leave, sanction, liberty, immunity, entitlement ≠ denial **3** = freedom, creativity, latitude, independence, liberty, deviation, leeway, free rein ≠ restraint **4** = laxity, excess, indulgence, irresponsibility, licentiousness, immoderation ≠ moderation
• PHRASES **under licence** = with permission, under a charter, under warrant, under a permit, with authorization, under a patent

license = permit, sanction, allow, warrant, authorize, empower, certify, accredit ≠ forbid

lick VERB **1** = taste, lap, tongue **2** (*Informal*) = beat, defeat, overcome, rout, outstrip, outdo, trounce, vanquish **3** (*of flames*) = flicker, touch, flick, dart, ripple, play over
• NOUN **1** = dab, bit, touch, stroke **2** (*Informal*) = pace, rate, speed, clip (*informal*)

lie¹ NOUN = falsehood, deceit, fabrication, fib, fiction, invention, deception, untruth
• VERB = fib, fabricate, falsify, prevaricate, not tell the truth, equivocate, dissimulate, tell untruths
• PHRASES **give the lie to something** = disprove, expose, discredit, contradict, refute, negate, invalidate, rebut

lie² 1 = recline, rest, lounge, sprawl, stretch out, loll, repose **2** = be placed, be, rest, exist, be situated **3** = be situated, sit, be located, be positioned **4** = be buried, remain, rest, be, be entombed

life 1 = being, existence, vitality, sentience **2** = existence, being, lifetime, time, days, span **3** = way of life, situation, conduct, behaviour, life style **4** = liveliness, energy, spirit, vitality, animation, vigour, verve, zest **5** = biography, story, history, profile, confessions, autobiography, memoirs, life story

RELATED WORDS
adjectives: animate, vital

lifelong = long-lasting, enduring, lasting, persistent, long-standing, perennial

lifetime = existence, time, day(s), span

lift VERB **1** = raise, pick up, hoist, draw up, elevate, uplift, heave up, upraise ≠ lower **2** = revoke, end, remove, withdraw, stop, cancel, terminate, rescind ≠ impose **3** = disappear, clear, vanish, disperse, dissipate, rise, be dispelled
• NOUN **1** = boost, encouragement, stimulus, pick-me-up, fillip, shot in the arm (*informal*), gee-up ≠ blow **2** = elevator (*chiefly U.S.*), hoist, paternoster **3** = ride, run, drive, hitch (*informal*)
• PHRASES **lift off** = take off, be launched, blast off, take to the air

light¹ NOUN **1** = brightness, illumination, luminosity, shining, glow, glare, gleam, brilliance ≠ dark **2** = lamp, torch, candle, flare, beacon, lantern, taper **3** = match, spark, flame, lighter **4** = aspect, context, angle, point of view, interpretation, viewpoint, slant, standpoint
• ADJECTIVE **1** = bright, brilliant, shining, illuminated, luminous, well-lit, lustrous, well-illuminated ≠ dark **2** = pale, fair, faded, blonde, blond, bleached, pastel, light-coloured ≠ dark
• VERB **1** = illuminate, light up, brighten ≠ darken **2** = ignite, inflame, kindle, touch off, set alight ≠ put out
• PHRASES **light up 1** = cheer, shine, blaze, sparkle, animate, brighten, lighten, irradiate **2** = shine, flash, beam, blaze, sparkle, flare, glare, gleam

light² ADJECTIVE **1** = insubstantial, thin, slight, portable, buoyant, airy, flimsy, underweight ≠ heavy **2** = weak, soft, gentle, moderate, slight, mild, faint, indistinct ≠ strong **3** = digestible, modest, frugal ≠ substantial **4** = insignificant, small, slight, petty, trivial, trifling, inconsequential, inconsiderable ≠ serious **5** = light-hearted, funny, entertaining, amusing, witty, humorous, frivolous, unserious ≠ serious **6** = nimble, graceful, deft, agile, sprightly, lithe, limber, lissom ≠ clumsy

• PHRASES **light on** *or* **upon something** **1** = settle, land, perch, alight **2** = come across, find, discover, encounter, stumble on, hit upon, happen upon

lighten[1] = brighten, illuminate, light up, irradiate, become light

lighten[2] **1** = ease, relieve, alleviate, allay, reduce, lessen, mitigate, assuage ≠ intensify **2** = cheer, lift, revive, brighten, perk up, buoy up ≠ depress

lightly **1** = moderately, thinly, slightly, sparsely, sparingly ≠ heavily **2** = gently, softly, slightly, faintly, delicately ≠ forcefully **3** = carelessly, breezily, thoughtlessly, flippantly, frivolously, heedlessly ≠ seriously **4** = easily, simply, readily, effortlessly, unthinkingly, without thought, flippantly, heedlessly ≠ with difficulty

lightweight **1** = thin, fine, delicate, sheer, flimsy, gossamer, diaphanous, filmy **2** = unimportant, shallow, trivial, insignificant, slight, petty, worthless, trifling ≠ significant

like[1] = similar to, same as, equivalent to, parallel to, identical to, alike, corresponding to, comparable to ≠ different

like[2] **1** = enjoy, love, delight in, go for, relish, savour, revel in, be fond of ≠ dislike **2** = admire, approve of, appreciate, prize, take to, esteem, cherish, hold dear ≠ dislike **3** = wish, want, choose, prefer, desire, fancy, care, feel inclined

likelihood = probability, chance, possibility, prospect

likely **1** = inclined, disposed, prone, liable, tending, apt **2** = probable, expected, anticipated, odds-on, on the cards, to be expected **3** = plausible, possible, reasonable, credible, feasible, believable

liken = compare, match, relate, parallel, equate, set beside

likewise = similarly, the same, in the same way, in similar fashion, in like manner

liking = fondness, love, taste, weakness, preference, affection, inclination, penchant ≠ dislike

limb **1** = part, member, arm, leg, wing, extremity, appendage **2** = branch, spur, projection, offshoot, bough

limelight = publicity, recognition, fame, the spotlight, attention, prominence, stardom, public eye

limit NOUN **1** = end, ultimate, deadline, breaking point, extremity **2** = boundary, edge, border, frontier, perimeter

• VERB = restrict, control, check, bound, confine, curb, restrain, ration

limitation **1** = restriction, control, check, curb, restraint, constraint **2** = weakness, failing, qualification, reservation, defect, flaw, shortcoming, imperfection

limited = restricted, controlled, checked, bounded, confined, curbed, constrained, finite ≠ unlimited

limp[1] VERB = hobble, stagger, stumble, shuffle, hop, falter, shamble, totter

• NOUN = lameness, hobble

limp[2] = floppy, soft, slack, drooping, flabby, pliable, flaccid ≠ stiff

line NOUN **1** = stroke, mark, score, band, scratch, slash, streak, stripe **2** = wrinkle, mark, crease, furrow, crow's foot **3** = row, queue, rank, file, column, convoy, procession **4** = string, cable, wire, rope, thread, cord **5** = trajectory, way, course, track, channel, direction, route, path **6** = boundary, limit, edge, border, frontier, partition, borderline **7** = occupation, work, calling, business, job, area, trade, field

• VERB **1** = border, edge, bound, fringe **2** = mark, crease, furrow, rule, score

• PHRASES **in line for** = due for, shortlisted for, in the running for

lined **1** = wrinkled, worn, furrowed, wizened **2** = ruled, feint

line-up = arrangement, team, row, selection, array

linger = stay, remain, stop, wait, delay, hang around, idle, dally

link NOUN **1** = connection, relationship, association, tie-up, affinity **2** = relationship, association, bond, connection, attachment, affinity **3** = component, part, piece, element, constituent

• VERB **1** = associate, relate, identify, connect, bracket **2** = connect, join, unite,

couple, tie, bind, attach, fasten ≠ separate
lip 1 = edge, rim, brim, margin, brink 2 (*Slang*) = impudence, insolence, impertinence, cheek (*informal*), effrontery, backchat (*informal*), brass neck (*informal*)
liquid NOUN = fluid, solution, juice, sap • ADJECTIVE 1 = fluid, running, flowing, melted, watery, molten, runny, aqueous 2 (*of assets*) = convertible, disposable, negotiable, realizable
liquor 1 = alcohol, drink, spirits, booze (*informal*), hard stuff (*informal*), strong drink 2 = juice, stock, liquid, extract, broth
list[1] NOUN = inventory, record, series, roll, index, register, catalogue, directory • VERB = itemize, record, enter, register, catalogue, enumerate, note down, tabulate
list[2] VERB = lean, tip, incline, tilt, heel over, careen • NOUN = tilt, leaning, slant, cant
listen 1 = hear, attend, pay attention, lend an ear, prick up your ears 2 = pay attention, observe, obey, mind, heed, take notice, take note of, take heed of
literacy = education, learning, knowledge
literal 1 = exact, close, strict, accurate, faithful, verbatim, word for word 2 = actual, real, true, simple, plain, genuine, bona fide, unvarnished
literally = exactly, really, closely, actually, truly, precisely, strictly, faithfully
literary = well-read, learned, formal, intellectual, scholarly, erudite, bookish
literate = educated, informed, knowledgeable
literature = writings, letters, compositions, lore, creative writing
litigation = lawsuit, case, action, prosecution
litter NOUN 1 = rubbish, refuse, waste, junk, debris, garbage (*chiefly U.S.*), trash, muck 2 = brood, young, offspring, progeny • VERB 1 = clutter, mess up, clutter up, be scattered about, disorder, disarrange, derange 2 = scatter, spread, shower, strew
little ADJECTIVE 1 = small, minute, short, tiny, wee, compact, miniature, diminutive ≠ big 2 = young, small, junior, infant, immature, undeveloped, babyish • ADVERB 1 = hardly, barely, scarcely ≠ much 2 = rarely, seldom, scarcely, not often, infrequently, hardly ever ≠ always • NOUN = bit, touch, spot, trace, hint, particle, fragment, speck ≠ lot • PHRASES **a little** = to a small extent, slightly, to some extent, to a certain extent, to a small degree
live[1] 1 = dwell, board, settle, lodge, occupy, abide, inhabit, reside 2 = exist, last, prevail, be, have being, breathe, persist, be alive 3 = survive, get along, make a living, make ends meet, subsist, eke out a living, support yourself, maintain yourself 4 = thrive, flourish, prosper, have fun, enjoy yourself, live life to the full
live[2] 1 = living, alive, breathing, animate 2 = active, unexploded 3 = topical, important, pressing, current, hot, burning, controversial, prevalent
livelihood = occupation, work, employment, living, job, bread and butter (*informal*)
lively 1 = animated, spirited, quick, keen, active, alert, dynamic, vigorous ≠ dull 2 = vivid, strong, striking, bright, exciting, stimulating, bold, colourful ≠ dull 3 = enthusiastic, strong, keen, stimulating, eager, formidable, vigorous, animated
living NOUN = lifestyle, ways, situation, conduct, behaviour, customs, lifestyle, way of life • ADJECTIVE 1 = alive, existing, moving, active, breathing, animate ≠ dead 2 = current, present, active, contemporary, in use, extant ≠ obsolete
load VERB 1 = fill, stuff, pack, pile, stack, heap, cram, freight 2 = make ready, charge, prime • NOUN 1 = cargo, delivery, haul, shipment, batch, freight, consignment 2 = oppression, charge, worry, trouble, weight, responsibility, burden, onus • PHRASES **load someone down** = burden, worry, oppress, weigh down, saddle with, encumber, snow under
loaded 1 = tricky, charged, sensitive, delicate, manipulative, emotive, insidious, artful 2 = biased, weighted, rigged, distorted 3 (*Slang*) = rich, wealthy, affluent, well off, flush (*informal*), well-heeled (*informal*), well-to-do, moneyed
loaf[1] 1 = lump, block, cake, cube, slab 2 (*Slang*) = head, mind, sense, common sense, nous (*Brit. slang*), gumption (*Brit. informal*)
loaf[2] = idle, hang around, take it easy, lie around, loiter, laze, lounge around

loan NOUN = advance, credit, overdraft
• VERB = lend, advance, let out
loathe = hate, dislike, despise, detest, abhor, abominate
loathing = hatred, hate, disgust, aversion, revulsion, antipathy, repulsion, abhorrence
lobby VERB = campaign, press, pressure, push, influence, promote, urge, persuade
• NOUN 1 = pressure group, group, camp, faction, lobbyists, interest group, special-interest group, ginger group 2 = corridor, passage, entrance, porch, hallway, foyer, entrance hall, vestibule
lobola (*S. African*) = dowry, portion, marriage settlement, dot (*archaic*)
local ADJECTIVE 1 = community, regional 2 = confined, limited, restricted
• NOUN = resident, native, inhabitant
locate 1 = find, discover, detect, come across, track down, pinpoint, unearth, pin down 2 = place, put, set, position, seat, site, establish, settle
location = place, point, setting, position, situation, spot, venue, locale
lock[1] VERB 1 = fasten, close, secure, shut, bar, seal, bolt 2 = unite, join, link, engage, clench, entangle, interlock, entwine 3 = embrace, press, grasp, clutch, hug, enclose, clasp, encircle
• NOUN = fastening, catch, bolt, clasp, padlock
• PHRASES **lock someone up** = imprison, jail, confine, cage, detain, shut up, incarcerate, send down (*informal*)
lock[2] = strand, curl, tuft, tress, ringlet
lodge NOUN 1 = cabin, shelter, cottage, hut, chalet, gatehouse 2 = society, group, club, section, wing, chapter, branch
• VERB 1 = register, enter, file, submit, put on record 2 = stay, room, board, reside 3 = stick, remain, implant, come to rest, imbed
lodging *often plural* = accommodation, rooms, apartments, quarters, digs (*Brit. informal*), shelter, residence, abode
lofty 1 = noble, grand, distinguished, renowned, elevated, dignified, illustrious, exalted ≠ humble 2 = high, raised, towering, soaring, elevated ≠ low 3 = haughty, proud, arrogant, patronizing, condescending, disdainful, supercilious ≠ modest
log NOUN 1 = stump, block, branch, chunk, trunk 2 = record, account, register, journal, diary, logbook
• VERB = record, enter, note, register, chart, put down, set down
logic = reason, reasoning, sense, good sense
logical 1 = rational, clear, reasoned, sound, consistent, valid, coherent, well-organized ≠ illogical 2 = reasonable, sensible, natural, wise, plausible ≠ unlikely
lone = solitary, single, one, only, sole, unaccompanied
loneliness = solitude, isolation, desolation, seclusion
lonely 1 = solitary, alone, isolated, abandoned, lone, withdrawn, single, forsaken ≠ accompanied 2 = desolate, deserted, remote, isolated, out-of-the-way, secluded, uninhabited, godforsaken ≠ crowded
lonesome (*Chiefly U.S. & Canad.*) = lonely, gloomy, dreary, desolate, forlorn, friendless, companionless
long[1] 1 = elongated, extended, stretched, expanded, extensive, lengthy, far-reaching, spread out ≠ short 2 = prolonged, sustained, lengthy, lingering, protracted, interminable, spun out, long-drawn-out ≠ brief
long[2] = desire, want, wish, burn, pine, lust, crave, yearn
longing = desire, hope, wish, burning, urge, ambition, hunger, yen (*informal*) ≠ indifference
long-standing = established, fixed, enduring, abiding, long-lasting, long-established, time-honoured
look VERB 1 = see, view, consider, watch, eye, study, survey, examine 2 = search, seek, hunt, forage, fossick (*Austral. & N.Z.*) 3 = consider, contemplate 4 = face, overlook 5 = hope, expect, await, anticipate, reckon on 6 = seem, appear, look like, strike you as
• NOUN 1 = glimpse, view, glance, observation, sight, examination, gaze, inspection 2 = appearance, bearing, air, style, aspect, manner, expression, impression
• PHRASES **look after something** *or* **someone** = take care of, mind, protect, tend, guard, nurse, care for, supervise
◆ **look down on** *or* **upon someone** = disdain, despise, scorn, sneer at, spurn,

contemn (*formal*) ◆ **look forward to something** = anticipate, expect, look for, wait for, await, hope for, long for ◆ **look out for something** = be careful of, beware, watch out for, pay attention to, be wary of, keep an eye out for ◆ **look someone up** = visit, call on, drop in on (*informal*), look in on ◆ **look something up** = research, find, search for, hunt for, track down, seek out ◆ **look up** = improve, develop, advance, pick up, progress, get better, shape up (*informal*), perk up ◆ **look up to someone** = respect, honour, admire, esteem, revere, defer to, think highly of

lookout 1 = watchman, guard, sentry, sentinel 2 = watch, guard, vigil 3 = watchtower, post, observatory, observation post 4 (*Informal*) = concern, business, worry

loom = appear, emerge, hover, take shape, threaten, bulk, menace, come into view

loop NOUN = curve, ring, circle, twist, curl, spiral, coil, twirl
• VERB = twist, turn, roll, knot, curl, spiral, coil, wind round

loophole = let-out, escape, excuse

loose ADJECTIVE 1 = free, detached, insecure, unfettered, unrestricted, untied, unattached, unfastened 2 = slack, easy, relaxed, sloppy, loose-fitting ≠ tight 3 (*Old-fashioned*) = promiscuous, fast, abandoned, immoral, dissipated, profligate, debauched, dissolute ≠ chaste 4 = vague, random, inaccurate, rambling, imprecise, ill-defined, indistinct, inexact ≠ precise
• VERB = free, release, liberate, detach, unleash, disconnect, set free, untie ≠ fasten

loosen VERB = untie, undo, release, separate, detach, unloose
• PHRASES **loosen up** = relax, chill (*slang*), soften, unwind, go easy (*informal*), hang loose, outspan (*S. African*), ease up *or* off

loot VERB = plunder, rob, raid, sack, rifle, ravage, ransack, pillage
• NOUN = plunder, goods, prize, haul, spoils, booty, swag (*slang*)

lord NOUN 1 = peer, nobleman, count, duke, gentleman, earl, noble, baron 2 = ruler, leader, chief, master, governor, commander, superior, liege
• PHRASES **lord it over someone** = boss around *or* about (*informal*), order around, threaten, bully, menace, intimidate, hector, bluster ◆ **the Lord** *or* **Our Lord** = Jesus Christ, God, Christ, Messiah, Jehovah, the Almighty

lose 1 = be defeated, be beaten, lose out, come to grief 2 = mislay, drop, forget, be deprived of, lose track of, misplace 3 = forfeit, miss, yield, be deprived of, pass up (*informal*)

loser = failure, flop (*informal*), also-ran, no-hoper (*Austral. slang*), dud (*informal*), non-achiever

loss NOUN 1 = losing, waste, squandering, forfeiture ≠ gain 2 *sometimes plural* = deficit, debt, deficiency, debit, depletion ≠ gain 3 = damage, cost, injury, hurt, harm ≠ advantage
• PHRASES **at a loss** = confused, puzzled, baffled, bewildered, helpless, stumped, perplexed, mystified

lost = missing, disappeared, vanished, wayward, misplaced, mislaid

lot NOUN 1 = bunch (*informal*), group, crowd, crew, set, band, quantity, assortment 2 = destiny, situation, circumstances, fortune, chance, accident, fate, doom
• PHRASES **a lot** *or* **lots** 1 = plenty, scores, masses (*informal*), load(s) (*informal*), wealth, piles (*informal*), a great deal, stack(s) 2 = often, regularly, a great deal, frequently, a good deal

lotion = cream, solution, balm, salve, liniment, embrocation

lottery 1 = raffle, draw, lotto (*Brit., N.Z., & S. African*), sweepstake 2 = gamble, chance, risk, hazard, toss-up (*informal*)

loud 1 = noisy, booming, roaring, thundering, forte (*Music*), resounding, deafening, thunderous ≠ quiet 2 = garish, bold, glaring, flamboyant, brash, flashy, lurid, gaudy ≠ sombre

loudly = noisily, vigorously, vehemently, vociferously, uproariously, lustily, shrilly, fortissimo (*Music*)

lounge VERB = relax, loaf, sprawl, lie about, take it easy, loiter, loll, laze, outspan (*S. African*)
• NOUN = sitting room, living room, parlour, drawing room, front room, reception room, television room

love VERB 1 = adore, care for, treasure, cherish, prize, worship, be devoted to,

dote on ≠ hate **2** = enjoy, like, appreciate, relish, delight in, savour, take pleasure in, have a soft spot for ≠ dislike
• **NOUN 1** = passion, affection, warmth, attachment, intimacy, devotion, tenderness, adoration, aroha (*N.Z.*) ≠ hatred **2** = liking, taste, bent for, weakness for, relish for, enjoyment, devotion to, penchant for **3** = beloved, dear, dearest, lover, darling, honey, sweetheart, truelove ≠ enemy **4** = sympathy, understanding, pity, humanity, warmth, mercy, sorrow, kindness, aroha (*N.Z.*)
• **PHRASES make love** = have sexual intercourse, have sex, go to bed, sleep together, do it (*informal*), mate, have sexual relations, have it off (*slang*)

love affair = romance, relationship, affair, intrigue, liaison, amour

lovely 1 = beautiful, appealing, attractive, charming, pretty, handsome, good-looking, exquisite ≠ ugly **2** = wonderful, pleasing, nice, pleasant, engaging, marvellous, delightful, enjoyable ≠ horrible

lover = sweetheart, beloved, loved one, flame (*informal*), mistress, admirer, suitor, woman friend

loving 1 = affectionate, dear, devoted, tender, fond, doting, amorous, warm-hearted ≠ cruel **2** = tender, kind, caring, warm, gentle, sympathetic, considerate

low 1 = small, little, short, stunted, squat ≠ tall **2** = inferior, bad, poor, inadequate, unsatisfactory, deficient, second-rate, shoddy, half-pie (*N.Z. informal*), bodger *or* bodgie (*Austral. slang*) **3** = quiet, soft, gentle, whispered, muted, subdued, hushed, muffled ≠ loud **4** = dejected, depressed, miserable, fed up, moody, gloomy, glum, despondent ≠ happy **5** = coarse, common, rough, crude, rude, vulgar, undignified, disreputable **6** = ill, weak, frail, stricken, debilitated ≠ strong

lower ADJECTIVE 1 = subordinate, under, smaller, junior, minor, secondary, lesser, inferior **2** = reduced, cut, diminished, decreased, lessened, curtailed ≠ increased
• **VERB 1** = drop, sink, depress, let down, submerge, take down, let fall ≠ raise **2** = lessen, cut, reduce, diminish, slash, decrease, prune, minimize ≠ increase

low-key = subdued, quiet, restrained, muted, understated, toned down

loyal = faithful, true, devoted, dependable, constant, staunch, trustworthy, trusty ≠ disloyal

loyalty = faithfulness, commitment, devotion, allegiance, fidelity, homage, obedience, constancy

luck NOUN 1 = good fortune, success, advantage, prosperity, blessing, windfall, godsend, serendipity **2** = fortune, lot, stars, chance, accident, fate, destiny, twist of fate
• **PHRASES in luck** = fortunate, successful, favoured, well-off, jammy (*Brit. slang*)
◆ **out of luck** = unfortunate, cursed, unlucky, unsuccessful

luckily = fortunately, happily, opportunely

lucky = fortunate, successful, favoured, charmed, blessed, jammy (*Brit. slang*), serendipitous ≠ unlucky

lucrative = profitable, rewarding, productive, fruitful, well-paid, advantageous, remunerative

ludicrous = ridiculous, crazy, absurd, preposterous, silly, laughable, farcical, outlandish ≠ sensible

luggage = baggage, things, cases, bags, gear, suitcases, paraphernalia, impedimenta

lull NOUN = respite, pause, quiet, silence, calm, hush, let-up (*informal*)
• **VERB** = calm, soothe, subdue, quell, allay, pacify, tranquillize

lumber[1] VERB (*Brit. informal*) = burden, land, load, saddle, encumber
• **NOUN** (*Brit.*) = junk, refuse, rubbish, trash, clutter, jumble

lumber[2] = plod, shuffle, shamble, trudge, stump, waddle, trundle

lumbering = awkward, heavy, hulking, ponderous, ungainly

lump NOUN 1 = piece, ball, block, mass, chunk, hunk, nugget **2** = swelling, growth, bump, tumour, bulge, hump, protrusion
• **VERB** = group, throw, mass, combine, collect, pool, consolidate, conglomerate

lunatic NOUN = madman, maniac, psychopath, nutcase (*slang*)
• **ADJECTIVE** = mad, crazy, insane, irrational, daft, deranged, crackpot (*informal*), crackbrained, off the air (*Austral. slang*)

lunge VERB = pounce, charge, dive, leap, plunge, thrust
• **NOUN** = thrust, charge, pounce, spring, swing, jab

lurch 1 = tilt, roll, pitch, list, rock, lean, heel 2 = stagger, reel, stumble, weave, sway, totter

lure VERB = tempt, draw, attract, invite, trick, seduce, entice, allure
• NOUN = temptation, attraction, incentive, bait, carrot (*informal*), inducement, enticement, allurement

lurk = hide, sneak, prowl, lie in wait, slink, skulk, conceal yourself

lush 1 = abundant, green, flourishing, dense, rank, verdant 2 = luxurious, grand, elaborate, lavish, extravagant, sumptuous, plush (*informal*), ornate

lust NOUN 1 = lechery, sensuality, lewdness, lasciviousness 2 = desire, longing, passion, appetite, craving, greed, thirst
• PHRASES **lust for** *or* **after someone** = desire, want, crave, yearn for, covet, hunger for *or* after ♦ **lust for** *or* **after something** = desire, crave, yearn for, covet

luxurious = sumptuous, expensive, comfortable, magnificent, splendid, lavish, plush (*informal*), opulent

luxury 1 = opulence, splendour, richness, extravagance, affluence, hedonism, a bed of roses, the life of Riley ≠ poverty 2 = extravagance, treat, extra, indulgence, frill ≠ necessity

lying NOUN = dishonesty, perjury, deceit, misrepresentation, mendacity, untruthfulness
• ADJECTIVE = deceitful, false, deceiving, treacherous, dishonest, two-faced, mendacious, perfidious ≠ truthful

lyrical = enthusiastic, inspired, poetic, impassioned, effusive, rhapsodic

m

machine 1 = appliance, device, apparatus, engine, tool, instrument, mechanism, gadget 2 = system, structure, organization, machinery, setup (*informal*)

machinery = equipment, gear, instruments, apparatus, technology, tackle, tools, gadgetry

macho = manly, masculine, chauvinist, virile

mad 1 = insane, crazy (*informal*), nuts (*slang*), raving, unstable, psychotic, demented, deranged, off the air (*Austral. slang*) ≠ sane 2 = foolish, absurd, wild, stupid, daft (*informal*), irrational, senseless, preposterous ≠ sensible 3 (*Informal*) = angry, furious, incensed, enraged, livid (*informal*), berserk, berko (*Austral. slang*), tooshie (*Austral. slang*), off the air (*Austral. slang*) ≠ calm 4 = enthusiastic, wild, crazy (*informal*), ardent, fanatical, avid, impassioned, infatuated ≠ nonchalant 5 = frenzied, wild, excited, frenetic, uncontrolled, unrestrained

madden = infuriate, irritate, incense, enrage, upset, annoy, inflame, drive you crazy ≠ calm

madly 1 (*Informal*) = passionately, wildly, desperately, intensely, to distraction, devotedly 2 = foolishly, wildly, absurdly, ludicrously, irrationally, senselessly 3 = energetically, wildly, furiously, excitedly, recklessly, speedily, like mad (*informal*) 4 = insanely, frantically, hysterically, crazily, deliriously, distractedly, frenziedly

madness 1 = insanity, mental illness, delusion, mania, dementia, distraction, aberration, psychosis 2 = foolishness, nonsense, folly, absurdity, idiocy, wildness, daftness (*informal*), foolhardiness

magazine = journal, publication, supplement, rag (*informal*), issue, glossy (*informal*), pamphlet, periodical

magic NOUN 1 = sorcery, wizardry, witchcraft, enchantment, black art, necromancy 2 = conjuring, illusion, trickery, sleight of hand, legerdemain, prestidigitation 3 = charm, power, glamour, fascination, magnetism, enchantment, allurement
• ADJECTIVE = miraculous, entrancing, charming, fascinating, marvellous, magical, enchanting, bewitching

magician 1 = conjuror, illusionist, prestidigitator 2 = sorcerer, witch, wizard, illusionist, warlock, necromancer, enchanter *or* enchantress

magistrate = judge, justice, justice of the

peace, J.P.
magnetic = attractive, irresistible, seductive, captivating, charming, fascinating, charismatic, hypnotic ≠ repulsive
magnificent 1 = splendid, impressive, imposing, glorious, gorgeous, majestic, regal, sublime ≠ ordinary 2 = brilliant, fine, excellent, outstanding, superb, splendid
magnify 1 = enlarge, increase, boost, expand, intensify, blow up (*informal*), heighten, amplify ≠ reduce 2 = make worse, exaggerate, intensify, worsen, exacerbate, increase, inflame 3 = exaggerate, overstate, inflate, overplay, overemphasize ≠ understate
magnitude 1 = importance, consequence, significance, moment, note, weight, greatness ≠ unimportance 2 = immensity, size, extent, enormity, volume, vastness ≠ smallness 3 = intensity, amplitude
maid 1 = servant, chambermaid, housemaid, menial, maidservant, female servant, domestic (*archaic*), parlourmaid 2 (*Literary*) = girl, maiden, lass, damsel, lassie (*informal*), wench
maiden NOUN (*Literary*) = girl, maid, lass, damsel, virgin, lassie (*informal*), wench
• ADJECTIVE 1 = first, initial, inaugural, introductory 2 = unmarried, unwed
mail NOUN = letters, post, correspondence
• VERB = post, send, forward, e-mail, dispatch
main ADJECTIVE = chief, leading, head, central, essential, primary, principal, foremost ≠ minor
• PLURAL NOUN 1 = pipeline, channel, pipe, conduit, duct 2 = cable, line, electricity supply, mains supply
• PHRASES **in the main** = on the whole, generally, mainly, mostly, in general, for the most part
mainly = chiefly, mostly, largely, principally, primarily, on the whole, predominantly, in the main
mainstream = conventional, general, established, received, accepted, current, prevailing, orthodox ≠ unconventional
maintain 1 = continue, retain, preserve, sustain, carry on, keep up, prolong, perpetuate ≠ end 2 = assert, state, claim, insist, declare, contend, profess, avow ≠ disavow 3 = look after, care for, take care of, conserve, keep in good condition
maintenance 1 = upkeep, keeping, care, repairs, conservation, nurture, preservation 2 = allowance, support, keep, alimony 3 = continuation, carrying-on, perpetuation, prolongation
majestic = grand, magnificent, impressive, superb, splendid, regal, stately, monumental ≠ modest
majesty = grandeur, glory, splendour, magnificence, nobility ≠ triviality
major 1 = important, critical, significant, great, serious, crucial, outstanding, notable 2 = main, higher, greater, bigger, leading, chief, senior, supreme ≠ minor
majority 1 = most, mass, bulk, best part, better part, lion's share, preponderance, greater number 2 = adulthood, maturity, age of consent, seniority, manhood *or* womanhood
make VERB 1 = produce, cause, create, effect, lead to, generate, bring about, give rise to 2 = perform, do, effect, carry out, execute 3 = force, cause, compel, drive, require, oblige, induce, constrain 4 = create, build, produce, manufacture, form, fashion, construct, assemble 5 = earn, get, gain, net, win, clear, obtain, bring in 6 = amount to, total, constitute, add up to, count as, tot up to (*informal*)
• NOUN = brand, sort, style, model, kind, type, variety, marque
• PHRASES **make for something** = head for, aim for, head towards, be bound for ◆ **make it** (*Informal*) = succeed, prosper, arrive (*informal*), get on, crack it (*informal*) ◆ **make off** = flee, clear out (*informal*), bolt, take to your heels, run away *or* off ◆ **make something up** = invent, create, construct, compose, frame, coin, devise, originate ◆ **make up** = settle your differences, bury the hatchet, call it quits, declare a truce, be friends again ◆ **make up for something** = compensate for, make amends for, atone for, balance out, offset, make recompense for ◆ **make up something** 1 = form, account for, constitute, compose, comprise 2 = complete, supply, fill, round off
maker = manufacturer, producer, builder, constructor
makeshift = temporary, provisional, substitute, expedient, stopgap
make-up 1 = cosmetics, paint (*informal*),

powder, face (*informal*), greasepaint (*Theatre*) **2** = nature, character, constitution, temperament, disposition **3** = structure, organization, arrangement, construction, assembly, constitution, format, composition

making NOUN = creation, production, manufacture, construction, assembly, composition, fabrication
• PLURAL NOUN = beginnings, potential, capacity, ingredients

male = masculine, manly, macho, virile ≠ female

malicious = spiteful, malevolent, resentful, vengeful, rancorous, ill-disposed, ill-natured ≠ benevolent

mammoth = colossal, huge, giant, massive, enormous, immense, gigantic, monumental ≠ tiny

man NOUN **1** = male, guy (*informal*), fellow (*informal*), gentleman, bloke (*Brit. informal*), chap (*Brit. informal*), dude (*U.S. informal*), geezer (*informal*) **2** = human, human being, person, individual, soul **3** = mankind, humanity, people, human race, humankind, Homo sapiens
• VERB = staff, people, crew, occupy, garrison

mana (*N.Z.*) = authority, influence, power, might, standing, status, importance, eminence

manage **1** = be in charge of, run, handle, direct, conduct, command, administer, supervise **2** = organize, use, handle, regulate **3** = cope, survive, succeed, carry on, make do, get by (*informal*), muddle through **4** = perform, do, achieve, carry out, undertake, cope with, accomplish, contrive **5** = control, handle, manipulate

management **1** = administration, control, running, operation, handling, direction, command, supervision **2** = directors, board, executive(s), administration, employers

manager = supervisor, head, director, executive, boss (*informal*), governor, administrator, organizer, baas (*S. African*)

mandate = command, order, commission, instruction, decree, directive, edict

mandatory = compulsory, required, binding, obligatory, requisite ≠ optional

manhood = manliness, masculinity, virility

manifest ADJECTIVE = obvious, apparent, patent, evident, clear, glaring, noticeable, blatant ≠ concealed
• VERB = display, show, reveal, express, demonstrate, expose, exhibit ≠ conceal

manifestation **1** = sign, symptom, indication, mark, example, evidence, proof, testimony **2** = display, show, exhibition, expression, demonstration

manipulate **1** = influence, control, direct, negotiate, exploit, manoeuvre **2** = work, use, operate, handle

mankind = people, man, humanity, human race, humankind, Homo sapiens

manly = virile, masculine, strong, brave, bold, strapping, vigorous, courageous ≠ effeminate

man-made = artificial, manufactured, mock, synthetic, ersatz

manner NOUN **1** = style, way, fashion, method, custom, mode **2** = behaviour, air, bearing, conduct, aspect, demeanour **3** = type, form, sort, kind, variety, brand, category
• PLURAL NOUN **1** = conduct, behaviour, demeanour **2** = politeness, courtesy, etiquette, refinement, decorum, p's and q's **3** = protocol, customs, social graces

mannered = affected, artificial, pretentious, stilted, arty-farty (*informal*) ≠ natural

manoeuvre VERB **1** = scheme, wangle (*informal*), machinate **2** = manipulate, arrange, organize, set up, engineer, fix, orchestrate, contrive
• NOUN **1** = stratagem, scheme, trick, tactic, intrigue, dodge, ploy, ruse **2** *often plural* = movement, operation, exercise, war game

mansion = residence, manor, hall, villa, seat

mantle **1** = covering, screen, curtain, blanket, veil, shroud, canopy, pall **2** = cloak, wrap, cape, hood, shawl

manual ADJECTIVE **1** = physical, human **2** = hand-operated, hand, non-automatic
• NOUN = handbook, guide, instructions, bible

manufacture VERB **1** = make, build, produce, construct, create, turn out, assemble, put together **2** = concoct, make up, invent, devise, fabricate, think up, cook up (*informal*), trump up
• NOUN = making, production, construction, assembly, creation

manufacturer = maker, producer,

builder, creator, industrialist, constructor
many DETERMINER = numerous, various, countless, abundant, myriad, innumerable, manifold, umpteen (*informal*)
• PRONOUN = a lot, lots (*informal*), plenty, scores, heaps (*informal*)
mar 1 = harm, damage, hurt, spoil, stain, taint, tarnish 2 = ruin, spoil, scar, flaw, impair, detract from, deform, blemish ≠ improve
march VERB 1 = parade, walk, file, pace, stride, swagger 2 = walk, strut, storm, sweep, stride, flounce
• NOUN 1 = walk, trek, slog, yomp (*Brit. informal*), routemarch 2 = progress, development, advance, evolution, progression
margin = edge, side, border, boundary, verge, brink, rim, perimeter
marginal 1 = insignificant, small, minor, slight, minimal, negligible 2 = borderline, bordering, on the edge, peripheral
marijuana = cannabis, pot (*slang*), dope (*slang*), grass (*slang*), hemp, dagga (*S. African*)
marine = nautical, maritime, naval, seafaring, seagoing
mariner = sailor, seaman, sea dog, seafarer, salt
marital = matrimonial, nuptial, conjugal, connubial
maritime 1 = nautical, marine, naval, oceanic, seafaring 2 = coastal, seaside, littoral
mark NOUN 1 = spot, stain, streak, smudge, line, scratch, scar, blot 2 = characteristic, feature, standard, quality, measure, stamp, attribute, criterion 3 = indication, sign, symbol, token 4 = brand, impression, label, device, flag, symbol, token, emblem 5 = target, goal, aim, purpose, object, objective
• VERB 1 = scar, scratch, stain, streak, blot, smudge, blemish 2 = label, identify, brand, flag, stamp, characterize 3 = grade, correct, assess, evaluate, appraise 4 = distinguish, show, illustrate, exemplify, denote 5 = observe, mind, note, notice, attend to, pay attention to, pay heed to
marked = noticeable, clear, decided, striking, obvious, prominent, patent, distinct ≠ imperceptible
markedly = noticeably, clearly, obviously, considerably, distinctly, decidedly, strikingly, conspicuously
market NOUN = fair, mart, bazaar, souk (*Arabic*)
• VERB = sell, promote, retail, peddle, vend
maroon = abandon, leave, desert, strand, leave high and dry (*informal*)
marriage = wedding, match, nuptials, wedlock, matrimony

RELATED WORDS
adjectives: conjugal, marital, nuptial

marry 1 = tie the knot (*informal*), wed, get hitched (*slang*) 2 = unite, join, link, bond, ally, merge, knit, unify
marsh = swamp, bog, slough, fen, quagmire, morass
marshal 1 = conduct, take, lead, guide, steer, escort, shepherd, usher 2 = arrange, group, order, line up, organize, deploy, array, draw up
martial = military, belligerent, warlike, bellicose
marvel VERB = be amazed, wonder, gape, be awed
• NOUN 1 = wonder, phenomenon, miracle, portent 2 = genius, prodigy
marvellous = excellent, great (*informal*), wonderful, brilliant, amazing, extraordinary, superb, spectacular, booshit (*Austral. slang*), exo (*Austral. slang*), sik (*Austral. slang*) ≠ terrible
masculine = male, manly, mannish, manlike, virile
mask NOUN = façade, disguise, front, cover, screen, veil, guise, camouflage
• VERB = disguise, hide, conceal, obscure, cover (up), screen, blanket, veil
mass NOUN 1 = lot, collection, load, pile, quantity, bunch, stack, heap 2 = piece, block, lump, chunk, hunk 3 = size, matter, weight, extent, bulk, magnitude, greatness
• ADJECTIVE = large-scale, general, widespread, extensive, universal, wholesale, indiscriminate
• VERB = gather, assemble, accumulate, collect, rally, swarm, throng, congregate
massacre NOUN = slaughter, murder, holocaust, carnage, extermination, annihilation, butchery, blood bath
• VERB = slaughter, kill, murder, butcher, wipe out, exterminate, mow down, cut to pieces
massage NOUN = rub-down, manipulation
• VERB 1 = rub down, manipulate, knead 2 = manipulate, alter, distort, doctor,

cook (*informal*), fix (*informal*), rig, fiddle (*informal*)

massive = huge, big, enormous, immense, hefty, gigantic, monumental, mammoth ≠ tiny

master NOUN **1** = lord, ruler, commander, chief, director, manager, boss (*informal*), head, baas (*S. African*) ≠ servant **2** = expert, maestro, ace (*informal*), genius, wizard, virtuoso, doyen, past master, fundi (*S. African*) ≠ amateur **3** = teacher, tutor, instructor ≠ student
• ADJECTIVE = main, principal, chief, prime, foremost, predominant ≠ lesser
• VERB **1** = learn, understand, pick up, grasp, get the hang of (*informal*), know inside out, know backwards **2** = overcome, defeat, conquer, tame, triumph over, vanquish ≠ give in to

masterly = skilful, expert, crack (*informal*), supreme, world-class, consummate, first-rate, masterful

mastermind VERB = plan, manage, direct, organize, devise, conceive
• NOUN = organizer, director, manager, engineer, brain(s) (*informal*), architect, planner

masterpiece = classic, tour de force (*French*), pièce de résistance (*French*), magnum opus, jewel

mastery **1** = understanding, skill, know-how, expertise, prowess, finesse, proficiency, virtuosity **2** = control, command, domination, superiority, supremacy, upper hand, ascendancy, mana (*N.Z.*), whip hand

match NOUN **1** = game, test, competition, trial, tie, contest, fixture, bout **2** = marriage, pairing, alliance, partnership **3** = equal, rival, peer, counterpart
• VERB **1** = correspond with, go with, fit with, harmonize with **2** = correspond, agree, accord, square, coincide, tally, conform, match up **3** = rival, equal, compete with, compare with, emulate, measure up to

matching = identical, like, twin, equivalent, corresponding, coordinating ≠ different

mate NOUN **1** (*Informal*) = friend, pal (*informal*), companion, buddy (*informal*), comrade, chum (*informal*), mucker (*Brit. informal*), crony, cobber (*Austral. & N.Z. old-fashioned informal*), E hoa (*N.Z.*) **2** = partner, lover, companion, spouse, consort, helpmeet, husband *or* wife **3** = assistant, subordinate, apprentice, helper, accomplice, sidekick (*informal*) **4** = colleague, associate, companion
• VERB = pair, couple, breed

material NOUN **1** = substance, matter, stuff **2** = cloth, fabric, textile **3** = information, details, facts, notes, evidence, particulars, data, info (*informal*)
• ADJECTIVE **1** = physical, solid, substantial, concrete, bodily, tangible, palpable, corporeal **2** = relevant, important, significant, essential, vital, serious, meaningful, applicable

materially = significantly, much, greatly, essentially, seriously, gravely, substantially ≠ insignificantly

maternal = motherly, protective, nurturing, maternalistic

maternity = motherhood, parenthood, motherliness

matted = tangled, knotted, unkempt, knotty, tousled, ratty, uncombed

matter NOUN **1** = situation, concern, business, question, event, subject, affair, incident **2** = substance, material, body, stuff
• VERB = be important, make a difference, count, be relevant, make any difference, carry weight, cut any ice (*informal*), be of account

matter-of-fact = unsentimental, plain, sober, down-to-earth, mundane, prosaic, deadpan, unimaginative

mature VERB = develop, grow up, bloom, blossom, come of age, age
• ADJECTIVE **1** = matured, seasoned, ripe, mellow **2** = grown-up, adult, of age, fully fledged, full-grown ≠ immature

maturity **1** = adulthood, puberty, coming of age, pubescence, manhood *or* womanhood ≠ immaturity **2** = ripeness

maul **1** = mangle, claw, lacerate, tear, mangulate (*Austral. slang*) **2** = ill-treat, abuse, batter, molest, manhandle

maverick NOUN = rebel, radical, dissenter, individualist, protester, eccentric, heretic, nonconformist ≠ traditionalist
• ADJECTIVE = rebel, radical, dissenting, individualistic, eccentric, heretical, iconoclastic, nonconformist

maximum ADJECTIVE = greatest, highest, supreme, paramount, utmost, most,

topmost ≠ minimal
• NOUN = top, peak, ceiling, utmost, upper limit ≠ minimum

maybe = perhaps, possibly, perchance (*archaic*)

mayhem = chaos, trouble, violence, disorder, destruction, confusion, havoc, fracas

maze = web, confusion, tangle, labyrinth, imbroglio, complex network

meadow = field, pasture, grassland, lea (*poetic*)

mean[1] 1 = signify, indicate, represent, express, stand for, convey, spell out, symbolize 2 = imply, suggest, intend, hint at, insinuate 3 = intend, want, plan, expect, design, aim, wish, think

mean[2] 1 = miserly, stingy, parsimonious, niggardly, mercenary, penny-pinching, ungenerous, tight-fisted, snoep (*S. African informal*) ≠ generous 2 = dishonourable, petty, shameful, shabby, vile, callous, sordid, despicable, scungy (*Austral. & N.Z.*) ≠ honourable

mean[3] NOUN = average, middle, balance, norm, midpoint
• ADJECTIVE = average, middle, standard

meaning 1 = significance, message, substance, drift, connotation, gist 2 = definition, sense

meaningful = significant, important, material, useful, relevant, valid, worthwhile, purposeful ≠ trivial

meaningless = nonsensical, senseless, inconsequential, inane ≠ worthwhile

means PLURAL NOUN 1 = method, way, process, medium, agency, instrument, mode 2 = money, funds, capital, income, resources, fortune, wealth, affluence
• PHRASES **by all means** = certainly, surely, of course, definitely, doubtlessly
◆ **by no means** = in no way, definitely not, not in the least, on no account

meantime *or* **meanwhile** = at the same time, simultaneously, concurrently

meanwhile *or* **meantime** = for now, in the interim

measure VERB = quantify, determine, assess, weigh, calculate, evaluate, compute, gauge
• NOUN 1 = quantity, share, amount, allowance, portion, quota, ration, allotment 2 = action, act, step, procedure, means, control, initiative, manoeuvre 3 = gauge, rule, scale, metre, ruler, yardstick 4 = law, act, bill, legislation, resolution, statute

measured 1 = steady, even, slow, regular, dignified, stately, solemn, leisurely 2 = considered, reasoned, studied, calculated, deliberate, sober, well-thought-out

measurement = calculation, assessment, evaluation, valuation, computation, calibration, mensuration

meat = food, flesh, kai (*N.Z. informal*)

mechanical 1 = automatic, automated, mechanized, power-driven, motor-driven ≠ manual 2 = unthinking, routine, automatic, instinctive, involuntary, impersonal, cursory, perfunctory ≠ conscious

mechanism 1 = process, way, means, system, operation, agency, method, technique 2 = machine, device, tool, instrument, appliance, apparatus, contrivance

mediate = intervene, step in (*informal*), intercede, referee, umpire, reconcile, arbitrate, conciliate

mediation = arbitration, intervention, reconciliation, conciliation, intercession

mediator = negotiator, arbitrator, referee, umpire, intermediary, middleman, arbiter, peacemaker

medicine = remedy, drug, cure, prescription, medication, nostrum, medicament

mediocre = second-rate, average, ordinary, indifferent, middling, pedestrian, inferior, so-so (*informal*), half-pie (*N.Z. informal*) ≠ excellent

meditation = reflection, thought, study, musing, pondering, contemplation, rumination, cogitation

medium ADJECTIVE = average, mean, middle, middling, fair, intermediate, midway, mediocre ≠ extraordinary
• NOUN 1 = spiritualist, seer, clairvoyant, fortune teller, channeller 2 = middle, mean, centre, average, compromise, midpoint

meet 1 = encounter, come across, run into, happen on, find, contact, confront, bump into (*informal*) ≠ avoid 2 = gather, collect, assemble, get together, come together, muster, convene, congregate ≠ disperse 3 = fulfil, match (up to), answer, satisfy, discharge, comply with, come up to, conform to ≠ fall short of **4** = experience, face, suffer, bear, go through, encounter, endure, undergo **5** = converge, join, cross, touch, connect, come together, link up, intersect ≠ diverge

meeting **1** = conference, gathering, assembly, congress, session, convention, get-together (*informal*), reunion, hui (*N.Z.*) **2** = encounter, introduction, confrontation, engagement, rendezvous, tryst, assignation

melancholy ADJECTIVE = sad, depressed, miserable, gloomy, glum, mournful, despondent, dispirited ≠ happy
• NOUN = sadness, depression, misery, gloom, sorrow, unhappiness, despondency, dejection ≠ happiness

mellow ADJECTIVE **1** = full-flavoured, rich, sweet, delicate **2** = ripe, mature, ripened ≠ unripe
• VERB **1** = relax, improve, settle, calm, mature, soften, sweeten **2** = season, develop, improve, ripen

melody **1** = tune, song, theme, air, music, strain **2** = tunefulness, harmony, musicality, euphony, melodiousness

melt **1** = dissolve, run, soften, fuse, thaw, defrost, liquefy, unfreeze **2** *often with* ***away*** = disappear, fade, vanish, dissolve, disperse, evaporate, evanesce **3** = soften, relax, disarm, mollify

member = representative, associate, supporter, fellow, subscriber, comrade, disciple

membership **1** = participation, belonging, fellowship, enrolment **2** = members, body, associates, fellows

memoir = account, life, record, journal, essay, biography, narrative, monograph

memoirs = autobiography, diary, life story, experiences, memories, journals, recollections, reminiscences

memorable = noteworthy, celebrated, historic, striking, famous, significant, remarkable, notable ≠ forgettable

memorandum = note, minute, message, communication, reminder, memo, jotting

memorial NOUN = monument, shrine, plaque, cenotaph
• ADJECTIVE = commemorative, remembrance, monumental

memory **1** = recall, mind, retention, ability to remember, powers of recall, powers of retention **2** = recollection, reminder, reminiscence, impression, echo, remembrance **3** = commemoration, respect, honour, recognition, tribute, remembrance, observance

menace NOUN **1** (*Informal*) = nuisance, plague, pest, annoyance, troublemaker **2** = threat, warning, intimidation, ill-omen, ominousness
• VERB = bully, threaten, intimidate, terrorize, frighten, scare

menacing = threatening, frightening, forbidding, looming, intimidating, ominous, louring *or* lowering ≠ encouraging

mend VERB **1** = repair, fix, restore, renew, patch up, renovate, refit, retouch **2** = darn, repair, patch, stitch, sew **3** = heal, improve, recover, get better, be all right, be cured, recuperate, pull through **4** = improve, reform, correct, revise, amend, rectify, ameliorate, emend
• PHRASES **on the mend** = convalescent, improving, recovering, getting better, recuperating

mental **1** = intellectual, rational, theoretical, cognitive, brain, conceptual, cerebral **2** (*Informal*) = insane, mad, disturbed, unstable, mentally ill, psychotic, unbalanced, deranged

mentality = attitude, character, personality, psychology, make-up, outlook, disposition, cast of mind

mentally = psychologically, intellectually, inwardly

mention VERB = refer to, point out, bring up, state, reveal, declare, disclose, intimate
• NOUN **1** *often with* ***of*** = reference to, observation, indication, remark on, allusion to **2** = acknowledgment, recognition, tribute, citation, honourable mention

mentor = guide, teacher, coach, adviser, tutor, instructor, counsellor, guru

menu = bill of fare, tariff (*chiefly Brit.*), set menu, table d'hôte, carte du jour (*French*)

merchandise = goods, produce, stock, products, commodities, wares

merchant = tradesman, dealer, trader, broker, retailer, supplier, seller, salesman

mercy **1** = compassion, pity, forgiveness, grace, kindness, clemency, leniency, forbearance ≠ cruelty **2** = blessing, boon, godsend

mere 1 = simple, nothing more than, common, plain, pure 2 = bare, slender, trifling, meagre, just, only, basic, no more than

merge 1 = combine, blend, fuse, amalgamate, unite, join, mix, mingle ≠ separate 2 = join, unite, combine, fuse ≠ separate 3 = melt, blend, mingle

merger = union, fusion, consolidation, amalgamation, combination, coalition, incorporation

merit NOUN = advantage, value, quality, worth, strength, asset, virtue, strong point
• VERB = deserve, warrant, be entitled to, earn, have a right to, be worthy of

merry 1 = cheerful, happy, carefree, jolly, festive, joyous, convivial, blithe ≠ gloomy 2 (*Brit. informal*) = tipsy, happy, mellow, tiddly (*slang, chiefly Brit.*), squiffy (*Brit. informal*)

mesh NOUN = net, netting, network, web, tracery
• VERB = engage, combine, connect, knit, coordinate, interlock, dovetail, harmonize

mess NOUN 1 = untidiness, disorder, confusion, chaos, litter, clutter, disarray, jumble 2 = shambles 3 = difficulty, dilemma, plight, hole (*informal*), fix (*informal*), jam (*informal*), muddle, pickle (*informal*), uphill (*S. African*)
• PHRASES **mess about** *or* **around** = potter about, dabble, amuse yourself, fool about *or* around, muck about *or* around (*informal*), play about *or* around, trifle ◆ **mess something up** 1 = botch, muck something up (*Brit. slang*), muddle something up 2 = dirty, pollute, clutter, disarrange, dishevel ◆ **mess with something** *or* **someone** = interfere, play, fiddle (*informal*), tamper, tinker, meddle

message 1 = communication, note, bulletin, word, letter, dispatch, memorandum, communiqué 2 = point, meaning, idea, moral, theme, import, purport

messenger = courier, runner, carrier, herald, envoy, go-between, emissary, delivery boy

messy 1 = disorganized, sloppy (*informal*), untidy 2 = dirty 3 = untidy, disordered, chaotic, muddled, cluttered, shambolic, disorganized ≠ tidy 4 = dishevelled, ruffled, untidy, rumpled, bedraggled, tousled, uncombed 5 = confusing, difficult, complex, confused, tangled, chaotic, tortuous

metaphor = figure of speech, image, symbol, analogy, conceit (*literary*), allegory, trope, figurative expression

method 1 = manner, process, approach, technique, way, system, style, procedure 2 = orderliness, planning, order, system, purpose, pattern, organization, regularity

midday = noon, twelve o'clock, noonday

middle NOUN = centre, heart, midst, halfway point, midpoint, midsection
• ADJECTIVE 1 = central, medium, mid, intervening, halfway, intermediate, median 2 = intermediate, intervening

middle-class = bourgeois, traditional, conventional

middling 1 = mediocre, all right, indifferent, so-so (*informal*), unremarkable, tolerable, run-of-the-mill, passable, half-pie (*N.Z. informal*) 2 = moderate, medium, average, fair, ordinary, modest, adequate

midnight = twelve o'clock, middle of the night, dead of night, the witching hour

midst
PHRASES **in the midst of** = among, during, in the middle of, surrounded by, amidst, in the thick of

midway ADJECTIVE *or* ADVERB = halfway, in the middle of, part-way, equidistant, at the midpoint, betwixt and between

might NOUN = power, force, energy, strength, vigour
• PHRASES **with all your might** = forcefully, vigorously, mightily, manfully, lustily

mighty = powerful, strong, strapping, robust, vigorous, sturdy, forceful, lusty ≠ weak

migrant NOUN = wanderer, immigrant, traveller, rover, nomad, emigrant, itinerant, drifter
• ADJECTIVE = itinerant, wandering, drifting, roving, travelling, shifting, immigrant, transient

migrate = move, travel, journey, wander, trek, voyage, roam, emigrate

migration = wandering, journey, voyage, travel, movement, trek, emigration, roving

mild 1 = gentle, calm, easy-going, meek, placid, docile, peaceable, equable ≠ harsh 2 = temperate, warm, calm, moderate,

tranquil, balmy ≠ cold **3** = bland, thin, smooth, tasteless, insipid, flavourless
militant = aggressive, active, vigorous, assertive, combative ≠ peaceful
military ADJECTIVE = warlike, armed, soldierly, martial
• NOUN = armed forces, forces, services, army
milk = exploit, pump, take advantage of
RELATED WORD
adjective: lactic
mill NOUN **1** = grinder, crusher, quern **2** = factory, works, plant, workshop, foundry
• VERB = grind, pound, crush, powder, grate
• PHRASES **mill about** *or* **around** = swarm, crowd, stream, surge, throng
mimic VERB = imitate, do (*informal*), take off (*informal*), ape, parody, caricature, impersonate
• NOUN = imitator, impressionist, copycat (*informal*), impersonator, caricaturist
mince 1 = cut, grind, crumble, dice, hash, chop up **2** = tone down, spare, moderate, weaken, soften
mincing = affected, camp (*informal*), precious, pretentious, dainty, sissy, effeminate, foppish
mind NOUN **1** = memory, recollection, remembrance, powers of recollection **2** = intelligence, reason, reasoning, understanding, sense, brain(s) (*informal*), wits, intellect **3** = intention, wish, desire, urge, fancy, leaning, notion, inclination **4** = sanity, reason, senses, judgment, wits, marbles (*informal*), rationality, mental balance
• VERB **1** = take offence at, dislike, care about, object to, resent, disapprove of, be bothered by, be affronted by **2** = be careful, watch, take care, be wary, be cautious, be on your guard **3** = look after, watch, protect, tend, guard, take care of, attend to, keep an eye on **4** = pay attention to, mark, note, listen to, observe, obey, heed, take heed of
RELATED WORD
adjective: mental
mine NOUN **1** = pit, deposit, shaft, colliery, excavation **2** = source, store, fund, stock, supply, reserve, treasury, wealth
• VERB = dig up, extract, quarry, unearth, excavate, hew, dig for
miner = coalminer, pitman (*Brit.*), collier (*Brit.*)
mingle 1 = mix, combine, blend, merge, unite, join, interweave, intermingle ≠ separate **2** = associate, consort, socialize, rub shoulders (*informal*), hobnob, fraternize, hang about *or* around ≠ dissociate
miniature = small, little, minute, tiny, toy, scaled-down, diminutive, minuscule ≠ giant
minimal = minimum, smallest, least, slightest, token, nominal, negligible, least possible
minimize 1 = reduce, decrease, shrink, diminish, prune, curtail, miniaturize ≠ increase **2** = play down, discount, belittle, disparage, decry, underrate, deprecate, make light *or* little of ≠ praise
minimum ADJECTIVE = lowest, smallest, least, slightest, minimal, least possible ≠ maximum
• NOUN = lowest, least, lowest level, nadir
minister NOUN = clergyman, priest, vicar, parson, preacher, pastor, cleric, rector
• VERB *often with* ***to*** = attend, serve, tend, take care of, cater to, pander to, administer to
ministry 1 = department, office, bureau, government department **2** = administration, council **3** = the priesthood, the church, the cloth, holy orders
minor = small, lesser, slight, petty, trivial, insignificant, unimportant, inconsequential ≠ major
mint = make, produce, strike, cast, stamp, punch, coin
minute[1] NOUN = moment, second, bit, flash, instant, tick (*Brit. informal*), sec (*informal*), short time
• PLURAL NOUN = record, notes, proceedings, transactions, transcript, memorandum
minute[2] **1** = small, little, tiny, miniature, microscopic, diminutive, minuscule, infinitesimal ≠ huge **2** = precise, close, detailed, critical, exact, meticulous, exhaustive, painstaking ≠ imprecise
miracle = wonder, phenomenon, sensation, marvel, amazing achievement, astonishing feat
miraculous = wonderful, amazing, extraordinary, incredible, astonishing,

unbelievable, phenomenal, astounding ≠ ordinary

mirror NOUN = looking-glass, glass (*Brit.*), reflector
• VERB = reflect, follow, copy, echo, emulate

miscarriage = failure, error, breakdown, mishap, perversion

misconduct = immorality, wrongdoing, mismanagement, malpractice, impropriety

miserable 1 = sad, depressed, gloomy, forlorn, dejected, despondent, sorrowful, wretched ≠ happy 2 = pathetic, sorry, shameful, despicable, deplorable, lamentable ≠ respectable

misery 1 = unhappiness, distress, despair, grief, suffering, depression, gloom, torment ≠ happiness 2 (*Brit. informal*) = moaner, pessimist, killjoy, spoilsport, prophet of doom, wet blanket (*informal*), sourpuss (*informal*), wowser (*Austral. & N.Z. slang*)

misfortune 1 *often plural* = bad luck, adversity, hard luck, ill luck, infelicity 2 = mishap, trouble, disaster, reverse, tragedy, setback, calamity, affliction ≠ good luck

misguided = unwise, mistaken, misplaced, deluded, ill-advised, imprudent, injudicious

mislead = deceive, fool, delude, take someone in (*informal*), misdirect, misinform, hoodwink, misguide

misleading = confusing, false, ambiguous, deceptive, evasive, disingenuous ≠ straightforward

miss VERB 1 = fail to notice, overlook, pass over 2 = long for, yearn for, pine for, long to see, ache for, feel the loss of, regret the absence of 3 = not go to, skip, cut, omit, be absent from, fail to attend, skive off (*informal*), play truant from, bludge (*Austral. & N.Z. informal*) 4 = avoid, beat, escape, skirt, duck, cheat, bypass, dodge
• NOUN = mistake, failure, error, blunder, omission, oversight

missile = projectile, weapon, shell, rocket

missing = lost, misplaced, not present, astray, unaccounted for, mislaid

mission = task, job, commission, duty, undertaking, quest, assignment, vocation

missionary = evangelist, preacher, apostle

mist = fog, cloud, steam, spray, film, haze, vapour, smog

mistake NOUN 1 = error, blunder, oversight, slip, gaffe (*informal*), miscalculation, faux pas 2 = oversight, error, slip, fault, howler (*informal*), erratum
• VERB 1 = confuse with, take for, mix up with 2 = misunderstand, misinterpret, misjudge, misread, misconstrue, misapprehend

mistaken 1 = wrong, incorrect, misguided, wide of the mark ≠ correct 2 = inaccurate, false, faulty, erroneous, unsound ≠ accurate

mistress = lover, girlfriend, concubine, kept woman, paramour

misunderstand 1 = misinterpret, misread, mistake, misjudge, misconstrue, misapprehend, be at cross-purposes with 2 = miss the point, get the wrong end of the stick

misunderstanding = mistake, error, mix-up, misconception, misinterpretation, misjudgment

misuse NOUN 1 = waste, squandering 2 = abuse 3 = misapplication, abuse, illegal use, wrong use 4 = perversion, desecration 5 = misapplication
• VERB 1 = abuse, misapply, prostitute 2 = waste, squander, embezzle, misappropriate

mix VERB 1 = combine, blend, merge, join, cross, fuse, mingle, jumble 2 = socialize, associate, hang out (*informal*), mingle, circulate, consort, hobnob, fraternize 3 *often with* ***up*** = combine, marry, blend, integrate, amalgamate, coalesce, meld
• NOUN = mixture, combination, blend, fusion, compound, assortment, alloy, medley
• PHRASES **mix something up** 1 = confuse, scramble, muddle, confound 2 = blend, beat, mix, stir, fold

mixed 1 = varied, diverse, different, differing, cosmopolitan, assorted, jumbled, disparate ≠ homogeneous 2 = combined, blended, united, compound, composite, mingled, amalgamated ≠ pure

mixed-up = confused, disturbed, puzzled, bewildered, at sea, upset, distraught, muddled

mixture 1 = blend, mix, variety, fusion, assortment, brew, jumble, medley 2 = composite, compound 3 = cross, combination, blend **4** = concoction, compound, blend, brew, amalgam

mix-up = confusion, mistake, misunderstanding, mess, tangle, muddle

moan VERB **1** = groan, sigh, sob, whine, lament **2** (*Informal*) = grumble, complain, groan, whine, carp, grouse, whinge (*informal*), bleat
• NOUN **1** = groan, sigh, sob, lament, wail, grunt, whine **2** (*Informal*) = complaint, protest, grumble, whine, grouse, gripe (*informal*), grouch (*informal*)

mob NOUN **1** = crowd, pack, mass, host, drove, flock, swarm, horde **2** (*Slang*) = gang, group, set, lot, crew (*informal*)
• VERB = surround, besiege, jostle, fall on, set upon, crowd around, swarm around

mobile = movable, moving, travelling, wandering, portable, itinerant, peripatetic

mobilize **1** = rally, organize, stimulate, excite, prompt, marshal, activate, awaken **2** = deploy, prepare, ready, rally, assemble, call up, marshal, muster

mock VERB = laugh at, tease, ridicule, taunt, scorn, sneer, scoff, deride ≠ respect
• ADJECTIVE = imitation, pretended, artificial, fake, false, dummy, sham, feigned ≠ genuine

mocking = scornful, scoffing, satirical, contemptuous, sarcastic, sardonic, disrespectful, disdainful

mode **1** = method, way, system, form, process, style, technique, manner **2** = fashion, style, trend, rage, vogue, look, craze

model NOUN **1** = representation, image, copy, miniature, dummy, replica, imitation, duplicate **2** = pattern, example, standard, original, ideal, prototype, paradigm, archetype **3** = sitter, subject, poser
• VERB **1** = show off (*informal*), wear, display, sport **2** = shape, form, design, fashion, carve, mould, sculpt

moderate ADJECTIVE **1** = mild, reasonable, controlled, limited, steady, modest, restrained, middle-of-the-road ≠ extreme **2** = average, middling, fair, ordinary, indifferent, mediocre, so-so (*informal*), passable, half-pie (*N.Z. informal*)
• VERB **1** = soften, control, temper, regulate, curb, restrain, subdue, lessen **2** = lessen, ease ≠ intensify

modern **1** = current, contemporary, recent, present-day, latter-day **2** = up-to-date, fresh, new, novel, newfangled ≠ old-fashioned

modest **1** = moderate, small, limited, fair, ordinary, middling, meagre, frugal **2** = unpretentious, reserved, retiring, shy, coy, reticent, self-effacing, demure

modesty = reserve, humility, shyness, reticence, timidity, diffidence, coyness, bashfulness ≠ conceit

modification = change, variation, qualification, adjustment, revision, alteration, refinement

modify **1** = change, reform, convert, alter, adjust, adapt, revise, remodel **2** = tone down, lower, qualify, ease, moderate, temper, soften, restrain

mogul = tycoon, baron, magnate, big shot (*informal*), big noise (*informal*), big hitter (*informal*), heavy hitter (*informal*), V.I.P.

moist = damp, wet, soggy, humid, clammy, dewy

moisture = damp, water, liquid, dew, wetness

molecule = particle, jot, speck

moment **1** = instant, second, flash, twinkling, split second, jiffy (*informal*), trice **2** = time, point, stage, juncture

momentous = significant, important, vital, critical, crucial, historic, pivotal, fateful ≠ unimportant

momentum = impetus, force, power, drive, push, energy, strength, thrust

monarch = ruler, king *or* queen, sovereign, tsar, potentate, emperor *or* empress, prince *or* princess

monarchy **1** = sovereignty, autocracy, kingship, royalism, monocracy **2** = kingdom, empire, realm, principality

monastery = abbey, convent, priory, cloister, nunnery, friary

monetary = financial, money, economic, capital, cash, fiscal, budgetary, pecuniary

money = cash, capital, currency, hard cash, readies (*informal*), riches, silver, coin

monitor VERB = check, follow, watch, survey, observe, keep an eye on, keep track of, keep tabs on
• NOUN **1** = guide, observer, supervisor, invigilator **2** = prefect (*Brit.*), head girl, head boy, senior boy, senior girl

monk (*Loosely*) = friar, brother
RELATED WORD
adjective: monastic

monkey **1** = simian, ape, primate

2 = rascal, horror, devil, rogue, imp, tyke, scallywag, scamp, nointer (*Austral. slang*)

RELATED WORD

adjective: simian

monster NOUN 1 = giant, mammoth, titan, colossus, monstrosity 2 = brute, devil, beast, demon, villain, fiend

• ADJECTIVE = huge, massive, enormous, tremendous, immense, gigantic, mammoth, colossal

monstrous 1 = outrageous, shocking, foul, intolerable, disgraceful, scandalous, inhuman, diabolical ≠ decent 2 = huge, massive, enormous, tremendous, immense, mammoth, colossal, prodigious ≠ tiny 3 = unnatural, horrible, hideous, grotesque, gruesome, frightful, freakish, fiendish ≠ normal

monument = memorial, cairn, marker, shrine, tombstone, mausoleum, commemoration, headstone

monumental 1 = important, significant, enormous, historic, memorable, awesome, majestic, unforgettable ≠ unimportant 2 (*Informal*) = immense, great, massive, staggering, colossal ≠ tiny

mood = state of mind, spirit, humour, temper, disposition, frame of mind

moody 1 = changeable, volatile, unpredictable, erratic, fickle, temperamental, impulsive, mercurial ≠ stable 2 = sulky, irritable, temperamental, touchy, ill-tempered, tooshie (*Austral. slang*) ≠ cheerful 3 = gloomy, sad, sullen, glum, morose ≠ cheerful 4 = sad, gloomy, melancholy, sombre

moon NOUN = satellite

• VERB = idle, drift, loaf, languish, waste time, daydream, mope

RELATED WORD

adjective: lunar

moor[1] = moorland, fell (*Brit.*), heath

moor[2] = tie up, secure, anchor, dock, lash, berth, make fast

mop NOUN 1 = squeegee, sponge, swab 2 = mane, shock, mass, tangle, mat, thatch

• VERB = clean, wash, wipe, sponge, swab

moral ADJECTIVE = good, just, right, principled, decent, noble, ethical, honourable ≠ immoral

• NOUN = lesson, meaning, point, message, teaching, import, significance, precept

• PLURAL NOUN = morality, standards, conduct, principles, behaviour, manners, habits, ethics

morale = confidence, heart, spirit, self-esteem, team spirit, esprit de corps

morality 1 = virtue, justice, morals, honour, integrity, goodness, honesty, decency 2 = ethics, conduct, principles, morals, manners, philosophy, mores 3 = rights and wrongs, ethics

moratorium = postponement, freeze, halt, suspension, standstill

more ADJECTIVE = extra, additional, new, other, added, further, new-found, supplementary

• ADVERB 1 = to a greater extent, longer, better, further, some more 2 = moreover, also, in addition, besides, furthermore, what's more, on top of that, to boot

moreover = furthermore, also, further, in addition, too, as well, besides, additionally

morning 1 = before noon, forenoon, morn (*poetic*), a.m. 2 = dawn, sunrise, first light, daybreak, break of day

mortal ADJECTIVE 1 = human, worldly, passing, fleshly, temporal, transient, ephemeral, perishable 2 = fatal, killing, terminal, deadly, destructive, lethal, murderous, death-dealing

• NOUN = human being, being, man, woman, person, human, individual, earthling

mortality 1 = humanity, transience, impermanence, corporeality, impermanency 2 = death, dying, fatality

mostly 1 = mainly, largely, chiefly, principally, primarily, on the whole, predominantly 2 = generally, usually, on the whole, as a rule

mother NOUN = female parent, mum (*Brit. informal*), ma (*informal*), mater, dam, mummy (*Brit. informal*), foster mother, biological mother

• VERB = nurture, raise, protect, tend, nurse, rear, care for, cherish

• ADJECTIVE = native, natural, innate, inborn

RELATED WORD

adjective: maternal

motherly = maternal, loving, caring, comforting, sheltering, protective, affectionate

motif 1 = design, shape, decoration, ornament 2 = theme, idea, subject, concept, leitmotif

motion NOUN 1 = movement,

mobility, travel, progress, flow, locomotion **2** = proposal, suggestion, recommendation, proposition, submission
• VERB = gesture, direct, wave, signal, nod, beckon, gesticulate

motivate 1 = inspire, drive, stimulate, move, cause, prompt, stir, induce **2** = stimulate, drive, inspire, stir, arouse, galvanize, incentivize

motivation = incentive, inspiration, motive, stimulus, reason, spur, inducement, incitement

motive = reason, ground(s), purpose, object, incentive, inspiration, stimulus, rationale

motto = saying, slogan, maxim, rule, adage, proverb, dictum, precept

mould[1] NOUN **1** = cast, shape, pattern **2** = design, style, fashion, build, form, kind, shape, pattern **3** = nature, character, sort, kind, quality, type, stamp, calibre
• VERB **1** = shape, make, work, form, create, model, fashion, construct **2** = influence, make, form, control, direct, affect, shape

mould[2] = fungus, blight, mildew

mound 1 = heap, pile, drift, stack, rick **2** = hill, bank, rise, dune, embankment, knoll, hillock, kopje *or* koppie (*S. African*)

mount VERB **1** = increase, build, grow, swell, intensify, escalate, multiply ≠ decrease **2** = accumulate, increase, collect, gather, build up, pile up, amass **3** = ascend, scale, climb (up), go up, clamber up ≠ descend **4** = get (up) on, jump on, straddle, climb onto, hop on to, bestride, get on the back of ≠ get off **5** = display, present, prepare, put on, organize, put on display
• NOUN **1** = horse, steed (*literary*) **2** = backing, setting, support, stand, base, frame

mountain 1 = peak, mount, horn, ridge, fell (*Brit.*), berg (*S. African*), alp, pinnacle **2** = heap, mass, masses, pile, a great deal, ton, stack, abundance

mourn 1 *often with* ***for*** = grieve for, lament, weep for, wail for **2** = bemoan, rue, deplore, bewail

mourning 1 = grieving, grief, bereavement, weeping, woe, lamentation **2** = black, sackcloth and ashes, widow's weeds

mouth 1 = lips, jaws, gob (*slang, esp. Brit.*), maw, cakehole (*Brit. slang*) **2** = entrance, opening, gateway, door, aperture, orifice **3** = opening **4** = inlet, outlet, estuary, firth, outfall, debouchment
RELATED WORD
adjective: oral

move VERB **1** = transfer, change, switch, shift, transpose **2** = go, advance, progress, shift, proceed, stir, budge, make a move **3** = relocate, leave, remove, quit, migrate, emigrate, decamp, up sticks (*Brit. informal*) **4** = drive, cause, influence, persuade, shift, inspire, prompt, induce ≠ discourage **5** = touch, affect, excite, impress, stir, disquiet **6** = propose, suggest, urge, recommend, request, advocate, submit, put forward
• NOUN **1** = action, step, manoeuvre **2** = ploy, action, measure, step, initiative, stroke, tactic, manoeuvre **3** = transfer, posting, shift, removal, relocation **4** = turn, go, play, chance, shot (*informal*), opportunity

movement 1 = group, party, organization, grouping, front, faction **2** = campaign, drive, push, crusade **3** = move, action, motion, manoeuvre **4** = activity, moving, stirring, bustle **5** = advance, progress, flow **6** = transfer, transportation, displacement **7** = development, change, variation, fluctuation **8** = progression, progress **9** (*Music*) = section, part, division, passage

movie = film, picture, feature, flick (*slang*)

moving 1 = emotional, touching, affecting, inspiring, stirring, poignant ≠ unemotional **2** = mobile, running, active, going, operational, in motion, driving, kinetic ≠ stationary

mow VERB = cut, crop, trim, shear, scythe
• PHRASES **mow something** *or* **someone down** = massacre, butcher, slaughter, cut down, shoot down, cut to pieces

much ADVERB **1** = greatly, a lot, considerably, decidedly, exceedingly, appreciably ≠ hardly **2** = often, a lot, routinely, a great deal, many times, habitually, on many occasions, customarily
• DETERMINER = great, a lot of, plenty of, considerable, substantial, piles of (*informal*), ample, abundant ≠ little
• PRONOUN = a lot, plenty, a great deal, lots (*informal*), masses (*informal*), loads (*informal*), tons (*informal*), heaps (*informal*) ≠ little

muck 1 = dirt, mud, filth, ooze, sludge, mire, slime, gunge (*informal*), kak (*S. African informal*) 2 = manure, dung, ordure
mud = dirt, clay, ooze, silt, sludge, mire, slime
muddle NOUN = confusion, mess, disorder, chaos, tangle, mix-up, disarray, predicament
• VERB 1 = jumble, disorder, scramble, tangle, mix up 2 = confuse, bewilder, daze, confound, perplex, disorient, stupefy, befuddle
muddy 1 = boggy, swampy, marshy, quaggy 2 = dirty, soiled, grimy, mucky, mud-caked, bespattered
mug[1] = cup, pot, beaker, tankard
mug[2] (*Informal*) 1 = face, features, countenance, visage 2 = fool, sucker (*slang*), chump (*informal*), simpleton, easy *or* soft touch (*slang*), dorba *or* dorb (*Austral. slang*), bogan (*Austral. slang*)
mug[3] VERB = attack, assault, beat up, rob, set about *or* upon
• PHRASES **mug up (on) something** = study, cram (*informal*), bone up on (*informal*), swot up on (*Brit. informal*)
multiple = many, several, various, numerous, sundry, manifold, multitudinous
multiply 1 = increase, extend, expand, spread, build up, proliferate ≠ decrease 2 = reproduce, breed, propagate
multitude 1 = great number, host, army, mass, horde, myriad 2 = crowd, host, mass, mob, swarm, horde, throng
mundane 1 = ordinary, routine, commonplace, banal, everyday, day-to-day, prosaic, humdrum ≠ extraordinary 2 = earthly, worldly, secular, mortal, terrestrial, temporal ≠ spiritual
municipal = civic, public, local, council, district, urban, metropolitan
murder NOUN = killing, homicide, massacre, assassination, slaying, bloodshed, carnage, butchery
• VERB = kill, massacre, slaughter, assassinate, eliminate (*slang*), butcher, slay, bump off (*slang*)
murderer = killer, assassin, slayer, butcher, slaughterer, cut-throat, hit man (*slang*)
murderous = deadly, savage, brutal, cruel, lethal, ferocious, cut-throat, bloodthirsty
murky 1 = dark, gloomy, grey, dull, dim, cloudy, misty, overcast ≠ bright 2 = dark, cloudy
murmur VERB = mumble, whisper, mutter
• NOUN = whisper, drone, purr
muscle NOUN 1 = tendon, sinew 2 = strength, might, power, weight, stamina, brawn
• PHRASES **muscle in** (*Informal*) = impose yourself, encroach, butt in, force your way in
muscular = strong, powerful, athletic, strapping, robust, vigorous, sturdy, sinewy
muse = ponder, consider, reflect, contemplate, deliberate, brood, meditate, mull over
musical = melodious, lyrical, harmonious, melodic, tuneful, dulcet, sweet-sounding, euphonious ≠ discordant
must = necessity, essential, requirement, fundamental, imperative, requisite, prerequisite, sine qua non (*Latin*)
muster VERB 1 = summon up, marshal 2 = rally, gather, assemble, marshal, mobilize, call together 3 = assemble, convene
• NOUN = assembly, meeting, collection, gathering, rally, convention, congregation, roundup, hui (*N.Z.*), runanga (*N.Z.*)
mutation 1 = anomaly, variation, deviant, freak of nature 2 = change, variation, evolution, transformation, modification, alteration, metamorphosis, transfiguration
mute 1 = close-mouthed, silent 2 = silent, dumb, unspoken, tacit, wordless, voiceless, unvoiced 3 = dumb, speechless, voiceless
mutter = grumble, complain, murmur, rumble, whine, mumble, grouse, bleat
mutual = shared, common, joint, returned, reciprocal, interchangeable, requited
myriad NOUN = multitude, host, army, swarm, horde
• ADJECTIVE = innumerable, countless, untold, incalculable, immeasurable, multitudinous
mysterious 1 = strange, puzzling, secret, weird, perplexing, uncanny, mystifying, arcane ≠ clear 2 = secretive, enigmatic, evasive, discreet, covert, reticent, furtive, inscrutable
mystery = puzzle, problem, question, secret, riddle, enigma, conundrum, teaser
mystic *or* **mystical** = supernatural, mysterious, transcendental, occult, metaphysical, paranormal, inscrutable,

otherworldly
myth **1** = legend, story, fiction, saga, fable, allegory, fairy story, folk tale **2** = illusion, story, fancy, fantasy, imagination, invention, delusion, superstition
mythology = legend, folklore, tradition, lore

n

nab = catch, arrest, apprehend, seize, grab, capture, collar (*informal*), snatch
nag¹ VERB = scold, harass, badger, pester, worry, plague, hassle (*informal*), upbraid
• NOUN = scold, complainer, grumbler, virago, shrew, tartar, moaner, harpy
nag² = horse (*U.S.*), hack
nagging **1** = continuous, persistent, continual, niggling, repeated, constant, endless, perpetual **2** = scolding, shrewish
nail NOUN **1** = tack, spike, rivet, hobnail, brad (*technical*) **2** = fingernail, toenail, talon, thumbnail, claw
• VERB **1** = fasten, fix, secure, attach, pin, hammer, tack **2** (*informal*) = catch, arrest, capture, apprehend, trap, snare, ensnare, entrap
naive *or* **naïve** = gullible, trusting, credulous, unsuspicious, green, simple, innocent, callow ≠ worldly
naked = nude, stripped, exposed, bare, undressed, starkers (*informal*), stark-naked, unclothed ≠ dressed
name NOUN = title, nickname, designation, term, handle (*slang*), epithet, sobriquet, moniker *or* monicker (*slang*)
• VERB **1** = call, christen, baptize, dub, term, style, label, entitle **2** = nominate, choose, select, appoint, specify, designate
namely = specifically, to wit, viz.
nap¹ NOUN = sleep, rest, kip (*Brit. slang*), siesta, catnap, forty winks (*informal*)
• VERB = sleep, rest, drop off (*informal*), doze, kip (*Brit. slang*), snooze (*informal*), nod off (*informal*), catnap
nap² = pile, down, fibre, weave, grain
napkin = serviette, cloth
narcotic NOUN = drug, anaesthetic, painkiller, sedative, opiate, tranquillizer, anodyne, analgesic
• ADJECTIVE = sedative, calming, hypnotic, analgesic, soporific, painkilling
narrative = story, report, history, account, statement, tale, chronicle
narrator = storyteller, writer, author, reporter, commentator, chronicler
narrow ADJECTIVE **1** = thin, fine, slim, slender, tapering, attenuated ≠ broad **2** = limited, restricted, confined, tight, close, meagre, constricted ≠ wide **3** = insular, prejudiced, partial, dogmatic, intolerant, narrow-minded, small-minded, illiberal ≠ broad-minded
• VERB **1** = restrict, limit, reduce, constrict **2** = get narrower, taper, shrink, tighten, constrict
narrowly = just, barely, only just, scarcely, by the skin of your teeth
nasty **1** = unpleasant, ugly, disagreeable ≠ pleasant **2** = spiteful, mean, offensive, vicious, unpleasant, vile, malicious, despicable ≠ pleasant **3** = disgusting, unpleasant, offensive, vile, distasteful, obnoxious, objectionable, disagreeable, festy (*Austral. slang*), yucko (*Austral. slang*) **4** = serious, bad, dangerous, critical, severe, painful
nation **1** = country, state, realm **2** = public, people, society
national ADJECTIVE = nationwide, public, widespread, countrywide
• NOUN = citizen, subject, resident, native, inhabitant
nationalism = patriotism, loyalty to your country, chauvinism, jingoism, allegiance
nationality **1** = citizenship, birth **2** = race, nation
nationwide = national, general, widespread, countrywide
native ADJECTIVE = mother, indigenous, vernacular
• NOUN = inhabitant, national, resident, citizen, countryman, aborigine (*often offensive*), dweller
natural **1** = logical, valid, legitimate **2** = normal, common, regular, usual, ordinary, typical, everyday ≠ abnormal **3** = innate, native, characteristic, inherent, instinctive, intuitive, inborn,

essential **4** = unaffected, open, genuine, spontaneous, unpretentious, unsophisticated, dinkum (*Austral. & N.Z. informal*), ingenuous, real ≠ affected **5** = pure, plain, organic, whole, unrefined ≠ processed

naturally **1** = of course, certainly **2** = typically, simply, normally, spontaneously

nature **1** = creation, world, earth, environment, universe, cosmos, natural world **2** = quality, character, make-up, constitution, essence, complexion **3** = temperament, character, personality, disposition, outlook, mood, humour, temper **4** = kind, sort, style, type, variety, species, category, description

naughty **1** = disobedient, bad, mischievous, badly behaved, wayward, wicked, impish, refractory ≠ good **2** = obscene, vulgar, improper, lewd, risqué, smutty, ribald ≠ clean

nausea = sickness, vomiting, retching, squeamishness, queasiness, biliousness

naval = nautical, marine, maritime

navigation = sailing, voyaging, seamanship, helmsmanship

navy = fleet, flotilla, armada

near **1** = close, neighbouring, nearby, adjacent, adjoining ≠ far **2** = imminent, forthcoming, approaching, looming, impending, upcoming, nigh, in the offing ≠ far-off

nearby = neighbouring, adjacent, adjoining

nearly **1** = practically, almost, virtually, just about, as good as, well-nigh **2** = almost, approaching, roughly, just about, approximately

neat **1** = tidy, trim, orderly, spruce, shipshape, spick-and-span ≠ untidy **2** = methodical, tidy, systematic, fastidious ≠ disorganized **3** = smart, trim, tidy, spruce, dapper, natty (*informal*), well-groomed, well-turned out **4** = graceful, elegant, adept, nimble, adroit, efficient ≠ clumsy **5** = clever, efficient, handy, apt, well-judged ≠ inefficient **6** = cool, great (*informal*), excellent, brilliant, superb, fantastic (*informal*), tremendous, fabulous (*informal*), booshit (*Austral. slang*), exo (*Austral. slang*), sik (*Austral. slang*) ≠ terrible **7** (*of alcoholic drinks*) = undiluted, straight, pure, unmixed

neatly **1** = tidily, smartly, systematically, methodically, fastidiously **2** = smartly, elegantly, tidily, nattily **3** = gracefully, expertly, efficiently, adeptly, skilfully, nimbly, adroitly, dexterously **4** = cleverly, efficiently

necessarily **1** = automatically, naturally, definitely, undoubtedly, certainly **2** = inevitably, of necessity, unavoidably, incontrovertibly, nolens volens (*Latin*)

necessary **1** = needed, required, essential, vital, compulsory, mandatory, imperative, indispensable ≠ unnecessary **2** = inevitable, certain, unavoidable, inescapable ≠ avoidable

necessity NOUN **1** = essential, need, requirement, fundamental, requisite, prerequisite, sine qua non (*Latin*), desideratum **2** = inevitability, certainty
• PLURAL NOUN = essentials, needs, requirements, fundamentals

need VERB **1** = want, miss, require, lack, have to have, demand **2** = require, want, demand, call for, entail, necessitate **3** = have to, be obliged to
• NOUN **1** = requirement, demand, essential, necessity, requisite, desideratum **2** = necessity, call, demand, obligation **3** = emergency, want, necessity, urgency, exigency **4** = poverty, deprivation, destitution, penury

needed = necessary, wanted, required, lacked, called for, desired

needle = irritate, provoke, annoy, harass, taunt, nag, goad, rile

needless = unnecessary, pointless, gratuitous, useless, unwanted, redundant, superfluous, groundless ≠ essential

needy = poor, deprived, disadvantaged, impoverished, penniless, destitute, poverty-stricken, underprivileged ≠ wealthy

negative ADJECTIVE **1** = pessimistic, cynical, unwilling, gloomy, jaundiced, uncooperative ≠ optimistic **2** = dissenting, contradictory, refusing, denying, rejecting, opposing, resisting, contrary ≠ assenting
• NOUN = denial, no, refusal, rejection, contradiction

neglect VERB **1** = disregard, ignore, fail to look after ≠ look after **2** = shirk, forget, overlook, omit, evade, pass over, skimp, be remiss in *or* about **3** = fail, forget, omit
• NOUN **1** = negligence, inattention

≠ care 2 = shirking, failure, oversight, carelessness, dereliction, slackness, laxity
neglected 1 = uncared-for, abandoned, underestimated, disregarded, undervalued, unappreciated 2 = run down, derelict, overgrown, uncared-for
negligence = carelessness, neglect, disregard, dereliction, slackness, inattention, laxity, thoughtlessness
negotiate 1 = bargain, deal, discuss, debate, mediate, hold talks, cut a deal, conciliate 2 = arrange, work out, bring about, transact 3 = get round, clear, pass, cross, get over, get past, surmount
negotiation 1 = bargaining, debate, discussion, transaction, dialogue, mediation, arbitration, wheeling and dealing (*informal*) 2 = arrangement, working out, transaction, bringing about
negotiator = mediator, ambassador, diplomat, delegate, intermediary, moderator, honest broker
neighbourhood 1 = district, community, quarter, region, locality, locale 2 = vicinity, environs
neighbouring = nearby, next, near, bordering, surrounding, connecting, adjacent, adjoining ≠ remote
neighbourly = helpful, kind, friendly, obliging, harmonious, considerate, sociable, hospitable
nerve NOUN 1 = bravery, courage, bottle (*Brit. slang*), resolution, daring, guts (*informal*), pluck, grit 2 (*Informal*) = impudence, cheek (*informal*), audacity, boldness, temerity, insolence, impertinence, brazenness
• PLURAL NOUN = tension, stress, strain, anxiety, butterflies (in your stomach) (*informal*), nervousness, cold feet (*informal*), worry
• PHRASES **nerve yourself** = brace yourself, prepare yourself, steel yourself, fortify yourself, gear yourself up, gee yourself up
nervous = apprehensive, anxious, uneasy, edgy, worried, tense, fearful, uptight (*informal*), toey (*Austral. slang*) ≠ calm
nest = refuge, retreat, haunt, den, hideaway
nestle = snuggle, cuddle, huddle, curl up, nuzzle
nestling = chick, fledgling, baby bird
net[1] NOUN = mesh, netting, network, web, lattice, openwork
• VERB = catch, bag, capture, trap, entangle, ensnare, enmesh
net[2] *or* **nett** ADJECTIVE = after taxes, final, clear, take-home
• VERB = earn, make, clear, gain, realize, bring in, accumulate, reap
network 1 = web, system, arrangement, grid, lattice 2 = maze, warren, labyrinth
neurotic = unstable, nervous, disturbed, abnormal, obsessive, compulsive, manic, unhealthy ≠ rational
neutral 1 = unbiased, impartial, disinterested, even-handed, uninvolved, nonpartisan, unprejudiced, nonaligned ≠ biased 2 = expressionless, dull 3 = uncontroversial *or* noncontroversial, inoffensive 4 = colourless
never 1 = at no time, not once, not ever ≠ always 2 = under no circumstances, not at all, on no account, not ever
nevertheless = even so, still, however, yet, regardless, nonetheless, notwithstanding, in spite of that
new 1 = modern, recent, contemporary, up-to-date, latest, current, original, fresh ≠ old-fashioned 2 = brand new 3 = extra, more, added, new-found, supplementary 4 = unfamiliar, strange 5 = renewed, changed, improved, restored, altered, revitalized
newcomer 1 = new arrival, stranger 2 = beginner, novice, new arrival, parvenu, Johnny-come-lately (*informal*)
news = information, latest (*informal*), report, story, exposé, intelligence, rumour, revelation
next ADJECTIVE 1 = following, later, succeeding, subsequent 2 = adjacent, closest, nearest, neighbouring, adjoining
• ADVERB = afterwards, then, later, following, subsequently, thereafter
nice 1 = pleasant, delightful, agreeable, good, attractive, charming, pleasurable, enjoyable ≠ unpleasant 2 = kind, helpful, obliging, considerate ≠ unkind 3 = likable *or* likeable, friendly, engaging, charming, pleasant, agreeable 4 = polite, courteous, well-mannered ≠ vulgar 5 = precise, fine, careful, strict, subtle, delicate, meticulous, fastidious ≠ vague
nicely 1 = pleasantly, well, delightfully, attractively, charmingly, agreeably, acceptably, pleasurably ≠ unpleasantly

2 = kindly, politely, thoughtfully, amiably, courteously
niche 1 = recess, opening, corner, hollow, nook, alcove 2 = position, calling, place, slot (*informal*), vocation, pigeonhole (*informal*)
nick VERB 1 (*Slang*) = steal, pinch (*informal*), swipe (*slang*), pilfer 2 = cut, mark, score, chip, scratch, scar, notch, dent
• NOUN = cut, mark, scratch, chip, scar, notch, dent
nickname = pet name, label, diminutive, epithet, sobriquet, moniker *or* monicker (*slang*)
night = darkness, dark, night-time
RELATED WORD
adjective: nocturnal
nightly ADJECTIVE = nocturnal, night-time
• ADVERB = every night, nights (*informal*), each night, night after night
nightmare 1 = bad dream, hallucination 2 = ordeal, trial, hell, horror, torture, torment, tribulation, purgatory
nil 1 = nothing, love, zero 2 = zero, nothing, none, naught
nip[1] VERB 1 = pop, go, run, rush, dash 2 = bite 3 = pinch, squeeze, tweak
• PHRASES **nip something in the bud** = thwart, check, frustrate
nip[2] = dram, shot (*informal*), drop, sip, draught, mouthful, snifter (*informal*)
nirvana = paradise, peace, joy, bliss, serenity, tranquillity
no INTERJECTION = not at all, certainly not, of course not, absolutely not, never, no way, nay ≠ yes
• NOUN = refusal, rejection, denial, negation ≠ consent
noble ADJECTIVE 1 = worthy, generous, upright, honourable, virtuous, magnanimous ≠ despicable 2 = dignified, great, imposing, impressive, distinguished, splendid, stately ≠ lowly 3 = aristocratic, lordly, titled, patrician, blue-blooded, highborn ≠ humble
• NOUN = lord, peer, aristocrat, nobleman ≠ commoner
nobody PRONOUN = no-one
• NOUN = nonentity, lightweight (*informal*), zero, cipher ≠ celebrity
nod VERB 1 = incline, bow 2 = signal, indicate, motion, gesture 3 = salute, acknowledge
• NOUN 1 = signal, sign, motion, gesture, indication 2 = salute, greeting, acknowledgment
noise = sound, row, racket, clamour, din, uproar, commotion, hubbub ≠ silence, calm
noisy 1 = rowdy, strident, boisterous, vociferous, uproarious, clamorous ≠ quiet 2 = loud, piercing, deafening, tumultuous, ear-splitting, cacophonous, clamorous ≠ quiet
nominal 1 = titular, formal, purported, in name only, supposed, so-called, theoretical, professed 2 = token, small, symbolic, minimal, trivial, trifling, insignificant, inconsiderable
nominate 1 = propose, suggest, recommend, put forward 2 = appoint, name, choose, select, elect, assign, designate
nomination 1 = proposal, suggestion, recommendation 2 = appointment, election, selection, designation, choice
nominee = candidate, applicant, entrant, contestant, aspirant, runner
none 1 = not any, nothing, zero, not one, nil 2 = no-one, nobody, not one
nonetheless = nevertheless, however, yet, even so, despite that, in spite of that
non-existent *or* **nonexistent** = imaginary, fictional, mythical, unreal, hypothetical, illusory ≠ real
nonsense 1 = rubbish, hot air (*informal*), twaddle, drivel, tripe (*informal*), gibberish, claptrap (*informal*), double Dutch (*Brit. informal*), bizzo (*Austral. slang*), bull's wool (*Austral. & N.Z. slang*) ≠ sense 2 = idiocy, stupidity
non-stop *or* **nonstop** ADJECTIVE = continuous, constant, relentless, uninterrupted, endless, unbroken, interminable, incessant ≠ occasional
• ADVERB = continuously, constantly, endlessly, relentlessly, perpetually, incessantly, ceaselessly, interminably
noon NOUN = midday, high noon, noonday, twelve noon, noontide
• ADJECTIVE = midday, noonday, noontide
norm = standard, rule, pattern, average, par, criterion, benchmark, yardstick
normal 1 = usual, common, standard, average, natural, regular, ordinary, typical ≠ unusual 2 = sane, reasonable, rational, well-adjusted, compos mentis (*Latin*), in your right mind, mentally sound

normally 1 = usually, generally, commonly, regularly, typically, ordinarily, as a rule, habitually 2 = as usual, naturally, properly, conventionally, in the usual way

north ADJECTIVE = northern, polar, arctic, boreal, northerly
• ADVERB = northward(s), in a northerly direction

nose NOUN = snout, bill, beak, hooter (*slang*), proboscis
• VERB = ease forward, push, edge, shove, nudge

RELATED WORD
adjective: nasal

nostalgia = reminiscence, longing, pining, yearning, remembrance, homesickness, wistfulness

nostalgic = sentimental, longing, emotional, homesick, wistful, maudlin, regretful

notable ADJECTIVE 1 = remarkable, striking, unusual, extraordinary, outstanding, memorable, uncommon, conspicuous ≠ imperceptible 2 = prominent, famous ≠ unknown
• NOUN = celebrity, big name, dignitary, luminary, personage, V.I.P.

notably = remarkably, unusually, extraordinarily, noticeably, strikingly, singularly, outstandingly, uncommonly

notch NOUN 1 = level (*Informal*), step, degree, grade 2 = cut, nick, incision, indentation, mark, score, cleft
• VERB = cut, mark, score, nick, scratch, indent

note NOUN 1 = message, letter, communication, memo, memorandum, epistle 2 = record, reminder, memo, memorandum, jotting, minute 3 = annotation, comment, remark 4 = document, form, record, certificate 5 = symbol, mark, sign, indication, token 6 = tone, touch, trace, hint, sound
• VERB 1 = notice, see, observe, perceive 2 = bear in mind, be aware, take into account 3 = mention, record, mark, indicate, register, remark 4 = write down, record, scribble, set down, jot down

notebook = notepad, exercise book, journal, diary

noted = famous, celebrated, distinguished, well-known, prominent, acclaimed, notable, renowned ≠ unknown

nothing 1 = nought, zero, nil, not a thing, zilch (*slang*) 2 = a trifle 3 = nobody, cipher, nonentity 4 = void, emptiness, nothingness, nullity

notice VERB = observe, see, note, spot, distinguish, perceive, detect, discern ≠ overlook
• NOUN 1 = notification, warning, advice, intimation, news, communication, announcement, instruction 2 = attention, interest, note, regard, consideration, observation, scrutiny, heed ≠ oversight 3 = the sack (*informal*), dismissal, the boot (*slang*), the push (*slang*), marching orders (*informal*)

noticeable = obvious, clear, striking, plain, evident, manifest, conspicuous, perceptible

notify = inform, tell, advise, alert to, announce, warn, make known to

notion 1 = idea, view, opinion, belief, concept, impression, sentiment, inkling 2 = whim, wish, desire, fancy, impulse, inclination, caprice

notorious = infamous, disreputable, opprobrious

notoriously = infamously, disreputably

notwithstanding = despite, in spite of, regardless of

nought or (*Archaic or literary*) **naught** = zero, nothing, nil

nourish 1 = feed, supply, sustain, nurture 2 = encourage, support, maintain, promote, sustain, foster

nourishing = nutritious, beneficial, wholesome, nutritive

novel[1] = story, tale, fiction, romance, narrative

novel[2] = new, different, original, fresh, unusual, innovative, uncommon ≠ ordinary

novelty 1 = newness, originality, freshness, innovation, surprise, uniqueness, strangeness, unfamiliarity 2 = curiosity, rarity, oddity, wonder 3 = trinket, souvenir, memento, bauble, trifle, knick-knack

novice = beginner, pupil, amateur, newcomer, trainee, apprentice, learner, probationer ≠ expert

now ADVERB 1 = nowadays, at the moment 2 = immediately, promptly, instantly, at once, straightaway
• PHRASES **now and then** *or* **again** = occasionally, sometimes, from time

to time, on and off, intermittently, infrequently, sporadically
nowadays = now, today, at the moment, in this day and age
nucleus = centre, heart, focus, basis, core, pivot, kernel, nub
nude = naked, stripped, bare, undressed, stark-naked, disrobed, unclothed, unclad ≠ dressed
nudge VERB 1 = push, touch, dig, jog, prod, elbow, shove, poke 2 = prompt, influence, persuade, spur, prod, coax
• NOUN 1 = push, touch, dig, elbow, bump, shove, poke, jog 2 = prompting, push, encouragement, prod
nuisance = trouble, problem, trial, drag (*informal*), bother, pest, irritation, hassle (*informal*) ≠ benefit
numb ADJECTIVE 1 = unfeeling, dead, frozen, paralysed, insensitive, deadened, immobilized, torpid ≠ sensitive 2 = stupefied, deadened, unfeeling
• VERB 1 = stun, knock out, paralyse, daze 2 = deaden, freeze, dull, paralyse, immobilize, benumb
number NOUN 1 = numeral, figure, character, digit, integer 2 = amount, quantity, collection, aggregate ≠ shortage 3 = crowd, horde, multitude, throng 4 = group, set, band, crowd, gang 5 = issue, copy, edition, imprint, printing
• VERB 1 = amount to, come to, total, add up to 2 = calculate, account, reckon, compute, enumerate ≠ guess 3 = include, count
numerous = many, several, countless, lots, abundant, plentiful, innumerable, copious ≠ few
nurse 1 = look after, treat, tend, care for, take care of, minister to 2 = harbour, have, maintain, preserve, entertain, cherish 3 = breast-feed, feed, nurture, nourish, suckle, wet-nurse
nursery = crèche, kindergarten, playgroup
nurture VERB = bring up, raise, look after, rear, care for, develop ≠ neglect
• NOUN = upbringing, training, education, instruction, rearing, development
nut 1 (*Slang*) = madman, psycho (*slang*), crank (*informal*), lunatic, maniac, nutcase (*slang*) 2 (*Slang*) = head, skull
nutrition = food, nourishment, sustenance, nutriment

O

oath 1 = promise, bond, pledge, vow, word, affirmation, avowal 2 = swear word, curse, obscenity, blasphemy, expletive, four-letter word, profanity
obedience = compliance, respect, reverence, observance, subservience, submissiveness, docility ≠ disobedience
obey 1 = submit to, surrender (to), give way to, bow to, give in to, yield to, do what you are told by ≠ disobey 2 = carry out, follow, implement, act upon, carry through ≠ disregard 3 = abide by, keep, follow, comply with, observe, heed, conform to, keep to
object[1] 1 = thing, article, body, item, entity 2 = purpose, aim, end, point, plan, idea, goal, design 3 = target, victim, focus, recipient
object[2] 1 *with* ***to*** = protest against, oppose, argue against, draw the line at, take exception to, cry out against, complain against, expostulate against ≠ accept 2 = disagree, demur, remonstrate, express disapproval ≠ agree
objection = protest, opposition, complaint, doubt, dissent, outcry, protestation, scruple ≠ agreement
objective NOUN = purpose, aim, goal, end, plan, hope, idea, target
• ADJECTIVE 1 = factual, real 2 = unbiased, detached, fair, open-minded, impartial, impersonal, disinterested, even-handed ≠ subjective
objectively = impartially, neutrally, fairly, justly, without prejudice, dispassionately, with an open mind, equitably
obligation 1 = duty, compulsion 2 = task, job, duty, work, charge, role, function, mission 3 = responsibility, duty, liability, accountability, answerability
oblige 1 = compel, make, force, require, bind, constrain, necessitate, impel 2 = help, assist, benefit, please, humour, accommodate, indulge, gratify ≠ bother
obliged 1 = forced, required, bound,

compelled, duty-bound **2** = grateful, in (someone's) debt, thankful, indebted, appreciative, beholden

obliging = accommodating, kind, helpful, willing, polite, cooperative, agreeable, considerate ≠ unhelpful

obscene **1** = indecent, dirty, offensive, filthy, improper, immoral, pornographic, lewd ≠ decent **2** = offensive, shocking, evil, disgusting, outrageous, revolting, sickening, vile

obscure ADJECTIVE **1** = unknown, little-known, humble, unfamiliar, out-of-the-way, lowly, unheard-of, undistinguished ≠ famous **2** = abstruse, complex, confusing, mysterious, vague, unclear, ambiguous, enigmatic ≠ straightforward **3** = unclear, uncertain, confused, mysterious, doubtful, indeterminate ≠ well-known **4** = indistinct, vague, blurred, dark, faint, dim, gloomy, murky ≠ clear
• VERB **1** = obstruct, hinder **2** = hide, screen, mask, disguise, conceal, veil, cloak, camouflage ≠ expose

observation **1** = watching, study, survey, review, investigation, monitoring, examination, inspection **2** = comment, thought, note, statement, opinion, remark, explanation, reflection **3** = remark, comment, statement, reflection, utterance **4** = observance of, compliance with, honouring of, fulfilment of, carrying out of

observe **1** = watch, study, view, look at, check, survey, monitor, keep an eye on (*informal*) **2** = notice, see, note, discover, spot, regard, witness, distinguish **3** = remark, say, comment, state, note, reflect, mention, opine **4** = comply with, keep, follow, respect, carry out, honour, discharge, obey ≠ disregard

observer **1** = witness, viewer, spectator, looker-on, watcher, onlooker, eyewitness, bystander **2** = commentator, reporter, special correspondent **3** = monitor, watchdog, supervisor, scrutineer

obsessed = absorbed, dominated, gripped, haunted, distracted, hung up (*slang*), preoccupied ≠ indifferent

obsession = preoccupation, thing (*informal*), complex, hang-up (*informal*), mania, phobia, fetish, fixation

obsessive = compulsive, gripping, consuming, haunting, irresistible, neurotic, besetting, uncontrollable

obsolete = outdated, old, passé, old-fashioned, discarded, extinct, out of date, archaic ≠ up-to-date

obstacle **1** = obstruction, block, barrier, hurdle, snag, impediment, blockage, hindrance **2** = hindrance, bar, difficulty, barrier, handicap, hurdle, hitch, drawback, uphill (*S. African*) ≠ help

obstruct **1** = block, close, bar, plug, barricade, stop up, bung up (*informal*) **2** = hold up, stop, check, block, restrict, slow down, hamper, hinder **3** = impede, hamper, hold back, thwart, hinder ≠ help **4** = obscure, screen, cover

obtain **1** = get, gain, acquire, land, net, pick up, secure, procure ≠ lose **2** = achieve, get, gain, accomplish, attain **3** (*Formal*) = prevail, hold, exist, be the case, abound, predominate, be in force, be current

obvious = clear, plain, apparent, evident, distinct, manifest, noticeable, conspicuous ≠ unclear

obviously **1** = clearly, of course, without doubt, assuredly **2** = plainly, patently, undoubtedly, evidently, manifestly, markedly, without doubt, unquestionably

occasion NOUN **1** = time, moment, point, stage, instance, juncture **2** = function, event, affair, do (*informal*), happening, experience, gathering, celebration **3** = opportunity, chance, time, opening, window **4** = reason, cause, call, ground(s), excuse, incentive, motive, justification
• VERB (*Formal*) = cause, produce, lead to, inspire, result in, generate, prompt, provoke

occasional = infrequent, odd, rare, irregular, sporadic, intermittent, few and far between, periodic ≠ constant

occasionally = sometimes, at times, from time to time, now and then, irregularly, now and again, periodically, once in a while ≠ constantly

occult NOUN = magic, witchcraft, sorcery, wizardry, enchantment, black art, necromancy
• ADJECTIVE = supernatural, magical, mysterious, psychic, mystical, unearthly, esoteric, uncanny

occupant = occupier, resident, tenant, inmate, inhabitant, incumbent, dweller, lessee

occupation **1** = job, calling, business,

line (of work), trade, career, employment, profession **2** = hobby, pastime, diversion, relaxation, leisure pursuit, (leisure) activity **3** = invasion, seizure, conquest, incursion, subjugation **4** = occupancy, residence, holding, control, possession, tenure, tenancy

occupied 1 = in use, taken, full, engaged, unavailable **2** = inhabited, peopled, lived-in, settled, tenanted ≠ uninhabited **3** = busy, engaged, employed, working, active, hard at work, rushed off your feet

occupy 1 = inhabit, own, live in, dwell in, reside in, abide in ≠ vacate **2** = invade, take over, capture, seize, conquer, overrun, annex, colonize ≠ withdraw **3** = hold, control, dominate, possess **4** = take up, consume, tie up, use up, monopolize **5** *often passive* = engage, involve, employ, divert, preoccupy, engross **6** = fill, take up, cover, fill up, pervade, permeate, extend over

occur VERB **1** = happen, take place, come about, turn up (*informal*), crop up (*informal*), transpire (*informal*), befall **2** = exist, appear, be found, develop, turn up, be present, manifest itself, present itself

• PHRASES **occur to someone** = come to mind, strike someone, dawn on someone, spring to mind, cross someone's mind, enter someone's head, suggest itself to someone

occurrence 1 = incident, happening, event, fact, matter, affair, circumstance, episode **2** = existence, instance, appearance, manifestation, materialization

odd 1 = peculiar, strange, unusual, extraordinary, bizarre, offbeat, freakish **2** = unusual, strange, rare, extraordinary, remarkable, bizarre, peculiar, irregular ≠ normal **3** = occasional, various, random, casual, irregular, periodic, sundry, incidental ≠ regular **4** = spare, remaining, extra, surplus, solitary, leftover, unmatched, unpaired ≠ matched

odds PLURAL NOUN **1** = probability, chances, likelihood

• PHRASES **at odds 1** = in conflict, arguing, quarrelling, at loggerheads, at daggers drawn **2** = at variance, conflicting, contrary to, at odds, out of line, out of step, at sixes and sevens (*informal*)

◆ **odds and ends** = scraps, bits, remains, fragments, debris, remnants, bits and pieces, bric-a-brac

odour = smell, scent, perfume, fragrance, stink, bouquet, aroma, stench

odyssey = journey, tour, trip, quest, trek, expedition, voyage, crusade

off ADVERB = away, out, apart, elsewhere, aside, hence, from here

• ADJECTIVE **1** = absent, gone, unavailable **2** = cancelled, abandoned, postponed, shelved **3** = bad, rotten, rancid, mouldy, turned, spoiled, sour, decayed

offence 1 = crime, sin, fault, violation, wrongdoing, trespass, felony, misdemeanour **2** = outrage, shock, anger, trouble, bother, resentment, irritation, hassle (*informal*) **3** = insult, slight, hurt, outrage, injustice, snub, affront, indignity

offend 1 = distress, upset, outrage, wound, slight, insult, annoy, snub ≠ please **2** = break the law, sin, err, do wrong, fall, go astray

offended = upset, hurt, bothered, disturbed, distressed, outraged, stung, put out (*informal*), tooshie (*Austral. slang*)

offender = criminal, convict, crook, villain, culprit, sinner, delinquent, felon

offensive ADJECTIVE **1** = insulting, rude, abusive, degrading, contemptuous, disparaging, objectionable, disrespectful ≠ respectful **2** = disgusting, gross, foul, unpleasant, revolting, vile, repellent, obnoxious, festy (*Austral. slang*), yucko (*Austral. slang*) ≠ pleasant **3** = attacking, threatening, aggressive, striking, hostile, invading, combative ≠ defensive

• NOUN = attack, charge, campaign, strike, push (*informal*), assault, raid, drive

offer VERB **1** = provide, present, furnish, afford ≠ withhold **2** = volunteer, come forward, offer your services **3** = propose, suggest, advance, submit **4** = give, show, bring, provide, render, impart **5** = put up for sale, sell **6** = bid, submit, propose, tender, proffer

• NOUN **1** = proposal, suggestion, proposition, submission **2** = bid, tender, bidding price

offering 1 = contribution, gift, donation, present, subscription, hand-out **2** = sacrifice, tribute, libation, burnt offering

office 1 = place of work, workplace, base,

workroom, place of business **2** = branch, department, division, section, wing, subdivision, subsection **3** = post, place, role, situation, responsibility, function, occupation

officer **1** = official, executive, agent, representative, appointee, functionary, office-holder, office bearer **2** = police officer, detective, PC, police constable, police man, police woman

official ADJECTIVE **1** = authorized, formal, sanctioned, licensed, proper, legitimate, authentic, certified ≠ unofficial **2** = formal, bureaucratic, ceremonial, solemn, ritualistic
• NOUN = officer, executive, agent, representative, bureaucrat, appointee, functionary, office-holder

offset = cancel out, balance, set off, make up for, compensate for, counteract, neutralize, counterbalance

offspring **1** = child, baby, kid (*informal*), youngster, infant, successor, babe, toddler, littlie (*Austral. informal*), ankle-biter (*Austral. slang*), tacker (*Austral. slang*) ≠ parent **2** = children, young, family, issue, stock, heirs, descendants, brood

often = frequently, generally, commonly, repeatedly, time and again, habitually, not infrequently ≠ never

oil VERB = lubricate, grease
• NOUN **1** = lubricant, grease, lubrication, fuel oil **2** = lotion, cream, balm, salve, liniment, embrocation, solution

oily = greasy, slimy, fatty, slippery, oleaginous

OK *or* **okay** ADJECTIVE (*Informal*) **1** = all right, fine, fitting, in order, permitted, suitable, acceptable, allowable ≠ unacceptable **2** = fine, good, average, fair, all right, acceptable, adequate, satisfactory ≠ unsatisfactory **3** = well, all right, safe, sound, healthy, unharmed, uninjured
• INTERJECTION = all right, right, yes, agreed, very good, roger, very well, ya (*S. African*), righto (*Brit. informal*), yebo (*S. African informal*)
• VERB = approve, allow, agree to, permit, sanction, endorse, authorize, rubber-stamp (*informal*)
• NOUN = authorization, agreement, sanction, approval, go-ahead (*informal*), blessing, permission, consent

old **1** = aged, elderly, ancient, mature, venerable, antiquated, senile, decrepit ≠ young **2** = former, earlier, past, previous, prior, one-time, erstwhile **3** = long-standing, established, fixed, enduring, abiding, long-lasting, long-established, time-honoured **4** = stale, worn-out, banal, threadbare, trite, overused, timeworn

old-fashioned **1** = out of date, dated, outdated, unfashionable, outmoded, passé, old hat, behind the times ≠ up-to-date **2** = oldfangled, square (*informal*), outdated, unfashionable, obsolescent

ominous = threatening, sinister, grim, fateful, foreboding, unpromising, portentous, inauspicious ≠ promising

omission **1** = exclusion, removal, elimination, deletion, excision ≠ inclusion **2** = gap, space, exclusion, lacuna **3** = failure, neglect, negligence, oversight, carelessness, dereliction, slackness, laxity

omit **1** = leave out, drop, exclude, eliminate, skip ≠ include **2** = forget, overlook, neglect, pass over, lose sight of

once ADVERB **1** = on one occasion, one time, one single time **2** = at one time, previously, formerly, long ago, once upon a time
• CONJUNCTION = as soon as, when, after, the moment, immediately, the instant
• PHRASES **at once** **1** = immediately, now, straight away, directly, promptly, instantly, right away, forthwith **2** = simultaneously, together, at the same time, concurrently

one-sided **1** = unequal, unfair, uneven, unjust, unbalanced, lopsided, ill-matched ≠ equal **2** = biased, prejudiced, weighted, unfair, partial, distorted, partisan, slanted ≠ unbiased

ongoing = in progress, developing, progressing, evolving, unfolding, unfinished

onlooker = spectator, witness, observer, viewer, looker-on, watcher, eyewitness, bystander

only ADJECTIVE = sole, one, single, individual, exclusive, unique, lone, solitary
• ADVERB **1** = just, simply, purely, merely **2** = hardly, just, barely, only just, scarcely, at a push

onset = beginning, start, birth, outbreak, inception, commencement ≠ end

onslaught = attack, charge, campaign, strike, assault, raid, invasion, offensive

≠ retreat
onward *or* **onwards** = forward, on, forwards, ahead, beyond, in front, forth
ooze[1] 1 = seep, well, escape, leak, drain, filter, drip, trickle 2 = emit, release, leak, drip, dribble, give off, pour forth 3 = exude, emit
ooze[2] = mud, clay, dirt, silt, sludge, mire, slime, alluvium
open VERB 1 = unfasten, unlock ≠ close 2 = unwrap, uncover, undo, unravel, untie ≠ wrap 3 = uncork 4 = unfold, spread (out), expand, unfurl, unroll ≠ fold 5 = clear, unblock ≠ block 6 = undo, unbutton, unfasten ≠ fasten 7 = begin business 8 = start, begin, launch, trigger, kick off (*informal*), initiate, commence, get going ≠ end 9 = begin, start, commence ≠ end
• ADJECTIVE 1 = unclosed, unlocked, ajar, unfastened, yawning ≠ closed 2 = unsealed, unstoppered ≠ unopened 3 = extended, unfolded, stretched out, unfurled, straightened out, unrolled ≠ shut 4 = frank, direct, straightforward, sincere, transparent, honest, candid, truthful ≠ sly 5 = receptive, sympathetic, responsive, amenable 6 = unresolved, unsettled, undecided, debatable, moot, arguable 7 = clear, passable, unhindered, unimpeded, navigable, unobstructed ≠ obstructed 8 = available, to hand, accessible, handy, at your disposal 9 = general, public, free, universal, blanket, across-the-board, unrestricted, overarching ≠ restricted 10 = vacant, free, available, empty, unoccupied, unfilled
open-air = outdoor, outside, out-of-door(s), alfresco
opening ADJECTIVE = first, earliest, beginning, premier, primary, initial, maiden, inaugural
• NOUN 1 = beginning, start, launch, dawn, outset, initiation, inception, commencement ≠ ending 2 = hole, space, tear, crack, gap, slot, puncture, aperture ≠ blockage 3 = opportunity, chance, time, moment, occasion, look-in (*informal*) 4 = job, position, post, situation, opportunity, vacancy
openly = frankly, plainly, honestly, overtly, candidly, unreservedly, unhesitatingly, forthrightly ≠ privately
open-minded = unprejudiced, liberal, balanced, objective, reasonable, tolerant, impartial, receptive ≠ narrow-minded
operate 1 = manage, run, direct, handle, supervise, be in charge of 2 = function, work, act 3 = run, work, use, control, manoeuvre 4 = work, go, run, perform, function ≠ break down
operation = performance, action, movement, motion
operational = working, going, running, ready, functioning, operative, viable, functional ≠ inoperative
operative ADJECTIVE = in force, effective, functioning, active, in effect, operational, in operation ≠ inoperative
• NOUN 1 = worker, employee, labourer, workman, artisan 2 (*U.S. & Canad.*) = spy, undercover agent, mole, nark (*Brit., Austral., & N.Z. slang*)
operator = worker, driver, mechanic, operative, conductor, technician, handler
opinion 1 = belief, feeling, view, idea, theory, conviction, point of view, sentiment 2 = estimation, view, impression, assessment, judgment, appraisal, considered opinion
opponent 1 = adversary, rival, enemy, competitor, challenger, foe, contestant, antagonist ≠ ally 2 = opposer, dissident, objector ≠ supporter
opportunity = chance, opening, time, turn, moment, possibility, occasion, slot
oppose = be against, fight (against), block, take on, counter, contest, resist, combat ≠ support
opposed 1 *with* ***to*** = against, hostile, adverse, in opposition, averse, antagonistic, (dead) set against 2 = contrary, conflicting, clashing, counter, adverse, contradictory, dissentient
opposing 1 = conflicting, different, contrasting, opposite, differing, contrary, contradictory, incompatible 2 = rival, conflicting, competing, enemy, opposite, hostile
opposite PREPOSITION = facing, face to face with, across from, eyeball to eyeball (*informal*)
• ADJECTIVE 1 = facing, other, opposing 2 = different, conflicting, contrasted, contrasting, unlike, contrary, dissimilar, divergent ≠ alike 3 = rival, conflicting, opposing, competing
• NOUN = reverse, contrary, converse,

antithesis, contradiction, inverse, obverse
opposition **1** = hostility, resistance, resentment, disapproval, obstruction, animosity, antagonism, antipathy ≠ support **2** = opponent(s), competition, rival(s), enemy, competitor(s), other side, challenger(s), foe
oppress **1** = subjugate, abuse, suppress, wrong, master, overcome, subdue, persecute ≠ liberate **2** = depress, burden, discourage, torment, harass, afflict, sadden, vex
oppression = persecution, control, abuse, injury, injustice, cruelty, domination, repression ≠ justice
oppressive **1** = tyrannical, severe, harsh, cruel, brutal, authoritarian, unjust, repressive ≠ merciful **2** = stifling, close, sticky, stuffy, humid, sultry, airless, muggy
opt VERB = choose, decide, prefer, select, elect ≠ reject
• PHRASES **opt for something** *or* **someone** = choose, pick, select, adopt, go for, designate, decide on, plump for
optimistic **1** = hopeful, positive, confident, encouraged, cheerful, rosy, buoyant, sanguine ≠ pessimistic **2** = encouraging, promising, bright, good, reassuring, rosy, heartening, auspicious ≠ discouraging
optimum *or* **optimal** = ideal, best, highest, finest, perfect, supreme, peak, outstanding ≠ worst
option = choice, alternative, selection, preference, freedom of choice, power to choose
optional = voluntary, open, discretionary, possible, extra, elective ≠ compulsory
opus = work, piece, production, creation, composition, work of art, brainchild, oeuvre (*French*)
oral = spoken, vocal, verbal, unwritten
orbit NOUN **1** = path, course, cycle, circle, revolution, rotation, trajectory, sweep **2** = sphere of influence, reach, range, influence, province, scope, domain, compass
• VERB = circle, ring, go round, revolve around, encircle, circumscribe, circumnavigate
orchestrate **1** = organize, plan, run, set up, arrange, put together, marshal, coordinate **2** = score, set, arrange, adapt
ordain **1** = appoint, name, commission, select, invest, nominate, anoint, consecrate **2** (*Formal*) = order, will, rule, demand, require, direct, command, dictate
ordeal = hardship, trial, difficulty, test, suffering, nightmare, torture, agony ≠ pleasure
order VERB **1** = command, instruct, direct, charge, demand, require, bid, compel ≠ forbid **2** = decree, rule, demand, prescribe, pronounce, ordain ≠ ban **3** = request, ask (for), book, seek, reserve, apply for, solicit, send away for **4** = arrange, group, sort, position, line up, organize, catalogue, sort out ≠ disarrange
• NOUN **1** = instruction, ruling, demand, direction, command, dictate, decree, mandate **2** = request, booking, demand, commission, application, reservation, requisition **3** = sequence, grouping, series, structure, chain, arrangement, line-up, array **4** = organization, system, method, pattern, symmetry, regularity, neatness, tidiness ≠ chaos **5** = peace, control, law, quiet, calm, discipline, law and order, tranquillity **6** = society, company, group, club, community, association, institute, organization **7** = class, set, rank, grade, caste **8** = kind, group, class, family, sort, type, variety, category
orderly **1** = well-behaved, controlled, disciplined, quiet, restrained, law-abiding, peaceable ≠ disorderly **2** = well-organized, regular, in order, organized, precise, neat, tidy, systematic ≠ disorganized
ordinary **1** = usual, standard, normal, common, regular, typical, conventional, routine **2** = commonplace, plain, modest, humble, mundane, banal, unremarkable, run-of-the-mill ≠ extraordinary
organ **1** = body part, part of the body, element, biological structure **2** = newspaper, medium, voice, vehicle, gazette, mouthpiece
organic **1** = natural, biological, living, live, animate **2** = systematic, ordered, structured, organized, integrated, orderly, methodical
organism = creature, being, thing, body, animal, structure, beast, entity
organization **1** = group, company, party, body, association, band, institution, corporation **2** = management, running, planning, control, operation, handling, structuring, administration **3** = structure,

form, pattern, make-up, arrangement, construction, format, formation

organize 1 = arrange, run, plan, prepare, set up, devise, put together, take care of, jack up (*N.Z. informal*) ≠ disrupt 2 = put in order, arrange, group, list, file, index, classify, inventory ≠ muddle

orient *or* **orientate** 1 = adjust, adapt, alter, accustom, align, familiarize, acclimatize 2 = get your bearings, establish your location

orientation 1 = inclination, tendency, disposition, predisposition, predilection, proclivity, partiality 2 = induction, introduction, adjustment, settling in, adaptation, assimilation, familiarization, acclimatization 3 = position, situation, location, bearings, direction, arrangement, whereabouts

origin 1 = beginning, start, birth, launch, foundation, creation, emergence, onset ≠ end 2 = root, source, basis, base, seed, foundation, nucleus, derivation

original ADJECTIVE 1 = first, earliest, initial 2 = initial, first, starting, opening, primary, introductory ≠ final 3 = new, fresh, novel, unusual, unprecedented, innovative, unfamiliar, seminal ≠ unoriginal 4 = creative, inspired, imaginative, artistic, fertile, ingenious, visionary, inventive
• NOUN = prototype, master, pattern ≠ copy

originally = initially, first, firstly, at first, primarily, to begin with, in the beginning

originate 1 = begin, start, emerge, come, happen, rise, appear, spring ≠ end 2 = invent, create, design, launch, introduce, institute, generate, pioneer

ornament NOUN 1 = decoration, trimming, accessory, festoon, trinket, bauble, knick-knack 2 = embellishment, decoration, embroidery, elaboration, adornment, ornamentation
• VERB = decorate, adorn, array, do up (*informal*), embellish, festoon, beautify, prettify

orthodox 1 = established, official, accepted, received, common, traditional, normal, usual ≠ unorthodox 2 = conformist, conservative, traditional, strict, devout, observant ≠ nonconformist

orthodoxy 1 = doctrine, teaching, opinion, principle, belief, convention, creed, dogma 2 = conformity, received wisdom, traditionalism, conventionality ≠ nonconformity

other 1 = additional, more, further, new, added, extra, fresh, spare 2 = different, alternative, contrasting, distinct, diverse, dissimilar, separate, alternative

otherwise 1 = or else, or, if not, or then 2 = apart from that, in other ways, in (all) other respects 3 = differently, any other way, contrarily

ounce = shred, bit, drop, trace, scrap, grain, fragment, atom

oust = expel, turn out, dismiss, exclude, exile, throw out, displace, topple

out ADJECTIVE 1 = not in, away, elsewhere, outside, gone, abroad, from home, absent 2 = extinguished, ended, finished, dead, exhausted, expired, used up, at an end ≠ alight 3 = in bloom, opening, open, flowering, blooming, in flower, in full bloom 4 = available, on sale, in the shops, to be had, purchasable 5 = revealed, exposed, common knowledge, public knowledge, (out) in the open ≠ kept secret
• VERB = expose

outbreak 1 = eruption, burst, explosion, epidemic, rash, outburst, flare-up, upsurge 2 = onset, beginning, outset, opening, dawn, commencement

outburst = explosion, fit, surge, outbreak, flare-up, eruption, spasm, outpouring

outcome = result, end, consequence, conclusion, payoff (*informal*), upshot

outcry = protest, complaint, objection, dissent, outburst, clamour, uproar, commotion

outdated = old-fashioned, dated, obsolete, out of date, passé, archaic, unfashionable, antiquated ≠ modern

outdoor = open-air, outside, out-of-door(s), alfresco ≠ indoor

outer 1 = external, outside, outward, exterior, exposed, outermost ≠ inner 2 = surface 3 = outlying, distant, provincial, out-of-the-way, peripheral, far-flung ≠ central

outfit 1 = costume, dress, clothes, clothing, suit, get-up (*informal*), kit, ensemble 2 (*Informal*) = group, company, team, party, unit, crowd, squad, organization

outgoing 1 = leaving, former, previous, retiring, withdrawing, prior, departing, erstwhile ≠ incoming 2 = sociable, open, social, warm, friendly, expansive, affable, extrovert ≠ reserved

outgoings = expenses, costs, payments, expenditure, overheads, outlay

outing = journey, run, trip, tour, expedition, excursion, spin (*informal*), jaunt

outlaw VERB **1** = ban, bar, veto, forbid, exclude, prohibit, disallow, proscribe ≠ legalise **2** = banish, put a price on (someone's) head
• NOUN (*History*) = bandit, criminal, thief, robber, fugitive, outcast, felon, highwayman

outlet 1 = shop, store, supermarket, market, boutique, emporium, hypermarket **2** = channel, release, medium, avenue, vent, conduit **3** = pipe, opening, channel, exit, duct

outline VERB **1** = summarize, draft, plan, trace, sketch (in), sum up, encapsulate, delineate **2** = silhouette, etch
• NOUN **1** = summary, review, résumé, rundown, synopsis, précis, thumbnail sketch, recapitulation **2** = shape, lines, form, figure, profile, silhouette, configuration, contour(s)

outlook 1 = attitude, opinion, position, approach, mood, perspective, point of view, stance **2** = prospect(s), future, expectations, forecast, prediction, probability, prognosis

out of date 1 = old-fashioned, dated, outdated, obsolete, démodé (*French*), antiquated, outmoded, passé ≠ modern **2** = invalid, expired, lapsed, void, null and void

output = production, manufacture, manufacturing, yield, productivity

outrage VERB = offend, shock, upset, wound, insult, infuriate, incense, madden
• NOUN = indignation, shock, anger, rage, fury, hurt, resentment, scorn

outrageous 1 = atrocious, shocking, terrible, offensive, appalling, cruel, savage, horrifying ≠ mild **2** = unreasonable, unfair, steep (*informal*), shocking, extravagant, scandalous, preposterous, unwarranted ≠ reasonable

outright ADJECTIVE **1** = absolute, complete, total, perfect, sheer, thorough, unconditional, unqualified **2** = definite, clear, certain, flat, absolute, black-and-white, straightforward, unequivocal
• ADVERB **1** = openly, frankly, plainly, overtly, candidly, unreservedly, unhesitatingly, forthrightly **2** = absolutely, completely, totally, fully, entirely, thoroughly, wholly, utterly

outset = beginning, start, opening, onset, inauguration, inception, commencement, kickoff (*informal*) ≠ finish

outside NOUN = exterior, face, front, covering, skin, surface, shell, coating
• ADJECTIVE **1** = external, outer, exterior, outward, extraneous ≠ inner **2** = remote, small, unlikely, slight, slim, distant, faint, marginal
• ADVERB = outdoors, out of the house, out-of-doors

outsider = stranger, incomer, visitor, newcomer, intruder, interloper, odd one out

outskirts = edge, boundary, suburbs, fringe, perimeter, periphery, suburbia, environs

outspan (*S. African*) = relax, chill out (*slang, chiefly U.S.*), take it easy, loosen up, put your feet up

outspoken = forthright, open, frank, straightforward, blunt, explicit, upfront (*informal*), unequivocal ≠ reserved

outstanding 1 = excellent, good, great, important, special, fine, brilliant, impressive, booshit (*Austral. slang*), exo (*Austral. slang*), sik (*Austral. slang*) ≠ mediocre **2** = unpaid, remaining, due, pending, payable, unsettled, uncollected **3** = undone, left, omitted, unfinished, unfulfilled, unperformed

outward = apparent, seeming, surface, ostensible ≠ inward

outwardly = apparently, externally, seemingly, it seems that, on the surface, it appears that, ostensibly, on the face of it

outweigh = override, cancel (out), eclipse, offset, compensate for, supersede, neutralize, counterbalance

oval = elliptical, egg-shaped, ovoid

ovation = applause, hand, cheers, praise, tribute, acclaim, clapping, accolade ≠ derision

over PREPOSITION **1** = above, on top of **2** = on top of, on, across, upon **3** = across, (looking) onto **4** = more than, above, exceeding, in excess of, upwards of **5** = about, regarding, relating to, concerning, apropos of
• ADVERB **1** = above, overhead, in the sky, on high, aloft, up above **2** = extra, more,

further, beyond, additional, in addition, surplus, in excess
• ADJECTIVE = finished, done (with), through, ended, closed, past, completed, complete

RELATED WORDS
prefixes: hyper-, super-

overall ADJECTIVE = total, full, whole, general, complete, entire, global, comprehensive
• ADVERB = in general, generally, mostly, all things considered, on average, on the whole, predominantly, in the main

overcome VERB 1 = defeat, beat, conquer, master, overwhelm, subdue, rout, overpower 2 = conquer, beat, master, subdue, triumph over, vanquish
• ADJECTIVE = overwhelmed, moved, affected, emotional, choked, speechless, bowled over (*informal*), at a loss for words

overdue 1 = delayed, belated, late, behind schedule, tardy, unpunctual, behindhand ≠ early 2 = unpaid, owing

overflow VERB = spill over, well over, run over, pour over, bubble over, brim over
• NOUN 1 = flood, spilling over 2 = surplus, extra, excess, overspill, overabundance, additional people *or* things

overhaul VERB 1 = check, service, maintain, examine, restore, tune (up), repair, go over 2 = overtake, pass, leave behind, catch up with, get past, outstrip, get ahead of, outdistance
• NOUN = check, service, examination, going-over (*informal*), inspection, once-over (*informal*), checkup, reconditioning

overhead ADJECTIVE = raised, suspended, elevated, aerial, overhanging
• ADVERB = above, in the sky, on high, aloft, up above ≠ underneath

overheads = running costs, expenses, outgoings, operating costs

overlook 1 = look over *or* out on, have a view of 2 = miss, forget, neglect, omit, disregard, pass over ≠ notice 3 = ignore, excuse, forgive, pardon, disregard, condone, turn a blind eye to, wink at

overpower 1 = overcome, master, overwhelm, overthrow, subdue, quell, subjugate, prevail over 2 defeat, crush, triumph over, vanquish 3 = overwhelm, overcome, bowl over (*informal*), stagger

override 1 = outweigh, eclipse, supersede, take precedence over, prevail over 2 = overrule, cancel, overturn, repeal, rescind, annul, nullify, countermand 3 = ignore, reject, discount, overlook, disregard, pass over, take no notice of

overrun 1 = overwhelm, attack, assault, occupy, raid, invade, penetrate, rout 2 = spread over, overwhelm, choke, swamp, infest, inundate, permeate, swarm over 3 = exceed, go beyond, surpass, overshoot, run over *or* on

overshadow 1 = spoil, ruin, mar, wreck, blight, crool *or* cruel (*Austral. slang*), mess up, put a damper on 2 = outshine, eclipse, surpass, dwarf, tower above, leave *or* put in the shade

overt = open, obvious, plain, public, manifest, blatant, observable, undisguised ≠ hidden

overtake 1 = pass, leave behind, overhaul, catch up with, get past, outdistance, go by *or* past 2 = outdo, top, exceed, eclipse, surpass, outstrip, get the better of, outclass 3 = befall, hit, happen to, catch off guard, catch unawares 4 = engulf, overwhelm, hit, strike, swamp, envelop, swallow up

overthrow VERB = defeat, overcome, conquer, bring down, oust, topple, rout, overpower ≠ uphold
• NOUN = downfall, fall, defeat, collapse, destruction, ousting, undoing, unseating ≠ preservation

overturn 1 = tip over, topple, upturn, capsize, upend, keel over, overbalance 2 = knock over *or* down, upturn, tip over, upend 3 = reverse, change, cancel, abolish, overthrow, set aside, repeal, quash 4 = overthrow, defeat, destroy, overcome, bring down, oust, topple, depose

overweight = fat, heavy, stout, hefty, plump, bulky, chunky, chubby ≠ underweight

overwhelm 1 = overcome, devastate, stagger, bowl over (*informal*), knock (someone) for six (*informal*), sweep (someone) off his *or* her feet, take (someone's) breath away 2 = destroy, defeat, overcome, crush, massacre, conquer, wipe out, overthrow

overwhelming 1 = overpowering, strong, powerful, towering, stunning, crushing, devastating, shattering ≠ negligible 2 = vast, huge, massive, enormous, tremendous, immense, very large

≠ insignificant
owe = be in debt (to), be in arrears (to), be overdrawn (by), be obligated *or* indebted (to)
owing to = because of, thanks to, as a result of, on account of, by reason of
own ADJECTIVE = personal, special, private, individual, particular, exclusive
• VERB = possess, have, keep, hold, enjoy, retain, be in possession of, have to your name
owner = possessor, holder, proprietor, titleholder, landlord *or* landlady
ownership = possession, occupation, tenure, dominion

p

pace NOUN **1** = speed, rate, tempo, velocity **2** = step, walk, stride, tread, gait **3** = footstep, step, stride
• VERB = stride, walk, pound, patrol, march up and down
pack VERB **1** = package, load, store, bundle, stow **2** = cram, crowd, press, fill, stuff, jam, ram, compress
• NOUN **1** = packet, box, package, carton **2** = bundle, parcel, load, burden, rucksack, knapsack, back pack, kitbag **3** = group, crowd, company, band, troop, gang, bunch, mob
• PHRASES **pack someone off** = send away, dismiss, send packing (*informal*) ♦ **pack something in 1** (*Brit. informal*) = resign from, leave, give up, quit (*informal*), chuck (*informal*), jack in (*informal*) **2** = stop, give up, kick (*informal*), cease, chuck (*informal*)
package NOUN **1** = parcel, box, container, packet, carton **2** = collection, lot, unit, combination, compilation
• VERB = pack, box, parcel (up)
packet 1 = container, box, package, carton **2** = package, parcel **3** (*Slang*) = a fortune, a bomb (*Brit. slang*), a pile (*informal*), a small fortune, a tidy sum (*informal*), a king's ransom (*informal*)
pact = agreement, alliance, treaty, deal, understanding, bargain, covenant
pad[1] NOUN **1** = wad, dressing, pack, padding, compress, wadding **2** = cushion, filling, stuffing, pillow, bolster, upholstery **3** = notepad, block, notebook, jotter, writing pad **4** (*Slang*) = home, flat, apartment, place **5** = paw, foot, sole
• VERB = pack, fill, protect, stuff, cushion
pad[2] = sneak, creep, steal, go barefoot
padding 1 = filling, stuffing, packing, wadding **2** = waffle (*informal, chiefly Brit.*), hot air (*informal*), verbiage, wordiness, verbosity
paddle[1] NOUN = oar, scull
• VERB = row, pull, scull
paddle[2] = wade, splash (about), slop
pagan ADJECTIVE = heathen, infidel, polytheistic, idolatrous
• NOUN = heathen, infidel, polytheist, idolater
page[1] = folio, side, leaf, sheet
page[2] VERB = call, summon, send for
• NOUN **1** = attendant, pageboy **2** = servant, attendant, squire, pageboy
pain NOUN **1** = suffering, discomfort, hurt, irritation, tenderness, soreness **2** = ache, stinging, aching, cramp, throb, throbbing, pang, twinge **3** = sorrow, suffering, torture, distress, despair, misery, agony, sadness
• PLURAL NOUN = trouble, effort, care, bother, diligence
• VERB **1** = distress, hurt, torture, grieve, torment, sadden, agonize, cut to the quick **2** = hurt
painful 1 = sore, smarting, aching, tender ≠ painless **2** = distressing, unpleasant, grievous, distasteful, agonizing, disagreeable ≠ pleasant **3** = difficult, arduous, trying, hard, troublesome, laborious ≠ easy
painfully = distressingly, clearly, sadly, unfortunately, dreadfully
paint NOUN = colouring, colour, stain, dye, tint, pigment, emulsion
• VERB **1** = colour, cover, coat, stain, whitewash, daub, distemper, apply paint to **2** = depict, draw, portray, picture, represent, sketch
pair NOUN **1** = set **2** = couple, brace, duo
• VERB = team, match (up), join, couple, twin, bracket
pal (*Informal*) = friend, companion, mate (*informal*), buddy (*informal*), comrade,

chum (*informal*), crony, cobber (*Austral. & N.Z. old-fashioned informal*), E hoa (*N.Z.*)

pale ADJECTIVE **1** = light, soft, faded, subtle, muted, bleached, pastel, light-coloured **2** = dim, weak, faint, feeble, thin, wan, watery **3** = white, pasty, bleached, wan, colourless, pallid, ashen ≠ rosy-cheeked
• VERB = become pale, blanch, whiten, go white, lose colour

pamper = spoil, indulge, pet, cosset, coddle, mollycoddle

pamphlet = booklet, leaflet, brochure, circular, tract

pan[1] NOUN = pot, container, saucepan
• VERB **1** (*Informal*) = criticize, knock, slam (*slang*), censure, tear into (*informal*) **2** = sift out, look for, search for

pan[2] = move along *or* across, follow, track, sweep

panic NOUN = fear, alarm, terror, anxiety, hysteria, fright, trepidation, a flap (*informal*)
• VERB **1** = go to pieces, become hysterical, lose your nerve **2** = alarm, scare, unnerve

panorama **1** = view, prospect, vista **2** = survey, perspective, overview, overall picture

pant = puff, blow, breathe, gasp, wheeze, heave

pants **1** (*Brit.*) = underpants, briefs, drawers, knickers, panties, boxer shorts, broekies (*S. African*), underdaks (*Austral. slang*) **2** (*U.S.*) = trousers, slacks

paper NOUN **1** = newspaper, daily, journal, gazette **2** = essay, article, treatise, dissertation **3** = examination, test, exam **4** = report
• PLURAL NOUN **1** = letters, records, documents, file, diaries, archive, paperwork, dossier **2** = documents, records, certificates, identification, deeds, identity papers, I.D. (*informal*)
• VERB = wallpaper, hang

parade NOUN **1** = procession, march, pageant, cavalcade **2** = show, display, spectacle
• VERB **1** = march, process, promenade **2** = flaunt, display, exhibit, show off (*informal*) **3** = strut, show off (*informal*), swagger, swank

paradigm = model, example, pattern, ideal

paradise **1** = heaven, Promised Land, Happy Valley (*Islam*), Elysian fields **2** = bliss, delight, heaven, felicity, utopia

paradox = contradiction, puzzle, anomaly, enigma, oddity

paragraph = section, part, item, passage, clause, subdivision

parallel NOUN **1** = equivalent, counterpart, match, equal, twin, analogue ≠ opposite **2** = similarity, comparison, analogy, resemblance, likeness ≠ difference
• ADJECTIVE **1** = matching, corresponding, like, similar, resembling, analogous ≠ different **2** = equidistant, alongside, side by side ≠ divergent

paralyse **1** = disable, cripple, lame, incapacitate **2** = freeze, stun, numb, petrify, halt, immobilize **3** = immobilize, freeze, halt, disable, cripple, incapacitate, bring to a standstill

paralysis **1** = immobility, palsy **2** = standstill, breakdown, stoppage, halt

parameter (*Informal*) *usually plural* = limit, restriction, framework, limitation, specification

paramount = principal, prime, first, chief, main, primary, supreme, cardinal ≠ secondary

paranoid **1** (*Informal*) = suspicious, worried, nervous, fearful, antsy (*informal*) **2** = obsessive, disturbed, manic, neurotic, mentally ill, psychotic, deluded, paranoiac

parasite = sponger (*informal*), leech, hanger-on, scrounger (*informal*), bloodsucker (*informal*), quandong (*Austral. slang*)

parcel NOUN = package, case, box, pack, bundle
• VERB *often with* ***up*** = wrap, pack, package, tie up, do up, gift-wrap, box up, fasten together

pardon VERB **1** = forgive, excuse ≠ condemn **2** = acquit, let off (*informal*), exonerate, absolve ≠ punish
• NOUN **1** = forgiveness, absolution ≠ condemnation **2** = acquittal, amnesty, exoneration ≠ punishment

parent = father *or* mother, sire, progenitor, procreator, old (*Austral. & N.Z. informal*), patriarch

parish **1** = district, community **2** = community, flock, church, congregation

park **1** = recreation ground, garden, playground, pleasure garden, playpark, domain (*N.Z.*), forest park (*N.Z.*)

2 = parkland, grounds, estate, lawns, woodland, grassland **3** = field, pitch, playing field

parliament 1 = assembly, council, congress, senate, convention, legislature **2** = sitting

parliamentary = governmental, legislative, law-making

parlour or (*U.S.*) **parlor** 1 (*Old-fashioned*) = sitting room, lounge, living room, drawing room, front room **2** = establishment, shop, store, salon

parody NOUN = takeoff (*informal*), satire, caricature, send-up (*Brit. informal*), spoof (*informal*), skit, burlesque
• VERB = take off (*informal*), caricature, send up (*Brit. informal*), burlesque, satirize, do a takeoff of (*informal*)

parrot = repeat, echo, imitate, copy, mimic

parry 1 = evade, avoid, dodge, sidestep **2** = ward off, block, deflect, repel, rebuff, repulse

parson = clergyman, minister, priest, vicar, preacher, pastor, cleric, churchman

part NOUN 1 = piece, share, proportion, percentage, bit, section, scrap, portion ≠ entirety **2** *often plural* = region, area, district, neighbourhood, quarter, vicinity **3** = component, bit, unit, constituent **4** = branch, division, office, section, wing, subdivision, subsection **5** = organ, member, limb **6** (*Theatre*) = role, representation, persona, portrayal, depiction, character part **7** (*Theatre*) = lines, words, script, dialogue **8** = side, behalf
• VERB 1 = divide, separate, break, tear, split, rend, detach, sever ≠ join **2** = part company, separate, split up ≠ meet
• PHRASES **in good part** = good-naturedly, well, cheerfully, without offence

partial 1 = incomplete, unfinished, imperfect, uncompleted ≠ complete **2** = biased, prejudiced, discriminatory, partisan, unfair, one-sided, unjust ≠ unbiased

partially = partly, somewhat, in part, not wholly, fractionally, incompletely

participant = participator, member, player, contributor, stakeholder

participate = take part, be involved, perform, join, partake ≠ refrain from

participation = taking part, contribution, involvement, sharing in, joining in, partaking

particle = bit, piece, scrap, grain, shred, mite, jot, speck

particular ADJECTIVE 1 = specific, special, exact, precise, distinct, peculiar ≠ general **2** = special, exceptional, notable, uncommon, marked, unusual, remarkable, singular **3** = fussy, demanding, fastidious, choosy (*informal*), picky (*informal*), finicky, pernickety (*informal*) ≠ indiscriminate
• NOUN *usually plural* = detail, fact, feature, item, circumstance, specification

particularly 1 = specifically, expressly, explicitly, especially, in particular, distinctly **2** = especially, notably, unusually, exceptionally, singularly, uncommonly

parting 1 = farewell, goodbye **2** = division, breaking, split, separation, rift, rupture

partisan ADJECTIVE = prejudiced, one-sided, biased, partial, sectarian ≠ unbiased
• NOUN 1 = supporter, devotee, adherent, upholder ≠ opponent **2** = underground fighter, guerrilla, freedom fighter, resistance fighter

partition NOUN 1 = screen, wall, barrier **2** = division, separation, segregation
• VERB = separate, screen, divide

partly = partially, somewhat, slightly ≠ completely

partner 1 = spouse, consort, significant other (*U.S. informal*), mate, husband or wife **2** = companion, ally, colleague, associate, mate, comrade **3** = associate, colleague, collaborator

partnership 1 = cooperation, alliance, sharing, union, connection, participation, copartnership **2** = company, firm, house, interest, society, cooperative

party 1 = faction, set, side, league, camp, clique, coterie **2** = get-together (*informal*), celebration, do (*informal*), gathering, function, reception, festivity, social gathering **3** = group, team, band, company, unit, squad, crew, gang

pass VERB 1 = go by or past, overtake, drive past, lap, leave behind, pull ahead of ≠ stop **2** = go, move, travel, progress, flow, proceed **3** = run, move, stroke **4** = give, hand, send, transfer, deliver, convey **5** = be left, come, be bequeathed, be inherited by **6** = kick, hit, loft, head, lob **7** = elapse, progress, go by, lapse, wear on, go past, tick by **8** = end, go, cease, blow over **9** = spend, fill, occupy, while away

10 = exceed, beat, overtake, go beyond, surpass, outstrip, outdo **11** = be successful in, qualify (in), succeed (in), graduate (in), get through, do, gain a pass in ≠ fail **12** = approve, accept, decree, enact, ratify, ordain, legislate (for) ≠ ban

• NOUN **1** = licence, ticket, permit, passport, warrant, authorization **2** = gap, route, canyon, gorge, ravine

• PHRASES **pass away** *or* **on** (*Euphemistic*) = die, pass on, expire, pass over, snuff it (*informal*), kick the bucket (*slang*), shuffle off this mortal coil, cark it (*Austral. & N.Z. informal*) ◆ **pass out** (*Informal*) = faint, black out (*informal*), lose consciousness, become unconscious ◆ **pass something over** = disregard, ignore, not dwell on ◆ **pass something up** (*Informal*) = miss, let slip, decline, neglect, forgo, abstain from, give (something) a miss (*informal*)

passage 1 = corridor, hall, lobby, vestibule **2** = alley, way, close (*Brit.*), course, road, channel, route, path **3** = extract, reading, piece, section, text, excerpt, quotation **4** = journey, crossing, trip, trek, voyage **5** = safe-conduct, right to travel, freedom to travel, permission to travel

passenger = traveller, rider, fare, commuter, fare payer

passer-by = bystander, witness, observer, viewer, spectator, looker-on, watcher, onlooker

passing 1 = momentary, fleeting, short-lived, transient, ephemeral, brief, temporary, transitory **2** = superficial, short, quick, glancing, casual, summary, cursory, perfunctory

passion 1 = love, desire, lust, infatuation, ardour **2** = emotion, feeling, fire, heat, excitement, intensity, warmth, zeal ≠ indifference **3** = mania, enthusiasm, obsession, bug (*informal*), craving, fascination, craze **4** = rage, fit, storm, anger, fury, outburst, frenzy, paroxysm

passionate 1 = emotional, eager, strong, intense, fierce, ardent, fervent, heartfelt ≠ unemotional **2** = loving, erotic, hot, ardent, amorous, lustful ≠ cold

passive 1 = submissive, compliant, receptive, docile, quiescent ≠ spirited **2** = inactive, uninvolved ≠ active

past NOUN **1** = former times, long ago, days gone by, the olden days ≠ future **2** = background, life, history, past life, life story, career to date

• ADJECTIVE **1** = former, early, previous, ancient, bygone, olden ≠ future **2** = previous, former, one-time, ex- **3** = last, previous **4** = over, done, ended, finished, gone

• PREPOSITION **1** = after, beyond, later than **2** = by, across, in front of

• ADVERB = on, by, along

paste NOUN **1** = adhesive, glue, cement, gum **2** = purée, pâté, spread

• VERB = stick, glue, cement, gum

pastel = pale, light, soft, delicate, muted ≠ bright

pastime = activity, game, entertainment, hobby, recreation, amusement, diversion

pastor = clergyman, minister, priest, vicar, parson, rector, curate, churchman

pastoral 1 = ecclesiastical, priestly, ministerial, clerical **2** = rustic, country, rural, bucolic

pasture = grassland, grass, meadow, grazing

pat VERB = stroke, touch, tap, pet, caress, fondle

• NOUN = tap, stroke, clap

patch NOUN **1** = spot, bit, scrap, shred, small piece **2** = plot, area, ground, land, tract **3** = reinforcement, piece of fabric, piece of cloth, piece of material, piece sewn on

• VERB *often with* ***up*** = mend, cover, repair, reinforce, stitch (up), sew (up)

patent NOUN = copyright, licence, franchise, registered trademark

• ADJECTIVE = obvious, apparent, evident, clear, glaring, manifest

path 1 = way, road, walk, track, trail, avenue, footpath, berm (*N.Z.*) **2** = route, way, course, direction **3** = course, way, road, route

pathetic = sad, moving, touching, affecting, distressing, tender, poignant, plaintive ≠ funny

patience 1 = forbearance, tolerance, serenity, restraint, calmness, sufferance ≠ impatience **2** = endurance, resignation, submission, fortitude, long-suffering, perseverance, stoicism, constancy

patient NOUN = sick person, case, sufferer, invalid

• ADJECTIVE **1** = forbearing, understanding, forgiving, mild, tolerant, indulgent, lenient, even-tempered ≠ impatient **2** = long-suffering, resigned, calm, enduring, philosophical, persevering, stoical, submissive

patriot = nationalist, loyalist, chauvinist

patriotic = nationalistic, loyal, chauvinistic, jingoistic

patriotism = nationalism, jingoism

patrol VERB = police, guard, keep watch (on), inspect, safeguard, keep guard (on)
• NOUN = guard, watch, watchman, sentinel, patrolman

patron **1** = supporter, friend, champion, sponsor, backer, helper, benefactor, philanthropist **2** = customer, client, buyer, frequenter, shopper, habitué

patronage = support, promotion, sponsorship, backing, help, aid, assistance

pattern **1** = order, plan, system, method, sequence **2** = design, arrangement, motif, figure, device, decoration **3** = plan, design, original, guide, diagram, stencil, template

pause VERB = stop briefly, delay, break, wait, rest, halt, cease, interrupt ≠ continue
• NOUN = stop, break, interval, rest, gap, halt, respite, lull ≠ continuance

pave = cover, floor, surface, concrete, tile

paw (*Informal*) = manhandle, grab, maul, molest, handle roughly

pay VERB **1** = reward, compensate, reimburse, recompense, requite, remunerate **2** = spend, give, fork out (*informal*), remit, shell out (*informal*) **3** = settle **4** = bring in, earn, return, net, yield **5** = be profitable, make money, make a return **6** = benefit, repay, be worthwhile **7** = give, extend, present with, grant, hand out, bestow
• NOUN = wages, income, payment, earnings, fee, reward, salary, allowance
• PHRASES **pay off** = succeed, work, be effective ◆ **pay something off** = settle, clear, square, discharge, pay in full

payable = due, outstanding, owed, owing

payment **1** = remittance, advance, deposit, premium, instalment **2** = settlement, paying, discharge, remittance **3** = wages, fee, reward, hire, remuneration

peace **1** = truce, ceasefire, treaty, armistice ≠ war **2** = stillness, rest, quiet, silence, calm, hush, tranquillity, seclusion **3** = serenity, calm, composure, contentment, repose, equanimity, peacefulness, harmoniousness **4** = harmony, accord, agreement, concord

peaceful **1** = at peace, friendly, harmonious, amicable, nonviolent ≠ hostile **2** = peace-loving, conciliatory, peaceable, unwarlike ≠ belligerent **3** = calm, still, quiet, tranquil, restful ≠ agitated **4** = serene, placid, undisturbed

peak NOUN **1** = high point, crown, climax, culmination, zenith, acme **2** = point, top, tip, summit, brow, crest, pinnacle, apex
• VERB = culminate, climax, come to a head

peasant = rustic, countryman

peck VERB **1** = pick, hit, strike, tap, poke, jab, prick **2** = kiss, plant a kiss, give someone a smacker, give someone a peck *or* kiss
• NOUN = kiss, smacker, osculation (*rare*)

peculiar **1** = odd, strange, unusual, bizarre, funny, extraordinary, curious, weird ≠ ordinary **2** = special, particular, unique, characteristic ≠ common

peddle = sell, trade, push (*informal*), market, hawk, flog (*slang*)

pedestrian NOUN = walker, foot-traveller ≠ driver
• ADJECTIVE = dull, ordinary, boring, commonplace, mundane, mediocre, banal, prosaic, half-pie (*N.Z. informal*) ≠ exciting

pedigree ADJECTIVE = purebred, thoroughbred, full-blooded
• NOUN = lineage, family, line, race, stock, blood, breed, descent

peel NOUN = rind, skin, peeling
• VERB = skin, scale, strip, pare, shuck, flake off, take the skin *or* rind off

peep VERB = peek, look, eyeball (*slang*), sneak a look, steal a look
• NOUN = look, glimpse, peek, look-see (*slang*)

peer[1] = squint, look, spy, gaze, scan, inspect, peep, peek

peer[2] **1** = noble, lord, aristocrat, nobleman **2** = equal, like, fellow, contemporary, compeer

peg NOUN = pin, spike, rivet, skewer, dowel, spigot
• VERB = fasten, join, fix, secure, attach

pen[1] = write (down), draft, compose, pencil, draw up, scribble, take down, inscribe

pen[2] NOUN = enclosure, pound, fold, cage, coop, hutch, sty
• VERB = enclose, confine, cage, fence in,

coop up, hedge in, shut up *or* in
penalty = punishment, price, fine, handicap, forfeit
pending ADJECTIVE **1** = undecided, unsettled, in the balance, undetermined **2** = forthcoming, imminent, prospective, impending, in the wind
• PREPOSITION = awaiting, until, waiting for, till
penetrate **1** = pierce, enter, go through, bore, stab, prick **2** = grasp, work out, figure out (*informal*), comprehend, fathom, decipher, suss (out) (*slang*), get to the bottom of
penetrating **1** = sharp, harsh, piercing, carrying, piping, loud, strident, shrill ≠ sweet **2** = pungent **3** = piercing **4** = intelligent, quick, sharp, keen, acute, shrewd, astute, perceptive ≠ dull **5** = perceptive, sharp, keen ≠ unperceptive
penetration **1** = piercing, entry, entrance, puncturing, incision **2** = entry, entrance
pension = allowance, benefit, welfare, annuity, superannuation
pensioner = senior citizen, retired person, retiree (*U.S.*), old-age pensioner, O.A.P.
people PLURAL NOUN **1** = persons, individuals, folk (*informal*), men and women, humanity, mankind, mortals, the human race **2** = nation, public, community, subjects, population, residents, citizens, folk **3** = race, tribe **4** = family, parents, relations, relatives, folk, folks (*informal*), clan, kin
• VERB = inhabit, occupy, settle, populate, colonize
pepper NOUN = seasoning, flavour, spice
• VERB **1** = pelt, hit, shower, blitz, rake, bombard, assail, strafe **2** = sprinkle, spot, scatter, dot, fleck, intersperse, speck, spatter
perceive **1** = see, notice, note, identify, discover, spot, observe, recognize **2** = understand, gather, see, learn, realize, grasp, comprehend, suss (out) (*slang*) **3** = consider, believe, judge, suppose, rate, deem, adjudge
perception **1** = awareness, understanding, sense, impression, feeling, idea, notion, consciousness **2** = understanding, intelligence, observation, discrimination, insight, sharpness, cleverness, keenness
perch VERB **1** = sit, rest, balance, settle **2** = place, put, rest, balance **3** = land, alight, roost
• NOUN = resting place, post, branch, pole
perennial = continual, lasting, constant, enduring, persistent, abiding, recurrent, incessant
perfect ADJECTIVE **1** = faultless, correct, pure, impeccable, exemplary, flawless, foolproof ≠ deficient **2** = excellent, ideal, supreme, superb, splendid, sublime, superlative **3** = immaculate, impeccable, flawless, spotless, unblemished ≠ flawed **4** = complete, absolute, sheer, utter, consummate, unmitigated ≠ partial **5** = exact, true, accurate, precise, correct, faithful, unerring
• VERB = improve, develop, polish, refine ≠ mar
perfection = excellence, integrity, superiority, purity, wholeness, sublimity, exquisiteness, faultlessness
perfectly **1** = completely, totally, absolutely, quite, fully, altogether, thoroughly, wholly ≠ partially **2** = flawlessly, ideally, wonderfully, superbly, supremely, impeccably, faultlessly ≠ badly
perform **1** = do, achieve, carry out, complete, fulfil, accomplish, execute, pull off **2** = fulfil, carry out, execute, discharge **3** = present, act (out), stage, play, produce, represent, put on, enact **4** = appear on stage, act **5** = function, go, work, run, operate, handle, respond, behave
performance **1** = presentation, playing, acting (out), staging, production, exhibition, rendering, portrayal **2** = show, appearance, concert, gig (*informal*), recital **3** = work, acts, conduct, exploits, feats **4** = carrying out, practice, achievement, execution, completion, accomplishment, fulfilment
performer = artiste, player, Thespian, trouper, actor *or* actress
perfume **1** = fragrance, scent **2** = scent, smell, fragrance, bouquet, aroma, odour
perhaps = maybe, possibly, it may be, it is possible (that), conceivably, perchance (*archaic*), feasibly, happen (*Northern English dialect*)
peril **1** = danger, risk, threat, hazard,

menace, jeopardy, perilousness **2** *often plural* = pitfall, problem, risk, hazard ≠ safety
perimeter = boundary, edge, border, bounds, limit, margin, confines, periphery ≠ centre
period = time, term, season, space, run, stretch, spell, phase
periodic = recurrent, regular, repeated, occasional, cyclical, sporadic, intermittent
peripheral **1** = secondary, minor, marginal, irrelevant, unimportant, incidental, inessential **2** = outermost, outside, external, outer, exterior
perish **1** = die, be killed, expire, pass away, lose your life, cark it (*Austral. & N.Z. slang*) **2** = be destroyed, fall, decline, collapse, disappear, vanish **3** = rot, waste away, decay, disintegrate, decompose, moulder
perk (*Brit. informal*) = bonus, benefit, extra, plus, fringe benefit, perquisite
permanent **1** = lasting, constant, enduring, persistent, eternal, abiding, perpetual, everlasting ≠ temporary **2** = long-term, established, secure, stable, steady ≠ temporary
permission = authorization, sanction, licence, approval, leave, go-ahead (*informal*), liberty, consent ≠ prohibition
permit VERB **1** = allow, grant, sanction, let, entitle, license, authorize, consent to ≠ forbid **2** = enable, let, allow, cause
• NOUN = licence, pass, document, certificate, passport, visa, warrant, authorization ≠ prohibition
perpetual **1** = everlasting, permanent, endless, eternal, lasting, perennial, infinite, never-ending ≠ temporary **2** = continual, repeated, constant, endless, continuous, persistent, recurrent, never-ending ≠ brief
perpetuate = maintain, preserve, keep going, immortalize ≠ end
persecute **1** = victimize, torture, torment, oppress, pick on, ill-treat, maltreat ≠ mollycoddle **2** = harass, bother, annoy, tease, hassle (*informal*), badger, pester ≠ leave alone
persist **1** = continue, last, remain, carry on, keep up, linger **2** = persevere, continue, go on, carry on, keep on, keep going, press on, not give up
persistence = determination, resolution, grit, endurance, tenacity, perseverance, doggedness, pertinacity
persistent **1** = continuous, constant, repeated, endless, perpetual, continual, never-ending, incessant ≠ occasional **2** = determined, dogged, steady, stubborn, persevering, tireless, tenacious, steadfast ≠ irresolute
person NOUN = individual, being, body, human, soul, creature, mortal, man *or* woman
• PHRASES **in person** **1** = personally, yourself **2** = in the flesh, actually, physically, bodily
personal **1** = own, special, private, individual, particular, peculiar **2** = individual, special, particular, exclusive **3** = private **4** = offensive, nasty, insulting, disparaging, derogatory
personality **1** = nature, character, make-up, identity, temperament, disposition, individuality **2** = character, charm, attraction, charisma, magnetism **3** = celebrity, star, notable, household name, famous name, personage, megastar (*informal*)
personally **1** = in your opinion, in your book, for your part, from your own viewpoint, in your own view **2** = by yourself, alone, independently, solely, on your own **3** = individually, specially, subjectively, individualistically **4** = privately, in private, off the record
personnel = employees, people, staff, workers, workforce, human resources, helpers
perspective **1** = outlook, attitude, context, angle, frame of reference **2** = objectivity, proportion, relation, relativity, relative importance
persuade **1** = talk (someone) into, urge, influence, win (someone) over, induce, sway, entice, coax ≠ dissuade **2** = cause, lead, move, influence, motivate, induce, incline, dispose **3** = convince, satisfy, assure, cause to believe
persuasion **1** = urging, inducement, wheedling, enticement, cajolery **2** = belief, views, opinion, party, school, side, camp, faith
persuasive = convincing, telling, effective, sound, compelling, influential, valid, credible ≠ unconvincing
pervasive = widespread, general, common, extensive, universal, prevalent, ubiquitous, rife

perverse 1 = <u>stubborn</u>, contrary, dogged, troublesome, rebellious, wayward, intractable, wilful ≠ cooperative 2 = <u>ill-natured</u>, cross, surly, fractious, churlish, ill-tempered, stroppy (*Brit. slang*), peevish ≠ good-natured 3 = <u>abnormal</u>, unhealthy, improper, deviant

pervert VERB 1 = <u>distort</u>, abuse, twist, misuse, warp, misrepresent, falsify 2 = <u>corrupt</u>, degrade, deprave, debase, debauch, lead astray
• NOUN = <u>deviant</u>, degenerate, sicko (*informal*), weirdo *or* weirdie (*informal*)

pessimistic = <u>gloomy</u>, dark, despairing, bleak, depressed, cynical, hopeless, glum ≠ optimistic

pest 1 = <u>infection</u>, bug, insect, plague, epidemic, blight, scourge, pestilence, gogga (*S. African informal*) 2 = <u>nuisance</u>, trial, pain (*informal*), drag (*informal*), bother, irritation, annoyance, bane

pet ADJECTIVE = <u>favourite</u>, favoured, dearest, cherished, fave (*informal*), dear to your heart
• NOUN = <u>favourite</u>, treasure, darling, jewel, idol
• VERB 1 = <u>fondle</u>, pat, stroke, caress 2 = <u>pamper</u>, spoil, indulge, cosset, baby, dote on, coddle, mollycoddle 3 (*Informal*) = <u>cuddle</u>, kiss, snog (*Brit. slang*), smooch (*informal*), neck (*informal*), canoodle (*slang*)

petition NOUN 1 = <u>appeal</u>, round robin, list of signatures 2 = <u>entreaty</u>, appeal, suit, application, request, prayer, plea, solicitation
• VERB = <u>appeal</u>, plead, ask, pray, beg, solicit, beseech, entreat

petty 1 = <u>trivial</u>, insignificant, little, small, slight, trifling, negligible, unimportant ≠ important 2 = <u>small-minded</u>, mean, shabby, spiteful, ungenerous, mean-minded ≠ broad-minded

phantom = <u>spectre</u>, ghost, spirit, shade (*literary*), spook (*informal*), apparition, wraith, phantasm

phase NOUN = <u>stage</u>, time, point, position, step, development, period, chapter
• PHRASES **phase something in** = <u>introduce</u>, incorporate, ease in, start ◆ **phase something out** = <u>eliminate</u>, close, remove, withdraw, pull out, wind up, run down, terminate

phenomenal = <u>extraordinary</u>, outstanding, remarkable, fantastic, unusual, marvellous, exceptional, miraculous ≠ unremarkable

phenomenon 1 = <u>occurrence</u>, happening, fact, event, incident, circumstance, episode 2 = <u>wonder</u>, sensation, exception, miracle, marvel, prodigy, rarity

philosopher = <u>thinker</u>, theorist, sage, wise man, logician, metaphysician

philosophical *or* **philosophic** 1 = <u>theoretical</u>, abstract, wise, rational, logical, thoughtful, sagacious ≠ practical 2 = <u>stoical</u>, calm, composed, cool, collected, serene, tranquil, unruffled ≠ emotional

philosophy 1 = <u>thought</u>, knowledge, thinking, reasoning, wisdom, logic, metaphysics 2 = <u>outlook</u>, values, principles, convictions, thinking, beliefs, doctrine, ideology

phone NOUN 1 = <u>telephone</u>, blower (*informal*) 2 = <u>call</u>, ring (*informal, chiefly Brit.*), tinkle (*Brit. informal*)
• VERB = <u>call</u>, telephone, ring (up) (*informal, chiefly Brit.*), give someone a call, give someone a ring (*informal, chiefly Brit.*), make a call, give someone a tinkle (*Brit. informal*), get on the blower (*informal*)

photograph NOUN = <u>picture</u>, photo (*informal*), shot, print, snap (*informal*), snapshot, transparency
• VERB = <u>take a picture of</u>, record, film, shoot, snap (*informal*), take (someone's) picture

photographic 1 = <u>pictorial</u>, visual, graphic, cinematic, filmic 2 = <u>accurate</u>, exact, precise, faithful, retentive

phrase NOUN = <u>expression</u>, saying, remark, construction, quotation, maxim, idiom, adage
• VERB = <u>express</u>, say, word, put, voice, communicate, convey, put into words

physical 1 = <u>corporal</u>, fleshly, bodily, corporeal 2 = <u>earthly</u>, fleshly, mortal, incarnate 3 = <u>material</u>, real, substantial, natural, solid, tangible, palpable

physician = <u>doctor</u>, doc (*informal*), medic (*informal*), general practitioner, medical practitioner, doctor of medicine, G.P., M.D.

pick VERB 1 = <u>select</u>, choose, identify, elect, nominate, specify, opt for, single out ≠ reject 2 = <u>gather</u>, pull, collect, take in,

harvest, pluck, garner **3** = provoke, start, cause, stir up, incite, instigate **4** = open, force, crack (*informal*), break into, break open
• NOUN **1** = choice, decision, option, selection, preference **2** = best, prime, finest, elect, elite, cream, jewel in the crown, crème de la crème (*French*)
• PHRASES **pick on someone** **1** = torment, bully, bait, tease, get at (*informal*), badger, persecute, hector **2** = choose, select, prefer, elect, single out, fix on, settle upon ◆ **pick something** *or* **someone out** = identify, recognize, distinguish, perceive, discriminate, make someone *or* something out, tell someone *or* something apart ◆ **pick something** *or* **someone up** **1** = lift, raise, gather, take up, grasp, uplift **2** = collect, get, call for ◆ **pick something up** **1** = learn, master, acquire, get the hang of (*informal*), become proficient in **2** = obtain, get, find, buy, discover, purchase, acquire, locate ◆ **pick up** **1** = improve, recover, rally, get better, bounce back, make progress, perk up, turn the corner **2** = recover, improve, rally, get better, mend, turn the corner, be on the mend, take a turn for the better

picket VERB = blockade, boycott, demonstrate outside
• NOUN **1** = demonstration, strike, blockade **2** = protester, demonstrator, picketer **3** = lookout, watch, guard, patrol, sentry, sentinel **4** = stake, post, pale, paling, upright, stanchion

pickle VERB = preserve, marinade, steep
• NOUN **1** = chutney, relish, piccalilli **2** (*Informal*) = predicament, fix (*informal*), difficulty, bind (*informal*), jam (*informal*), dilemma, scrape (*informal*), hot water (*informal*), uphill (*S. African*)

pick-up = improvement, recovery, rise, rally, strengthening, revival, upturn, change for the better

picnic = excursion, barbecue, barbie (*informal*), cookout (*U.S. & Canad.*), alfresco meal, clambake (*U.S. & Canad.*), outdoor meal, outing

picture NOUN **1** = representation, drawing, painting, portrait, image, print, illustration, sketch **2** = photograph, photo, still, shot, image, print, frame, slide **3** = film, movie (*U.S. informal*), flick (*slang*), feature film, motion picture **4** = idea, vision, concept, impression, notion, visualization, mental picture, mental image **5** = description, impression, explanation, report, account, image, sketch, depiction **6** = personification, embodiment, essence, epitome
• VERB **1** = imagine, see, envision, visualize, conceive of, fantasize about, conjure up an image of **2** = represent, show, draw, paint, illustrate, sketch, depict **3** = show, photograph, capture on film

picturesque **1** = interesting, pretty, beautiful, attractive, charming, scenic, quaint ≠ unattractive **2** = vivid, striking, graphic, colourful, memorable ≠ dull

piece **1** = bit, slice, part, block, quantity, segment, portion, fragment **2** = component, part, section, bit, unit, segment, constituent, module **3** = item, report, story, study, review, article **4** = composition, work, production, opus **5** = work of art, work, creation **6** = share, cut (*informal*), slice, percentage, quantity, portion, quota, fraction

pier **1** = jetty, wharf, quay, promenade, landing place **2** = pillar, support, post, column, pile, upright, buttress

pierce = penetrate, stab, spike, enter, bore, drill, puncture, prick

piercing **1** (*of sound*) = penetrating, sharp, loud, shrill, high-pitched, ear-splitting ≠ low **2** = perceptive, sharp, keen, alert, penetrating, shrewd, perspicacious, quick-witted ≠ unperceptive **3** = sharp, acute, severe, intense, painful, stabbing, excruciating, agonizing **4** (*of weather*) = cold, biting, freezing, bitter, arctic, wintry, nippy

pig **1** = hog, sow, boar, swine, porker **2** (*Informal*) = slob, glutton **3** (*Informal*) = brute, monster, scoundrel, rogue, swine, rotter, boor

pigment = colour, colouring, paint, stain, dye, tint, tincture

pile[1] NOUN **1** = heap, collection, mountain, mass, stack, mound, accumulation, hoard **2** (*Informal*) *often plural* = lot(s), mountain(s), load(s) (*informal*), oceans, wealth, great deal, stack(s), abundance **3** = mansion, building, residence, manor, country house, seat, big house, stately home
• VERB **1** = load, stuff, pack, stack, charge, heap, cram, lade **2** = crowd, pack, rush,

climb, flood, stream, crush, squeeze
• PHRASES **pile up** = accumulate, collect, gather (up), build up, amass

pile[2] = foundation, support, post, column, beam, upright, pillar

pile[3] = nap, fibre, down, hair, fur, plush

pile-up (*Informal*) = collision, crash, accident, smash, smash-up (*informal*), multiple collision

pilgrim = traveller, wanderer, devotee, wayfarer

pilgrimage = journey, tour, trip, mission, expedition, excursion

pill = tablet, capsule, pellet

pillar 1 = support, post, column, prop, shaft, upright, pier, stanchion 2 = supporter, leader, mainstay, leading light (*informal*), upholder

pilot NOUN 1 = airman, flyer, aviator, aeronaut 2 = helmsman, navigator, steersman
• VERB 1 = fly, operate, be at the controls of 2 = navigate, drive, direct, guide, handle, conduct, steer 3 = direct, conduct, steer
• ADJECTIVE = trial, test, model, sample, experimental

pin NOUN 1 = tack, nail, needle, safety pin 2 = peg, rod, brace, bolt
• VERB 1 = fasten, stick, attach, join, fix, secure, nail, clip 2 = hold fast, hold down, constrain, immobilize, pinion
• PHRASES **pin someone down** = force, pressure, compel, put pressure on, pressurize, nail someone down, make someone commit themselves ◆ **pin something down** = determine, identify, locate, name, specify, pinpoint

pinch VERB 1 = nip, press, squeeze, grasp, compress 2 = hurt, crush, squeeze, pain, cramp 3 (*Brit. informal*) = steal, lift (*informal*), nick (*slang, chiefly Brit.*), swipe (*slang*), knock off (*slang*), pilfer, purloin, filch
• NOUN 1 = nip, squeeze 2 = dash, bit, mite, jot, speck, soupçon (*French*) 3 = emergency, crisis, difficulty, plight, scrape (*informal*), strait, uphill (*S. African*), predicament

pine VERB = waste, decline, sicken, fade, languish
• PHRASES **pine for something** *or* **someone** 1 = long, ache, crave, yearn, eat your heart out over 2 = hanker after, crave, wish for, yearn for, thirst for, hunger for

pink NOUN *or* ADJECTIVE = rosy, rose, salmon, flushed, reddish, roseate

pinnacle 1 = summit, top, height, peak 2 = height, top, crown, crest, zenith, apex, vertex

pinpoint 1 = identify, discover, define, distinguish, put your finger on 2 = locate, find, identify, zero in on

pioneer NOUN 1 = founder, leader, developer, innovator, trailblazer 2 = settler, explorer, colonist
• VERB = develop, create, establish, start, discover, institute, invent, initiate

pipe NOUN = tube, drain, canal, pipeline, line, main, passage, cylinder
• VERB = convey, channel, conduct
• PHRASES **pipe down** (*Informal*) = be quiet, shut up (*informal*), hush, stop talking, quieten down, shush, shut your mouth, hold your tongue

pipeline = tube, passage, pipe, conduit, duct

pirate NOUN = buccaneer, raider, marauder, corsair, freebooter
• VERB = copy, steal, reproduce, bootleg, appropriate, poach, crib (*informal*), plagiarize

pit NOUN 1 = coal mine, mine, shaft, colliery, mine shaft 2 = hole, depression, hollow, crater, trough, cavity, abyss, chasm
• VERB = scar, mark, dent, indent, pockmark

pitch NOUN 1 = sports field, ground, stadium, arena, park, field of play 2 = tone, sound, key, frequency, timbre, modulation 3 = level, point, degree, summit, extent, height, intensity, high point 4 = talk, patter, spiel (*informal*)
• VERB 1 = throw, cast, toss, hurl, fling, chuck (*informal*), sling, lob (*informal*) 2 = fall, drop, plunge, dive, tumble, topple, plummet, fall headlong 3 = set up, raise, settle, put up, erect 4 = toss (about), roll, plunge, lurch
• PHRASES **pitch in** = help, contribute, participate, join in, cooperate, chip in (*informal*), get stuck in (*Brit. informal*), lend a hand

pitfall *usually plural* = danger, difficulty, peril, catch, trap, hazard, drawback, snag, uphill (*S. African*)

pity NOUN 1 = compassion, charity, sympathy, kindness, fellow feeling ≠ mercilessness 2 = shame, sin (*informal*), misfortune, bummer (*slang*), crying

shame **3** = mercy, kindness, clemency, forbearance
• VERB = feel sorry for, feel for, sympathize with, grieve for, weep for, bleed for, have compassion for

pivotal = crucial, central, vital, critical, decisive

place NOUN **1** = spot, point, position, site, area, location, venue, whereabouts **2** = region, quarter, district, neighbourhood, vicinity, locality, locale, dorp (*S. African*) **3** = position, point, spot, location **4** = space, position, seat, chair **5** = rank, standing, position, footing, station, status, grade, niche **6** = situation, position, circumstances, shoes (*informal*) **7** = job, position, post, situation, office, employment, appointment **8** = home, house, room, property, accommodation, pad (*slang*), residence, dwelling **9** (In this context, the construction is always negative) = duty, right, job, charge, concern, role, affair, responsibility
• VERB **1** = lay (down), put (down), set (down), stand, position, rest, station, stick (*informal*) **2** = put, lay, set, invest, pin **3** = classify, class, group, put, order, sort, rank, arrange **4** = entrust to, give to, assign to, appoint to, allocate to, find a home for **5** = identify, remember, recognize, pin someone down, put your finger on, put a name to
• PHRASES **take place** = happen, occur, go on, go down (*U.S. & Canad.*), arise, come about, crop up, transpire (*informal*)

plague NOUN **1** = disease, infection, epidemic, pestilence **2** = infestation, invasion, epidemic, influx, host, swarm, multitude
• VERB **1** = torment, trouble, torture **2** = pester, trouble, bother, annoy, tease, harry, harass, hassle

plain ADJECTIVE **1** = unadorned, simple, basic, severe, bare, stark, austere, spartan ≠ ornate **2** = clear, obvious, patent, evident, visible, distinct, understandable, manifest ≠ hidden **3** = straightforward, open, direct, frank, blunt, outspoken, honest, downright ≠ roundabout **4** = ugly, unattractive, homely (*U.S. & Canad.*), unlovely, unprepossessing, not beautiful, no oil painting (*informal*), ill-favoured ≠ attractive **5** = ordinary, common, simple, everyday, commonplace, unaffected, unpretentious ≠ sophisticated
• NOUN = flatland, plateau, prairie, grassland, steppe, veld

plan NOUN **1** = scheme, system, design, programme, proposal, strategy, method, suggestion **2** = diagram, map, drawing, chart, representation, sketch, blueprint, layout
• VERB **1** = devise, arrange, scheme, plot, draft, organize, outline, formulate **2** = intend, aim, mean, propose, purpose **3** = design, outline, draw up a plan of

plane NOUN **1** = aeroplane, aircraft, jet, airliner, jumbo jet **2** = flat surface, the flat, horizontal, level surface **3** = level, position, stage, condition, standard, degree, rung, echelon
• ADJECTIVE = level, even, flat, regular, smooth, horizontal
• VERB = skim, sail, skate, glide

plant[1] NOUN = flower, bush, vegetable, herb, weed, shrub
• VERB **1** = sow, scatter, transplant, implant, put in the ground **2** = seed, sow, implant **3** = place, put, set, fix **4** = hide, put, place, conceal **5** = place, put, establish, found, fix, insert

plant[2] **1** = factory, works, shop, yard, mill, foundry **2** = machinery, equipment, gear, apparatus

plaster NOUN **1** = mortar, stucco, gypsum, plaster of Paris **2** = bandage, dressing, sticking plaster, Elastoplast®, adhesive plaster
• VERB = cover, spread, coat, smear, overlay, daub

plastic = pliant, soft, flexible, supple, pliable, ductile, mouldable ≠ rigid

plate NOUN **1** = platter, dish, dinner plate, salver, trencher (*archaic*) **2** = helping, course, serving, dish, portion, platter, plateful **3** = layer, panel, sheet, slab **4** = illustration, picture, photograph, print, engraving, lithograph
• VERB = coat, gild, laminate, cover, overlay

plateau **1** = upland, table, highland, tableland **2** = levelling off, level, stage, stability

platform **1** = stage, stand, podium, rostrum, dais, soapbox **2** = policy, programme, principle, objective(s), manifesto, party line

plausible **1** = believable, possible, likely, reasonable, credible, probable, persuasive, conceivable ≠ unbelievable **2** = glib, smooth, specious, smooth-talking, smooth-tongued

play VERB **1** = amuse yourself, have fun, sport, fool, romp, revel, trifle, entertain yourself **2** = take part in, be involved in, engage in, participate in, compete in **3** = compete against, challenge, take on, oppose, contend against **4** = perform, carry out **5** = act, portray, represent, perform, act the part of **6** = perform on, strum, make music on
• NOUN **1** = amusement, pleasure, leisure, games, sport, fun, entertainment, relaxation **2** = drama, show, piece, comedy, tragedy, farce, soapie (*Austral. slang*), pantomime
• PHRASES **play on** *or* **upon something** = take advantage of, abuse, exploit, impose on, trade on, capitalize on ◆ **play something down** = minimize, make light of, gloss over, talk down, underrate, underplay, pooh-pooh (*informal*), soft-pedal (*informal*) ◆ **play something up** = emphasize, highlight, underline, stress, accentuate ◆ **play up 1** (*Brit. informal*) = hurt, be painful, bother you, trouble you, be sore, pain you **2** (*Brit. informal*) = malfunction, not work properly, be on the blink (*slang*) **3** (*Brit. informal*) = be awkward, misbehave, give trouble, be disobedient, be stroppy (*Brit. slang*)

playboy = womanizer, philanderer, rake, lady-killer (*informal*), roué, ladies' man

player 1 = sportsman *or* sportswoman, competitor, participant, contestant **2** = musician, artist, performer, virtuoso, instrumentalist **3** = performer, entertainer, Thespian, trouper, actor *or* actress

plea 1 = appeal, request, suit, prayer, petition, entreaty, intercession, supplication **2** = excuse, defence, explanation, justification

plead = appeal, ask, request, beg, petition, implore, beseech, entreat

pleasant 1 = pleasing, nice, fine, lovely, amusing, delightful, enjoyable, agreeable, lekker (*S. African slang*) ≠ horrible **2** = friendly, nice, agreeable, likable *or* likeable, engaging, charming, amiable, genial ≠ disagreeable

please = delight, entertain, humour, amuse, suit, satisfy, indulge, gratify ≠ annoy

pleased = happy, delighted, contented, satisfied, thrilled, glad, gratified, over the moon (*informal*)

pleasing 1 = enjoyable, satisfying, charming, delightful, gratifying, agreeable, pleasurable ≠ unpleasant **2** = likable *or* likeable, engaging, charming, delightful, agreeable ≠ disagreeable

pleasure 1 = happiness, delight, satisfaction, enjoyment, bliss, gratification, gladness, delectation ≠ displeasure **2** = amusement, joy ≠ duty

pledge NOUN **1** = promise, vow, assurance, word, undertaking, warrant, oath, covenant **2** = guarantee, security, deposit, bail, collateral, pawn, surety
• VERB = promise, vow, swear, contract, engage, give your word, give your oath

plentiful = abundant, liberal, generous, lavish, ample, overflowing, copious, bountiful ≠ scarce

plenty 1 = abundance, wealth, prosperity, fertility, profusion, affluence, plenitude, fruitfulness **2** *usually with* **of** = lots of (*informal*), enough, a great deal of, masses of, piles of (*informal*), stacks of, heaps of (*informal*), an abundance of

plight = difficulty, condition, state, situation, trouble, predicament

plot¹ NOUN **1** = plan, scheme, intrigue, conspiracy, cabal, stratagem, machination **2** = story, action, subject, theme, outline, scenario, narrative, story line
• VERB **1** = plan, scheme, conspire, intrigue, manoeuvre, contrive, collude, machinate **2** = devise, design, lay, conceive, hatch, contrive, concoct, cook up (*informal*) **3** = chart, mark, map, locate, calculate, outline

plot² = patch, lot, area, ground, parcel, tract, allotment

plough VERB = turn over, dig, till, cultivate
• PHRASES **plough through something** = forge, cut, drive, press, push, plunge, wade

ploy = tactic, move, trick, device, scheme, manoeuvre, dodge, ruse

pluck VERB **1** = pull out *or* off, pick, draw, collect, gather, harvest **2** = tug, catch, snatch, clutch, jerk, yank, tweak, pull at **3** = strum, pick, finger, twang
• NOUN = courage, nerve, bottle (*Brit. slang*), guts (*informal*), grit, bravery, backbone, boldness

plug NOUN **1** = stopper, cork, bung, spigot **2** (*Informal*) = mention, advertisement, advert (*Brit. informal*), push, publicity, hype
• VERB **1** = seal, close, stop, fill, block, stuff, pack, cork **2** (*Informal*) = mention, push, promote, publicize, advertise, build up, hype
• PHRASES **plug away** (*Informal*) = slog away, labour, toil away, grind away (*informal*), peg away, plod away

plum = choice, prize, first-class

plumb VERB = delve into, explore, probe, go into, penetrate, gauge, unravel, fathom
• ADVERB = exactly, precisely, bang, slap, spot-on (*Brit. informal*)

plummet **1** = drop, fall, crash, nose-dive, descend rapidly **2** = plunge, fall, drop, crash, tumble, nose-dive, descend rapidly

plump = chubby, fat, stout, round, tubby, dumpy, roly-poly, rotund ≠ scrawny

plunder VERB **1** = loot, strip, sack, rob, raid, rifle, ransack, pillage **2** = steal, rob, take, nick (*informal*), pinch (*informal*), embezzle, pilfer, thieve
• NOUN **1** = pillage **2** = loot, spoils, booty, swag (*slang*), ill-gotten gains

plunge VERB **1** = descend, fall, drop, crash, pitch, sink, dive, tumble **2** = hurtle, charge, career, jump, tear, rush, dive, dash **3** = submerge, dip **4** = throw, cast, pitch, propel **5** = fall steeply, drop, crash (*informal*), slump, plummet, take a nosedive (*informal*)
• NOUN **1** = dive, jump, duck, descent **2** = fall, crash (*informal*), slump, drop, tumble

plus PREPOSITION = and, with, added to, coupled with
• NOUN (*Informal*) = advantage, benefit, asset, gain, extra, bonus, good point
• ADJECTIVE = additional, added, extra, supplementary, add-on

plush = luxurious, luxury, lavish, rich, sumptuous, opulent, de luxe

ply = work at, follow, exercise, pursue, carry on, practise

pocket NOUN = pouch, bag, sack, compartment, receptacle
• ADJECTIVE = small, compact, miniature, portable, little
• VERB = steal, take, lift (*informal*), appropriate, pilfer, purloin, filch

pod = shell, case, hull, husk, shuck

podium = platform, stand, stage, rostrum, dais

poem = verse, song, lyric, rhyme, sonnet, ode, verse composition

poet = bard, rhymer, lyricist, lyric poet, versifier, elegist

poetic **1** = figurative, creative, lyric, symbolic, lyrical **2** = lyrical, lyric, elegiac, metrical

poetry = verse, poems, rhyme, rhyming, verse composition

poignant = moving, touching, sad, bitter, intense, painful, distressing, pathetic

point NOUN **1** = essence, meaning, subject, question, heart, import, drift, thrust **2** = purpose, aim, object, end, reason, goal, intention, objective **3** = aspect, detail, feature, quality, particular, respect, item, characteristic **4** = place, area, position, site, spot, location, locality, locale **5** = moment, time, stage, period, phase, instant, juncture, moment in time **6** = stage, level, position, condition, degree, pitch, circumstance, extent **7** = end, tip, sharp end, top, spur, spike, apex, prong **8** = score, tally, mark **9** = pinpoint, mark, spot, dot, fleck
• VERB **1** = aim, level, train, direct **2** = indicate, show, signal, point to, gesture towards **3** = face, look, direct
• PHRASES **point at** *or* **to something** *or* **someone** = indicate, point out, specify, designate, gesture towards

pointed **1** = sharp, edged, acute, barbed **2** = cutting, telling, biting, sharp, keen, acute, penetrating, pertinent

pointer **1** = hint, tip, suggestion, recommendation, caution, piece of information, piece of advice **2** = indicator, hand, guide, needle, arrow

pointless = senseless, meaningless, futile, fruitless, stupid, silly, useless, absurd ≠ worthwhile

poised **1** = ready, waiting, prepared, standing by, all set **2** = composed, calm, together (*informal*), collected, dignified, self-confident, self-possessed ≠ agitated

poison NOUN = toxin, venom, bane (*archaic*)
• VERB **1** = murder, kill, give someone poison, administer poison to **2** = contaminate, foul, infect, spoil, pollute, blight, taint, befoul **3** = corrupt, colour, undermine, bias, sour, pervert, warp, taint

poisonous **1** = toxic, fatal, deadly, lethal,

mortal, virulent, noxious, venomous **2** = evil, malicious, corrupting, pernicious, baleful

poke VERB **1** = jab, push, stick, dig, stab, thrust, shove, nudge **2** = protrude, stick, thrust, jut
• NOUN = jab, dig, thrust, nudge, prod

pole = rod, post, support, staff, bar, stick, stake, paling

police NOUN = the law (*informal*), police force, constabulary, fuzz (*slang*), boys in blue (*informal*), the Old Bill (*slang*), rozzers (*slang*)
• VERB = control, patrol, guard, watch, protect, regulate

policy **1** = procedure, plan, action, practice, scheme, code, custom **2** = line, rules, approach

polish NOUN **1** = varnish, wax, glaze, lacquer, japan **2** = sheen, finish, glaze, gloss, brightness, lustre **3** = style, class (*informal*), finish, breeding, grace, elegance, refinement, finesse
• VERB **1** = shine, wax, smooth, rub, buff, brighten, burnish **2** *often with* ***up*** = perfect, improve, enhance, refine, finish, brush up, touch up

polished **1** = elegant, sophisticated, refined, polite, cultivated, suave, well-bred ≠ unsophisticated **2** = accomplished, professional, masterly, fine, expert, skilful, adept, superlative ≠ amateurish **3** = shining, bright, smooth, gleaming, glossy, burnished ≠ dull

polite **1** = mannerly, civil, courteous, gracious, respectful, well-behaved, complaisant, well-mannered ≠ rude **2** = refined, cultured, civilized, polished, sophisticated, elegant, genteel, well-bred ≠ uncultured

politic = wise, diplomatic, sensible, prudent, advisable, expedient, judicious

political = governmental, government, state, parliamentary, constitutional, administrative, legislative, ministerial

politician = statesman *or* stateswoman, representative, senator (*U.S.*), congressman (*U.S.*), Member of Parliament, legislator, public servant, congresswoman (*U.S.*)

politics **1** = affairs of state, government, public affairs, civics **2** = political beliefs, party politics, political allegiances, political leanings, political sympathies **3** = political science, statesmanship, civics, statecraft

poll NOUN **1** = survey, figures, count, sampling, returns, ballot, tally, census **2** = election, vote, voting, referendum, ballot, plebiscite
• VERB **1** = question, interview, survey, sample, ballot, canvass **2** = gain, return, record, register, tally

pollute **1** = contaminate, dirty, poison, soil, foul, infect, spoil, stain ≠ decontaminate **2** = defile, corrupt, sully, deprave, debase, profane, desecrate, dishonour ≠ honour

pollution **1** = contamination, dirtying, corruption, taint, foulness, defilement, uncleanness **2** = waste, poisons, dirt, impurities

pond = pool, tarn, small lake, fish pond, duck pond, millpond

ponder = think about, consider, reflect on, contemplate, deliberate about, muse on, brood on, meditate on

pool[1] **1** = swimming pool, lido, swimming bath(s) (*Brit.*), bathing pool (*archaic*) **2** = pond, lake, mere, tarn **3** = puddle, drop, patch

pool[2] NOUN **1** = supply, reserve, fall-back **2** = kitty, bank, fund, stock, store, pot, jackpot, stockpile
• VERB = combine, share, merge, put together, amalgamate, lump together, join forces on

poor **1** = impoverished, broke (*informal*), hard up (*informal*), short, needy, penniless, destitute, poverty-stricken ≠ rich **2** = unfortunate, unlucky, hapless, pitiful, luckless, wretched, ill-starred, pitiable ≠ fortunate **3** = inferior, unsatisfactory, mediocre, second-rate, rotten (*informal*), low-grade, below par, substandard, half-pie (*N.Z. informal*), bodger *or* bodgie (*Austral. slang*) ≠ excellent **4** = meagre, inadequate, insufficient, lacking, incomplete, scant, deficient, skimpy ≠ ample

poorly ADVERB = badly, incompetently, inadequately, unsuccessfully, insufficiently, unsatisfactorily, inexpertly ≠ well
• ADJECTIVE (*Informal*) = ill, sick, unwell, crook (*Austral. & N.Z. informal*), seedy (*informal*), below par, off colour, under the weather (*informal*), feeling rotten (*informal*) ≠ healthy

pop NOUN = bang, report, crack, noise, burst, explosion
• VERB 1 = burst, crack, snap, bang, explode, go off (with a bang) 2 = put, insert, push, stick, slip, thrust, tuck, shove

pope = Holy Father, pontiff, His Holiness, Bishop of Rome, Vicar of Christ

popular 1 = well-liked, liked, in, accepted, favourite, approved, in favour, fashionable ≠ unpopular 2 = common, general, prevailing, current, conventional, universal, prevalent ≠ rare

popularity 1 = favour, esteem, acclaim, regard, approval, vogue 2 = currency, acceptance, circulation, vogue, prevalence

populate 1 = inhabit, people, live in, occupy, reside in, dwell in (*formal*) 2 = settle, occupy, pioneer, colonize

population = inhabitants, people, community, society, residents, natives, folk, occupants

pore = opening, hole, outlet, orifice

pornography = obscenity, porn (*informal*), dirt, filth, indecency, smut

port = harbour, haven, anchorage, seaport

portable = light, compact, convenient, handy, manageable, movable, easily carried

porter[1] (*Chiefly Brit.*) = doorman, caretaker, janitor, concierge, gatekeeper

porter[2] = baggage attendant, carrier, bearer, baggage-carrier

portion 1 = part, bit, piece, section, scrap, segment, fragment, chunk 2 = helping, serving, piece, plateful 3 = share, allowance, lot, measure, quantity, quota, ration, allocation

portrait 1 = picture, painting, image, photograph, representation, likeness 2 = description, profile, portrayal, depiction, characterization, thumbnail sketch

portray 1 = play, take the role of, act the part of, represent, personate (*rare*) 2 = describe, present, depict, evoke, delineate, put in words 3 = represent, draw, paint, illustrate, sketch, figure, picture, depict 4 = characterize, represent, depict

portrayal 1 = performance, interpretation, characterization 2 = depiction, picture, representation, sketch, rendering 3 = description, account, representation 4 = characterization, representation, depiction

pose VERB 1 = position yourself, sit, model, arrange yourself 2 = put on airs, posture, show off (*informal*)
• NOUN 1 = posture, position, bearing, attitude, stance 2 = act, façade, air, front, posturing, pretence, mannerism, affectation
• PHRASES **pose as something** *or* **someone** = impersonate, pretend to be, profess to be, masquerade as, pass yourself off as

posh (*Informal, chiefly Brit.*) 1 = smart, grand, stylish, luxurious, classy (*slang*), swish (*informal, chiefly Brit.*), up-market, swanky (*informal*) 2 = upper-class, high-class

position NOUN 1 = location, place, point, area, post, situation, station, spot 2 = posture, attitude, arrangement, pose, stance 3 = status, place, standing, footing, station, rank, reputation, importance 4 = job, place, post, opening, office, role, situation, duty 5 = place, standing, rank, status 6 = attitude, view, perspective, point of view, opinion, belief, stance, outlook
• VERB = place, put, set, stand, arrange, locate, lay out

positive 1 = beneficial, useful, practical, helpful, progressive, productive, worthwhile, constructive ≠ harmful 2 = certain, sure, convinced, confident, satisfied, assured, free from doubt ≠ uncertain 3 = definite, real, clear, firm, certain, express, absolute, decisive ≠ inconclusive 4 (*Informal*) = absolute, complete, perfect, right (*Brit. informal*), real, total, sheer, utter

positively 1 = definitely, surely, firmly, certainly, absolutely, emphatically, unquestionably, categorically 2 = really, completely, simply, plain (*informal*), absolutely, thoroughly, utterly, downright

possess 1 = own, have, hold, be in possession of, be the owner of, have in your possession 2 = be endowed with, have, enjoy, benefit from, be possessed of, be gifted with 3 = seize, hold, control, dominate, occupy, take someone over, have power over, have mastery over

possession NOUN = ownership, control, custody, hold, hands, tenure

• PLURAL NOUN = property, things, effects, estate, assets, belongings, chattels

possibility 1 = feasibility, likelihood, potentiality, practicability, workableness 2 = likelihood, chance, risk, odds, prospect, liability, probability 3 *often plural* = potential, promise, prospects, talent, capabilities, potentiality

possible 1 = feasible, viable, workable, achievable, practicable, attainable, doable, realizable ≠ unfeasible 2 = likely, potential, anticipated, probable, odds-on, on the cards ≠ improbable 3 = conceivable, likely, credible, plausible, hypothetical, imaginable, believable, thinkable ≠ inconceivable 4 = aspiring, would-be, promising, hopeful, prospective, wannabe (*informal*)

possibly = perhaps, maybe, perchance (*archaic*)

post[1] NOUN 1 = mail, collection, delivery, postal service, snail mail (*informal*) 2 = correspondence, letters, cards, mail
• VERB = send (off), forward, mail, get off, transmit, dispatch, consign
• PHRASES **keep someone posted** = notify, brief, advise, inform, report to, keep someone informed, keep someone up to date, apprise

post[2] NOUN 1 = job, place, office, position, situation, employment, appointment, assignment 2 = position, place, base, beat, station
• VERB = station, assign, put, place, position, situate, put on duty

post[3] NOUN = support, stake, pole, column, shaft, upright, pillar, picket
• VERB = put something up, display, affix, pin something up

poster = notice, bill, announcement, advertisement, sticker, placard, public notice

postpone = put off, delay, suspend, adjourn, shelve, defer, put back, put on the back burner (*informal*) ≠ go ahead with

posture NOUN = bearing, set, attitude, stance, carriage, disposition
• VERB = show off (*informal*), pose, affect, put on airs

pot = container, bowl, pan, vessel, basin, cauldron, skillet

potent 1 = powerful, commanding, dynamic, dominant, influential, authoritative 2 = strong, powerful, mighty, vigorous, forceful ≠ weak

potential ADJECTIVE 1 = possible, future, likely, promising, probable 2 = hidden, possible, inherent, dormant, latent
• NOUN = ability, possibilities, capacity, capability, aptitude, wherewithal, potentiality

potter *usually with **around** or **about*** = mess about, tinker, dabble, footle (*informal*)

pottery = ceramics, terracotta, crockery, earthenware, stoneware

pounce = attack, strike, jump, leap, swoop

pound[1] = enclosure, yard, pen, compound, kennels

pound[2] 1 *sometimes with **on*** = beat, strike, hammer, batter, thrash, thump, clobber (*slang*), pummel 2 = crush, powder, pulverize 3 = pulsate, beat, pulse, throb, palpitate 4 = stomp, tramp, march, thunder (*informal*)

pour 1 = let flow, spill, splash, dribble, drizzle, slop (*informal*), slosh (*informal*), decant 2 = flow, stream, run, course, rush, emit, cascade, gush 3 = rain, pelt (down), teem, bucket down (*informal*) 4 = stream, crowd, flood, swarm, gush, throng, teem

pout VERB = sulk, glower, look petulant, pull a long face
• NOUN = sullen look, glower, long face

poverty 1 = pennilessness, want, need, hardship, insolvency, privation, penury, destitution ≠ wealth 2 = scarcity, lack, absence, want, deficit, shortage, deficiency, inadequacy ≠ abundance

powder NOUN = dust, talc, fine grains, loose particles
• VERB = dust, cover, scatter, sprinkle, strew, dredge

power 1 = control, authority, influence, command, dominance, domination, mastery, dominion, mana (*N.Z.*) 2 = ability, capacity, faculty, property, potential, capability, competence, competency ≠ inability 3 = authority, right, licence, privilege, warrant, prerogative, authorization 4 = strength, might, energy, muscle, vigour, potency, brawn ≠ weakness 5 = forcefulness, force, strength, punch (*informal*), intensity, potency, eloquence, persuasiveness

powerful 1 = influential, dominant,

controlling, commanding, prevailing, authoritative ≠ powerless **2** = strong, strapping, mighty, vigorous, potent, energetic, sturdy ≠ weak **3** = persuasive, convincing, telling, moving, striking, storming, dramatic, impressive

powerless **1** = defenceless, vulnerable, dependent, subject, tied, ineffective, unarmed **2** = weak, disabled, helpless, incapable, frail, feeble, debilitated, impotent ≠ strong

practical **1** = functional, realistic, pragmatic ≠ impractical **2** = empirical, real, applied, actual, hands-on, in the field, experimental, factual ≠ theoretical **3** = sensible, ordinary, realistic, down-to-earth, matter-of-fact, businesslike, hard-headed ≠ impractical **4** = feasible, possible, viable, workable, practicable, doable ≠ impractical **5** = useful, ordinary, appropriate, sensible, everyday, functional, utilitarian, serviceable **6** = skilled, experienced, efficient, accomplished, proficient ≠ inexperienced

practically **1** = almost, nearly, essentially, virtually, basically, fundamentally, all but, just about **2** = sensibly, reasonably, matter-of-factly, realistically, rationally, pragmatically

practice **1** = custom, way, system, rule, method, tradition, habit, routine, tikanga (*N.Z.*) **2** = training, study, exercise, preparation, drill, rehearsal, repetition **3** = profession, work, business, career, occupation, pursuit, vocation **4** = business, company, office, firm, enterprise, partnership, outfit (*informal*) **5** = use, experience, action, operation, application, enactment

practise **1** = rehearse, study, prepare, perfect, repeat, go through, go over, refine **2** = do, train, exercise, drill **3** = carry out, follow, apply, perform, observe, engage in **4** = work at, pursue, carry on

practised = skilled, trained, experienced, seasoned, able, expert, accomplished, proficient ≠ inexperienced

pragmatic = practical, sensible, realistic, down-to-earth, utilitarian, businesslike, hard-headed ≠ idealistic

praise VERB **1** = acclaim, approve of, honour, cheer, admire, applaud, compliment, congratulate ≠ criticize **2** = give thanks to, bless, worship, adore, glorify, exalt
• NOUN **1** = approval, acclaim, tribute, compliment, congratulations, eulogy, commendation, approbation ≠ criticism **2** = thanks, glory, worship, homage, adoration

pray **1** = say your prayers, offer a prayer, recite the rosary **2** = beg, ask, plead, petition, request, solicit, implore, beseech

prayer **1** = supplication, devotion **2** = orison, litany, invocation, intercession **3** = plea, appeal, request, petition, entreaty, supplication

preach **1** *often with* ***to*** = deliver a sermon, address, evangelize, preach a sermon **2** = urge, teach, champion, recommend, advise, counsel, advocate, exhort

preacher = clergyman, minister, parson, missionary, evangelist

precarious **1** = insecure, dangerous, tricky, risky, dodgy (*Brit., Austral., & N.Z. informal*), unsure, hazardous, shaky ≠ secure **2** = dangerous, shaky, insecure, unsafe, unreliable ≠ stable

precaution **1** = safeguard, insurance, protection, provision, safety measure **2** = forethought, care, caution, prudence, providence, wariness

precede **1** = go before, antedate **2** = go ahead of, lead, head, go before **3** = preface, introduce, go before

precedent = instance, example, standard, model, pattern, prototype, paradigm, antecedent

precinct = area, quarter, section, sector, district, zone

precious **1** = valuable, expensive, fine, prized, dear, costly, invaluable, priceless ≠ worthless **2** = loved, prized, dear, treasured, darling, beloved, adored, cherished **3** = affected, artificial, twee (*Brit. informal*), overrefined, overnice

precipitate VERB **1** = quicken, trigger, accelerate, advance, hurry, speed up, bring on, hasten **2** = throw, launch, cast, hurl, fling, let fly
• ADJECTIVE **1** = hasty, rash, reckless, impulsive, precipitous, impetuous, heedless **2** = sudden, quick, brief, rushing, rapid, unexpected, swift, abrupt

precise **1** = exact, specific, particular, express, correct, absolute, accurate, explicit ≠ vague **2** = strict, particular, exact, formal, careful, stiff, rigid, meticulous ≠ inexact

precisely 1 = exactly, squarely, correctly, absolutely, strictly, accurately, plumb (*informal*), square on 2 = just so, yes, absolutely, exactly, quite so, you bet (*informal*), without a doubt, indubitably 3 = just, entirely, absolutely, altogether, exactly, in all respects 4 = word for word, literally, exactly, to the letter

precision = exactness, care, accuracy, particularity, meticulousness, preciseness

predecessor 1 = previous job holder, precursor, forerunner, antecedent 2 = ancestor, forebear, antecedent, forefather, tupuna *or* tipuna (*N.Z.*)

predicament = fix (*informal*), situation, spot (*informal*), hole (*slang*), mess, jam (*informal*), dilemma, pinch

predict = foretell, forecast, divine, prophesy, augur, portend

predictable = likely, expected, sure, certain, anticipated, reliable, foreseeable ≠ unpredictable

prediction = prophecy, forecast, prognosis, divination, prognostication, augury

predominantly = mainly, largely, chiefly, mostly, generally, principally, primarily, for the most part

prefer 1 = like better, favour, go for, pick, fancy, opt for, incline towards, be partial to 2 = choose, opt for, pick, desire, would rather, would sooner, incline towards

preferable = better, best, chosen, preferred, recommended, favoured, superior, more suitable ≠ undesirable

preferably = ideally, if possible, rather, sooner, by choice, in *or* for preference

preference 1 = liking, wish, taste, desire, leaning, bent, bias, inclination 2 = first choice, choice, favourite, pick, option, selection 3 = priority, first place, precedence, favouritism, favoured treatment

pregnant 1 = expectant, expecting (*informal*), with child, in the club (*Brit. slang*), big *or* heavy with child 2 = meaningful, pointed, charged, significant, telling, loaded, expressive, eloquent

prejudice NOUN 1 = discrimination, injustice, intolerance, bigotry, unfairness, chauvinism, narrow-mindedness 2 = bias, preconception, partiality, preconceived notion, prejudgment

• VERB 1 = bias, influence, colour, poison, distort, slant, predispose 2 = harm, damage, hurt, injure, mar, undermine, spoil, impair, crool *or* cruel (*Austral. slang*)

prejudiced = biased, influenced, unfair, one-sided, bigoted, intolerant, opinionated, narrow-minded ≠ unbiased

preliminary ADJECTIVE 1 = first, opening, trial, initial, test, pilot, prior, introductory 2 = qualifying, eliminating

• NOUN = introduction, opening, beginning, start, prelude, preface, overture, preamble

prelude 1 = introduction, beginning, start 2 = overture, opening, introduction, introductory movement

premature 1 = early, untimely, before time, unseasonable 2 = hasty, rash, too soon, untimely, ill-timed, overhasty

premier NOUN = head of government, prime minister, chancellor, chief minister, P.M.

• ADJECTIVE = chief, leading, first, highest, head, main, prime, primary

premiere = first night, opening, debut

premise = assumption, proposition, argument, hypothesis, assertion, supposition, presupposition, postulation

premises = building(s), place, office, property, site, establishment

premium NOUN 1 = fee, charge, payment, instalment 2 = surcharge, extra charge, additional fee *or* charge 3 = bonus, reward, prize, perk (*Brit. informal*), bounty, perquisite

• PHRASES **at a premium** = in great demand, rare, scarce, in short supply, hard to come by

preoccupation 1 = obsession, fixation, bee in your bonnet 2 = absorption, abstraction, daydreaming, immersion, reverie, absent-mindedness, engrossment, woolgathering

preoccupied 1 = absorbed, lost, wrapped up, immersed, engrossed, rapt 2 = lost in thought, distracted, oblivious, absent-minded

preparation 1 = groundwork, preparing, getting ready 2 *usually plural* = arrangement, plan, measure, provision 3 = mixture, medicine, compound, concoction

prepare 1 = make *or* get ready, arrange, jack up (*N.Z. informal*) 2 = train, guide, prime, direct, brief, discipline, put someone in the picture 3 = make, cook, put together, get, produce, assemble, muster, concoct 4 = get ready 5 = practise, get ready, train, exercise, warm up, get into shape

prepared 1 = willing, inclined, disposed 2 = ready, set 3 = fit, primed, in order, arranged, in readiness

prescribe 1 = specify, order, direct, stipulate, write a prescription for 2 = ordain, set, order, rule, recommend, dictate, lay down, decree

prescription 1 = instruction, direction, formula, script (*informal*), recipe 2 = medicine, drug, treatment, preparation, cure, mixture, dose, remedy

presence NOUN 1 = being, existence, residence, attendance, showing up, occupancy, inhabitance 2 = personality, bearing, appearance, aspect, air, carriage, aura, poise
• PHRASES **presence of mind** = level-headedness, assurance, composure, poise, cool (*slang*), wits, countenance, coolness

present[1] ADJECTIVE 1 = current, existing, immediate, contemporary, present-day, existent 2 = here, there, near, ready, nearby, at hand ≠ absent 3 = in existence, existing, existent, extant
• PHRASES **the present** = now, today, the time being, here and now, the present moment

present[2] NOUN = gift, offering, grant, donation, hand-out, endowment, boon, gratuity, bonsela (*S. African*), koha (*N.Z.*)
• VERB 1 = give, award, hand over, grant, hand out, confer, bestow 2 = put on, stage, perform, give, show, render 3 = launch, display, parade, exhibit, unveil 4 = introduce, make known, acquaint someone with

presentation 1 = giving, award, offering, donation, bestowal, conferral 2 = appearance, look, display, packaging, arrangement, layout 3 = performance, production, show

presently 1 = at present, currently, now, today, these days, nowadays, at the present time, in this day and age 2 = soon, shortly, directly, before long, momentarily (*U.S. & Canad.*), by and by, in a jiffy (*informal*)

preservation 1 = upholding, support, maintenance 2 = protection, safety, maintenance, conservation, salvation, safeguarding, safekeeping

preserve VERB 1 = maintain, keep, continue, sustain, keep up, prolong, uphold, conserve ≠ end 2 = protect, keep, save, maintain, defend, shelter, shield, care for ≠ attack
• NOUN = area, department, field, territory, province, arena, sphere

preside = officiate, chair, moderate, be chairperson

press 1 = push (down), depress, lean on, press down, force down 2 = push, squeeze, jam, thrust, ram, wedge, shove 3 = hug, squeeze, embrace, clasp, crush, hold close, fold in your arms 4 = urge, beg, petition, exhort, implore, pressurize, entreat 5 = plead, present, lodge, submit, tender, advance insistently 6 = steam, iron, smooth, flatten 7 = compress, grind, reduce, mill, crush, pound, squeeze, tread 8 = crowd, push, gather, surge, flock, herd, swarm, seethe

pressing = urgent, serious, vital, crucial, imperative, important, high-priority, importunate ≠ unimportant

pressure 1 = force, crushing, squeezing, compressing, weight, compression 2 = power, influence, force, constraint, sway, compulsion, coercion 3 = stress, demands, strain, heat, load, burden, urgency, hassle (*informal*), uphill (*S. African*)

prestige = status, standing, credit, reputation, honour, importance, fame, distinction, mana (*N.Z.*)

prestigious = celebrated, respected, prominent, great, important, esteemed, notable, renowned ≠ unknown

presumably = it would seem, probably, apparently, seemingly, on the face of it, in all probability, in all likelihood

presume 1 = believe, think, suppose, assume, guess (*informal, chiefly U.S. & Canad.*), take for granted, infer, conjecture 2 = dare, venture, go so far as, take the liberty, make so bold as

pretend 1 = feign, affect, assume, allege, fake, simulate, profess, sham 2 = make believe, suppose, imagine, act, make up

pretty ADJECTIVE = attractive, beautiful,

lovely, charming, fair, good-looking, bonny, comely ≠ plain
• ADVERB (*Informal*) = fairly, rather, quite, kind of (*informal*), somewhat, moderately, reasonably

prevail 1 = win, succeed, triumph, overcome, overrule, be victorious 2 = be widespread, abound, predominate, be current, be prevalent, exist generally

prevailing 1 = widespread, general, established, popular, common, current, usual, ordinary 2 = predominating, ruling, main, existing, principal

prevalent = common, established, popular, general, current, usual, widespread, universal ≠ rare

prevent = stop, avoid, frustrate, hamper, foil, inhibit, avert, thwart ≠ help

prevention = elimination, safeguard, precaution, thwarting, avoidance, deterrence

preview = sample, sneak preview, trailer, taster, foretaste, advance showing

previous 1 = earlier, former, past, prior, preceding, erstwhile ≠ later 2 = preceding, past, prior, foregoing

previously = before, earlier, once, in the past, formerly, hitherto, beforehand

prey 1 = quarry, game, kill 2 = victim, target, mug (*Brit. slang*), dupe, fall guy (*informal*)

price NOUN 1 = cost, value, rate, charge, figure, worth, damage (*informal*), amount 2 = consequences, penalty, cost, result, toll, forfeit
• VERB = evaluate, value, estimate, rate, cost, assess

priceless = valuable, expensive, precious, invaluable, dear, costly ≠ worthless

prick VERB = pierce, stab, puncture, punch, lance, jab, perforate
• NOUN = puncture, hole, wound, perforation, pinhole

prickly 1 = spiny, barbed, thorny, bristly 2 = itchy, sharp, smarting, stinging, crawling, tingling, scratchy

pride 1 = satisfaction, achievement, fulfilment, delight, content, pleasure, joy, gratification 2 = self-respect, honour, ego, dignity, self-esteem, self-image, self-worth 3 = conceit, vanity, arrogance, pretension, hubris, self-importance, egotism, self-love ≠ humility

priest = clergyman, minister, father, divine, vicar, pastor, cleric, curate

primarily 1 = chiefly, largely, generally, mainly, essentially, mostly, principally, fundamentally 2 = at first, originally, initially, in the first place, in the beginning, first and foremost, at *or* from the start

primary = chief, main, first, highest, greatest, prime, principal, cardinal ≠ subordinate

prime ADJECTIVE 1 = main, leading, chief, central, major, key, primary, supreme 2 = best, top, select, highest, quality, choice, excellent, first-class
• NOUN = peak, flower, bloom, height, heyday, zenith
• VERB 1 = inform, tell, train, coach, brief, fill in (*informal*), notify, clue in (*informal*) 2 = prepare, set up, load, equip, get ready, make ready

primitive 1 = early, first, earliest, original, primary, elementary, primordial, primeval ≠ modern 2 = crude, simple, rough, rudimentary, unrefined ≠ elaborate

prince = ruler, lord, monarch, sovereign, crown prince, liege, prince regent, crowned head

princely 1 = substantial, considerable, large, huge, massive, enormous, sizable *or* sizeable 2 = regal, royal, imperial, noble, sovereign, majestic

princess = ruler, lady, monarch, sovereign, liege, crowned head, crowned princess, dynast

principal ADJECTIVE = main, leading, chief, prime, first, key, essential, primary ≠ minor
• NOUN 1 = headmaster *or* headmistress, head (*informal*), dean, head teacher, rector, master *or* mistress 2 = star, lead, leader, prima ballerina, leading man *or* lady, coryphée 3 = capital, money, assets, working capital

principally = mainly, largely, chiefly, especially, mostly, primarily, above all, predominantly

principle NOUN 1 = morals, standards, ideals, honour, virtue, ethics, integrity, conscience, kaupapa (*N.Z.*) 2 = rule, law, truth, precept
• PHRASES **in principle** 1 = in general 2 = in theory, ideally, on paper, theoretically, in an ideal world, en principe (*French*)

print VERB 1 = run off, publish, copy, reproduce, issue, engrave 2 = publish,

release, circulate, issue, disseminate **3** = mark, impress, stamp, imprint
● NOUN **1** = photograph, photo, snap **2** = picture, plate, etching, engraving, lithograph, woodcut, linocut **3** = copy, photo (*informal*), picture, reproduction, replica

prior ADJECTIVE = earlier, previous, former, preceding, foregoing, pre-existing, pre-existent
● PHRASES **prior to** = before, preceding, earlier than, in advance of, previous to

priority 1 = prime concern **2** = precedence, preference, primacy, predominance **3** = supremacy, rank, precedence, seniority, right of way, pre-eminence

prison = jail, confinement, nick (*Brit. slang*), cooler (*slang*), jug (*slang*), dungeon, clink (*slang*), gaol, boob (*Austral. slang*)

prisoner 1 = convict, con (*slang*), lag (*slang*), jailbird **2** = captive, hostage, detainee, internee

privacy = seclusion, isolation, solitude, retirement, retreat

private 1 = exclusive, individual, privately owned, own, special, reserved ≠ public **2** = secret, confidential, covert, unofficial, clandestine, off the record, hush-hush (*informal*) ≠ public **3** = personal, individual, secret, intimate, undisclosed, unspoken, innermost, unvoiced **4** = secluded, secret, separate, isolated, sequestered ≠ busy **5** = solitary, reserved, retiring, withdrawn, discreet, secretive, self-contained, reclusive ≠ sociable

privilege = right, due, advantage, claim, freedom, liberty, concession, entitlement

privileged = special, advantaged, favoured, honoured, entitled, elite

prize[1] NOUN **1** = reward, cup, award, honour, medal, trophy, accolade **2** = winnings, haul, jackpot, stakes, purse
● ADJECTIVE = champion, best, winning, top, outstanding, award-winning, first-rate

prize[2] = value, treasure, esteem, cherish, hold dear

prize[3] *or* **prise 1** = force, pull, lever **2** = drag, force, draw, wring, extort

probability 1 = likelihood, prospect, chance, odds, expectation, liability, likeliness **2** = chance, odds, possibility, likelihood

probable = likely, possible, apparent, reasonable to think, credible, plausible, feasible, presumable ≠ unlikely

probably = likely, perhaps, maybe, possibly, presumably, most likely, doubtless, perchance (*archaic*)

probation = trial period, trial, apprenticeship

probe VERB **1** *often with* ***into*** = examine, go into, investigate, explore, search, look into, analyze, dissect **2** = explore, examine, poke, prod, feel around
● NOUN = investigation, study, inquiry, analysis, examination, exploration, scrutiny, scrutinization

problem 1 = difficulty, trouble, dispute, plight, obstacle, dilemma, headache (*informal*), complication **2** = puzzle, question, riddle, enigma, conundrum, poser

problematic = tricky, puzzling, doubtful, dubious, debatable, problematical ≠ clear

procedure = method, policy, process, course, system, action, practice, strategy

proceed 1 = begin, go ahead **2** = continue, go on, progress, carry on, go ahead, press on ≠ discontinue **3** = go on, continue, progress, carry on, go ahead, move on, move forward, press on ≠ stop **4** = arise, come, issue, result, spring, flow, stem, derive

proceeding = action, process, procedure, move, act, step, measure, deed

proceeds = income, profit, revenue, returns, products, gain, earnings, yield

process NOUN **1** = procedure, means, course, system, action, performance, operation, measure **2** = development, growth, progress, movement, advance, evolution, progression **3** = method, system, practice, technique, procedure
● VERB = handle, manage, action, deal with, fulfil

procession = parade, train, march, file, cavalcade, cortege

proclaim 1 = announce, declare, advertise, publish, indicate, herald, circulate, profess ≠ keep secret **2** = pronounce, announce, declare

prod VERB **1** = poke, push, dig, shove, nudge, jab **2** = prompt, move, urge, motivate, spur, stimulate, rouse, incite
● NOUN **1** = poke, push, dig, shove, nudge, jab **2** = prompt, signal, cue, reminder, stimulus

prodigy = genius, talent, wizard, mastermind, whizz (*informal*)

produce VERB **1** = cause, effect, generate, bring about, give rise to **2** = make, create, develop, manufacture, construct, invent, fabricate **3** = create, develop, write, turn out, compose, originate, churn out (*informal*) **4** = yield, provide, grow, bear, give, supply, afford, render **5** = bring forth, bear, deliver, breed, give birth to, beget, bring into the world **6** = show, provide, present, advance, demonstrate, offer, come up with, exhibit **7** = display, show, present, proffer **8** = present, stage, direct, put on, do, show, mount, exhibit
• NOUN = fruit and vegetables, goods, food, products, crops, yield, harvest, greengrocery (*Brit.*)

producer **1** = director, promoter, impresario **2** = maker, manufacturer, builder, creator, fabricator **3** = grower, farmer

product **1** = goods, produce, creation, commodity, invention, merchandise, artefact **2** = result, consequence, effect, outcome, upshot

production **1** = producing, making, manufacture, manufacturing, construction, formation, fabrication **2** = creation, development, fashioning, composition, origination **3** = management, administration, direction **4** = presentation, staging, mounting

productive **1** = fertile, rich, prolific, plentiful, fruitful, fecund ≠ barren **2** = creative, inventive **3** = useful, rewarding, valuable, profitable, effective, worthwhile, beneficial, constructive ≠ useless

productivity = output, production, capacity, yield, efficiency, work rate

profess **1** = claim, allege, pretend, fake, make out, purport, feign **2** = state, admit, announce, declare, confess, assert, proclaim, affirm

professed **1** = supposed, would-be, alleged, so-called, pretended, purported, self-styled, ostensible **2** = declared, confirmed, confessed, proclaimed, self-confessed, avowed, self-acknowledged

profession = occupation, calling, business, career, employment, office, position, sphere

professional ADJECTIVE **1** = qualified, trained, skilled, white-collar **2** = expert, experienced, skilled, masterly, efficient, competent, adept, proficient ≠ amateurish
• NOUN = expert, master, pro (*informal*), specialist, guru, adept, maestro, virtuoso, fundi (*S. African*)

professor = don (*Brit.*), fellow (*Brit.*), prof (*informal*)

profile **1** = outline, lines, form, figure, silhouette, contour, side view **2** = biography, sketch, vignette, characterization, thumbnail sketch

profit NOUN **1** *often plural* = earnings, return, revenue, gain, yield, proceeds, receipts, takings ≠ loss **2** = benefit, good, use, value, gain, advantage, advancement ≠ disadvantage
• VERB **1** = make money, gain, earn **2** = benefit, help, serve, gain, promote, be of advantage to

profitable **1** = money-making, lucrative, paying, commercial, worthwhile, cost-effective, fruitful, remunerative **2** = beneficial, useful, rewarding, valuable, productive, worthwhile, fruitful, advantageous ≠ useless

profound **1** = sincere, acute, intense, great, keen, extreme, heartfelt, deeply felt ≠ insincere **2** = wise, learned, deep, penetrating, philosophical, sage, abstruse, sagacious ≠ uninformed

programme **1** = schedule, plan, agenda, timetable, listing, list, line-up, calendar **2** = course, curriculum, syllabus **3** = show, performance, production, broadcast, episode, presentation, transmission, telecast

progress NOUN **1** = development, growth, advance, gain, improvement, breakthrough, headway ≠ regression **2** = movement forward, passage, advancement, course, advance, headway ≠ movement backward
• VERB **1** = move on, continue, travel, advance, proceed, go forward, make headway ≠ move back **2** = develop, improve, advance, grow, gain ≠ get behind
• PHRASES **in progress** = going on, happening, continuing, being done, occurring, taking place, proceeding, under way

progression **1** = progress, advance,

advancement, gain, headway, furtherance, movement forward **2** = sequence, course, series, chain, cycle, string, succession

progressive **1** = enlightened, liberal, modern, advanced, radical, revolutionary, avant-garde, reformist **2** = growing, continuing, increasing, developing, advancing, ongoing

prohibit **1** = forbid, ban, veto, outlaw, disallow, proscribe, debar ≠ permit **2** = prevent, restrict, stop, hamper, hinder, impede ≠ allow

prohibition = ban, boycott, embargo, bar, veto, prevention, exclusion, injunction

project **NOUN** **1** = scheme, plan, job, idea, campaign, operation, activity, venture **2** = assignment, task, homework, piece of research

• **VERB** **1** = forecast, expect, estimate, predict, reckon, calculate, gauge, extrapolate **2** = stick out, extend, stand out, bulge, protrude, overhang, jut

projection = forecast, estimate, reckoning, calculation, estimation, computation, extrapolation

proliferation = multiplication, increase, spread, expansion

prolific **1** = productive, creative, fertile, inventive, copious **2** = fruitful, fertile, abundant, luxuriant, profuse, fecund ≠ unproductive

prolong = lengthen, continue, perpetuate, draw out, extend, delay, stretch out, spin out ≠ shorten

prominence **1** = fame, name, reputation, importance, celebrity, distinction, prestige, eminence **2** = conspicuousness, markedness

prominent **1** = famous, leading, top, important, main, distinguished, well-known, notable ≠ unknown **2** = noticeable, obvious, outstanding, pronounced, conspicuous, eye-catching, obtrusive ≠ inconspicuous

promise **VERB** **1** = guarantee, pledge, vow, swear, contract, assure, undertake, warrant **2** = seem likely, look like, show signs of, augur, betoken

• **NOUN** **1** = guarantee, word, bond, vow, commitment, pledge, undertaking, assurance **2** = potential, ability, talent, capacity, capability, aptitude

promising **1** = encouraging, likely, bright, reassuring, hopeful, favourable, rosy, auspicious ≠ unpromising **2** = talented, able, gifted, rising

promote **1** = help, back, support, aid, forward, encourage, advance, boost ≠ impede **2** = advertise, sell, hype, publicize, push, plug (*informal*) **3** = raise, upgrade, elevate, exalt ≠ demote

promotion **1** = rise, upgrading, move up, advancement, elevation, exaltation, preferment **2** = publicity, advertising, plugging (*informal*) **3** = encouragement, support, boosting, advancement, furtherance

prompt **VERB** **1** = cause, occasion, provoke, give rise to, elicit **2** = remind, assist, cue, help out

• **ADJECTIVE** = immediate, quick, rapid, instant, timely, early, swift, speedy ≠ slow

• **ADVERB** (*Informal*) = exactly, sharp, promptly, on the dot, punctually

promptly **1** = immediately, swiftly, directly, quickly, at once, speedily **2** = punctually, on time, spot on (*informal*), bang on (*informal*), on the dot, on the button (*U.S.*), on the nail

prone **1** = liable, given, subject, inclined, tending, bent, disposed, susceptible ≠ disinclined **2** = face down, flat, horizontal, prostrate, recumbent ≠ face up

pronounce **1** = say, speak, sound, articulate, enunciate **2** = declare, announce, deliver, proclaim, decree, affirm

pronounced = noticeable, decided, marked, striking, obvious, evident, distinct, definite ≠ imperceptible

proof **NOUN** = evidence, demonstration, testimony, confirmation, verification, corroboration, authentication, substantiation

• **ADJECTIVE** = impervious, strong, resistant, impenetrable, repellent

prop **VERB** **1** = lean, place, set, stand, position, rest, lay, balance **2** *often with* ***up*** = support, sustain, hold up, brace, uphold, bolster, buttress

• **NOUN** **1** = support, stay, brace, mainstay, buttress, stanchion **2** = mainstay, support, sustainer, anchor, backbone, cornerstone, upholder

propaganda = information, advertising, promotion, publicity, hype, disinformation

propel **1** = drive, launch, force, send, shoot, push, thrust, shove ≠ stop **2** = impel, drive, push, prompt, spur, motivate ≠ hold back

proper 1 = real, actual, genuine, true, bona fide, dinkum (*Austral. & N.Z. informal*) 2 = correct, accepted, established, appropriate, right, formal, conventional, precise ≠ improper 3 = polite, right, becoming, seemly, fitting, fit, mannerly, suitable ≠ unseemly

properly 1 = correctly, rightly, fittingly, appropriately, accurately, suitably, aptly ≠ incorrectly 2 = politely, decently, respectably ≠ badly

property 1 = possessions, goods, effects, holdings, capital, riches, estate, assets 2 = land, holding, estate, real estate, freehold 3 = quality, feature, characteristic, attribute, trait, hallmark

prophecy 1 = prediction, forecast, prognostication, augury 2 = second sight, divination, augury, telling the future, soothsaying

prophet *or* **prophetess** = soothsayer, forecaster, diviner, oracle, seer, sibyl, prophesier

proportion NOUN 1 = part, share, amount, division, percentage, segment, quota, fraction 2 = relative amount, relationship, ratio 3 = balance, harmony, correspondence, symmetry, concord, congruity

• PLURAL NOUN = dimensions, size, volume, capacity, extent, expanse

proportional *or* **proportionate** = correspondent, corresponding, even, balanced, consistent, compatible, equitable, in proportion ≠ disproportionate

proposal = suggestion, plan, programme, scheme, offer, project, bid, recommendation

propose 1 = put forward, present, suggest, advance, submit 2 = intend, mean, plan, aim, design, scheme, have in mind 3 = nominate, name, present, recommend 4 = offer marriage, pop the question (*informal*), ask for someone's hand (in marriage)

proposition NOUN 1 = task, problem, activity, job, affair, venture, undertaking 2 = theory, idea, argument, concept, thesis, hypothesis, theorem, premiss 3 = proposal, plan, suggestion, scheme, bid, recommendation 4 = advance, pass (*informal*), proposal, overture, improper suggestion, come-on (*informal*)

• VERB = make a pass at, solicit, accost, make an improper suggestion to

proprietor *or* **proprietress** = owner, titleholder, landlord *or* landlady

prosecute (*Law*) = take someone to court, try, sue, indict, arraign, put someone on trial, litigate, bring someone to trial

prospect NOUN 1 = likelihood, chance, possibility, hope, promise, odds, expectation, probability 2 = idea, outlook 3 = view, landscape, scene, sight, outlook, spectacle, vista

• PLURAL NOUN = possibilities, chances, future, potential, expectations, outlook, scope

• VERB = look, search, seek, dowse

prospective 1 = potential, possible 2 = expected, coming, future, likely, intended, anticipated, forthcoming, imminent

prospectus = catalogue, list, programme, outline, syllabus, synopsis

prosper = succeed, advance, progress, thrive, get on, do well, flourish

prosperity = success, riches, plenty, fortune, wealth, luxury, good fortune, affluence ≠ poverty

prosperous 1 = wealthy, rich, affluent, well-off, well-heeled (*informal*), well-to-do, moneyed ≠ poor 2 = successful, booming, thriving, flourishing, doing well ≠ unsuccessful

prostitute NOUN = whore, hooker (*U.S. slang*), pro (*slang*), tart (*informal*), call girl, harlot, streetwalker, loose woman

• VERB = cheapen, sell out, pervert, degrade, devalue, squander, demean, debase

protagonist 1 = supporter, champion, advocate, exponent 2 = leading character, principal, central character, hero *or* heroine

protect = keep someone safe, defend, support, save, guard, preserve, look after, shelter ≠ endanger

protection 1 = safety, care, defence, protecting, security, custody, safeguard, aegis 2 = safeguard, cover, guard, shelter, screen, barrier, shield, buffer 3 = armour, cover, screen, barrier, shelter, shield

protective 1 = protecting 2 = caring, defensive, motherly, fatherly, maternal, vigilant, watchful, paternal

protector 1 = defender, champion, guard,

guardian, patron, bodyguard **2** = guard, screen, protection, shield, pad, cushion, buffer

protest VERB **1** = object, demonstrate, oppose, complain, disagree, cry out, disapprove, demur **2** = assert, insist, maintain, declare, affirm, profess, attest, avow
• NOUN **1** = demonstration, march, rally, sit-in, demo (*informal*), hikoi (*N.Z.*)
2 = objection, complaint, dissent, outcry, protestation, remonstrance

protocol = code of behaviour, manners, conventions, customs, etiquette, propriety, decorum

prototype = original, model, first, example, standard

protracted = extended, prolonged, drawn-out, spun out, dragged out, long-drawn-out

proud 1 = satisfied, pleased, content, thrilled, glad, gratified, joyful, well-pleased ≠ dissatisfied **2** = conceited, arrogant, lordly, imperious, overbearing, haughty, snobbish, self-satisfied ≠ humble

prove 1 = turn out, come out, end up **2** = verify, establish, determine, show, confirm, demonstrate, justify, substantiate ≠ disprove

proven = established, proved, confirmed, tested, reliable, definite, verified, attested

provide VERB **1** = supply, give, distribute, outfit, equip, donate, furnish, dispense ≠ withhold **2** = give, bring, add, produce, present, serve, afford, yield
• PHRASES **provide for someone** = support, care for, keep, maintain, sustain, take care of, fend for ◆ **provide for something** = take precautions against, plan for, prepare for, anticipate, plan ahead for, forearm for

provided *often with* ***that*** = if, given, on condition, as long as

provider 1 = supplier, giver, source, donor **2** = breadwinner, supporter, earner, wage earner

providing *often with* ***that*** = on condition that, given that, as long as

province 1 = region, section, district, zone, patch, colony, domain **2** = area, business, concern, responsibility, line, role, department, field

provincial ADJECTIVE **1** = regional, state, local, county, district, territorial, parochial **2** = rural, country, local, rustic, homespun, hick (*informal, chiefly U.S. & Canad.*), backwoods ≠ urban **3** = parochial, insular, narrow-minded, unsophisticated, limited, narrow, small-town (*chiefly U.S.*), inward-looking ≠ cosmopolitan

provision NOUN **1** = supplying, giving, providing, supply, delivery, distribution, catering, presentation **2** = condition, term, requirement, demand, rider, restriction, qualification, clause
• PLURAL NOUN = food, supplies, stores, fare, rations, foodstuff, kai (*N.Z. informal*), victuals, edibles

provisional 1 = temporary, interim ≠ permanent **2** = conditional, limited, qualified, contingent, tentative ≠ definite

provocation 1 = cause, reason, grounds, motivation, stimulus, incitement **2** = offence, challenge, insult, taunt, injury, dare, grievance, annoyance

provocative = offensive, provoking, insulting, stimulating, annoying, galling, goading

provoke 1 = anger, annoy, irritate, infuriate, hassle (*informal*), aggravate (*informal*), incense, enrage ≠ pacify **2** = rouse, cause, produce, promote, occasion, prompt, stir, induce ≠ curb

prowess 1 = skill, ability, talent, expertise, genius, excellence, accomplishment, mastery ≠ inability **2** = bravery, daring, courage, heroism, mettle, valour, fearlessness, valiance ≠ cowardice

proximity = nearness, closeness

proxy = representative, agent, deputy, substitute, factor, delegate

prudent 1 = cautious, careful, wary, discreet, vigilant ≠ careless **2** = wise, politic, sensible, shrewd, discerning, judicious ≠ unwise **3** = thrifty, economical, sparing, careful, canny, provident, frugal, far-sighted ≠ extravagant

prune 1 = cut, trim, clip, dock, shape, shorten, snip **2** = reduce, cut, cut back, trim, cut down, pare down, make reductions in

psyche = soul, mind, self, spirit, personality, individuality, anima, wairua (*N.Z.*)

psychiatrist = psychotherapist, analyst, therapist, psychologist, shrink (*slang*), psychoanalyst, headshrinker (*slang*)

psychic ADJECTIVE **1** = supernatural,

mystic, occult **2** = mystical, spiritual, magical, other-worldly, paranormal, preternatural **3** = psychological, emotional, mental, spiritual, inner, psychiatric, cognitive
• NOUN = clairvoyant, fortune teller

psychological **1** = mental, emotional, intellectual, inner, cognitive, cerebral **2** = imaginary, psychosomatic, irrational, unreal, all in the mind

psychology **1** = behaviourism, study of personality, science of mind **2** (*Informal*) = way of thinking, attitude, behaviour, temperament, mentality, thought processes, mental processes, what makes you tick

pub *or* **public house** = tavern, bar, inn, saloon

public NOUN = people, society, community, nation, everyone, citizens, electorate, populace
• ADJECTIVE **1** = civic, government, state, national, local, official, community, social **2** = general, popular, national, shared, common, widespread, universal, collective **3** = open, accessible, communal, unrestricted ≠ private **4** = well-known, leading, important, respected, famous, celebrated, recognized, distinguished **5** = known, open, obvious, acknowledged, plain, patent, overt ≠ secret

publication **1** = pamphlet, newspaper, magazine, issue, title, leaflet, brochure, periodical **2** = announcement, publishing, broadcasting, reporting, declaration, disclosure, proclamation, notification

publicity **1** = advertising, press, promotion, hype, boost, plug (*informal*) **2** = attention, exposure, fame, celebrity, fuss, public interest, limelight, notoriety

publish **1** = put out, issue, produce, print **2** = announce, reveal, spread, advertise, broadcast, disclose, proclaim, circulate

pudding = dessert, afters (*Brit. informal*), sweet, pud (*informal*)

puff VERB **1** = smoke, draw, drag (*slang*), suck, inhale, pull at *or* on **2** = breathe heavily, pant, exhale, blow, gasp, gulp, wheeze, fight for breath
• NOUN **1** = drag, pull (*slang*), moke **2** = blast, breath, whiff, draught, gust

pull VERB **1** = draw, haul, drag, trail, tow, tug, jerk, yank ≠ push **2** = extract, pick, remove, gather, take out, pluck, uproot, draw out ≠ insert **3** (*Informal*) = attract, draw, bring in, tempt, lure, interest, entice, pull in ≠ repel **4** = strain, tear, stretch, rip, wrench, dislocate, sprain
• NOUN **1** = tug, jerk, yank, twitch, heave ≠ shove **2** = puff, drag (*slang*), inhalation **3** (*Informal*) = influence, power, weight, muscle, clout (*informal*), kai (*N.Z. informal*)
• PHRASES **pull out (of)** **1** = withdraw, quit **2** = leave, abandon, get out, quit, retreat from, depart, evacuate ♦ **pull someone up** = reprimand, rebuke, admonish, read the riot act to, tell someone off (*informal*), reprove, bawl someone out (*informal*), tear someone off a strip (*Brit. informal*) ♦ **pull something off** (*Informal*) = succeed in, manage, carry out, accomplish ♦ **pull something out** = produce, draw, bring out, draw out ♦ **pull up** = stop, halt, brake

pulp NOUN **1** = paste, mash, mush **2** = flesh, meat, soft part
• ADJECTIVE = cheap, lurid, trashy, rubbishy
• VERB = crush, squash, mash, pulverize

pulse NOUN = beat, rhythm, vibration, beating, throb, throbbing, pulsation
• VERB = beat, throb, vibrate, pulsate

pump **1** = supply, send, pour, inject **2** = interrogate, probe, quiz, cross-examine

punch[1] VERB = hit, strike, box, smash, belt (*informal*), sock (*slang*), swipe (*informal*), bop (*informal*)
• NOUN **1** = blow, hit, sock (*slang*), jab, swipe (*informal*), bop (*informal*), wallop (*informal*) **2** (*Informal*) = effectiveness, bite, impact, drive, vigour, verve, forcefulness

punch[2] = pierce, cut, bore, drill, stamp, puncture, prick, perforate

punctuate = interrupt, break, pepper, sprinkle, intersperse

puncture NOUN **1** = flat tyre, flat, flattie (*N.Z.*) **2** = hole, opening, break, cut, nick, leak, slit
• VERB = pierce, cut, nick, penetrate, prick, rupture, perforate, bore a hole

punish = discipline, correct, castigate, chastise, sentence, chasten, penalize

punishing = hard, taxing, wearing, tiring, exhausting, gruelling, strenuous, arduous ≠ easy

punishment **1** = penalizing, discipline, correction, retribution, chastening,

chastisement **2** = penalty, penance
punitive = retaliatory, in reprisal, retaliative
punt VERB = bet, back, stake, gamble, lay, wager
• NOUN = bet, stake, gamble, wager
punter **1** = gambler, better, backer **2** (*Informal*) = person, man in the street
pupil **1** = student, schoolboy *or* schoolgirl, schoolchild ≠ teacher **2** = learner, novice, beginner, disciple ≠ instructor
puppet **1** = marionette, doll, glove puppet, finger puppet **2** = pawn, tool, instrument, mouthpiece, stooge, cat's-paw
purchase VERB = buy, pay for, obtain, get, score (*slang*), gain, pick up, acquire ≠ sell
• NOUN **1** = acquisition, buy, investment, property, gain, asset, possession **2** = grip, hold, support, leverage, foothold
pure **1** = unmixed, real, simple, natural, straight, genuine, neat, authentic ≠ adulterated **2** = clean, wholesome, sanitary, spotless, sterilized, squeaky-clean, untainted, uncontaminated ≠ contaminated **3** = complete, total, perfect, absolute, sheer, patent, utter, outright ≠ qualified **4** = innocent, modest, good, moral, impeccable, righteous, virtuous, squeaky-clean ≠ corrupt
purely = absolutely, just, only, completely, simply, entirely, exclusively, merely
purge VERB **1** = rid, clear, cleanse, strip, empty, void **2** = get rid of, remove, expel, wipe out, eradicate, do away with, exterminate
• NOUN = removal, elimination, expulsion, eradication, ejection
purity **1** = cleanness, cleanliness, wholesomeness, pureness, faultlessness, immaculateness ≠ impurity **2** = innocence, virtue, integrity, honesty, decency, virginity, chastity, chasteness ≠ immorality
purport = claim, allege, assert, profess
purpose NOUN **1** = reason, point, idea, aim, object, intention **2** = aim, end, plan, hope, goal, wish, desire, object **3** = determination, resolve, will, resolution, ambition, persistence, tenacity, firmness
• PHRASES **on purpose** = deliberately, purposely, intentionally, knowingly, designedly
purposely = deliberately, expressly, consciously, intentionally, knowingly, with intent, on purpose ≠ accidentally
purse NOUN **1** = pouch, wallet, money-bag **2** (*U.S.*) = handbag, bag, shoulder bag, pocket book, clutch bag **3** = funds, means, money, resources, treasury, wealth, exchequer
• VERB = pucker, contract, tighten, pout, press together
pursue **1** = engage in, perform, conduct, carry on, practise **2** = try for, seek, desire, search for, aim for, work towards, strive for **3** = continue, maintain, carry on, keep on, persist in, proceed in, persevere in **4** = follow, track, hunt, chase, dog, shadow, tail (*informal*), hound ≠ flee
pursuit **1** = quest, seeking, search, aim of, aspiration for, striving towards **2** = pursuing, seeking, search, hunt, chase, trailing **3** = occupation, activity, interest, line, pleasure, hobby, pastime
push VERB **1** = shove, force, press, thrust, drive, knock, sweep, plunge ≠ pull **2** = press, operate, depress, squeeze, activate, hold down **3** = make *or* force your way, move, shoulder, inch, squeeze, thrust, elbow, shove **4** = urge, encourage, persuade, spur, press, incite, impel ≠ discourage
• NOUN **1** = shove, thrust, butt, elbow, nudge ≠ pull **2** (*Informal*) = drive, go (*informal*), energy, initiative, enterprise, ambition, vitality, vigour
• PHRASES **the push** (*Informal, chiefly Brit.*) = dismissal, the sack (*informal*), discharge, the boot (*slang*), your cards (*informal*)
put VERB **1** = place, leave, set, position, rest, park (*informal*), plant, lay **2** = express, state, word, phrase, utter
• PHRASES **put someone off** **1** = discourage, intimidate, deter, daunt, dissuade, demoralize, scare off, dishearten **2** = disconcert, confuse, unsettle, throw (*informal*), dismay, perturb, faze, discomfit ◆ **put someone up** **1** = accommodate, house, board, lodge, quarter, take someone in, billet **2** = nominate, put forward, offer, present, propose, recommend, submit ◆ **put something across** *or* **over** = communicate, explain, convey, make clear, get across, make yourself understood ◆ **put something off** = postpone, delay, defer, adjourn, hold over, put on the back burner (*informal*),

take a rain check on (*U.S. & Canad. informal*) ◆ **put something up** 1 = build, raise, set up, construct, erect, fabricate 2 = offer, present, mount, put forward

puzzle VERB = perplex, confuse, baffle, stump, bewilder, confound, mystify, faze • NOUN 1 = problem, riddle, question, conundrum, poser 2 = mystery, problem, paradox, enigma, conundrum

puzzling = perplexing, baffling, bewildering, involved, enigmatic, incomprehensible, mystifying, abstruse ≠ simple

q

quake = shake, tremble, quiver, move, rock, shiver, shudder, vibrate

qualification 1 = eligibility, quality, ability, skill, fitness, attribute, capability, aptitude 2 = condition, proviso, requirement, rider, reservation, limitation, modification, caveat

qualified 1 = capable, trained, experienced, seasoned, able, fit, expert, chartered ≠ untrained 2 = restricted, limited, provisional, conditional, reserved, bounded, adjusted, moderated ≠ unconditional

qualify 1 = certify, equip, empower, train, prepare, fit, ready, permit ≠ disqualify 2 = restrict, limit, reduce, ease, moderate, regulate, diminish, temper

quality 1 = standard, standing, class, condition, rank, grade, merit, classification 2 = excellence, status, merit, position, value, worth, distinction, virtue 3 = characteristic, feature, attribute, point, side, mark, property, aspect 4 = nature, character, make, sort, kind

quantity 1 = amount, lot, total, sum, part, number 2 = size, measure, mass, volume, length, capacity, extent, bulk

quarrel NOUN = disagreement, fight, row, argument, dispute, controversy, breach, contention, biffo (*Austral. slang*) ≠ accord • VERB = disagree, fight, argue, row, clash, dispute, differ, fall out (*informal*) ≠ get on *or* along (with)

quarry = prey, victim, game, goal, aim, prize, objective

quarter NOUN 1 = district, region, neighbourhood, place, part, side, area, zone 2 = mercy, pity, compassion, charity, sympathy, tolerance, kindness, forgiveness • PLURAL NOUN = lodgings, rooms, chambers, residence, dwelling, barracks, abode, habitation • VERB = accommodate, house, lodge, place, board, post, station, billet

quash 1 = annul, overturn, reverse, cancel, overthrow, revoke, overrule, rescind 2 = suppress, crush, put down, beat, overthrow, squash, subdue, repress

queen 1 = sovereign, ruler, monarch, leader, Crown, princess, majesty, head of state 2 = leading light, star, favourite, celebrity, darling, mistress, big name

queer 1 = strange, odd, funny, unusual, extraordinary, curious, weird, peculiar ≠ normal 2 = faint, dizzy, giddy, queasy, light-headed

query NOUN 1 = question, inquiry, problem 2 = doubt, suspicion, objection • VERB 1 = question, challenge, doubt, suspect, dispute, object to, distrust, mistrust 2 = ask, inquire *or* enquire, question

quest 1 = search, hunt, mission, enterprise, crusade 2 = expedition, journey, adventure

question NOUN 1 = inquiry, enquiry, query, investigation, examination, interrogation ≠ answer 2 = difficulty, problem, doubt, argument, dispute, controversy, query, contention 3 = issue, point, matter, subject, problem, debate, proposal, theme • VERB 1 = interrogate, cross-examine, interview, examine, probe, quiz, ask questions 2 = dispute, challenge, doubt, suspect, oppose, query, mistrust, disbelieve ≠ accept • PHRASES **out of the question** = impossible, unthinkable, inconceivable, not on (*informal*), hopeless, unimaginable, unworkable, unattainable

questionable = dubious, suspect, doubtful, controversial, suspicious, dodgy (*Brit., Austral., & N.Z. informal*), debatable, moot ≠ indisputable

queue = line, row, file, train, series, chain, string, column

quick **1** = fast, swift, speedy, express, cracking (*Brit. informal*), smart, rapid, fleet ≠ slow **2** = brief, passing, hurried, flying, fleeting, summary, lightning, short-lived ≠ long **3** = immediate, instant, prompt, sudden, abrupt, instantaneous **4** = excitable, passionate, irritable, touchy, irascible, testy ≠ calm **5** = intelligent, bright (*informal*), alert, sharp, acute, smart, clever, shrewd ≠ stupid

quicken **1** = speed up, hurry, accelerate, hasten, gee up (*informal*) **2** = stimulate, inspire, arouse, excite, revive, incite, energize, invigorate

quickly **1** = swiftly, rapidly, hurriedly, fast, hastily, briskly, apace ≠ slowly **2** = soon, speedily, as soon as possible, momentarily (*U.S.*), instantaneously, pronto (*informal*), a.s.a.p. (*informal*) **3** = immediately, at once, directly, promptly, abruptly, without delay

quiet **ADJECTIVE** **1** = soft, low, muted, lowered, whispered, faint, suppressed, stifled ≠ loud **2** = peaceful, silent, hushed, soundless, noiseless ≠ noisy **3** = calm, peaceful, tranquil, mild, serene, placid, restful ≠ exciting **4** = still, calm, peaceful, tranquil ≠ troubled **5** = undisturbed, isolated, secluded, private, sequestered, unfrequented ≠ crowded **6** = silent **7** = reserved, retiring, shy, gentle, mild, sedate, meek ≠ excitable
• **NOUN** = peace, rest, tranquillity, ease, silence, solitude, serenity, stillness ≠ noise

quietly **1** = noiselessly, silently **2** = softly, inaudibly, in an undertone, under your breath **3** = calmly, serenely, placidly, patiently, mildly **4** = silently, mutely

quilt = bedspread, duvet, coverlet, eiderdown, counterpane, doona (*Austral.*), continental quilt

quip = joke, sally, jest, riposte, wisecrack (*informal*), retort, pleasantry, gibe

quirky = odd, unusual, eccentric, idiosyncratic, peculiar, offbeat

quit **1** = resign (from), leave, retire (from), pull out (of), step down (from) (*informal*), abdicate **2** = stop, give up, cease, end, drop, abandon, halt, discontinue ≠ continue **3** = leave, depart from, go out of, go away from, pull out from

quite **1** = somewhat, rather, fairly, reasonably, relatively, moderately **2** = absolutely, perfectly, completely, totally, fully, entirely, wholly

quiz **NOUN** = examination, questioning, interrogation, interview, investigation, grilling (*informal*), cross-examination, cross-questioning
• **VERB** = question, ask, interrogate, examine, investigate

quota = share, allowance, ration, part, limit, slice, quantity, portion

quotation **1** = passage, quote (*informal*), excerpt, reference, extract, citation **2** (*Commerce*) = estimate, price, tender, rate, cost, charge, figure, quote (*informal*)

quote **1** = repeat, recite, recall **2** = refer to, cite, give, name, detail, relate, mention, instance

r

race[1] **NOUN** **1** = competition, contest, chase, dash, pursuit **2** = contest, competition, rivalry
• **VERB** **1** = compete against, run against **2** = compete, run, contend, take part in a race **3** = run, fly, career, speed, tear, dash, hurry, dart

race[2] = people, nation, blood, stock, type, folk, tribe

racial = ethnic, ethnological, national, folk, genetic, tribal, genealogical

rack **NOUN** = frame, stand, structure, framework
• **VERB** = torture, torment, afflict, oppress, harrow, crucify, agonize, pain

racket **1** = noise, row, fuss, disturbance, outcry, clamour, din, pandemonium **2** = fraud, scheme

radiate **1** = emit, spread, send out, pour, shed, scatter **2** = shine, be diffused **3** = show, display, demonstrate, exhibit, emanate, give off *or* out **4** = spread out, diverge, branch out

radical **ADJECTIVE** **1** = extreme, complete, entire, sweeping, severe, thorough, drastic **2** = revolutionary, extremist, fanatical **3** = fundamental, natural, basic, profound, innate, deep-seated ≠ superficial
• **NOUN** = extremist, revolutionary, militant,

fanatic ≠ conservative

rage NOUN **1** = fury, temper, frenzy, rampage, tantrum, foulie (*Austral. slang*) ≠ calmness **2** = anger, passion, madness, wrath, ire **3** = craze, fashion, enthusiasm, vogue, fad (*informal*), latest thing
• VERB = be furious, blow up (*informal*), fume, lose it (*informal*), seethe, lose the plot (*informal*), go ballistic (*slang, chiefly U.S.*), lose your temper ≠ stay calm

ragged **1** = tatty, worn, torn, run-down, shabby, seedy, scruffy, in tatters ≠ smart **2** = rough, rugged, unfinished, uneven, jagged, serrated

raid VERB **1** = steal from, plunder, pillage, sack **2** = attack, invade, assault **3** = make a search of, search, bust (*informal*), make a raid on, make a swoop on
• NOUN **1** = attack, invasion, foray, sortie, incursion, sally, inroad **2** = bust (*informal*), swoop **3** = robbery, sacking

raider = attacker, thief, robber, plunderer, invader, marauder

railing = fence, rails, barrier, paling, balustrade

rain NOUN = rainfall, fall, showers, deluge, drizzle, downpour, raindrops, cloudburst
• VERB **1** = pour, pelt (down), teem, bucket down (*informal*), drizzle, come down in buckets (*informal*) **2** = fall, shower, be dropped, sprinkle, be deposited

rainy = wet, damp, drizzly, showery ≠ dry

raise **1** = lift, elevate, uplift, heave **2** = set upright, lift, elevate **3** = increase, intensify, heighten, advance, boost, strengthen, enhance, enlarge ≠ reduce **4** = make louder, heighten, amplify, louden **5** = collect, gather, obtain **6** = cause, start, produce, create, occasion, provoke, originate, engender **7** = put forward, suggest, introduce, advance, broach, moot **8** = bring up, develop, rear, nurture **9** = build, construct, put up, erect ≠ demolish

rake[1] **1** = gather, collect, remove **2** = search, comb, scour, scrutinize, fossick (*Austral. & N.Z.*)

rake[2] = libertine, playboy, swinger (*slang*), lecher, roué, debauchee ≠ puritan

rally NOUN **1** = gathering, convention, meeting, congress, assembly, hui (*N.Z.*) **2** = recovery, improvement, revival, recuperation ≠ relapse
• VERB **1** = gather together, unite, regroup, reorganize, reassemble **2** = recover, improve, revive, get better, recuperate ≠ get worse

ram **1** = hit, force, drive into, crash, impact, smash, dash, butt **2** = cram, force, stuff, jam, thrust

ramble NOUN = walk, tour, stroll, hike, roaming, roving, saunter
• VERB **1** = walk, range, wander, stroll, stray, roam, rove, saunter, go walkabout (*Austral.*) **2** *often with* ***on*** = babble, rabbit (on) (*Brit. informal*), waffle (*informal, chiefly Brit.*), witter on (*informal*)

ramp = slope, incline, gradient, rise

rampage VERB = go berserk, storm, rage, run riot, run amok
• PHRASES **on the rampage** = berserk, wild, violent, raging, out of control, amok, riotous, berko (*Austral. slang*)

rampant **1** = widespread, prevalent, rife, uncontrolled, unchecked, unrestrained, profuse, spreading like wildfire **2** (*Heraldry*) = upright, standing, rearing, erect

random ADJECTIVE **1** = chance, casual, accidental, incidental, haphazard, fortuitous, hit or miss, adventitious ≠ planned **2** = casual
• PHRASES **at random** = haphazardly, randomly, arbitrarily, by chance, willy-nilly, unsystematically

randy (*Informal*) = lustful, hot, turned-on (*slang*), aroused, horny (*slang*), amorous, lascivious

range NOUN **1** = series, variety, selection, assortment, lot, collection, gamut **2** = limits, reach **3** = scope, area, bounds, province, orbit, radius
• VERB **1** = vary, run, reach, extend, stretch **2** = roam, wander, rove, ramble, traverse

rank[1] NOUN **1** = status, level, position, grade, order, sort, type, division **2** = class, caste **3** = row, line, file, column, group, range, series, tier
• VERB **1** = order, dispose **2** = arrange, sort, line up, array, align

rank[2] **1** = absolute, complete, total, gross, sheer, utter, thorough, blatant **2** = foul, bad, offensive, disgusting, revolting, stinking, noxious, rancid, festy (*Austral. slang*) **3** = abundant, lush, luxuriant, dense, profuse

ransom = payment, money, price, payoff

rant = shout, roar, yell, rave, cry, declaim

rap VERB = hit, strike, knock, crack, tap
• NOUN **1** = blow, knock, crack, tap, clout (*informal*) **2** (*Slang*) = rebuke, blame, responsibility, punishment

rape VERB = sexually assault, violate, abuse, ravish, force, outrage
• NOUN = sexual assault, violation, ravishment, outrage

rapid **1** = sudden, prompt, speedy, express, swift ≠ gradual **2** = quick, fast, hurried, swift, brisk, hasty ≠ slow

rapidly = quickly, fast, swiftly, briskly, promptly, hastily, hurriedly, speedily

rare **1** = uncommon, unusual, few, strange, scarce, singular, sparse, infrequent ≠ common **2** = superb, great, fine, excellent, superlative, choice, peerless

rarely = seldom, hardly, hardly ever, infrequently ≠ often

raring (in construction *raring to do something*) = eager, impatient, longing, ready, keen, desperate, enthusiastic

rarity **1** = curio, find, treasure, gem, collector's item **2** = uncommonness, scarcity, infrequency, unusualness, shortage, strangeness, sparseness

rash¹ = reckless, hasty, impulsive, imprudent, careless, ill-advised, foolhardy, impetuous ≠ cautious

rash² **1** = outbreak of spots, (skin) eruption **2** = spate, series, wave, flood, plague, outbreak

rate NOUN **1** = speed, pace, tempo, velocity, frequency **2** = degree, standard, scale, proportion, ratio **3** = charge, price, cost, fee, figure
• VERB **1** = evaluate, consider, rank, reckon, value, measure, estimate, count **2** = deserve, merit, be entitled to, be worthy of
• PHRASES **at any rate** = in any case, anyway, anyhow, at all events

rather **1** = preferably, sooner, more readily, more willingly **2** = to some extent, quite, a little, fairly, relatively, somewhat, moderately, to some degree

ratify = approve, establish, confirm, sanction, endorse, uphold, authorize, affirm ≠ annul

rating = position, placing, rate, order, class, degree, rank, status

ratio = proportion, rate, relation, percentage, fraction

ration NOUN = allowance, quota, allotment, helping, part, share, measure, portion
• VERB = limit, control, restrict, budget

rational = sensible, sound, wise, reasonable, intelligent, realistic, logical, sane ≠ insane

rationale = reason, grounds, theory, principle, philosophy, logic, motivation, raison d'être (*French*)

rattle **1** = clatter, bang, jangle **2** = shake, jolt, vibrate, bounce, jar **3** (*Informal*) = fluster, shake, upset, disturb, disconcert, perturb, faze

ravage VERB = destroy, ruin, devastate, spoil, demolish, ransack, lay waste, despoil
• PLURAL NOUN = damage, destruction, devastation, ruin, havoc, ruination, spoliation

rave **1** = rant, rage, roar, go mad (*informal*), babble, be delirious **2** (*Informal*) = enthuse, praise, gush, be mad about (*informal*), be wild about (*informal*)

raving = mad, wild, crazy, hysterical, insane, irrational, crazed, delirious, berko (*Austral. slang*), off the air (*Austral. slang*)

raw **1** = unrefined, natural, crude, unprocessed, basic, rough, coarse, unfinished ≠ refined **2** = uncooked, natural, fresh ≠ cooked **3** = inexperienced, new, green, immature, callow ≠ experienced **4** = chilly, biting, cold, freezing, bitter, piercing, parky (*Brit. informal*)

ray = beam, bar, flash, shaft, gleam

re = concerning, about, regarding, with regard to, with reference to, apropos

reach VERB **1** = arrive at, get to, make, attain **2** = attain, get to **3** = touch, grasp, extend to, stretch to, contact **4** = contact, get in touch with, get through to, communicate with, get hold of
• NOUN **1** = grasp, range, distance, stretch, capacity, extent, extension, scope **2** = jurisdiction, power, influence

react = respond, act, proceed, behave

reaction **1** = response, answer, reply **2** = counteraction, backlash, recoil **3** = conservatism, the right

reactionary ADJECTIVE = conservative,

right-wing
• NOUN = conservative, die-hard, right-winger ≠ radical

read 1 = scan, study, look at, pore over, peruse 2 = understand, interpret, comprehend, construe, decipher, see, discover 3 = register, show, record, display, indicate

readily 1 = willingly, freely, quickly, gladly, eagerly ≠ reluctantly 2 = promptly, quickly, easily, smoothly, effortlessly, speedily, unhesitatingly ≠ with difficulty

readiness 1 = willingness, eagerness, keenness 2 = promptness, facility, ease, dexterity, adroitness

reading 1 = perusal, study, examination, inspection, scrutiny 2 = learning, education, knowledge, scholarship, erudition 3 = recital, performance, lesson, sermon 4 = interpretation, version, impression, grasp

ready 1 = prepared, set, primed, organized ≠ unprepared 2 = completed, arranged 3 = mature, ripe, mellow, ripened, seasoned 4 = willing, happy, glad, disposed, keen, eager, inclined, prone ≠ reluctant 5 = prompt, smart, quick, bright, sharp, keen, alert, clever ≠ slow 6 = available, handy, present, near, accessible, convenient ≠ unavailable

real 1 = true, genuine, sincere, factual, dinkum (*Austral. & N.Z. informal*), unfeigned 2 = genuine, authentic, dinkum (*Austral. & N.Z. informal*) ≠ fake 3 = proper, true, valid 4 = true, actual 5 = typical, true, genuine, sincere, dinkum (*Austral. & N.Z. informal*), unfeigned 6 = complete, total, perfect, utter, thorough

realistic 1 = practical, real, sensible, common-sense, down-to-earth, matter-of-fact, level-headed ≠ impractical 2 = attainable, sensible 3 = lifelike, true to life, authentic, true, natural, genuine, faithful

reality 1 = fact, truth, realism, validity, verity, actuality 2 = truth, fact, actuality

realization 1 = awareness, understanding, recognition, perception, grasp, conception, comprehension, cognizance 2 = achievement, accomplishment, fulfilment

realize 1 = become aware of, understand, take in, grasp, comprehend, get the message 2 = fulfil, achieve, accomplish, make real 3 = achieve, do, effect, complete, perform, fulfil, accomplish, carry out *or* through

really 1 = certainly, genuinely, positively, surely 2 = truly, actually, in fact, indeed, in actuality

realm 1 = field, world, area, province, sphere, department, branch, territory 2 = kingdom, country, empire, land, domain, dominion

reap 1 = get, gain, obtain, acquire, derive 2 = collect, gather, bring in, harvest, garner, cut

rear[1] NOUN 1 = back part, back ≠ front 2 = back, end, tail, rearguard, tail end
• ADJECTIVE = back, hind, last, following ≠ front

rear[2] 1 = bring up, raise, educate, train, foster, nurture 2 = breed, keep 3 = rise, tower, soar, loom

reason NOUN 1 = cause, grounds, purpose, motive, goal, aim, object, intention 2 = sense, mind, understanding, judgment, logic, intellect, sanity, rationality ≠ emotion
• VERB = deduce, conclude, work out, make out, infer, think
• PHRASES **reason with someone** = persuade, bring round, urge, win over, prevail upon (*informal*), talk into *or* out of

reasonable 1 = sensible, sound, practical, wise, logical, sober, plausible, sane ≠ irrational 2 = fair, just, right, moderate, equitable, tenable ≠ unfair 3 = within reason, fit, proper ≠ impossible 4 = low, cheap, competitive, moderate, modest, inexpensive 5 = average, fair, moderate, modest, O.K. *or* okay (*informal*)

reassure = encourage, comfort, hearten, gee up, restore confidence to, put *or* set your mind at rest

rebate = refund, discount, reduction, bonus, allowance, deduction

rebel NOUN 1 = revolutionary, insurgent, secessionist, revolutionist 2 = nonconformist, dissenter, heretic, apostate, schismatic
• VERB 1 = revolt, resist, rise up, mutiny 2 = defy, dissent, disobey
• ADJECTIVE = rebellious, revolutionary, insurgent, insurrectionary

rebellion 1 = resistance, rising, revolution, revolt, uprising, mutiny 2 = nonconformity, defiance, heresy, schism

rebellious 1 = defiant, difficult, resistant, unmanageable, refractory ≠ obedient 2 = revolutionary, rebel, disorderly, unruly, insurgent, disloyal, seditious, mutinous ≠ obedient
rebound 1 = bounce, ricochet, recoil 2 = misfire, backfire, recoil, boomerang
rebuff VERB = reject, refuse, turn down, cut, slight, snub, spurn, knock back (*slang*) ≠ encourage
• NOUN = rejection, snub, knock-back, slight, refusal, repulse, cold shoulder, slap in the face (*informal*) ≠ encouragement
rebuke VERB = scold, censure, reprimand, castigate, chide, dress down (*informal*), admonish, tell off (*informal*) ≠ praise
• NOUN = scolding, censure, reprimand, row, dressing down (*informal*), telling-off (*informal*), admonition ≠ praise
recall VERB 1 = recollect, remember, evoke, call to mind 2 = call back 3 = annul, withdraw, cancel, repeal, revoke, retract, countermand
• NOUN 1 = recollection, memory, remembrance 2 = annulment, withdrawal, repeal, cancellation, retraction, rescindment
recede = fall back, withdraw, retreat, return, retire, regress
receipt 1 = sales slip, proof of purchase, counterfoil 2 = receiving, delivery, reception, acceptance
receive 1 = get, accept, be given, pick up, collect, obtain, acquire, take 2 = experience, suffer, bear, encounter, sustain, undergo 3 = greet, meet, admit, welcome, entertain, accommodate
recent = new, modern, up-to-date, late, current, fresh, novel, present-day ≠ old
recently = not long ago, newly, lately, currently, freshly, of late, latterly
reception 1 = party, gathering, get-together, social gathering, function, celebration, festivity, soirée 2 = response, reaction, acknowledgment, treatment, welcome, greeting
recess 1 = break, rest, holiday, interval, vacation, respite, intermission 2 = alcove, corner, bay, hollow, niche, nook
recession = depression, drop, decline, slump ≠ boom
recipe = directions, instructions, ingredients
recital 1 = performance, rendering, rehearsal, reading 2 = account, telling, statement, relation, narrative 3 = recitation
recite = perform, deliver, repeat, declaim
reckless = careless, wild, rash, precipitate, hasty, mindless, headlong, thoughtless ≠ cautious
reckon 1 (*Informal*) = think, believe, suppose, imagine, assume, guess (*informal, chiefly U.S. & Canad.*) 2 = consider, rate, account, judge, regard, count, esteem, deem 3 = count, figure, total, calculate, compute, add up, tally, number
reckoning = count, estimate, calculation, addition
reclaim 1 = retrieve, regain 2 = regain, salvage, recapture
recognition 1 = identification, recollection, discovery, remembrance 2 = acceptance, admission, allowance, confession
recognize 1 = identify, know, place, remember, spot, notice, recall, recollect 2 = acknowledge, allow, accept, admit, grant, concede ≠ ignore 3 = appreciate, respect, notice
recollection = memory, recall, impression, remembrance, reminiscence
recommend 1 = advocate, suggest, propose, approve, endorse, commend ≠ disapprove of 2 = put forward, approve, endorse, commend, praise 3 = advise, suggest, advance, propose, counsel, advocate, prescribe, put forward
recommendation 1 = advice, proposal, suggestion, counsel 2 = commendation, reference, praise, sanction, approval, endorsement, advocacy, testimonial
reconcile 1 = resolve, settle, square, adjust, compose, rectify, put to rights 2 = reunite, bring back together, conciliate 3 = make peace between, reunite, propitiate
reconciliation = reunion, conciliation, pacification, reconcilement ≠ separation
reconsider = rethink, review, revise, think again, reassess
reconstruct 1 = rebuild, restore, recreate, remake, renovate, remodel, regenerate 2 = build up a picture of, build up, piece together, deduce
record NOUN 1 = document, file, register, log, report, account, entry, journal

2 = evidence, trace, documentation, testimony, witness 3 = disc, single, album, LP, vinyl 4 = background, history, performance, career
• VERB 1 = set down, minute, note, enter, document, register, log, chronicle 2 = make a recording of, video, tape, video-tape, tape-record 3 = register, show, indicate, give evidence of

recorder = chronicler, archivist, historian, clerk, scribe, diarist

recording = record, video, tape, disc

recount = tell, report, describe, relate, repeat, depict, recite, narrate

recover 1 = get better, improve, get well, recuperate, heal, revive, mend, convalesce ≠ relapse 2 = rally 3 = save, rescue, retrieve, salvage, reclaim ≠ abandon 4 = recoup, restore, get back, regain, retrieve, reclaim, redeem, recapture ≠ lose

recovery 1 = improvement, healing, revival, mending, recuperation, convalescence 2 = retrieval, repossession, reclamation, restoration

recreation = leisure, play, sport, fun, entertainment, relaxation, enjoyment, amusement

recruit VERB 1 = gather, obtain, engage, procure 2 = assemble, raise, levy, muster, mobilize 3 = enlist, draft, enrol ≠ dismiss
• NOUN = beginner, trainee, apprentice, novice, convert, initiate, helper, learner

recur = happen again, return, repeat, persist, revert, reappear, come again

recycle = reprocess, reuse, salvage, reclaim, save

red NOUN *or* ADJECTIVE 1 = crimson, scarlet, ruby, vermilion, cherry, coral, carmine 2 = flushed, embarrassed, blushing, florid, shamefaced 3 (*of hair*) = chestnut, reddish, flame-coloured, sandy, Titian, carroty
• PHRASES **in the red** (*Informal*) = in debt, insolvent, in arrears, overdrawn ◆ **see red** (*Informal*) = lose your temper, lose it (*informal*), go mad (*informal*), crack up (*informal*), lose the plot (*informal*), go ballistic (*slang, chiefly U.S.*), fly off the handle (*informal*), blow your top

redeem 1 = reinstate, absolve, restore to favour 2 = make up for, compensate for, atone for, make amends for 3 = buy back, recover, regain, retrieve, reclaim, repurchase 4 = save, free, deliver, liberate, ransom, emancipate

redemption 1 = compensation, amends, reparation, atonement 2 = salvation, release, rescue, liberation, emancipation, deliverance

redress VERB 1 = make amends for, make up for, compensate for 2 = put right, balance, correct, adjust, regulate, rectify, even up
• NOUN = amends, payment, compensation, reparation, atonement, recompense

reduce 1 = lessen, cut, lower, moderate, weaken, diminish, decrease, cut down ≠ increase 2 = degrade, downgrade, break, humble, bring low ≠ promote

redundancy 1 = layoff, sacking, dismissal 2 = unemployment, the sack (*informal*), the axe (*informal*), joblessness

redundant = superfluous, extra, surplus, unnecessary, unwanted, inessential, supernumerary ≠ essential

reel 1 = stagger, rock, roll, pitch, sway, lurch 2 = whirl, spin, revolve, swirl

refer VERB = direct, point, send, guide
• PHRASES **refer to something** *or* **someone** 1 = allude to, mention, cite, speak of, bring up 2 = relate to, concern, apply to, pertain to, be relevant to 3 = consult, go, apply, turn to, look up

referee NOUN = umpire, judge, ref (*informal*), arbiter, arbitrator, adjudicator
• VERB = umpire, judge, mediate, adjudicate, arbitrate

reference 1 = allusion, note, mention, quotation 2 = citation 3 = testimonial, recommendation, credentials, endorsement, character reference

referendum = public vote, popular vote, plebiscite

refine 1 = purify, process, filter, cleanse, clarify, distil 2 = improve, perfect, polish, hone

refined 1 = purified, processed, pure, filtered, clean, clarified, distilled ≠ unrefined 2 = cultured, polished, elegant, polite, cultivated, civilized, well-bred ≠ coarse 3 = discerning, fine, sensitive, delicate, precise, discriminating, fastidious

reflect 1 = show, reveal, display, indicate, demonstrate, manifest 2 = throw back, return, mirror, echo, reproduce 3 = consider, think, muse, ponder,

meditate, ruminate, cogitate, wonder
reflection 1 = image, echo, mirror image 2 = consideration, thinking, thought, idea, opinion, observation, musing, meditation
reflective = thoughtful, contemplative, meditative, pensive
reform NOUN = improvement, amendment, rehabilitation, betterment
• VERB 1 = improve, correct, restore, amend, mend, rectify 2 = mend your ways, go straight (*informal*), shape up (*informal*), turn over a new leaf, clean up your act (*informal*), pull your socks up (*Brit. informal*)
refrain[1] = stop, avoid, cease, renounce, abstain, leave off, desist, forbear
refrain[2] = chorus, tune, melody
refresh 1 = revive, freshen, revitalize, stimulate, brace, enliven, invigorate 2 = stimulate, prompt, renew, jog
refreshing 1 = new, original, novel 2 = stimulating, fresh, bracing, invigorating ≠ tiring
refreshment = food and drink, drinks, snacks, titbits, kai (*N.Z. informal*)
refuge 1 = protection, shelter, asylum 2 = haven, retreat, sanctuary, hide-out
refugee = exile, émigré, displaced person, escapee
refund NOUN = repayment, reimbursement, return
• VERB = repay, return, restore, pay back, reimburse
refurbish = renovate, restore, repair, clean up, overhaul, revamp, mend, do up (*informal*)
refusal = rejection, denial, rebuff, knock-back (*slang*)
refuse[1] 1 = decline, reject, turn down, say no to 2 = deny, decline, withhold ≠ allow
refuse[2] = rubbish, waste, junk (*informal*), litter, garbage, trash
regain 1 = recover, get back, retrieve, recapture, win back, take back, recoup 2 = get back to, return to, reach again
regal = royal, majestic, kingly *or* queenly, noble, princely, magnificent
regard VERB 1 = consider, see, rate, view, judge, think of, esteem, deem 2 = look at, view, eye, watch, observe, clock (*Brit. slang*), check out (*informal*), gaze at
• NOUN 1 = respect, esteem, thought, concern, care, consideration 2 = look, gaze, scrutiny, stare, glance
• PLURAL NOUN = good wishes, respects, greetings, compliments, best wishes
• PHRASES **as regards** = concerning, regarding, relating to, pertaining to
regarding = concerning, about, on the subject of, re, respecting, as regards, with reference to, in *or* with regard to
regardless 1 = in spite of everything, anyway, nevertheless, in any case 2 *with* **of** = irrespective of, heedless of, unmindful of
regime 1 = government, rule, management, leadership, reign 2 = plan, course, system, policy, programme, scheme, regimen
region = area, place, part, quarter, section, sector, district, territory
regional = local, district, provincial, parochial, zonal
register NOUN = list, record, roll, file, diary, catalogue, log, archives
• VERB 1 = enrol, enlist, list, note, enter 2 = record, catalogue, chronicle 3 = indicate, show 4 = show, mark, indicate, manifest 5 = express, show, reveal, display, exhibit
regret VERB 1 = be *or* feel sorry about, rue, deplore, bemoan, repent (of), bewail ≠ be satisfied with 2 = mourn, miss, grieve for *or* over
• NOUN 1 = remorse, compunction, bitterness, repentance, contrition, penitence 2 = sorrow ≠ satisfaction
regular 1 = frequent 2 = normal, common, usual, ordinary, typical, routine, customary, habitual ≠ infrequent 3 = steady, consistent 4 = even, level, balanced, straight, flat, fixed, smooth, uniform ≠ uneven
regulate 1 = control, run, rule, manage, direct, guide, handle, govern 2 = moderate, control, modulate, fit, tune, adjust
regulation 1 = rule, order, law, dictate, decree, statute, edict, precept 2 = control, government, management, direction, supervision
rehearsal = practice, rehearsing, run-through, preparation, drill
rehearse = practise, prepare, run through, go over, train, repeat, drill, recite
reign VERB 1 = be supreme, prevail, predominate, hold sway 2 = rule, govern, be in power, influence, command

• NOUN = rule, power, control, command, monarchy, dominion
rein = control, harness, bridle, hold, check, brake, curb, restraint
reincarnation = rebirth, transmigration of souls
reinforce 1 = support, strengthen, fortify, toughen, stress, prop, supplement, emphasize 2 = increase, extend, add to, strengthen, supplement
reinforcement NOUN 1 = strengthening, increase, fortification, augmentation 2 = support, stay, prop, brace, buttress
• PLURAL NOUN = reserves, support, auxiliaries, additional *or* fresh troops
reinstate = restore, recall, re-establish, return
reiterate (*Formal*) = repeat, restate, say again, do again
reject VERB 1 = rebuff, jilt, turn down, spurn, refuse, say no to, repulse ≠ accept 2 = deny, exclude, veto, relinquish, renounce, disallow, forsake, disown ≠ approve 3 = discard, decline, eliminate, scrap, jettison, throw away *or* out ≠ accept
• NOUN 1 = castoff, second, discard ≠ treasure 2 = failure, loser, flop
rejection 1 = denial, veto, dismissal, exclusion, disowning, thumbs down, renunciation, repudiation ≠ approval 2 = rebuff, refusal, knock-back (*slang*), kick in the teeth (*slang*), brushoff (*slang*) ≠ acceptance
rejoice = be glad, celebrate, be happy, glory, be overjoyed, exult ≠ lament
rejoin = reply, answer, respond, retort, riposte
relate VERB = tell, recount, report, detail, describe, recite, narrate
• PHRASES **relate to something** *or* **someone** 1 = concern, refer to, apply to, have to do with, pertain to, be relevant to 2 = connect with, associate with, link with, couple with, join with, correlate to
related 1 = associated, linked, joint, connected, affiliated, akin, interconnected ≠ unconnected 2 = akin, kindred ≠ unrelated
relation NOUN 1 = similarity, link, bearing, bond, comparison, correlation, connection 2 = relative, kin, kinsman *or* kinswoman
• PLURAL NOUN 1 = dealings, relationship, affairs, contact, connections, interaction, intercourse 2 = family, relatives, tribe, clan, kin, kindred, kinsmen, kinsfolk, ainga (*N.Z.*)
relationship 1 = association, bond, connection, affinity, rapport, kinship 2 = affair, romance, liaison, amour, intrigue 3 = connection, link, parallel, similarity, tie-up, correlation
relative NOUN = relation, kinsman *or* kinswoman, member of your *or* the family
• ADJECTIVE 1 = comparative 2 = corresponding 3 *with* **to** = in proportion to, proportionate to
relatively = comparatively, rather, somewhat
relax 1 = be *or* feel at ease, chill out (*slang, chiefly U.S.*), take it easy, lighten up (*slang*), outspan (*S. African*) ≠ be alarmed 2 = calm down, calm, unwind 3 = make less tense, rest 4 = lessen, reduce, ease, relieve, weaken, loosen, let up, slacken ≠ tighten 5 = moderate, ease, relieve, weaken, slacken ≠ tighten up
relaxation = leisure, rest, fun, pleasure, recreation, enjoyment
relay = broadcast, carry, spread, communicate, transmit, send out
release VERB 1 = set free, free, discharge, liberate, drop, loose, undo, extricate ≠ imprison 2 = acquit, let go, let off, exonerate, absolve 3 = issue, publish, make public, make known, launch, distribute, put out, circulate ≠ withhold
• NOUN 1 = liberation, freedom, liberty, discharge, emancipation, deliverance ≠ imprisonment 2 = acquittal, exemption, absolution, exoneration 3 = issue, publication, proclamation
relegate = demote, degrade, downgrade
relentless 1 = merciless, fierce, cruel, ruthless, unrelenting, implacable, remorseless, pitiless ≠ merciful 2 = unremitting, persistent, unrelenting, incessant, nonstop, unrelieved
relevant = significant, appropriate, related, fitting, to the point, apt, pertinent, apposite ≠ irrelevant
reliable 1 = dependable, trustworthy, sure, sound, true, faithful, staunch ≠ unreliable 2 = safe, dependable 3 = definitive, sound, dependable, trustworthy
reliance 1 = dependency, dependence 2 = trust, confidence, belief, faith
relic = remnant, vestige, memento, trace, fragment, souvenir, keepsake

relief **1** = <u>ease</u>, release, comfort, cure, remedy, solace, deliverance, mitigation **2** = <u>rest</u>, respite, relaxation, break, breather (*informal*) **3** = <u>aid</u>, help, support, assistance, succour

relieve **1** = <u>ease</u>, soothe, alleviate, relax, comfort, calm, cure, soften ≠ intensify **2** = <u>help</u>, support, aid, sustain, assist, succour

religion = <u>belief</u>, faith, theology, creed

religious **1** = <u>spiritual</u>, holy, sacred, devotional **2** = <u>conscientious</u>, faithful, rigid, meticulous, scrupulous, punctilious

relinquish (*Formal*) = <u>give up</u>, leave, drop, abandon, surrender, let go, renounce, forsake

relish VERB **1** = <u>enjoy</u>, like, savour, revel in ≠ dislike **2** = <u>look forward to</u>, fancy, delight in
• NOUN **1** = <u>enjoyment</u>, liking, love, taste, fancy, penchant, fondness, gusto ≠ distaste **2** = <u>condiment</u>, seasoning, sauce

reluctance = <u>unwillingness</u>, dislike, loathing, distaste, aversion, disinclination, repugnance

reluctant = <u>unwilling</u>, hesitant, loath, disinclined, unenthusiastic ≠ willing

rely on **1** = <u>depend on</u>, lean on **2** = <u>be confident of</u>, bank on, trust, count on, bet on

remain **1** = <u>stay</u>, continue, go on, stand, dwell **2** = <u>stay behind</u>, wait, delay ≠ go **3** = <u>continue</u>, be left, linger

remainder = <u>rest</u>, remains, balance, excess, surplus, remnant, residue, leavings

remains **1** = <u>remnants</u>, leftovers, rest, debris, residue, dregs, leavings **2** = <u>corpse</u>, body, carcass, cadaver **3** = <u>relics</u>

remark VERB **1** = <u>comment</u>, say, state, reflect, mention, declare, observe, pass comment **2** = <u>notice</u>, note, observe, perceive, see, mark, make out, espy
• NOUN = <u>comment</u>, observation, reflection, statement, utterance

remarkable = <u>extraordinary</u>, striking, outstanding, wonderful, rare, unusual, surprising, notable ≠ ordinary

remedy NOUN = <u>cure</u>, treatment, medicine, nostrum
• VERB = <u>put right</u>, rectify, fix, correct, set to rights

remember **1** = <u>recall</u>, think back to, recollect, reminisce about, call to mind ≠ forget **2** = <u>bear in mind</u>, keep in mind **3** = <u>look back (on)</u>, commemorate

remembrance **1** = <u>commemoration</u>, memorial **2** = <u>souvenir</u>, token, reminder, monument, memento, keepsake **3** = <u>memory</u>, recollection, thought, recall, reminiscence

remind = <u>jog your memory</u>, prompt, make you remember

reminiscent = <u>suggestive</u>, evocative, similar

remnant = <u>remainder</u>, remains, trace, fragment, end, rest, residue, leftovers

remorse = <u>regret</u>, shame, guilt, grief, sorrow, anguish, repentance, contrition

remote **1** = <u>distant</u>, far, isolated, out-of-the-way, secluded, inaccessible, in the middle of nowhere ≠ nearby **2** = <u>far</u>, distant **3** = <u>slight</u>, small, outside, unlikely, slim, faint, doubtful, dubious ≠ strong **4** = <u>aloof</u>, cold, reserved, withdrawn, distant, abstracted, detached, uncommunicative ≠ outgoing

removal **1** = <u>extraction</u>, withdrawal, uprooting, eradication, dislodgment, taking away *or* off *or* out **2** = <u>dismissal</u>, expulsion, elimination, ejection **3** = <u>move</u>, transfer, departure, relocation, flitting (*Scot. & Northern English dialect*)

remove **1** = <u>take out</u>, withdraw, extract ≠ insert **2** = <u>take off</u> ≠ put on **3** = <u>erase</u>, eliminate, take out **4** = <u>dismiss</u>, eliminate, get rid of, discharge, abolish, expel, throw out, oust ≠ appoint **5** = <u>get rid of</u>, erase, eradicate, expunge **6** = <u>take away</u>, detach, displace ≠ put back **7** = <u>delete</u>, get rid of, erase, excise **8** = <u>move</u>, depart, relocate, flit (*Scot. & Northern English dialect*)

renaissance *or* **renascence** = <u>rebirth</u>, revival, restoration, renewal, resurgence, reappearance, reawakening

rend (*Literary*) = <u>tear</u>, rip, separate, wrench, rupture

render **1** = <u>make</u>, cause to become, leave **2** = <u>provide</u>, give, pay, present, supply, submit, tender, hand out **3** = <u>represent</u>, portray, depict, do, give, play, act, perform

renew **1** = <u>recommence</u>, continue, extend, repeat, resume, reopen, recreate, reaffirm **2** = <u>reaffirm</u>, resume, recommence **3** = <u>replace</u>, refresh, replenish, restock **4** = <u>restore</u>, repair, overhaul, mend, refurbish, renovate, refit, modernize

renounce **1** = <u>disown</u>, quit, forsake,

recant, forswear, abjure **2** = disclaim, deny, give up, relinquish, waive, abjure ≠ assert

renovate = restore, repair, refurbish, do up (*informal*), renew, overhaul, refit, modernize

renowned = famous, noted, celebrated, well-known, distinguished, esteemed, notable, eminent ≠ unknown

rent[1] **VERB 1** = hire, lease **2** = let, lease
• **NOUN** = hire, rental, lease, fee, payment

rent[2] **1** = tear, split, rip, slash, slit, gash, hole **2** = opening, hole

repair VERB 1 = mend, fix, restore, heal, patch, renovate, patch up ≠ damage **2** = put right, make up for, compensate for, rectify, redress
• **NOUN 1** = mend, restoration, overhaul **2** = darn, mend, patch **3** = condition, state, form, shape (*informal*)

repay = pay back, refund, settle up, return, square, compensate, reimburse, recompense

repeal VERB = abolish, reverse, revoke, annul, recall, cancel, invalidate, nullify ≠ pass
• **NOUN** = abolition, cancellation, annulment, invalidation, rescindment ≠ passing

repeat VERB 1 = reiterate, restate **2** = retell, echo, replay, reproduce, rerun, reshow
• **NOUN 1** = repetition, echo, reiteration **2** = rerun, replay, reshowing

repeatedly = over and over, often, frequently, many times

repel 1 = drive off, fight, resist, parry, hold off, rebuff, ward off, repulse ≠ submit to **2** = disgust, offend, revolt, sicken, nauseate, gross out (*U.S. slang*) ≠ delight

repertoire = range, list, stock, supply, store, collection, repertory

repetition 1 = recurrence, repeating, echo **2** = repeating, replication, restatement, reiteration, tautology

replace 1 = take the place of, follow, succeed, oust, take over from, supersede, supplant **2** = substitute, change, exchange, switch, swap **3** = put back, restore

replacement 1 = replacing **2** = successor, double, substitute, stand-in, proxy, surrogate, understudy

replica 1 = reproduction, model, copy, imitation, facsimile, carbon copy ≠ original **2** = duplicate, copy, carbon copy

replicate = copy, reproduce, recreate, mimic, duplicate, reduplicate

reply VERB = answer, respond, retort, counter, rejoin, retaliate, reciprocate
• **NOUN** = answer, response, reaction, counter, retort, retaliation, counterattack, rejoinder

report VERB 1 = inform of, communicate, recount **2** *often with* ***on*** = communicate, tell, state, detail, describe, relate, broadcast, pass on **3** = present yourself, come, appear, arrive, turn up
• **NOUN 1** = article, story, piece, write-up **2** = account, record, statement, communication, description, narrative **3** *often plural* = news, word **4** = bang, sound, crack, noise, blast, boom, explosion, discharge **5** = rumour, talk, buzz, gossip, hearsay

reporter = journalist, writer, correspondent, hack (*derogatory*), pressman, journo (*slang*)

represent 1 = act for, speak for **2** = stand for, serve as **3** = express, correspond to, symbolize, mean **4** = exemplify, embody, symbolize, typify, personify, epitomize **5** = depict, show, describe, picture, illustrate, outline, portray, denote

representation 1 = picture, model, image, portrait, illustration, likeness **2** = portrayal, depiction, account, description

representative NOUN 1 = delegate, member, agent, deputy, proxy, spokesman *or* spokeswoman **2** = agent, salesman, rep, commercial traveller
• **ADJECTIVE 1** = typical, characteristic, archetypal, exemplary ≠ uncharacteristic **2** = symbolic

repress 1 = control, suppress, hold back, bottle up, check, curb, restrain, inhibit ≠ release **2** = hold back, suppress, stifle **3** = subdue, abuse, wrong, persecute, quell, subjugate, maltreat ≠ liberate

repression 1 = subjugation, control, constraint, domination, tyranny, despotism **2** = suppression, crushing, quashing **3** = inhibition, control, restraint, bottling up

reprieve VERB = grant a stay of execution to, pardon, let off the hook (*slang*)
• **NOUN** = stay of execution, amnesty, pardon, remission, deferment, postponement of punishment

reproduce 1 = copy, recreate, replicate, duplicate, match, mirror, echo, imitate 2 = print, copy 3 (*Biology*) = breed, procreate, multiply, spawn, propagate

reproduction 1 = copy, picture, print, replica, imitation, duplicate, facsimile ≠ original 2 (*Biology*) = breeding, increase, generation, multiplication

Republican ADJECTIVE = right-wing, Conservative
• NOUN = right-winger, Conservative

reputation = name, standing, character, esteem, stature, renown, repute

request VERB 1 = ask for, appeal for, put in for, demand, desire 2 = invite, entreat 3 = seek, ask (for), solicit
• NOUN 1 = appeal, call, demand, plea, desire, entreaty, suit 2 = asking, plea

require 1 = need, crave, want, miss, lack, wish, desire 2 = order, demand, command, compel, exact, oblige, call upon, insist upon 3 = ask

requirement = necessity, demand, stipulation, want, need, must, essential, prerequisite

rescue VERB 1 = save, get out, release, deliver, recover, liberate ≠ desert 2 = salvage, deliver, redeem
• NOUN = saving, salvage, deliverance, release, recovery, liberation, salvation, redemption

research NOUN = investigation, study, analysis, examination, probe, exploration
• VERB = investigate, study, examine, explore, probe, analyse

resemblance = similarity, correspondence, parallel, likeness, kinship, sameness, similitude ≠ dissimilarity

resemble = be like, look like, mirror, parallel, be similar to, bear a resemblance to

resent = be bitter about, object to, grudge, begrudge, take exception to, take offence at ≠ be content with

resentment = bitterness, indignation, ill feeling, ill will, grudge, animosity, pique, rancour

reservation 1 *often plural* = doubt, scruples, hesitancy 2 = reserve, territory, preserve, sanctuary

reserve VERB 1 = book, prearrange, engage 2 = put by, secure 3 = keep, hold, save, store, retain, set aside, stockpile, hoard
• NOUN 1 = store, fund, savings, stock, supply, reservoir, hoard, cache 2 = park, reservation, preserve, sanctuary, tract, forest park (*N.Z.*) 3 = shyness, silence, restraint, constraint, reticence, secretiveness, taciturnity 4 = reservation, doubt, delay, uncertainty, indecision, hesitancy, vacillation, irresolution
• ADJECTIVE = substitute, extra, spare, secondary, fall-back, auxiliary

reserved 1 = uncommunicative, retiring, silent, shy, restrained, secretive, reticent, taciturn ≠ uninhibited 2 = set aside, taken, kept, held, booked, retained, engaged, restricted

reservoir 1 = lake, pond, basin 2 = store, stock, source, supply, reserves, pool

reside (*Formal*) = live, lodge, dwell, stay, abide ≠ visit

residence = home, house, dwelling, place, flat, lodging, abode, habitation

resident 1 = inhabitant, citizen, local ≠ nonresident 2 = tenant, occupant, lodger 3 = guest, lodger

residue = remainder, remains, remnant, leftovers, rest, extra, excess, surplus

resign VERB 1 = quit, leave, step down (*informal*), vacate, abdicate, give *or* hand in your notice 2 = give up, abandon, yield, surrender, relinquish, renounce, forsake, forgo
• PHRASES **resign yourself to something** = accept, succumb to, submit to, give in to, yield to, acquiesce to

resignation 1 = leaving, departure, abandonment, abdication 2 = acceptance, patience, submission, compliance, endurance, passivity, acquiescence, sufferance ≠ resistance

resigned = stoical, patient, subdued, long-suffering, compliant, unresisting

resist 1 = oppose, battle against, combat, defy, stand up to, hinder ≠ accept 2 = refrain from, avoid, keep from, forgo, abstain from, forbear ≠ indulge in 3 = withstand, be proof against

resistance 1 = opposition, hostility, aversion 2 = fighting, fight, battle, struggle, defiance, obstruction, impediment, hindrance

resistant 1 = opposed, hostile, unwilling, intractable, antagonistic, intransigent 2 = impervious, hard, strong, tough, unaffected

resolution 1 = declaration 2 = decision, resolve, intention, aim, purpose, determination, intent 3 = determination, purpose, resolve, tenacity, perseverance, willpower, firmness, steadfastness

resolve VERB 1 = work out, answer, clear up, crack, fathom 2 = decide, determine, agree, purpose, intend, fix, conclude
• NOUN 1 = determination, resolution, willpower, firmness, steadfastness, resoluteness ≠ indecision 2 = decision, resolution, objective, purpose, intention

resort 1 = holiday centre, spot, retreat, haunt, tourist centre 2 = recourse to, reference to

resound 1 = echo, resonate, reverberate, re-echo 2 = ring

resounding = echoing, full, ringing, powerful, booming, reverberating, resonant, sonorous

resource NOUN 1 = facility 2 = means, course, resort, device, expedient
• PLURAL NOUN 1 = funds, holdings, money, capital, riches, assets, wealth 2 = reserves, supplies, stocks

respect VERB 1 = think highly of, value, honour, admire, esteem, look up to, defer to, have a good *or* high opinion of 2 = show consideration for, honour, observe, heed 3 = abide by, follow, observe, comply with, obey, heed, keep to, adhere to ≠ disregard
• NOUN 1 = regard, honour, recognition, esteem, admiration, estimation ≠ contempt 2 = consideration, kindness, deference, tact, thoughtfulness, considerateness 3 = particular, way, point, matter, sense, detail, feature, aspect

respectable 1 = honourable, good, decent, worthy, upright, honest, reputable, estimable ≠ disreputable 2 = decent, neat, spruce 3 = reasonable, considerable, substantial, fair, ample, appreciable, sizable *or* sizeable ≠ small

respective = specific, own, individual, particular, relevant

respite = pause, break, rest, relief, halt, interval, recess, lull

respond 1 = answer, return, reply, counter, retort, rejoin ≠ remain silent 2 *often with to* = reply to, answer 3 = react, retaliate, reciprocate

response = answer, return, reply, reaction, feedback, retort, counterattack, rejoinder

responsibility 1 = duty, business, job, role, task, accountability, answerability 2 = fault, blame, liability, guilt, culpability 3 = obligation, duty, liability, charge, care 4 = authority, power, importance, mana (*N.Z.*) 5 = job, task, function, role 6 = level-headedness, rationality, dependability, trustworthiness, conscientiousness, sensibleness

responsible 1 = to blame, guilty, at fault, culpable 2 = in charge, in control, in authority 3 = accountable, liable, answerable ≠ unaccountable 4 = sensible, reliable, rational, dependable, trustworthy, level-headed ≠ unreliable

responsive = sensitive, open, alive, susceptible, receptive, reactive, impressionable ≠ unresponsive

rest[1] VERB 1 = relax, take it easy, sit down, be at ease, put your feet up, outspan (*S. African*) ≠ work 2 = stop, have a break, break off, take a breather (*informal*), halt, cease ≠ keep going 3 = place, repose, sit, lean, prop 4 = be placed, sit, lie, be supported, recline
• NOUN 1 = relaxation, repose, leisure ≠ work 2 = pause, break, stop, halt, interval, respite, lull, interlude 3 = refreshment, release, relief, ease, comfort, cure, remedy, solace 4 = inactivity 5 = support, stand, base, holder, prop 6 = calm, tranquillity, stillness

rest[2] = remainder, remains, excess, remnants, others, balance, surplus, residue

restaurant = café, diner (*chiefly U.S. & Canad.*), bistro, cafeteria, tearoom, eatery *or* eaterie

restless 1 = unsettled, nervous, edgy, fidgeting, on edge, restive, jumpy, fidgety ≠ relaxed 2 = moving, wandering, unsettled, unstable, roving, transient, nomadic ≠ settled

restoration 1 = reinstatement, return, revival, restitution, re-establishment, replacement ≠ abolition 2 = repair, reconstruction, renewal, renovation, revitalization ≠ demolition

restore 1 = reinstate, re-establish, reintroduce ≠ abolish 2 = revive, build up, strengthen, refresh, revitalize ≠ make worse 3 = re-establish, replace, reinstate, give back 4 = repair, refurbish, renovate, reconstruct, fix (up), renew, rebuild, mend ≠ demolish 5 = return, replace, recover,

bring back, send back, hand back
restrain **1** = hold back, control, check, contain, restrict, curb, hamper, hinder ≠ encourage **2** = control, inhibit
restrained **1** = controlled, moderate, self-controlled, calm, mild, undemonstrative ≠ hot-headed **2** = unobtrusive, discreet, subdued, tasteful, quiet ≠ garish
restraint **1** = limitation, limit, check, ban, embargo, curb, rein, interdict ≠ freedom **2** = self-control, self-discipline, self-restraint, self-possession ≠ self-indulgence **3** = constraint, limitation, inhibition, control, restriction
restrict **1** = limit, regulate, curb, ration ≠ widen **2** = hamper, handicap, restrain, inhibit
restriction **1** = control, rule, regulation, curb, restraint, confinement **2** = limitation, handicap, inhibition
result NOUN **1** = consequence, effect, outcome, end result, product, sequel, upshot ≠ cause **2** = outcome, end
• VERB = arise, follow, issue, happen, appear, develop, spring, derive
resume = begin again, continue, go on with, proceed with, carry on, reopen, restart ≠ discontinue
résumé = summary, synopsis, précis, rundown, recapitulation
resumption = continuation, carrying on, reopening, renewal, restart, resurgence, re-establishment
resurgence = revival, return, renaissance, resurrection, resumption, rebirth, re-emergence
resurrect **1** = revive, renew, bring back, reintroduce **2** = restore to life, raise from the dead
resurrection **1** = revival, restoration, renewal, resurgence, return, renaissance, rebirth, reappearance ≠ killing off **2** *usually caps* = raising *or* rising from the dead, return from the dead ≠ demise
retain **1** = maintain, reserve, preserve, keep up, continue to have **2** = keep, save ≠ let go
retaliate = pay someone back, hit back, strike back, reciprocate, take revenge, get even with (*informal*), get your own back (*informal*) ≠ turn the other cheek
retaliation = revenge, repayment, vengeance, reprisal, an eye for an eye, reciprocation, requital, counterblow
retard = slow down, check, arrest, delay, handicap, hinder, impede, set back ≠ speed up
retire **1** = stop working, give up work **2** = withdraw, leave, exit, go away, depart **3** = go to bed, turn in (*informal*), hit the sack (*slang*), hit the hay (*slang*)
retirement = withdrawal, retreat, privacy, solitude, seclusion
retiring = shy, reserved, quiet, timid, unassuming, self-effacing, bashful, unassertive ≠ outgoing
retort VERB = reply, return, answer, respond, counter, come back with, riposte
• NOUN = reply, answer, response, comeback, riposte, rejoinder
retreat VERB = withdraw, back off, draw back, leave, go back, depart, fall back, pull back ≠ advance
• NOUN **1** = flight, retirement, departure, withdrawal, evacuation ≠ advance **2** = refuge, haven, shelter, sanctuary, hideaway, seclusion
retrieve **1** = get back, regain, recover, restore, recapture **2** = redeem, save, win back, recoup
retrospect = hindsight, review, re-examination ≠ foresight
return VERB **1** = come back, go back, retreat, turn back, revert, reappear ≠ depart **2** = put back, replace, restore, reinstate ≠ keep **3** = give back, repay, refund, pay back, reimburse, recompense ≠ keep **4** = recur, repeat, persist, revert, happen again, reappear, come again **5** = elect, choose, vote in
• NOUN **1** = reappearance ≠ departure **2** = restoration, reinstatement, re-establishment ≠ removal **3** = recurrence, repetition, reappearance, reversion, persistence **4** = profit, interest, gain, income, revenue, yield, proceeds, takings **5** = statement, report, form, list, account, summary
revamp = renovate, restore, overhaul, refurbish, do up (*informal*), recondition
reveal **1** = make known, disclose, give away, make public, tell, announce, proclaim, let out ≠ keep secret **2** = show, display, exhibit, unveil, uncover, manifest, unearth, unmask ≠ hide
revel VERB = celebrate, carouse, live it up (*informal*), make merry
• NOUN *often plural* = merrymaking, party,

celebration, spree, festivity, carousal
revelation 1 = disclosure, news, announcement, publication, leak, confession, divulgence 2 = exhibition, publication, exposure, unveiling, uncovering, unearthing, proclamation
revenge NOUN = retaliation, vengeance, reprisal, retribution, an eye for an eye
• VERB = avenge, repay, take revenge for, get your own back for (*informal*)
revenue = income, returns, profits, gain, yield, proceeds, receipts, takings ≠ expenditure
revere = be in awe of, respect, honour, worship, reverence, exalt, look up to, venerate ≠ despise
reverse VERB 1 (*Law*) = change, cancel, overturn, overthrow, undo, repeal, quash, revoke ≠ implement 2 = turn round, turn over, turn upside down, upend 3 = transpose, change, move, exchange, transfer, switch, shift, alter 4 = go backwards, retreat, back up, turn back, move backwards, back ≠ go forward
• NOUN 1 = opposite, contrary, converse, inverse 2 = misfortune, blow, failure, disappointment, setback, hardship, reversal, adversity 3 = back, rear, other side, wrong side, underside ≠ front
• ADJECTIVE = opposite, contrary, converse
revert 1 = go back, return, come back, resume 2 = return
review NOUN 1 = survey, study, analysis, examination, scrutiny 2 = critique, commentary, evaluation, notice, criticism, judgment 3 = inspection, parade, march past 4 = magazine, journal, periodical, zine (*informal*)
• VERB 1 = reconsider, revise, rethink, reassess, re-examine, re-evaluate, think over 2 = assess, study, judge, evaluate, criticize 3 = inspect, check, survey, examine, vet 4 = look back on, remember, recall, reflect on, recollect
reviewer = critic, judge, commentator
revise 1 = change, review 2 = edit, correct, alter, update, amend, rework, redo, emend 3 = study, go over, run through, cram (*informal*), swot up on (*Brit. informal*)
revision 1 = emendation, updating, correction 2 = change, amendment 3 = studying, cramming (*informal*), swotting (*Brit. informal*), homework
revival 1 = resurgence ≠ decline 2 = reawakening, renaissance, renewal, resurrection, rebirth, revitalization
revive 1 = revitalize, restore, renew, rekindle, invigorate, reanimate 2 = bring round, awaken 3 = come round, recover 4 = refresh ≠ exhaust
revolt NOUN = uprising, rising, revolution, rebellion, mutiny, insurrection, insurgency
• VERB 1 = rebel, rise up, resist, mutiny 2 = disgust, sicken, repel, repulse, nauseate, gross out (*U.S. slang*), turn your stomach, make your flesh creep
revolting = disgusting, foul, horrible, sickening, horrid, repellent, repulsive, nauseating, yucko (*Austral. slang*) ≠ delightful
revolution 1 = revolt, rising, coup, rebellion, uprising, mutiny, insurgency 2 = transformation, shift, innovation, upheaval, reformation, sea change 3 = rotation, turn, cycle, circle, spin, lap, circuit, orbit
revolutionary ADJECTIVE 1 = rebel, radical, extremist, subversive, insurgent ≠ reactionary 2 = innovative, new, different, novel, radical, progressive, drastic, ground-breaking ≠ conventional
• NOUN = rebel, insurgent, revolutionist ≠ reactionary
revolve 1 = go round, circle, orbit 2 = rotate, turn, wheel, spin, twist, whirl
reward NOUN 1 = punishment, retribution, comeuppance (*slang*), just deserts 2 = payment, return, prize, wages, compensation, bonus, premium, repayment ≠ penalty
• VERB = compensate, pay, repay, recompense, remunerate ≠ penalize
rewarding = satisfying, fulfilling, valuable, profitable, productive, worthwhile, beneficial, enriching ≠ unrewarding
rhetoric 1 = hyperbole, bombast, wordiness, verbosity, grandiloquence, magniloquence 2 = oratory, eloquence, public speaking, speech-making, elocution, declamation, grandiloquence, whaikorero (*N.Z.*)
rhetorical = high-flown, bombastic, verbose, oratorical, grandiloquent, declamatory, arty-farty (*informal*), magniloquent
rhyme = poem, song, verse, ode
rhythm 1 = beat, swing, accent, pulse, tempo, cadence, lilt 2 = metre, time

rich 1 = wealthy, affluent, well-off, loaded (*slang*), prosperous, well-heeled (*informal*), well-to-do, moneyed ≠ poor 2 = well-stocked, full, productive, ample, abundant, plentiful, copious, well-supplied ≠ scarce 3 = full-bodied, sweet, fatty, tasty, creamy, luscious, succulent ≠ bland 4 = fruitful, productive, fertile, prolific ≠ barren 5 = abounding, luxurious, lush, abundant

riches 1 = wealth, assets, plenty, fortune, substance, treasure, affluence ≠ poverty 2 = resources, treasures

richly 1 = elaborately, lavishly, elegantly, splendidly, exquisitely, expensively, luxuriously, gorgeously 2 = fully, well, thoroughly, amply, appropriately, properly, suitably

rid VERB = free, clear, deliver, relieve, purge, unburden, make free, disencumber
• PHRASES **get rid of something** *or* **someone** = dispose of, throw away *or* out, dump, remove, eliminate, expel, eject

riddle[1] 1 = puzzle, problem, conundrum, poser 2 = enigma, question, secret, mystery, puzzle, conundrum, teaser, problem

riddle[2] 1 = pierce, pepper, puncture, perforate, honeycomb 2 = pervade, fill, spread through

riddled = filled, spoilt, pervaded, infested, permeated

ride VERB 1 = control, handle, manage 2 = travel, be carried, go, move
• NOUN = journey, drive, trip, lift, outing, jaunt

ridicule VERB = laugh at, mock, make fun of, sneer at, jeer at, deride, poke fun at, chaff
• NOUN = mockery, scorn, derision, laughter, jeer, chaff, gibe, raillery

ridiculous = laughable, stupid, silly, absurd, ludicrous, farcical, comical, risible ≠ sensible

rife = widespread, rampant, general, common, universal, frequent, prevalent, ubiquitous

rifle = ransack, rob, burgle, loot, strip, sack, plunder, pillage

rift 1 = breach, division, split, separation, falling out (*informal*), disagreement, quarrel 2 = split, opening, crack, gap, break, fault, flaw, cleft

rig VERB 1 = fix, engineer (*informal*), arrange, manipulate, tamper with, gerrymander 2 (*Nautical*) = equip, fit out, kit out, outfit, supply, furnish
• PHRASES **rig something up** = set up, build, construct, put up, arrange, assemble, put together, erect

right ADJECTIVE 1 = correct, true, genuine, accurate, exact, precise, valid, factual, dinkum (*Austral. & N.Z. informal*) ≠ wrong 2 = proper, done, becoming, seemly, fitting, fit, appropriate, suitable ≠ inappropriate 3 = just, good, fair, moral, proper, ethical, honest, equitable ≠ unfair
• ADVERB 1 = correctly, truly, precisely, exactly, genuinely, accurately ≠ wrongly 2 = suitably, fittingly, appropriately, properly, aptly ≠ improperly 3 = exactly, squarely, precisely 4 = directly, straight, precisely, exactly, unswervingly, without deviation, by the shortest route, in a beeline 5 = straight, directly, quickly, promptly, straightaway ≠ indirectly
• NOUN 1 = prerogative, business, power, claim, authority, due, freedom, licence 2 = justice, truth, fairness, legality, righteousness, lawfulness ≠ injustice
• VERB = rectify, settle, fix, correct, sort out, straighten, redress, put right

right away = immediately, now, directly, instantly, at once, straightaway, forthwith, pronto (*informal*)

righteous = virtuous, good, just, fair, moral, pure, ethical, upright ≠ wicked

rigid 1 = strict, set, fixed, exact, rigorous, stringent ≠ flexible 2 = inflexible, uncompromising, unbending 3 = stiff, inflexible, inelastic ≠ pliable

rigorous = strict, hard, demanding, tough, severe, exacting, harsh, stern ≠ soft

rim 1 = edge, lip, brim 2 = border, edge, trim 3 = margin, border, verge, brink

ring[1] VERB 1 = phone, call, telephone, buzz (*informal, chiefly Brit.*) 2 = chime, sound, toll, reverberate, clang, peal 3 = reverberate
• NOUN 1 = call, phone call, buzz (*informal, chiefly Brit.*) 2 = chime, knell, peal

ring[2] NOUN 1 = circle, round, band, circuit, loop, hoop, halo 2 = arena, enclosure, circus, rink 3 = gang, group, association, band, circle, mob, syndicate, cartel
• VERB = encircle, surround, enclose, girdle, gird

rinse VERB = wash, clean, dip, splash, cleanse, bathe

• NOUN = wash, dip, splash, bath
riot NOUN 1 = disturbance, disorder, confusion, turmoil, upheaval, strife, turbulence, lawlessness 2 = display, show, splash, extravaganza, profusion 3 = laugh, joke, scream (*informal*), hoot (*informal*), lark
• VERB = rampage, run riot, go on the rampage
• PHRASES **run riot** 1 = rampage, go wild, be out of control 2 = grow profusely, spread like wildfire
rip VERB 1 = tear, cut, split, burst, rend, slash, claw, slit 2 = be torn, tear, split, burst
• NOUN = tear, cut, hole, split, rent, slash, slit, gash
• PHRASES **rip someone off** (*Slang*) = cheat, rob, con (*informal*), skin (*slang*), fleece, defraud, swindle
ripe 1 = ripened, seasoned, ready, mature, mellow ≠ unripe 2 = right, suitable 3 = mature 4 = suitable, timely, ideal, favourable, auspicious, opportune ≠ unsuitable
rip-off *or* **ripoff** (*Slang*) = cheat, con (*informal*), scam (*slang*), con trick (*informal*), fraud, theft, swindle
rise VERB 1 = get up, stand up, get to your feet 2 = arise 3 = go up, climb, ascend ≠ descend 4 = loom, tower 5 = get steeper, ascend, go uphill, slope upwards ≠ drop 6 = increase, mount ≠ decrease 7 = grow, go up, intensify 8 = rebel, revolt, mutiny 9 = advance, progress, get on, prosper
• NOUN 1 = upward slope, incline, elevation, ascent, kopje *or* koppie (*S. African*) 2 = increase, upturn, upswing, upsurge ≠ decrease 3 = pay increase, raise (*U.S.*), increment 4 = advancement, progress, climb, promotion
• PHRASES **give rise to something** = cause, produce, effect, result in, bring about
risk NOUN 1 = danger, chance, possibility, hazard 2 = gamble, chance, speculation, leap in the dark 3 = peril, jeopardy
• VERB 1 = stand a chance of 2 = dare, endanger, jeopardize, imperil, venture, gamble, hazard
risky = dangerous, hazardous, unsafe, perilous, uncertain, dodgy (*Brit., Austral., & N.Z. informal*), dicey (*informal, chiefly Brit.*), chancy (*informal*) ≠ safe
rite = ceremony, custom, ritual, practice, procedure, observance
ritual NOUN 1 = ceremony, rite, observance 2 = custom, tradition, routine, convention, practice, procedure, habit, protocol, tikanga (*N.Z.*)
• ADJECTIVE = ceremonial, conventional, routine, customary, habitual
rival NOUN = opponent, competitor, contender, contestant, adversary ≠ supporter
• VERB = compete with, match, equal, compare with, come up to, be a match for
• ADJECTIVE = competing, conflicting, opposing
rivalry = competition, opposition, conflict, contest, contention
river 1 = stream, brook, creek, waterway, tributary, burn (*Scot.*) 2 = flow, rush, flood, spate, torrent
riveting = enthralling, gripping, fascinating, absorbing, captivating, hypnotic, engrossing, spellbinding
road 1 = roadway, highway, motorway, track, route, path, lane, pathway 2 = way, path
roam = wander, walk, range, travel, stray, ramble, prowl, rove
roar VERB 1 = thunder 2 = guffaw, laugh heartily, hoot, split your sides (*informal*) 3 = cry, shout, yell, howl, bellow, bawl, bay
• NOUN 1 = guffaw, hoot 2 = cry, shout, yell, howl, outcry, bellow
rob 1 = steal from, hold up, mug (*informal*) 2 = raid, hold up, loot, plunder, burgle, pillage 3 = dispossess, con (*informal*), cheat, defraud 4 = deprive, do out of (*informal*)
robber = thief, raider, burglar, looter, fraud, cheat, bandit, plunderer
robbery 1 = burglary, raid, hold-up, rip-off (*slang*), stick-up (*slang, chiefly U.S.*) 2 = theft, stealing, mugging (*informal*), plunder, swindle, pillage, larceny
robe = gown, costume, habit
robot = machine, automaton, android, mechanical man
robust = strong, tough, powerful, fit, healthy, strapping, hardy, vigorous ≠ weak
rock[1] = stone, boulder
rock[2] 1 = sway, pitch, swing, reel, toss, lurch, roll 2 = shock, surprise, shake, stun, astonish, stagger, astound
rocky[1] = rough, rugged, stony, craggy

rocky² = unstable, shaky, wobbly, rickety, unsteady
rod 1 = stick, bar, pole, shaft, cane 2 = staff, baton, wand
rogue 1 = scoundrel, crook (*informal*), villain, fraud, blackguard, skelm (*S. African*), rorter (*Austral. slang*) 2 = scamp, rascal, scally (*Northwest English dialect*), nointer (*Austral. slang*)
role 1 = job, part, position, post, task, duty, function, capacity 2 = part, character, representation, portrayal
roll VERB 1 = turn, wheel, spin, go round, revolve, rotate, whirl, swivel 2 = trundle, go, move 3 = flow, run, course 4 *often with up* = wind, bind, wrap, swathe, envelop, furl, enfold 5 = level, even, press, smooth, flatten 6 = toss, rock, lurch, reel, tumble, sway
• NOUN 1 = rumble, boom, roar, thunder, reverberation 2 = register, record, list, index, census 3 = turn, spin, rotation, cycle, wheel, revolution, reel, whirl
romance 1 = love affair, relationship, affair, attachment, liaison, amour 2 = excitement, colour, charm, mystery, glamour, fascination 3 = story, tale, fantasy, legend, fairy tale, love story, melodrama
romantic ADJECTIVE 1 = loving, tender, passionate, fond, sentimental, amorous, icky (*informal*) ≠ unromantic 2 = idealistic, unrealistic, impractical, dreamy, starry-eyed ≠ realistic 3 = exciting, fascinating, mysterious, colourful, glamorous ≠ unexciting
• NOUN = idealist, dreamer, sentimentalist
romp VERB = frolic, sport, have fun, caper, cavort, frisk, gambol
• NOUN = frolic, lark (*informal*), caper
room 1 = chamber, office, apartment 2 = space, area, capacity, extent, expanse 3 = opportunity, scope, leeway, chance, range, occasion, margin
root¹ NOUN 1 = stem, tuber, rhizome 2 = source, cause, heart, bottom, base, seat, seed, foundation
• PLURAL NOUN = sense of belonging, origins, heritage, birthplace, home, family, cradle
• PHRASES **root something** *or* **someone out** = get rid of, remove, eliminate, abolish, eradicate, do away with, weed out, exterminate
root² = dig, burrow, ferret
rope NOUN = cord, line, cable, strand, hawser
• PHRASES **know the ropes** = be experienced, be knowledgeable, be an old hand ◆ **rope someone in** *or* **into something** (*Brit.*) = persuade, involve, engage, enlist, talk into, inveigle
rosy ADJECTIVE 1 = glowing, blooming, radiant, ruddy, healthy-looking ≠ pale 2 = promising, encouraging, bright, optimistic, hopeful, cheerful, favourable, auspicious ≠ gloomy
• NOUN = pink, red
rot VERB 1 = decay, spoil, deteriorate, perish, decompose, moulder, go bad, putrefy 2 = crumble 3 = deteriorate, decline, waste away
• NOUN 1 = decay, decomposition, corruption, mould, blight, canker, putrefaction 2 (*Informal*) = nonsense, rubbish, drivel, twaddle, garbage (*chiefly U.S.*), trash, tripe (*informal*), claptrap (*informal*), bizzo (*Austral. slang*), bull's wool (*Austral. & N.Z. slang*)
RELATED WORD
adjective: putrid
rotate 1 = revolve, turn, wheel, spin, reel, go round, swivel, pivot 2 = follow in sequence, switch, alternate, take turns
rotation 1 = revolution, turning, turn, wheel, spin, spinning, reel, orbit 2 = sequence, switching, cycle, succession, alternation
rotten 1 = decaying, bad, rank, corrupt, sour, stinking, perished, festering, festy (*Austral. slang*) ≠ fresh 2 = crumbling, perished 3 (*Informal*) = despicable, mean, base, dirty, nasty, contemptible 4 (*Informal*) = inferior, poor, inadequate, duff (*Brit. informal*), unsatisfactory, lousy (*slang*), substandard, crummy (*slang*), bodger *or* bodgie (*Austral. slang*) 5 = corrupt, immoral, crooked (*informal*), dishonest, dishonourable, perfidious ≠ honourable
rough ADJECTIVE 1 = uneven, broken, rocky, irregular, jagged, bumpy, stony, craggy ≠ even 2 = boisterous, hard, tough, arduous 3 = ungracious, blunt, rude, coarse, brusque, uncouth, impolite, uncivil ≠ refined 4 = unpleasant, hard, difficult, tough, uncomfortable ≠ easy 5 = approximate, estimated ≠ exact 6 = vague, general, sketchy, imprecise,

inexact **7** = basic, crude, unfinished, incomplete, imperfect, rudimentary, sketchy, unrefined ≠ complete **8** = stormy, wild, turbulent, choppy, squally ≠ calm **9** = harsh, tough, nasty, cruel, unfeeling ≠ gentle
• NOUN = outline, draft, mock-up, preliminary sketch
• PHRASES **rough and ready** **1** = makeshift, crude, provisional, improvised, sketchy, stopgap **2** = unrefined, shabby, untidy, unkempt, unpolished, ill-groomed ◆ **rough something out** = outline, plan, draft, sketch

round NOUN **1** = series, session, cycle, sequence, succession **2** = stage, turn, level, period, division, session, lap **3** = sphere, ball, band, ring, circle, disc, globe, orb **4** = course, tour, circuit, beat, series, schedule, routine
• ADJECTIVE **1** = spherical, rounded, curved, circular, cylindrical, rotund, globular **2** = plump, full, ample, fleshy, rotund, full-fleshed
• VERB = go round, circle, skirt, flank, bypass, encircle, turn
• PHRASES **round something** *or* **someone up** = gather, muster, group, drive, collect, rally, herd, marshal

roundabout **1** = indirect, devious, tortuous, circuitous, evasive, discursive ≠ direct **2** = oblique, implied, indirect, circuitous

roundup = muster, collection, rally, assembly, herding

rouse **1** = wake up, call, wake, awaken **2** = excite, move, stir, provoke, anger, animate, agitate, inflame **3** = stimulate, provoke, incite

rousing = lively, moving, spirited, exciting, inspiring, stirring, stimulating ≠ dull

rout VERB = defeat, beat, overthrow, thrash, destroy, crush, conquer, wipe the floor with (*informal*)
• NOUN = defeat, beating, overthrow, thrashing, pasting (*slang*), debacle, drubbing

route **1** = way, course, road, direction, path, journey, itinerary **2** = beat, circuit

routine NOUN = procedure, programme, order, practice, method, pattern, custom
• ADJECTIVE **1** = usual, standard, normal, customary, ordinary, typical, everyday, habitual ≠ unusual **2** = boring, dull, predictable, tedious, tiresome, humdrum

row[1] NOUN = line, bank, range, series, file, string, column
• PHRASES **in a row** = consecutively, running, in turn, one after the other, successively, in sequence

row[2] NOUN (*Informal*) **1** = quarrel, dispute, argument, squabble, tiff, trouble, brawl **2** = disturbance, noise, racket, uproar, commotion, rumpus, tumult
• VERB = quarrel, fight, argue, dispute, squabble, wrangle

royal **1** = regal, kingly, queenly, princely, imperial, sovereign **2** = splendid, grand, impressive, magnificent, majestic, stately

rub VERB **1** = stroke, massage, caress **2** = polish, clean, shine, wipe, scour **3** = chafe, scrape, grate, abrade
• NOUN **1** = massage, caress, kneading **2** = polish, stroke, shine, wipe
• PHRASES **rub something out** = erase, remove, cancel, wipe out, delete, obliterate, efface

rubbish **1** = waste, refuse, scrap, junk (*informal*), litter, garbage (*chiefly U.S.*), trash, lumber **2** = nonsense, garbage (*chiefly U.S.*), twaddle, rot, trash, hot air (*informal*), tripe (*informal*), claptrap (*informal*), bizzo (*Austral. slang*), bull's wool (*Austral. & N.Z. slang*)

rude **1** = impolite, insulting, cheeky, abusive, disrespectful, impertinent, insolent, impudent ≠ polite **2** = uncivilized, rough, coarse, brutish, boorish, uncouth, loutish, graceless **3** = vulgar ≠ refined **4** = unpleasant, sharp, sudden, harsh, startling, abrupt **5** = roughly-made, simple, rough, raw, crude, primitive, makeshift, artless ≠ well-made

rue (*Literary*) = regret, mourn, lament, repent, be sorry for, kick yourself for

ruffle **1** = disarrange, disorder, mess up, rumple, tousle, dishevel **2** = annoy, upset, irritate, agitate, nettle, fluster, peeve (*informal*) ≠ calm

rugged **1** = rocky, broken, rough, craggy, difficult, ragged, irregular, uneven ≠ even **2** = strong-featured, rough-hewn, weather-beaten ≠ delicate **3** = well-built, strong, tough, robust, sturdy **4** = tough, strong, robust, muscular, sturdy, burly, husky (*informal*), brawny ≠ delicate

ruin VERB **1** = destroy, devastate, wreck, defeat, smash, crush, demolish, lay waste ≠ create **2** = bankrupt, break, impoverish, beggar, pauperize **3** = spoil, damage, mess up, blow (*slang*), screw up (*informal*), botch, make a mess of, crool *or* cruel (*Austral. slang*) ≠ improve
• NOUN **1** = bankruptcy, insolvency, destitution **2** = disrepair, decay, disintegration, ruination, wreckage **3** = destruction, fall, breakdown, defeat, collapse, wreck, undoing, downfall ≠ preservation

rule NOUN **1** = regulation, law, direction, guideline, decree **2** = precept, principle, canon, maxim, tenet, axiom **3** = custom, procedure, practice, routine, tradition, habit, convention **4** = government, power, control, authority, command, regime, reign, jurisdiction, mana (*N.Z.*)
• VERB **1** = govern, control, direct, have power over, command over, have charge of **2** = reign, govern, be in power, be in authority **3** = decree, decide, judge, settle, pronounce **4** = be prevalent, prevail, predominate, be customary, preponderate
• PHRASES **as a rule** = usually, generally, mainly, normally, on the whole, ordinarily ◆ **rule someone out** = exclude, eliminate, disqualify, ban, reject, dismiss, prohibit, leave out ◆ **rule something out** = reject, exclude, eliminate

ruler **1** = governor, leader, lord, commander, controller, monarch, sovereign, head of state **2** = measure, rule, yardstick

ruling ADJECTIVE **1** = governing, reigning, controlling, commanding **2** = predominant, dominant, prevailing, preponderant, chief, main, principal, pre-eminent ≠ minor
• NOUN = decision, verdict, judgment, decree, adjudication, pronouncement

rumour = story, news, report, talk, word, whisper, buzz, gossip

run VERB **1** = race, rush, dash, hurry, sprint, bolt, gallop, hare (*Brit. informal*) ≠ dawdle **2** = flee, escape, take off (*informal*), bolt, beat it (*slang*), leg it (*informal*), take flight, do a runner (*slang*) ≠ stay **3** = take part, compete **4** = continue, go, stretch, reach, extend, proceed ≠ stop **5** (*Chiefly U.S. & Canad.*) = compete, stand, contend, be a candidate, put yourself up for, take part **6** = manage, lead, direct, be in charge of, head, control, operate, handle **7** = go, work, operate, perform, function **8** = perform, carry out **9** = work, go, operate, function **10** = pass, go, move, roll, glide, skim **11** = flow, pour, stream, go, leak, spill, discharge, gush **12** = publish, feature, display, print **13** = melt, dissolve, liquefy, go soft **14** = smuggle, traffic in, bootleg
• NOUN **1** = race, rush, dash, sprint, gallop, jog, spurt **2** = ride, drive, trip, spin (*informal*), outing, excursion, jaunt **3** = sequence, period, stretch, spell, course, season, series, string **4** = enclosure, pen, coop
• PHRASES **run away** = flee, escape, bolt, abscond, do a runner (*slang*), make a run for it, scram (*informal*), fly the coop (*U.S. & Canad. informal*) ◆ **run into someone** = meet, encounter, bump into, run across, come across *or* upon ◆ **run into something 1** = be beset by, encounter, come across *or* upon, face, experience **2** = collide with, hit, strike ◆ **run out 1** = be used up, dry up, give out, fail, finish, be exhausted **2** = expire, end, terminate ◆ **run over something 1** = exceed, overstep, go over the top of, go over the limit of **2** = review, check, go through, go over, run through, rehearse ◆ **run over something** *or* **someone** = knock down, hit, run down, knock over ◆ **run something** *or* **someone down 1** = criticize, denigrate, belittle, knock (*informal*), rubbish (*informal*), slag (off) (*slang*), disparage, decry **2** = downsize, cut, reduce, trim, decrease, cut back, curtail **3** = knock down, hit, run into, run over, knock over

run-down *or* **rundown 1** = exhausted, weak, drained, weary, unhealthy, worn-out, debilitated, below par ≠ fit **2** = dilapidated, broken-down, shabby, worn-out, seedy, ramshackle, decrepit

runner 1 = athlete, sprinter, jogger **2** = messenger, courier, errand boy, dispatch bearer

running NOUN **1** = management, control, administration, direction, leadership, organization, supervision **2** = working, performance, operation, functioning, maintenance
• ADJECTIVE **1** = continuous, constant, perpetual, uninterrupted, incessant **2** = in succession, unbroken **3** = flowing, moving,

streaming, coursing
rupture NOUN = break, tear, split, crack, rent, burst, breach, fissure
• VERB = break, separate, tear, split, crack, burst, sever
rural 1 = agricultural, country 2 = rustic, country, pastoral, sylvan ≠ urban
rush VERB 1 = hurry, run, race, shoot, fly, career, speed, tear ≠ dawdle 2 = push, hurry, press, hustle 3 = attack, storm, charge at
• NOUN 1 = dash, charge, race, scramble, stampede 2 = hurry, haste, hustle 3 = surge, flow, gush 4 = attack, charge, assault, onslaught
• ADJECTIVE = hasty, fast, quick, hurried, rapid, urgent, swift ≠ leisurely
rust NOUN 1 = corrosion, oxidation 2 = mildew, must, mould, rot, blight
• VERB = corrode, oxidize
rusty 1 = corroded, rusted, oxidized, rust-covered 2 = out of practice, weak, stale, unpractised 3 = reddish-brown, chestnut, reddish, russet, coppery, rust-coloured
ruthless = merciless, harsh, cruel, brutal, relentless, callous, heartless, remorseless ≠ merciful

S

sabotage VERB = damage, destroy, wreck, disable, disrupt, subvert, incapacitate, vandalize
• NOUN = damage, destruction, wrecking
sack[1] NOUN 1 = bag, pocket, sac, pouch, receptacle 2 = dismissal, discharge, the boot (*slang*), the axe (*informal*), the push (*slang*)
• VERB (*Informal*) = dismiss, fire (*informal*), axe (*informal*), discharge, kiss off (*slang, chiefly U.S. & Canad.*), give (someone) the push (*informal*)
sack[2] VERB = plunder, loot, pillage, strip, rob, raid, ruin
• NOUN = plundering, looting, pillage
sacred 1 = holy, hallowed, blessed, divine, revered, sanctified ≠ secular 2 = religious, holy, ecclesiastical, hallowed ≠ unconsecrated 3 = inviolable, protected, sacrosanct, hallowed, inalienable, unalterable
sacrifice VERB 1 = offer, offer up, immolate 2 = give up, abandon, relinquish, lose, surrender, let go, do without, renounce
• NOUN 1 = offering, oblation 2 = surrender, loss, giving up, rejection, abdication, renunciation, repudiation, forswearing
sad 1 = unhappy, down, low blue, depressed, melancholy, mournful, dejected ≠ happy 2 = tragic, moving, upsetting, depressing, dismal, pathetic, poignant, harrowing 3 = deplorable, bad, sorry, terrible, unfortunate, regrettable, lamentable, wretched ≠ good
sadden = upset, depress, distress, grieve, make sad, deject
saddle = burden, load, lumber (*Brit. informal*), encumber
sadness = unhappiness, sorrow, grief, depression, the blues, misery, melancholy, poignancy ≠ happiness
safe ADJECTIVE 1 = protected, secure, impregnable, out of danger, safe and sound, in safe hands, out of harm's way ≠ endangered 2 = all right, intact, unscathed, unhurt, unharmed, undamaged, O.K. *or* okay (*informal*) 3 = risk-free, sound, secure, certain, impregnable
• NOUN = strongbox, vault, coffer, repository, deposit box, safe-deposit box
safeguard VERB = protect, guard, defend, save, preserve, look after, keep safe
• NOUN = protection, security, defence, guard
safely = in safety, with impunity, without risk, safe and sound
safety 1 = security, protection, safeguards, precautions, safety measures, impregnability ≠ risk 2 = shelter, haven, protection, cover, retreat, asylum, refuge, sanctuary
sag 1 = sink, bag, droop, fall, slump, dip, give way, hang loosely 2 = drop, sink, slump, flop, droop, loll 3 = decline, tire, flag, weaken, wilt, wane, droop
saga 1 = carry-on (*informal, chiefly Brit.*), performance (*informal*), pantomime (*informal*) 2 = epic, story, tale, narrative, yarn

sage NOUN = wise man, philosopher, guru, master, elder, tohunga (*N.Z.*)
• ADJECTIVE = wise, sensible, judicious, sagacious, sapient

sail NOUN = sheet, canvas
• VERB 1 = go by water, cruise, voyage, ride the waves, go by sea 2 = set sail, embark, get under way, put to sea, put off, leave port, hoist sail, cast *or* weigh anchor 3 = pilot, steer 4 = glide, sweep, float, fly, wing, soar, drift, skim

sailor = mariner, marine, seaman, sea dog, seafarer

sake NOUN = purpose, interest, reason, end, aim, objective, motive
• PHRASES **for someone's sake** = in someone's interests, to someone's advantage, on someone's account, for the benefit of, for the good of, for the welfare of, out of respect for, out of consideration for

salary = pay, income, wage, fee, payment, wages, earnings, allowance

sale 1 = selling, marketing, dealing, transaction, disposal 2 = auction, fair, mart, bazaar

salt NOUN = seasoning
• ADJECTIVE = salty, saline, brackish, briny

salute VERB 1 = greet, welcome, acknowledge, address, hail, mihi (*N.Z.*) 2 = honour, acknowledge, recognize, pay tribute *or* homage to
• NOUN = greeting, recognition, salutation, address

salvage = save, recover, rescue, get back, retrieve, redeem

salvation = saving, rescue, recovery, salvage, redemption, deliverance ≠ ruin

same 1 = identical, similar, alike, equal, twin, corresponding, duplicate ≠ different 2 = the very same, one and the same, selfsame 3 = aforementioned, aforesaid 4 = unchanged, consistent, constant, unaltered, invariable, unvarying, changeless ≠ altered

sample NOUN 1 = specimen, example, model, pattern, instance 2 = cross section
• VERB = test, try, experience, taste, inspect
• ADJECTIVE = test, trial, specimen, representative

sanction VERB = permit, allow, approve, endorse, authorize ≠ forbid
• NOUN 1 *often plural* = ban, boycott, embargo, exclusion, penalty, coercive measures ≠ permission 2 = permission, backing, authority, approval, authorization, O.K. *or* okay (*informal*), stamp *or* seal of approval ≠ ban

sanctuary 1 = protection, shelter, refuge, haven, retreat, asylum 2 = reserve, park, preserve, reservation, national park, tract, nature reserve, conservation area

sane 1 = rational, all there (*informal*), of sound mind, compos mentis (*Latin*), in your right mind, mentally sound ≠ insane 2 = sensible, sound, reasonable, balanced, judicious, level-headed ≠ foolish

sap[1] 1 = juice, essence, vital fluid, lifeblood 2 (*Slang*) = fool, jerk (*slang, chiefly U.S. & Canad.*), idiot, wally (*slang*), twit (*informal*), simpleton, ninny, dorba *or* dorb (*Austral. slang*), bogan (*Austral. slang*)

sap[2] = weaken, drain, undermine, exhaust, deplete

satanic = evil, demonic, hellish, black, wicked, devilish, infernal, fiendish ≠ godly

satire 1 = mockery, irony, ridicule 2 = parody, mockery, caricature, lampoon, burlesque

satisfaction 1 = fulfilment, pleasure, achievement, relish, gratification, pride ≠ dissatisfaction 2 = contentment, content, comfort, pleasure, happiness, enjoyment, satiety, repletion ≠ discontent

satisfactory = adequate, acceptable, good enough, average, fair, all right, sufficient, passable ≠ unsatisfactory

satisfy 1 = content, please, indulge, gratify, pander to, assuage, pacify, quench ≠ dissatisfy 2 = convince, persuade, assure, reassure ≠ dissuade 3 = comply with, meet, fulfil, answer, serve, fill, observe, obey ≠ fail to meet

saturate 1 = flood, overwhelm, swamp, overrun 2 = soak, steep, drench, imbue, suffuse, wet through, waterlog, souse

saturated = soaked, soaking (wet), drenched, sodden, dripping, waterlogged, sopping (wet), wet through

sauce = dressing, dip, relish, condiment

savage ADJECTIVE 1 = cruel, brutal, vicious, fierce, harsh, ruthless, ferocious, sadistic ≠ gentle 2 = wild, fierce, ferocious, unbroken, feral, untamed, undomesticated ≠ tame 3 = primitive, undeveloped, uncultivated, uncivilized 4 = uncultivated, rugged, unspoilt, uninhabited, rough, uncivilized

≠ cultivated
• NOUN = lout, yob (*Brit. slang*), barbarian, yahoo, hoon (*Austral. & N.Z.*), boor, cougan (*Austral. slang*), scozza (*Austral. slang*), bogan (*Austral. slang*)
• VERB = maul, tear, claw, attack, mangle, lacerate, mangulate (*Austral. slang*)

save 1 = rescue, free, release, deliver, recover, get out, liberate, salvage ≠ endanger 2 = keep, reserve, set aside, store, collect, gather, hold, hoard ≠ spend 3 = protect, keep, guard, preserve, look after, safeguard, salvage, conserve 4 = put aside, keep, reserve, collect, retain, set aside, put by

saving NOUN = economy, discount, reduction, bargain
• PLURAL NOUN = nest egg, fund, store, reserves, resources

saviour = rescuer, deliverer, defender, protector, liberator, redeemer, preserver

Saviour = Christ, Jesus, the Messiah, the Redeemer

savour VERB 1 = relish, delight in, revel in, luxuriate in 2 = enjoy, appreciate, relish, delight in, revel in, luxuriate in
• NOUN = flavour, taste, smell, relish, smack, tang, piquancy

say VERB 1 = state, declare, remark, announce, maintain, mention, assert, affirm 2 = speak, utter, voice, express, pronounce 3 = suggest, express, imply, communicate, disclose, give away, convey, divulge 4 = suppose, supposing, imagine, assume, presume 5 = estimate, suppose, guess, conjecture, surmise
• NOUN 1 = influence, power, control, authority, weight, clout (*informal*), mana (*N.Z.*) 2 = chance to speak, vote, voice

saying = proverb, maxim, adage, dictum, axiom, aphorism

scale[1] = flake, plate, layer, lamina

scale[2] NOUN 1 = degree, size, range, extent, dimensions, scope, magnitude, breadth 2 = system of measurement, measuring system 3 = ranking, ladder, hierarchy, series, sequence, progression 4 = ratio, proportion
• VERB = climb up, mount, ascend, surmount, clamber up, escalade

scan 1 = glance over, skim, look over, eye, check, examine, check out (*informal*), run over 2 = survey, search, investigate, sweep, scour, scrutinize

scandal 1 = disgrace, crime, offence, sin, embarrassment, wrongdoing, dishonourable behaviour, discreditable behaviour 2 = gossip, talk, rumours, dirt, slander, tattle, aspersion 3 = shame, disgrace, stigma, infamy, opprobrium 4 = outrage, shame, insult, disgrace, injustice, crying shame

scant = inadequate, meagre, sparse, little, minimal, barely sufficient ≠ adequate

scapegoat = fall guy, whipping boy

scar NOUN 1 = mark, injury, wound, blemish 2 = trauma, suffering, pain, torture, anguish
• VERB = mark, disfigure, damage, mar, mutilate, blemish, deface

scarce 1 = in short supply, insufficient ≠ plentiful 2 = rare, few, uncommon, few and far between, infrequent ≠ common

scarcely 1 = hardly, barely 2 (*Often used ironically*) = by no means, hardly, definitely not

scare VERB = frighten, alarm, terrify, panic, shock, startle, intimidate, dismay
• NOUN 1 = fright, shock, start 2 = panic, hysteria 3 = alert, warning, alarm

scared = afraid, alarmed, frightened, terrified, shaken, startled, fearful, petrified

scary (*Informal*) = frightening, alarming, terrifying, chilling, horrifying, spooky (*informal*), creepy (*informal*), spine-chilling

scatter 1 = throw about, spread, sprinkle, strew, shower, fling, diffuse, disseminate ≠ gather 2 = disperse, dispel, disband, dissipate ≠ assemble

scenario 1 = situation 2 = story line, résumé, outline, summary, synopsis

scene 1 = act, part, division, episode 2 = setting, set, background, location, backdrop 3 = site, place, setting, area, position, spot, locality 4 (*Informal*) = world, business, environment, arena 5 = view, prospect, panorama, vista, landscape, outlook 6 = fuss, to-do, row, performance, exhibition, carry-on (*informal, chiefly Brit.*), tantrum, commotion

scenery 1 = landscape, view, surroundings, terrain, vista 2 (*Theatre*) = set, setting, backdrop, flats, stage set

scenic = picturesque, beautiful, spectacular, striking, panoramic
scent NOUN **1** = fragrance, smell, perfume, bouquet, aroma, odour **2** = trail, track, spoor
• VERB = smell, sense, detect, sniff, discern, nose out
scented = fragrant, perfumed, aromatic, sweet-smelling, odoriferous
sceptic **1** = doubter, cynic, disbeliever **2** = agnostic, doubter, unbeliever, doubting Thomas
sceptical = doubtful, cynical, dubious, unconvinced, disbelieving, incredulous, mistrustful ≠ convinced
scepticism = doubt, suspicion, disbelief, cynicism, incredulity
schedule NOUN = plan, programme, agenda, calendar, timetable
• VERB = plan, set up, book, programme, arrange, organize
scheme NOUN **1** = plan, programme, strategy, system, project, proposal, tactics **2** = plot, ploy, ruse, intrigue, conspiracy, manoeuvre, subterfuge, stratagem
• VERB = plot, plan, intrigue, manoeuvre, conspire, contrive, collude, machinate
scheming = calculating, cunning, sly, tricky, wily, artful, conniving, underhand ≠ straightforward
scholar **1** = intellectual, academic, savant, acca (*Austral. slang*) **2** = student, pupil, learner, schoolboy *or* schoolgirl
scholarly = learned, academic, intellectual, lettered, erudite, scholastic, bookish ≠ uneducated
scholarship **1** = grant, award, payment, endowment, fellowship, bursary **2** = learning, education, knowledge, erudition, book-learning
school NOUN **1** = academy, college, institution, institute, seminary **2** = group, set, circle, faction, followers, disciples, devotees, denomination
• VERB = train, coach, discipline, educate, drill, tutor, instruct
science = discipline, body of knowledge, branch of knowledge
scientific = systematic, accurate, exact, precise, controlled, mathematical
scientist = researcher, inventor, boffin (*informal*), technophile
scoff[1] = scorn, mock, laugh at, ridicule, knock (*informal*), despise, sneer, jeer
scoff[2] = gobble (up), wolf, devour, bolt, guzzle, gulp down, gorge yourself on
scoop VERB = win, get, land, gain, achieve, earn, secure, obtain
• NOUN **1** = ladle, spoon, dipper **2** = exclusive, exposé, revelation, sensation
• PHRASES **scoop something** *or* **someone up** = gather up, lift, pick up, take up, sweep up *or* away ◆ **scoop something out** **1** = take out, empty, spoon out, bail *or* bale out **2** = dig, shovel, excavate, gouge, hollow out
scope **1** = opportunity, room, freedom, space, liberty, latitude **2** = range, capacity, reach, area, outlook, orbit, span, sphere
scorch = burn, sear, roast, wither, shrivel, parch, singe
scorching = burning, boiling, baking, flaming, roasting, searing, fiery, red-hot
score VERB **1** = gain, win, achieve, make, get, attain, notch up (*informal*), chalk up (*informal*) **2** (*Music*) = arrange, set, orchestrate, adapt **3** = cut, scratch, mark, slash, scrape, graze, gouge, deface
• NOUN **1** = rating, mark, grade, percentage **2** = points, result, total, outcome **3** = composition, soundtrack, arrangement, orchestration **4** = grievance, wrong, injury, injustice, grudge
• PLURAL NOUN = lots, loads, many, millions, hundreds, masses, swarms, multitudes
• PHRASES **score something out** *or* **through** = cross out, delete, strike out, cancel, obliterate
scorn NOUN = contempt, disdain, mockery, derision, sarcasm, disparagement ≠ respect
• VERB = despise, reject, disdain, slight, be above, spurn, deride, flout ≠ respect
scour[1] = scrub, clean, polish, rub, buff, abrade
scour[2] = search, hunt, comb, ransack
scout NOUN = vanguard, lookout, precursor, outrider, reconnoitrer, advance guard
• VERB = reconnoitre, investigate, watch, survey, observe, spy, probe, recce (*slang*)
scramble VERB **1** = struggle, climb, crawl, swarm, scrabble **2** = strive, rush, contend, vie, run, push, jostle **3** = jumble, mix up, muddle, shuffle
• NOUN **1** = clamber, ascent **2** = race, competition, struggle, rush, confusion, commotion, melee *or* mêlée

scrap[1] **NOUN 1** = piece, fragment, bit, grain, particle, portion, part, crumb **2** = waste, junk, off cuts
• **PLURAL NOUN** = leftovers, remains, bits, leavings
• **VERB** = get rid of, drop, abandon, ditch (*slang*), discard, write off, jettison, throw away *or* out ≠ bring back

scrap[2] (*Informal*) **NOUN** = fight, battle, row, argument, dispute, disagreement, quarrel, squabble, biffo (*Austral. slang*)
• **VERB** = fight, argue, row, squabble, wrangle

scrape VERB 1 = rake, sweep, drag, brush **2** = grate, grind, scratch, squeak, rasp **3** = graze, skin, scratch, bark, scuff, rub **4** = clean, remove, scour
• **NOUN** (*Informal*) = predicament, difficulty, fix (*informal*), mess, dilemma, plight, tight spot, awkward situation

scratch VERB 1 = rub, scrape, claw at **2** = mark, cut, score, damage, grate, graze, etch, lacerate
• **NOUN** = mark, scrape, graze, blemish, gash, laceration, claw mark
• **PHRASES up to scratch** (*Informal*) = adequate, acceptable, satisfactory, sufficient, up to standard

scream VERB = cry, yell, shriek, screech, bawl, howl
• **NOUN** = cry, yell, howl, shriek, screech, yelp

screen NOUN = cover, guard, shade, shelter, shield, partition, cloak, canopy
• **VERB 1** = broadcast, show, put on, present, air, cable, beam, transmit **2** = cover, hide, conceal, shade, mask, veil, cloak **3** = investigate, test, check, examine, scan **4** = process, sort, examine, filter, scan, evaluate, gauge, sift **5** = protect, guard, shield, defend, shelter

screw NOUN = nail, pin, tack, rivet, fastener, spike
• **VERB 1** = fasten, fix, attach, bolt, clamp, rivet **2** = turn, twist, tighten **3** (*Informal*) = cheat, do (*slang*), rip (someone) off (*slang*), skin (*slang*), trick, con, sting (*informal*), fleece **4** (*Informal*) *often with* ***out of*** = squeeze, wring, extract, wrest
• **PHRASES screw something up 1** = contort, wrinkle, distort, pucker **2** (*Informal*) = bungle, botch, mess up, spoil, mishandle, make a mess of (*slang*), make a hash of (*informal*), crool *or* cruel (*Austral. slang*)

scribble = scrawl, write, jot dash off

script NOUN 1 = text, lines, words, book, copy, dialogue, libretto **2** = handwriting, writing, calligraphy, penmanship
• **VERB** = write, draft

scripture = The Bible, The Gospels, The Scriptures, The Good Book, Holy Scripture, Holy Writ, Holy Bible

scrub 1 = scour, clean, polish rub, wash, cleanse, buff **2** (*Informal*) = cancel, drop, give up, abolish, forget about, call off, delete

scrutiny = examination, study, investigation, search, analysis, inspection, exploration, perusal

sculpture NOUN = statue, figure, model, bust, effigy, figurine, statuette
• **VERB** = carve, form, model, fashion, shape, mould, sculpt, chisel

sea NOUN 1 = ocean, the deep, the waves, main **2** = mass, army, host, crowd, mob, abundance, swarm, horde
• **PHRASES at sea** = bewildered, lost, confused, puzzled, baffled, perplexed, mystified, flummoxed

RELATED WORDS
adjectives: marine, maritime

seal VERB = settle, clinch, conclude, consummate, finalize
• **NOUN 1** = sealant, sealer, adhesive **2** = authentication, stamp, confirmation, ratification, insignia, imprimatur

seam 1 = joint, closure **2** = layer, vein, stratum, lode

sear = wither, burn scorch, sizzle

search VERB = examine, investigate, explore, inspect, comb, scour, ransack, scrutinize, fossick (*Austral. & N.Z.*)
• **NOUN** = hunt, look, investigation, examination, pursuit, quest, inspection, exploration
• **PHRASES search for something** *or* **someone** = look for, hunt for, pursue

searching = keen, sharp, probing, close, intent, piercing, penetrating, quizzical ≠ superficial

searing 1 = acute, intense, shooting, severe, painful, stabbing, piercing, gut-wrenching **2** = cutting, biting, bitter, harsh, barbed, hurtful, caustic

season NOUN = period, time, term, spell
• **VERB** = flavour, salt, spice, enliven, pep up

seasoned = experienced, veteran, practised, hardened, time-served ≠ inexperienced
seasoning = flavouring, spice, salt and pepper, condiment
seat NOUN **1** = chair, bench, stall, stool, pew, settle **2** = membership, place, constituency, chair, incumbency **3** = centre, place, site, heart, capital, situation, source, hub **4** = mansion, house, residence, abode, ancestral hall • VERB **1** = sit, place, settle, set, fix, locate, install **2** = hold, take, accommodate, sit, contain, cater for
second[1] ADJECTIVE **1** = next, following, succeeding, subsequent **2** = additional, other, further, extra, alternative **3** = inferior, secondary, subordinate, lower, lesser • NOUN = supporter, assistant, aide, colleague, backer, helper, right-hand man • VERB = support, back, endorse, approve, go along with
second[2] = moment, minute, instant, flash, sec (*informal*), jiffy (*informal*), trice
secondary **1** = subordinate, minor, lesser, lower, inferior, unimportant ≠ main **2** = resultant, contingent, derived, indirect ≠ original
second-hand = used, old, hand-me-down (*informal*), nearly new
secondly = next, second, moreover, furthermore, also, in the second place
secrecy **1** = mystery, stealth, concealment, furtiveness, secretiveness, clandestineness, covertness **2** = confidentiality, privacy **3** = privacy, silence, seclusion
secret ADJECTIVE **1** = undisclosed, unknown, confidential, underground, undercover, unrevealed **2** = concealed, hidden, disguised ≠ unconcealed **3** = undercover, furtive ≠ open **4** = secretive, reserved, close ≠ frank **5** = mysterious, cryptic, abstruse, occult, clandestine, arcane ≠ straightforward • NOUN = private affair • PHRASES **in secret** = secretly, surreptitiously, slyly
secretive = reticent, reserved, close, deep, uncommunicative, tight-lipped ≠ open
secretly = in secret, privately, surreptitiously, quietly, covertly, furtively, stealthily, clandestinely
sect = group, division, faction, party, camp, denomination, schism
section **1** = part, piece, portion, division, slice, passage, segment, fraction **2** = district, area, region, sector, zone
sector **1** = part, division **2** = area, part, region, district, zone, quarter
secular = worldly, lay, earthly, civil, temporal, nonspiritual ≠ religious
secure VERB **1** = obtain, get, acquire, score (*slang*), gain, procure ≠ lose **2** = attach, stick, fix, bind, fasten ≠ detach • ADJECTIVE **1** = safe, protected, immune, unassailable ≠ unprotected **2** = fast, firm, fixed, stable, steady, fastened, immovable ≠ insecure **3** = confident, sure, easy, certain, assured, reassured ≠ uneasy
security **1** = precautions, defence, safeguards, protection, safety measures **2** = assurance, confidence, conviction, certainty, reliance, sureness, positiveness ≠ insecurity **3** = pledge, insurance, guarantee, hostage, collateral, pawn, gage, surety **4** = protection, safety, custody, refuge, sanctuary, safekeeping ≠ vulnerability
sediment = dregs, grounds, residue, lees, deposit
seduce **1** = tempt, lure, entice, mislead, deceive, beguile, lead astray, inveigle **2** = corrupt, deprave, dishonour, debauch, deflower
seductive = tempting, inviting, attractive, enticing, provocative, alluring, bewitching
see VERB **1** = perceive, spot, notice, sight, witness, observe, distinguish, glimpse **2** = understand, get, follow, realize, appreciate, grasp, comprehend, fathom **3** = find out, learn, discover, determine, verify, ascertain **4** = consider, decide, reflect, deliberate, think over **5** = make sure, ensure, guarantee, make certain, see to it **6** = accompany, show, escort, lead, walk, usher **7** = speak to, receive, interview, consult, confer with **8** = meet, come across, happen on, bump into, run across, chance on **9** = go out with, court, date (*informal*, *chiefly U.S.*), go steady with (*informal*) • PHRASES **seeing as** = since, as, in view of the fact that, inasmuch as
seed NOUN **1** = grain, pip, germ, kernel, egg, embryo, spore, ovum **2** = beginning, start, germ **3** = origin, source, nucleus **4** (*Chiefly Bible*) = offspring, children,

descendants, issue, progeny
• PHRASES **go** *or* **run to seed** = decline, deteriorate, degenerate, decay, go downhill (*informal*), let yourself go, go to pot

seek **1** = look for, pursue, search for, be after, hunt **2** = try, attempt, aim, strive, endeavour, essay, aspire to

seem = appear, give the impression of being, look

seep = ooze, well, leak, soak, trickle, exude, permeate

seethe **1** = be furious, rage, fume, simmer, see red (*informal*), be livid, go ballistic (*slang, chiefly U.S.*) **2** = boil, bubble, foam, fizz, froth

segment = section, part, piece, division, slice, portion, wedge

segregate = set apart, divide, separate, isolate, discriminate against, dissociate ≠ unite

segregation = separation, discrimination, apartheid, isolation

seize **1** = grab, grip, grasp, take, snatch, clutch, snap up, pluck ≠ let go **2** = take by storm, take over, acquire, occupy, conquer **3** = capture, catch, arrest, apprehend, take captive ≠ release

seizure **1** = attack, fit, spasm, convulsion, paroxysm **2** = taking, grabbing, annexation, confiscation, commandeering **3** = capture, arrest, apprehension

seldom = rarely, not often, infrequently, hardly ever ≠ often

select VERB = choose, take, pick, opt for, decide on, single out, adopt, settle upon ≠ reject
• ADJECTIVE **1** = choice, special, excellent, superior, first-class, hand-picked, top-notch (*informal*) ≠ ordinary **2** = exclusive, elite, privileged, cliquish ≠ indiscriminate

selection **1** = choice, choosing, pick, option, preference **2** = anthology, collection, medley, choice

selective = particular, discriminating, careful, discerning, tasteful, fastidious ≠ indiscriminate

selfish = self-centred, self-interested, greedy, ungenerous, egoistic *or* egoistical, egotistic *or* egoistical ≠ unselfish

sell VERB **1** = trade, exchange, barter ≠ buy **2** = deal in, market, trade in, stock, handle, retail, peddle, traffic in ≠ buy
• PHRASES **sell out of something** = run out of, be out of stock of

seller = dealer, merchant, vendor, agent, retailer, supplier, purveyor, salesman *or* saleswoman

send VERB **1** = dispatch, forward, direct, convey, remit **2** = propel, hurl, fling, shoot, fire, cast, let fly
• PHRASES **send something** *or* **someone up** (*Brit. informal*) = mock, mimic, parody, spoof (*informal*), imitate, take off (*informal*), make fun of, lampoon

send-off = farewell, departure, leave-taking, valediction

senior **1** = higher ranking, superior ≠ subordinate **2** = the elder, major (*Brit.*) ≠ junior

sensation **1** = feeling, sense, impression, perception, awareness, consciousness **2** = excitement, thrill, stir, furore, commotion

sensational **1** = amazing, dramatic, thrilling, astounding ≠ dull **2** = shocking, exciting, melodramatic, shock-horror (*facetious*) ≠ unexciting **3** (*Informal*) = excellent, superb, mean (*slang*), impressive, smashing (*informal*), fabulous (*informal*), marvellous, out of this world (*informal*), booshit (*Austral. slang*), exo (*Austral. slang*), sik (*Austral. slang*) ≠ ordinary

sense NOUN **1** = faculty **2** = feeling, impression, perception, awareness, consciousness, atmosphere, aura **3** = understanding, awareness **4** *sometimes plural* = intelligence, reason, understanding, brains (*informal*), judgment, wisdom, wit(s), common sense ≠ foolishness **5** = meaning, significance, import, implication, drift, gist
• VERB = perceive, feel, understand, pick up, realize, be aware of, discern, get the impression ≠ be unaware of

sensibility *often plural* = feelings, emotions, sentiments, susceptibilities, moral sense

sensible **1** = wise, practical, prudent, shrewd, judicious ≠ foolish **2** = intelligent, practical, rational, sound, realistic, sage, shrewd, down-to-earth ≠ senseless

sensitive **1** = thoughtful, kindly, concerned, patient, attentive, tactful, unselfish **2** = delicate, tender **3** = susceptible to, responsive to, easily affected by **4** = touchy, oversensitive, easily upset, easily offended, easily hurt ≠ insensitive **5** = precise, fine, acute, keen, responsive ≠ imprecise

sensitivity **1** = susceptibility, responsiveness, receptiveness, sensitiveness **2** = consideration, patience, thoughtfulness **3** = touchiness, oversensitivity **4** = responsiveness, precision, keenness, acuteness

sensual **1** = sexual, erotic, raunchy (*slang*), lewd, lascivious, lustful, lecherous **2** = physical, bodily, voluptuous, animal, luxurious, fleshly, carnal

sentence NOUN **1** = punishment, condemnation **2** = verdict, order, ruling, decision, judgment, decree
• VERB **1** = condemn, doom **2** = convict, condemn, penalize

sentiment **1** = feeling, idea, view, opinion, attitude, belief, judgment **2** = sentimentality, emotion, tenderness, romanticism, sensibility, emotionalism, mawkishness

sentimental = romantic, touching, emotional, nostalgic, maudlin, weepy (*informal*), slushy (*informal*), schmaltzy (*slang*) ≠ unsentimental

separate ADJECTIVE **1** = unconnected, individual, particular, divided, divorced, isolated, detached, disconnected ≠ connected **2** = individual, independent, apart, distinct ≠ joined
• VERB **1** = divide, detach, disconnect, disjoin ≠ combine **2** = come apart, split, come away ≠ connect **3** = sever, break apart, split in two, divide in two ≠ join **4** = split up, part, divorce, break up, part company, get divorced, be estranged **5** = distinguish, mark, single out, set apart ≠ link

separated **1** = estranged, parted, separate, apart, disunited **2** = disconnected, parted, divided, separate, disassociated, disunited, sundered

separately **1** = alone, apart, not together, severally ≠ together **2** = individually, singly

separation **1** = division, break, dissociation, disconnection, disunion **2** = split-up, parting, split, divorce, break-up, rift

sequel **1** = follow-up, continuation, development **2** = consequence, result, outcome, conclusion, end, upshot

sequence = succession, course, series, order, chain, cycle, arrangement, progression

series **1** = sequence, course, chain, succession, run, set, order, train **2** = drama, serial, soap (*informal*), sitcom (*informal*), soap opera, soapie (*Austral. slang*), situation comedy

serious **1** = grave, bad, critical, dangerous, acute, severe **2** = important, crucial, urgent, pressing, worrying, significant, grim, momentous ≠ unimportant **3** = thoughtful, detailed, careful, deep, profound, in-depth **4** = deep, sophisticated **5** = solemn, earnest, grave, sober, staid, humourless, unsmiling ≠ light-hearted **6** = sincere, earnest, genuine, honest, in earnest ≠ insincere

seriously **1** = truly, in earnest, all joking aside **2** = badly, severely, gravely, critically, acutely, dangerously

seriousness **1** = importance, gravity, urgency, significance **2** = solemnity, gravity, earnestness, gravitas

sermon = homily, address

servant = attendant, domestic, slave, maid, help, retainer, skivvy (*chiefly Brit.*)

serve **1** = work for, help, aid, assist, be in the service of **2** = perform, do, complete, fulfil, discharge **3** = be adequate, do, suffice, suit, satisfy, be acceptable, answer the purpose **4** = present, provide, supply, deliver, set out, dish up

service NOUN **1** = facility, system, resource, utility, amenity **2** = ceremony, worship, rite, observance **3** = work, labour, employment, business, office, duty **4** = check, maintenance check
• VERB = overhaul, check, maintain, tune (up), go over, fine tune

session = meeting, hearing, sitting, period, conference, congress, discussion, assembly

set[1] VERB **1** = put, place, lay, position, rest, plant, station, stick **2** = arrange, decide (upon), settle, establish, determine, fix, schedule, appoint **3** = assign, give, allot, prescribe **4** = harden, stiffen, solidify, cake, thicken, crystallize, congeal **5** = go down, sink, dip, decline, disappear, vanish, subside **6** = prepare, lay, spread, arrange, make ready
• ADJECTIVE **1** = established, planned,

decided, agreed, arranged, rigid, definite, inflexible **2** = strict, rigid, stubborn, inflexible ≠ flexible **3** = conventional, traditional, stereotyped, unspontaneous
• NOUN **1** = scenery, setting, scene, stage set **2** = position, bearing, attitude, carriage, posture
• PHRASES **be set on** *or* **upon something** = be determined to, be intent on, be bent on, be resolute about ◆ **set something up 1** = arrange, organize, prepare, prearrange **2** = establish, begin, found, institute, initiate **3** = build, raise, construct, put up, assemble, put together, erect **4** = assemble, put up

set² **1** = series, collection, assortment, batch, compendium, ensemble **2** = group, company, crowd, circle, band, gang, faction, clique

setback = hold-up, check, defeat, blow, reverse, disappointment, hitch, misfortune

setting = surroundings, site, location, set, scene, background, context, backdrop

settle 1 = resolve, work out, put an end to, straighten out **2** = pay, clear, square (up), discharge **3** = move to, take up residence in, live in, dwell in, inhabit, reside in, set up home in, put down roots in **4** = colonize, populate, people, pioneer **5** = land, alight, descend, light, come to rest **6** = calm, quiet, relax, relieve, reassure, soothe, lull, quell ≠ disturb

settlement 1 = agreement, arrangement, working out, conclusion, establishment, confirmation **2** = payment, clearing, discharge **3** = colony, community, outpost, encampment, kainga *or* kaika (*N.Z.*)

settler = colonist, immigrant, pioneer, frontiersman

set-up (*Informal*) = arrangement, system, structure, organization, conditions, regime

sever 1 = cut, separate, split, part, divide, detach, disconnect, cut in two ≠ join **2** = discontinue, terminate, break off, put an end to, dissociate ≠ continue

several ADJECTIVE = some, a few, a number of, a handful of
• PRONOUN = various, different, diverse, sundry

severe 1 = serious, critical, terrible, desperate, extreme, awful, drastic, catastrophic **2** = acute, intense, violent, piercing, harrowing, unbearable, agonizing, insufferable **3** = strict, hard, harsh, cruel, rigid, drastic, oppressive, austere ≠ lenient **4** = grim, serious, grave, forbidding, stern, unsmiling, tight-lipped ≠ genial **5** = plain, simple, austere, classic, restrained, Spartan, unadorned, unfussy ≠ fancy

severely 1 = seriously, badly, extremely, gravely, acutely **2** = strictly, harshly, sternly, sharply

severity = strictness, harshness, toughness, hardness, sternness, severeness

sew = stitch, tack, seam, hem

sex 1 = gender **2** (*Informal*) = lovemaking, sexual relations, copulation, fornication, coitus, coition

sexual 1 = carnal, erotic, intimate **2** = sexy, erotic, sensual, arousing, naughty, provocative, seductive, sensuous

sexuality = desire, lust, eroticism, sensuality, sexiness (*informal*), carnality

sexy = erotic, sensual, seductive, arousing, naughty, provocative, sensuous, suggestive

shabby 1 = tatty, worn, ragged, scruffy, tattered, threadbare ≠ smart **2** = run-down, seedy, mean, dilapidated **3** = mean, low, rotten (*informal*), cheap, dirty, despicable, contemptible, scurvy ≠ fair

shack = hut, cabin, shanty, whare (*N.Z.*)

shade NOUN **1** = hue, tone, colour, tint **2** = shadow **3** = dash, trace, hint, suggestion **4** = nuance, difference, degree **5** = screen, covering, cover, blind, curtain, shield, veil, canopy **6** (*Literary*) = ghost, spirit, phantom, spectre, apparition, kehua (*N.Z.*)
• VERB **1** = darken, shadow, cloud, dim **2** = cover, protect, screen, hide, shield, conceal, obscure, veil

shadow NOUN **1** = silhouette, shape, outline, profile **2** = shade, dimness, darkness, gloom, cover, dusk
• VERB **1** = shade, screen, shield, darken, overhang **2** = follow, tail (*informal*), trail, stalk

shady 1 = shaded, cool, dim ≠ sunny **2** (*Informal*) = crooked, dodgy (*Brit., Austral., & N.Z. informal*), unethical, suspect, suspicious, dubious, questionable, shifty ≠ honest

shaft 1 = tunnel, hole, passage, burrow, passageway, channel **2** = handle, staff, pole, rod, stem, baton, shank **3** = ray, beam, gleam

shake VERB 1 = jiggle, agitate 2 = tremble, shiver, quake, quiver 3 = rock, totter 4 = wave, wield, flourish, brandish 5 = upset, shock, frighten, disturb, distress, rattle (*informal*), unnerve, traumatize • NOUN = vibration, trembling, quaking, jerk, shiver, shudder, jolt, tremor

shaky 1 = unstable, weak, precarious, rickety ≠ stable 2 = unsteady, faint, trembling, faltering, quivery 3 = uncertain, suspect, dubious, questionable, iffy (*informal*) ≠ reliable

shallow = superficial, surface, empty, slight, foolish, trivial, meaningless, frivolous ≠ deep

sham NOUN = fraud, imitation, hoax, pretence, forgery, counterfeit, humbug, impostor ≠ the real thing • ADJECTIVE = false, artificial, bogus, pretended, mock, imitation, simulated, counterfeit ≠ real

shambles 1 = chaos, mess, disorder, confusion, muddle, havoc, disarray, madhouse 2 = mess, jumble, untidiness

shame NOUN 1 = embarrassment, humiliation, ignominy, mortification, abashment ≠ shamelessness 2 = disgrace, scandal, discredit, smear, disrepute, reproach, dishonour, infamy ≠ honour • VERB 1 = embarrass, disgrace, humiliate, humble, mortify, abash ≠ make proud 2 = dishonour, degrade, stain, smear, blot, debase, defile ≠ honour

shameful = disgraceful, outrageous, scandalous, mean, low, base, wicked, dishonourable ≠ admirable

shape NOUN 1 = appearance, form, aspect, guise, likeness, semblance 2 = form, profile, outline, lines, build, figure, silhouette, configuration 3 = pattern, model, frame, mould 4 = condition, state, health, trim, fettle • VERB 1 = form, make, produce, create, model, fashion, mould 2 = mould, form, make, fashion, model, frame

share NOUN = part, portion, quota, ration, lot, due, contribution, allowance • VERB 1 = divide, split, distribute, assign 2 = go halves on, go fifty-fifty on (*informal*)

sharp ADJECTIVE 1 = keen, jagged, serrated ≠ blunt 2 = quick-witted, clever, astute, knowing, quick, bright, alert, penetrating ≠ dim 3 = cutting, biting, bitter, harsh, barbed, hurtful, caustic ≠ gentle 4 = sudden, marked, abrupt, extreme, distinct ≠ gradual 5 = clear, distinct, well-defined, crisp ≠ indistinct 6 = sour, tart, pungent, hot, acid, acrid, piquant ≠ bland 7 = acute, severe, intense, painful, shooting, stabbing, piercing, gut-wrenching • ADVERB = promptly, precisely, exactly, on time, on the dot, punctually ≠ approximately

sharpen = make sharp, hone, whet, grind, edge

shatter 1 = smash, break, burst, crack, crush, pulverize 2 = destroy, ruin, wreck, demolish, torpedo

shattered 1 = devastated, crushed, gutted (*slang*) 2 (*Informal*) = exhausted, drained, worn out, done in (*informal*), all in (*slang*), knackered (*slang*), tired out, ready to drop

shave 1 = trim, crop 2 = scrape, trim, shear, pare

shed[1] = hut, shack, outhouse, whare (*N.Z.*)

shed[2] 1 = drop, spill, scatter 2 = cast off, discard, moult, slough off 3 = give out, cast, emit, give, radiate

sheen = shine, gleam, gloss, polish, brightness, lustre

sheer 1 = total, complete, absolute, utter, pure, downright, out-and-out, unmitigated ≠ moderate 2 = steep, abrupt, precipitous ≠ gradual 3 = fine, thin, transparent, see-through, gossamer, diaphanous, gauzy ≠ thick

sheet 1 = page, leaf, folio, piece of paper 2 = plate, piece, panel, slab 3 = coat, film, layer, surface, stratum, veneer, overlay, lamina 4 = expanse, area, stretch, sweep, covering, blanket

shell NOUN 1 = husk, case, pod 2 = carapace 3 = frame, structure, hull, framework, chassis • VERB = bomb, bombard, attack, blitz, strafe • PHRASES **shell something out** (with money or a specified sum of money as object) = pay out, fork out (*slang*), give, hand over

shelter NOUN 1 = cover, screen 2 = protection, safety, refuge, cover 3 = refuge, haven, sanctuary, retreat, asylum

• **VERB 1** = take shelter, hide, seek refuge, take cover **2** = protect, shield, harbour, safeguard, cover, hide, guard, defend ≠ endanger

sheltered 1 = screened, covered, protected, shielded, secluded ≠ exposed **2** = protected, screened, shielded, quiet, isolated, secluded, cloistered

shelve = postpone, defer, freeze, suspend, put aside, put on ice, put on the back burner (*informal*), take a rain check on (*U.S. & Canad. informal*)

shepherd NOUN = drover, stockman, herdsman, grazier
• **VERB** = guide, conduct, steer, herd, usher

RELATED WORD
adjective: pastoral

shield NOUN = protection, cover, defence, screen, guard, shelter, safeguard
• **VERB** = protect, cover, screen, guard, defend, shelter, safeguard

shift VERB 1 = move, move around, budge **2** = remove, move, displace, relocate, rearrange, reposition
• **NOUN 1** = change, shifting, displacement **2** = move, rearrangement

shimmer VERB = gleam, twinkle, glisten, scintillate
• **NOUN** = gleam, iridescence

shine VERB 1 = gleam, flash, beam, glow, sparkle, glitter, glare, radiate **2** = polish, buff, burnish, brush **3** = be outstanding, stand out, excel, be conspicuous
• **NOUN 1** = polish, gloss, sheen, lustre **2** = brightness, light, sparkle, radiance

shining = bright, brilliant, gleaming, beaming, sparkling, shimmering, radiant, luminous

shiny = bright, gleaming, glossy, glistening, polished, lustrous

ship = vessel, boat, craft

shiver VERB = shudder, shake, tremble, quake, quiver
• **NOUN** = tremble, shudder, quiver, trembling, flutter, tremor

shock NOUN 1 = upset, blow, trauma, bombshell, turn (*informal*), distress, disturbance **2** = impact, blow, clash, collision **3** = start, scare, fright, turn, jolt
• **VERB 1** = shake, stun, stagger, jolt, stupefy **2** = horrify, appal, disgust, revolt, sicken, nauseate, scandalize

shocking 1 (*Informal*) = terrible, appalling, dreadful, bad, horrendous, ghastly, deplorable, abysmal **2** = appalling, outrageous, disgraceful, disgusting, dreadful, horrifying, revolting, sickening ≠ wonderful

shoot VERB 1 = open fire on, blast (*slang*), hit, kill, plug (*slang*), bring down **2** = fire, launch, discharge, project, hurl, fling, propel, emit **3** = speed, race, rush, charge, fly, tear, dash, barrel (along) (*informal, chiefly U.S. & Canad.*)
• **NOUN** = sprout, branch, bud, sprig, offshoot

shop = store, supermarket, boutique, emporium, hypermarket, dairy (*N.Z.*)

shore = beach, coast, sands, strand (*poetic*), seashore

short ADJECTIVE 1 = brief, fleeting, momentary ≠ long **2** = concise, brief, succinct, summary, compressed, terse, laconic, pithy ≠ lengthy **3** = small, little, squat, diminutive, petite, dumpy ≠ tall **4** = abrupt, sharp, terse, curt, brusque, impolite, discourteous, uncivil ≠ polite **5** = scarce, wanting, low, limited, lacking, scant, deficient ≠ plentiful
• **ADVERB** = abruptly, suddenly, without warning ≠ gradually

shortage = deficiency, want, lack, scarcity, dearth, paucity, insufficiency ≠ abundance

shortcoming = failing, fault, weakness, defect, flaw, imperfection

shorten 1 = cut, reduce, decrease, diminish, lessen, curtail, abbreviate, abridge ≠ increase **2** = turn up

shortly = soon, presently, before long, in a little while

shot 1 = discharge, gunfire, crack, blast, explosion, bang **2** = ammunition, bullet, slug, pellet, projectile, lead, ball **3** = marksman, shooter, markswoman **4** (*Informal*) = strike, throw, lob **5** = attempt, go (*informal*), try, turn, effort, stab (*informal*), endeavour

shoulder 1 = bear, carry, take on, accept, assume, be responsible for **2** = push, elbow, shove, jostle, press

shout VERB = cry (out), call (out), yell, scream, roar, bellow, bawl, holler (*informal*)
• **NOUN** = cry, call, yell, scream, roar, bellow
• **PHRASES shout someone down** = drown out, overwhelm, drown, silence

shove VERB = push, thrust, elbow, drive, press, propel, jostle, impel

• NOUN = push, knock, thrust, elbow, bump, nudge, jostle
• PHRASES **shove off** (*Informal*) = go away, leave, clear off (*informal*), depart, push off (*informal*), scram (*informal*)

shovel 1 = move, scoop, dredge, load, heap 2 = stuff, ladle

show VERB 1 = indicate, demonstrate, prove, reveal, display, point out, manifest, testify to ≠ disprove 2 = display, exhibit 3 = guide, lead, conduct, accompany, direct, escort 4 = demonstrate, describe, explain, teach, illustrate, instruct 5 = be visible ≠ be invisible 6 = express, display, reveal, indicate, register, demonstrate, manifest ≠ hide 7 = turn up, appear, attend 8 = broadcast, transmit, air, beam, relay, televise, put on the air
• NOUN 1 = display, sight, spectacle, array 2 = exhibition, fair, display, parade, pageant 3 = appearance, display, pose, parade 4 = pretence, appearance, illusion, affectation 5 = programme, broadcast, presentation, production 6 = entertainment, production, presentation
• PHRASES **show off** (*Informal*) = boast, brag, blow your own trumpet, swagger ◆ **show someone up** (*Informal*) = embarrass, let down, mortify, put to shame ◆ **show something off** = exhibit, display, parade, demonstrate, flaunt ◆ **show something up** = reveal, expose, highlight, lay bare

showdown (*Informal*) = confrontation, clash, face-off (*slang*)

shower NOUN = deluge
• VERB 1 = cover, dust, spray, sprinkle 2 = inundate, heap, lavish, pour, deluge

show-off (*Informal*) = exhibitionist, boaster, poseur, braggart

shred 1 = strip, bit, piece, scrap, fragment, sliver, tatter 2 = particle, trace, scrap, grain, atom, jot, iota

shrewd = astute, clever, sharp, keen, smart, calculating, intelligent, cunning ≠ naive

shriek VERB = scream, cry, yell, screech, squeal
• NOUN = scream, cry, yell, screech, squeal

shrink = decrease, dwindle, lessen, grow *or* get smaller, contract, narrow, diminish, shorten ≠ grow

shroud NOUN 1 = winding sheet, grave clothes 2 = covering, veil, mantle, screen, pall
• VERB = conceal, cover, screen, hide, blanket, veil, cloak, envelop

shudder VERB = shiver, shake, tremble, quake, quiver, convulse
• NOUN = shiver, tremor, quiver, spasm

shuffle 1 = shamble, stagger, stumble, dodder 2 = scuffle, drag, scrape 3 = rearrange, jumble, mix, disorder, disarrange

shun = avoid, steer clear of, keep away from

shut VERB = close, secure, fasten, seal, slam ≠ open
• ADJECTIVE = closed, fastened, sealed, locked ≠ open
• PHRASES **shut down** = stop work, halt work, close down

shuttle = go back and forth, commute, go to and fro, alternate

shy ADJECTIVE 1 = timid, self-conscious, bashful, retiring, shrinking, coy, self-effacing, diffident ≠ confident 2 = cautious, wary, hesitant, suspicious, distrustful, chary ≠ reckless
• VERB *sometimes with* ***off*** *or* ***away*** = recoil, flinch, draw back, start, balk

sick 1 = unwell, ill, poorly (*informal*), diseased, crook (*Austral. & N.Z. informal*), ailing, under the weather, indisposed ≠ well 2 = nauseous, ill, queasy, nauseated 3 = tired, bored, fed up, weary, jaded 4 (*Informal*) = morbid, sadistic, black, macabre, ghoulish

sicken 1 = disgust, revolt, nauseate, repel, gross out (*U.S. slang*), turn your stomach 2 = fall ill, take sick, ail

sickening = disgusting, revolting, offensive, foul, distasteful, repulsive, nauseating, loathsome, yucko (*Austral. slang*) ≠ delightful

sickness 1 = illness, disorder, ailment, disease, complaint, bug (*informal*), affliction, malady 2 = nausea, queasiness 3 = vomiting

side NOUN 1 = border, margin, boundary, verge, flank, rim, perimeter, edge ≠ middle 2 = face, surface, facet 3 = party, camp, faction, cause 4 = point of view, viewpoint, position, opinion, angle, slant, standpoint 5 = team, squad, line-up 6 = aspect, feature, angle, facet
• ADJECTIVE = subordinate, minor,

secondary, subsidiary, lesser, marginal, incidental, ancillary ≠ main
• PHRASES **side with someone** = support, agree with, stand up for, favour, go along with, take the part of, ally yourself with

sidewalk (*U.S. & Canad.*) = pavement, footpath (*Austral. & N.Z.*)

sideways ADVERB 1 = indirectly, obliquely 2 = to the side, laterally
• ADJECTIVE = sidelong, oblique

sift 1 = part, filter, strain, separate, sieve 2 = examine, investigate, go through, research, analyse, work over, scrutinize

sight NOUN 1 = vision, eyes, eyesight, seeing, eye 2 = spectacle, show, scene, display, exhibition, vista, pageant 3 = view, range of vision, visibility 4 (*Informal*) = eyesore, mess, monstrosity
• VERB = spot, see, observe, distinguish, perceive, make out, discern, behold
RELATED WORDS
adjectives: optical, visual

sign NOUN 1 = symbol, mark, device, logo, badge, emblem 2 = figure 3 = notice, board, warning, placard 4 = indication, evidence, mark, signal, symptom, hint, proof, gesture 5 = omen, warning, portent, foreboding, augury, auspice
• VERB 1 = gesture, indicate, signal, beckon, gesticulate 2 = autograph, initial, inscribe

signal NOUN 1 = flare, beam, beacon 2 = cue, sign, prompting, reminder 3 = sign, gesture, indication, mark, note, expression, token
• VERB = gesture, sign, wave, indicate, motion, beckon, gesticulate

significance = importance, consequence, moment, weight

significant 1 = important, serious, material, vital, critical, momentous, weighty, noteworthy ≠ insignificant 2 = meaningful, expressive, eloquent, indicative, suggestive ≠ meaningless

signify = indicate, mean, suggest, imply, intimate, be a sign of, denote, connote

silence NOUN 1 = quiet, peace, calm, hush, lull, stillness ≠ noise 2 = reticence, dumbness, taciturnity, muteness ≠ speech
• VERB = quieten, still, quiet, cut off, stifle, cut short, muffle, deaden ≠ make louder

silent 1 = mute, dumb, speechless, wordless, voiceless ≠ noisy 2 = uncommunicative, quiet, taciturn 3 = quiet, still, hushed, soundless, noiseless, muted ≠ loud

silently 1 = quietly, in silence, soundlessly, noiselessly, inaudibly, without a sound 2 = mutely, in silence, wordlessly

silhouette NOUN = outline, form, shape, profile
• VERB = outline, etch

silly 1 = stupid, ridiculous, absurd, daft, inane, senseless, idiotic, fatuous ≠ clever 2 = foolish, stupid, unwise, rash, irresponsible, thoughtless, imprudent ≠ sensible

similar 1 = alike, resembling, comparable ≠ different 2 *with* ***to*** = like, comparable to, analogous to, close to

similarity = resemblance, likeness, sameness, agreement, correspondence, analogy, affinity, closeness ≠ difference

simmer VERB 1 = bubble, boil gently, seethe 2 = fume, seethe, smoulder, rage, be angry
• PHRASES **simmer down** (*Informal*) = calm down, control yourself, cool off *or* down

simple 1 = uncomplicated, clear, plain, understandable, lucid, recognizable, comprehensible, intelligible ≠ complicated 2 = easy, straightforward, not difficult, effortless, painless, uncomplicated, undemanding 3 = plain, natural, classic, unfussy, unembellished ≠ elaborate 4 = pure, mere, sheer, unalloyed 5 = artless, innocent, naive, natural, sincere, unaffected, childlike, unsophisticated ≠ sophisticated 6 = unpretentious, modest, humble, homely, unfussy, unembellished ≠ fancy

simplicity 1 = straightforwardness, ease, clarity, clearness ≠ complexity 2 = plainness, restraint, purity, lack of adornment ≠ elaborateness

simplify = make simpler, streamline, disentangle, dumb down, reduce to essentials

simply 1 = just, only, merely, purely, solely 2 = totally, really, completely, absolutely, wholly, utterly 3 = clearly, straightforwardly, directly, plainly, intelligibly 4 = plainly, naturally, modestly, unpretentiously 5 = without doubt, surely, certainly, definitely, beyond question

simulate = pretend, act, feign, affect, put

on, sham
simultaneous = coinciding, concurrent, contemporaneous, coincident, synchronous, happening at the same time
simultaneously = at the same time, together, concurrently
sin NOUN **1** = wickedness, evil, crime, error, transgression, iniquity **2** = crime, offence, error, wrongdoing, misdeed, transgression, act of evil, guilt
• VERB = transgress, offend, lapse, err, go astray, do wrong
sincere = honest, genuine, real, true, serious, earnest, frank, candid, dinkum (*Austral. & N.Z. informal*) ≠ false
sincerely = honestly, truly, genuinely, seriously, earnestly, wholeheartedly, in earnest
sincerity = honesty, truth, candour, frankness, seriousness, genuineness
sing 1 = croon, carol, chant, warble, yodel, pipe **2** = trill, chirp, warble
singer = vocalist, crooner, minstrel, soloist, chorister, balladeer
single ADJECTIVE **1** = one, sole, lone, solitary, only, only one **2** = individual, separate, distinct **3** = unmarried, free, unattached, unwed **4** = separate, individual, exclusive, undivided, unshared **5** = simple, unmixed, unblended
• PHRASES **single something** *or* **someone out** = pick, choose, select, separate, distinguish, fix on, set apart, pick on *or* out
singly = one by one, individually, one at a time, separately
singular 1 = single, individual **2** = remarkable, outstanding, exceptional, notable, eminent, noteworthy ≠ ordinary **3** = unusual, odd, strange, extraordinary, curious, peculiar, eccentric, queer ≠ conventional
sinister = threatening, evil, menacing, dire, ominous, malign, disquieting ≠ reassuring
sink 1 = go down, founder, go under, submerge, capsize **2** = slump, drop **3** = fall, drop, slip, plunge, subside, abate **4** = drop, fall **5** = stoop, be reduced to, lower yourself **6** = decline, fade, fail, flag, weaken, diminish, decrease, deteriorate ≠ improve **7** = dig, bore, drill, drive, excavate
sip VERB = drink, taste, sample, sup
• NOUN = swallow, drop, taste, thimbleful
sit 1 = take a seat, perch, settle down **2** = place, set, put, position, rest, lay, settle, deposit **3** = be a member of, serve on, have a seat on, preside on **4** = convene, meet, assemble, officiate
site NOUN **1** = area, plot **2** = location, place, setting, point, position, situation, spot
• VERB = locate, put, place, set, position, establish, install, situate
situation 1 = position, state, case, condition, circumstances, equation, plight, state of affairs **2** = scenario, state of affairs **3** = location, place, setting, position, site, spot
size NOUN = dimensions, extent, range, amount, mass, volume, proportions, bulk
• PHRASES **size something** *or* **someone up** (*Informal*) = assess, evaluate, appraise, take stock of
sizeable *or* **sizable** = large, considerable, substantial, goodly, decent, respectable, largish
sizzle = hiss, spit, crackle, fry, frizzle
skeleton = bones, bare bones
sketch NOUN = drawing, design, draft, delineation
• VERB = draw, outline, represent, draft, depict, delineate, rough out
skilful = expert, skilled, masterly, able, professional, clever, practised, competent ≠ clumsy
skill = expertise, ability, proficiency, art, technique, facility, talent, craft ≠ clumsiness
skilled = expert, professional, able, masterly, skilful, proficient ≠ unskilled
skim 1 = remove, separate, cream **2** = glide, fly, coast, sail, float **3** *usually with* ***over*** *or* ***through*** = scan, glance, run your eye over
skin NOUN **1** = hide, pelt, fell **2** = peel, rind, husk, casing, outside, crust **3** = film, coating
• VERB **1** = peel **2** = scrape, flay
skinny = thin, lean, scrawny, emaciated, undernourished ≠ fat
skip 1 = hop, dance, bob, trip, bounce, caper, prance, frisk **2** = miss out, omit, leave out, overlook, pass over, eschew, give (something) a miss
skirt 1 = border, edge, flank **2** *often with* ***around*** *or* ***round*** = go round, circumvent

3 *often with* ***around*** *or* ***round*** = avoid, evade, steer clear of, circumvent
sky = heavens, firmament, rangi (*N.Z.*)
RELATED WORD
adjective: celestial
slab = piece, slice, lump, chunk, wedge, portion
slack ADJECTIVE **1** = limp, relaxed, loose, lax **2** = loose, baggy ≠ taut **3** = slow, quiet, inactive, dull, sluggish, slow-moving ≠ busy **4** = negligent, lazy, lax, idle, inactive, slapdash, neglectful, slipshod ≠ strict
• VERB = shirk, idle, dodge, skive (*Brit. slang*), bludge (*Austral. & N.Z. informal*)
• NOUN **1** = surplus, excess, glut, surfeit, superabundance, superfluity **2** = room, excess, leeway, give (*informal*)
slam **1** = bang, crash, smash **2** = throw, dash, hurl, fling
slant VERB **1** = slope, incline, tilt, list, bend, lean, heel, cant **2** = bias, colour, twist, angle, distort
• NOUN **1** = slope, incline, tilt, gradient, camber **2** = bias, emphasis, prejudice, angle, point of view, one-sidedness
slanting = sloping, angled, inclined, tilted, tilting, bent, diagonal, oblique
slap VERB = smack, beat, clap, cuff, swipe, spank, clobber (*slang*), wallop (*informal*)
• NOUN = smack, blow, cuff, swipe, spank
slash VERB **1** = cut, slit, gash, lacerate, score, rend, rip, hack **2** = reduce, cut, decrease, drop, lower, moderate, diminish, cut down
• NOUN = cut, slit, gash, rent, rip, incision, laceration
slate (*Informal, chiefly Brit.*) = criticize, censure, rebuke, scold, tear into (*informal*)
slaughter VERB **1** = kill, murder, massacre, destroy, execute, assassinate **2** = butcher, kill, slay, massacre
• NOUN = slaying, killing, murder, massacre, bloodshed, carnage, butchery
slave NOUN **1** = servant, serf, vassal **2** = drudge, skivvy (*chiefly Brit.*)
• VERB = toil, drudge, slog
slavery = enslavement, servitude, subjugation, captivity, bondage ≠ freedom
slay **1** (*Archaic or literary*) = kill, slaughter, massacre, butcher **2** = murder, kill, massacre, slaughter, mow down
sleaze (*Informal*) = corruption, fraud, dishonesty, bribery, extortion, venality, unscrupulousness
sleek = glossy, shiny, lustrous, smooth ≠ shaggy
sleep NOUN = slumber(s), nap, doze, snooze (*informal*), hibernation, siesta, forty winks (*informal*), zizz (*Brit. informal*)
• VERB = slumber, doze, snooze (*informal*), hibernate, take a nap, catnap, drowse
sleepy = drowsy, sluggish, lethargic, heavy, dull, inactive ≠ wide-awake
slender **1** = slim, narrow, slight, lean, willowy ≠ chubby **2** = faint, slight, remote, slim, thin, tenuous ≠ strong **3** = meagre, little, small, scant, scanty ≠ large
slice NOUN = piece, segment, portion, wedge, sliver, helping, share, cut
• VERB = cut, divide, carve, sever, dissect, bisect
slick ADJECTIVE **1** = skilful, deft, adroit, dexterous, professional, polished ≠ clumsy **2** = glib, smooth, plausible, polished, specious
• VERB = smooth, sleek, plaster down
slide = slip, slither, glide, skim, coast
slight ADJECTIVE **1** = small, minor, insignificant, trivial, feeble, trifling, meagre, unimportant ≠ large **2** = slim, small, delicate, spare, fragile, lightly-built ≠ sturdy
• VERB = snub, insult, ignore, affront, scorn, disdain ≠ compliment
• NOUN = insult, snub, affront, rebuff, slap in the face (*informal*), (the) cold shoulder ≠ compliment
slightly = a little, a bit, somewhat
slim ADJECTIVE **1** = slender, slight, trim, thin, narrow, lean, svelte, willowy ≠ chubby **2** = slight, remote, faint, slender ≠ strong
• VERB = lose weight, diet ≠ put on weight
sling **1** (*Informal*) = throw, cast, toss, hurl, fling, chuck (*informal*), lob (*informal*), heave **2** = hang, suspend
slip VERB **1** = fall, skid **2** = slide, slither **3** = sneak, creep, steal
• NOUN = mistake, failure, error, blunder, lapse, omission, oversight
• PHRASES **give someone the slip** = escape from, get away from, evade, elude, lose (someone), flee, dodge
◆ **slip up** = make a mistake, blunder, err, miscalculate
slippery **1** = smooth, icy, greasy, glassy, slippy (*informal, dialect*), unsafe

2 = untrustworthy, tricky, cunning, dishonest, devious, crafty, evasive, shifty

slit VERB = cut (open), rip, slash, knife, pierce, lance, gash
• NOUN 1 = cut, gash, incision, tear, rent 2 = opening, split

slogan = catch phrase, motto, tag-line, catchword

slope NOUN = inclination, rise, incline, tilt, slant, ramp, gradient
• VERB = slant, incline, drop away, fall, rise, lean, tilt
• PHRASES **slope off** (*Informal*) = slink away, slip away, creep away

sloping = slanting, leaning, inclined, oblique

sloppy 1 (*Informal*) = careless, slovenly, slipshod, messy, untidy 2 (*Informal*) = sentimental, soppy (*Brit. informal*), slushy (*informal*), gushing, mawkish, icky (*informal*)

slot NOUN 1 = opening, hole, groove, vent, slit, aperture 2 (*Informal*) = place, time, space, opening, position, vacancy
• VERB = fit, insert

slow ADJECTIVE 1 = unhurried, sluggish, leisurely, lazy, ponderous, dawdling, laggard, lackadaisical ≠ quick 2 = prolonged, protracted, long-drawn-out, lingering, gradual 3 = late, behind, tardy 4 = stupid, dim, dense, thick, retarded, dozy (*Brit. informal*), obtuse, braindead (*informal*) ≠ bright
• VERB 1 *often with* ***down*** = decelerate, brake 2 *often with* ***down*** = delay, hold up, handicap, retard ≠ speed up

slowly = gradually, unhurriedly ≠ quickly

sluggish = inactive, slow, lethargic, heavy, dull, inert, indolent, torpid ≠ energetic

slum = hovel, ghetto, shanty

slump VERB 1 = fall, sink, plunge, crash, collapse, slip ≠ increase 2 = sag, hunch, droop, slouch, loll
• NOUN 1 = fall, drop, decline, crash, collapse, reverse, downturn, trough ≠ increase 2 = recession, depression, stagnation, inactivity, hard *or* bad times

slur = insult, stain, smear, affront, innuendo, calumny, insinuation, aspersion

sly ADJECTIVE 1 = roguish, knowing, arch, mischievous, impish 2 = cunning, scheming, devious, secret, clever, subtle, wily, crafty ≠ open
• PHRASES **on the sly** = secretly, privately, covertly, surreptitiously, on the quiet

smack VERB 1 = slap, hit, strike, clap, cuff, swipe, spank 2 = drive, hit, strike
• NOUN = slap, blow, cuff, swipe, spank
• ADVERB (*Informal*) = directly, right, straight, squarely, precisely, exactly, slap (*informal*)

small 1 = little, minute, tiny, mini, miniature, minuscule, diminutive, petite ≠ big 2 = young, little, junior, wee, juvenile, youthful, immature 3 = unimportant, minor, trivial, insignificant, little, petty, trifling, negligible ≠ important 4 = modest, humble, unpretentious ≠ grand

smart ADJECTIVE 1 = chic, trim, neat, stylish, elegant, spruce, snappy, natty (*informal*) ≠ scruffy 2 = clever, bright, intelligent, quick, sharp, keen, acute, shrewd ≠ stupid 3 = brisk, quick, lively, vigorous
• VERB = sting, burn, hurt

smash VERB 1 = break, crush, shatter, crack, demolish, pulverize 2 = shatter, break, disintegrate, crack, splinter 3 = collide, crash, meet head-on, clash, come into collision 4 = destroy, ruin, wreck, trash (*slang*), lay waste
• NOUN = collision, crash, accident

smashing (*Informal, chiefly Brit.*) = excellent, mean (*slang*), great (*informal*), wonderful, brilliant (*informal*), cracking (*Brit. informal*), superb, fantastic (*informal*), booshit (*Austral. slang*), exo (*Austral. slang*), sik (*Austral. slang*) ≠ awful

smear VERB 1 = spread over, daub, rub on, cover, coat, bedaub 2 = slander, malign, blacken, besmirch 3 = smudge, soil, dirty, stain, sully
• NOUN 1 = smudge, daub, streak, blot, blotch, splotch 2 = slander, libel, defamation, calumny

smell NOUN 1 = odour, scent, fragrance, perfume, bouquet, aroma 2 = stink, stench, pong (*Brit. informal*), fetor
• VERB 1 = stink, reek, pong (*Brit. informal*) 2 = sniff, scent

smile VERB = grin, beam, smirk, twinkle, grin from ear to ear
• NOUN = grin, beam, smirk

smooth ADJECTIVE 1 = even, level, flat, plane, flush, horizontal ≠ uneven 2 = sleek, polished, shiny, glossy, silky, velvety ≠ rough 3 = mellow, pleasant, mild, agreeable 4 = flowing, steady, regular,

uniform, rhythmic **5** = <u>easy</u>, effortless, well-ordered **6** = <u>suave</u>, slick, persuasive, urbane, glib, facile, unctuous, smarmy (*Brit. informal*)
• **VERB 1** = <u>flatten</u>, level, press, plane, iron **2** = <u>ease</u>, facilitate ≠ hinder

smother 1 = <u>extinguish</u>, put out, stifle, snuff **2** = <u>suffocate</u>, choke, strangle, stifle **3** = <u>suppress</u>, stifle, repress, hide, conceal, muffle

smug = <u>self-satisfied</u>, superior, complacent, conceited

snack = <u>light meal</u>, bite, refreshment(s)

snag NOUN = <u>difficulty</u>, hitch, problem, obstacle, catch, disadvantage, complication, drawback
• **VERB** = <u>catch</u>, tear, rip

snake = <u>serpent</u>
RELATED WORD
adjective: serpentine

snap VERB 1 = <u>break</u>, crack, separate **2** = <u>pop</u>, click, crackle **3** = <u>speak sharply</u>, bark, lash out at, jump down (someone's) throat (*informal*) **4** = <u>bite at</u>, bite, nip
• **ADJECTIVE** = <u>instant</u>, immediate, sudden, spur-of-the-moment
• **PHRASES snap something up** = <u>grab</u>, seize, take advantage of, pounce upon

snare NOUN = <u>trap</u>, net, wire, gin, noose
• **VERB** = <u>trap</u>, catch, net, wire, seize, entrap

snatch VERB 1 = <u>grab</u>, grip, grasp, clutch **2** = <u>steal</u>, take, nick (*slang, chiefly Brit.*), pinch (*informal*), lift (*informal*), pilfer, filch, thieve **3** = <u>win</u> **4** = <u>save</u>, recover, get out, salvage
• **NOUN** = <u>bit</u>, part, fragment, piece, snippet

sneak VERB 1 = <u>slink</u>, slip, steal, pad, skulk **2** = <u>slip</u>, smuggle, spirit
• **NOUN** = <u>informer</u>, betrayer, telltale, Judas, accuser, stool pigeon, nark (*Brit., Austral., & N.Z. slang*), fizgig (*Austral. slang*)

sneaking 1 = <u>nagging</u>, worrying, persistent, uncomfortable **2** = <u>secret</u>, private, hidden, unexpressed, unvoiced, undivulged

sneer VERB 1 = <u>scorn</u>, mock, ridicule, laugh, jeer, disdain, deride **2** = <u>say contemptuously</u>, snigger
• **NOUN** = <u>scorn</u>, ridicule, mockery, derision, jeer, gibe

sniff 1 = <u>breathe in</u>, inhale **2** = <u>smell</u>, scent **3** = <u>inhale</u>, breathe in, suck in, draw in

snub VERB = <u>insult</u>, slight, put down, humiliate, cut (*informal*), rebuff, cold-shoulder
• **NOUN** = <u>insult</u>, put-down, affront, slap in the face

so = <u>therefore</u>, thus, hence, consequently, then, as a result, accordingly, thence

soak VERB 1 = <u>steep</u> **2** = <u>wet</u>, damp, saturate, drench, moisten, suffuse, wet through, waterlog **3** = <u>penetrate</u>, permeate, seep
• **PHRASES soak something up** = <u>absorb</u>, suck up, assimilate

soaking = <u>soaked</u>, dripping, saturated, drenched, sodden, streaming, sopping, wet through

soar 1 = <u>rise</u>, increase, grow, mount, climb, go up, rocket, escalate **2** = <u>fly</u>, wing, climb, ascend ≠ plunge **3** = <u>tower</u>, climb, go up

sob VERB = <u>cry</u>, weep, howl, shed tears
• **NOUN** = <u>cry</u>, whimper, howl

sober 1 = <u>abstinent</u>, temperate, abstemious, moderate ≠ drunk **2** = <u>serious</u>, cool, grave, reasonable, steady, composed, rational, solemn ≠ frivolous **3** = <u>plain</u>, dark, sombre, quiet, subdued, drab ≠ bright

so-called = <u>alleged</u>, supposed, professed, pretended, self-styled

social ADJECTIVE 1 = <u>communal</u>, community, collective, group, public, general, common **2** = <u>organized</u>, gregarious
• **NOUN** = <u>get-together</u> (*informal*), party, gathering, function, reception, social gathering

society 1 = <u>the community</u>, people, the public, humanity, civilization, mankind **2** = <u>culture</u>, community, population **3** = <u>organization</u>, group, club, union, league, association, institute, circle **4** = <u>upper classes</u>, gentry, elite, high society, beau monde **5** (*Old-fashioned*) = <u>companionship</u>, company, fellowship, friendship

sofa = <u>couch</u>, settee, divan, chaise longue

soft 1 = <u>velvety</u>, smooth, silky, feathery, downy, fleecy ≠ rough **2** = <u>yielding</u>, elastic ≠ hard **3** = <u>soggy</u>, swampy, marshy, boggy **4** = <u>squashy</u>, sloppy, mushy, spongy, gelatinous, pulpy **5** = <u>pliable</u>, flexible, supple, malleable, plastic, elastic, bendable, mouldable **6** = <u>quiet</u>, gentle, murmured, muted, dulcet, soft-toned ≠ loud **7** = <u>lenient</u>, easy-going, lax, indulgent, permissive, spineless, overindulgent ≠ harsh **8** = kind, tender, sentimental, compassionate, sensitive, gentle, tenderhearted, touchy-feely (*informal*) **9** (*Informal*) = easy, comfortable, undemanding, cushy (*informal*) **10** = pale, light, subdued, pastel, bland, mellow ≠ bright **11** = dim, faint, dimmed ≠ bright **12** = mild, temperate, balmy

soften **1** = melt, tenderize **2** = lessen, moderate, temper, ease, cushion, subdue, allay, mitigate

soil[1] **1** = earth, ground, clay, dust, dirt **2** = territory, country, land

soil[2] = dirty, foul, stain, pollute, tarnish, sully, defile, besmirch ≠ clean

soldier = fighter, serviceman, trooper, warrior, man-at-arms, squaddie *or* squaddy (*Brit. slang*)

sole = only, one, single, individual, alone, exclusive, solitary

solely = only, completely, entirely, exclusively, alone, merely

solemn **1** = serious, earnest, grave, sober, sedate, staid ≠ cheerful **2** = formal, grand, grave, dignified, ceremonial, stately, momentous ≠ informal

solid **1** = firm, hard, compact, dense, concrete ≠ unsubstantial **2** = strong, stable, sturdy, substantial, unshakable ≠ unstable **3** = reliable, dependable, upstanding, worthy, upright, trusty ≠ unreliable **4** = sound, real, reliable, good, genuine, dinkum (*Austral. & N.Z. informal*) ≠ unsound

solidarity = unity, unification, accord, cohesion, team spirit, unanimity, concordance, like-mindedness, kotahitanga (*N.Z.*)

solitary **1** = unsociable, reclusive, unsocial, isolated, lonely, cloistered, lonesome, friendless ≠ sociable **2** = lone, alone **3** = isolated, remote, out-of-the-way, hidden, unfrequented ≠ busy

solution **1** = answer, key, result, explanation **2** (*Chemistry*) = mixture, mix, compound, blend, solvent

solve = answer, work out, resolve, crack, clear up, unravel, decipher, suss (out) (*slang*)

sombre **1** = gloomy, sad, sober, grave, dismal, mournful, lugubrious, joyless ≠ cheerful **2** = dark, dull, gloomy, sober, drab ≠ bright

somebody = celebrity, name, star, notable, household name, dignitary, luminary, personage ≠ nobody

somehow = one way or another, come what may, come hell or high water (*informal*), by fair means or foul, by hook or (by) crook, by some means or other

sometimes = occasionally, at times, now and then ≠ always

song = ballad, air, tune, carol, chant, chorus, anthem, number, waiata (*N.Z.*)

soon = before long, shortly, in the near future

soothe **1** = calm, still, quiet, hush, appease, lull, pacify, mollify ≠ upset **2** = relieve, ease, alleviate, assuage ≠ irritate

soothing **1** = calming, relaxing, peaceful, quiet, calm, restful **2** = emollient, palliative

sophisticated **1** = complex, advanced, complicated, subtle, delicate, elaborate, refined, intricate ≠ simple **2** = cultured, refined, cultivated, worldly, cosmopolitan, urbane ≠ unsophisticated

sophistication = poise, worldliness, savoir-faire, urbanity, finesse, worldly wisdom

sore **1** = painful, smarting, raw, tender, burning, angry, sensitive, irritated **2** = annoyed, cross, angry, pained, hurt, upset, stung, irritated, tooshie (*Austral. slang*), hoha (*N.Z.*) **3** = annoying, troublesome **4** (*Literary*) = urgent, desperate, extreme, dire, pressing, critical, acute

sorrow NOUN **1** = grief, sadness, woe, regret, distress, misery, mourning, anguish ≠ joy **2** = hardship, trial, tribulation, affliction, trouble, woe, misfortune ≠ good fortune
• VERB = grieve, mourn, lament, be sad, bemoan, agonize, bewail ≠ rejoice

sorry **1** = regretful, apologetic, contrite, repentant, remorseful, penitent, shamefaced, conscience-stricken ≠ unapologetic **2** = sympathetic, moved, full of pity, compassionate, commiserative ≠ unsympathetic **3** = wretched, miserable, pathetic, mean, poor, sad, pitiful, deplorable

sort NOUN = kind, type, class, make, order, style, quality, nature
• VERB = arrange, group, order, rank, divide, grade, classify, categorize

soul **1** = spirit, essence, life, vital force,

wairua (*N.Z.*) **2** = embodiment, essence, epitome, personification, quintessence, type **3** = person, being, individual, body, creature, man *or* woman

sound[1] NOUN **1** = noise, din, report, tone, reverberation **2** = idea, impression, drift **3** = cry, noise, peep, squeak **4** = tone, music, note
• VERB **1** = toll, set off **2** = resound, echo, go off, toll, set off, chime, reverberate, clang **3** = seem, seem to be, appear to be
RELATED WORDS
adjectives: sonic, acoustic

sound[2] **1** = fit, healthy, perfect, intact, unhurt, uninjured, unimpaired ≠ frail **2** = sturdy, strong, solid, stable **3** = sensible, wise, reasonable, right, correct, proper, valid, rational ≠ irresponsible **4** = deep, unbroken, undisturbed, untroubled ≠ troubled

sour **1** = sharp, acid, tart, bitter, pungent, acetic ≠ sweet **2** = rancid, turned, gone off, curdled, gone bad, off ≠ fresh **3** = bitter, tart, acrimonious, embittered, disagreeable, ill-tempered, waspish, ungenerous ≠ good-natured

source **1** = cause, origin, derivation, beginning, author **2** = informant, authority **3** = origin, fount

souvenir = keepsake, reminder, memento

sovereign ADJECTIVE **1** = supreme, ruling, absolute, royal, principal, imperial, kingly *or* queenly **2** = excellent, efficient, effectual
• NOUN = monarch, ruler, king *or* queen, chief, potentate, emperor *or* empress, prince *or* princess

sovereignty = supreme power, domination, supremacy, primacy, kingship, rangatiratanga (*N.Z.*)

sow = scatter, plant, seed, implant

space **1** = room, capacity, extent, margin, scope, play, expanse, leeway **2** = period, interval, time, while, span, duration **3** = outer space, the universe, the galaxy, the solar system, the cosmos **4** = blank, gap, interval

spacious = roomy, large, huge, broad, extensive, ample, expansive, capacious ≠ limited

span NOUN **1** = period, term, duration, spell **2** = extent, reach, spread, length, distance, stretch
• VERB = extend across, cross, bridge, cover, link, traverse

spar = argue, row, squabble, scrap (*informal*), wrangle, bicker

spare ADJECTIVE **1** = back-up, reserve, second, extra, additional, auxiliary **2** = extra, surplus, leftover, over, free, odd, unwanted, unused ≠ necessary **3** = free, leisure, unoccupied **4** = thin, lean, meagre, gaunt, wiry ≠ plump
• VERB **1** = afford, give, grant, do without, part with, manage without, let someone have **2** = have mercy on, pardon, leave, let off (*informal*), go easy on (*informal*), save (from harm) ≠ show no mercy to

sparing = economical, frugal, thrifty, saving, careful, prudent ≠ lavish

spark NOUN **1** = flicker, flash, gleam, glint, flare **2** = trace, hint, scrap, atom, jot, vestige
• VERB *often with* ***off*** = start, stimulate, provoke, inspire, trigger (off), set off, precipitate

sparkle VERB = glitter, flash, shine, gleam, shimmer, twinkle, dance, glint
• NOUN **1** = glitter, flash, gleam, flicker, brilliance, twinkle, glint **2** = vivacity, life, spirit, dash, vitality, élan, liveliness

spate = flood, flow, torrent, rush, deluge, outpouring

speak **1** = talk, say something **2** = articulate, say, pronounce, utter, tell, state, talk, express **3** = converse, talk, chat, discourse, confer, commune, exchange views, korero (*N.Z.*) **4** = lecture, address an audience

speaker = orator, public speaker, lecturer, spokesperson, spokesman *or* spokeswoman

spearhead = lead, head, pioneer, launch, set off, initiate, set in motion

special **1** = exceptional, important, significant, particular, unique, unusual, extraordinary, memorable ≠ ordinary **2** = specific, particular, distinctive, individual, appropriate, precise ≠ general

specialist = expert, authority, professional, master, consultant, guru, buff (*informal*), connoisseur, fundi (*S. African*)

speciality = forte, métier, specialty, bag (*slang*), pièce de résistance (*French*)

species = kind, sort, type, group, class, variety, breed, category

specific **1** = particular, special, characteristic, distinguishing ≠ general

2 = precise, exact, explicit, definite, express, clear-cut, unequivocal ≠ vague 3 = peculiar, appropriate, individual, particular, unique

specification = requirement, detail, particular, stipulation, condition, qualification

specify = state, designate, stipulate, name, detail, mention, indicate, define

specimen 1 = sample, example, model, type, pattern, instance, representative, exemplification 2 = example, model, type

spectacle 1 = show, display, exhibition, event, performance, extravaganza, pageant 2 = sight, wonder, scene, phenomenon, curiosity, marvel

spectacular ADJECTIVE = impressive, striking, dramatic, stunning (*informal*), grand, magnificent, splendid, dazzling ≠ unimpressive

• NOUN = show, display, spectacle

spectator = onlooker, observer, viewer, looker-on, watcher, bystander ≠ participant

spectre = ghost, spirit, phantom, vision, apparition, wraith, kehua (*N.Z.*)

speculate 1 = conjecture, consider, wonder, guess, surmise, theorize, hypothesize 2 = gamble, risk, venture, hazard

speculation 1 = theory, opinion, hypothesis, conjecture, guess, surmise, guesswork, supposition 2 = gamble, risk, hazard

speculative = hypothetical, academic, theoretical, notional, conjectural, suppositional

speech 1 = communication, talk, conversation, discussion, dialogue 2 = diction, pronunciation, articulation, delivery, fluency, inflection, intonation, elocution 3 = language, tongue, jargon, dialect, idiom, parlance, articulation, diction 4 = talk, address, lecture, discourse, homily, oration, spiel (*informal*), whaikorero (*N.Z.*)

speed NOUN 1 = rate, pace 2 = swiftness, rush, hurry, haste, rapidity, quickness ≠ slowness

• VERB 1 = race, rush, hurry, zoom, career, tear, barrel (along) (*informal*, *chiefly U.S. & Canad.*), gallop ≠ crawl 2 = help, advance, aid, boost, assist, facilitate, expedite ≠ hinder

speedy = quick, fast, rapid, swift, express, immediate, prompt, hurried ≠ slow

spell¹ = indicate, mean, signify, point to, imply, augur, portend

spell² 1 = incantation, charm, makutu (*N.Z.*) 2 = enchantment, magic, fascination, glamour, allure, bewitchment

spell³ = period, time, term, stretch, course, season, interval, bout

spend 1 = pay out, fork out (*slang*), expend, disburse ≠ save 2 = pass, fill, occupy, while away 3 = use up, waste, squander, empty, drain, exhaust, consume, run through ≠ save

sphere 1 = ball, globe, orb, globule, circle 2 = field, department, function, territory, capacity, province, patch, scope

spice 1 = seasoning 2 = excitement, zest, colour, pep, zing (*informal*), piquancy

spicy 1 = hot, seasoned, aromatic, savoury, piquant 2 (*Informal*) = risqué, racy, ribald, hot (*informal*), suggestive, titillating, indelicate

RELATED WORD

fear of: arachnophobia

spike NOUN = point, stake, spine, barb, prong

• VERB = impale, spit, spear, stick

spill 1 = tip over, overturn, capsize, knock over 2 = shed, discharge, disgorge 3 = slop, flow, pour, run, overflow

spin VERB 1 = revolve, turn, rotate, reel, whirl, twirl, gyrate, pirouette 2 = reel, swim, whirl

• NOUN 1 (*Informal*) = drive, ride, joy ride (*informal*) 2 = revolution, roll, whirl, gyration

• PHRASES **spin something out** = prolong, extend, lengthen, draw out, drag out, delay, amplify

spine 1 = backbone, vertebrae, spinal column, vertebral column 2 = barb, spur, needle, spike, ray, quill

spiral ADJECTIVE = coiled, winding, whorled, helical

• NOUN = coil, helix, corkscrew, whorl

spirit NOUN 1 = soul, life 2 = life force, vital spark, mauri (*N.Z.*) 3 = ghost, phantom, spectre, apparition, atua (*N.Z.*), kehua (*N.Z.*) 4 = courage, guts (*informal*), grit, backbone, spunk (*informal*), gameness 5 = liveliness, energy, vigour, life, force, fire, enthusiasm, animation 6 = attitude, character, temper, outlook, temperament,

disposition **7** = heart, sense, nature, soul, core, substance, essence, quintessence **8** = intention, meaning, purpose, purport, gist **9** = feeling, atmosphere, character, tone, mood, tenor, ambience
• **PLURAL NOUN** = mood, feelings, morale, temper, disposition, state of mind, frame of mind

spirited = lively, energetic, animated, active, feisty (*informal, chiefly U.S. & Canad.*), vivacious, mettlesome ≠ lifeless

spiritual **1** = nonmaterial, immaterial, incorporeal ≠ material **2** = sacred, religious, holy, divine, devotional

spit **VERB 1** = expectorate **2** = eject, throw out
• **NOUN** = saliva, dribble, spittle, drool, slaver

spite **NOUN** = malice, malevolence, ill will, hatred, animosity, venom, spleen, spitefulness ≠ kindness
• **VERB** = annoy, hurt, injure, harm, vex ≠ benefit
• **PHRASES in spite of** = despite, regardless of, notwithstanding, (even) though

splash **VERB 1** = paddle, plunge, bathe, dabble, wade, wallow **2** = scatter, shower, spray, sprinkle, wet, spatter, slop **3** = spatter, mark, stain, speck, speckle
• **NOUN 1** = dash, touch, spattering **2** = spot, burst, patch, spurt **3** = blob, spot, smudge, stain, smear, fleck, speck

splendid **1** = excellent, wonderful, marvellous, great (*informal*), cracking (*Brit. informal*), fantastic (*informal*), first-class, glorious, booshit (*Austral. slang*), exo (*Austral. slang*), sik (*Austral. slang*) ≠ poor **2** = magnificent, grand, impressive, rich, superb, costly, gorgeous, lavish ≠ squalid

splendour = magnificence, grandeur, show, display, spectacle, richness, nobility, pomp ≠ squalor

splinter **NOUN** = sliver, fragment, chip, flake
• **VERB** = shatter, split, fracture, disintegrate

split **VERB 1** = break, crack, burst, open, give way, come apart, come undone **2** = cut, break, crack, snap, chop **3** = divide, separate, disunite, disband, cleave **4** = diverge, separate, branch, fork, part **5** = tear, rend, rip **6** = share out, divide, distribute, halve, allocate, partition, allot, apportion
• **NOUN 1** = division, breach, rift, rupture, discord, schism, estrangement, dissension **2** = separation, break-up, split-up **3** = crack, tear, rip, gap, rent, breach, slit, fissure
• **ADJECTIVE 1** = divided **2** = broken, cracked, fractured, ruptured, cleft

spoil **VERB 1** = ruin, destroy, wreck, damage, injure, harm, mar, trash (*slang*), crool *or* cruel (*Austral. slang*) ≠ improve **2** = overindulge, indulge, pamper, cosset, coddle, mollycoddle ≠ deprive **3** = indulge, pamper, satisfy, gratify, pander to **4** = go bad, turn, go off (*Brit. informal*), rot, decay, decompose, curdle, addle
• **PLURAL NOUN** = booty, loot, plunder, prey, swag (*slang*)

spoken = verbal, voiced, expressed, uttered, oral, said, told, unwritten

spokesperson = speaker official, spokesman *or* spokeswoman, voice, spin doctor (*informal*), mouthpiece

sponsor **VERB** = back, fund, finance, promote, subsidize, patronize
• **NOUN** = backer, patron, promoter

spontaneous = unplanned, impromptu, unprompted, willing, natural, voluntary, instinctive, impulsive ≠ planned

sport **NOUN 1** = game, exercise, recreation, play, amusement, diversion, pastime **2** = fun, joking, teasing, banter, jest, badinage
• **VERB** (*Informal*) = wear, display, flaunt, exhibit, flourish, show off, vaunt

sporting = fair, sportsmanlike, game (*informal*) ≠ unfair

sporty = athletic, outdoor, energetic

spot **NOUN 1** = mark, stain, speck, scar, blot, smudge, blemish, speckle **2** = pimple, pustule, zit (*slang*) **3** = place, site, point, position, scene, location **4** (*Informal*) = predicament, trouble, difficulty, mess, plight, hot water (*informal*), quandary, tight spot
• **VERB 1** = see, observe, catch sight of, sight, recognize, detect, make out, discern **2** = mark, stain, soil, dirty, fleck, spatter, speckle, splodge

spotlight **NOUN** = attention, limelight, public eye, fame
• **VERB** = highlight, draw attention to, accentuate

spotted = speckled, dotted, flecked,

mottled, dappled
spouse = partner, mate, husband *or* wife, consort, significant other (*U.S. informal*)
sprawl = loll, slump, lounge, flop, slouch
spray[1] NOUN 1 = droplets, fine mist, drizzle 2 = aerosol, sprinkler, atomizer
• VERB = scatter, shower, sprinkle, diffuse
spray[2] = sprig, floral arrangement, branch, corsage
spread VERB 1 = open (out), extend, stretch, unfold, sprawl, unroll 2 = extend, open, stretch 3 = grow, increase, expand, widen, escalate, proliferate, multiply, broaden 4 = circulate, broadcast, propagate, disseminate, make known ≠ suppress 5 = diffuse, cast, shed, radiate
• NOUN 1 = increase, development, advance, expansion, proliferation, dissemination, dispersal 2 = extent, span, stretch, sweep
spree = fling, binge (*informal*), orgy
spring NOUN = flexibility, bounce, resilience, elasticity, buoyancy
• VERB 1 = jump, bound, leap, bounce, vault 2 *often with* ***from*** = originate, come, derive, start, issue, proceed, arise, stem
RELATED WORD
adjective: vernal
sprinkle = scatter, dust, strew, pepper, shower, spray, powder, dredge
sprinkling = scattering, dusting, few, dash, handful, sprinkle
sprint = run, race, shoot, tear, dash, dart, hare (*Brit. informal*)
sprout 1 = germinate, bud, shoot, spring 2 = grow, develop, ripen
spur VERB = incite, drive, prompt, urge, stimulate, animate, prod, prick
• NOUN = stimulus, incentive, impetus, motive, impulse, inducement, incitement
• PHRASES **on the spur of the moment** = on impulse, impulsively, on the spot, impromptu, without planning
spurn = reject, slight, scorn, rebuff, snub, despise, disdain, repulse ≠ accept
spy NOUN = undercover agent, mole, nark (*Brit., Austral., & N.Z. slang*)
• VERB = catch sight of, spot, notice, observe, glimpse, espy
squabble VERB = quarrel, fight, argue, row, dispute, wrangle, bicker
• NOUN = quarrel, fight, row, argument, dispute, disagreement, tiff
squad = team, group, band, company, force, troop, crew, gang
squander = waste, spend, fritter away, blow (*slang*), misuse, expend, misspend ≠ save
square ADJECTIVE = fair, straight, genuine, ethical, honest, on the level (*informal*), kosher (*informal*), dinkum (*Austral. & N.Z. informal*), above board
• VERB *often with* ***with*** = agree, match, fit, correspond, tally, reconcile
squash 1 = crush, press, flatten, mash, smash, distort, pulp, compress 2 = suppress, quell, silence, crush, annihilate 3 = embarrass, put down, shame, degrade, mortify
squeeze VERB 1 = press, crush, squash, pinch 2 = clutch, press, grip, crush, pinch, squash, compress, wring 3 = cram, press, crowd, force, stuff, pack, jam, ram 4 = hug, embrace, cuddle, clasp, enfold
• NOUN 1 = press, grip, clasp, crush, pinch, squash, wring 2 = crush, jam, squash, press, crowd, congestion 3 = hug, embrace, clasp
stab VERB = pierce, stick, wound, knife, thrust, spear, jab, transfix
• NOUN 1 (*Informal*) = attempt, go, try, endeavour 2 = twinge, prick, pang, ache
stability = firmness, strength, soundness, solidity, steadiness ≠ instability
stable 1 = secure, lasting, strong, sound, fast, sure, established, permanent ≠ insecure 2 = well-balanced, balanced, sensible, reasonable, rational 3 = solid, firm, fixed, substantial, durable, well-made, well-built, immovable ≠ unstable
stack NOUN 1 = pile, heap, mountain, mass, load, mound 2 = lot, mass, load (*informal*), ton (*informal*), heap (*informal*), great amount
• VERB = pile, heap up, load, assemble, accumulate, amass
staff 1 = workers, employees, personnel, workforce, team 2 = stick, pole, rod, crook, cane, stave, wand, sceptre
stage = step, leg, phase, point, level, period, division, lap
stagger 1 = totter, reel, sway, lurch, wobble 2 = astound, amaze, stun, shock, shake, overwhelm, astonish, confound
stain NOUN 1 = mark, spot, blot, blemish, discoloration, smirch 2 = stigma, shame, disgrace, slur, dishonour 3 = dye, colour, tint

• VERB 1 = mark, soil, discolour, dirty, tinge, spot, blot, blemish 2 = dye, colour, tint

stake[1] = pole, post, stick, pale, paling, picket, palisade

stake[2] NOUN = bet, ante, wager

• VERB 1 = bet, gamble, wager, chance, risk, venture, hazard 2 = interest, share, involvement, concern, investment

stale 1 = old, hard, dry, decayed ≠ fresh 2 = musty, fusty 3 = tasteless, flat, sour 4 = unoriginal, banal, trite, stereotyped, worn-out, threadbare, hackneyed, overused ≠ original

stalk = pursue, follow, track, hunt, shadow, haunt

stall VERB 1 = play for time, delay, hedge, temporize 2 = stop dead, jam, seize up, catch, stick, stop short

• NOUN = stand, table, counter, booth, kiosk

stalwart 1 = loyal, faithful, firm, true, dependable, steadfast 2 = strong, strapping, sturdy, stout ≠ puny

stamina = staying power, endurance, resilience, force, power, energy, strength

stammer = stutter, falter, pause, hesitate, stumble over your words

stamp NOUN = imprint, mark, brand, signature, earmark, hallmark

• VERB 1 = print, mark, impress 2 = trample, step, tread, crush 3 = identify, mark, brand, label, reveal, show to be, categorize

• PHRASES **stamp something out** = eliminate, destroy, eradicate, crush, suppress, put down, scotch, quell

stance 1 = attitude, stand, position, viewpoint, standpoint 2 = posture, carriage, bearing, deportment

stand VERB 1 = be upright, be erect, be vertical 2 = get to your feet, rise, stand up, straighten up 3 = be located, be, sit, be positioned, be situated *or* located 4 = be valid, continue, exist, prevail, remain valid 5 = put, place, position, set, mount 6 = sit, mellow 7 = resist, endure, tolerate, stand up to 8 = tolerate, bear, abide, stomach, endure, brook 9 = take, bear, handle, endure, put up with (*informal*), countenance

• NOUN 1 = position, attitude, stance, opinion, determination 2 = stall, booth, kiosk, table

• PHRASES **stand by** = be prepared, wait ♦ **stand for something** 1 = represent, mean, signify, denote, indicate, symbolize, betoken 2 (*Informal*) = tolerate, bear, endure, put up with, brook ♦ **stand in for someone** = be a substitute for, represent, cover for, take the place of, deputize for ♦ **stand up for something** *or* **someone** = support, champion, defend, uphold, stick up for (*informal*)

standard NOUN 1 = level, grade 2 = criterion, measure, guideline, example, model, average, norm, gauge 3 *often plural* = principles, ideals, morals, ethics 4 = flag, banner, ensign

• ADJECTIVE 1 = usual, normal, customary, average, basic, regular, typical, orthodox ≠ unusual 2 = accepted, official, established, approved, recognized, definitive, authoritative ≠ unofficial

stand-in = substitute, deputy, replacement, reserve, surrogate, understudy, locum, stopgap

standing NOUN 1 = status, position, footing, rank, reputation, eminence, repute 2 = duration, existence, continuance

• ADJECTIVE 1 = permanent, lasting, fixed, regular 2 = upright, erect, vertical

staple = principal, chief, main, key, basic, fundamental, predominant

star NOUN 1 = heavenly body, celestial body 2 = celebrity, big name, megastar (*informal*), name, luminary 3 = leading man *or* lady, hero *or* heroine, principal, main attraction

• VERB = play the lead, appear, feature, perform

• ADJECTIVE = leading, major, celebrated, brilliant, well-known, prominent

RELATED WORDS

adjectives: astral, stellar

stare = gaze, look, goggle, watch, gape, eyeball (*slang*), gawp (*Brit. slang*), gawk

stark ADJECTIVE 1 = plain, harsh, basic, grim, straightforward, blunt 2 = sharp, clear, striking, distinct, clear-cut 3 = austere, severe, plain, bare, harsh 4 = bleak, grim, barren, hard 5 = absolute, pure, sheer, utter, downright, out-and-out, unmitigated

• ADVERB = absolutely, quite, completely, entirely, altogether, wholly, utterly

start VERB 1 = set about, begin, proceed, embark upon, take the first step, make

a beginning ≠ stop **2** = begin, arise, originate, issue, appear, commence ≠ end **3** = set in motion, initiate, instigate, open, trigger, originate, get going, kick-start ≠ stop **4** = establish, begin, found, create, launch, set up, institute, pioneer ≠ terminate **5** = start up, activate, get something going ≠ turn off **6** = jump, shy, jerk, flinch, recoil
• NOUN **1** = beginning, outset, opening, birth, foundation, dawn, onset, initiation ≠ end **2** = jump, spasm, convulsion

startle = surprise, shock, frighten, scare, make (someone) jump

starving = hungry, starved, ravenous, famished

state NOUN **1** = country, nation, land, republic, territory, federation, commonwealth, kingdom **2** = government, ministry, administration, executive, regime, powers-that-be **3** = condition, shape **4** = frame of mind, condition, spirits, attitude, mood, humour **5** = ceremony, glory, grandeur, splendour, majesty, pomp **6** = circumstances, situation, position, predicament
• VERB = say, declare, specify, present, voice, express, assert, utter

stately = grand, majestic, dignified, royal, august, noble, regal, lofty ≠ lowly

statement **1** = announcement, declaration, communication, communiqué, proclamation **2** = account, report

station NOUN **1** = railway station, stop, stage, halt, terminal, train station, terminus **2** = headquarters, base, depot **3** = position, rank, status, standing, post, situation **4** = post, place, location, position, situation
• VERB = assign, post, locate, set, establish, install

stature **1** = height, build, size **2** = importance, standing, prestige, rank, prominence, eminence

status **1** = position, rank, grade **2** = prestige, standing, authority, influence, weight, honour, importance, fame, mana (*N.Z.*) **3** = state of play, development, progress, condition, evolution

staunch = loyal, faithful, stalwart, firm, sound, true, trusty, steadfast

stay VERB **1** = remain, continue to be, linger, stop, wait, halt, pause, abide ≠ go **2** *often with* ***at*** = lodge, visit, sojourn, put up at, be accommodated at **3** = continue, remain, go on, survive, endure
• NOUN **1** = visit, stop, holiday, stopover, sojourn **2** = postponement, delay, suspension, stopping, halt, deferment

steady **1** = continuous, regular, constant, consistent, persistent, unbroken, uninterrupted, incessant ≠ irregular **2** = stable, fixed, secure, firm, safe ≠ unstable **3** = regular, established **4** = dependable, sensible, reliable, secure, calm, supportive, sober, level-headed ≠ undependable

steal **1** = take, nick (*slang, chiefly Brit.*), pinch (*informal*), lift (*informal*), embezzle, pilfer, misappropriate, purloin **2** = copy, take, appropriate, pinch (*informal*) **3** = sneak, slip, creep, tiptoe, slink

stealth = secrecy, furtiveness, slyness, sneakiness, unobtrusiveness, stealthiness, surreptitiousness

steep¹ **1** = sheer, precipitous, abrupt, vertical ≠ gradual **2** = sharp, sudden, abrupt, marked, extreme, distinct **3** (*Informal*) = high, exorbitant, extreme, unreasonable, overpriced, extortionate ≠ reasonable

steep² = soak, immerse, marinate (*Cookery*), submerge, drench, moisten, souse

steeped = saturated, pervaded, permeated, filled, infused, imbued, suffused

steer **1** = drive, control, direct, handle, pilot **2** = direct, lead, guide, conduct, escort

stem¹ NOUN = stalk, branch, trunk, shoot, axis
• PHRASES **stem from something** = originate from, be caused by, derive from, arise from

stem² = stop, hold back, staunch, check, dam, curb

step NOUN **1** = pace, stride, footstep **2** = footfall **3** = move, measure, action, means, act, deed, expedient **4** = stage, point, phase **5** = level, rank, degree
• VERB = walk, pace, tread, move
• PHRASES **step in** (*Informal*) = intervene, take action, become involved ◆ **step something up** = increase, intensify, raise

stereotype NOUN = formula, pattern
• VERB = categorize, typecast, pigeonhole,

standardize

sterile 1 = germ-free, sterilized, disinfected, aseptic ≠ unhygienic 2 = barren, infertile, unproductive, childless ≠ fertile

sterling = excellent, sound, fine, superlative

stern 1 = strict, harsh, hard, grim, rigid, austere, inflexible ≠ lenient 2 = severe, serious, forbidding ≠ friendly

stick[1] 1 = twig, branch 2 = cane, staff, pole, rod, crook, baton 3 (*Slang*) = abuse, criticism, flak (*informal*), fault-finding

stick[2] VERB 1 (*Informal*) = put, place, set, lay, deposit 2 = poke, dig, stab, thrust, pierce, penetrate, spear, prod 3 = fasten, fix, bind, hold, bond, attach, glue, paste 4 = adhere, cling, become joined, become welded 5 = stay, remain, linger, persist 6 (*Slang*) = tolerate, take, stand, stomach, abide

• PHRASES **stick out** = protrude, stand out, jut out, show, project, bulge, obtrude ◆ **stick up for someone** (*Informal*) = defend, support, champion, stand up for

sticky 1 = adhesive, gummed, adherent 2 = gooey, tacky (*informal*), viscous, glutinous, gummy, icky (*informal*), gluey, clinging 3 (*Informal*) = difficult, awkward, tricky, embarrassing, nasty, delicate, unpleasant, barro (*Austral. slang*) 4 = humid, close, sultry, oppressive, sweltering, clammy, muggy

stiff 1 = inflexible, rigid, unyielding, hard, firm, tight, solid, tense ≠ flexible 2 = formal, constrained, forced, unnatural, stilted, unrelaxed ≠ informal 3 = vigorous, great, strong 4 = severe, strict, harsh, hard, heavy, extreme, drastic 5 = difficult, hard, tough, exacting, arduous

stifle 1 = suppress, repress, stop, check, silence, restrain, hush, smother 2 = restrain, suppress, repress, smother

stigma = disgrace, shame, dishonour, stain, slur, smirch

still ADJECTIVE 1 = motionless, stationary, calm, peaceful, serene, tranquil, undisturbed, restful ≠ moving 2 = silent, quiet, hushed ≠ noisy

• VERB = quieten, calm, settle, quiet, silence, soothe, hush, lull ≠ get louder

• ADVERB = however, but, yet, nevertheless, notwithstanding

stimulate = encourage, inspire, prompt, fire, spur, provoke, arouse, rouse

stimulating = exciting, inspiring, stirring, rousing, provocative, exhilarating ≠ boring

stimulus = incentive, spur, encouragement, impetus, inducement, goad, incitement, fillip

sting 1 = hurt, burn, wound 2 = smart, burn, pain, hurt, tingle

stink VERB = reek, pong (*Brit. informal*)

• NOUN = stench, pong (*Brit. informal*), foul smell, fetor

stint NOUN = term, time, turn, period, share, shift, stretch, spell

• VERB = be mean, hold back, be sparing, skimp on, be frugal

stipulate = specify, agree, require, contract, settle, covenant, insist upon

stir VERB 1 = mix, beat, agitate 2 = stimulate, move, excite, spur, provoke, arouse, awaken, rouse ≠ inhibit 3 = spur, drive, prompt, stimulate, prod, urge, animate, prick

• NOUN = commotion, excitement, activity, disorder, fuss, disturbance, bustle, flurry

stock NOUN 1 = shares, holdings, securities, investments, bonds, equities 2 = property, capital, assets, funds 3 = goods, merchandise, wares, range, choice, variety, selection, commodities 4 = supply, store, reserve, fund, stockpile, hoard 5 = livestock, cattle, beasts, domestic animals

• VERB 1 = sell, supply, handle, keep, trade in, deal in 2 = fill, supply, provide with, equip, furnish, fit out

• ADJECTIVE 1 = hackneyed, routine, banal, trite, overused 2 = regular, usual, ordinary, conventional, customary

stomach NOUN 1 = belly, gut (*informal*), abdomen, tummy (*informal*), puku (*N.Z.*) 2 = tummy, pot 3 = inclination, taste, desire, appetite, relish

• VERB = bear, take, tolerate, endure, swallow, abide

RELATED WORD

adjective: gastric

stone 1 = masonry, rock 2 = rock, pebble 3 = pip, seed, pit, kernel

stoop VERB 1 = hunch 2 = bend, lean, bow, duck, crouch

• NOUN = slouch, bad posture, round-shoulderedness

stop VERB 1 = quit, cease, refrain, put an end to, discontinue, desist ≠ start

2 = prevent, cut short, arrest, restrain, hold back, hinder, repress, impede ≠ facilitate 3 = end, conclude, finish, terminate ≠ continue 4 = cease, shut down, discontinue, desist ≠ continue 5 = halt, pause ≠ keep going 6 = pause, wait, rest, take a break, have a breather (*informal*), stop briefly 7 = stay, rest, lodge

• NOUN 1 = halt, standstill 2 = station, stage, depot, terminus 3 = stay, break, rest

store NOUN 1 = shop, outlet, market, mart 2 = supply, stock, reserve, fund, quantity, accumulation, stockpile, hoard 3 = repository, warehouse, depository, storeroom

• VERB 1 *often with* ***away*** *or* ***up*** = put by, save, hoard, keep, reserve, deposit, garner, stockpile 2 = put away, put in storage, put in store 3 = keep, hold, preserve, maintain, retain, conserve

storm NOUN 1 = tempest, hurricane, gale, blizzard, squall 2 = outburst, row, outcry, furore, outbreak, turmoil, disturbance, strife

• VERB 1 = rush, stamp, flounce, fly 2 = rage, rant, thunder, rave, bluster 3 = attack, charge, rush, assault, assail

stormy 1 = wild, rough, raging, turbulent, windy, blustery, inclement, squally 2 = rough, wild, turbulent, raging 3 = angry, heated, fierce, passionate, fiery, impassioned

story 1 = tale, romance, narrative, history, legend, yarn 2 = anecdote, account, tale, report 3 = report, news, article, feature, scoop, news item

stout 1 = fat, big, heavy, overweight, plump, bulky, burly, fleshy ≠ slim 2 = strong, strapping, muscular, robust, sturdy, stalwart, brawny, able-bodied ≠ puny 3 = brave, bold, courageous, fearless, resolute, gallant, intrepid, valiant ≠ timid

straight ADJECTIVE 1 = direct ≠ indirect 2 = level, even, right, square, true, smooth, aligned, horizontal ≠ crooked 3 = frank, plain, straightforward, blunt, outright, honest, candid, forthright ≠ evasive 4 = successive, consecutive, continuous, running, solid, nonstop ≠ discontinuous 5 (*Slang*) = conventional, conservative, bourgeois ≠ fashionable 6 = honest, just, fair, reliable, respectable, upright, honourable, law-abiding ≠ dishonest 7 = undiluted, pure, neat, unadulterated, unmixed 8 = in order, organized, arranged, neat, tidy, orderly, shipshape ≠ untidy

• ADVERB 1 = directly, precisely, exactly, unswervingly, by the shortest route, in a beeline 2 = immediately, directly, promptly, instantly, at once, straight away, without delay, forthwith

straight away = immediately, now, at once, directly, instantly, right away

straighten = neaten, arrange, tidy (up), order, put in order

straightforward 1 (*Chiefly Brit.*) = simple, easy, uncomplicated, routine, elementary, easy-peasy (*slang*) ≠ complicated 2 = honest, open, direct, genuine, sincere, candid, truthful, forthright, dinkum (*Austral. & N.Z. informal*) ≠ devious

strain[1] NOUN 1 = pressure, stress, demands, burden 2 = stress, anxiety 3 = worry, effort, struggle ≠ ease 4 = burden, tension 5 = injury, wrench, sprain, pull

• VERB 1 = stretch, tax, overtax 2 = strive, struggle, endeavour, labour, go for it (*informal*), bend over backwards (*informal*), give it your best shot (*informal*), knock yourself out (*informal*) ≠ relax 3 = sieve, filter, sift, purify

strain[2] 1 = trace, suggestion, tendency, streak 2 = breed, family, race, blood, descent, extraction, ancestry, lineage

strained 1 = tense, difficult, awkward, embarrassed, stiff, uneasy ≠ relaxed 2 = forced, put on, false, artificial, unnatural ≠ natural

strait NOUN *often plural* = channel, sound, narrows

• PLURAL NOUN = difficulty, dilemma, plight, hardship, uphill (*S. African*), predicament, extremity

strand = filament, fibre, thread, string

stranded 1 = beached, grounded, marooned, ashore, shipwrecked, aground 2 = helpless, abandoned, high and dry

strange 1 = odd, curious, weird, wonderful, extraordinary, bizarre, peculiar, abnormal ≠ ordinary 2 = unfamiliar, new, unknown, foreign, novel, alien, exotic, untried ≠ familiar

stranger 1 = unknown person 2 = newcomer, incomer, foreigner, guest, visitor, alien, outlander

strangle 1 = throttle, choke, asphyxiate, strangulate 2 = suppress, inhibit, subdue, stifle, repress, overpower, quash, quell

strap NOUN = tie, thong, belt
• VERB = fasten, tie, secure, bind, lash, buckle

strapping = well-built, big, powerful, robust, sturdy, husky (*informal*), brawny

strategic 1 = tactical, calculated, deliberate, planned, politic, diplomatic 2 = crucial, important, key, vital, critical, decisive, cardinal

strategy 1 = policy, procedure, approach, scheme 2 = plan, approach, scheme

stray VERB 1 = wander, go astray, drift 2 = drift, wander, roam, meander, rove 3 = digress, diverge, deviate, get off the point
• ADJECTIVE 1 = lost, abandoned, homeless, roaming, vagrant 2 = random, chance, accidental

streak NOUN 1 = band, line, strip, stroke, layer, slash, vein, stripe 2 = trace, touch, element, strain, dash, vein
• VERB = speed, fly, tear, flash, sprint, dart, zoom, whizz (*informal*)

stream NOUN 1 = river, brook, burn (*Scot.*), beck, tributary, bayou, rivulet 2 = flow, current, rush, run, course, drift, surge, tide
• VERB 1 = flow, run, pour, issue, flood, spill, cascade, gush 2 = rush, fly, speed, tear, flood, pour

streamlined = efficient, organized, rationalized, slick, smooth-running

street = road, lane, avenue, terrace, row, roadway

strength 1 = might, muscle, brawn ≠ weakness 2 = will, resolution, courage, character, nerve, determination, pluck, stamina 3 = health, fitness, vigour 4 = mainstay 5 = toughness, soundness, robustness, sturdiness 6 = force, power, intensity ≠ weakness 7 = potency, effectiveness, efficacy 8 = strong point, skill, asset, advantage, talent, forte, speciality ≠ failing

strengthen 1 = fortify, harden, toughen, consolidate, stiffen, gee up, brace up ≠ weaken 2 = reinforce, support, intensify, bolster, buttress 3 = bolster, harden, reinforce 4 = heighten, intensify 5 = make stronger, build up, invigorate, restore, give strength to 6 = support, brace, reinforce, consolidate, harden, bolster, augment, buttress 7 = become stronger, intensify, gain strength

stress VERB 1 = emphasize, underline, dwell on 2 = place the emphasis on, emphasize, give emphasis to, lay emphasis upon
• NOUN 1 = emphasis, significance, force, weight 2 = strain, pressure, worry, tension, burden, anxiety, trauma 3 = accent, beat, emphasis, accentuation

stretch VERB 1 = extend, cover, spread, reach, put forth, unroll 2 = last, continue, go on, carry on, reach 3 = expand 4 = pull, distend, strain, tighten, draw out, elongate
• NOUN 1 = expanse, area, tract, spread, distance, extent 2 = period, time, spell, stint, term, space

strict 1 = severe, harsh, stern, firm, stringent ≠ easy-going 2 = stern, firm, severe, harsh, authoritarian 3 = exact, accurate, precise, close, true, faithful, meticulous, scrupulous 4 = absolute, total, utter

strife = conflict, battle, clash, quarrel, friction, discord, dissension

strike NOUN = walkout, industrial action, mutiny, revolt
• VERB 1 = walk out, down tools, revolt, mutiny 2 = hit, smack, thump, beat, knock, punch, hammer, slap 3 = drive, hit, smack, wallop (*informal*) 4 = collide with, hit, run into, bump into 5 = knock, smack, thump, beat 6 = affect, touch, devastate, overwhelm, leave a mark on 7 = attack, assault someone, set upon someone, lay into someone (*informal*) 8 = occur to, hit, come to, register (*informal*), dawn on *or* upon 9 = seem to, appear to, look to, give the impression to 10 = move, touch, hit, affect, overcome, stir, disturb, perturb

striking = impressive, dramatic, outstanding, noticeable, conspicuous, jaw-dropping ≠ unimpressive

string 1 = cord, twine, fibre 2 = series, line, row, file, sequence, succession, procession 3 = sequence, run, series, chain, succession

stringent = strict, tough, rigorous, tight, severe, rigid, inflexible ≠ lax

strip[1] 1 = undress, disrobe, unclothe 2 = plunder, rob, loot, empty, sack, ransack, pillage, divest

strip[2] 1 = piece, shred, band, belt 2 = stretch, area, tract, expanse, extent

strive = try, labour, struggle, attempt, toil, go all out (*informal*), bend over backwards (*informal*), do your best

stroke VERB = caress, rub, fondle, pet
• NOUN 1 = apoplexy, fit, seizure, attack, collapse 2 = blow, hit, knock, pat, rap, thump, swipe

stroll VERB = walk, ramble, amble, promenade, saunter
• NOUN = walk, promenade, constitutional, ramble, breath of air

strong 1 = powerful, muscular, tough, athletic, strapping, hardy, sturdy, burly ≠ weak 2 = fit, robust, lusty 3 = durable, substantial, sturdy, heavy-duty, well-built, hard-wearing ≠ flimsy 4 = extreme, radical, drastic, strict, harsh, rigid, forceful, uncompromising 5 = decisive, firm, forceful, decided, determined, resolute, incisive 6 = persuasive, convincing, compelling, telling, sound, effective, potent, weighty 7 = keen, deep, acute, fervent, zealous, vehement 8 = intense, deep, passionate, ardent, fierce, fervent, vehement, fervid 9 = staunch, firm, fierce, ardent, enthusiastic, passionate, fervent 10 = distinct, marked, clear, unmistakable ≠ slight 11 = bright, brilliant, dazzling, bold ≠ dull

stronghold 1 = bastion, fortress, bulwark 2 = refuge, haven, retreat, sanctuary, hide-out

structure NOUN 1 = arrangement, form, make-up, design, organization, construction, formation, configuration 2 = building, construction, erection, edifice
• VERB = arrange, organize, design, shape, build up, assemble

struggle VERB 1 = strive, labour, toil, work, strain, go all out (*informal*), give it your best shot (*informal*), exert yourself 2 = fight, battle, wrestle, grapple, compete, contend
• NOUN 1 = effort, labour, toil, work, pains, scramble, exertion 2 = fight, battle, conflict, clash, contest, brush, combat, tussle, biffo (*Austral. slang*)

strut = swagger, parade, peacock, prance

stubborn = obstinate, dogged, inflexible, persistent, intractable, tenacious, recalcitrant, unyielding ≠ compliant

stuck 1 = fastened, fast, fixed, joined, glued, cemented 2 (*Informal*) = baffled, stumped, beaten

student 1 = undergraduate, scholar 2 = pupil, scholar, schoolchild, schoolboy *or* schoolgirl 3 = learner, trainee, apprentice, disciple

studied = planned, deliberate, conscious, intentional, premeditated ≠ unplanned

studio = workshop, workroom, atelier

study VERB 1 = learn, cram (*informal*), swot (up) (*Brit. informal*), read up, mug up (*Brit. slang*) 2 = examine, survey, look at, scrutinize 3 = contemplate, read, examine, consider, go into, pore over
• NOUN 1 = examination, investigation, analysis, consideration, inspection, scrutiny, contemplation 2 = piece of research, survey, report, review, inquiry, investigation 3 = learning, lessons, school work, reading, research, swotting (*Brit. informal*)

stuff NOUN 1 = things, gear, possessions, effects, equipment, objects, tackle, kit 2 = substance, material, essence, matter
• VERB 1 = shove, force, push, squeeze, jam, ram 2 = cram, fill, pack, crowd

stuffing = wadding, filling, packing

stumble VERB 1 = trip, fall, slip, reel, stagger, falter, lurch 2 = totter, reel, lurch, wobble
• PHRASES **stumble across** *or* **on** *or* **upon something** *or* **someone** = discover, find, come across, chance upon

stump NOUN = tail end, end, remnant, remainder
• VERB = baffle, confuse, puzzle, bewilder, perplex, mystify, flummox, nonplus

stun 1 = overcome, shock, confuse, astonish, stagger, bewilder, astound, overpower 2 = daze, knock out, stupefy, numb, benumb

stunning (*Informal*) = wonderful, beautiful, impressive, striking, lovely, spectacular, marvellous, splendid ≠ unimpressive

stunt = feat, act, trick, exploit, deed

stunted = undersized, little, small, tiny, diminutive

stupid 1 = unintelligent, thick, simple, slow, dim, dense, simple-minded, moronic ≠ intelligent 2 = silly, foolish, daft (*informal*), rash, pointless, senseless, idiotic, fatuous ≠ sensible 3 = senseless, dazed, groggy, insensate, semiconscious

sturdy 1 = robust, hardy, powerful, athletic, muscular, lusty, brawny ≠ puny 2 = substantial, solid, durable, well-made, well-built ≠ flimsy

style NOUN **1** = manner, way, method, approach, technique, mode **2** = elegance, taste, chic, flair, polish, sophistication, panache, élan **3** = design, form, cut **4** = type, sort, kind, variety, category, genre **5** = fashion, trend, mode, vogue, rage **6** = luxury, ease, comfort, elegance, grandeur, affluence
• VERB **1** = design, cut, tailor, fashion, shape, arrange, adapt **2** = call, name, term, label, entitle, dub, designate

stylish = smart, chic, fashionable, trendy (*Brit. informal*), modish, dressy (*informal*), voguish ≠ scruffy

subdue **1** = overcome, defeat, master, break, control, crush, conquer, tame **2** = moderate, suppress, soften, mellow, tone down, quieten down ≠ arouse

subdued **1** = quiet, serious, sad, chastened, dejected, downcast, crestfallen, down in the mouth ≠ lively **2** = hushed, soft, quiet, muted ≠ loud

subject NOUN **1** = topic, question, issue, matter, point, business, affair, object **2** = citizen, resident, native, inhabitant, national **3** = dependant, subordinate
• ADJECTIVE = subordinate, dependent, satellite, inferior, obedient
• VERB = put through, expose, submit, lay open
• PHRASES **subject to** **1** = liable to, open to, exposed to, vulnerable to, prone to, susceptible to **2** = bound by **3** = dependent on, contingent on, controlled by, conditional on

subjective = personal, prejudiced, biased, nonobjective ≠ objective

sublime = noble, glorious, high, great, grand, elevated, lofty, exalted ≠ lowly

submerge **1** = flood, swamp, engulf, overflow, inundate, deluge **2** = immerse, plunge, duck **3** = sink, plunge, go under water **4** = overwhelm, swamp, engulf, deluge

submission **1** = surrender, yielding, giving in, cave-in (*informal*), capitulation **2** = presentation, handing in, entry, tendering **3** = compliance, obedience, meekness, resignation, deference, passivity, docility

submit **1** = surrender, yield, give in, agree, endure, tolerate, comply, succumb **2** = present, hand in, tender, put forward, table, proffer

subordinate NOUN = inferior, junior, assistant, aide, second, attendant ≠ superior
• ADJECTIVE = inferior, lesser, lower, junior, subject, minor, secondary, dependent ≠ superior

subscribe **1** = support, advocate, endorse **2** = contribute, give, donate

subscription (*Chiefly Brit.*) = membership fee, dues, annual payment

subsequent = following, later, succeeding, after, successive, ensuing ≠ previous

subsequently = later, afterwards

subside **1** = decrease, diminish, lessen, ease, wane, ebb, abate, slacken ≠ increase **2** = collapse, sink, cave in, drop, lower, settle

subsidiary NOUN = branch, division, section, office, department, wing, subdivision, subsection
• ADJECTIVE = secondary, lesser, subordinate, minor, supplementary, auxiliary, ancillary ≠ main

subsidy = aid, help, support, grant, assistance, allowance

substance **1** = material, body, stuff, fabric **2** = importance, significance, concreteness **3** = meaning, main point, gist, import, significance, essence **4** = wealth, means, property, assets, resources, estate

substantial = big, significant, considerable, large, important, ample, sizable *or* sizeable ≠ small

substitute VERB = replace, exchange, swap, change, switch, interchange
• NOUN = replacement, reserve, surrogate, deputy, sub, proxy, locum
• ADJECTIVE = replacement, reserve, surrogate, second, alternative, fall-back, proxy

subtle **1** = faint, slight, implied, delicate, understated ≠ obvious **2** = crafty, cunning, sly, shrewd, ingenious, devious, wily, artful ≠ straightforward **3** = muted, soft, subdued, low-key, toned down **4** = fine, minute, narrow, tenuous, hair-splitting

subtlety **1** = fine point, refinement, sophistication, delicacy **2** = skill, ingenuity, cleverness, deviousness, craftiness, artfulness, slyness, wiliness

subversive ADJECTIVE = seditious, riotous, treasonous
• NOUN = dissident, terrorist, saboteur, fifth

columnist

succeed 1 = triumph, win, prevail 2 = work out, work, be successful 3 = make it (*informal*), do well, be successful, triumph, thrive, flourish, make good, prosper ≠ fail 4 = take over from, assume the office of 5 *with* ***to*** = take over, assume, attain, come into, inherit, accede to, come into possession of 6 = follow, come after, follow after ≠ precede

success 1 = victory, triumph ≠ failure 2 = prosperity, fortune, luck, fame 3 = hit (*informal*), winner, smash (*informal*), triumph, sensation ≠ flop (*informal*) 4 = big name, star, hit (*informal*), celebrity, sensation, megastar (*informal*) ≠ nobody

successful 1 = triumphant, victorious, lucky, fortunate 2 = thriving, profitable, rewarding, booming, flourishing, fruitful ≠ unprofitable 3 = top, prosperous, wealthy

successfully = well, favourably, with flying colours, victoriously

succession 1 = series, run, sequence, course, order, train, chain, cycle 2 = taking over, assumption, inheritance, accession

successive = consecutive, following, in succession

succumb 1 *often with* ***to*** = surrender, yield, submit, give in, cave in (*informal*), capitulate ≠ beat 2 *with* ***to*** (with an illness as object) = catch, fall ill with

suck 1 = drink, sip, draw 2 = take, draw, pull, extract

sudden = quick, rapid, unexpected, swift, hurried, abrupt, hasty ≠ gradual

suddenly = abruptly, all of a sudden, unexpectedly

sue (*Law*) = take (someone) to court, prosecute, charge, summon, indict

suffer 1 = be in pain, hurt, ache 2 = be affected, have trouble with, be afflicted, be troubled with 3 = undergo, experience, sustain, bear, go through, endure 4 = tolerate, stand, put up with (*informal*), bear, endure

suffering = pain, distress, agony, misery, ordeal, discomfort, torment, hardship

suffice = be enough, do, be sufficient, be adequate, serve, meet requirements

sufficient = adequate, enough, ample, satisfactory ≠ insufficient

suggest 1 = recommend, propose, advise, advocate, prescribe 2 = indicate 3 = hint at, imply, intimate 4 = bring to mind, evoke

suggestion 1 = recommendation, proposal, proposition, plan, motion 2 = hint, insinuation, intimation 3 = trace, touch, hint, breath, indication, whisper, intimation

suit NOUN 1 = outfit, costume, ensemble, dress, clothing, habit 2 = lawsuit, case, trial, proceeding, cause, action, prosecution • VERB 1 = be acceptable to, please, satisfy, do, gratify 2 = agree with, become, match, go with, harmonize with

suitable 1 = appropriate, right, fitting, fit, becoming, satisfactory, apt, befitting ≠ inappropriate 2 = seemly, fitting, becoming, proper, correct ≠ unseemly 3 = suited, appropriate, in keeping with ≠ out of keeping 4 = pertinent, relevant, applicable, fitting, appropriate, to the point, apt ≠ irrelevant 5 = convenient, timely, appropriate, well-timed, opportune ≠ inopportune

suite = rooms, apartment

sum 1 = amount, quantity, volume 2 = calculation, figures, arithmetic, mathematics, maths (*Brit. informal*), tally, math (*U.S. informal*), arithmetical problem 3 = total, aggregate 4 = totality, whole

summarize = sum up, condense, encapsulate, epitomize, abridge, précis

summary = synopsis, résumé, précis, review, outline, rundown, abridgment

summit 1 = peak, top, tip, pinnacle, apex, head ≠ base 2 = height, pinnacle, peak, zenith, acme ≠ depths

summon 1 = send for, call, bid, invite 2 *often with* ***up*** = gather, muster, draw on

sumptuous = luxurious, grand, superb, splendid, gorgeous, lavish, opulent ≠ plain

sunny 1 = bright, clear, fine, radiant, sunlit, summery, unclouded ≠ dull 2 = cheerful, happy, cheery, buoyant, joyful, light-hearted ≠ gloomy

sunset = nightfall, dusk, eventide, close of (the) day

superb 1 = splendid, excellent, magnificent, fine, grand, superior, marvellous, world-class, booshit (*Austral. slang*), exo (*Austral. slang*), sik (*Austral. slang*) ≠ inferior 2 = magnificent, superior, marvellous, exquisite, superlative ≠ terrible

superficial 1 = shallow, frivolous, empty-headed, silly, trivial ≠ serious **2** = hasty, cursory, perfunctory, hurried, casual, sketchy, desultory, slapdash ≠ thorough **3** = slight, surface, external, on the surface, exterior ≠ profound

superintendent = supervisor, director, manager, chief, governor, inspector, controller, overseer

superior ADJECTIVE **1** = better, higher, greater, grander, surpassing, unrivalled ≠ inferior **2** = first-class, excellent, first-rate, choice, exclusive, exceptional, de luxe, booshit (*Austral. slang*), exo (*Austral. slang*), sik (*Austral. slang*) ≠ average **3** = supercilious, patronizing, condescending, haughty, disdainful, lordly, lofty, pretentious

• NOUN = boss, senior, director, manager, chief (*informal*), principal, supervisor, baas (*S. African*) ≠ subordinate

superiority = supremacy, lead, advantage, excellence, ascendancy, predominance

supernatural = paranormal, unearthly, uncanny, ghostly, psychic, mystic, miraculous, occult

supervise **1** = observe, guide, monitor, oversee, keep an eye on **2** = oversee, run, manage, control, direct, handle, look after, superintend

supervision = superintendence, direction, control, charge, care, management, guidance

supervisor = boss (*informal*), manager, chief, inspector, administrator, foreman, overseer, baas (*S. African*)

supplement VERB = add to, reinforce, augment, extend

• NOUN **1** = pull-out, insert **2** = appendix, add-on, postscript **3** = addition, extra

supply VERB **1** = provide, give, furnish, produce, stock, grant, contribute, yield **2** = furnish, provide, equip, endow

• NOUN = store, fund, stock, source, reserve, quantity, hoard, cache

• PLURAL NOUN = provisions, necessities, stores, food, materials, equipment, rations

support VERB **1** = help, back, champion, second, aid, defend, assist, side with ≠ oppose **2** = provide for, maintain, look after, keep, fund, finance, sustain ≠ live off **3** = bear out, confirm, verify, substantiate, corroborate ≠ refute **4** = bear, carry, sustain, prop (up), reinforce, hold, brace, buttress

• NOUN **1** = furtherance, backing, promotion, assistance, encouragement **2** = help, loyalty ≠ opposition **3** = aid, help, benefits, relief, assistance **4** = prop, post, foundation, brace, pillar **5** = supporter, prop, mainstay, tower of strength, second, backer ≠ antagonist **6** = upkeep, maintenance, keep, subsistence, sustenance

supporter = follower, fan, advocate, friend, champion, sponsor, patron, helper ≠ opponent

supportive = helpful, encouraging, understanding, sympathetic

suppose **1** = imagine, consider, conjecture, postulate, hypothesize **2** = think, imagine, expect, assume, guess (*informal, chiefly U.S. & Canad.*), presume, conjecture

supposed **1** *usually with* ***to*** = meant, expected, required, obliged **2** = presumed, alleged, professed, accepted, assumed

supposedly = presumably, allegedly, ostensibly, theoretically, hypothetically ≠ actually

suppress **1** = stamp out, stop, check, crush, conquer, subdue, put an end to, overpower ≠ encourage **2** = check, inhibit, subdue, stop, quell **3** = restrain, stifle, contain, silence, conceal, curb, repress, smother

suppression **1** = elimination, crushing, check, quashing **2** = inhibition, blocking, restraint, smothering

supremacy = domination, sovereignty, sway, mastery, primacy, predominance, supreme power

supreme **1** = paramount ≠ least **2** = chief, leading, principal, highest, head, top, prime, foremost ≠ lowest **3** = ultimate, highest, greatest

supremo (*Brit. informal*) = head, leader, boss (*informal*), director, master, governor, commander, principal, baas (*S. African*)

sure **1** = certain, positive, decided, convinced, confident, assured, definite ≠ uncertain **2** = inevitable, guaranteed, bound, assured, inescapable ≠ unsure **3** = reliable, accurate, dependable, undoubted, undeniable, foolproof, infallible, unerring ≠ unreliable

surely **1** = it must be the case that **2** = undoubtedly, certainly, definitely, without doubt, unquestionably, indubitably, doubtlessly

surface NOUN **1** = covering, face, exterior, side, top, veneer **2** = façade
• VERB **1** = emerge, come up, come to the surface **2** = appear, emerge, arise, come to light, crop up (*informal*), transpire, materialize

surge NOUN **1** = rush, flood **2** = flow, wave, rush, roller, gush, outpouring **3** = tide, swell, billowing **4** = rush, wave, storm, torrent, eruption
• VERB **1** = rush, pour, rise, gush **2** = roll, rush, heave **3** = sweep, rush, storm

surpass = outdo, beat, exceed, eclipse, excel, transcend, outstrip, outshine

surpassing = supreme, extraordinary, outstanding, exceptional, unrivalled, incomparable, matchless

surplus NOUN = excess, surfeit ≠ shortage
• ADJECTIVE = extra, spare, excess, remaining, odd, superfluous ≠ insufficient

surprise NOUN **1** = shock, revelation, jolt, bombshell, eye-opener (*informal*) **2** = amazement, astonishment, wonder, incredulity
• VERB **1** = amaze, astonish, stun, startle, stagger, take aback **2** = catch unawares *or* off-guard, spring upon

surprised = amazed, astonished, speechless, thunderstruck

surprising = amazing, remarkable, incredible, astonishing, unusual, extraordinary, unexpected, staggering

surrender VERB **1** = give in, yield, submit, give way, succumb, cave in (*informal*), capitulate ≠ resist **2** = give up, abandon, relinquish, yield, concede, part with, renounce, waive
• NOUN = submission, cave-in (*informal*), capitulation, resignation, renunciation, relinquishment

surround = enclose, ring, encircle, encompass, envelop, hem in

surrounding ADJECTIVE = nearby, neighbouring
• PLURAL NOUN = environment, setting, background, location, milieu

surveillance = observation, watch, scrutiny, supervision, inspection

survey NOUN **1** = poll, study, research, review, inquiry, investigation **2** = examination, inspection, scrutiny **3** = valuation, estimate, assessment, appraisal
• VERB **1** = interview, question, poll, research, investigate **2** = look over, view, examine, observe, contemplate, inspect, eyeball (*slang*), scrutinize **3** = measure, estimate, assess, appraise

survive 1 = remain alive, last, live on, endure **2** = continue, last, live on **3** = live longer than, outlive, outlast

susceptible 1 = responsive, sensitive, receptive, impressionable, suggestible ≠ unresponsive **2** *usually with* ***to*** = liable, inclined, prone, given, subject, vulnerable, disposed ≠ resistant

suspect VERB **1** = believe, feel, guess, consider, suppose, speculate ≠ know **2** = distrust, doubt, mistrust ≠ trust
• ADJECTIVE = dubious, doubtful, questionable, iffy (*informal*) ≠ innocent

suspend 1 = postpone, put off, cease, interrupt, shelve, defer, cut short, discontinue ≠ continue **2** = hang, attach, dangle

suspension = postponement, break, breaking off, interruption, abeyance, deferment, discontinuation

suspicion 1 = distrust, scepticism, mistrust, doubt, misgiving, qualm, wariness, dubiety **2** = idea, notion, hunch, guess, impression **3** = trace, touch, hint, suggestion, shade, streak, tinge, soupçon (*French*)

suspicious 1 = distrustful, sceptical, doubtful, unbelieving, wary ≠ trusting **2** = suspect, dubious, questionable, doubtful, dodgy (*Brit., Austral., & N.Z. informal*), fishy (*informal*) ≠ beyond suspicion

sustain 1 = maintain, continue, keep up, prolong, protract **2** = suffer, experience, undergo, feel, bear, endure, withstand **3** = help, aid, assist **4** = keep alive, nourish, provide for **5** = support, bear, uphold

sustained = continuous, constant, steady, prolonged, perpetual, unremitting, nonstop ≠ periodic

swallow 1 = eat, consume, devour, swig (*informal*) **2** = gulp, drink

swamp NOUN = bog, marsh, quagmire, slough, fen, mire, morass, pakihi (*N.Z.*)
• VERB **1** = flood, engulf, submerge, inundate **2** = overload, overwhelm, inundate

swap *or* **swop** = exchange, trade, switch,

interchange, barter
swarm NOUN = multitude, crowd, mass, army, host, flock, herd, horde
• VERB 1 = crowd, flock, throng, mass, stream 2 = teem, crawl, abound, bristle
swathe NOUN = area, section, tract
• VERB = wrap, drape, envelop, cloak, shroud, bundle up
sway VERB 1 = move from side to side, rock, roll, swing, bend, lean 2 = influence, affect, guide, persuade, induce
• NOUN = power, control, influence, authority, clout (*informal*)
swear 1 = curse, blaspheme, be foul-mouthed 2 = vow, promise, testify, attest 3 = declare, assert, affirm
swearing = bad language, cursing, profanity, blasphemy, foul language
sweat NOUN 1 = perspiration 2 (*Informal*) = panic, anxiety, worry, distress, agitation
• VERB 1 = perspire, glow 2 (*Informal*) = worry, fret, agonize, torture yourself
sweep VERB 1 = brush, clean 2 = clear, remove, brush, clean 3 = sail, pass, fly, tear, zoom, glide, skim
• NOUN 1 = movement, move, swing, stroke 2 = extent, range, stretch, scope
sweeping 1 = indiscriminate, blanket, wholesale, exaggerated, overstated, unqualified 2 = wide-ranging, global, comprehensive, wide, broad, extensive, all-inclusive, all-embracing ≠ limited
sweet ADJECTIVE 1 = sugary, cloying, saccharine, icky (*informal*) ≠ sour 2 = fragrant, aromatic ≠ stinking 3 = fresh, clean, pure 4 = melodious, musical, harmonious, mellow, dulcet ≠ harsh 5 = charming, kind, agreeable ≠ nasty 6 = delightful, appealing, cute, winning, engaging, lovable, likable *or* likeable ≠ unpleasant
• NOUN 1 *usually plural* = confectionery, candy (*U.S.*), lolly (*Austral. & N.Z.*), bonbon 2 (*Brit.*) = dessert, pudding
sweetheart 1 = dearest, beloved, sweet, angel, treasure, honey, dear, sweetie (*informal*) 2 = love, boyfriend *or* girlfriend, beloved, lover, darling
swell VERB 1 = increase, rise, grow, mount, expand, accelerate, escalate, multiply ≠ decrease 2 = expand, increase, grow, rise, balloon, enlarge, bulge, dilate ≠ shrink
• NOUN = wave, surge, billow
swelling = enlargement, lump, bump, bulge, inflammation, protuberance, distension
swift 1 = quick, prompt, rapid 2 = fast, quick, rapid, hurried, speedy ≠ slow
swiftly 1 = quickly, rapidly, speedily 2 = fast, promptly, hurriedly
swing VERB 1 = brandish, wave, shake, flourish, wield, dangle 2 = sway, rock, wave, veer, oscillate 3 *usually with* ***round*** = turn, swivel, curve, rotate, pivot 4 = hit out, strike, swipe, lash out at, slap 5 = hang, dangle, suspend
• NOUN 1 = swaying, sway 2 = fluctuation, change, shift, switch, variation
swirl = whirl, churn, spin, twist, eddy
switch NOUN 1 = control, button, lever, on/off device 2 = change, shift, reversal
• VERB 1 = change, shift, divert, deviate 2 = exchange, swap, substitute
swollen = enlarged, bloated, inflamed, puffed up, distended
swoop 1 = pounce, attack, charge, rush, descend 2 = drop, plunge, dive, sweep, descend, pounce, stoop
symbol 1 = metaphor, image, sign, representation, token 2 = representation, sign, figure, mark, image, token, logo, badge
symbolic 1 = representative, emblematic, allegorical 2 = representative, figurative
sympathetic 1 = caring, kind, understanding, concerned, interested, warm, pitying, supportive ≠ uncaring 2 = like-minded, compatible, agreeable, friendly, congenial, companionable ≠ uncongenial
sympathy 1 = compassion, understanding, pity, commiseration, aroha (*N.Z.*) ≠ indifference 2 = affinity, agreement, rapport, fellow feeling ≠ opposition
symptom 1 = sign, mark, indication, warning 2 = manifestation, sign, indication, mark, evidence, expression, proof, token
synthetic = artificial, fake, man-made ≠ real
system 1 = arrangement, structure, organization, scheme, classification 2 = method, practice, technique, procedure, routine
systematic = methodical, organized, efficient, orderly ≠ unmethodical

t

table NOUN **1** = counter, bench, stand, board, surface, work surface **2** = list, chart, tabulation, record, roll, register, diagram, itemization
• VERB (*Brit.*) = submit, propose, put forward, move, suggest, enter, file, lodge

taboo NOUN = prohibition, ban, restriction, anathema, interdict, proscription, tapu (*N.Z.*)
• ADJECTIVE = forbidden, banned, prohibited, unacceptable, outlawed, anathema, proscribed, unmentionable ≠ permitted

tack NOUN = nail, pin, drawing pin
• VERB **1** = fasten, fix, attach, pin, nail, affix **2** (*Brit.*) = stitch, sew, hem, bind, baste
• PHRASES **tack something on to something** = append, add, attach, tag

tackle VERB **1** = deal with, set about, get stuck into (*informal*), come *or* get to grips with **2** = undertake, attempt, embark upon, get stuck into (*informal*), have a go *or* stab at (*informal*) **3** = intercept, stop, challenge
• NOUN **1** = block, challenge **2** = rig, apparatus

tactic NOUN = policy, approach, move, scheme, plans, method, manoeuvre, ploy
• PLURAL NOUN = strategy, campaigning, manoeuvres, generalship

tactical = strategic, shrewd, smart, diplomatic, cunning ≠ impolitic

tag NOUN = label, tab, note, ticket, slip, identification, marker, flap
• VERB = label, mark

tail NOUN **1** = extremity, appendage, brush, rear end, hindquarters, hind part **2** = train, end, trail, tailpiece
• VERB (*Informal*) = follow, track, shadow, trail, stalk
• PHRASES **turn tail** = run away, flee, run off, retreat, cut and run, take to your heels

tailor NOUN = outfitter, couturier, dressmaker, seamstress, clothier, costumier
• VERB = adapt, adjust, modify, style, fashion, shape, alter, mould

taint = spoil, ruin, contaminate, damage, stain, corrupt, pollute, tarnish ≠ purify

take VERB **1** = grip, grab, seize, catch, grasp, clasp, take hold of **2** = carry, bring, bear, transport, ferry, haul, convey, fetch ≠ send **3** = accompany, lead, bring, guide, conduct, escort, convoy, usher **4** = remove, draw, pull, fish, withdraw, extract **5** = steal, appropriate, pocket, pinch (*informal*), misappropriate, purloin ≠ return **6** = capture, seize, take into custody, lay hold of ≠ release **7** = tolerate, stand, bear, stomach, endure, abide, put up with (*informal*), withstand ≠ avoid **8** = require, need, involve, demand, call for, entail, necessitate **9** = understand, follow, comprehend, get, see, grasp, apprehend **10** = regard as, believe to be, consider to be, perceive to be, presume to be **11** = have room for, hold, contain, accommodate, accept
• PHRASES **take off 1** = lift off, take to the air **2** (*Informal*) = depart, go, leave, disappear, abscond, decamp, slope off
◆ **take someone in** = deceive, fool, con (*informal*), trick, cheat, mislead, dupe, swindle ◆ **take someone off** (*Informal*) = parody, imitate, mimic, mock, caricature, send up (*Brit. informal*), lampoon, satirize
◆ **take something in** = understand, absorb, grasp, digest, comprehend, assimilate, get the hang of (*informal*)
◆ **take something up 1** = start, begin, engage in, adopt, become involved in **2** = occupy, absorb, consume, use up, cover, fill, waste, squander

takeover = merger, coup, incorporation

tale = story, narrative, anecdote, account, legend, saga, yarn (*informal*), fable

talent = ability, gift, aptitude, capacity, genius, flair, knack

talented = gifted, able, expert, master, masterly, brilliant, ace (*informal*), consummate

talk VERB **1** = speak, chat, chatter, converse, communicate, natter **2** = discuss, confer, negotiate, parley, confabulate, korero (*N.Z.*) **3** = inform, grass (*Brit. slang*), tell all, give the game away, blab, let the cat out of the bag
• NOUN = speech, lecture, presentation, report, address, discourse, sermon,

symposium, whaikorero (*N.Z.*)
talking-to (*Informal*) = reprimand, lecture, rebuke, scolding, criticism, reproach, ticking-off (*informal*), dressing-down (*informal*) ≠ praise
tall **1** = lofty, big, giant, long-legged, lanky, leggy **2** = high, towering, soaring, steep, elevated, lofty ≠ short **3** (*Informal*) = implausible, incredible, far-fetched, exaggerated, absurd, unbelievable, preposterous, cock-and-bull (*informal*) ≠ plausible **4** = difficult, hard, demanding, unreasonable, well-nigh impossible
tally NOUN = record, score, total, count, reckoning, running total
• VERB = agree, match, accord, fit, square, coincide, correspond, conform ≠ disagree
tame ADJECTIVE **1** = domesticated, docile, broken, gentle, obedient, amenable, tractable ≠ wild **2** = submissive, meek, compliant, subdued, manageable, obedient, docile, unresisting ≠ stubborn **3** = unexciting, boring, dull, bland, uninspiring, humdrum, uninteresting, insipid ≠ exciting
• VERB **1** = domesticate, train, break in, house-train ≠ make fiercer **2** = subdue, suppress, master, discipline, humble, conquer, subjugate ≠ arouse
tangible = definite, real, positive, material, actual, concrete, palpable, perceptible ≠ intangible
tangle NOUN **1** = knot, twist, web, jungle, coil, entanglement **2** = mess, jam, fix (*informal*), confusion, complication, mix-up, shambles, entanglement
• VERB = twist, knot, mat, coil, mesh, entangle, interweave, ravel ≠ disentangle
• PHRASES **tangle with someone** = come into conflict with, come up against, cross swords with, dispute with, contend with, contest with, lock horns with
tantrum = outburst, temper, hysterics, fit, flare-up, foulie (*Austral. slang*)
tap[1] VERB = knock, strike, pat, rap, beat, touch, drum
• NOUN = knock, pat, rap, touch, drumming
tap[2] NOUN = valve, stopcock
• VERB = listen in on, monitor, bug (*informal*), spy on, eavesdrop on, wiretap
• PHRASES **on tap** **1** (*Informal*) = available, ready, standing by, to hand, on hand, at hand, in reserve **2** = on draught, cask-conditioned, from barrels, not bottled *or* canned
tape NOUN = binding, strip, band, string, ribbon
• VERB **1** = record, video, tape-record, make a recording of **2** *sometimes with* ***up*** = bind, secure, stick, seal, wrap
target **1** = mark, goal **2** = goal, aim, objective, end, mark, object, intention, ambition **3** = victim, butt, prey, scapegoat
tariff **1** = tax, duty, toll, levy, excise **2** = price list, schedule
tarnish VERB **1** = damage, taint, blacken, sully, smirch ≠ enhance **2** = stain, discolour, darken, blot, blemish ≠ brighten
• NOUN = stain, taint, discoloration, spot, blot, blemish
tart[1] = pie, pastry, pasty, tartlet, patty
tart[2] = sharp, acid, sour, bitter, pungent, tangy, piquant, vinegary ≠ sweet
tart[3] (*Informal*) = slut, prostitute, whore, call girl, trollop, floozy (*slang*)
task NOUN = job, duty, assignment, exercise, mission, enterprise, undertaking, chore
• PHRASES **take someone to task** = criticize, blame, censure, rebuke, reprimand, reproach, scold, tell off (*informal*)
taste NOUN **1** = flavour, savour, relish, smack, tang ≠ blandness **2** = bit, bite, mouthful, sample, dash, spoonful, morsel, titbit **3** = liking, preference, penchant, fondness, partiality, fancy, appetite, inclination ≠ dislike **4** = refinement, style, judgment, discrimination, appreciation, elegance, sophistication, discernment ≠ lack of judgment
• VERB **1** = have a flavour of, smack of, savour of **2** = sample, try, test, sip, savour **3** = distinguish, perceive, discern, differentiate **4** = experience, know, undergo, partake of, encounter, meet with ≠ miss
tasty = delicious, luscious, palatable, delectable, savoury, full-flavoured, scrumptious (*informal*), appetizing, lekker (*S. African slang*), yummo (*Austral. slang*) ≠ bland
taunt VERB = jeer, mock, tease, ridicule, provoke, insult, torment, deride
• NOUN = jeer, dig, insult, ridicule, teasing, provocation, derision, sarcasm
tavern = inn, bar, pub (*informal*, *chiefly*

Brit.), public house, hostelry, alehouse (*archaic*)
tax NOUN = charge, duty, toll, levy, tariff, excise, tithe
• VERB **1** = charge, rate, assess **2** = strain, stretch, try, test, load, burden, exhaust, weaken
teach VERB = instruct, train, coach, inform, educate, drill, tutor, enlighten
• VERB = show, train
teacher = instructor, coach, tutor, guide, trainer, lecturer, mentor, educator
team NOUN **1** = side, squad **2** = group, company, set, body, band, gang, line-up, bunch
• PHRASES **team up** = join, unite, work together, cooperate, couple, link up, get together, band together
tear VERB **1** = rip, split, rend, shred, rupture **2** = run **3** = scratch, cut (open), gash, lacerate, injure, mangle, cut to pieces, cut to ribbons, mangulate (*Austral. slang*) **4** = pull apart, claw, lacerate, mutilate, mangle, mangulate (*Austral. slang*) **5** = rush, run, charge, race, fly, speed, dash, hurry
• NOUN = hole, split, rip, rent, snag, rupture
tears PLURAL NOUN = crying, weeping, sobbing, wailing, blubbering
• PHRASES **in tears** = weeping, crying, sobbing, blubbering
tease 1 = mock, provoke, torment, taunt, goad, pull someone's leg (*informal*), make fun of **2** = tantalize, lead on, flirt with, titillate
technical = scientific, technological, skilled, specialist, specialized, hi-tech *or* high-tech
technique 1 = method, way, system, approach, means, style, manner, procedure **2** = skill, performance, craft, touch, execution, artistry, craftsmanship, proficiency
tedious = boring, dull, dreary, monotonous, drab, tiresome, laborious, humdrum ≠ exciting
teenager = youth, minor, adolescent, juvenile, girl, boy
telephone NOUN = phone, mobile (phone), handset, dog and bone (*slang*)
• VERB = call, phone, ring (*chiefly Brit.*), dial
telescope NOUN = glass, scope (*informal*), spyglass
• VERB = shorten, contract, compress, shrink, condense, abbreviate, abridge ≠ lengthen
television = TV, telly (*Brit. informal*), small screen (*informal*), the box (*Brit. informal*), the tube (*slang*)
tell VERB **1** = inform, notify, state to, reveal to, express to, disclose to, proclaim to, divulge **2** = describe, relate, recount, report, portray, depict, chronicle, narrate **3** = instruct, order, command, direct, bid **4** = distinguish, discriminate, discern, differentiate, identify **5** = have *or* take effect, register, weigh, count, take its toll, carry weight, make its presence felt
• PHRASES **tell someone off** = reprimand, rebuke, scold, lecture, censure, reproach, berate, chide
telling = effective, significant, considerable, marked, striking, powerful, impressive, influential ≠ unimportant
temper NOUN **1** = irritability, irascibility, passion, resentment, petulance, surliness, hot-headedness ≠ good humour **2** = frame of mind, nature, mind, mood, constitution, humour, temperament, disposition **3** = rage, fury, bad mood, passion, tantrum, foulie (*Austral. slang*) **4** = self-control, composure, cool (*slang*), calmness, equanimity ≠ anger
• VERB **1** = moderate, restrain, tone down, soften, soothe, lessen, mitigate, assuage ≠ intensify **2** = strengthen, harden, toughen, anneal ≠ soften
temperament 1 = nature, character, personality, make-up, constitution, bent, humour, temper **2** = moods, anger, volatility, petulance, excitability, moodiness, hot-headedness
temple = shrine, church, sanctuary, house of God
temporarily = briefly, for the time being, momentarily, fleetingly, pro tem
temporary 1 = impermanent, transitory, brief, fleeting, interim, short-lived, momentary, ephemeral ≠ permanent **2** = short-term, acting, interim, supply, stand-in, fill-in, caretaker, provisional
tempt 1 = attract, allure **2** = entice, lure, lead on, invite, seduce, coax ≠ discourage
temptation 1 = enticement, lure, inducement, pull, seduction, allurement, tantalization **2** = appeal, attraction
tempting = inviting, enticing, seductive, alluring, attractive, mouthwatering,

appetizing ≠ uninviting

tenant = leaseholder, resident, renter, occupant, inhabitant, occupier, lodger, boarder

tend[1] = be inclined, be liable, have a tendency, be apt, be prone, lean, incline, gravitate

tend[2] **1** = take care of, look after, keep, attend, nurture, watch over ≠ neglect **2** = maintain, take care of, nurture, cultivate, manage ≠ neglect

tendency = inclination, leaning, liability, disposition, propensity, susceptibility, proclivity, proneness

tender[1] **1** = gentle, loving, kind, caring, sympathetic, affectionate, compassionate, considerate ≠ harsh **2** = vulnerable, young, sensitive, raw, youthful, inexperienced, immature, impressionable ≠ experienced **3** = sensitive, painful, sore, raw, bruised, inflamed

tender[2] **NOUN** = offer, bid, estimate, proposal, submission
• **VERB** = offer, present, submit, give, propose, volunteer, hand in, put forward

tense **ADJECTIVE** **1** = strained, uneasy, stressful, fraught, charged, difficult, worrying, exciting **2** = nervous, edgy, strained, anxious, apprehensive, uptight (*informal*), on edge, jumpy ≠ calm **3** = rigid, strained, taut, stretched, tight ≠ relaxed
• **VERB** = tighten, strain, brace, stretch, flex, stiffen ≠ relax

tension **1** = strain, stress, nervousness, pressure, anxiety, unease, apprehension, suspense ≠ calmness **2** = friction, hostility, unease, antagonism, antipathy, enmity **3** = rigidity, tightness, stiffness, pressure, stress, stretching, tautness

tentative **1** = unconfirmed, provisional, indefinite, test, trial, pilot, preliminary, experimental ≠ confirmed **2** = hesitant, cautious, uncertain, doubtful, faltering, unsure, timid, undecided ≠ confident

term **NOUN** **1** = word, name, expression, title, label, phrase **2** = period, time, spell, while, season, interval, span, duration
• **PLURAL NOUN** **1** = conditions, particulars, provisions, provisos, stipulations, qualifications, specifications **2** = relationship, standing, footing, relations, status
• **VERB** = call, name, label, style, entitle, tag, dub, designate

terminal **ADJECTIVE** **1** = fatal, deadly, lethal, killing, mortal, incurable, inoperable, untreatable **2** = final, last, closing, finishing, concluding, ultimate, terminating ≠ initial
• **NOUN** = terminus, station, depot, end of the line

terminate **1** = end, stop, conclude, finish, complete, discontinue ≠ begin **2** = cease, end, close, finish **3** = abort, end

terrain = ground, country, land, landscape, topography, going

terrestrial = earthly, worldly, global

terrible **1** = awful, shocking, terrifying, horrible, dreadful, horrifying, fearful, horrendous **2** (*Informal*) = bad, awful, dreadful, dire, abysmal, poor, rotten (*informal*) ≠ wonderful **3** = serious, desperate, severe, extreme, dangerous, insufferable ≠ mild

terribly **1** = very much, very, dreadfully, seriously, extremely, desperately, thoroughly, decidedly **2** = extremely, very, dreadfully, seriously, desperately, thoroughly, decidedly, awfully (*informal*)

terrific **1** (*Informal*) = excellent, wonderful, brilliant, amazing, outstanding, superb, fantastic (*informal*), magnificent, booshit (*Austral. slang*), exo (*Austral. slang*), sik (*Austral. slang*), ka pai (*N.Z.*) ≠ awful **2** = intense, great, huge, enormous, tremendous, fearful, gigantic

terrified = frightened, scared, petrified, alarmed, panic-stricken, horror-struck

terrify = frighten, scare, alarm, terrorize

territory = district, area, land, region, country, zone, province, patch

terror **1** = fear, alarm, dread, fright, panic, anxiety **2** = nightmare, monster, bogeyman, devil, fiend, bugbear

test **VERB** **1** = check, investigate, assess, research, analyse, experiment with, try out, put something to the test **2** = examine, put someone to the test
• **NOUN** **1** = trial, research, check, investigation, analysis, assessment, examination, evaluation **2** = examination, paper, assessment, evaluation

testament **1** = proof, evidence, testimony, witness, demonstration, tribute **2** = will, last wishes

testify = bear witness, state, swear, certify, assert, affirm, attest, corroborate

≠ disprove
testimony 1 = evidence, statement, submission, affidavit, deposition 2 = proof, evidence, demonstration, indication, support, manifestation, verification, corroboration
testing = difficult, demanding, taxing, challenging, searching, tough, exacting, rigorous ≠ undemanding
text 1 = contents, words, content, wording, body, subject matter 2 = words, wording 3 = transcript, script
texture = feel, consistency, structure, surface, tissue, grain
thank = say thank you to, show your appreciation to
thanks PLURAL NOUN = gratitude, appreciation, credit, recognition, acknowledgment, gratefulness
• PHRASES **thanks to** = because of, through, due to, as a result of, owing to
thaw = melt, dissolve, soften, defrost, warm, liquefy, unfreeze ≠ freeze
theatrical 1 = dramatic, stage, Thespian 2 = exaggerated, dramatic, melodramatic, histrionic, affected, mannered, showy, ostentatious ≠ natural
theft = stealing, robbery, thieving, fraud, embezzlement, pilfering, larceny, purloining
theme 1 = motif, leitmotif 2 = subject, idea, topic, essence, subject matter, keynote, gist
theological = religious, ecclesiastical, doctrinal
theoretical 1 = abstract, speculative ≠ practical 2 = hypothetical, academic, notional, unproven, conjectural, postulatory
theory = belief, feeling, speculation, assumption, hunch, presumption, conjecture, surmise
therapeutic = beneficial, healing, restorative, good, corrective, remedial, salutary, curative ≠ harmful
therapist = psychologist, analyst, psychiatrist, shrink (*informal*), counsellor, healer, psychotherapist, psychoanalyst
therapy = remedy, treatment, cure, healing, method of healing
therefore = consequently, so, thus, as a result, hence, accordingly, thence, ergo
thesis 1 = proposition, theory, hypothesis, idea, view, opinion, proposal, contention 2 = dissertation, paper, treatise, essay, monograph
thick 1 = bulky, broad, big, large, fat, solid, substantial, hefty ≠ thin 2 = wide, across, deep, broad, in extent *or* diameter 3 = dense, close, heavy, compact, impenetrable, lush 4 = heavy, heavyweight, dense, chunky, bulky, woolly 5 = opaque, heavy, dense, impenetrable 6 = viscous, concentrated, stiff, condensed, gelatinous, semi-solid, viscid ≠ runny 7 = crowded, full, covered, bursting, bristling, brimming ≠ empty 8 (*Informal*) = stupid, slow, dense, dopey (*informal*), moronic, obtuse, brainless, dumb-ass (*informal*) ≠ clever 9 (*Informal*) = friendly, close, intimate, familiar, pally (*informal*), devoted, inseparable ≠ unfriendly
thicken = set, condense, congeal, clot, jell, coagulate ≠ thin
thief = robber, burglar, stealer, plunderer, shoplifter, embezzler, pickpocket, pilferer
thin 1 = narrow, fine, attenuated ≠ thick 2 = slim, spare, lean, slight, slender, skinny, skeletal, bony ≠ fat 3 = meagre, sparse, scanty, poor, scattered, inadequate, insufficient, deficient ≠ plentiful 4 = fine, delicate, flimsy, sheer, skimpy, gossamer, diaphanous, filmy ≠ thick 5 = unconvincing, inadequate, feeble, poor, weak, superficial, lame, flimsy ≠ convincing 6 = wispy, thinning, sparse, scarce, scanty
thing NOUN 1 = substance, stuff, being, body, material, fabric, entity 2 (*Informal*) = phobia, fear, complex, horror, terror, hang-up (*informal*), aversion, neurosis 3 (*Informal*) = obsession, liking, preoccupation, mania, fetish, fixation, soft spot, predilection
• PLURAL NOUN 1 = possessions, stuff, gear, belongings, effects, luggage, clobber (*Brit. slang*), chattels 2 = equipment, gear, tools, stuff, tackle, implements, kit, apparatus 3 = circumstances, the situation, the state of affairs, matters, life, affairs
think VERB 1 = believe, be of the opinion, be of the view 2 = judge, consider, estimate, reckon, deem, regard as 3 = ponder, reflect, contemplate, deliberate, meditate, ruminate, cogitate, be lost in thought
• PHRASES **think something up** = devise, create, come up with, invent, contrive,

visualize, concoct, dream something up
thinker = philosopher, intellect (*informal*), wise man, sage, brain (*informal*), theorist, mastermind
thinking NOUN = reasoning, idea, view, position, theory, opinion, judgment, conjecture
• ADJECTIVE = thoughtful, intelligent, reasoning, rational, philosophical, reflective, contemplative, meditative
thirst **1** = dryness, thirstiness, drought **2** = craving, appetite, longing, desire, passion, yearning, hankering, keenness ≠ aversion
thorn = prickle, spike, spine, barb
thorough **1** = comprehensive, full, complete, sweeping, intensive, in-depth, exhaustive ≠ cursory **2** = careful, conscientious, painstaking, efficient, meticulous, exhaustive, assiduous ≠ careless **3** = complete, total, absolute, utter, perfect, outright, unqualified, out-and-out ≠ partial
thoroughly **1** = carefully, fully, efficiently, meticulously, painstakingly, scrupulously, assiduously, intensively ≠ carelessly **2** = fully **3** = completely, quite, totally, perfectly, absolutely, utterly, downright, to the hilt ≠ partly
though CONJUNCTION = although, while, even if, even though, notwithstanding
• ADVERB = nevertheless, still, however, yet, nonetheless, for all that, notwithstanding
thought **1** = thinking, consideration, reflection, deliberation, musing, meditation, rumination, cogitation **2** = opinion, view, idea, concept, notion, judgment **3** = consideration, study, attention, care, regard, scrutiny, heed **4** = intention, plan, idea, design, aim, purpose, object, notion **5** = hope, expectation, prospect, aspiration, anticipation
thoughtful **1** = reflective, pensive, contemplative, meditative, serious, studious, deliberative, ruminative ≠ shallow **2** = considerate, kind, caring, kindly, helpful, attentive, unselfish, solicitous ≠ inconsiderate
thrash VERB **1** = defeat, beat, crush, slaughter (*informal*), rout, trounce, run rings around (*informal*), wipe the floor with (*informal*) **2** = beat, wallop, whip, belt (*informal*), cane, flog, scourge, spank **3** = thresh, flail, jerk, writhe, toss and turn
• PHRASES **thrash something out** = settle, resolve, discuss, debate, solve, argue out, have something out, talk something over
thrashing **1** = defeat, beating, hammering (*informal*), hiding (*informal*), rout, trouncing, drubbing **2** = beating, hiding (*informal*), belting (*informal*), whipping, flogging
thread NOUN **1** = strand, fibre, yarn, filament, line, string, twine **2** = theme, train of thought, direction, plot, drift, story line
• VERB = move, pass, ease, thrust, squeeze through, pick your way
threat **1** = danger, risk, hazard, menace, peril **2** = threatening remark, menace **3** = warning, foreshadowing, foreboding
threaten **1** = intimidate, bully, menace, terrorize, lean on (*slang*), pressurize, browbeat ≠ defend **2** = endanger, jeopardize, put at risk, imperil, put in jeopardy, put on the line ≠ protect **3** = be imminent, impend
threshold **1** = entrance, doorway, door, doorstep **2** = start, beginning, opening, dawn, verge, brink, outset, inception ≠ end **3** = limit, margin, starting point, minimum
thrift = economy, prudence, frugality, saving, parsimony, carefulness, thriftiness ≠ extravagance
thrill NOUN = pleasure, kick (*informal*), buzz (*slang*), high, stimulation, tingle, titillation ≠ tedium
• VERB = excite, stimulate, arouse, move, stir, electrify, titillate, give someone a kick
thrilling = exciting, gripping, stimulating, stirring, sensational, rousing, riveting, electrifying ≠ boring
thrive = prosper, do well, flourish, increase, grow, develop, succeed, get on ≠ decline
thriving = successful, flourishing, healthy, booming, blooming, prosperous, burgeoning ≠ unsuccessful
throb VERB **1** = pulsate, pound, beat, pulse, thump, palpitate **2** = vibrate, pulsate, reverberate, shake, judder (*informal*)
• NOUN **1** = pulse, pounding, beat, thump, thumping, pulsating, palpitation **2** = vibration, throbbing, reverberation, judder (*informal*), pulsation

throng NOUN = crowd, mob, horde, host, pack, mass, crush, swarm
• VERB 1 = crowd, flock, congregate, converge, mill around, swarm around ≠ disperse 2 = pack, crowd

throttle = strangle, choke, garrotte, strangulate

through PREPOSITION 1 = via, by way of, by, between, past, from one side to the other of 2 = because of, by way of, by means of 3 = using, via, by way of, by means of, by virtue of, with the assistance of 4 = during, throughout, for the duration of, in
• ADJECTIVE = completed, done, finished, ended
• PHRASES **through and through** = completely, totally, fully, thoroughly, entirely, altogether, wholly, utterly

throughout PREPOSITION 1 = right through, everywhere in, during the whole of, through the whole of 2 = all over, everywhere in, through the whole of
• ADVERB 1 = from start to finish, right through 2 = all through, right through

throw VERB 1 = hurl, toss, fling, send, launch, cast, pitch, chuck (*informal*) 2 = toss, fling, chuck (*informal*), cast, hurl, sling 3 (*Informal*) = confuse, baffle, faze, astonish, confound, disconcert, dumbfound
• NOUN = toss, pitch, fling, sling, lob (*informal*), heave

thrust VERB = push, force, shove, drive, plunge, jam, ram, propel
• NOUN 1 = stab, pierce, lunge 2 = push, shove, poke, prod 3 = momentum, impetus, drive

thug = ruffian, hooligan, tough, heavy (*slang*), gangster, bully boy, bruiser (*informal*), tsotsi (*S. African*)

thump VERB = strike, hit, punch, pound, beat, knock, smack, clout (*informal*)
• NOUN 1 = blow, knock, punch, rap, smack, clout (*informal*), whack, swipe 2 = thud, crash, bang, clunk, thwack

thunder NOUN = rumble, crash, boom, explosion
• VERB 1 = rumble, crash, boom, roar, resound, reverberate, peal 2 = shout, roar, yell, bark, bellow

thus 1 = therefore, so, hence, consequently, accordingly, for this reason, ergo, on that account 2 = in this way, so, like this, as follows

thwart = frustrate, foil, prevent, snooker, hinder, obstruct, outwit, stymie ≠ assist

tick NOUN 1 = check mark, mark, line, stroke, dash 2 = click, tapping, clicking, ticktock 3 (*Brit. informal*) = moment, second, minute, flash, instant, twinkling, split second, trice
• VERB 1 = mark, indicate, check off 2 = click, tap, ticktock

ticket 1 = voucher, pass, coupon, card, slip, certificate, token, chit 2 = label, tag, marker, sticker, card, slip, tab, docket

tide 1 = current, flow, stream, ebb, undertow, tideway 2 = course, direction, trend, movement, tendency, drift

tidy ADJECTIVE 1 = neat, orderly, clean, spruce, well-kept, well-ordered, shipshape ≠ untidy 2 = organized, neat, methodical 3 (*Informal*) = considerable, large, substantial, goodly, healthy, generous, handsome, ample ≠ small
• VERB = neaten, straighten, order, clean, groom, spruce up ≠ disorder

tie VERB 1 = fasten, bind, join, link, connect, attach, knot ≠ unfasten 2 = tether, secure 3 = restrict, limit, confine, bind, restrain, hamper, hinder ≠ free 4 = draw, be level, match, equal
• NOUN 1 = fastening, binding, link, bond, knot, cord, fetter, ligature 2 = bond, relationship, connection, commitment, liaison, allegiance, affiliation 3 = draw, dead heat, deadlock, stalemate

tier = row, bank, layer, line, level, rank, storey, stratum

tight 1 = close-fitting, narrow, cramped, snug, constricted, close ≠ loose 2 = secure, firm, fast, fixed 3 = taut, stretched, rigid ≠ slack 4 = close, even, well-matched, hard-fought, evenly-balanced ≠ uneven 5 (*Informal*) = miserly, mean, stingy, grasping, parsimonious, niggardly, tightfisted ≠ generous 6 (*Informal*) = drunk, intoxicated, plastered (*slang*), under the influence (*informal*), tipsy, paralytic (*informal*), inebriated, out to it (*Austral. & N.Z. slang*) ≠ sober

tighten = close, narrow, strengthen, squeeze, harden, constrict ≠ slacken

till[1] = cultivate, dig, plough, work

till[2] = cash register, cash box

tilt VERB = slant, tip, slope, list, lean, heel, incline
• NOUN 1 = slope, angle, inclination, list,

pitch, incline, slant, camber **2** (*Medieval history*) = joust, fight, tournament, lists, combat, duel
timber 1 = beams, boards, planks **2** = wood, logs
time NOUN **1** = period, term, space, stretch, spell, span **2** = occasion, point, moment, stage, instance, point in time, juncture **3** = age, duration **4** = tempo, beat, rhythm, measure
• VERB = schedule, set, plan, book, programme, set up, fix, arrange
timeless = eternal, lasting, permanent, enduring, immortal, everlasting, ageless, changeless ≠ temporary
timely = opportune, appropriate, well-timed, suitable, convenient, judicious, propitious, seasonable ≠ untimely
timetable 1 = schedule, programme, agenda, list, diary, calendar **2** = syllabus, course, curriculum, programme, teaching programme
tinge NOUN **1** = tint, colour, shade **2** = trace, bit, drop, touch, suggestion, dash, sprinkling, smattering
• VERB = tint, colour
tinker = meddle, play, potter, fiddle (*informal*), dabble, mess about
tint NOUN **1** = shade, colour, tone, hue **2** = dye, wash, rinse, tinge, tincture
• VERB = dye, colour
tiny = small, little, minute, slight, miniature, negligible, microscopic, diminutive ≠ huge
tip¹ NOUN **1** = end, point, head, extremity, sharp end, nib, prong **2** = peak, top, summit, pinnacle, zenith, spire, acme, vertex
• VERB = cap, top, crown, surmount, finish
tip² VERB **1** = reward, remunerate, give a tip to, sweeten (*informal*) **2** = predict, back, recommend, think of
• NOUN **1** = gratuity, gift, reward, present, sweetener (*informal*) **2** = hint, suggestion, piece of advice, pointer
tip³ VERB **1** = pour, drop, empty, dump, drain, discharge, unload, jettison **2** (*Brit.*) = dump, empty, unload, pour out
• NOUN (*Brit.*) = dump, midden, rubbish heap, refuse heap
tire 1 = exhaust, drain, fatigue, weary, wear out ≠ refresh **2** = flag, become tired, fail **3** = bore, weary, exasperate, irritate, irk
tired 1 = exhausted, fatigued, weary, flagging, drained, sleepy, worn out, drowsy, tuckered out (*Austral. & N.Z. informal*) ≠ energetic **2** = bored, fed up, weary, sick, hoha (*N.Z.*) ≠ enthusiastic about **3** = hackneyed, stale, well-worn, old, corny (*slang*), threadbare, trite, clichéd ≠ original
tiring = exhausting, demanding, wearing, tough, exacting, strenuous, arduous, laborious
title 1 = name, designation, term, handle (*slang*), moniker *or* monicker (*slang*) **2** (*Sport*) = championship, trophy, bays, crown, honour **3** (*Law*) = ownership, right, claim, privilege, entitlement, tenure, prerogative, freehold
toast¹ 1 = brown, grill, crisp, roast **2** = warm (up), heat (up), thaw, bring back to life
toast² NOUN **1** = tribute, compliment, salute, health, pledge, salutation **2** = favourite, celebrity, darling, talk, pet, focus of attention, hero *or* heroine, blue-eyed boy *or* girl (*Brit. informal*)
• VERB = drink to, honour, salute, drink (to) the health of
together ADVERB **1** = collectively, jointly, as one, with each other, in conjunction, side by side, mutually, in partnership ≠ separately **2** = at the same time, simultaneously, concurrently, contemporaneously, at one fell swoop
• ADJECTIVE (*Informal*) = self-possessed, composed, well-balanced, well-adjusted
toil VERB **1** = labour, work, struggle, strive, sweat (*informal*), slave, graft (*informal*), slog **2** = struggle, trek, slog, trudge, fight your way, footslog
• NOUN = hard work, effort, application, sweat, graft (*informal*), slog, exertion, drudgery ≠ idleness
toilet 1 = lavatory, bathroom, loo (*Brit. informal*), privy, cloakroom (*Brit.*), urinal, latrine, washroom, dunny (*Austral. & N.Z. old-fashioned informal*), bogger (*Austral. slang*), brasco (*Austral. slang*) **2** = bathroom, gents *or* ladies (*Brit. informal*), privy, latrine, water closet, ladies' room, W.C.
token NOUN = symbol, mark, sign, note, expression, indication, representation, badge
• ADJECTIVE = nominal, symbolic, minimal, hollow, superficial, perfunctory

tolerance 1 = broad-mindedness, indulgence, forbearance, permissiveness, open-mindedness ≠ intolerance 2 = endurance, resistance, stamina, fortitude, resilience, toughness, staying power, hardiness 3 = resistance, immunity, resilience, non-susceptibility

tolerant = broad-minded, understanding, open-minded, catholic, long-suffering, permissive, forbearing, unprejudiced ≠ intolerant

tolerate 1 = endure, stand, take, stomach, put up with (*informal*) 2 = allow, accept, permit, take, brook, put up with (*informal*), condone ≠ forbid

toll[1] VERB = ring, sound, strike, chime, knell, clang, peal
• NOUN = ringing, chime, knell, clang, peal

toll[2] 1 = charge, tax, fee, duty, payment, levy, tariff 2 = damage, cost, loss, roll, penalty, sum, number, roster 3 = adverse effects, price, cost, suffering, damage, penalty, harm

tomb = grave, vault, crypt, mausoleum, sarcophagus, catacomb, sepulchre

tone NOUN 1 = pitch, inflection, intonation, timbre, modulation 2 = volume, timbre 3 = character, style, feel, air, spirit, attitude, manner, mood 4 = colour, shade, tint, tinge, hue
• VERB = harmonize, match, blend, suit, go well with
• PHRASES **tone something down** = moderate, temper, soften, restrain, subdue, play down = reduce, moderate

tongue = language, speech, dialect, parlance

tonic = stimulant, boost, pick-me-up (*informal*), fillip, shot in the arm (*informal*), restorative

too 1 = also, as well, further, in addition, moreover, besides, likewise, to boot 2 = excessively, very, extremely, overly, unduly, unreasonably, inordinately, immoderately

tool 1 = implement, device, appliance, machine, instrument, gadget, utensil, contraption 2 = puppet, creature, pawn, stooge (*slang*), minion, lackey, flunkey, hireling

top NOUN 1 = peak, summit, head, crown, height, ridge, brow, crest ≠ bottom 2 = lid, cover, cap, plug, stopper, bung 3 = first place, head, peak, lead, high point
• ADJECTIVE 1 = highest, loftiest, furthest up, uppermost 2 = leading, best, first, highest, head, finest, elite, foremost ≠ lowest 3 = chief, most important, principal, most powerful, highest, head, leading, main 4 = prime, best, select, first-class, quality, choice, excellent, premier
• VERB 1 = lead, head, be at the top of, be first in 2 = cover, garnish, finish, crown, cap 3 = surpass, better, beat, improve on, cap, exceed, eclipse, excel ≠ not be as good as

topic = subject, point, question, issue, matter, theme, subject matter

topical = current, popular, contemporary, up-to-date, up-to-the-minute, newsworthy

topple 1 = fall over, fall, collapse, tumble, overturn, totter, keel over, overbalance 2 = knock over 3 = overthrow, overturn, bring down, oust, unseat, bring low

torment NOUN = suffering, distress, misery, pain, hell, torture, agony, anguish ≠ bliss
• VERB 1 = torture, distress, rack, crucify ≠ comfort 2 = tease, annoy, bother, irritate, harass, hassle (*informal*), pester, vex

torn 1 = cut, split, rent, ripped, ragged, slit, lacerated 2 = undecided, uncertain, unsure, wavering, vacillating, in two minds (*informal*), irresolute

tornado = whirlwind, storm, hurricane, gale, cyclone, typhoon, tempest, squall

torture VERB 1 = torment, abuse, persecute, afflict, scourge, molest, crucify, mistreat ≠ comfort 2 = distress, torment, worry, trouble, rack, afflict, harrow, inflict anguish on
• NOUN 1 = ill-treatment, abuse, torment, persecution, maltreatment, harsh treatment 2 = agony, suffering, anguish, distress, torment, heartbreak ≠ bliss

toss VERB 1 = throw, pitch, hurl, fling, launch, cast, flip, sling 2 = shake 3 = thrash (about), twitch, wriggle, squirm, writhe
• NOUN = throw, pitch, lob (*informal*)

tot NOUN 1 = infant, child, baby, toddler, mite, littlie (*Austral. informal*), ankle-biter (*Austral. slang*), tacker (*Austral. slang*) 2 = measure, shot (*informal*), finger, nip, slug, dram, snifter (*informal*)
• PHRASES **tot something up** = add up, calculate, total, reckon, compute, tally, enumerate, count up

total NOUN = sum, entirety, grand total, whole, aggregate, totality, full amount,

sum total ≠ part
• ADJECTIVE = complete, absolute, utter, whole, entire, undivided, overarching, thoroughgoing ≠ partial
• VERB 1 = amount to, make, come to, reach, equal, run to, number, add up to 2 = add up, work out, compute, reckon, tot up ≠ subtract

totally = completely, entirely, absolutely, fully, comprehensively, thoroughly, wholly, utterly ≠ partly

touch VERB 1 = feel, handle, finger, stroke, brush, make contact with, caress, fondle 2 = come into contact, meet, contact, border, graze, adjoin, be in contact, abut 3 = tap 4 = affect, influence, inspire, impress 5 = consume, take, drink, eat, partake of 6 = move, stir, disturb 7 = match, rival, equal, compare with, parallel, hold a candle to (*informal*)
• NOUN 1 = contact, push, stroke, brush, press, tap, poke, nudge 2 = feeling, handling, physical contact 3 = bit, spot, trace, drop, dash, small amount, jot, smattering 4 = style, method, technique, way, manner, trademark
• PHRASES **touch and go** = risky, close, near, critical, precarious, nerve-racking
◆ **touch on** *or* **upon something** = refer to, cover, raise, deal with, mention, bring in, speak of, hint at

touching = moving, affecting, sad, stirring, pathetic, poignant, emotive, pitiable

tough ADJECTIVE 1 = strong ≠ weak 2 = hardy, strong, seasoned, strapping, vigorous, sturdy, stout 3 = violent, rough, ruthless, pugnacious, hard-bitten 4 = strict, severe, stern, hard, firm, resolute, merciless, unbending ≠ lenient 5 = hard, difficult, troublesome, uphill, strenuous, arduous, laborious 6 = resilient, hard, resistant, durable, strong, solid, rugged, sturdy ≠ fragile
• NOUN = ruffian, bully, thug, hooligan, bruiser (*informal*), roughneck (*slang*), tsotsi (*S. African*)

tour NOUN = journey, expedition, excursion, trip, outing, jaunt, junket
• VERB 1 = travel round, travel through, journey round, trek round, go on a trip through 2 = visit, explore, go round, inspect, walk round, drive round, sightsee

tourist = traveller, voyager, tripper, globetrotter, holiday-maker, sightseer, excursionist

tournament = competition, meeting, event, series, contest

tow = drag, draw, pull, haul, tug, yank, lug

towards 1 = in the direction of, to, for, on the way to, en route for 2 = regarding, about, concerning, respecting, in relation to, with regard to, with respect to, apropos

tower = column, pillar, turret, belfry, steeple, obelisk

toxic = poisonous, deadly, lethal, harmful, pernicious, noxious, septic, pestilential ≠ harmless

toy NOUN = plaything, game, doll
• PHRASES **toy with something** = play with, consider, trifle with, dally with, entertain the possibility of, amuse yourself with, think idly of

trace VERB 1 = search for, track, unearth, hunt down 2 = find, track (down), discover, detect, unearth, hunt down, ferret out, locate 3 = outline, sketch, draw 4 = copy, map, draft, outline, sketch, reproduce, draw over
• NOUN 1 = bit, drop, touch, shadow, suggestion, hint, suspicion, tinge 2 = remnant, sign, record, mark, evidence, indication, vestige 3 = track, trail, footstep, path, footprint, spoor, footmark

track NOUN 1 = path, way, road, route, trail, pathway, footpath 2 = course, line, path, orbit, trajectory 3 = line, tramline
• VERB = follow, pursue, chase, trace, tail (*informal*), shadow, trail, stalk
• PHRASES **track something** *or* **someone down** = find, discover, trace, unearth, dig up, hunt down, sniff out, run to earth *or* ground

tract[1] = area, region, district, stretch, territory, extent, plot, expanse

tract[2] = treatise, essay, booklet, pamphlet, dissertation, monograph, homily

trade NOUN 1 = commerce, business, transactions, dealing, exchange, traffic, truck, barter 2 = job, employment, business, craft, profession, occupation, line of work, métier
• VERB 1 = deal, do business, traffic, truck, bargain, peddle, transact, cut a deal 2 = exchange, switch, swap, barter 3 = operate, run, deal, do business

trader = dealer, supplier, merchant, seller, purveyor

tradition 1 = customs, institution, ritual,

folklore, lore, tikanga (*N.Z.*) **2** = established practice, custom, convention, habit, ritual
traditional **1** = old-fashioned, old, established, conventional, usual, accustomed, customary, time-honoured ≠ revolutionary **2** = folk, old
traffic **NOUN** **1** = transport, vehicles, transportation, freight **2** = trade, commerce, business, exchange, truck, dealings, peddling
• **VERB** = trade, deal, exchange, bargain, do business, peddle, cut a deal, have dealings
tragedy = disaster, catastrophe, misfortune, adversity, calamity ≠ fortune
tragic **1** = distressing, sad, appalling, deadly, unfortunate, disastrous, dreadful, dire ≠ fortunate **2** = sad, miserable, pathetic, mournful ≠ happy
trail **NOUN** **1** = path, track, route, way, course, road, pathway, footpath **2** = tracks, path, marks, wake, trace, scent, footprints, spoor **3** = wake, stream, tail
• **VERB** **1** = follow, track, chase, pursue, dog, hunt, shadow, trace **2** = drag, draw, pull, sweep, haul, tow, dangle, droop **3** = lag, follow, drift, wander, linger, trudge, plod, meander
train **VERB** **1** = instruct, school, prepare, coach, teach, guide, educate, drill **2** = exercise, prepare, work out, practise, do exercise, get into shape **3** = aim, point, level, position, direct, focus, sight, zero in
• **NOUN** = sequence, series, chain, string, set, cycle, trail, succession
trainer = coach, manager, guide, adviser, tutor, instructor, counsellor, guru
trait = characteristic, feature, quality, attribute, quirk, peculiarity, mannerism, idiosyncrasy
traitor = betrayer, deserter, turncoat, renegade, defector, Judas, quisling, apostate, fizgig (*Austral. slang*) ≠ loyalist
tramp **VERB** **1** = trudge, stump, toil, plod, traipse (*informal*) **2** = hike, walk, trek, roam, march, ramble, slog, rove
• **NOUN** **1** = vagrant, derelict, drifter, down-and-out, derro (*Austral. slang*) **2** = tread, stamp, footstep, footfall **3** = hike, march, trek, ramble, slog
trample *often with* ***on*** = stamp, crush, squash, tread, flatten, run over, walk over
trance = daze, dream, abstraction, rapture, reverie, stupor, unconsciousness
transaction = deal, negotiation, business, enterprise, bargain, undertaking
transcend = surpass, exceed, go beyond, rise above, eclipse, excel, outstrip, outdo
transcript = copy, record, manuscript, reproduction, duplicate, transcription
transfer **VERB** = move, transport, shift, relocate, transpose, change
• **NOUN** = transference, move, handover, change, shift, transmission, translation, relocation
transform **1** = change, convert, alter, transmute **2** = make over, remodel, revolutionize
transformation **1** = change, conversion, alteration, metamorphosis, transmutation **2** = revolution, sea change
transit = movement, transfer, transport, passage, crossing, transportation, carriage, conveyance
transition = change, passing, development, shift, conversion, alteration, progression, metamorphosis
transitional **1** = changing, passing, fluid, intermediate, unsettled, developmental **2** = temporary, working, acting, short-term, interim, fill-in, caretaker, provisional
translate = render, put, change, convert, interpret, decode, construe, paraphrase
translation = interpretation, version, rendering, rendition, decoding, paraphrase
transmission **1** = transfer, spread, spreading, passing on, circulation, dispatch, relaying, mediation **2** = broadcasting, showing, putting out, relaying, sending **3** = programme, broadcast, show, production, telecast
transmit **1** = broadcast, televise, relay, air, radio, send out, disseminate, beam out **2** = pass on, carry, spread, send, bear, transfer, hand on, convey
transparent **1** = clear, sheer, see-through, lucid, translucent, crystalline, limpid, diaphanous ≠ opaque **2** = obvious, plain, patent, evident, explicit, manifest, recognizable, unambiguous ≠ uncertain
transplant **1** = implant, transfer, graft **2** = transfer, take, bring, carry, remove, transport, shift, convey
transport **NOUN** **1** = vehicle, transportation, conveyance **2** = transference, carrying, delivery, distribution, transportation, shipment, freight, haulage **3** *often plural* = ecstasy,

delight, heaven, bliss, euphoria, rapture, enchantment, ravishment ≠ despondency • VERB 1 = convey, take, move, bring, send, carry, bear, transfer 2 = enrapture, move, delight, entrance, enchant, captivate, ravish 3 (*History*) = exile, banish, deport

trap NOUN 1 = snare, net, gin, pitfall, noose 2 = ambush, set-up (*informal*) 3 = trick, set-up (*informal*), deception, ploy, ruse, trickery, subterfuge, stratagem • VERB 1 = catch, snare, ensnare, entrap, take, corner, bag, lay hold of 2 = trick, fool, cheat, lure, seduce, deceive, dupe, beguile 3 = capture, catch, arrest, seize, take, secure, collar (*informal*), apprehend

trash 1 = nonsense, rubbish, rot, drivel, twaddle, tripe (*informal*), moonshine, hogwash, kak (*S. African taboo slang*), bizzo (*Austral. slang*), bull's wool (*Austral. & N.Z. slang*) ≠ sense 2 (*Chiefly U.S. & Canad.*) = litter, refuse, waste, rubbish, junk (*informal*), garbage, dross

trauma 1 = shock, suffering, pain, torture, ordeal, anguish 2 = injury, damage, hurt, wound, agony

traumatic = shocking, upsetting, alarming, awful, disturbing, devastating, painful, distressing ≠ calming

travel VERB = go, journey, move, tour, progress, wander, trek, voyage • NOUN *usually plural* = journey, wandering, expedition, globetrotting, tour, trip, voyage, excursion

traveller *or* (*U.S.*) **traveler** = voyager, tourist, explorer, globetrotter, holiday-maker, wayfarer

tread VERB = step, walk, march, pace, stamp, stride, hike • NOUN = step, walk, pace, stride, footstep, gait, footfall

treason = disloyalty, mutiny, treachery, duplicity, sedition, perfidy, lese-majesty, traitorousness ≠ loyalty

treasure NOUN 1 = riches, money, gold, fortune, wealth, valuables, jewels, cash 2 (*Informal*) = angel, darling, jewel, gem, paragon, nonpareil • VERB = prize, value, esteem, adore, cherish, revere, hold dear, love

treasury = storehouse, bank, store, vault, hoard, cache, repository

treat VERB 1 = behave towards, deal with, handle, act towards, use, consider, serve, manage 2 = take care of, minister to, attend to, give medical treatment to, doctor (*informal*), nurse, care for, prescribe medicine for 3 = provide, stand (*informal*), entertain, lay on, regale • NOUN 1 = entertainment, party, surprise, gift, celebration, feast, outing, excursion 2 = pleasure, delight, joy, thrill, satisfaction, enjoyment, source of pleasure, fun

treatment 1 = care, medical care, nursing, medicine, surgery, therapy, healing, medication 2 = cure, remedy, medication, medicine 3 *often with* ***of*** = handling, dealings with, behaviour towards, conduct towards, management, manipulation, action towards

treaty = agreement, pact, contract, alliance, convention, compact, covenant, entente

trek VERB 1 = journey, march, hike, tramp, rove, go walkabout (*Austral.*) 2 = trudge, traipse (*informal*), footslog, slog • NOUN 1 = slog, tramp 2 = journey, hike, expedition, safari, march, odyssey

tremble VERB 1 = shake, shiver, quake, shudder, quiver, totter 2 = vibrate, shake, quake, wobble • NOUN = shake, shiver, quake, shudder, wobble, tremor, quiver, vibration

tremendous 1 = huge, great, enormous, terrific, formidable, immense, gigantic, colossal ≠ tiny 2 = excellent, great, wonderful, brilliant, amazing, extraordinary, fantastic (*informal*), marvellous, booshit (*Austral. slang*), exo (*Austral. slang*), sik (*Austral. slang*) ≠ terrible

trench = ditch, channel, drain, gutter, trough, furrow, excavation

trend 1 = tendency, swing, drift, inclination, current, direction, flow, leaning 2 = fashion, craze, fad (*informal*), mode, thing, style, rage, vogue

trendy (*Brit. informal*) = fashionable, with it (*informal*), stylish, in fashion, in vogue, modish, voguish

trial 1 (*Law*) = hearing, case, court case, inquiry, tribunal, lawsuit, appeal, litigation 2 = test, experiment, evaluation, audition, dry run (*informal*), assessment, probation, appraisal 3 = hardship, suffering, trouble, distress, ordeal, adversity, affliction, tribulation

tribe = race, people, family, clan, hapu (*N.Z.*), iwi (*N.Z.*)

tribunal = hearing, court, trial
tribute = accolade, testimonial, eulogy, recognition, compliment, commendation, panegyric ≠ criticism
trick NOUN **1** = joke, stunt, spoof (*informal*), prank, practical joke, antic, jape, leg-pull (*Brit. informal*) **2** = deception, trap, fraud, manoeuvre, ploy, hoax, swindle, ruse **3** = sleight of hand, stunt, legerdemain **4** = secret, skill, knack, hang (*informal*), technique, know-how (*informal*) **5** = mannerism, habit, characteristic, trait, quirk, peculiarity, foible, idiosyncrasy
• VERB = deceive, trap, take someone in (*informal*), fool, cheat, con (*informal*), kid (*informal*), mislead
trickle VERB = dribble, run, drop, stream, drip, ooze, seep, exude
• NOUN = dribble, drip, seepage, thin stream
tricky 1 = difficult, sensitive, complicated, delicate, risky, hairy (*informal*), problematic, thorny ≠ simple **2** = crafty, scheming, cunning, slippery, sly, devious, wily, artful ≠ open
trifle = knick-knack, toy, plaything, bauble, bagatelle
trifling = insignificant, trivial, worthless, negligible, unimportant, paltry, measly ≠ significant
trigger = bring about, start, cause, produce, generate, prompt, provoke, set off ≠ prevent
trim ADJECTIVE **1** = neat, smart, tidy, spruce, dapper, natty (*informal*), well-groomed, shipshape ≠ untidy **2** = slender, fit, slim, sleek, streamlined, shapely, svelte, willowy
• VERB **1** = cut, crop, clip, shave, tidy, prune, pare, even up **2** = decorate, dress, array, adorn, ornament, embellish, deck out, beautify
• NOUN **1** = decoration, edging, border, piping, trimming, frill, embellishment, adornment **2** = condition, health, shape (*informal*), fitness, wellness, fettle **3** = cut, crop, clipping, shave, pruning, shearing, tidying up
trimming NOUN = decoration, edging, border, piping, frill, embellishment, adornment, ornamentation
• PLURAL NOUN = extras, accessories, ornaments, accompaniments, frills, trappings, paraphernalia
trinity = threesome, trio, triad, triumvirate
trio = threesome, trinity, trilogy, triad, triumvirate
trip NOUN **1** = journey, outing, excursion, day out, run, drive, tour, spin (*informal*) **2** = stumble, fall, slip, misstep
• VERB **1** = stumble, fall, fall over, slip, tumble, topple, stagger, misstep **2** = skip, dance, hop, gambol
• PHRASES **trip someone up** = catch out, trap, wrongfoot
triple ADJECTIVE **1** = treble, three times **2** = three-way, threefold, tripartite
• VERB = treble, increase threefold
triumph NOUN **1** = success, victory, accomplishment, achievement, coup, feat, conquest, attainment ≠ failure **2** = joy, pride, happiness, rejoicing, elation, jubilation, exultation
• VERB **1** *often with* ***over*** = succeed, win, overcome, prevail, prosper, vanquish ≠ fail **2** = rejoice, celebrate, glory, revel, gloat, exult, crow
triumphant 1 = victorious, winning, successful, conquering ≠ defeated **2** = celebratory, jubilant, proud, elated, exultant, cock-a-hoop
trivial = unimportant, small, minor, petty, meaningless, worthless, trifling, insignificant ≠ important
troop NOUN = group, company, team, body, unit, band, crowd, squad
• PLURAL NOUN = soldiers, men, armed forces, servicemen, army, soldiery
• VERB = flock, march, stream, swarm, throng, traipse (*informal*)
trophy 1 = prize, cup, award, laurels **2** = souvenir, spoils, relic, memento, booty, keepsake
tropical = hot, stifling, steamy, torrid, sultry, sweltering ≠ cold
trot VERB = run, jog, scamper, lope, canter
• NOUN = run, jog, lope, canter
trouble NOUN **1** = bother, problems, concern, worry, stress, difficulty (*informal*), anxiety, distress **2** *usually plural* = distress, problem, worry, pain, anxiety, grief, torment, sorrow ≠ pleasure **3** = ailment, disease, failure, complaint, illness, disorder, defect, malfunction **4** = disorder, fighting, conflict, bother, unrest, disturbance, to-do (*informal*), furore, biffo (*Austral. slang*) ≠ peace **5** = effort, work, thought, care, labour, pains, hassle (*informal*), inconvenience ≠ convenience

• VERB 1 = bother, worry, upset, disturb, distress, plague, pain, sadden ≠ please 2 = afflict, hurt, bother, cause discomfort to, pain, grieve 3 = inconvenience, disturb, burden, put out, impose upon, incommode ≠ relieve 4 = take pains, take the time, make an effort, exert yourself ≠ avoid

troublesome 1 = bothersome, trying, taxing, demanding, difficult, worrying, annoying, tricky ≠ simple 2 = disorderly, violent, turbulent, rebellious, unruly, rowdy, undisciplined, uncooperative ≠ well-behaved

trough = manger, water trough

truce = ceasefire, peace, moratorium, respite, lull, cessation, let-up (*informal*), armistice

true 1 = correct, right, accurate, precise, factual, truthful, veracious ≠ false 2 = actual, real, genuine, proper, authentic, dinkum (*Austral. & N.Z. informal*) 3 = faithful, loyal, devoted, dedicated, steady, reliable, staunch, trustworthy ≠ unfaithful 4 = exact, perfect, accurate, precise, spot-on (*Brit. informal*), on target, unerring ≠ inaccurate

truly 1 = genuinely, correctly, truthfully, rightly, precisely, exactly, legitimately, authentically ≠ falsely 2 = really, very, greatly, indeed, extremely 3 = faithfully, steadily, sincerely, staunchly, dutifully, loyally, devotedly

trumpet NOUN = horn, clarion, bugle
• VERB = proclaim, advertise, tout (*informal*), announce, broadcast, shout from the rooftops ≠ keep secret

trunk 1 = stem, stalk, bole 2 = chest, case, box, crate, coffer, casket 3 = body, torso 4 = snout, nose, proboscis

trust VERB 1 = believe in, have faith in, depend on, count on, bank on, rely upon ≠ distrust 2 = entrust, commit, assign, confide, consign, put into the hands of, allow to look after, hand over 3 = expect, hope, suppose, assume, presume, surmise
• NOUN = confidence, credit, belief, faith, expectation, conviction, assurance, certainty ≠ distrust

trusting *or* **trustful** = unsuspecting, naive, gullible, unwary, credulous, unsuspicious ≠ suspicious

truth 1 = reality, fact(s), real life 2 = truthfulness, fact, accuracy, precision, validity, legitimacy, veracity, genuineness ≠ inaccuracy

try VERB 1 = attempt, seek, aim, strive, struggle, endeavour, have a go, make an effort 2 = experiment with, try out, put to the test, test, taste, examine, investigate, sample
• NOUN = attempt, go (*informal*), shot (*informal*), effort, crack (*informal*), stab (*informal*), bash (*informal*), whack (*informal*)

trying = annoying, hard, taxing, difficult, tough, stressful, exasperating, tiresome ≠ straightforward

tuck VERB = push, stick, stuff, slip, ease, insert, pop (*informal*)
• NOUN 1 (*Brit. informal*) = food, grub (*slang*), kai (*N.Z. informal*), nosh (*slang*) 2 = fold, gather, pleat, pinch

tug VERB 1 = pull, pluck, jerk, yank, wrench 2 = drag, pull, haul, tow, lug, heave, draw
• NOUN = pull, jerk, yank

tuition = training, schooling, education, teaching, lessons, instruction, tutoring, tutelage

tumble VERB = fall, drop, topple, plummet, stumble, flop
• NOUN = fall, drop, trip, plunge, spill, stumble

tumour = growth, cancer, swelling, lump, carcinoma (*Pathology*), sarcoma (*Medical*)

tune NOUN 1 = melody, air, song, theme, strain(s), jingle, ditty 2 = harmony, pitch, euphony
• VERB 1 = tune up, adjust 2 = regulate, adapt, modulate, harmonize, attune, pitch

tunnel NOUN = passage, underpass, passageway, subway, channel, hole, shaft
• VERB = dig, burrow, mine, bore, drill, excavate

turbulent = stormy, rough, raging, tempestuous, furious, foaming, agitated, tumultuous ≠ calm

turf NOUN 1 = grass, sward 2 = sod
• PHRASES **the turf** = horse-racing, the flat, racing

turmoil = confusion, disorder, chaos, upheaval, disarray, uproar, agitation, commotion ≠ peace

turn VERB 1 = change course, swing round, wheel round, veer, move, switch, shift, swerve 2 = rotate, spin, go round (and round), revolve, roll, circle, twist, spiral 3 = change, transform, shape, convert,

alter, mould, remodel, mutate **4** = shape, form, fashion, cast, frame, mould, make **5** = go bad, go off (*Brit. informal*), curdle **6** = make rancid, spoil, sour, taint
• **NOUN 1** = rotation, cycle, circle, revolution, spin, twist, whirl, swivel **2** = change of direction, shift, departure, deviation **3** = direction, course, tack, tendency, drift **4** = opportunity, go, time, try, chance, crack (*informal*), stint **5** = deed, service, act, action, favour, gesture
• **PHRASES turn on someone** = attack, assault, fall on, round on, lash out at, assail, lay into (*informal*), let fly at ◆ **turn someone on** (*Informal*) = arouse, attract, excite, thrill, stimulate, please, titillate ◆ **turn something down 1** = refuse, decline, reject, spurn, rebuff, repudiate **2** = lower, soften, mute, lessen, muffle, quieten ◆ **turn something in** = hand in, return, deliver, give up, hand over, submit, surrender, tender ◆ **turn something off** = switch off, turn out, put out, stop, cut out, shut down, unplug, flick off ◆ **turn something on** = switch on, activate, start, start up, ignite, kick-start ◆ **turn something up 1** = find, reveal, discover, expose, disclose, unearth, dig up **2** = increase, raise, boost, enhance, intensify, amplify ◆ **turn up 1** = arrive, come, appear, show up (*informal*), attend, put in an appearance, show your face **2** = come to light, show up, pop up, materialize

turning = turn-off, turn, bend, curve, junction, crossroads, side road, exit

turning point = crossroads, change, crisis, crux, moment of truth

turnout = attendance, crowd, audience, gate, assembly, congregation, number, throng

turnover 1 = output, business, productivity **2** = movement, coming and going, change

tutor NOUN = teacher, coach, instructor, educator, guide, guardian, lecturer, guru
• **VERB** = teach, educate, school, train, coach, guide, drill, instruct

twig = branch, stick, sprig, shoot, spray

twilight 1 = dusk, evening, sunset, early evening, nightfall, sundown, gloaming (*Scot. poetic*), close of day, evo (*Austral. slang*) ≠ dawn **2** = half-light, gloom, dimness, semi-darkness

twin NOUN = double, counterpart, mate, match, fellow, clone, duplicate, lookalike
• **VERB** = pair, match, join, couple, link, yoke

twinkle VERB = sparkle, flash, shine, glitter, gleam, blink, flicker, shimmer
• **NOUN** = sparkle, flash, spark, gleam, flicker, shimmer, glimmer

twist VERB 1 = coil, curl, wind, wrap, screw, twirl **2** = intertwine **3** = distort, screw up, contort, mangle, mangulate (*Austral. slang*) ≠ straighten
• **NOUN 1** = surprise, change, turn, development, revelation **2** = development, emphasis, variation, slant **3** = wind, turn, spin, swivel, twirl **4** = curve, turn, bend, loop, arc, kink, zigzag, dog-leg

twitch VERB 1 = jerk, flutter, jump, squirm **2** = pull (at), tug (at), pluck (at), yank (at)
• **NOUN** = jerk, tic, spasm, jump, flutter

tycoon = magnate, capitalist, baron, industrialist, financier, fat cat (*slang, chiefly U.S.*), mogul, plutocrat

type = kind, sort, class, variety, group, order, style, species

typical 1 = archetypal, standard, model, normal, stock, representative, usual, regular ≠ unusual **2** = characteristic **3** = average, normal, usual, routine, regular, orthodox, predictable, run-of-the-mill

tyranny = oppression, cruelty, dictatorship, authoritarianism, despotism, autocracy, absolutism, high-handedness ≠ liberality

U

ubiquitous = ever-present, pervasive, omnipresent, everywhere, universal

ugly 1 = unattractive, homely (*chiefly U.S.*), plain, unsightly, unlovely, unprepossessing, ill-favoured ≠ beautiful **2** = unpleasant, shocking, terrible, nasty, distasteful, horrid, objectionable, disagreeable ≠ pleasant **3** = bad-

tempered, dangerous, menacing, sinister, baleful
ulcer = sore, abscess, peptic ulcer, gumboil
ultimate **1** = final, last, end **2** = supreme, highest, greatest, paramount, superlative **3** = worst, greatest, utmost, extreme **4** = best, greatest, supreme, optimum, quintessential
ultimately **1** = finally, eventually, in the end, after all, at last, sooner or later, in due time **2** = fundamentally, essentially, basically, primarily, at heart, deep down
umpire NOUN = referee, judge, arbiter, arbitrator
• VERB = referee, judge, adjudicate, arbitrate
unable = incapable, powerless, unfit, impotent, unqualified, ineffectual ≠ able
unanimous **1** = agreed, united, in agreement, harmonious, like-minded, of the same mind ≠ divided **2** = united, common, concerted, solid, consistent, harmonious, undivided, congruent ≠ split
unarmed = defenceless, helpless, unprotected ≠ armed
unaware = ignorant, unconscious, oblivious, uninformed, unknowing, not in the loop (*informal*) ≠ aware
unbearable = intolerable, insufferable, too much (*informal*), unacceptable ≠ tolerable
unborn = expected, awaited, embryonic
uncertain = unsure, undecided, vague, unclear, dubious, hazy, irresolute ≠ sure
uncertainty **1** = unpredictability, precariousness, ambiguity, unreliability, fickleness, chanciness, changeableness ≠ predictability **2** = doubt, confusion ≠ confidence **3** = hesitancy, indecision
uncomfortable **1** = uneasy, troubled, disturbed, embarrassed, awkward, discomfited ≠ comfortable **2** = painful, awkward, rough
uncommon **1** = rare, unusual, odd, novel, strange, peculiar, scarce, queer ≠ common **2** = extraordinary, remarkable, special, outstanding, distinctive, exceptional, notable ≠ ordinary
uncompromising = inflexible, strict, rigid, firm, tough, inexorable, intransigent, unbending
unconditional = absolute, full, complete, total, positive, entire, outright, unlimited ≠ qualified
unconscious **1** = senseless, knocked out, out cold (*informal*), out, stunned, dazed, in a coma, stupefied ≠ awake **2** = unaware, ignorant, oblivious, unknowing ≠ aware **3** = unintentional, unwitting, inadvertent, accidental ≠ intentional
uncover **1** = reveal, expose, disclose, divulge, make known ≠ conceal **2** = open, unveil, unwrap, show, strip, expose, bare, lay bare
under PREPOSITION **1** = below, beneath, underneath ≠ over **2** = subordinate to, subject to, governed by, secondary to
• ADVERB = below, down, beneath ≠ up
undercover = secret, covert, private, hidden, concealed ≠ open
underdog = weaker party, little fellow (*informal*), outsider
underestimate **1** = undervalue, understate, diminish, play down, minimize, downgrade, miscalculate, trivialize ≠ overestimate **2** = underrate, undervalue, belittle ≠ overrate
undergo = experience, go through, stand, suffer, bear, sustain, endure
underground ADJECTIVE **1** = subterranean, basement, lower-level, sunken, covered, buried, subterrestrial **2** = secret, covert, hidden, guerrilla, revolutionary, confidential, dissident, closet
• PHRASES **the underground** **1** = the tube (*Brit.*), the subway, the metro **2** = the Resistance, partisans, freedom fighters
underline **1** = emphasize, stress, highlight, accentuate ≠ minimize **2** = underscore, mark
underlying = fundamental, basic, prime, primary, elementary, intrinsic
undermine = weaken, sabotage, subvert, compromise, disable ≠ reinforce
understand **1** = comprehend, get, take in, perceive, grasp, see, follow, realize **2** = believe, gather, think, see, suppose, notice, assume, fancy
understandable = reasonable, natural, justified, expected, inevitable, legitimate, predictable, accountable
understanding NOUN **1** = perception, knowledge, grasp, sense, know-how (*informal*), judgment, awareness, appreciation ≠ ignorance **2** = agreement, deal, promise, arrangement, accord, contract, bond, pledge ≠ disagreement

3 = belief, view, opinion, impression, interpretation, feeling, idea, notion
• ADJECTIVE = sympathetic, kind, compassionate, considerate, patient, sensitive, tolerant ≠ unsympathetic

undertake = agree, promise, contract, guarantee, engage, pledge

undertaking **1** = task, business, operation, project, attempt, effort, affair, venture **2** = promise, commitment, pledge, word, vow, assurance

underwear = underclothes, lingerie, undies (*informal*), undergarments, underthings, broekies (*S. African informal*), underdaks (*Austral. slang*)

underworld **1** = criminals, gangsters, organized crime, gangland (*informal*) **2** = nether world, Hades, nether regions

underwrite = finance, back, fund, guarantee, sponsor, insure, ratify, subsidize

undesirable = unwanted, unwelcome, disagreeable, objectionable, unacceptable, unsuitable, unattractive, distasteful ≠ desirable

undo **1** = open, unfasten, loose, untie, unbutton, disentangle **2** = reverse, cancel, offset, neutralize, invalidate, annul **3** = ruin, defeat, destroy, wreck, shatter, upset, undermine, overturn

undone = unfinished, left, neglected, omitted, unfulfilled, unperformed ≠ finished

undoubtedly = certainly, definitely, surely, doubtless, without doubt, assuredly

unearth **1** = discover, find, reveal, expose, uncover **2** = dig up, excavate, exhume, dredge up

unearthly = eerie, strange, supernatural, ghostly, weird, phantom, uncanny, spooky (*informal*)

uneasy **1** = anxious, worried, troubled, nervous, disturbed, uncomfortable, edgy, perturbed ≠ relaxed **2** = precarious, strained, uncomfortable, tense, awkward, shaky, insecure

unemployed = out of work, redundant, laid off, jobless, idle ≠ working

unfair **1** = biased, prejudiced, unjust, one-sided, partial, partisan, bigoted **2** = unscrupulous, dishonest, unethical, wrongful, unsporting ≠ ethical

unfit **1** = out of shape, feeble, unhealthy, flabby, in poor condition ≠ healthy **2** = incapable, inadequate, incompetent, no good, useless, unqualified ≠ capable **3** = unsuitable, inadequate, useless, unsuited ≠ suitable

unfold **1** = reveal, tell, present, show, disclose, uncover, divulge, make known **2** = open, spread out, undo, expand, unfurl, unwrap, unroll

unfortunate **1** = disastrous, calamitous, adverse, ill-fated ≠ opportune **2** = regrettable, deplorable, lamentable, unsuitable, unbecoming ≠ becoming **3** = unlucky, unhappy, doomed, cursed, unsuccessful, hapless, wretched ≠ fortunate

unhappy **1** = sad, depressed, miserable, blue, melancholy, mournful, dejected, despondent ≠ happy **2** = unlucky, unfortunate, hapless, cursed, wretched, ill-fated ≠ fortunate

unhealthy **1** = harmful, detrimental, unwholesome, insanitary, insalubrious ≠ beneficial **2** = sick, sickly, unwell, delicate, crook (*Austral. & N.Z. informal*), ailing, frail, feeble, invalid ≠ well **3** = weak, ailing ≠ strong

unification = union, uniting, alliance, coalition, federation, confederation, amalgamation, coalescence

uniform NOUN **1** = regalia, suit, livery, colours, habit **2** = outfit, dress, costume, attire, gear (*informal*), get-up (*informal*), ensemble, garb
• ADJECTIVE **1** = consistent, unvarying, similar, even, same, matching, regular, constant ≠ varying **2** = alike, similar, like, same, equal

unify = unite, join, combine, merge, consolidate, confederate, amalgamate ≠ divide

union **1** = joining, uniting, unification, combination, coalition, merger, mixture, blend **2** = alliance, league, association, coalition, federation, confederacy

unique **1** = distinct, special, exclusive, peculiar, only, single, lone, solitary **2** = unparalleled, unmatched, unequalled, matchless, without equal

unit **1** = entity, whole, item, feature **2** = section, company, group, force, detail, division, cell, squad **3** = measure, quantity, measurement **4** = part, section, segment, class, element, component, constituent, tutorial

unite 1 = join, link, combine, couple, blend, merge, unify, fuse ≠ separate 2 = cooperate, ally, join forces, band, pool, collaborate ≠ split

unity 1 = union, unification, coalition, federation, integration, confederation, amalgamation 2 = wholeness, integrity, oneness, union, entity, singleness ≠ disunity 3 = agreement, accord, consensus, harmony, solidarity, unison, assent, concord ≠ disagreement

universal 1 = widespread, general, common, whole, total, unlimited, overarching 2 = global, worldwide, international, pandemic

universally = without exception, everywhere, always, invariably

universe = cosmos, space, creation, nature, heavens, macrocosm, all existence

unknown 1 = strange, new, undiscovered, uncharted, unexplored, virgin, remote, alien 2 = unidentified, mysterious, anonymous, unnamed, nameless, incognito 3 = obscure, humble, unfamiliar ≠ famous

unlike 1 = different from, dissimilar to, distinct from, unequal to ≠ similar to 2 = contrasted with, not like, in contradiction to, in contrast with *or* to, as opposed to, differently from, opposite to

unlikely 1 = improbable, doubtful, remote, slight, faint ≠ probable 2 = unbelievable, incredible, implausible, questionable ≠ believable

unload 1 = empty, clear, unpack, dump, discharge 2 = unburden

unnatural 1 = abnormal, odd, strange, unusual, extraordinary, perverted, queer, irregular ≠ normal 2 = false, forced, artificial, affected, stiff, feigned, stilted, insincere ≠ genuine

unpleasant 1 = nasty, bad, horrid, distasteful, displeasing, objectionable, disagreeable ≠ nice 2 = obnoxious, rude ≠ likable *or* likeable

unravel 1 = solve, explain, work out, resolve, figure out (*informal*) 2 = undo, separate, disentangle, free, unwind, untangle

unrest = discontent, rebellion, protest, strife, agitation, discord, sedition, dissension ≠ peace

unsettled 1 = unstable, shaky, insecure, disorderly, unsteady 2 = restless, tense, shaken, confused, disturbed, anxious, agitated, flustered 3 = inconstant, changing, variable, uncertain

unstable 1 = changeable, volatile, unpredictable, variable, fluctuating, fitful, inconstant ≠ constant 2 = insecure, shaky, precarious, unsettled, wobbly, tottering, unsteady 3 = unpredictable, irrational, erratic, inconsistent, temperamental, capricious, changeable ≠ level-headed

unthinkable 1 = impossible, out of the question, inconceivable, absurd, unreasonable 2 = inconceivable, incredible, unimaginable

untold 1 = indescribable, unthinkable, unimaginable, undreamed of, unutterable, inexpressible 2 = countless, incalculable, innumerable, myriad, numberless, uncountable

untrue 1 = false, lying, wrong, mistaken, incorrect, inaccurate, dishonest, deceptive ≠ true 2 = unfaithful, disloyal, deceitful, treacherous, faithless, false, untrustworthy, inconstant ≠ faithful

unusual 1 = rare, odd, strange, extraordinary, different, curious, queer, uncommon ≠ common 2 = extraordinary, unique, remarkable, exceptional, uncommon, singular, unconventional ≠ average

upbeat (*Informal*) = cheerful, positive, optimistic, encouraging, hopeful, cheery

upbringing = education, training, breeding, rearing, raising

update = bring up to date, improve, correct, renew, revise, upgrade, amend, overhaul

upgrade 1 = improve, better, update, reform, add to, enhance, refurbish, renovate 2 = promote, raise, advance, boost, move up, elevate, kick upstairs (*informal*), give promotion to ≠ demote

upheaval = disturbance, revolution, disorder, turmoil, disruption

uphill 1 = ascending, rising, upward, mounting, climbing ≠ descending 2 = arduous, hard, taxing, difficult, tough, exhausting, gruelling, strenuous

uphold 1 = support, back, defend, aid, champion, maintain, promote, sustain 2 = confirm, endorse

uplift VERB = improve, better, raise, advance, inspire, refine, edify
• NOUN = improvement, enlightenment,

advancement, refinement, enhancement, enrichment, edification

upper 1 = topmost, top ≠ bottom 2 = higher, high ≠ lower 3 = superior, senior, higher-level, greater, top, important, chief, most important ≠ inferior

upper class = aristocratic, upper-class, noble, high-class, patrician, blue-blooded, highborn

upright 1 = vertical, straight, standing up, erect, perpendicular, bolt upright ≠ horizontal 2 = honest, good, principled, just, ethical, honourable, righteous, conscientious ≠ dishonourable

uprising = rebellion, rising, revolution, revolt, disturbance, mutiny, insurrection, insurgence

uproar 1 = commotion, noise, racket, riot, turmoil, mayhem, din, pandemonium 2 = protest, outrage, complaint, objection, fuss, stink (*informal*), outcry, furore

upset ADJECTIVE 1 = distressed, shaken, disturbed, worried, troubled, hurt, bothered, unhappy 2 = sick, queasy, bad, ill 3 = overturned, upside down, capsized, spilled
• VERB 1 = distress, trouble, disturb, worry, alarm, bother, grieve, agitate 2 = tip over, overturn, capsize, knock over, spill 3 = mess up, spoil, disturb, change, confuse, disorder, unsettle, disorganize
• NOUN 1 = distress, worry, trouble, shock, bother, disturbance, agitation 2 = reversal, shake-up (*informal*), defeat 3 = illness, complaint, disorder, bug (*informal*), sickness, malady

upside down *or* **upside-down** ADVERB = wrong side up
• ADJECTIVE 1 = inverted, overturned, upturned 2 (*Informal*) = confused, disordered, chaotic, muddled, topsy-turvy, higgledy-piggledy (*informal*)

up-to-date = modern, fashionable, trendy (*Brit. informal*), current, stylish, in vogue, up-to-the-minute ≠ out of date

urban = civic, city, town, metropolitan, municipal, dorp (*S. African*)

urge VERB 1 = beg, exhort, plead, implore, beseech, entreat 2 = advocate, recommend, advise, support, counsel ≠ discourage
• NOUN = impulse, longing, wish, desire, drive, yearning, itch (*informal*), thirst ≠ reluctance

urgency = importance, need, necessity, gravity, pressure, hurry, seriousness, extremity

urgent = crucial, desperate, pressing, great, important, crying, critical, immediate ≠ unimportant

usage 1 = use, operation, employment, running, control, management, handling 2 = practice, method, procedure, habit, regime, custom, routine, convention

use VERB 1 = employ, utilize, work, apply, operate, exercise, practise, resort to 2 *sometimes with* ***up*** = consume, exhaust, spend, run through, expend 3 = take advantage of, exploit, manipulate
• NOUN 1 = usage, employment, operation, application 2 = purpose, end, reason, object 3 = good, point, help, service, value, benefit, profit, advantage

used = second-hand, cast-off, nearly new, shopsoiled ≠ new

used to = accustomed to, familiar with

useful = helpful, effective, valuable, practical, profitable, worthwhile, beneficial, fruitful ≠ useless

useless 1 = worthless, valueless, impractical, fruitless, unproductive, ineffectual, unsuitable ≠ useful 2 = pointless, futile, vain ≠ worthwhile 3 (*Informal*) = inept, no good, hopeless, incompetent, ineffectual

usher VERB = escort, lead, direct, guide, conduct
• NOUN = attendant, guide, doorman, escort, doorkeeper

usual = normal, customary, regular, general, common, standard, ordinary, typical ≠ unusual

usually = normally, generally, mainly, commonly, mostly, on the whole, as a rule, habitually

utility = usefulness, benefit, convenience, practicality, efficacy, serviceableness

utilize = use, employ, deploy, take advantage of, make use of, put to use, bring into play, avail yourself of

utmost ADJECTIVE 1 = greatest, highest, maximum, supreme, paramount, pre-eminent 2 = farthest, extreme, last, final
• NOUN = best, greatest, maximum, highest, hardest

utter[1] = say, state, speak, voice, express, deliver, declare, mouth

utter[2] = absolute, complete, total,

sheer, outright, thorough, downright, unmitigated

utterly = totally, completely, absolutely, perfectly, fully, entirely, extremely, thoroughly

V

vacancy 1 = opening, job, post, place, position, role, situation, opportunity 2 = room, space, available accommodation, unoccupied room

vacant 1 = empty, free, available, abandoned, deserted, for sale, on the market, void ≠ occupied 2 = unfilled, unoccupied ≠ taken 3 = blank, vague, dreamy, empty, abstracted, idle, vacuous, inane ≠ thoughtful

vacuum 1 = gap, lack, absence, space, deficiency, void 2 = emptiness, space, void, gap, nothingness, vacuity

vague 1 = unclear, indefinite, hazy, confused, loose, uncertain, unsure, superficial ≠ clear 2 = imprecise, unspecified, generalized, rough, loose, ambiguous, hazy, equivocal 3 = absent-minded, distracted, vacant, preoccupied, oblivious, inattentive 4 = indistinct, unclear, faint, hazy, indeterminate, nebulous, ill-defined ≠ distinct

vain ADJECTIVE 1 = futile, useless, pointless, unsuccessful, idle, worthless, senseless, fruitless ≠ successful 2 = conceited, narcissistic, proud, arrogant, swaggering, egotistical, self-important ≠ modest
• PHRASES **in vain** 1 = useless, to no avail, unsuccessful, fruitless, vain 2 = uselessly, to no avail, unsuccessfully, fruitlessly, vainly, ineffectually

valid 1 = sound, good, reasonable, telling, convincing, rational, logical, viable ≠ unfounded 2 = legal, official, legitimate, genuine, authentic, lawful, bona fide ≠ invalid

validity 1 = soundness, force, power, weight, strength, cogency 2 = legality, authority, legitimacy, right, lawfulness

valley = hollow, dale, glen, vale, depression, dell

valuable ADJECTIVE 1 = useful, important, profitable, worthwhile, beneficial, helpful ≠ useless 2 = treasured, prized, precious 3 = precious, expensive, costly, dear, high-priced, priceless, irreplaceable ≠ worthless
• PLURAL NOUN = treasures, prized possessions, precious items, heirlooms, personal effects, costly article

value NOUN 1 = importance, benefit, worth, merit, point, service, sense, profit ≠ worthlessness 2 = cost, price, worth, rate, market price, face value, asking price, selling price
• PLURAL NOUN = principles, morals, ethics, mores, standards of behaviour, (moral) standards
• VERB 1 = appreciate, rate, prize, regard highly, respect, admire, treasure, esteem ≠ undervalue 2 = evaluate, price, estimate, rate, cost, assess, set at, appraise

vanish 1 = disappear, dissolve, evaporate, fade away, melt away, evanesce ≠ appear 2 = die out, disappear, pass away, end, fade, dwindle, cease to exist, become extinct

vanity = pride, arrogance, conceit, narcissism, egotism, conceitedness ≠ modesty

variable = changeable, unstable, fluctuating, shifting, flexible, uneven, temperamental, unsteady ≠ constant

variant NOUN = variation, form, version, development, alternative, adaptation, revision, modification
• ADJECTIVE = different, alternative, modified, divergent

variation 1 = alternative, variety, modification, departure, innovation, variant 2 = variety, change, deviation, difference, diversity, diversion, novelty ≠ uniformity

varied = different, mixed, various, diverse, assorted, miscellaneous, sundry, motley ≠ unvarying

variety 1 = diversity, change, variation, difference, diversification, heterogeneity, multifariousness ≠ uniformity 2 = range, selection, assortment, mix, collection, line-up, mixture, array 3 = type, sort, kind, class, brand, species, breed, strain

various 1 = different, assorted, miscellaneous, varied, distinct, diverse, disparate, sundry ≠ similar 2 = many, numerous, countless, several, abundant, innumerable, sundry, profuse

varnish NOUN = lacquer, polish, glaze, gloss
• VERB = lacquer, polish, glaze, gloss

vary 1 = differ, be different, be dissimilar, disagree, diverge 2 = change, shift, swing, alter, fluctuate, oscillate, see-saw 3 = alternate

vast = huge, massive, enormous, great, wide, immense, gigantic, monumental ≠ tiny

vault[1] 1 = strongroom, repository, depository 2 = crypt, tomb, catacomb, cellar, mausoleum, charnel house, undercroft

vault[2] = jump, spring, leap, clear, bound, hurdle

veer = change direction, turn, swerve, shift, sheer, change course

vehicle 1 = conveyance, machine, motor vehicle 2 = medium, means, channel, mechanism, organ, apparatus

veil NOUN 1 = mask, cover, shroud, film, curtain, cloak 2 = screen, mask, disguise, blind 3 = film, cover, curtain, cloak, shroud
• VERB = cover, screen, hide, mask, shield, disguise, conceal, obscure ≠ reveal

veiled = disguised, implied, hinted at, covert, masked, concealed, suppressed

vein 1 = blood vessel 2 = mood, style, note, tone, mode, temper, tenor 3 = seam, layer, stratum, course, current, bed, deposit, streak

velocity = speed, pace, rapidity, quickness, swiftness

vengeance = revenge, retaliation, reprisal, retribution, requital ≠ forgiveness

vent NOUN = outlet, opening, aperture, duct, orifice
• VERB = express, release, voice, air, discharge, utter, emit, pour out ≠ hold back

venture NOUN = undertaking, project, enterprise, campaign, risk, operation, activity, scheme
• VERB 1 = go, travel, journey, set out, wander, stray, plunge into, rove 2 = dare, presume, have the courage to, be brave enough, hazard, go out on a limb (*informal*), take the liberty, go so far as 3 = put forward, volunteer

verbal = spoken, oral, word-of-mouth, unwritten

verdict = decision, finding, judgment, opinion, sentence, conclusion, conviction, adjudication

verge NOUN 1 = brink, point, edge, threshold 2 = border, edge, margin, limit, boundary, threshold, brim
• PHRASES **verge on something** = come near to, approach, border on, resemble, incline to, be similar to, touch on, be more or less

verify 1 = check, make sure, examine, monitor, inspect 2 = confirm, prove, substantiate, support, validate, bear out, corroborate, authenticate ≠ disprove

versatile 1 = adaptable, flexible, all-round, resourceful, multifaceted ≠ unadaptable 2 = all-purpose, variable, adjustable ≠ limited

versed = knowledgeable, experienced, seasoned, familiar, practised, acquainted, well-informed, proficient ≠ ignorant

version 1 = form, variety, variant, sort, class, design, style, model 2 = adaptation, edition, interpretation, form, copy, rendering, reproduction, portrayal 3 = account, report, description, record, reading, story, view, understanding

vertical = upright sheer, perpendicular, straight (up and down), erect, plumb, on end, precipitous, vertiginous ≠ horizontal

very ADVERB = extremely, highly, greatly, really, deeply, unusually, profoundly, decidedly
• ADJECTIVE 1 = exact, precise, selfsame 2 = ideal

vessel 1 = ship, boat, craft 2 = container, receptacle, can, bowl, tank, pot, drum, barrel

vest VERB
• PHRASES **vest in something** *or* **someone** *usually passive* = place, invest, entrust, settle, confer, endow, bestow, consign ◆ **vest with something** *usually passive* = endow with, entrust with

vet = check, examine, investigate, review, appraise, scrutinize

veteran NOUN = old hand, past master, warhorse (*informal*), old stager ≠ novice
• ADJECTIVE = long-serving, seasoned, experienced, old, established, qualified, mature, practised

veto VERB = ban, block, reject, rule out, turn down, forbid, boycott, prohibit ≠ pass
• NOUN = ban, dismissal, rejection, vetoing, boycott, embargo, prohibiting, prohibition ≠ ratification
viable = workable, practical, feasible, suitable, realistic, operational, applicable, usable ≠ unworkable
vibrant 1 = energetic, dynamic, sparkling, vivid, spirited, storming, alive, vigorous 2 = vivid, bright, brilliant, intense, clear, rich, glowing
vice 1 = fault, failing, weakness, limitation, defect, deficiency, flaw, shortcoming ≠ good point 2 = wickedness, evil, corruption, sin, depravity, immorality, iniquity, turpitude ≠ virtue
vice versa = the other way round, conversely, in reverse, contrariwise
vicious 1 = savage, brutal, violent, cruel, ferocious, barbarous ≠ gentle 2 = malicious, vindictive, spiteful, mean, cruel, venomous
victim 1 = casualty, sufferer, fatality ≠ survivor 2 = scapegoat, sacrifice, martyr
victor = winner, champion, conqueror, vanquisher, prizewinner ≠ loser
victorious = winning, successful, triumphant, first, champion, conquering, vanquishing, prizewinning ≠ losing
victory = win, success, triumph, conquest, walkover (*informal*) ≠ defeat
vie = compete, struggle, contend, strive
view NOUN 1 *sometimes plural* = opinion, belief, feeling, attitude, impression, conviction, point of view, sentiment 2 = scene, picture, sight, prospect, perspective, landscape, outlook, spectacle 3 = vision, sight, visibility, perspective, eyeshot
• VERB = regard, see, consider, perceive, treat, estimate, reckon, deem
viewer = watcher, observer, spectator, onlooker
vigorous 1 = strenuous, energetic, arduous, hard, taxing, active, rigorous 2 = spirited, lively, energetic, active, dynamic, animated, forceful, feisty (*informal*) ≠ lethargic 3 = strong, powerful, lively, lusty ≠ weak
vigorously 1 = energetically, hard, forcefully, strongly, strenuously, lustily 2 = forcefully, strongly, vehemently, strenuously
vigour *or* (*U.S.*) **vigor** = energy, vitality, power, spirit, strength, animation, verve, gusto ≠ weakness
vile 1 = wicked, evil, corrupt, perverted, degenerate, depraved, nefarious ≠ honourable 2 = disgusting, foul, revolting, offensive, nasty, sickening, horrid, repulsive, yucko (*Austral. slang*) ≠ pleasant
villain 1 = evildoer, criminal, rogue, scoundrel, wretch, reprobate, miscreant, blackguard 2 = baddy (*informal*), antihero ≠ hero
vindicate 1 = clear, acquit, exonerate, absolve, let off the hook, exculpate ≠ condemn 2 = support, defend, excuse, justify
vintage NOUN (always used of wines) = harvest
• ADJECTIVE 1 (always used of wines) = high-quality, best, prime, quality, choice, select, superior 2 = classic, old, veteran, historic, heritage, enduring, antique, timeless
violate 1 = break, infringe, disobey, transgress, ignore, defy, disregard, flout ≠ obey 2 = invade, infringe on, disturb, upset, shatter, disrupt, impinge on, encroach on 3 = desecrate, profane, defile, abuse, pollute, deface, dishonour, vandalize ≠ honour 4 = rape, molest, sexually assault, ravish, abuse, assault, interfere with, sexually abuse
violation 1 = breach, abuse, infringement, contravention, abuse, trespass, transgression, infraction 2 = invasion, intrusion, trespass, breach, disturbance, disruption, interruption, encroachment 3 = desecration, sacrilege, defilement, profanation, spoliation 4 = rape, sexual assault, molesting, ravishing (*old-fashioned*), abuse, sexual abuse, indecent assault, molestation
violence 1 = brutality, bloodshed, savagery, fighting, terrorism 2 = force, power, strength, might, ferocity, forcefulness, powerfulness 3 = intensity, force, cruelty, severity, fervour, vehemence
violent 1 = brutal, aggressive, savage, wild, fierce, bullying, cruel, vicious ≠ gentle 2 = sharp 3 = passionate, uncontrollable, unrestrained 4 = fiery, fierce, passionate
VIP = celebrity, big name, star, somebody, luminary, big hitter (*informal*), heavy

hitter (*informal*)
virgin NOUN = maiden, girl (*archaic*)
• ADJECTIVE = pure, chaste, immaculate, virginal, vestal, uncorrupted, undefiled ≠ corrupted
virtual = practical, essential, in all but name
virtually = practically, almost, nearly, in effect, in essence, as good as, in all but name
virtue 1 = goodness, integrity, worth, morality, righteousness, probity, rectitude, incorruptibility ≠ vice 2 = merit, strength, asset, plus (*informal*), attribute, good point, strong point ≠ failing 3 = advantage, benefit, merit, credit, usefulness, efficacy
visible = perceptible, observable, clear, apparent, evident, manifest, in view, discernible ≠ invisible
vision 1 = image, idea, dream, plans, hopes, prospect, ideal, concept 2 = hallucination, illusion, apparition, revelation, delusion, mirage, chimera 3 = sight, seeing, eyesight, view, perception 4 = foresight, imagination, perception, insight, awareness, inspiration, innovation, creativity
visionary NOUN 1 = idealist, romantic, dreamer, daydreamer ≠ realist 2 = prophet, diviner, mystic, seer, soothsayer, sibyl, scryer, spaewife (*Scot.*)
• ADJECTIVE 1 = idealistic, romantic, unrealistic, utopian, speculative, impractical, unworkable, quixotic ≠ realistic 2 = prophetic, mystical, predictive, oracular, sibylline
visit VERB 1 = call on, drop in on (*informal*), stay at, stay with, stop by, spend time with, look someone up, go see (*U.S.*) 2 = stay in, stop by
• NOUN 1 = call, social call 2 = trip, stop, stay, break, tour, holiday, vacation (*informal*), stopover
visitor = guest, caller, company, manu(w)hiri (*N.Z.*)
vista = view, scene, prospect, landscape, panorama, perspective
visual 1 = optical, optic, ocular 2 = observable, visible, perceptible, discernible ≠ imperceptible
vital 1 = essential, important, necessary, key, basic, significant, critical, crucial ≠ unnecessary 2 = lively, vigorous, energetic, spirited, dynamic, animated, vibrant, vivacious ≠ lethargic
vitality = energy, vivacity, life, strength, animation, vigour, exuberance, liveliness ≠ lethargy
vivid 1 = clear, detailed, realistic, telling, moving, affecting, arresting, powerful ≠ vague 2 = bright, brilliant, intense, clear, rich, glowing, colourful ≠ dull
vocabulary 1 = language, words, lexicon 2 = wordbook, dictionary, glossary, lexicon
vocal 1 = outspoken, frank, forthright, strident, vociferous, articulate, expressive, eloquent ≠ quiet 2 = spoken, voiced, uttered, oral, said
vocation = profession, calling, job, trade, career, mission, pursuit
vogue = fashion, trend, craze, style, mode, passing fancy, dernier cri (*French*)
voice NOUN 1 = tone, sound, articulation 2 = utterance 3 = opinion, will, feeling, wish, desire 4 = say, view, vote, comment, input
• VERB = express, declare, air, raise, reveal, mention, mouth, pronounce

RELATED WORD
adjective: vocal

void NOUN 1 = gap, space, lack, hole, emptiness 2 = emptiness, space, vacuum, oblivion, blankness, nullity, vacuity
• ADJECTIVE = invalid, null and void, inoperative, useless, ineffective, worthless
• VERB = invalidate, nullify, cancel, withdraw, reverse, undo, repeal, quash
volatile 1 = changeable, shifting, variable, unsettled, unstable, explosive, unreliable, unsteady ≠ stable 2 = temperamental, erratic, mercurial, up and down (*informal*), fickle, over-emotional ≠ calm
volley = barrage, blast, burst, shower, hail, bombardment, salvo, fusillade
volume 1 = amount, quantity, level, body, total, measure, degree, mass 2 = capacity, size, mass, extent, proportions, dimensions, bulk, measurements 3 = book, work, title, opus, publication, manual, tome, treatise 4 = loudness, sound, amplification
voluntarily = willingly, freely, by choice, off your own bat, of your own accord, of your own volition
voluntary 1 = intentional, deliberate, planned, calculated, wilful ≠ unintentional 2 = optional, discretionary, up to the

individual, open, unforced, at your discretion, open to choice ≠ obligatory **3** = unpaid, free, willing, pro bono (*Law*)
volunteer = offer, step forward ≠ refuse
vomit **1** = be sick, throw up (*informal*), spew, chuck (*Austral. & N.Z. informal*), heave (*slang*), retch **2** *often with* ***up*** = bring up, throw up, regurgitate, emit (*informal*), disgorge, spew out *or* up
vote NOUN = poll, election, ballot, referendum, popular vote, plebiscite, straw poll, show of hands
• VERB = cast your vote
voucher = ticket, token, coupon, pass, slip, chit, chitty (*Brit. informal*), docket
vow VERB = promise, pledge, swear, commit, engage, affirm, avow, bind yourself
• NOUN = promise, commitment, pledge, oath, profession, avowal
voyage NOUN = journey, trip, passage, expedition, crossing, sail, cruise, excursion
• VERB = travel, journey, tour, cruise, steam, take a trip, go on an expedition
vulgar **1** = tasteless, common ≠ tasteful **2** = crude, rude, coarse, indecent, tasteless, risqué, ribald **3** = uncouth, unrefined, impolite, ill-bred ≠ refined
vulnerable **1** = susceptible, helpless, unprotected, defenceless, exposed, weak, sensitive, tender ≠ immune **2** = exposed, open, unprotected, defenceless, accessible, wide open, assailable ≠ well-protected

W

waddle = shuffle, totter, toddle, sway, wobble
wade **1** = paddle, splash, splash about, slop **2** = walk through, cross, ford, travel across
wag VERB **1** = wave, shake, waggle, stir, quiver, vibrate, wiggle **2** = waggle, wave, shake, flourish, brandish, wobble, wiggle **3** = shake, bob, nod
• NOUN **1** = wave, shake, quiver, vibration, wiggle, waggle **2** = nod, bob, shake
wage NOUN *often plural* = payment, pay, remuneration, fee, reward, income, allowance, recompense
• VERB = engage in, conduct, pursue, carry on, undertake, practise, prosecute, proceed with
wail VERB = cry, weep, grieve, lament, howl, bawl, yowl
• NOUN = cry, moan, howl, lament, yowl
wait VERB **1** = stay, remain, stop, pause, rest, linger, loiter, tarry ≠ go **2** = stand by, hold back, hang fire **3** = be postponed, be suspended, be delayed, be put off, be put back, be deferred, be put on hold (*informal*), be shelved
• NOUN = delay, gap, pause, interval, stay, rest, halt, hold-up
waiter *or* **waitress** = attendant, server, flunkey, steward *or* stewardess, servant
waive **1** = give up, relinquish, renounce, forsake, drop, abandon, set aside, dispense with ≠ claim **2** = disregard, ignore, discount, overlook, set aside, pass over, dispense with, brush aside
wake[1] VERB **1** = awake, stir, awaken, come to, arise, get up, rouse, get out of bed ≠ fall asleep **2** = awaken, arouse, rouse, waken **3** = evoke, recall, renew, stimulate, revive, induce, arouse, call up
• NOUN = vigil, watch, funeral, deathwatch, tangi (*N.Z.*)
wake[2] NOUN = slipstream, wash, trail, backwash, train, track, waves, path
• PHRASES **in the wake of** = in the aftermath of, following, because of, as a result of, on account of, as a consequence of
walk VERB **1** = stride, stroll, go, move, step, march, pace, hike **2** = travel on foot **3** = escort, take, see, show, partner, guide, conduct, accompany
• NOUN **1** = stroll, hike, ramble, march, trek, trudge, promenade, saunter **2** = gait, step, bearing, carriage, tread **3** = path, footpath, track, way, road, lane, trail, avenue, berm (*N.Z.*)
• PHRASES **walk of life** = area, calling, business, line, trade, class, field, career
walker = hiker, rambler, wayfarer, pedestrian
wall **1** = partition, screen, barrier,

enclosure **2** = barrier, obstacle, barricade, obstruction, check, bar, fence, impediment

wallet = purse, pocketbook, pouch, case, holder, money-bag

wander VERB = roam, walk, drift, stroll, range, stray, ramble, prowl
• NOUN = excursion, walk, stroll, cruise, ramble, meander, promenade, mosey (*informal*)

wanderer = traveller, rover, nomad, drifter, gypsy, explorer, rambler, voyager

wane **1** = decline, weaken, diminish, fail, fade, decrease, dwindle, lessen ≠ grow **2** = diminish, decrease, dwindle ≠ wax

want VERB **1** = wish for, desire, long for, crave, covet, hope for, yearn for, thirst for ≠ have **2** = need, demand, require, call for **3** = should, need, must, ought **4** = desire, long for, crave, wish for, yearn for, thirst for, hanker after, burn for **5** = lack, need, require, miss
• NOUN **1** = lack, need, absence, shortage, deficiency, famine, scarcity, dearth ≠ abundance **2** = poverty, hardship, privation, penury, destitution, neediness, pennilessness ≠ wealth **3** = wish, will, need, desire, requirement, longing, appetite, craving

wanting **1** = deficient, poor, inadequate, insufficient, faulty, defective, imperfect, unsound, bodger *or* bodgie (*Austral. slang*) ≠ adequate **2** = lacking, missing, absent, incomplete, short, shy ≠ complete

war NOUN **1** = conflict, drive, attack, fighting, fight, operation, battle, movement ≠ peace **2** = campaign, drive, attack, operation, movement, push, mission, offensive
• VERB = fight, battle, clash, wage war, campaign, combat, do battle, take up arms ≠ make peace

ward NOUN **1** = room, department, unit, quarter, division, section, apartment, cubicle **2** = district, constituency, area, division, zone, parish, precinct **3** = dependant, charge, pupil, minor, protégé
• PHRASES **ward someone off** = drive off, resist, fight off, hold off, repel, fend off ♦ **ward something off** **1** = avert, fend off, stave off, avoid, frustrate, deflect, repel **2** = parry, avert, deflect, avoid, repel, turn aside

warden **1** = steward, guardian, administrator, superintendent, caretaker, curator, custodian **2** = jailer, prison officer, guard, screw (*slang*) **3** = governor, head, leader, director, manager, chief, executive, commander, baas (*S. African*) **4** = ranger, keeper, guardian, protector, custodian, official

wardrobe **1** = clothes cupboard, cupboard, closet (*U.S.*), cabinet **2** = clothes, apparel, attire

warehouse = store, depot, storehouse, repository, depository, stockroom

wares = goods, produce, stock, products, stuff, commodities, merchandise

warfare = war, fighting, battle, conflict, combat, hostilities, enmity ≠ peace

warm ADJECTIVE **1** = balmy, mild, temperate, pleasant, fine, bright, sunny, agreeable ≠ cool **2** = cosy, snug, toasty (*informal*), comfortable, homely, comfy (*informal*) **3** = moderately hot, heated ≠ cool **4** = thermal, winter, thick, chunky, woolly ≠ cool **5** = mellow, relaxing, pleasant, agreeable, restful **6** = affable, kindly, friendly, affectionate, loving, tender, amicable, cordial ≠ unfriendly **7** = near, close, hot, near to the truth
• VERB = warm up, heat, thaw (out), heat up ≠ cool down
• PHRASES **warm something** *or* **someone up** = heat, thaw, heat up

warmth **1** = heat, snugness, warmness, comfort, homeliness, hotness ≠ coolness **2** = affection, feeling, love, goodwill, kindness, tenderness, cordiality, kindliness ≠ hostility

warn **1** = notify, tell, remind, inform, alert, tip off, give notice, make someone aware **2** = advise, urge, recommend, counsel, caution, commend, exhort, admonish

warning **1** = caution, information, advice, injunction, notification **2** = notice, notification, sign, alarm, announcement, alert, tip-off (*informal*) **3** = omen, sign, forecast, indication, prediction, prophecy, foreboding, portent, rahui (*N.Z.*) **4** = reprimand, admonition

warp VERB **1** = distort, bend, twist, buckle, deform, disfigure, contort, malform **2** = become distorted, bend, twist, contort, become deformed, become misshapen **3** = pervert, twist, corrupt, degrade, deprave, debase, debauch, lead astray
• NOUN = twist, bend, defect, flaw,

distortion, imperfection, kink, contortion
warrant VERB 1 = call for, demand, require, merit, rate, earn, deserve, permit 2 = guarantee, declare, pledge, promise, ensure, affirm, certify, attest
• NOUN 1 = authorization, permit, licence, permission, authority, sanction 2 = justification, reason, grounds, basis, licence, rationale, vindication, authority
warranty = guarantee, promise, contract, bond, pledge, certificate, assurance, covenant
warrior = soldier, combatant, fighter, gladiator, trooper, man-at-arms
wary 1 = suspicious, sceptical, guarded, distrustful, chary 2 = watchful, careful, alert, cautious, vigilant, circumspect, heedful ≠ careless
wash VERB 1 = clean, scrub, sponge, rinse, scour, cleanse 2 = launder, clean, rinse, dry-clean 3 = rinse, clean, scrub, lather 4 = bathe, bath, clean yourself, soak, douse, scrub yourself down 5 = move, overcome, touch, upset, stir, disturb, perturb, surge through 6 (*Informal*) (always used in negative constructions) = be plausible, stand up, hold up, pass muster, hold water, stick, carry weight, be convincing
• NOUN 1 = laundering, cleaning, clean, cleansing 2 = bathe, dip, soak, scrub, rinse 3 = backwash, slipstream, path, trail, train, track, waves, aftermath 4 = splash, surge, swell, rise and fall, undulation 5 = coat, film, covering, layer, coating, overlay
• PHRASES **wash something** *or* **someone away** = sweep away, carry off, bear away ◆ **wash something away** = erode, wear something away
waste VERB 1 = squander, throw away, blow (*slang*), lavish, misuse, dissipate, fritter away ≠ save 2 = wear out, wither
• NOUN 1 = squandering, misuse, extravagance, frittering away, dissipation, wastefulness, prodigality ≠ saving 2 = rubbish, refuse, debris, scrap, litter, garbage, trash, leftovers
• PLURAL NOUN = desert, wilderness, wasteland
• ADJECTIVE 1 = unwanted, useless, worthless, unused, leftover, superfluous, unusable, supernumerary ≠ necessary 2 = uncultivated, wild, bare, barren, empty, desolate, unproductive, uninhabited ≠ cultivated
• PHRASES **waste away** = decline, dwindle, wither, fade, crumble, decay, wane, wear out
watch VERB 1 = look at, observe, regard, eye, see, view, contemplate, eyeball (*slang*) 2 = spy on, follow, track, monitor, keep an eye on, stake out, keep tabs on (*informal*), keep watch on 3 = guard, keep, mind, protect, tend, look after, shelter, take care of
• NOUN 1 = wristwatch, timepiece, chronometer 2 = guard, surveillance, observation, vigil, lookout
watchdog 1 = guardian, monitor, protector, custodian, scrutineer 2 = guard dog
water NOUN = liquid, H_2O, wai (*N.Z.*)
• PLURAL NOUN = sea, main, waves, ocean, depths, briny
• VERB 1 = sprinkle, spray, soak, irrigate, hose, dampen, drench, douse 2 = get wet, cry, weep, become wet, exude water
• PHRASES **water something down** = dilute, weaken, water, doctor, thin
RELATED WORD
adjective: aquatic
waterfall = cascade, fall, cataract
wave VERB 1 = signal, sign, gesture, gesticulate 2 = guide, point, direct, indicate, signal, motion, gesture, nod 3 = brandish, swing, flourish, wag, shake 4 = flutter, flap, stir, shake, swing, wag, oscillate
• NOUN 1 = gesture, sign, signal, indication, gesticulation 2 = ripple, breaker, swell, ridge, roller, billow 3 = outbreak, rash, upsurge, flood, surge, ground swell 4 = stream, flood, surge, spate, current, flow, rush, tide
waver 1 = hesitate, dither (*chiefly Brit.*), vacillate, falter, fluctuate, seesaw, hum and haw ≠ be decisive 2 = flicker, shake, tremble, wobble, quiver, totter
wax 1 = increase, grow, develop, expand, swell, enlarge, magnify ≠ wane 2 = become fuller, enlarge
way 1 = method, means, system, process, technique, manner, procedure, mode 2 = manner, style, fashion, mode 3 *often plural* = custom, manner, habit, style, practice, nature, personality, wont, tikanga (*N.Z.*) 4 = route, direction, course, road, path 5 = access, road, track, channel, route,

path, trail, pathway **6** = journey, approach, passage **7** = distance, length, stretch

wayward = erratic, unruly, unmanageable, unpredictable, capricious, ungovernable, inconstant ≠ obedient

weak 1 = feeble, frail, debilitated, fragile, sickly, puny, unsteady, infirm ≠ strong **2** = slight, faint, feeble, pathetic, hollow **3** = fragile, brittle, flimsy, fine, delicate, frail, dainty, breakable **4** = unsafe, exposed, vulnerable, helpless, unprotected, defenceless, unguarded ≠ secure **5** = unconvincing, unsatisfactory, lame, flimsy, pathetic ≠ convincing **6** = tasteless, thin, diluted, watery, runny, insipid ≠ strong

weaken 1 = reduce, undermine, moderate, diminish, lessen, sap ≠ boost **2** = wane, diminish, dwindle, lower, flag, fade, lessen ≠ grow **3** = sap the strength of ≠ strengthen

weakness 1 = frailty, fatigue, exhaustion, fragility, infirmity, feebleness, decrepitude ≠ strength **2** = liking, appetite, penchant, soft spot, passion, inclination, fondness, partiality ≠ aversion **3** = powerlessness, vulnerability, meekness, spinelessness, timorousness, cravenness, cowardliness **4** = inadequacy, deficiency, transparency, lameness, hollowness, implausibility, flimsiness, unsoundness **5** = failing, fault, defect, deficiency, flaw, shortcoming, blemish, imperfection ≠ strong point

wealth 1 = riches, fortune, prosperity, affluence, money, opulence ≠ poverty **2** = property, capital, fortune **3** = abundance, plenty, richness, profusion, fullness, cornucopia, copiousness ≠ lack

wealthy = rich, prosperous, affluent, well-off, flush (*informal*), opulent, well-heeled (*informal*), well-to-do ≠ poor

wear VERB **1** = be dressed in, have on, sport (*informal*), put on **2** = show, present, bear, display, assume, put on, exhibit **3** = deteriorate, fray, wear thin
• NOUN **1** = clothes, things, dress, gear (*informal*), attire, costume, garments, apparel **2** = damage, wear and tear, erosion, deterioration, attrition, corrosion, abrasion ≠ repair
• PHRASES **wear off** = subside, disappear, fade, diminish, decrease, dwindle, wane, peter out

wearing = tiresome, trying, fatiguing, oppressive, exasperating, irksome, wearisome ≠ refreshing

weary ADJECTIVE **1** = tired, exhausted, drained, worn out, done in (*informal*), flagging, fatigued, sleepy, clapped out (*Austral. & N.Z. informal*) ≠ energetic **2** = tiring, arduous, tiresome, laborious, wearisome ≠ refreshing
• VERB = grow tired, tire, become bored ≠ invigorate

weather NOUN = climate, conditions, temperature, forecast, outlook, meteorological conditions, elements
• VERB = withstand, stand, survive, overcome, resist, brave, endure, come through ≠ surrender to

weave 1 = knit, intertwine, plait, braid, entwine, interlace **2** = zigzag, wind, crisscross **3** = create, tell, recount, narrate, build, relate, make up, spin

web 1 = cobweb, spider's web **2** = mesh, lattice **3** = tangle, network

wed 1 = get married to, be united to ≠ divorce **2** = get married, marry, be united, tie the knot (*informal*), take the plunge (*informal*) ≠ divorce **3** = unite, combine, join, link, ally, blend, merge, interweave ≠ divide

wedding = marriage, nuptials, wedding ceremony, marriage service, wedding service

wedge VERB = squeeze, force, lodge, jam, crowd, stuff, pack, thrust
• NOUN = block, lump, chunk

weep = cry, shed tears, sob, whimper, mourn, lament, blubber, snivel ≠ rejoice

weigh 1 = have a weight of, tip the scales at (*informal*) **2** *often with* ***up*** = consider, examine, contemplate, evaluate, ponder, think over, reflect upon, meditate upon **3** = compare, balance, contrast, juxtapose, place side by side **4** = matter, carry weight, count

weight NOUN **1** = heaviness, mass, poundage, load, tonnage **2** = importance, force, power, value, authority, influence, impact, import, mana (*N.Z.*)
• VERB **1** *often with* ***down*** = load **2** = bias, load, slant, unbalance

weird 1 = strange, odd, unusual, bizarre, mysterious, queer, eerie, unnatural ≠ normal **2** = bizarre, odd, strange, unusual, queer, unnatural, creepy (*informal*), freakish ≠ ordinary

welcome VERB 1 = greet, meet, receive, embrace, hail, karanga (*N.Z.*), mihi (*N.Z.*) ≠ reject 2 = accept gladly, appreciate, embrace, approve of, be pleased by, give the thumbs up to (*informal*), be glad about, express pleasure *or* satisfaction at
• NOUN = greeting, welcoming, reception, acceptance, hail, hospitality, salutation ≠ rejection
• ADJECTIVE 1 = pleasing, appreciated, acceptable, pleasant, desirable, refreshing, delightful, gratifying ≠ unpleasant 2 = wanted ≠ unwanted 3 = free

weld 1 = join, link, bond, bind, connect, fuse, solder 2 = unite, combine, blend, unify, fuse

welfare 1 = wellbeing, good, interest, health, security, benefit, safety, protection 2 = state benefit, support, benefits, pensions, dole (*slang*), social security, unemployment benefit, state benefits

well[1] ADVERB 1 = skilfully, expertly, adeptly, professionally, correctly, properly, efficiently, adequately ≠ badly 2 = satisfactorily, nicely, smoothly, successfully, pleasantly, splendidly, agreeably ≠ badly 3 = thoroughly, completely, fully, carefully, effectively, efficiently, rigorously 4 = intimately, deeply, fully, profoundly ≠ slightly 5 = favourably, highly, kindly, warmly, enthusiastically, approvingly, admiringly, with admiration ≠ unfavourably 6 = considerably, easily, very much, significantly, substantially, markedly 7 = fully, highly, greatly, amply, very much, thoroughly, considerably, substantially 8 = possibly, probably, certainly, reasonably, conceivably, justifiably 9 = decently, right, kindly, fittingly, fairly, properly, politely, suitably ≠ unfairly 10 = prosperously, comfortably, splendidly, in comfort, in (the lap of) luxury, without hardship
• ADJECTIVE 1 = healthy, sound, fit, blooming, in fine fettle, in good condition ≠ ill 2 = satisfactory, right, fine, pleasing, proper, thriving ≠ unsatisfactory 3 = advisable, proper, agreeable ≠ inadvisable

well[2] NOUN = hole, bore, pit, shaft
• VERB 1 = flow, spring, pour, jet, surge, gush, spurt, spout 2 = rise, increase, grow, mount, surge, intensify

wet ADJECTIVE 1 = damp, soaking, saturated, moist, watery, soggy, sodden, waterlogged ≠ dry 2 = rainy, damp, drizzly, showery, raining, pouring, drizzling, teeming ≠ sunny 3 (*Informal*) = feeble, soft, weak, ineffectual, weedy (*informal*), spineless, effete, timorous
• VERB = moisten, spray, dampen, water, soak, saturate, douse, irrigate ≠ dry
• NOUN 1 = rain, drizzle ≠ fine weather 2 = moisture, water, liquid, damp, humidity, condensation, dampness, wetness ≠ dryness

whack (*Informal*) VERB = strike, hit, belt (*informal*), bang, smack, thrash, thump, swipe
• NOUN 1 = blow, hit, stroke, belt (*informal*), bang, smack, thump, swipe 2 (*Informal*) = share, part, cut (*informal*), bit, portion, quota 3 (*Informal*) = attempt, go (*informal*), try, turn, shot (*informal*), crack (*informal*), stab (*informal*), bash (*informal*)

wharf = dock, pier, berth, quay, jetty, landing stage

wheel NOUN = disc, ring, hoop
• VERB 1 = push, trundle, roll 2 = turn, swing, spin, revolve, rotate, whirl, swivel 3 = circle, go round, twirl, gyrate

whereabouts = position, situation, site, location

whiff = smell, hint, scent, sniff, aroma, odour

whim = impulse, caprice, fancy, urge, notion

whine VERB 1 = cry, sob, wail, whimper, sniffle, snivel, moan 2 = complain, grumble, gripe (*informal*), whinge (*informal*), moan, grouse, grizzle (*informal, chiefly Brit.*), grouch (*informal*)
• NOUN 1 = cry, moan, sob, wail, whimper 2 = drone, note, hum 3 = complaint, moan, grumble, grouse, gripe (*informal*), whinge (*informal*), grouch (*informal*)

whip NOUN = lash, cane, birch, crop, scourge, cat-o'-nine-tails
• VERB 1 = lash, cane, flog, beat, strap, thrash, birch, scourge 2 (*Informal*) = dash, shoot, fly, tear, rush, dive, dart, whisk 3 = whisk, beat, mix vigorously, stir vigorously 4 = incite, drive, stir, spur, work up, get going, agitate, inflame

whirl VERB 1 = spin, turn, twist, rotate, twirl 2 = rotate, roll, twist, revolve, swirl, twirl, pirouette 3 = feel dizzy, swim, spin, reel,

go round
• NOUN 1 = revolution, turn, roll, spin, twist, swirl, rotation, twirl 2 = bustle, round, series, succession, flurry, merry-go-round 3 = confusion, daze, dither (*chiefly Brit.*), giddiness 4 = tumult, spin

whisk VERB 1 = flick, whip, sweep, brush 2 = beat, mix vigorously, stir vigorously, whip, fluff up
• NOUN 1 = flick, sweep, brush, whip 2 = beater, mixer, blender

whisper VERB 1 = murmur, breathe ≠ shout 2 = rustle, sigh, hiss, swish
• NOUN 1 = murmur, mutter, mumble, undertone 2 (*Informal*) = rumour, report, gossip, innuendo, insinuation 3 = rustle, sigh, hiss, swish

white = pale, wan, pasty, pallid, ashen

white-collar = clerical, professional, salaried, nonmanual

whittle VERB = carve, cut, hew, shape, trim, shave, pare
• PHRASES **whittle something** *or* **someone down** = reduce, cut down, cut, decrease, prune, scale down ◆ **whittle something away** = undermine, reduce, consume, erode, eat away, wear away

whole NOUN = unit, ensemble, entirety, totality ≠ part
• ADJECTIVE 1 = complete, full, total, entire, uncut, undivided, unabridged ≠ partial 2 = undamaged, intact, unscathed, unbroken, untouched, unharmed, in one piece ≠ damaged
• PHRASES **on the whole** 1 = all in all, altogether, all things considered, by and large 2 = generally, in general, as a rule, chiefly, mainly, mostly, principally, on average

wholesale ADJECTIVE = extensive, total, mass, sweeping, broad, comprehensive, wide-ranging, blanket ≠ limited
• ADVERB = extensively, comprehensively, across the board, indiscriminately

wholly = completely, totally, perfectly, fully, entirely, altogether, thoroughly, utterly ≠ partly

whore = prostitute, tart (*informal*), streetwalker, call girl

wide ADJECTIVE 1 = spacious, broad, extensive, roomy, commodious ≠ confined 2 = baggy, full, loose, ample, billowing, roomy, voluminous, capacious 3 = expanded, dilated, distended ≠ shut 4 = broad, extensive, wide-ranging, large, sweeping, vast, immense, expansive ≠ restricted 5 = extensive, general, far-reaching, overarching 6 = large, broad, vast, immense 7 = distant, remote, off course, off target
• ADVERB 1 = fully, completely ≠ partly 2 = off target, astray, off course, off the mark

widen 1 = broaden, expand, enlarge, dilate, spread, extend, stretch ≠ narrow 2 = get wider, spread, extend, expand, broaden ≠ narrow

widespread = common, general, popular, broad, extensive, universal, far-reaching, pervasive ≠ limited

width = breadth, extent, span, scope, diameter, compass, thickness, girth

wield 1 = brandish, flourish, manipulate, swing, use, manage, handle, employ 2 = exert, maintain, exercise, have, possess

wife = spouse, partner, mate, bride, better half (*humorous*), vrou (*S. African*), wahine (*N.Z.*)

wild ADJECTIVE 1 = untamed, fierce, savage, ferocious, unbroken, feral, undomesticated, free, warrigal (*Austral. literary*) ≠ tame 2 = uncultivated, natural ≠ cultivated 3 = stormy, violent, rough, raging, choppy, tempestuous, blustery 4 = excited, crazy (*informal*), enthusiastic, raving, hysterical ≠ unenthusiastic 5 = uncontrolled, disorderly, turbulent, wayward, unruly, rowdy, unfettered, riotous ≠ calm 6 = mad (*informal*), furious, fuming, infuriated, incensed, enraged, very angry, irate, tooshie (*Austral. slang*), off the air (*Austral. slang*) 7 = uncivilized, fierce, savage, primitive, ferocious, barbaric, brutish, barbarous ≠ civilized
• PLURAL NOUN = wilderness, desert, wasteland, middle of nowhere (*informal*), backwoods, back of beyond (*informal*)

wilderness = wilds, desert, wasteland, uncultivated region

will NOUN 1 = determination, drive, purpose, commitment, resolution, resolve, spine, backbone 2 = wish, mind, desire, intention, fancy, preference, inclination 3 = choice, prerogative, volition 4 = decree, wish, desire, command, dictate, ordinance 5 = testament, bequest(s), last wishes, last will and testament
• VERB 1 = wish, want, prefer, desire, see

fit **2** = bequeath, give, leave, transfer, gift, hand on, pass on, confer

willing 1 = inclined, prepared, consenting, agreeable, compliant, amenable ≠ unwilling **2** = ready, game (*informal*) ≠ reluctant

willingly = readily, freely, gladly, happily, eagerly, voluntarily, cheerfully, by choice ≠ unwillingly

willingness = inclination, will, agreement, wish, consent, volition ≠ reluctance

wilt 1 = droop, wither, sag, shrivel **2** = weaken, languish, droop **3** = wane, flag, fade

win VERB **1** = be victorious in, succeed in, prevail in, come first in, be the victor in ≠ lose **2** = be victorious, succeed, triumph, overcome, prevail, conquer, come first, sweep the board ≠ lose **3** = gain, get, land, achieve, earn, secure, obtain, acquire ≠ forfeit

• NOUN = victory, success, triumph, conquest ≠ defeat

• PHRASES **win someone over** *or* **round** = convince, influence, persuade, convert, sway, prevail upon, bring *or* talk round

wince VERB = flinch, start, shrink, cringe, quail, recoil, cower, draw back

• NOUN = flinch, start, cringe

wind¹ NOUN **1** = air, blast, hurricane, breeze, draught, gust, zephyr **2** = flatulence, gas **3** = breath, puff, respiration **4** = nonsense, talk, boasting, hot air, babble, bluster, humbug, twaddle (*informal*), bizzo (*Austral. slang*), bull's wool (*Austral. & N.Z. slang*)

• PHRASES **get wind of something** = hear about, learn of, find out about, become aware of, be told about, be informed of, be made aware of, hear tell of

wind² VERB **1** = meander, turn, bend, twist, curve, snake, ramble, twist and turn **2** = wrap, twist, reel, curl, loop, coil **3** = coil, curl, spiral, encircle

• PHRASES **wind someone up** (*Informal*) **1** = irritate, excite, anger, annoy, exasperate, nettle, work someone up, pique **2** = tease, kid (*informal*), have someone on (*informal*), annoy, rag (*informal*), rib (*informal*), josh (*informal*), vex ◆ **wind something up 1** = end, finish, settle, conclude, tie up, wrap up, finalize **2** = close down, close, dissolve, terminate, put something into liquidation ◆ **wind up** = end up, be left, finish up, fetch up (*informal*), land up

windfall = godsend, find, jackpot, bonanza, manna from heaven ≠ misfortune

windy = breezy, wild, stormy, windswept, blustery, gusty, squally, blowy ≠ calm

wing NOUN = faction, group, arm, section, branch

• VERB **1** = fly, soar, glide, take wing **2** = wound, hit, clip

wink VERB **1** = blink, bat, flutter **2** = twinkle, flash, shine, sparkle, gleam, shimmer, glimmer

• NOUN = blink, flutter

winner = victor, champion, master, champ (*informal*), conqueror, prizewinner ≠ loser

winning ADJECTIVE **1** = victorious, first, top, successful, unbeaten, conquering, triumphant, undefeated **2** = charming, pleasing, attractive, engaging, cute, disarming, enchanting, endearing ≠ unpleasant

• PLURAL NOUN = spoils, profits, gains, prize, proceeds, takings

wipe VERB **1** = clean, polish, brush, rub, sponge, mop, swab **2** = erase, remove

• NOUN = rub, brush

• PHRASES **wipe something** *or* **someone out** = destroy, massacre, erase, eradicate, obliterate, annihilate, exterminate, expunge

wisdom = understanding, learning, knowledge, intelligence, judgment, insight, enlightenment, erudition ≠ foolishness

wise 1 = sage, clever, intelligent, sensible, enlightened, discerning, perceptive, erudite ≠ foolish **2** = sensible, clever, intelligent, prudent, judicious ≠ unwise

wish NOUN = desire, want, hope, urge, intention, fancy (*informal*), ambition, yen (*informal*) ≠ aversion

• VERB = want, feel, choose, please, desire, think fit

• PHRASES **wish for something** = desire, want, hope for, long for, crave, aspire to, yearn for, hanker for

wit 1 = humour, quips, banter, puns, repartee, wordplay, witticisms, badinage ≠ seriousness **2** = humorist, card (*informal*), comedian, wag, joker, dag (*N.Z. informal*) **3** *often plural* = cleverness,

sense, brains, wisdom, common sense, intellect, ingenuity, acumen ≠ stupidity
witch = enchantress, magician, hag, crone, sorceress, Wiccan
witchcraft = magic, voodoo, wizardry, black magic, enchantment, occultism, sorcery, Wicca, makutu (*N.Z.*)
withdraw 1 = remove, take off, pull out, extract, take away, pull back, draw out, draw back 2 = take out, extract, draw out
withdrawal = removal, ending, stopping, taking away, abolition, elimination, cancellation, termination
withdrawn = uncommunicative, reserved, retiring, distant, shy, taciturn, introverted, unforthcoming ≠ outgoing
wither 1 = wilt, decline, decay, disintegrate, perish, shrivel ≠ flourish 2 = waste, decline, shrivel 3 = fade, decline, perish ≠ increase
withering = scornful, devastating, humiliating, snubbing, hurtful, mortifying
withhold 1 = keep secret, refuse, hide, reserve, retain, conceal, suppress, hold back ≠ reveal 2 = hold back, suppress, keep back ≠ release
withstand = resist, suffer, bear, oppose, cope with, endure, tolerate, stand up to ≠ give in to
witness NOUN 1 = observer, viewer, spectator, looker-on, watcher, onlooker, eyewitness, bystander 2 = testifier
• VERB 1 = see, view, watch, note, notice, observe, perceive 2 = countersign, sign, endorse, validate
witty = humorous, funny, clever, amusing, sparkling, whimsical, droll, piquant ≠ dull
wizard = magician, witch, shaman, sorcerer, occultist, magus, conjuror, warlock, tohunga (*N.Z.*)
wobble VERB 1 = shake, rock, sway, tremble, teeter, totter 2 = tremble, shake
• NOUN 1 = unsteadiness, shake, tremble 2 = unsteadiness, shake, tremor
woe 1 = misery, distress, grief, agony, gloom, sadness, sorrow, anguish ≠ happiness 2 = problem, grief, misery, sorrow
woman = lady, girl, female, sheila (*Austral. & N.Z. informal*), vrou (*S. African*), adult female, charlie (*Austral. slang*), chook (*Austral. slang*), wahine (*N.Z.*) ≠ man
womanly 1 = feminine, motherly, female, warm, tender, matronly, ladylike 2 = curvaceous, ample, voluptuous, shapely, curvy (*informal*), busty (*informal*), buxom, full-figured
wonder VERB 1 = think, question, puzzle, speculate, query, ponder, meditate, conjecture 2 = be amazed, stare, marvel, be astonished, gape
• NOUN 1 = amazement, surprise, admiration, awe, fascination, astonishment, bewilderment, wonderment 2 = phenomenon, sight, miracle, spectacle, curiosity, marvel, prodigy, rarity
wonderful 1 = excellent, great (*informal*), brilliant, outstanding, superb, fantastic (*informal*), tremendous, magnificent, booshit (*Austral. slang*), exo (*Austral. slang*), sik (*Austral. slang*) ≠ terrible 2 = remarkable, amazing, extraordinary, incredible, astonishing, staggering, startling, phenomenal ≠ ordinary
woo 1 = seek, cultivate 2 = court, pursue
wood 1 = timber, planks, planking, lumber (*U.S.*) 2 *or* **woods** = woodland, forest, grove, thicket, copse, coppice 3 = firewood, fuel, logs, kindling
wooded = tree-covered, forested, timbered, sylvan (*poetic*), tree-clad
wooden 1 = made of wood, timber, woody, ligneous 2 = expressionless, lifeless, deadpan, unresponsive
wool 1 = fleece, hair, coat 2 = yarn
word NOUN 1 = term, name, expression 2 = chat, tête-à-tête, talk, discussion, consultation, confab (*informal*), heart-to-heart, powwow (*informal*) 3 = comment, remark, utterance 4 = message, news, report, information, notice, intelligence, dispatch, communiqué 5 = promise, guarantee, pledge, vow, assurance, oath 6 = command, order, decree, bidding, mandate
• VERB = express, say, state, put, phrase, utter, couch, formulate

RELATED WORDS

adjectives: lexical, verbal

wording = phraseology, words, language, phrasing, terminology
work VERB 1 = be employed, be in work 2 = labour, sweat, slave, toil, slog (away), drudge, peg away, exert yourself ≠ relax 3 = function, go, run, operate, be in working order ≠ be out of order 4 = succeed, work out, pay off (*informal*), be successful, be effective, do the trick

(*informal*), do the business (*informal*), get results **5** = cultivate, farm, dig, till, plough **6** = operate, use, move, control, drive, manage, handle, manipulate **7** = manipulate, form, fashion, shape, mould, knead
• NOUN **1** = employment, business, job, trade, duty, profession, occupation, livelihood ≠ play **2** = effort, industry, labour, sweat, toil, exertion, drudgery, elbow grease (*facetious*) ≠ leisure **3** = task, jobs, projects, commissions, duties, assignments, chores, yakka (*Austral. & N.Z. informal*) **4** = handiwork, doing, act, feat, deed **5** = creation, piece, production, opus, achievement, composition, handiwork
• PLURAL NOUN **1** = factory, plant, mill, workshop **2** = writings, output, canon, oeuvre (*French*) **3** = mechanism, workings, parts, action, movement, machinery
• PHRASES **work something out** = solve, find out, calculate, figure out

worker = employee, hand, labourer, workman, craftsman, artisan, tradesman

workman = labourer, hand, worker, employee, mechanic, operative, craftsman, artisan

workshop **1** = factory, plant, mill **2** = workroom, studio

world **1** = earth, planet, globe **2** = mankind, man, everyone, the public, everybody, humanity, humankind **3** = sphere, area, field, environment, realm, domain **4** (usually used in phrase *a world of difference*) = huge amount, mountain, wealth, great deal, good deal, abundance, enormous amount, vast amount

worldly **1** = earthly, physical, secular, terrestrial, temporal, profane ≠ spiritual **2** = materialistic, grasping, selfish, greedy ≠ nonmaterialistic **3** = worldly-wise, knowing, experienced, sophisticated, cosmopolitan, urbane, blasé ≠ naive

worn = ragged, frayed, shabby, tattered, tatty, threadbare, the worse for wear

worried = anxious, concerned, troubled, afraid, frightened, nervous, tense, uneasy ≠ unworried

worry VERB **1** = be anxious, be concerned, be worried, obsess, brood, fret, agonize, get in a lather (*informal*) ≠ be unconcerned **2** = trouble, upset, bother, disturb, annoy, unsettle, pester, vex ≠ soothe
• NOUN **1** = anxiety, concern, fear, trouble, unease, apprehension, misgiving, trepidation ≠ peace of mind **2** = problem, care, trouble, bother, hassle (*informal*)

worsen **1** = deteriorate, decline, sink, decay, get worse, degenerate, go downhill (*informal*) ≠ improve **2** = aggravate, damage, exacerbate, make worse ≠ improve

worship VERB **1** = revere, praise, honour, adore, glorify, exalt, pray to, venerate ≠ dishonour **2** = love, adore, idolize, put on a pedestal ≠ despise
• NOUN = reverence, praise, regard, respect, honour, glory, devotion, adulation

worth **1** = value, price, rate, cost, estimate, valuation ≠ worthlessness **2** = merit, value, quality, importance, excellence, goodness, worthiness ≠ unworthiness **3** = usefulness, value, quality, importance, excellence, goodness ≠ uselessness

worthless **1** = valueless, rubbishy, negligible ≠ valuable **2** = useless, unimportant, ineffectual, negligible ≠ useful **3** = good-for-nothing, vile, despicable, contemptible ≠ honourable

worthwhile = useful, valuable, helpful, profitable, productive, beneficial, meaningful, constructive ≠ useless

worthy = praiseworthy, deserving, valuable, worthwhile, admirable, virtuous, creditable, laudable ≠ disreputable

would-be = budding, self-styled, wannabe (*informal*), unfulfilled, self-appointed

wound NOUN **1** = injury, cut, hurt, trauma (*Pathology*), gash, lesion, laceration **2** *often plural* = trauma, offence, slight, insult
• VERB **1** = injure, cut, wing, hurt, pierce, gash, lacerate **2** = offend, hurt, annoy, sting, mortify, cut to the quick

wrangle VERB = argue, fight, row, dispute, disagree, contend, quarrel, squabble
• NOUN = argument, row, dispute, quarrel, squabble, bickering, tiff, altercation

wrap VERB **1** = cover, enclose, shroud, swathe, encase, enfold, bundle up **2** = pack, package, parcel (up), tie up, giftwrap ≠ unpack **3** = bind, swathe ≠ unwind
• NOUN = cloak, cape, stole, mantle, shawl
• PHRASES **wrap something up** **1** = giftwrap, pack, package, bundle up **2** (*Informal*) = end, conclude, wind up, terminate, finish off, round off, polish off

wrath = anger, rage, temper, fury, resentment, indignation, ire, displeasure ≠ satisfaction

wreck VERB 1 = destroy, break, smash, ruin, devastate, shatter, spoil, demolish ≠ build 2 = spoil, ruin, devastate, shatter, crool *or* cruel (*Austral. slang*) ≠ save
• NOUN = shipwreck, hulk

wreckage = remains, pieces, ruin, fragments, debris, rubble

wrench VERB 1 = twist, force, pull, tear, rip, tug, jerk, yank 2 = sprain, strain, rick
• NOUN 1 = twist, pull, rip, tug, jerk, yank 2 = sprain, strain, twist 3 = blow, shock, upheaval, pang 4 = spanner, adjustable spanner

wrestle = fight, battle, struggle, combat, grapple, tussle, scuffle

wrinkle NOUN 1 = line, fold, crease, furrow, crow's-foot, corrugation 2 = crease, fold, crumple, furrow, crinkle, corrugation
• VERB = crease, gather, fold, crumple, furrow, rumple, pucker, corrugate ≠ smooth

writ = summons, document, decree, indictment, court order, subpoena, arraignment

write 1 = record, scribble, inscribe, set down, jot down 2 = compose, draft, pen, draw up 3 = correspond, get in touch, keep in touch, write a letter, drop a line, drop a note

writer = author, novelist, hack, scribbler, scribe, wordsmith, penpusher

writing = script, hand, printing, fist (*informal*), scribble, handwriting, scrawl, calligraphy

wrong ADJECTIVE 1 = amiss, faulty, unsatisfactory, not right, defective, awry 2 = incorrect, mistaken, false, inaccurate, untrue, erroneous, wide of the mark, fallacious 3 = inappropriate, incorrect, unsuitable, unacceptable, undesirable, incongruous, unseemly, unbecoming ≠ correct 4 = bad, criminal, illegal, evil, unlawful, immoral, unjust, dishonest ≠ moral 5 = defective, faulty, awry, askew
• ADVERB 1 = incorrectly, badly, wrongly, mistakenly, erroneously, inaccurately ≠ correctly 2 = amiss, astray, awry, askew
• NOUN = offence, injury, crime, error, sin, injustice, misdeed, transgression ≠ good deed
• VERB = mistreat, abuse, hurt, harm, cheat, take advantage of, oppress, malign ≠ treat well

X

X-ray = radiograph, x-ray image

Y

yank VERB = pull, tug, jerk, seize, snatch, pluck, hitch, wrench
• NOUN = pull, tug, jerk, snatch, hitch, wrench, tweak

yarn 1 = thread, fibre, cotton, wool 2 (*Informal*) = story, tale, anecdote, account, narrative, fable, reminiscence, urban myth

yawning = gaping, wide, huge, vast, cavernous

yearly ADJECTIVE = annual, each year, every year, once a year
• ADVERB = annually, every year, by the year, once a year, per annum

yearn *often with* ***for*** = long, desire, hunger, ache, crave, covet, itch, hanker after

yell VERB = scream, shout, cry out, howl, call out, wail, shriek, screech ≠ whisper
• NOUN = scream, cry, shout, roar, howl, shriek, whoop, screech ≠ whisper

yen = longing, desire, craving, yearning, passion, hunger, ache, itch

yet ADVERB 1 = so far, until now, up to now, still, as yet, even now, thus far, up till now 2 = now, right now, just now, so soon 3 = still, in addition, besides, to boot, into the bargain
• CONJUNCTION = nevertheless, still, however, for all that, notwithstanding, just the same, be that as it may

yield VERB 1 = bow, submit, give in, surrender, succumb, cave in (*informal*), capitulate 2 = relinquish, resign, hand

over, surrender, turn over, make over, give over, bequeath ≠ retain ≠ resist **3** = produce, give, provide, return, supply, bear, net, earn ≠ use up
• **NOUN 1** = produce, crop, harvest, output **2** = profit, return, income, revenue, earnings, takings ≠ loss

yielding 1 = soft, pliable, springy, elastic, supple, spongy, unresisting **2** = submissive, obedient, compliant, docile, flexible, accommodating, pliant, acquiescent ≠ obstinate

yob *or* **yobbo** = thug, hooligan, lout, hoon (*Austral. & N.Z. slang*), ruffian, roughneck (*slang*), tsotsi (*S. African*), cougan (*Austral. slang*), scozza (*Austral. slang*), bogan (*Austral. slang*)

young ADJECTIVE 1 = immature, juvenile, youthful, little, green, junior, infant, adolescent ≠ old **2** = early, new, undeveloped, fledgling ≠ advanced
• **PLURAL NOUN** = offspring, babies, litter, family, issue, brood, progeny ≠ parents

youngster = youth, girl, boy, kid (*informal*), lad, teenager, juvenile, lass

youth 1 = immaturity, adolescence, boyhood *or* girlhood, salad days ≠ old age **2** = boy, lad, youngster, kid (*informal*), teenager, young man, adolescent, teen (*informal*) ≠ adult

youthful = young, juvenile, childish, immature, boyish, girlish ≠ elderly

Z

zeal = enthusiasm, passion, zest, spirit, verve, fervour, eagerness, gusto ≠ apathy

zero 1 = nought, nothing, nil **2** = rock bottom, the bottom, an all-time low, a nadir, as low as you can get

zip VERB = speed, shoot, fly, flash, zoom, whizz (*informal*)
• **NOUN** (*Informal*) = energy, drive, vigour, verve, zest, gusto, liveliness ≠ lethargy

zone = area, region, section, sector, district, territory, belt, sphere

zoom = speed, shoot, fly, rush, flash, dash, whizz (*informal*), hurtle